Irish Law of Specific Performance

To Brenda

Irish Law of Specific Performance

by

John Farrell, M.A., S.C

Consultant Editor
Professor J.C.W. Wylie, LL.M, LL.D

BUTTERWORTHS
1994

Republic of Ireland	Butterworth (Ireland) Ltd, 26 Upper Ormond Quay, DUBLIN 7
United Kingdom	Butterworth & Co (Publishers) Ltd, Halsbury House, 35 Chancery Lane, LONDON WC2A 1EL and 4 Hill Street, EDINBURGH EH2 3JZ
Australia	Butterworths Pty Ltd, SYDNEY, MELBOURNE, BRISBANE, ADELAIDE, PERTH, CANBERRA and HOBART
Canada	Butterworths Canada Ltd, TORONTO and VANCOUVER
Malaysia	Malayan Law Journal Sdn Bhd, KUALA LUMPUR
New Zealand	Butterworths of New Zealand Ltd, WELLINGTON and AUCKLAND
Puerto Rico	Butterworth of Puerto Rico, Inc, SAN JUAN
Singapore	Butterworths Asia, SINGAPORE
South Africa	Butterworths Publishers (Pty) Ltd, DURBAN
USA	Butterworth Legal Publishers, Carlsbad, CALIFORNIA and Salem, NEW HAMPSHIRE

© Butterworth Ireland Ltd

A CIP Catalogue record for this book is available from the British Library.
ISBN 1 85475 0313
Typeset in Ireland by Typeform Ltd, Dublin
Printed in Ireland by Colourbooks Ltd, Dublin

Contents

Preface

The two main objects of this book are to examine the remedy of specific performance through the Irish case law and to try to make that case law more readily accessible. Many Irish lawyers may not be fully aware of the rich supply of Irish decisions in specific performance and other areas of possible interest to someone involved in or thinking about a claim for specific performance.

A few words of warning are needed. A reference in this book to a case is a distant second best to detailed consideration of the case and opening the case to a court. Most references are to *obiter* material and the book would be very tiresome if I set out every time whether I think something is *obiter* or not. Great care must be taken to see how far the facts of a decided case correspond with those of a client's case. As an Irish judge warned in 1813:

> "It is always unsatisfactory to abstract altogether the Reasoning of the Court, in any reported Case, from the Facts to which that Reasoning is meant to apply; it has a Tendency only to misrepresent one Judge, and to mislead another."[1]

It has been difficult at times to decide what to cover and what to omit. Obviously aspects of the remedy of specific performance covered in the Irish case law have been included. I have also covered other items which could interest persons involved in specific performance claims or choosing from possible courses of action. Hence, for example, the short chapter on injunctions viewed from a standpoint of the relief of specific performance. Also the material on the "sanction of voidness" in the Family Home Protection Act, 1976 (where amending legislation is pending).

Another example is the treatment of damages. Obviously the adequacy of damages as a relief must be considered in a book about specific performance. Damages in addition to or in lieu of specific performance are also relevant. Misrepresentation may be a good defence to a claim for specific performance or lead to the equitable relief of rescission; so it seemed useful to consider also the possibility of damages for negligent misrepresentation and the like. In general the law of damages is outside the scope of this book.

This book has emerged from a very happy working relationship with John Wylie on *his* book, *Irish Landlord and Tenant Law*. It has been a great pleasure to have him as my Consultant Editor here. His influence on the book has been immensely valuable and wide ranging. His friendly, non-pushy encouragement has been an example to any diplomat. I look forward with great interest to the revamped version of *Irish Conveyancing Law*; the 1978 version was a huge help to many of us.

A great help has been the kindness and efficiency of the Law Library staff in digging up obscure old reports and modern unreported cases. Special thanks also to my good-humoured Kerry wife for her tolerance and encouragement.

I have opted for simplicity in citing the reported cases where there is some room for choice. However, the book was written omitting square brackets in referring to those reports which use them. Butterworths, who have infinitely more experience in these matters, decided that the square brackets should be restored. I have referred to older Irish cases without "I" or "Ir" in their normal citation by spelling the names of the learned reporters in full. Thus, a citation of "Schoales and Lefroy" shows at once that it is an Irish case whereas "Sch and Lef" would mean that it was not Irish.

The case law has been included until roughly July 1994. Some judgments have become available faster than others. Thanks must go to all those engaged in producing the modern Irish reports and the unreported judgments. The raw material is much more readily available to a writer than used to be the case. That means unfortunately that omission of cases which ought to be mentioned is much more clearly my fault than it would have been twenty years ago!

John Farrell
The Law Library
The Four Courts
Dublin 7

20 October 1994

---

[1]   *Revell v Hussey* 2 Ball & Beatty 281 at 286.

Table of Cases

Table of Statutes

Chapter 1

The Nature of the Remedy

[1.01] The doctrine of specific performance rests on the ground that a person is entitled in equity to have in specie the specific thing for which he has contracted and is not bound to take damages instead.[1] In the circumstances of his case an award of damages would not give him the compensation to which he is entitled, that is, would not put him in a situation as beneficial to him as if the agreement were specifically performed.[2] If a plaintiff might have no remedy at law that could be an additional reason for giving him equitable relief.[3] The object of the court in exercising the jurisdiction is to do more complete justice.[4] Equity has been described as "a gloss on or an improvement and reform of the common law".[5] In Ireland prior to the Judicature Act 1877[6] (the "1877 Act") the relief of specific performance could be given by the courts of equity[7] to a plaintiff who formerly would have failed in a claim to damages in a court of law because he had not strictly performed his part of the deal.[8] Thus, a party who had not complied with a stipulation as to time in a contract could succeed on his claim or defence in a court of equity unless it was established that time was of the essence of the contract.[9] The result of the 1877 Act is that the law which was applied in the Court of Chancery before 1877 now prevails.[10]

[1.02] A claim for specific performance must be based on a submission that a contract exists and should be enforced.[11] If negotiations between the parties do not get as far as a complete contract a claim for specific performance must fail for the simple reason that there is no contract to be specifically enforced.[12] If a contract is void, is voidable and has been avoided, is unenforceable by action by reason of the Statute of Frauds, has been discharged for some reason, has been frustrated, is illegal or if some other defence succeeds[13] specific performance cannot be obtained. There must have been consideration if the remedy is to be available.[14] The relief is discretionary even where a plaintiff has

---

[1] *Per* Farwell J in *Hexter v Pearce* [1990] 1 Ch 341 at 346 approved by O'Connor J in *O'Regan v White* [1919] 2 IR 338 at 392.

[2] *Harnett v Yielding* (1805) 2 Schoales & Lefroy 549 at 553; *cf Revell v Hussey* [1813] 2 Ball & Beatty 280 at 289.

[3] *Revell v Hussey* (1813) 2 Ball & Beatty 280 at 289.

[4] *Harnett's* case at 554-5. *Cf Davis v Hone* (1805) 2 Schoales & Lefroy 341 at 347.

[5] *Hynes v Independent Newspapers Ltd* [1980] IR 204 at 218, *per* Kenny J.

[6] Supreme Court of Judicature (Ireland) Act 1877, para **1.05** *infra*.

[7] Ch 2 of Keane, *Equity and the Law of Trusts in the Republic of Ireland* (1988) Butterworth Ireland, discusses fully the background to equity and its history and development in Ireland; see also Wylie, *Irish Land Law* 2nd Ed (1986) Butterworth Ireland, para 3.001-6 and the discussion of the history of specific performance by Jones & Goodhart, *Specific Performance* (1986) at pp 3-7.

[8] *Lennon v Napper* (1802) 2 Schoales & Lefroy 682 at 684.

[9] The *Hynes* case at 218-9. *Cf* O'Higgins CJ at p 214. Time limits are discussed at paras **8.29-40** *post*.

[10] *Per* Kenny J in the *Hynes* case at 221.

[11] *Holohan v Ardmayle Estates* (SC) 1 May 1967, Walsh J, unrep at 4.

[12] *Lynch v O'Meara* (SC) 8 May 1975, Henchy J, unrep at 4. See discussion of consensus at paras **3.01-2** *post*, "subject to contract" in Ch 4 and the defence of "no contract" in paras **9.02-4**.

[13] On defences see Ch 9. Some defences prevent specific performance but leave other remedies open; others defeat all claims.

[14] *Re Wilson* [1933] IR 729 at 739; see defence of lack of consideration at para **9.05** *post*.

1

made out his case and has behaved properly.[15] The remedy usually must be mutual also as equity will not aid one party to an agreement unless it can likewise aid the other party if necessary.[16] A decree of specific performance is made for the benefit of both parties[17] even though almost always one side has been resisting the granting of the relief or has been seeking it on a basis different from that claimed by the successful party.

[1.03] As just now noted, equity is reluctant to aid one party to an agreement if it cannot also assist the other if necessary.[18] This may be a factor in a point which may appear anomalous at first sight. A vendor's claim for specific performance usually is in substance a claim for the purchase price so that damages might seem to be an adequate remedy but it is settled that he also is entitled to specific performance.[19] A modern Australian case has decided that where the contract is of such a kind that the purchaser can sue for specific performance the vendor can also sue for specific performance although the claim is merely to recover a sum of money.[20] Several reasons have been advanced in support of the vendor's right to specific performance. One is that where one party can get specific performance justice requires that the other party should equally be able to enforce the contract in specie even though damages would otherwise be regarded as adequate for him; a second is that the vendor is entitled to divest himself of the legal estate in the property and therefore damages are not adequate in fact.[21] It has also been suggested that the point is based upon the principle of mutuality.[22] Other similar situations can arise. For example, specific performance of a contract to advance money normally will not be ordered[23] but, if the loan has been advanced in fact, equity will decree specific performance of the agreement to provide the stipulated security.[24]

[1.04] The English courts have perceived some ambiguity in the use of the words "specific performance". A broad distinction has been drawn between specific performance in relation to *executory* contracts and *executed* contracts. Lord Selborne said:[25]

> "There is a class of suits in this Court, known as suits for specific performance of executory agreements, which agreements are not intended between the parties to be the final instruments regulating their mutual relations under their contracts. We call those executory contracts as distinct from executed contracts: and we call those contracts 'executed', in which that has been already done which will finally determine and settle the relative positions of the parties, so that nothing else remains to be done for that particular purpose. The common expression, 'specific performance', as applied to suits known by that name, presupposes an executory as distinct from an executed agreement,

---

[15] See paras **1.06-9** *infra.*
[16] *O'Regan's* case at 392-5; see want of mutuality at paras **9.70-73** *post.*
[17] *Bourke v Grimes* (1929) 63 ILTR 53 at 54, *per* Fitzgibbon J.
[18] Para **1.02** *supra.*
[19] *Abbott v Ryan* (1901) 1 NIJR 75; *Jessop v Smyth* [1895] 1 IR 508.
[20] *Turner v Bladin* (1951) 82 CLR 463 at 473.
[21] See Meagher, Gummow, Lehane, *Equity Doctrines & Remedies* 3rd Ed (1992) at para 2009, esp fn 12; Jones & Goodhart, *Specific Performance* (1986) at p 19.
[22] Wylie, *Irish Conveyancing Law* (1978) para 12.39, fn 95.
[23] See para **1.19** *infra.*
[24] *The Regina Coeli* [1976] 5 NIJB at 40.
[25] *Wolverhampton and Walsall Railway Co v London and North-Western Railway Co* (1873) LR 16 Eq 433 at 439.

something remaining to be done, such as the execution of a deed or a conveyance, in order to put the parties in the position relative to each other in which by the preliminary agreement they were intended to be placed."

He did not suggest that the jurisdiction to order specific performance was confined to one or other type of case.[26] More recently the Privy Council, while accepting that the distinction existed, felt that a court, when invited to order specific performance of an executed agreement or some part thereof, would be entitled to pay attention to considerations as to the conduct and position of the plaintiff in the same way as in cases of executory agreements.[27]

The distinction does not seem to have been an issue in any Irish case. An Irish writer has noted it but concluded that it is "not perhaps of great practical importance".[28] Most decided cases here relate to claims for specific performance of executory contracts for the sale of land. According to the distinction those are claims for specific performance "properly so-called" or "in the proper sense of the words".[29] However, having noted the distinction, we may let it lie and the words "specific performance" in the rest of this book will cover the relief in relation to both executory and executed contracts without regard to the distinction.

[1.05] Formerly the remedy of specific performance had been seen by the courts of equity as a remedy intended to make good what were supposed to be defects in the remedies available in courts of law.[30] However, the 1877 Act[31] brought the rules of equity into play in all courts.[32] This means, for example, that the doctrine of part performance[33] is now available to assist a plaintiff in an action for damages for breach of contract in a case where a court of equity would have sustained an action for specific performance prior to the statute.[34] Another effect of the 1877 Act is that a claimant's failure to show that there is power to give him the relief of specific performance does not prevent him getting damages in the same action for a breach of contract by the defendant.[35] Any necessity for a right to an order for specific performance to exist or to have existed when an action was commenced as a condition precedent to the granting of damages applied only at a time when the courts of equity were separated from and distinct in their powers and jurisdiction from the courts of common law.[36] When a party to a contract for the sale of land sues only for damages for its breach the court will approach stipulations as to time on the same basis as if equitable relief were being claimed.[37] It has been said also that the

---

[26] *Cf Australian Hardwoods Pty Ltd v Commissioner for Railways* [1961] 1 All ER 737 at 743. In the older case the court could compel the defendents by injunction to use the railway line as they had promised in their agreement confirmed by Act of Parliament provided the court could define that which they ought, or ought not, to do; p 441.
[27] The *Australian Hardwoods* case at 743.
[28] Keane, *Equity and the Law of Trusts in the Republic of Ireland* (1988) Butterworths, para 16.01. Maybe the distinction matters if part of the subject matter of a contract can be enforced by specific performance and the rest cannot: *Keane* at para 16.08 considering *Ogden v Fossick* (1862) 4 De GF & J 426.
[29] The *Wolverhampton & Walsall Railway Co* case at 439.
[30] *Harnett v Yielding* (1805) 2 Schoales & Lefroy 549 at 555.
[31] The Supreme Court of Judicature (Ireland) Act 1877; note s 28.
[32] *Somers v W* [1979] IR 94 at 108; *Guckian v Brennan* [1981] IR 478 at 487.
[33] Discussed in Ch 6 *post*.
[34] *Crowley v O'Sullivan* [1900] 2 IR 478 at 490, 492; *cf Lowry v Reid* [1927] NI 142 at 157.
[35] *Duggan v Allied Irish Building Society* (HC) 4 March 1976, Finlay P, unrep at 15.
[36] *Ibid* at 15-16.
[37] *Maye v Merriman* (HC) 13 February 1980, unrep at 19. The deal closed 14 days after the agreed completion date (time not of the essence). The purchaser sought damages. Hamilton J held at p 22 that he was trying "to make an unfair use of the letter of his contract".

powers of the court to grant an injunction, either at the hearing or on an interlocutory order, have been much extended by the 1877 Act.[38] A very important result of the "fusion of common-law and equitable rules"[39] is that the equitable rule as to time in contracts now applies[40] and time is originally of the essence of a contract only whenever it appears to have been part of the real intention of the parties that it should be so.[41]

The discretion

[1.06] Specific performance is an equitable remedy and as such it is discretionary. It is well established that the discretion to grant specific performance should not be exercised if the contract is not equal and fair.[42] Courts of equity have long applied the principle that specific performance should not be granted unless it appears that the party who seeks that particular relief has acted, not only fairly, but "in a manner clear of all suspicion".[43] The jurisdiction to grant specific performance has been described as delicate and to be exercised with discretion and care.[44] The relief may be withheld as an exercise of that discretion[45] even where a plaintiff proves a valid contract and no specific defence of any of the types discussed later[46] is established. In considering whether to grant the remedy fairness is vital. Finlay CJ noted the approach of equity:[47]

> "...the discretion which arises is not as to whether any relief will be given to the party who has a binding contract in law, at all, but rather as to what the form of relief will be: will it be specific performance, or is it one of the cases where the court of equity will say: 'It is not fair to specifically perform this contract; we will award damages instead'."

Once it is decided that an enforceable contract exists then equitable principles determine, not the validity of the contract, but the exercise of the court's discretion to grant equitable relief.[48] That relief may be refused even though there has been no improper conduct on the part of the plaintiff - it is enough if the facts as a whole make it inequitable to grant the relief.[49] The discretion to grant or refuse the relief will be exercised in a manner which is neither arbitrary nor capricious but which has regard to the essential fairness of the transaction involved.[50]

[1.07] Equity may set aside a contract which is not equal and fair.[51] In other cases, the

---

[38] *Cork Corporation v Rooney* (1881) 7 LRI 191 at 200. Injunctions are considered in Ch 2 *post*.
[39] The words of O'Higgins CJ in *Hynes v Independent Newspapers Ltd* [1980] IR 204 at 216. The fusion was initiated by the 1877 Act and completed by the Courts of Justice Act 1924 and the Courts (Establishment and Constitution) Act 1961. *Cf* discussion by Keane, *Equity and the Law of Trusts in the Republic of Ireland* (1988) at para 2.24.
[40] *Hynes Ltd v Independent Newspapers Ltd* [1980] IR 204 at 216, 219; note s 28(7) of the 1877 Act.
[41] The *Hynes* case at 219, Kenny J approving a passage from Fry, *Specific Performance* 6th Ed.
[42] *Smelter Corporation of Ireland Ltd v O'Driscoll* [1977] IR 305 at 311.
[43] *O'Rourke v Perceval* (1811) 2 Ball & Beatty 58 at 62.
[44] *Nolan v Graves* [1946] IR 376 at 391, per Haugh J.
[45] This is the second point considered at para **9.01** *post*.
[46] In Ch 9 below. Note that cases in which equity refuses specific performance do not fall within defined categories: para **9.01** *post*.
[47] *O'Neill v Ryan (No 3)* [1992] 1 IR 166 at 196. See also Costello J at 191.
[48] *Per* Costello J in *O'Neill's* case at 191.
[49] *Buckley v Irwin* [1960] NI 98 at 103.
[50] *Smelter Corporation of Ireland Ltd v O'Driscoll* [1977] IR 305 at 310-11; *McCrystal v O'Kane* [1986] NI 123 at 131-2. *Cf Smyth v Lynn* [1951] NI 69 at 76, 78.
[51] The *Smelter Corporation* case at 310-11. The Supreme Court did not formally set aside the contract but found "a fundamental unfairness" and ordered the return of all monies paid: p 311-2.

courts do not set aside the contract but in the exercise of the discretion do not decree specific performance of it either. Black LJ explained in *Conlon v Murray*:[52]

> "The remedy of specific performance still retains the character of an equitable remedy. It is not granted as of right but is a discretionary remedy which may be withheld in cases of a type where the court, having regard to the conduct of the parties and all the circumstances of the case, considers in its discretion that the remedy ought not to be granted. This discretion is not, of course, the arbitrary discretion of the individual judge but is a discretion to be exercised on the principles which have been worked out in a multitude of decided cases. And it is well established that there is a class of cases in which a contract may be such and entered into in such conditions that the court will not order it to be rescinded but, at the same time, looking to the substantial justice of the case, will not order it to be specifically performed."

It follows that when the aid of a court is sought by way of specific performance the principles of ethics have a more extensive sway than when a contract is sought to be rescinded.[53] By reason of the court's exercise of the discretion not to grant specific performance, a plaintiff may be denied specific performance but allowed the remedy of damages, although in practice this does not happen very often.[54] In ordinary cases of the sort where the remedy is available[55] justice is better done by carrying out the contract than by awarding damages.[56]

[1.08] In sales of land the "normal rule" is for the court to grant specific performance of a contract and in such a case the onus is on the defendant of establishing a ground or grounds upon which the relief should be refused.[57] The court must consider whether it should in the exercise of its discretion withhold from the plaintiff the "normal equitable remedy granted in this type of case, viz. specific performance of the contract".[58] The time at which the court should examine the contract for the purpose of considering which way to use its discretion is normally the time when the parties contracted.[59] If it thinks that the circumstances in which the contract was made were unfair, if they were in any way oppressive, if there was any advantage taken by one party of another the court has a jurisdiction and power to refuse to grant specific performance.[60] Changes occurring later making the contract less beneficial to one party are immaterial as a rule unless brought about by the action of the other party.[61] Thus, hardship arising after the date of the contract is unlikely to establish the type of case "in which the Court should intervene to deny the ordinary remedy to one of the contracting parties in what was, at the time, a perfectly fair and proper transaction".[62]

---

[52] [1958] NI 17 at 25.

[53] *Ibid*, citing Kerr on *Fraud and Mistake*, 7th Ed (1952) at 568. *Cf Buckley v Irwin* [1960] NI 98 at 103-5; *Smyth v Lynn* [1951] NI 69 at 76, 78.

[54] As in *White v McCooey* (HC) 26 April 1976, Gannon J, unrep at 33-35. It occurred in the High Court in *Holohan v Ardmayle Estates* (SC) 1 May 1967, unrep. See p 2 of the transcript. The Supreme Court was concerned only with issues about damages.

[55] On which see para **1.14-27** below.

[56] *Patrick v Williams* (1897) 31 ILTR 166 at 167.

[57] *McCrystal v O'Kane* [1986] NI 123 at 132.

[58] *Ibid* at 131.

[59] *Revell v Hussey* (1813) 2 Ball & Beatty 281 at 288-9.

[60] *Hoon v Nolan* (1966) 101 ILTR 99 at 104 (reversed on other grounds).

[61] *Lavan v Walsh* [1964] IR 87 at 102 (alleged hardship).

[62] *Roberts v O'Neill* [1983] IR 47 at 57, *per* McCarthy J.

Examples of points which may cause specific performance to be withheld include serious doubts about entitlement to use leasehold premises for the purpose for which they were being used in fact,[63] the facts that chattels are ordinary articles of commerce of no special value to the plaintiff and damages would fully compensate,[64] an undisclosed change of intention about access for traffic which would treble traffic interference with a vendor's retained lands,[65] suppression of a material ingredient in an agreement,[66] unfair statements or omissions in relation to a vendor's title,[67] and misleading material which may be less serious than that required to enable the misled party to rescind the contract.[68] Hardship may be a ground for exercising the discretion by refusing specific performance and leaving a plaintiff to his right to damages. In practice it is very difficult to prove the type of circumstances required.[69] The court will rarely take into account events occurring after the contract was made[70] and in any event it will have to balance the hardship alleged by the defendant against the hardship which the plaintiff would suffer if he is denied specific performance.[71] Laches is another important example of a factor which may lead a court to withhold specific performance.[72] It is very important to remember that the examples given are simply *examples*. The vital issue when the court is asked to exercise its discretion in favour of granting specific performance is likely to be whether it is fair to do so.[73] In considering that issue the court will have regard to the conduct of the parties and all the circumstances of the particular case.[74] It will reject any suggestion that the cases in which equity refuses the remedy of specific performance should be put into defined or rigid categories.[75] If the discretion is used in favour of the claimant and specific performance is granted the court has jurisdiction to attach conditions to the order.[76]

[1.09] Factors which have induced the courts to exercise the discretion by withholding the relief of specific performance while also dismissing the action, refusing damages or rescinding the contract have included an agreement by a defendant believing that she had no real option where the plaintiff accepted her agreement knowing that that was not so.[77] Other instances have been a snap bargain at an undervalue (not gross) from a vendor who needed some responsible independent advice,[78] a purchase from a 69-year-old woman in poor physical health rushed through with extraordinary haste,[79] concern about the policy

---

[63] *Ashe v Hogan* [1920] 1 IR 159 at 165 (V & P Summons).
[64] *Nesbitt & Co Ltd v McClure* (HC) NI 1970 No 267, Gibson J, at 9 (statutory right of specific performance under s 52 of the Sale of Goods Act 1893).
[65] *Minister for Education v North Star Ltd* (HC) Cir App, 12 January 1987, Lynch J, unrep at 5-6.
[66] *Ellard v Lord Llandaff* (1810) 1 Ball & Beatty 241 at 250-1.
[67] *Heffernan v Kavanagh* (HC) 14 November 1969, Pringle J, unrep at 14: on the facts the non-disclosure did not preclude the right to specific performance: p 15.
[68] *Molphy v Coyne* (1919) 53 ILTR 177 at 181 (V & P Summons).
[69] See the defence of hardship at para **9.38-41** *infra*.
[70] *Lavan v Walsh* [1964] IR 87 at 102.
[71] *O'Neill v Ryan (No 3)* [1992] 1 IR 166 at 192.
[72] This defence is considered at para **9.42-7** below.
[73] Note the passage quoted from Finlay CJ in para **1.05** above.
[74] *Conlon v Murray* [1958] NI 17 at 25.
[75] *Ibid* at 26.
[76] *McCrystal v O'Kane* [1986] NI 123 at 134.
[77] *Smelter Corporation of Ireland Ltd v O'Driscoll* [1977] IR 305 at 311-2, effective rescission by ordering the return of all money paid.
[78] *Buckley v Irwin* [1960] NI 98 at 104-5. The relief could have been refused even if the plaintiff and his associate were blameless: p 104.
[79] *Conlon v Murray* [1958] NI 17 at 26.

of acts of the Oireachtas[80] and abuse of confidence.[81] As in the last paragraph above, the point must be made that those instances are no more than examples. Also to be remembered is Black LJ's statement that there are cases where a court will not order the rescission of a contract but will not order it to be specifically performed either.[82] Where it is clear that the discretion would have to be used against granting specific performance, the court may take the drastic step of ordering the vacation of a *lis pendens*[83] and, probably, staying or striking out the claim as an abuse of the process of the court.[84]

Inadequacy of damages

[1.10] If adequate relief at law can be obtained, it is the duty of a court of equity to dismiss a claim for specific performance. As Plunkett LC explained:[85]

> "A number of cases have been cited on both sides, and the result of them all is, not that wherever there is a relief at Law, relief will be refused in Equity; but that when the relief at Law is equally beneficial and equally effectual with that which may be obtained in Equity, there the Court will refuse to interfere."

For example, it is much more satisfactory to decree specific performance of an agreement to pay a personal annuity than to leave the beneficiary to the remedies at law of either bringing four actions a year for quarterly payments of the annuity or recovering damages in a single action for all the breaches that might occur during the relevant life or lives.[86] The long established view of the courts that damages are an adequate remedy in certain types of case has been a major factor in making specific performance usually or always unavailable in such claims. Thus, specific performance of building contracts usually is not decreed although one major exception is recognised.[87] Also it would be very difficult indeed to persuade a court to give specific performance of a contract to make a loan.[88]

In most cases of those sorts where specific performance is likely to be available[89] the only relevant relief at law for purposes of comparison will be damages and the issue therefore will be whether damages will be equally beneficial and equally effectual as specific performance. The test as stated by Lord Redesdale in 1805 was whether the plaintiff could show "that satisfaction in the form of damages is not an adequate remedy for him"[90] or that damages "would not answer the intention of the parties in making the contract, and a specific performance, as far as the contract can be performed, is therefore essential to justice".[91]

Certainty of contract

[1.11] If a contract is "completely uncertain" it is equally void at law and in equity.[92] Occasionally there is a degree of uncertainty which will lose the right to specific

---

[80] *Traynor v Duffy* [1947] IJR 9 at 11.
[81] *Costigan v Hastler* (1804) 2 Schoales & Lefroy 160 at 165.
[82] *Conlon's* case at 25.
[83] *Culhane v Hewson* [1979] IR 8 at 14. See also para **10.10-14** *post*.
[84] On that relief see para **10.03-05** *post*.
[85] *Swift v Swift* (1841) 3 IR Eq 267 at 275.
[86] *Ibid* at 275-6; see comments on this case by Jones & Goodhart, *Specific Performance* (1986) at 126.
[87] See para **1.21-2** *infra*.
[88] Para **1.19** *infra*.
[89] On which see paras **1.14-27** *infra*.
[90] *Harnett v Yeilding* (1805) 2 Schoales & Lefroy 549 at 560; *cf* 553.
[91] *Davis v Hone* (1805) 2 Schoales & Lefroy 341 at 347.
[92] *Harnett v Yeilding* (1805) 2 Schoales and Lefroy 549 at 555.

performance without also destroying remedies at law. As Lord Redesdale pointed out in 1805,[93]

> "...if it is certain to a degree, but doubtful as to the extent, equity would, I think, act infinitely more wisely in leaving the party to the old remedy by action for damages, than to run the hazard of doing injustice, in doing what is said to be more complete justice, by decreeing a specific performance."

The burden is on the plaintiff to satisfy a court of an agreement, the terms of which "are sufficiently certain to justify a decree for specific performance".[94] He may expect to fail if he does not satisfy the court of the certainty of the material terms even though it may believe that *some* complete and binding agreement was reached.[95] Leaving a vital matter such as the price or method of ascertaining it "shrouded in doubt and ambiguities" makes it "quite inappropriate for the court to seek to enforce the contract which the parties have left so vague".[96] A court may accept that a clause should be construed in such a way as to give effect to the intention of the parties if at all possible[97] but if an agreed mechanism for fixing the price is unworkable there is no enforceable contract.[98] If there is no evidence on a vital term the court will not direct the trial of an issue to ascertain that term.[99] Lack of certainty can have widespread effects. For example, lack of definition of what needs to be done is a major factor in the reluctance of the courts to order specific performance of building contracts.[100]

Sometimes the uncertain element in a contract is a severable term entirely in favour of one party; that party may waive it[101] and ask for specific performance of the rest of the agreement.[102] In other cases it may be possible to avoid the problem by interpreting an ambiguous condition in favour of the purchaser.[103] The court also has jurisdiction to attach conditions to an order for specific performance and this power may be used in order to deal with a slight doubt arising over a term in a contract.[104] If an allegedly uncertain contract has been partially performed it is the duty of the court to struggle against the difficulty arising from the vagueness of the terms.[105] However, there is a limit to this duty and the struggle may not be successful. Even with part performance present, the terms of the contract must be made out satisfactorily to the court.[106]

Supervision by the Court

[1.12] The courts have been very slow in the past to decree specific performance where enforcement of the order would need much supervision by the courts. This has been a factor working against the granting of the relief in building contract cases.[107] The basis for

---

[93] *Ibid.*
[94] *Williams v Kenneally* (1912) 46 ILTR 292 at 294.
[95] *Ibid* (problems over commencement date and payment of rates).
[96] *Lonergan v McCartney* [1983] NI 129 at 135.
[97] *Carr v Phelan* [1976/7] ILRM 149 at 154.
[98] *Ibid* at 156; *Lonergan's* case at 134-5.
[99] *Savage v Carroll* (1810) 1 Ball & Beatty 265 at 283-4.
[100] *Rushbrooke v O'Sullivan* [1908] 1 IR 232 at 234-5; on building contracts see para **1.21-2** *post*.
[101] On this see para **3.29-30** and **5.14** *infra*.
[102] *Gordon v Gordon* [1951] IR 301 at 306 (security to be given).
[103] *Allman v McDaniel* [1912] 1 IR 467 at 472 - property sold pursuant to court order so the conditions of sale probably were treated as drafted by the vendor and the "contra proferentem" rule applied.
[104] *McCrystal v O'Kane* [1986] NI 123 at 134-5.
[105] *Hart v Hart* (1881) 18 Ch D 670 at 685.
[106] *Mortal v Lyons* (1858) 8 Ir Ch R 112 at 118.
[107] *Rushbrooke v O'Sullivan* [1908] 1 IR 232 at 234-5.

the attitude has been that the court cannot oversee the performance of the services but a modern Irish decision has shown that this is not a "rigid rule."[108] If, in fact, there is no reason for the court to oversee the performance the rule is not applicable anyway.[109] The modern tendency in England rejects the notion that there is any such rule.[110] A recent judgment suggests that whether or not an order for specific performance should be made depends on the following considerations:

(*a*) is there a sufficient definition of what has to be done in order to comply with the order of the court;

(*b*) whether enforcing compliance involves superintendence by the court to an unacceptable degree; and

(*c*) what are the respective prejudices or hardships that will be suffered by the parties if the order is made or not made?[111]

Pointless or unnecessary orders

[1.13] The court will not order specific performance if it is pointless to do so. It will not lend its assistance by granting specific performance of an agreement which the defendant is not able to perform but will leave the plaintiff to his right to damages.[112] Where a plaintiff was entitled to enforce an agreement for the grant of a lease but the term of the intended lease would have expired when judgment is given it may be pointless to make the order.[113] In such a case the court usually can do justice by an award of damages which may take into account breaches of the terms of the lease if it had been granted.[114] Perhaps specific performance might be given on special facts if the execution of a lease for the expired term or availability of agreed covenants made a significant difference. There is an Irish practice that when specific performance of an agreement for lease is granted, the court will direct that the lease be ante-dated so that the parties can rely on their rights at law on the covenants in the lease in case there has been a breach of them by anticipation.[115] A court may consider it unnecessary to order specific performance of an agreement to surrender a lease when the term had expired at the time of judgment.[116]

Usually a court will refuse specific performance of a partnership agreement. To compel an unwilling person to become a partner with another would hardly be conducive to the well being of the latter. If the partnership was to be at will the decree would be nugatory anyway because either party could dissolve the partnership the moment after the decree was made.[117] However, a partnership agreement which was to be incorporated in a deed or was not to be terminated earlier than a certain time can be the subject of

---

[108] *Lift Manufacturers Ltd v Irish Life Assurance Co Ltd* [1979] ILRM 277 at 280.
[109] *Ibid.*
[110] Snell's *Equity*, 29th Ed (1990) at 594-5; Jones & Goodhart, *Specific Performance* (1986) at 28-33; *cf* the discussion of authorities by Melvyn Davies J in *Posner v Scott-Lewis* [1986] 3 All ER 513 at 519-21.
[111] *Posner's* case at 521 (covenant to provide resident porter); *cf Ryan v Mutual Tontine Westminster Chambers Association* (1893) 1 Ch 116.
[112] *Bayly v Tyrrell* (1813) 2 Ball & Beatty 358 at 361.
[113] *Brownlee v Duggan* [1976] 5 NIJB at 11.
[114] In *Brownlee's* case Murray J gave damages for breach of covenants for quiet enjoyment which s 41 of Deasy's Act would imply: p 11-12.
[115] *McIlroy v Trail* [1898] IR 1 459 at 461.
[116] *Reg Armstrong Motors Ltd v Texaco (Ireland) Ltd* (HC) 21 December 1971, unrep, at 18. Pringle J seemed willing to order specific performance, if asked: *ibid.* The lease had valuable statutory rights (p 3-4) but the defendants seemed unaware of that (pp 16, 17-18).
[117] See Lindley & Banks, *Partnership*, 16th Ed (1990) at paras 23.40-44.

specific performance on suitable facts though the alternative remedy of damages often will be more appropriate.[118] An executed partnership agreement is unlikely to be enforced by specific performance if the relief sought is in substance a claim for money or for damages.[119] A factor in the unwillingness of the courts to decree specific performance in some cases of contracts for loans[120] is that it would be futile to do so if the lender could call in the money at once.[121] If there is no suggestion that a party will fail to pay money due or to become due from him it is unnecessary for the court to make any order in that connection.[122] The fact that a plaintiff succeeds on the only point in issue in an action for specific performance does not entitle him automatically to a decree; the court may still not feel satisfied on the facts that an order for specific performance is necessary or even appropriate.[123]

WHERE SPECIFIC PERFORMANCE IS AVAILABLE

[1.14] The remedy of specific performance is available only in certain types of case. It must not be assumed, however, that the relief will be obtained in every case within the relevant areas. Even in a case of a type suitable in principle for the remedy the claim may be defeated on one of many possible grounds, eg, by one of the defences mentioned later in Chapter 9, by the exercise of the discretion inherent in the nature of the remedy or[124] by a plea of the Statute of Frauds[125].

Sales, agreements for lease and options

[1.15] There is no doubt that the normal rule is for the court to grant specific performance of a contract for the sale of land.[126] In such a case the onus is on the defendant of establishing a ground or grounds on which the remedy should be refused.[127] Specific performance of a covenant for further assurance in an assignment of a leasehold interest may be decreed.[128] And the relief is available in the case of a contract for the exchange of land.[129] It is also available to the holder of an option to purchase land.[130] In some Irish cases options to purchase land have been protected by seeking declarations.[131] In another case an option for a "sale" to be carried out by way of a sublease at a fine of £1,720 and yearly rent of £12.50 for the entire of the residue of the landlord's 150-year term less one day was upheld by the Supreme Court.[132] Maguire CJ held that on payment of the agreed sum

---

118 *Crowley v O'Sullivan* [1900] 2 IR 478 at 485, 487-9.
119 *Bagnell v Edwards* (1876) IR 10 Eq 215 at 218.
120 See para **1.19** *infra.*
121 *Gorringe v Land Improvement Society* [1899] 1 IR 142 at 151.
122 *Kennedy v Mangan* (HC) 15 May 1986, Costello J, unrep at 8.
123 *Hickey v Keating* (HC) 25 January 1980, McWilliam J, unrep at 5: the point concerned the effect on a 28-day notice to complete of a Vendor & Purchaser Summons issued while the time was running.
124 On which see para **1.06-9** *supra.*
125 Considered in Ch 5 *post.*
126 *McCrystal v O'Kane* [1986] NI 123 at 132; cf *Roberts v O'Neill* [1983] IR 47 at 57. On the Statute of Frauds see para **5.06** *post.*
127 *McCrystal's* case at 132; *Broughton v Snook* [1938] Ch 505 at 513.
128 *Maguire v Armstrong* (1814) 2 Ball & Beatty 538.
129 *Lowry v Reid* [1927] NI 142 at 157; cf *Gervais v Edwards* (1842) 2 Drury & Warren 80 at 83-4.
130 *McCarthy & Stone Ltd v Hodge & Co Ltd* [1971] 2 All ER 973 at 980.
131 *Sunnybank Inn Ltd v East Coast Inns Ltd* (HC) 11 November 1979, Hamilton J, unrep at 10, 16; *Massarella v Massarella* (HC) 10 July 1980, Keane J, unrep at 27-8 (right of pre-emption); cf *Fitzachary v Phoenix Construction Co Ltd* (HC) 23 June 1970, Teevan J, unrep; *Cassidy v Baker* (1969) 103 ILTR 40.
132 *Jameson v Squire* [1948] IR 153 at 161, 163-4; 175.

the defendant should execute the agreed sublease[133] and the other three members of the court also held that the plaintiff was entitled to exercise the option.[134] An option to repurchase also may be enforced by specific performance.[135] The holder of an option to purchase his landlord's freehold reversion who exercises the option but then fails to complete may himself be sued for specific performance.[136] If he does not comply with that order he risks the usual steps being taken to enforce it[137] or perhaps an order rescinding the agreement brought into being by the exercise of the option.[138]

[1.16] Probably it is also the "normal rule" that specific performance will be granted to enforce an agreement for a lease or tenancy which, unlike a licence, creates an interest in land.[139] A contract for a lease has been held to be an agreement touching an interest in land and therefore one requiring compliance with the Statute of Frauds.[140] The special attractiveness of a piece of land for an intending lessee would seem generally similar to that of the same property to a purchaser and thus likely to make damages an inadequate remedy. In any event, specific performance of an agreement for a lease or tenancy is certainly *available*. Once there was a view that specific performance would not be granted to enforce the grant of tenancies for short terms. It was said in the Courts of Chancery that there could not be a decree for the specific performance of an agreement from year to year upon the ground that it was inconceivable that a case could be heard within a twelvemonth.[141] That notion has died and a court will now make an order in a case of a short tenancy, at any rate before the intended term would have expired.[142] Specific performance will also be decreed to force a landlord to renew a term of years where he has covenanted to do so as often as he gets a renewal himself from his own landlord.[143] The same applies to covenants for the grant of a new lease for the remainder of the lessor's term[144] and apparently also to an option for the "sale" of the landlord's reversion by a long sublease at a substantial fine and small yearly rent.[145]

Licences

[1.17] As we shall see later,[146] licences[147] have provided some good examples of the granting of injunctions[148] to protect parties' rights. The speed of the procedures for

---

[133] *Ibid* at 161.

[134] Murnaghan J at 163-4, O'Byrne J concurring and Black J at 175.

[135] *O'Hara v Flint* [1979] ILRM 156 (consent order noted at 158; the material in the judgment shows that the consent was right).

[136] *Croft Inns Ltd v Scott* [1982] NI 95.

[137] On which see para **8.28** *post*.

[138] As occurred in the *Croft Inns* case.

[139] *Irish Shell & BP Ltd v Costello* [1981] ILRM 66 at 70; see also Wylie, *Irish Landlord and Tenant Law*, paras 3.09-10.

[140] *Bentham v Hardy* (1843) 6 ILR 179 at 182-3. On contracts for leases and the Statute of Frauds see para **5.08** *post*.

[141] *Gilbey v Cossey* [1911-3] All ER Rep 644 at 645 (not the judge's view!).

[142] *Ibid*; *Verrall v Great Yarmouth BC* [1980] 1 All ER at 843; 846-7; see para **1.13** *supra* on the situation where the term would have expired.

[143] *Revell v Hussey* (1813) 2 Ball & Beatty 280 at 288-9; *cf Evans v Walshe* (1805) 2 Schoales & Lefroy 519.

[144] *Hughes Ltd v Hughes Dickson & Co Ltd* [1923] 1 IR 121 at 123-3.

[145] *Jameson v Squire* [1948] IR 153; see para **1.15** *supra*.

[146] Para **2.06** *post*.

[147] As distinct from tenancies: on drink licences see para **1.18** *infra*.

[148] As in *Woods v Donnelly* [1982] NI 257 at 263-4; *Whipp v Mackey* (1927) IR 372 at 388; *Millenium Productions Ltd v Winter Garden Theatre (London) Ltd* (1946) considered by Hutton J in the *Woods* case at 264-5.

seeking injunctions and in particular the scope for getting interlocutory injunctions[149] are very useful when the time for getting relief is limited or the duration of the proposed licence is short. In a recent Irish case[150] an injunction was granted on judicial review to restrain a local authority from breaking or refusing to fulfil a contract for the hiring of a town hall to a political party for its annual conference. The purported termination of the hiring contract by the town clerk was brought about by a resolution of the council which was political in nature and had no bearing on the contract *per se*. Since the political party was entitled to pursue any remedy lawfully open to it to enforce the contract the adequacy or otherwise of damages as an alternative remedy was irrelevant.[151] In a modern English case on very similar facts[152] specific performance was decreed. An argument by the defence that the hiring was only for two days for an annual conference and as such a "transient interest" in respect of which the relief should not be granted was rejected.[153] The Supreme Court has decreed specific performance of an agreement for a licence entitling a party to enter upon land for the purpose of building houses on it.[154] In another modern Irish case the plaintiff has been held entitled to specific performance of an agreement for a licence or franchise to use part of the defendant's property for a period of five years.[155] There is a difficulty over attempts to assign, charge or otherwise dispose of the benefit of the rights granted by a licence. A genuine licence is a personal privilege and not capable of being assigned or charged.[156] Accordingly the nature of a licence should make it impossible to get specific performance of any purported contract to deal with it.[157]

[1.18] Another type of licence well known to property lawyers is that permitting the sale of alcoholic drink. It has long been accepted that a licence to sell intoxicating liquor is inalienable and must be attached to premises.[158] It cannot be sold as an item of property with a viable existence separate from the premises.[159] Accordingly, specific performance of an agreement for the sale of a licence cannot be obtained. However, an agreement by the holder of a licence for its *extinguishment* is enforceable and, if no other problem arises, specific performance should be available. An agreement of that sort might recite the agreement of the parties, that the licensee holds the licence, that it is subsisting and will be kept in force, the intended application to the court for a new licence, the description of the premises to which it is attached and the agreement to consent to its extinguishment.[160] When licensed premises are sold, both parties normally take it for granted that whoever has the premises should have the licence. Therefore the contract is likely to be complete without an express term about the licence and it does not have to be covered in a note or memorandum to satisfy the Statute of Frauds.[161]

---

[149] On which see paras **2.09-15** (prohibitory), **2.16-7** (mandatory) and **2.18-20** (*Mareva*) *post.*
[150] *Browne v Dundalk UDC* [1993] 2 IR 512 at 522-3.
[151] *Ibid* at 523.
[152] *Verrall v Great Yarmouth BC* [1980] 1 All ER 839.
[153] Denning MR at 843 and Roskill LJ at 846.
[154] *Neville & Sons Ltd v Guardian Builders Ltd* 27 July 1994, unrep.
[155] *Kennedy v Mangan* (HC) 15 May 1986, Costello J, unrep at 7-8.
[156] *Irish Shell & BP Ltd v Costello* [1981] ILRM 66 at 70, 71.
[157] *Cf* the position about a drinks licence: para **1.18** *infra.*
[158] *Macklin v Graecen & Co Ltd* [1983] IR 61 at 66.
[159] *Re Sherry-Brennan* [1979] ILRM 113 at 118.
[160] *Per* Griffin J in *Macklin's* case at 66.
[161] *White v McCooey* [1976] ILRM 72 at 78. See also para **5.09** *post.*

Contracts for loans

[1.19] An Irish court was satisfied recently[162] based on old English case law[163] that the court cannot and should not grant specific performance of a contract to advance money even when that is in the form of a contract by the alleged intending lender to enter into a legal mortgage. A later Irish case held that a "Letter of Commitment" and ancillary documentation constituted an enforceable contract to advance money[164] but there was no question of specific performance as the only issues for the court were whether there was a valid subsisting contract and, if so, whether the defendants were liable in damages for breach of it.[165] The approach of the courts to this seems to be based largely on the view that damages would be an adequate remedy. Futility may be an element also. Porter MR explained:[166]

> "As a general proposition it is correct to say that a mere agreement to lend money, even upon security, will not be specifically performed. If money is lent, the lender may call it in again, and therefore specific performance would be futile. Money compensation in such a case affords an adequate, and, indeed, the best remedy, and goes nearer to a complete *restitutio in integrum* than the enforcement of a loan which the lender might straightaway proceed to require back, leaving the borrower in no better position after the interference of the court."[167]

Perhaps exceptions will be considered on special facts. An intending borrower might get specific performance if the intending lender has agreed to advance money on specified security, the terms of the deal do not let him call in the loan in the absence of default and the consequences of the money not being produced are serious enough for the borrower that damages are not an adequate remedy. Of course, a lender who has advanced his money can get specific performance against a borrower to make him grant the agreed security.[168]

Contracts for services

[1.20] The traditional view has been that specific performance of a contract for services will not be decreed on the ground that the court cannot oversee the performance of the services.[169] It has been said that a contract of hiring and service is of so personal and confidential a character that the court refuses to entertain jurisdiction on such contracts.[170] The rule has been described by an Irish judge as "not rigid".[171] If there is no reason for the court to oversee the performance of the services the rule is not applicable.[172] In England the "so-called rule" that contracts for personal services or involving the continuous performance of services will not be specifically enforced has been described as "plainly

---

[162] *Duggan v Allied Irish Building Society* (HC) 4 March 1976, Finlay P, unrep at 15.
[163] *Rogers v Challis* (1859) 27 Beav 175 and *Larios v Bonany & Gurety* (1873) LR 5 PC 346.
[164] *Shannonside Holdings (US) v Associated Mortgage Investors* (HC) 12 March 1980, Doyle J, unrep at 55.
[165] *Ibid* at 2.
[166] *Gorringe v Land Improvement Society* [1899] 1 IR 142 at 151.
[167] He goes on to consider the views of the House of Lords in *South African Territories (Limited) v Wallington* [1898] AC 309.
[168] *The Regina Coeli* [1976] 5 NIJB at 40; *cf Re Lynch Monahan & O'Brien Ltd* (HC) 14 October 1986, Costello J, unrep at 13-14.
[169] *Lift Manufacturers Ltd v Irish Life Assurance Co Ltd* [1979] ILRM 277 at 280.
[170] *Gillis v McGhee* (1862) 13 Ir Ch R 48 at 57 citing Fry on *Specific Performance*.
[171] The *Lift Manufacturers Ltd* case at 280.
[172] *Ibid.*

not absolute and without exception".[173] In general, no doubt, the "inconvenience and mischief" of decreeing specific performance of most contracts of personal service or for the continuous performance of services will greatly outweigh the advantages and specific performance will be refused.[174] Possibly it will be less difficult to get specific performance of an agreement to procure the provision of services than one which requires the performance of personal services or any continuous series of acts.[175]

Building contracts

[1.21] The views of courts of equity as to enforcing covenants to build and covenants to repair have not always been consistent. In earlier days they appear to have enforced them.[176] However, it became clearly settled[177] that usually the courts will not enforce such contracts though there is an important exception when a plaintiff establishes three vital points. As Romer LJ explained:[178]

> "There is no doubt that as a general rule the Court will not enforce specific performance of a building contract, but an exception from the rule has been recognised. It has, I think, for some time been held that, in order to bring himself within that exception, a plaintiff must establish three things. The first is that the building work, of which he seeks to enforce the performance is defined by the contract; that is to say, that the particulars of the work are so far definitely ascertained that the Court can sufficiently see what is the exact nature of the work of which it is asked to order the performance. The second is that the plaintiff has a substantial interest in having the contract performed, which is of such a nature that he cannot adequately be compensated for breach of the contract by damages."[179]

The third thing which Romer LJ said had to be established was that the defendant "has by the contract obtained possession of land on which the work is contracted to be done".[180] That reference to the contract probably was too restrictive. It has been clarified by a later English case[181] and it is clear in England now that the defendant need not have possession under the particular contract. If he has possession and the other two points are met specific performance will be granted. Indeed Farwell J has said that "the mere fact that the defendant has not got possession of land on which the work is contracted to be done is not necessarily a complete bar to the court's granting specific performance".[182] Presumably it suffices if the defendant can get possession. Of course, if he cannot get possession it may be impossible for him to carry out the contract and in such a case the court would not grant specific performance.[183] It has been suggested that the reason for

---

[173] *CH Giles & Co Ltd v Morris* [1972] 1 All ER 960 at 969, Megarry J.
[174] *Ibid* at 970.
[175] *Ibid*; *Posner v Scott-Lewis* [1986] 3 All ER 513 at 520-1.
[176] As noted by Meredith MR in *Rushbrooke v O'Sullivan* [1908] 1 IR 232 at 234. In *Treacy v Dwyer Nolan Developments Ltd* [1979] ILRM 163 it was accepted by the defendant that the plaintiff was to have a decree of specific performance of an agreement to build and sell a house - the only issue was the plaintiff's liability to pay interest at the contract rate.
[177] *Per* Meredith MR, *ibid.*
[178] *Wolverhampton Corporation v Emmons* [1901] 1 QB 515 at 524-5.
[179] That passage was approved by Meredith MR in *Rushbrooke v O'Sullivan* [1908] 1 IR 232 at 236.
[180] *Not* quoted by Meredith MR in *Rushbrooke's* case.
[181] *Carpenters Estates Ltd v Davies* [1940] 1 All ER 13 at 17-18.
[182] The *Carpenters Estates Ltd* case at 18.
[183] *Ibid* at 17.

the requirement that the defendant has possession is that otherwise there would be no reason why the plaintiff should not carry out the work himself.[184]

[1.22] The requirement that any works needing to be done are "so far definitely ascertained that the Court can sufficiently see what is the exact nature of the work of which it is asked to order the performance"[185] is not extremely demanding. If a plaintiff's architect prepared his plans and specifications and said "there is what you must do: you must take down here; you must rebuild and repair there" the works probably would be sufficiently ascertained.[186] A railway company has been ordered to perform its agreement to replace a siding and put it into working order where the ground on which the siding was to be reconstructed was clearly indicated in correspondence.[187] Sometimes injunctions have been granted to uphold certain rights given by building contracts.[188]

Shares

[1.23] The courts will not decree specific performance of a contract for the purchase of stocks or shares which are readily available on the market. If there is a free market in shares damages would normally be a fully adequate remedy.[189] However, specific performance has been ordered of a contract for the purchase of a substantial block of shares in a publicly quoted company in the course of a "take over battle"[190] and a purchase of all the issued share capital in a private company.[191] In the case of a sale of shares in a private company the court is likely to give directions about the observation of the provisions in the company's articles of association about transfers of shares including any duty to offer them first to other shareholders.[192] A vendor who is also a director of the relevant company probably will be bound to vote in favour of the transfer of the shares and the registration of the purchaser as holder.[193] However, a sale of shares by a vendor not having control of the company is unlikely to imply any undertaking by him that it would register the transfer.[194] Sales of shares in companies are outside the Statute of Frauds even if the only substantial asset of the company is land.[195] In deciding how to exercise its discretion to grant or withhold specific performance of a contract for the sale of shares, a court may take into account factors such as the hardship which would be suffered by one side or the other if an order for specific performance is granted or

---

[184] Keane, *Equity and the Law of Trusts in the Republic of Ireland* (1988) para 16.04.

[185] Romer LJ's first point in the *Wolverhampton Corporation* case.

[186] *Rushbrooke v O'Sullivan* [1908] 1 IR 232 at 236.

[187] *Todd & Co v Midland Great Western Railway of Ireland Co* (1881) 9 LRI 85 at 104-5. To an extent the courts have treated contracts by railway companies to take lands on terms that they will do certain works as a distinct class: see *Ryan v Mutual Tontine Westminster Chambers Assoc* [1893] 1 Ch 116 at 124, 128.

[188] See para **2.05** *post*; on interlocutory injunctions see para **2.09-15**.

[189] *Chinn v Collins* [1979] 2 All ER 529 at 538 (Buckley LJ) and 544 (Goff LJ). An appeal to the House of Lords succeeded on the facts of the case: [1981] 1 All ER 189.

[190] *Pernod Ricard v FII (Fyffes) Plc* (HC) 21 October 1988, Costello J, unrep, affirmed by (SC) 11 November 1988, unrep.

[191] *Lee & Co (Dublin) Ltd v Egan (Wholesale) Ltd* (HC) 27 April 1978, Kenny J, unrep at 8. In this case the secondnamed defendant could only sell 7,100 shares out of 8,802 and Kenny J held that the plaintiffs could either refuse to purchase the 7,100 and sue for damages or could take the 7,100 and claim damages for breach of warranty of authority in relation to the rest: p 9.

[192] *Lee & Co's* case at 9-10 and supplemental judgment of 23 May 1979.

[193] *Ibid* at 10.

[194] *Casey v Bentley* [1902] 1 IR 376.

[195] *Guardian Builders Ltd v Sleecon Ltd* (HC) 18 August 1988, Blayney J, unrep at 14-15. See also para **5.10** *post*.

withheld, the likelihood of fluctuations in the value of the shares, the fact that the plaintiff has been dismissed from his job with the relevant company and his lack of control over it.[196] It may also take into account the fact that the *defendant* has laid stress on the desirability of buying out the plaintiff.[197]

Arbitration

[1.24] Probably the courts of equity had no jurisdiction to compel a party to an arbitration agreement to actually go to arbitration.[198] However, the courts now have power to appoint an arbitrator, umpire or third arbitrator once there is an arbitration agreement.[199] In many cases there is a satisfactory indirect way of making sure that a party abides by his agreement. If he (or anyone claiming through or under him) institutes proceedings in any court in respect of any matter agreed to be referred to arbitration, any party to the proceedings may apply to the court to stay the proceedings.[200] The court must stay the proceedings unless it is satisfied that the arbitration agreement is null and void, inoperative or incapable of being performed or that there is not in fact any dispute between the parties with regard to the matter agreed to be referred to arbitration.[201] This provision curtails the court's discretion as to whether or not it should stay proceedings much more tightly than formerly.[202] It must stay the proceedings even though there has been "inexcusable delay" by the party seeking the stay but if that party continues his delay the arbitration might become inoperative or incapable of being performed in which event the stay could be removed.[203] The power to stay proceedings has been applied to a claim for specific performance.[204]

An arbitrator's award binds a party only by virtue of his contract to go to arbitration.[205] If the matter deals with an interest in land that contract must satisfy the Statute of Frauds.[206] However, not everything connected with land is necessarily an interest in it. For example, a claim for damages sustained by a party in consequence of a road having been made through his land is not one for an interest in land and therefore a submission to arbitration over that does not need to be in writing.[207] Unless a contrary intention appears in an arbitration agreement, an arbitrator himself has the same power as the High Court to order specific performance of any contract other than a contract relating to land or any interest in land.[208]

Other cases

[1.25] Specific performance has been decreed in a claim on foot of a contract for the creation of a rentcharge[209] and one on foot of an agreement for the payment of a personal

---

[196] *O'Neill v Ryan (No 3)* [1992] 1 IR 166 at 192.

[197] *Ibid* at 196.

[198] *Re Smith & Service and Nelson & Sons* (1890) 25 QBD 545; [1886-90] All ER Rep 1091. Lindley LJ could not see why specific performance of an obligation to appoint an arbitrator should have been always refused.

[199] Section 18 of the Arbitration Act 1954.

[200] Section 5 of the Arbitration Act 1980 replacing s 12 of the Arbitration Act 1954.

[201] *Ibid.*

[202] *O'Mahony v Lysaght* [1988] IR 29 at 30.

[203] *Ibid* at 30-31.

[204] *Geraghty v Rohan Industrial Estates Ltd* [1988] IR 419 at 432.

[205] *Johnston v McAllister* (1835) Jones 499 at 503.

[206] *Ibid*; *cf Gillanders v Lord Rossmore* (1835) Jones 504.

[207] *Gillanders'* case: oral extension of time for award valid: p 508.

[208] Section 26 of the 1954 Act.

[209] *Gorringe v The Land Improvement Society* [1899] 1 IR 142 at 155-6.

annuity.[210] A right to enter and remove timber has been protected by an injunction restraining a purchaser with notice of the right from interfering with the removal of the timber.[211] It seems that specific performance could be awarded in such a case.[212] An agreement to leave property by will can be enforced by compelling the personal representatives to deal with the property as if the promisor had made the agreed disposition by will.[213] Where a plaintiff gave up his own property to his detriment on the faith of his mother's representations that she would leave other property to him by will there was a "parol contract for the specific performance of which he was entitled in equity to a decree to carry those representations into execution".[214] The agreement relied on must be more than a mere expression of intention.[215] English case law shows that specific performance will be awarded in contracts for the sale of chattels only if there is something special about the articles.[216] The relief has been given in an Irish case involving a "trade in" of a motor car[217] possibly under a special statutory provision.[218] The relief will sometimes be available in partnership matters though the "general rule" is that the court will not order the specific performance of an agreement for partnership.[219] In some cases it would be futile[220] and in others an order for payment of money or for damages would be adequate.[221]

Composite contracts

[1.26] Difficulty may arise where a composite and indivisible contract for sale includes an item in respect of which specific performance is normally available and another in respect of which it is not. A court cannot give specific performance of a contract unless it can execute every part of it; it cannot give "a partial execution of the contract".[222] A sale of a farm and a tractor was considered in one modern Irish case but the case was decided on another point.[223] The defendant conceded that there was power to grant specific performance of the contract including the sale of the tractor but argued that the court should not do so in the absence of special circumstances. The plaintiff accepted that the court could not apportion part of the purchase price to the land and give specific performance of that part of the deal.[224] In an older English case[225] the plaintiff agreed to grant the defendant a lease of a coal wharf provided the latter employed him throughout the currency of the lease and paid him a commission on sales of coal. The court refused

---

210 *Swift v Swift* (1841) 3 IR Eq 267 at 275-7.
211 *O'Hanlon v Murdock* [1901] 1 IR 122 at 127-8.
212 *Jones v Earl of Tankerville* [1909] 2 Ch 440 at 445. A claim for specific performance was made in *McNeill v Richards* [1899] 1 IR 79 but the parties agreed at hearing that damages should be awarded: p 82.
213 *Lowry v Reid* [1927] NI 142 at 152-3, 160-1.
214 *Lowry's* case *per* Moore LCJ at 152 (part performance an issue).
215 *Mackey v Jones* (1958) 93 ILTR 177 at 178.
216 Jones & Goodhart *Specific Performance* (1986) p 112-7; Snell's *Equity* 29th Ed (1990) p 586-7.
217 *Clarke v Reilly & Sons* (1962) 96 ILTR 96; unusual facts.
218 Sale of Goods Act 1893 s 52; adequacy of damages not canvassed.
219 Lindley & Banks, *Partnership* 16th Ed (1990) at 23.40.
220 See para **1.13** above.
221 *Bagnell v Edwards* (1876) IR 10 Eq 215 at 218; *Crowley v O'Sullivan* [1900] 2 IR 478 at 485, 487-9. See Lindley & Banks, *op cit* para 23.41-4 for cases in which specific performance or an injunction may be available.
222 *Gervais v Edwards* (1842) 2 Drury & Warren 80 at 83.
223 *Buckley v Irwin* [1960] NI 98 at 105.
224 *Ibid. Cf Re Sherry-Brennan* [1979] ILRM 113 at 118.
225 *Ogden v Fossick* (1862) 4 De GF & J 426 considered by Keane, *Equity and the Law of Trusts in Ireland* (1988) at para 16.08.

specific performance; although the agreement for lease could have been specifically enforced if it had stood on its own the agreement to employ the plaintiff could not.[226] The modern tendency in England has been to apply this principle less rigidly.[227] It should not be assumed that as soon as any element of personal service or continuous services can be discerned in a contract the court will automatically refuse specific performance. Megarry J said this:[228]

> "The obligation to enter into a service agreement is merely one part of a contract which deals with many other matters; and that obligation is the only part of that complex which is said not to be specifically enforceable. Now there is authority for saying that the mere presence in a contract of one provision which by itself would not be specifically enforceable (because for example it requires the performance of personal services) does not prevent the contract as a whole from being specifically enforced... In such cases, the contract must be regarded as a whole, and the court may refuse to let the disadvantages and difficulties of specifically enforcing the obligation to perform personal services outweigh the suitability of the rest of the contract for specific performance, and the desirability of the contract as a whole being enforced. After all, *pacta sunt servanda*."[229]

And a little later:[230]

> "In general, no doubt, the inconvenience and mischief of decreeing specific performance of most of such contracts[231] will greatly outweigh the advantages, and specific performance will be refused. But I do not think that it should be assumed that as soon as any element of personal service or continuous services can be discerned in a contract the court will, without more, refuse specific performance. Of course, a requirement for the continuous performance of services has the disadvantage that repeated breaches may engender repeated applications to the court for enforcement. But so may many injunctions; and the prospects of repetition, although an important consideration, ought not to be allowed to negative a right. As is so often the case in equity, the matter is one of the balance of advantage and disadvantage in the particular obligations in question; and the fact that the balance will usually lie on one side does not turn this probability into a rule."[232]

[1.27] Where certain things are to be done at once and others are dependent on future contingencies the court is likely to find it impossible to give specific performance.[233] However, if there is agreement on a contract being performed by stages it is likely to be enforceable.[234] If payment of a purchase price is to be made by instalments the unpaid vendor's lien normally applies in relation to future payments even though he parts with possession and the courts may protect his interest by, eg, declaring him entitled to a lien on the property for the entirety of the purchase money including future instalments.[235]

---

[226] Keane, *ibid.*

[227] Jones & Goodhart, *Specific Performance* (1986) p 35-8.

[228] *CH Giles & Co Ltd v Morris* [1972] 1 All ER 960 at 969-70.

[229] That passage is quoted by Jones & Goodhart, *op cit* at p 35 in the course of a full discussion.

[230] At 970.

[231] *ie,* contracts of personal services or for the continuous performance of services.

[232] Quoted with agreement by Goff LJ in *Price v Strange* [1977] 3 All ER 371 at 385-6.

[233] *Gervais v Edwards* (1842) 2 Drury & Warren 80 at 84-5.

[234] *Lark Developments Ltd v Dublin Corporation* (HC) 10 February 1993, Murphy J, unrep; plaintiff was confined to damages in relation to second block due to laches: p 13-15.

[235] *Nives v Nives* (1880) 15 Ch D 649 at 650; *Langen & Wind Ltd v Bell* [1972] 1 All ER 296 at 299.

DAMAGES TO OR IN SUBSTITUTION FOR SPECIFIC PERFORMANCE

Lord Cairns' Act

[1.28] Jurisdiction to award damages in addition to or in substitution for specific performance was expressly conferred by statute on the Court of Chancery by s 2 of Lord Cairns' Act.[236] In a case where damages are given in substitution for specific performance there is power by virtue of that Act to award such damages as will put the plaintiff in as good a position as if the contract had been performed.[237] In earlier times there had been doubt about the jurisdiction of a court of equity to award damages; in some cases the courts awarded damages and in others they refused.[238] The right to award damages in lieu of specific performance is discretional in its exercise but this should be done only where "more complete and perfect justice can thereby be done".[239] A decree for specific performance should not be coupled with an alternative decree for damages in the event of inability or unwillingness on the part of the defendant to perform the agreement specifically.[240] Since the Judicature Act,[241] the jurisdiction to award damages when specific performance has been claimed does not depend on there having been any right to specific performance.[242] The courts have full power to make an award on foot of a claim for damages joined with a claim for specific performance irrespective of the merits of the latter claim and without any need to rely on the power given by Lord Cairns' Act.

[1.29] In a suitable case a party is entitled to damages in addition to a decree of specific performance and this "is expressly allowed under Lord Cairns' Act".[243] If a vendor or lessor is not able to give possession of the entire property the purchaser or lessee may accept possession of the part he can get and sue for damages in respect of the failure to give possession of the rest.[244] Where a sale is delayed by the vendor's default the general rule is that the vendor instead of getting interest must be satisfied with "the interim rents and profits" but he does not lose both ways.[245] The purchaser who has got specific performance and claims damages for the vendor's delay must set off the interest which he saved or earned during the period of delay against any damages he proves.[246] Thus it may not be proper to allow a plaintiff the whole of the rent he has had to pay for alternative accommodation while he has had the use of unpaid purchase money.[247] When the interest saved or earned exceeds the damages proved the vendor does not get any

---

[236] *Ie*, the Chancery Amendment Act 1858.
[237] *Brownlee v Duggan* [1976] 5 NIJB at 11.
[238] *Patrick v Williams* (1897) 31 ILTR 166 at 167. Note discussion by Jones and Goodhart, *Specific Performance* (1986) at p 222-3 of pre-1858 awards of damages by courts of equity.
[239] *Patrick's case, ibid.*
[240] *Ibid.*
[241] The Supreme Court of Judicature (Ireland) Act 1877. See para **1.05** above.
[242] *Duggan v Allied Irish Building Society*, (HC) 4 March 1976, Finlay P, unrep at 15-16.
[243] *Murphy v Quality Homes* (HC) 22 June 1976, McWilliam J, unrep at 4.
[244] *Fitzgerald v Browne* (1854) 4 ICLR 178 at 182-5.
[245] *Re Hewitt's Contract* [1963] 1 WLR 1298 at 1301; [1963] 3 All ER 419 at 422.
[246] *O'Brien v White-Spunner* [1979] ILRM 240 at 242-3. *Cf Malone v Malone* (HC) 9 June 1982, Costello J, unrep at 16-17.
[247] *Sheridan v Higgins* [1971] IR 291 at 304.

balance because that would enable him to profit by his own wrong.[248] So a purchaser who lost rental value of £7,560 due to the vendor's delay in completion but saved interest of £14,175 failed in that part of his claim; the vendor did not seek the balance of £6,615 and presumably would have failed if he had claimed it.[249] Damages will be assessed to the date of actual completion and outgoings will be apportioned to that date.[250] If the purchase price has been paid or placed on deposit in the names of the parties or their solicitors despite possession being retained by the vendor,[251] the interest it earns is likely to belong to the purchaser without obligation to set it off against damages proved by him.[252] It is important to remember that each party to a contract of sale has the right to expect the other to be reasonable in taking such necessary steps as may be incidental to the closing of the sale.[253] Thus a vendor who asks a purchaser to complete by bank draft[254] but then causes him to suffer loss in respect of the interest on money which he has borrowed to buy the bank draft may be liable in damages.[255] On the other hand it should be borne in mind that sometimes a party is entitled to delay closing while a claim *eg* for compensation by way of abatement of the purchase price is being determined.[256]

[1.30] The power to award damages in lieu of specific performance is likely to be used where there has been significant delay by the plaintiff which need not necessarily be enough to establish the defence of laches.[257] Thus a developer who delays due mainly to a downturn in the market is likely to be confined to damages.[258] When parties have accommodated themselves over a period of three years to the position arising under a broken contract and have been slow in bringing the claim for specific performance to trial the court may feel that it should grant the alternative relief of damages.[259] Delay held insufficient to set up the defence of laches has still affected the exercise of the court's discretion whether to grant specific performance.[260] The power has been used also in a case of an agreement for lease where the term of the intended lease had expired by the time judgment was given.[261] A party who is prevented from getting specific performance solely because of another contract having priority over his agreement will be held entitled to damages in lieu of specific performance.[262] He will be directed to vacate any lis pendens as the claim for damages does not warrant its retention.[263] If specific performance

---

[248] *Esdaile v Stephenson* (1822) 1 Sim & St 122 quoted in *Re Hewitt's Contract* and in *O'Brien's* case at 242.
[249] *O'Brien v White-Spunner* [1979] ILRM 240.
[250] *O'Gorman v Hudson* [1934] LJ Ir 45 at 46.
[251] This normally could not be recommended.
[252] *Malone v Malone* (HC) 9 June 1982, Costello J, unrep at 16-17; of course parties may agree any arrangements.
[253] *Neville v Slattery Estates Co Ltd* (HC) 15 February 1984, Barrington J, unrep at 16.
[254] Normal practice in itself.
[255] *Neville's* case at 12-18.
[256] *Keating v Bank of Ireland* [1983] ILRM 295 at 298-9.
[257] On which see para **9.42-7** *post.*
[258] *Lark Developments Ltd v Dublin Corporation* (HC) 10 February 1993, Murphy J, unrep at 13-15; no express finding of laches.
[259] *Murphy v Harrington* [1927] IR 339 at 345; laches not found.
[260] *White v McCooey* [1976-7] ILRM 72 at 86-7.
[261] *Brownlee v Duggan* [1976] 5 NIJB at 11; cf *Reg Armstrong Motors Ltd v Texaco (Ireland) Ltd* (HC) 21 December 1971, Pringle J, unrep at 18.
[262] *O'Connor v McCarthy* [1982] IR 161 at 178; the later judgment assessing the damages is at [1982] ILRM 201.

is decreed against a defendant who does not comply with the order and the plaintiff applies successfully to the court to dissolve the order and put an end to the contract he is entitled at that stage to damages in lieu of specific performance.[264] We will look at this in more detail later and consider the date by reference to which damages should be assessed.[265]

[1.31] The jurisdiction gives the court power to award such damages as will put the plaintiff in as good a position as if the contract had been performed.[266] If the facts of a case are such that the trial judge is of opinion that he could make an order for specific performance but in his discretion awards damages in lieu thereof he must take into account in assessing the damages not merely such items as the loss of bargain and other loss which flows from the breach but the out of pocket expenses and other money laid out by the plaintiff which would naturally include any part of the purchase money already paid.[267] The loss suffered by not getting the property agreed to be sold should be measured at the date of the judgment which decides that the claimant should have damages in lieu of specific performance.[268] The loss under that head is the difference between the value of the property at the date of that judgment and the contract price.[269] Possibly there should be adjustments to allow for the fact that the disappointed purchaser has retained the use of his money and the fact that if he had got the property and paid for it in the normal way he would have enjoyed the rents and profits. If there is no evidence on those points the court will not assume that the purchaser received any financial advantage from the vendor's wrongful repudiation of a contract.[270]

The normal rules as to the measure of damages established by the well known case of *Hadley v Baxendale*[271] will apply. The damages payable by the contractbreaker will be such as may fairly and reasonably be considered either arising naturally i.e. according to the usual course of things from such breach of contract itself or such as may reasonably be supposed to have been in the contemplation of both parties at the time they made the contract as the probable result of the breach of it.[272] It has been held that a builder ought to have contemplated that a plaintiff left with a defective house because the builder failed to perform an agreement to buy it back would suffer loss due to the rise in price of a suitable alternative house during the time the plaintiff neither had got the agreed sale price nor could raise money on the security of the defective house.[273] In the same case damages were awarded for the discomfort, inconvenience and distress in having to remain over the winter in the defective house. While parties may expect that a purchaser will have to borrow some money to complete the purchaser a vendor may

---

[263] *Ibid. Cf Dunville Investments Ltd v Kelly* (HC) 27 April 1979, Costello J, unrep at 4-5. On vacating a *lis pendens* see para **10.10-14** below.
[264] *Vandeleur v Dargan* [1979] ILRM 75 at 77.
[265] Para **8.28** *post*.
[266] *Brownlee v Duggan* [1976] 5 NIJB at 11, Murray J approving a passage from Megarry J in *Wroth v Tyler* [1974] Ch 30; *cf O'Connor v McCarthy* [1982] ILRM 201 at 203.
[267] *Holohan v Ardmayle Estates* (SC) 1 May 1967, Walsh J, unrep at 4.
[268] *O'Connor v McCarthy* [1982] ILRM 201 at 202.
[269] *Ibid* at 202-3. Costello J held that the property had risen in value by about 75% in a 3-year period from the contract to the initial judgment. *Cf Roberts v O'Neill* [1983] 1 R 47 at 50.
[270] *O'Connor's* case at 203.
[271] (1854) 9 Exch 341.
[272] *O'Connor's* case at 204, Costello J quoting from *Hadley's* case.
[273] *Murphy v Quality Homes* (HC) 22 June 1976, McWilliam J, unrep.

not be expected to contemplate any special liabilities of the purchase of which the vendor was not told.[274] A vendor who knows that his purchaser is buying timber in the course of his business is likely to be liable in damages for the loss resulting from failure to supply the timber.[275]

---

[274] *Malone v Malone* (HC) 9 June 1982, Costello J, unrep.
[275] *McNeill v Richards* [1899] 1 IR 79 at 85.

Chapter 2

Injunctions

[2.01] We look now at aspects of the very important equitable remedy of the injunction.[1] Like specific performance relief by way of injunction is a discretionary remedy[2] though, also like specific performance, the jurisdiction is exercised in accordance with established principles. An obvious difference is that injunctions have a much wider scope in terms of contracts and other relationships in connection with which they can be invoked. Claims for an injunction may come up against many of the same defences or grounds for refusal as claims for specific performance. Thus, for example, the courts have discretion to refuse an injunction to a party who comes to court otherwise than "with clean hands".[3] That phrase, however, would seem to require "an element of turpitude" and cannot necessarily be equated with a mere breach of contract.[4] However, an applicant who himself fails to comply with an important statutory requirement may lose his right to an injunction.[5] Claimants who move slowly may fail to get an interlocutory injunction[6] or may get it with conditions attached encouraging them to move faster.[7] It has been pointed out, however, that mere delay will not of itself disentitle a plaintiff to an injunction in aid of legal rights unless the claim to enforce the right is barred by a statute of limitations; there must be such delay and acquiescence as would make it in the nature of a fraud for a plaintiff afterwards to insist upon his legal right.[8] Other principles may be common to the reliefs of injunctions and specific performance. In both damages must be an inadequate remedy.[9] A court may have to consider whether a principle which usually would defeat a claim for specific performance must also defeat an application for an injunction in the same proceedings.[10]

Injunctions may be either prohibitory - ie, restraining the defendant from doing some particular thing - or mandatory - ordering him to do something specified.[11] The duration for which they are granted varies also. The courts may grant a perpetual injunction which is normally done at the trial. Three requirements normally must be met before a perpetual injunction is granted. These are (i) the injunction must be granted to protect a right of the plaintiff; (ii) that right must have been infringed already or there must be a probability of an infringement; and (iii) there must be no other adequate remedy.[12] Interlocutory

---

[1] See the much fuller consideration by Keane, *Equity and the Law of Trusts in Ireland* (1988) at Ch 15. At para 15.01 he shows why it is the "most potent" of equitable remedies

[2] *Patterson v Murphy* [1978] ILRM 85 at 99.

[3] *Curust Financial Services Ltd v Loewe* [1993] ILRM 723 at 731; *Ardent Fisheries Ltd v Minister for Tourism, Fisheries and Forestry* [1987] ILRM 528 at 533.

[4] *The Curust Financial Services* case at 731.

[5] *Irish Oil and Cake Mills Ltd v Donnelly*, (HC) 27 March 1983, Costello J, unrep at 14-15.

[6] *Lennon v Ganly* [1981] ILRM 84 at 86.

[7] *DJS Meats Ltd v Minister for Agriculture and Food*, (HC) 17 February 1993, Lynch J, unrep at 7-8.

[8] *Cahill v Irish Motor Traders Association* [1966] IR 430 at 449; a claim for a perpetual injunction and Budd J left open the possibility that different considerations would apply to an application for an interlocutory injunction. *Cf* defence of laches in paras **9.42-7** *post*.

[9] See para **1.10** *ante* in relation to specific performance and para **2.02** *infra* in respect of injunctions.

[10] *Eg, Lift Manufacturers Ltd v Irish Life Assurance Co Ltd* [1979] ILRM 277 at 280: interlocutory injunction restraining the employment of another sub-contractor to do work despite submission that specific performance of a contract for services cannot be decreed.

[11] Keane, *op cit*, para 15.02.

[12] See Keane, *op cit*, para 15.08. The inadequacy of damages is dealt with in the next para.

injunctions may also be granted and will be considered in some detail shortly.[13] When a matter is sufficiently urgent a court will grant an interim injunction on *ex parte* application; this is usually given for a short time until an interlocutory application can be brought. The court sometimes abridges the time for service of a motion for an interlocutory injunction.

[2.02] As in the case of specific performance[14] an injunction will not be granted if damages are an adequate remedy.[15] If a loss proved by a plaintiff in an action, no interlocutory injunction having been granted to him, is clearly and exclusively a commercial loss in a stable and well established market, that loss *prima facie* should be capable of being assessed in damages both under the heading of loss actually suffered up to the date of assessment and also under the heading of probable future loss.[16] Difficulty, as distinct from complete impossibility, in the assessment of damages should not be a ground for characterising the awarding of damages as an inadequate remedy.[17] On the other hand, the fact that the monetary amount claimed is easily ascertainable does not always mean that damages are an adequate remedy. For example, wages and salaries left unpaid are easy to quantify but the effect of the non-payment may still cause serious inconvenience and prejudice in the circumstances.[18]

[2.03] Damages may be awarded in addition to an injunction.[19] Also the court has a discretion to award damages in lieu of an injunction. Section 2 of Lord Cairns's Act[20] provided that in all cases where the Court of Chancery[21] has jurisdiction to entertain an application for an injunction against a breach of any covenant, contract or agreement or against the commission or continuance of any wrongful act, the court may, if it thinks fit, award damages to the party injured, either in addition to or in substitution for the injunction. The discretion to award damages in lieu of an injunction is exercised on well established principles[22] and the relevant ones were identified by Costello J for the purposes of a modern Irish case:[23]

> "1. When an infringement of the plaintiff's right and a threatened further infringement to a material extent has been established the plaintiff is *prima facie* entitled to an injunction. There may be circumstances, however, depriving the plaintiff of this *prima facie* right but generally speaking the plaintiff will only be deprived of an injunction in very exceptional circumstances.

---

[13] Interlocutory injunctions (prohibitory) are discussed at paras **2.09-15** *infra* and interlocutory mandatory injunctions at paras **2.16-7**.

[14] On which see para **1.10** *ante*.

[15] *Westman Holdings Ltd v McCormack* [1992] IR 151 at 158.

[16] *Curust Financial Services Ltd v Loewe* [1993] ILRM 723 at 733.

[17] *Ibid; cf Reno Engrais et Produits Chemiques SA v Irish Agricultural Wholesale Society Ltd* [1976/7] ILRM 179.

[18] *Boyle v An Post* [1992] 2 IR 437 at 442, 446.

[19] As in *Rabbette v Mayo County Council* [1984] ILRM 156.

[20] Its official title is the Chancery Amendment Act 1858.

[21] Now the unified courts since the Supreme Court of Judicature Act (Ireland) 1877.

[22] Note the detailed consideration by Kenny J in *Cullen v Cullen* [1962] IR 268 at 286-90 and the powerful reasons which led him to withhold the injunction realising that he was denying the plaintiff one of his fundamental rights of property.

[23] *Patterson v Murphy* [1978] ILRM 85 at 99-100.

2.   If the injury to the plaintiff's rights is small, and is one capable of being estimated in money, and is one which can be adequately compensated by a small money payment, and if the case is one in which it would be oppressive to the defendant to grant an injunction, then these are circumstances in which damages in lieu of an injunction may be granted.

3.   The conduct of the plaintiff may be such as to disentitle him to an injunction. The conduct of the defendant may be such as to disentitle him from seeking the substitution of damages for an injunction.

4.   The mere fact that a wrong-doer is able and willing to pay for the injury he has inflicted is not a ground for substituting damages."[24]

Substantial, and largely successful, efforts by a defendant to remove causes of complaint in a "thorough and conscientious way" may enable a court to award damages in lieu of continuing an injunction.[25]

[2.04] An injunction is often granted to compel parties to honour obligations and issues may arise whether the court is in substance being asked to decree specific performance in types of cases where the relief is not available. For example, the courts usually will not grant specific performance of contracts for services[26] so it could be a valid objection to the grant of an injunction that it would be an attempt to decree specific performance of such a contract. However, when parties enter into a negative agreement it is normally the court's duty to hold them to their bargain. As Lord Cairns explained in *Doherty v Allman*:[27]

> "If parties, for valuable consideration, with their eyes open, contract that a particular thing shall not be done, all that a Court of Equity has to do is to say, by way of injunction, that which the parties have already said by way of covenant, that the thing shall not be done; and in such case the injunction does nothing more than give the sanction of the process of the court to that which already is the contract between the parties. It is not then a question of the balance of convenience or inconvenience, or of the amount of damage or of injury - it is the specific performance, by the court, of that negative bargain which the parties have made, with their eyes open, between themselves."[28]

The second sentence in that passage is notable for two reasons. One is the recognition that an injunction to enforce a negative covenant may be described fairly as specific performance of a negative bargain. The other is that the reference to "the balance of convenience or inconvenience" may suggest nowadays that the passage did or could apply to an application for an interlocutory injunction. That may have led to doubts about the need to consider the balance of convenience in applications for interlocutory injunctions to restrain breaches of negative obligations when the claimant has shown a *prima facie* case. We return to this later when dealing in more detail with interlocutory injunctions.[29]

---

[24]   On this point Costello J cited *Shelfer v City of London Electric Co* [1895] 1 Ch 287 and Kerr on *Injunctions* 6th ed at 656-7.

[25]   *Halpin v Tara Mines Ltd* [1976/7] ILRM 28 at 40.

[26]   See para **1.20** *ante*.

[27]   (1878) 3 App Cas 709 at 720.

[28]   Approved by O'Dalaigh CJ giving the judgment of the Supreme Court in *Dublin Port & Docks Board v Brittania Dredging Co Ltd* [1968] IR 136 at 145. *Cf* discussion by Black J in *Belton v Nicholl* [1941] IR 230 at 241-3.

[29]   See para **2.13** *infra*.

[2.05] In another case where specific performance of a building contract[30] was sought, an interlocutory injunction was granted preventing the employer from nominating another contractor.[31] A submission that the injunction should be refused because specific performance of a contract for services cannot be decreed[32] was rejected on the ground that there was no need to oversee performance of the services.[33] In an older case, a contractor who failed to make requisite progress was restrained from preventing the employer taking up and completing the works in accordance with the contract.[34] However, as Chatterton VC pointed out in the actual case,[35] he had to assume the correctness of the engineer's decision as to the lack of sufficient progress so the decision probably does not assist in a case in which the contractor's default is *bona fide* disputed.[36] There are many cases in which it may not be appropriate to grant either side an injunction.[37] An injunction has been granted to restrain the erection of houses or felling of trees in breach of an assurance by a developer that an open space would be kept and trees preserved.[38] And injunctions including a *quia timet*[39] injunction have been granted to restrain breaches by a landlord of covenants for quiet enjoyment.[40]

[2.06] Licences[41] have provided some good examples of the use of injunctions to protect rights. The decisions mostly have concerned parties trying to break their licence agreements rather than instances of parties refusing to grant licences[42] though in some cases specific performance has been decreed.[43] The distinction has been made that an injunction restraining the revocation of a licence may in a sense be called relief by way of specific performance but it is not specific performance in the sense of compelling the party to do anything; it merely prevents him from breaking his contract.[44] Where a contractual licence is given to a person during his life to enter land to draw sand and gravel from it, equity will enforce that contract and will not permit the licensor or his personal representatives to act in disregard of that licence.[45] If a licensor is threatening to revoke a licence without having the right to do so, equity may grant an injunction to restrain him from carrying out that threat; if he has in fact purported to revoke the licence

---

[30] Paras **1.21-2** *ante*.
[31] *Lift Manufacturers Ltd v Irish Life Assurance Co Ltd* [1979] ILRM 277.
[32] On this point see para **1.20** *ante*.
[33] The *Lift Manufacturers* case at 280. McWilliam J saw that a number of difficult questions would be raised in the action but was not concerned with them at the interlocutory stage once he was satisfied that the plaintiff had a "genuine claim".
[34] *Cork Corporation v Rooney* (1881) 7 LRI 191 at 204-7.
[35] At 205.
[36] Note Megarry J's consideration of the *Cork Corporation* case in *London Borough of Hounslow v Twickenham Garden Developments Ltd* [1970] 3 All ER 326 at 345.
[37] *Per* Megarry J in the *London Borough of Hounslow* case at 345.
[38] *Browne v Viscount Securities Ltd* (SC) 12 June 1980, unrep (oral judgments).
[39] *Ie* because he (or she) fears. There must be a "well-grounded apprehension of injury - proof of actual and real danger - a strong probability almost amounting to a moral certainty": see Keane, *Equity and the Law of Trusts in the Republic of Ireland* (1988) para 15.32 and cases cited.
[40] *Whelan v Madigan* [1979] ILRM 136 at 144.
[41] On licences see further paras **1.17** *ante* and **5.09** *post*.
[42] Note the distinction made by Keane, *Equity and the Law of Trusts in the Republic of Ireland* (1988) para 16.01 between *executory contracts* and *executed contracts* and his point that specific performance of executed contracts is more akin to injunctive relief than true specific performance. See also para **1.04** *ante*.
[43] See para **1.17** *ante*.
[44] By Parker J in *Jones v Earl of Tankerville* [1909] 2 Ch 440 at 443 approved by Fitzgibbon J in *Whipp v Mackey* [1927] IR 372 at 388.
[45] *Woods v Donnelly* [1982] NI 257 at 263-4.

equity can prevent him from carrying that revocation into effect and restrain him from doing anything under it.[46] In Ireland a local authority has been restrained by injunction from refusing to fulfil a contract for hiring a town hall to a political party for its annual conference.[47] In a similar[48] English case specific performance was decreed.[49]

[2.07] Injunctions may also be granted in aid of or ancillary to a claim for specific performance. A decree of specific performance of a contract for the sale of shares has had added a perpetual injunction restraining the defendant from selling or disposing of any shares to any person other than the plaintiffs or their nominee.[50] A plaintiff who succeeded in a claim for specific performance of an agreement to execute a statutory mortgage of a boat also got an order restraining any dealings with the boat.[51] And one who was entitled to a lease of a plot from the defendants and also could get specific performance against another relevant party was given a perpetual injunction restraining the defendants from entering or doing any work on the site.[52] A sub-contractor seeking specific performance of a building contract was given an interlocutory injunction restraining the defendant from nominating another sub-contractor to do the work.[53] Decrees of specific performance of agreements for lease have directed the leases to be ante-dated and included an order restraining parties from claiming that the leases ran from any other dates.[54] The possibility of letting a party who claims to have a binding contract to purchase land apply for an interlocutory injunction to restrain the owner from dealing with the land until the trial of the action - an injunction which would be coupled with an undertaking to pay damages to the defendant owner if the claim ultimately failed - has been left open in Ireland.[55] English case law[56] indicates that a party may seek an interlocutory injunction to prevent a defendant in possession of property from damaging it[57] or taking it outside the jurisdiction, if movable.[58] He may also be directed to take positive steps to preserve the subject matter of the action, eg, by continuing to pump water out of a mine.[59] An injunction may also be granted after completion to restrain a person from derogating from his grant by, for example, acting so as to militate against the use and enjoyment of the property sold.[60]

---

[46] *Millenium Productions Ltd v Winter Garden Theatre (London) Ltd* [1946] 1 All ER 678 at 684-5 considered by Hutton J in the *Woods* case at 265. The *Millenium Productions* case was reversed by the House of Lords on the point of construction that the licensors had power to revoke the licence: see Hutton J in the *Woods* case at 264.

[47] *Browne v Dundalk UDC* [1993] 2 IR 512 at 522-3.

[48] In both cases the local authority tried to go back on a contract to hire a hall to a political party of which many would disapprove.

[49] *Verrall v Great Yarmouth BC* [1980] 1 All ER 839 CA.

[50] *Pernod Ricard Comrie plc v FII (Fyffes) plc* (HC) 21 October 1988, Costello J, unrep at 31, affirmed (SC) 11 November 1988, unrep.

[51] *The Regina Coeli* (HC) NI [1976] 5 NIJB at 40-41.

[52] *Lucey v Laurel Construction Ltd* (HC) 18 December 1970, Kenny J, unrep at 12-15 (interlocutory application treated as trial of action).

[53] *Lift Manufacturers Ltd v Irish Life Assurance Co Ltd* [1979] ILRM 277.

[54] *McIlroy v Traill* [1898] 1 IR 459 at 461. *Cf Browne v Marquis of Sligo* (1859) 10 IR Ch R 1 at 13 (in text of order).

[55] *Barry v Buckley* [1981] IR 306 at 311.

[56] Cited by Jones and Goodhart, *Specific Performance* (1986) at 189.

[57] *Crockford v Alexander* (1808) 15 Ves 138.

[58] *Hart v Herwig* (1873) 8 Ch App 860 (a ship).

[59] *Strelley v Pearson* (1880) 15 Ch D 113.

[60] *Connell v O'Malley* (HC) 28 July 1983, Barron J, unrep (recorded at [1984] ILRM 563).

A binding contract for purchase, with or without proceedings for specific performance being instituted, may give a person *locus standi* to seek an injunction in relation to the land. A plaintiff purchaser who has a binding contract but not a conveyance can get an injunction in a specific performance action restraining his vendor from selling to another person or demolishing buildings on the land.[61] He may also seek an injunction against a third party restraining the demolition of buildings on the land without having a conveyance or instituting an action for specific performance.[62]

[2.08] An injunction may also prevent a party from insisting on a contract which he might have appeared entitled to enforce. Thus, where there is a right to rectification of a document[63] the other party is likely to be restrained from trying to enforce it in its unreformed condition.[64] An injunction also will be granted to prevent attempts to enforce a contract obtained by fraudulent misrepresentation.[65] A purchaser of land who knew that someone else had bought the timber on it was restrained on the ground of fraud from relying on his conveyance obtained through the Landed Estates Court to prevent the buyer of the timber from entering to take it.[66] The position probably would be the same in the case of a purchase out of court.[67] The courts will restrain a party from suing in a foreign action if that party is bound in conscience in Ireland not to sue.[68] However, a court will decline to grant an injunction affecting a person's conduct in a foreign country when it has no means of supervising the enforcement of the order.[69]

An injunction may be granted to restrain a sale in an appropriate case. Thus, a liquidator may be restrained by injunction from proceeding with a sale where he has been in breach of his fiduciary duty to obtain the best available price or to investigate the genuineness of a new offer at a time when no binding contract to sell exists.[70] The same may happen to a mortgagee which agrees to sell property having refused to look into a basis of valuation which its own surveyors advised would show a higher price.[71] A receiver and manager may be restrained from preparing a sale by tender in breach of his duties.[72] It is important to remember that this type of claim should be directed at preventing a breach of duty, not at choosing between two possible methods of sale.[73] An interim and an interlocutory injunction may be granted to restrain completion of a sale by auction in the event of a dispute over who was the last bidder.[74]

---

[61] *Curtis v the Marquis of Buckingham* (1814) 3 Ves & B 168 applied in *O'Hara v Flint* [1979] ILRM 156 at 159.

[62] As in *O'Hara's* case (plaintiff lost on other grounds).

[63] On which see paras **10.15-24** *post.*

[64] *Young v Halahan* (1875) 9 IR Eq 70 at 82.

[65] *Costello v Martin* (1867) 1 Ir Eq R 50.

[66] *O'Hanlon v Murdock* [1901] 1 IR 122 at 127-8.

[67] *Ibid* at 128.

[68] *Lett v Lett* [1906] 1 IR 618 at 640-1 *per* FitzGibbon LJ; see also Walker C at 635. Holmes LJ dissented. Note also *Booth v Leycester* 3 M & C 459 where an English court restrained prosecution of a suit in Ireland (approved by FitzGibbon LJ in *Lett's* case at 640-1). *Cf Re Belfast Shipowners Co Ltd* [1894] 1 IR 321.

[69] *Lennon v Ganly* [1981] ILRM 84 at 86.

[70] *Re Brook Cottage Ltd* [1976] NI 78 at 114-7.

[71] *Holohan v Friends Provident and Century Life Office* [1966] IR 1 at 25.

[72] *Lambert Jones Estates Ltd v Donnelly* (HC) 5 November 1982, unrep at 11, (claim failed as on the facts the plaintiffs' action was "implausible": p 13). *Cf McGowan v Gannon* [1983] ILRM 516.

[73] *Ibid* at 11.

[74] *Tully v Irish Land Commission* (1961) 97 ILTR 94 at 97; the challenge failed at plenary hearing: (1961) 97 ILTR 174 at 179.

INTERLOCUTORY INJUNCTIONS

[2.09] Interlocutory relief is intended to maintain the status quo until the trial and to do no more.[75] The grant of an interlocutory injunction is a remedy that is both temporary and discretionary.[76] No rights are determined nor are issues decided.[77] The object of the injunction and other interlocutory relief is to permit the just realisation of the plaintiff's claim if he is successful.[78] In interfering by interlocutory injunction the court does not in general profess to anticipate the determination of the right, but merely gives the opinion that there is a substantial question to be tried and that a case has been made out for the preservation of the property *in statu quo* pending the trial.[79] The court's jurisdiction is not restricted to actual breaches of contract[80]; it also has jurisdiction to restrain an apprehended or threatened breach.[81] The application for an interlocutory injunction is often treated by consent as the trial of the action. When that happens, the rights of the parties are finally determined on the interlocutory motion. There seems to be no significant difference in the law in this country and that of England and Wales as to the principles that should be applied by the court in granting or withholding an interlocutory injunction save that the constitutional rights of any of the parties to the action under the Irish Constitution cannot be abridged by the order.[82]

[2.10] The first question for the court to determine in an application for an interlocutory injunction where the claimant's right or its violation is disputed is whether he has shown that "a fair question" arises for decision by the court on the trial of the action in due course.[83] It frequently happens that neither the applicant's right nor the fact of its violation is disputed by the person whose acts are sought to be restrained; in such a case an injunction may be given almost as of course.[84] There are cases where a breach of contract in issue is so clear or the party attempting to resist the application for the interlocutory injunction so devoid of merits that the court should immediately provide a remedy by way of injunction.[85] In very many other cases the right, the fact of its violation or both those points are contested. Then the issue of "a fair question" does arise. Tests applied by judges in recent times such as "that there is a fair question raised to be decided at the trial,"[86] "a serious question of law arose",[87] "that there is a substantial issue to be tried"[88]

---

[75] *Campus Oil v Minister for Industry (No 2)* [1983] IR 88 at 106, *per* O'Higgins CJ. Note that this was one of the unusual cases in which a mandatory interlocutory injunction was granted; see further paras **2.16-7** *infra*.

[76] *Per* Lord Diplock in *American Cyanamid Co v Ethicon Ltd* [1975] AC 396 at 405, said in a contested application.

[77] The *Campus Oil* case at 106.

[78] *Caudron v Air Zaire* [1985] IR 716 at 721.

[79] The *Campus Oil* case at 106-7, O'Higgins CJ approving a passage from the 6th Ed of Kerr, *Injunctions* at 2; *cf* Griffin J at 108-11.

[80] Of course the jurisdiction covers many other matters as well: see Keane, *Equity and the Law of Trusts in the Republic of Ireland,* para 15.32 on "Quia timet injunctions".

[81] *Dublin Port and Docks Board v Brittania Dredging Co Ltd* [1968] IR 136 at 145.

[82] *Oblique Financial Services Ltd v The Promise Productions Co Ltd* [1994] ILRM 74 at 76-7.

[83] *Per* Lynch J in *DJS Meats Ltd v Minister for Agriculture and Food* (HC) unrep at 4, 5.

[84] *Per* O'Higgins CJ in *Campus Oil Ltd v Minister for Industry & Energy* [1983] IR 88 at 106.

[85] *Per* O'Flaherty J in *Curust Financial Services Ltd v Loewe* [1993] ILRM 723 at 735; *cf Boyle v An Post* [1992] 2 IR 437 at 442.

[86] Lavery J in *Educational Company of Ireland Ltd v Fitzparick* [1961] IR 323 at 337.

[87] Kingsmill Moore J in the *Educational Company* case at 342.

[88] Walsh J in *Esso Petroleum Co (Ireland) Ltd v Fogarty* [1965] IR 531 at 541.

and "that there is a serious question to be tried"[89] are essentially the same.[90] In a later case Finlay CJ has used the phrases "whether the plaintiffs have... raised an arguable case" and "if it could be asserted as an arguable case"[91] while also making it clear[92] that he was applying the principles laid down by the court in the *Campus Oil* case. There is no inconsistency; whether there is an "arguable case" is to be judged in the light of the principles in the *Campus Oil* case.

Formerly the position was less clear on the "fair question" point and the majority opinion seems to have been that a plaintiff had to show on an interlocutory application that he probably would succeed at the trial.[93] In the *Campus Oil* case the probability test was rejected by O'Higgins CJ.[94] He pointed out that the application of that criterion on a motion for interlocutory relief would involve the court in a determination of an issue which properly arises for determination at the trial of the action.[95]

[2.11] When the party seeking an interlocutory injunction has raised a fair question to be tried at the hearing of an action in which, if he succeeded, he would be entitled to a permanent injunction the court should not express any view on the strength of the contending submissions, but should proceed to consider the other matters which then arise in regard to the granting of an interlocutory injunction.[96] Normally it is undesirable that a court should come to firm conclusions in its judgment on an interlocutory application.[97] In many cases where the courts have considered the principles applicable in granting or refusing an interlocutory injunction stress has been laid on the difficulties facing the court when the facts are disputed and it is not possible to resolve such conflict by a perusal of the affidavits.[98] In such circumstances it is inadvisable for the court to express a view as to the probable outcome of the proceedings when they go to plenary hearing or to base a decision as to interlocutory relief on a forecast of such probable outcome.[99] O'Higgins CJ explained the approach of the courts:[100]

> "In cases where rights are disputed and challenged and where a significant period must elapse before the trial, the court must exercise its discretion (to grant interlocutory relief) with due regard to certain well-established principles. Not only will the court have regard to what is complained of and whether damages would be an appropriate remedy but it will consider what inconvenience, loss and damage might be caused to the other party,

---

[89] Lord Diplock in *American Cyanamid v Ethicon Ltd* [1975] AC 396 at 407-8.

[90] *Per* Griffin J in the *Campus Oil* case at 111.

[91] *Mitchelstown Co-operative Society Ltd v Societe des produits Nestle SA* [1989] ILRM 582 at 585. On the same page he uses the words "a fair case" clearly equating that with "an arguable case" used by Egan J at first instance.

[92] At 587.

[93] In *Irish Shell Ltd v Elm Motors Ltd* [1984] IR 200 McCarthy J said at 227 that the *American Cyanamid* case "appears to have departed from an existing requirement of 'probable success' and to substitute for it that of there being a serious issue to be tried". See also Griffin J in *Campus Oil* at 108-111 and Keane, *op cit* at para 15.23-4.

[94] The *Campus Oil* case at 106, Griffin and Hederman JJ concurring.

[95] At 107; *cf* the *Irish Shell* case at 224-5.

[96] *Per* Finlay CJ giving the judgment of the Supreme Court in *Westman Holdings Ltd v McCormack* [1992] 1 IR 151 at 157-8.

[97] *Irish Shell Ltd v Elm Motors Ltd* [1984] IR 200 at 228.

[98] *Lambert Jones Estates Ltd v Donnelly* (HC) 5 November 1982, O'Hanlon J, unrep at 7.

[99] *Ibid* at 7-8.

[100] The *Campus Oil* case at 106.

and will enquire whether the applicant has shown that the balance of convenience is in his favour."

Lord Diplock has also explained: [101]

"The object of the interlocutory injunction is to protect the plaintiff against injury by violation of his right for which he could not be adequately compensated in damages recoverable in the action if the uncertainty were resolved in his favour at the trial; but the plaintiff's need for such protection must be weighed against the corresponding need of the defendant to be protected against injury resulting from his having been prevented from exercising his own legal rights for which he could not be adequately compensated under the plaintiff's undertaking in damages if the uncertainty were resolved in the defendant's favour at the trial. The court must weigh one against another and determine where 'the balance of convenience' lies."[102]

The potential inconvenience to the plaintiff must be greater than that to the defendant and the onus of proof is on the plaintiff.[103]The phrase "balance of convenience" has been described as "simply a useful shorthand expression" pointing out that a number of factors should be taken into account 'and these are usefully embraced under the general rubric 'the balance of convenience'[104]. Accordingly it may be said that the two material questions in the great majority of claims for interlocutory injunctions are whether the applicant has made a fair case and where the balance of convenience lies.[105]

[2.12] A vital matter for consideration in relation to the balance of convenience is whether, if the plaintiff is refused an interlocutory injunction but succeeds at the full hearing, he could be adequately compensated in damages.[106] That point itself may raise two questions. One is whether damages would be an adequate remedy; the second is whether there is a defendant liable to pay such damages who is able to pay them so that the compensation could actually be realised.[107] The facts that individuals might be unable to pay and that an organisation such as a trade union might have some immunity[108] or that the party expected to pay may show that in fact he has no liability in law for the loss[109] will be taken into account. The fact that a plaintiff's right to compensation in the event of his ultimate success is not conceded may be a factor in a decision to grant or withhold an interlocutory injunction.[110] A plaintiff usually has to establish the inadequacy of damages as a remedy "for the purposes of the interlocutory injunction"[111] and, if the case goes to plenary hearing, he must be able to discharge a similar onus then.[112] The fact that

---

[101] *American Cyanamid Co v Ethicon Ltd* [1975] AC 396 at 406.
[102] Approved by McWilliam J in *Lift Manufacturers Ltd v Irish Life Assurance Co Ltd* [1979] ILRM 277 at 280. *Cf* Lavery J in *Educational Company of Ireland Ltd v Fitzpatrick* [1961] IR 323 at 337-8.
[103] The *Educational Company* case at 337-8 approving a passage from Halsbury (Hailsham ed) vol 18 p 33. Note O'Higgins CJ "whether the applicant has shown that the balance of convenience is in his favour" in the *Campus Oil* case at 106 and also Finlay CJ in the *Mitchelstown Co-operative Society* case at 587-8.
[104] Keane, *Equity and the Law of Trusts in the Republic of Ireland* (1988) at para 15.24A.
[105] *Irish Shell Ltd v Elm Motors Ltd* [1984] IR 200 at 229; we return to this topic in para **2.13** *infra*.
[106] *Westman Holdings Ltd v McCormack* [1992] 1 IR 151 at 158.
[107] *Ibid.*
[108] As in the *Westman Holdings* case at 158.
[109] As in *DJS Meats Ltd v Minister for Agriculture and Food* (HC) 17 February 1993, Lynch J, unrep at 6.
[110] Per McCarthy J in *Pesca Valentia Ltd v Minister for Fisheries and Forestry* [1985] IR 193 at 204. The phrase must also be understood in the light of the guiding principle of doing justice to all parties according to law: *De Vos v Baxter* [1987] 11 NIJB 103 at 104.
[111] *Curust Financial Services Ltd v Loewe* [1993] ILRM 723 at 735.
[112] See para **2.02** *supra*.

a claim relates to ascertainable sums of money does not always make damages a sufficient remedy. For example, non-payment of plaintiffs' wages and salaries, having regard to their particular personal circumstances, may cause hardship, distress and anxiety constituting substantial prejudice and injury over and above the fact of non-payment.[113]

The next point to be considered is whether, if the interlocutory injunction is granted but the defendant succeeds at the full hearing, he can be compensated adequately for any loss suffered by a combination of the undertaking which must necessarily be given in order to obtain the interlocutory injunction and any separate claim he may have against the plaintiff by way of counterclaim or otherwise.[114] If the undertaking as to damages is not worthwhile, even without default on the plaintiff's part, that is an important factor against granting the interlocutory injunction.[115]

[2.13] There has been a view that in cases of alleged breaches of negative covenants it was unnecessary to consider the balance of convenience once a claimant showed that there was a fair question to be tried.[116] That seems to have been based on a perception of *Doherty v Allman*[117] and references to it in *Dublin Port and Docks Board v Brittania Dredging Co Ltd*.[118] In fact, as O'Dalaigh CJ pointed out,[119] the order in *Doherty v Allman* was made on the trial of the action and no case was brought to the notice of the Supreme Court in the *Dublin Port and Docks Board* case in which the principles stated by Lord Cairns had been applied on an interlocutory motion. Lord Cairns's remarks were made also on the footing that there was no dispute as to the validity of the covenant relied on and his reference to "balance of convenience" may well have referred in his time to considerations relevant to the granting of perpetual injunctions.[120]

In any event the principle stated in *Doherty v Allman*[121] was applied by the Supreme Court in the *Dublin Port and Docks Board* case[122] at an interlocutory stage to a clause in a dredging contract that the contractor would not remove constructional plant, temporary works or materials provided by it although the court appreciated that inability to remove plant and gear might deter a contractor from withdrawing from work.[123] As matters stood the defendant had not shown that it was not bound by the contract relied on by the plaintiff; therefore the position was not different from what it would be if at the trial the court reached the same conclusion.[124] Since the principle in *Doherty v Allman* applied the court was not concerned to examine either the balance of convenience or the amount of damage.[125] Enforcement of the clause did not amount to specific performance; the clause

---

[113] *Boyle v An Post* [1992] 2 IR 437 at 442, 446.
[114] The *Westman Holdings Ltd* case at 158.
[115] *Moloney v Laurib Investments Ltd* (HC) 20 July 1993, Lynch J, unrep at 5, 6 (a *Mareva* injunction case).
[116] Formerly (probably) a probability of success - see para **2.10** *supra*.
[117] (1878) 3 App Cas 709.
[118] [1968] IR 136 at 145-7.
[119] The *Dublin Port & Docks Board* case at 145.
[120] *Texaco Ltd v Mulberry Filling Station Ltd* [1972] 1 All ER 513 at 528-9.
[121] (1878) 3 App Cas 709 at 720.
[122] [1968] IR 136 at 147.
[123] The *Dublin Port & Docks* case at 145.
[124] *Ibid* at 147.
[125] *Ibid*.

envisaged that the employer would take over the work when the contractor left it, not that the contractor would continue the work.[126]

[2.14] Keane J later analysed the *Dublin Port and Docks Board* case and concluded: [127]

> "The defendants in that case were proposing to repudiate the contract in its entirety in circumstances where the court was satisfied that they were not entitled to do so. The circumstances of the present case are wholly different: the defendants strenuously contend that neither of the transactions which the company proposes to enter into will constitute a breach of their contractual obligations under the shareholders' agreement. I do not think that O'Dalaigh CJ in the passages to which I have referred, was laying down any general principle that, in all cases where the plaintiff establishes a *prima facie* case of a breach of a negative stipulation in a contract, the court could disregard any question of the balance of convenience as between the parties. His observations were clearly confined to a case where one party to a contract was proposing to act in breach of a negative contract (and indeed to repudiate the whole contract) in circumstances where the court was not satisfied on the evidence that they were entitled so to do. I do not think that the passage lends any support to the proposition that even where the violation of the plaintiff's right is denied, as it unquestionably is in the present case, the court can disregard the balance of convenience to the parties."[128]

The present state of the law appears to be that, save in the most exceptional circumstances[129] the determination of an application for an interlocutory injunction lies, and lies only, in the answers to the two material questions as to there being a fair case to be made and where the balance of convenience lies.[130] Exceptions may occur where, eg, both the applicant's right and its violation are undisputed, a case is clear for other reasons or a party attempting to resist an application for the interlocutory injunction is devoid of merits.[131]

Undertakings as to damages

[2.15] An undertaking as to damages is normally required as a condition of getting an interlocutory injunction.[132] A party who refuses to give such an undertaking or offers only a limited one ought not expect to get the interlocutory injunction.[133] One of the reasons for the introduction of the practice of requiring an undertaking as to damages upon the grant of an interlocutory injunction is that it assists the court in abstaining from expressing any opinion on the merits of the case until the hearing.[134] If the right sought to be protected is not in issue the court is unlikely to require any undertaking.[135]

---

[126] *Ibid* at 144-5.
[127] *TMG Group Ltd v Al Babtain* [1982] ILRM 349 at 353-4.
[128] That passage was approved by McCarthy J in *Irish Shell Ltd v Elm Motors Ltd* [1984] IR 200 at 228-9.
[129] Which McCarthy J thought it invidious to try to detail.
[130] The *Irish Shell* case at 229.
[131] See para **2.10** above. The judgment in the *Irish Shell* case accepts at p 225 that if the material before the court at the hearing of the interlocutory application fails to disclose that the defendant has any real prospect of succeeding in his defence to a claim for a permanent injunction at the trial the court need not go on to the balance of convenience.
[132] See Keane, *Equity and the Law of Trusts in the Republic of Ireland* (1988) para 15.26 on "the usual undertaking as to damages" and how it is enforced if necessary.
[133] *Keenan Brothers Ltd v CIE* (1963) 97 ILTR 54 at 59-60.
[134] *Per* Lord Diplock in *American Cyanamid Co v Ethicon Ltd* [1975] AC 396 at 407-8 referring to *Wakefield v Duke of Buccleugh* (1865) 12 LT 628 and approved by Griffin J in *Campus Oil Ltd v Minister for Industry and Energy (No. 2)* [1983] IR 88 at 111.
[135] *Boyle v An Post* [1992] 2 IR 437 at 448.

INTERLOCUTORY MANDATORY INJUNCTIONS

[2.16] A mandatory injunction does not usually issue prior to the trial of an action.[136] However, there are exceptions.[137] If the case is clear and one which the court thinks ought to be decided at once, if the act done is a simple and summary one which can be easily remedied or if the defendant attempts to steal a march on the plaintiff a mandatory interlocutory injunction will be granted.[138] Presumably the view of the Supreme Court[139] that, save in exceptional cases, the two material questions on an application for an interlocutory injunction are whether a fair case has been made and where the balance of convenience lies, applies also to applications for interlocutory mandatory injunctions though the mandatory nature of the relief may result in a very cautious approach.[140] While the authorities show that the granting or withholding of the injunction remains a matter of discretion[141] it has been said that the court must feel a high degree of assurance that at the trial it will appear that the injunction was rightly granted.[142] The court is generally less ready to grant a mandatory interlocutory injunction than a restrictive one.[143] It will also be wary of granting an interlocutory mandatory injunction which involves pre-judging a crucial issue in the action.[144] Certainty about what is to be done pursuant to a mandatory order is vital and a court would be very concerned about any difficulty in achieving that.[145] Save in very exceptional circumstances, a mandatory order ought to be granted in such terms that the person against whom it is granted ought to know exactly what he has to do.[146]

[2.17] In some cases two factors may lead a court to treat applications for mandatory injunctions with particular caution. Firstly, a mandatory injunction often is a means of undoing what has already been done as far as possible and, secondly, it may require the dismantling or destruction of something already constructed resulting in waste of time, money and materials if it is ultimately established that the defendant was entitled to retain anything removed.[147] The court is more likely to grant a mandatory injunction if what is required to be done by the defendant is simple and cheap than if it is expensive to carry out, eg, by pulling down an established building.[148] However, if in a particular case a mandatory interlocutory injunction does not require the undoing of things done or carrying out or undoing work involving disproportionate expense, waste of time or

---

[136] *Per* O'Higgins CJ in *Campus Oil Ltd v Minister for Industry and Energy (No. 2)* [1983] IR 88 at 107.
[137] *Ibid.*
[138] *Boyle v An Post* [1992] 2 IR 437 at 440 Lardner J, approving a passage from Halsbury's *Laws of England* 4th Ed, vol 24, para 9.48.
[139] *Irish Shell Ltd v Elm Motors Ltd* [1984] IR 200 at 229.
[140] In the *Irish Shell* case McCarthy J referred to difficult legal issues arising and instanced the fact that the covenants were in form affirmatory rather than negative: p 228.
[141] *Per* Keane J in the *Campus Oil* case at 95.
[142] *Irish Oil and Cake Mills Ltd v Donnelly* (HC) 27 March 1983, Costello J, unrep at 14; cf *Boyle v An Post* [1992] 2 IR 437 at 442.
[143] *De Vos v Baxter* [1987] 11 NIJB 103 at 106-7
[144] *Bula Ltd v Tara Mines Ltd (No 2)* [1987] IR 95 at 105.
[145] *Ibid* at 103-4.
[146] *Per* Maugham LJ in *Fishenden v Higgs & Hill Ltd* (1935) 153 LT 128 at 142, approved by Murphy J in the *Bula* case at 104.
[147] *Shepherd Homes Ltd v Sandham* [1971] Ch 340 at 348; [1970] 3 All ER 402 at 409, approved by Keane J in the *Campus Oil* case at 95-6.
[148] *De Vos v Baxter* [1987] 11 NIJB 103 at 106-7.

inconvenience, those two factors are missing and the party claiming the injunction does not have to show an "unusually sharp and clear" case for the injunction to be granted.[149] In special circumstances the court is not limited to the very stringent principles on which it normally gives interlocutory relief of a mandatory sort.[150] Accordingly the court has ordered a defendant to pay money by interlocutory mandatory injunction when faced with competing likelihoods that the plaintiff would go into liquidation if not paid and the defendant would not be able to get back the money if it succeeded on appeal in the related case.[151]

MAREVA INJUNCTIONS

[2.18] Until the *Mareva* case[152] the principle generally applicable was that "you cannot get an injunction to restrain a man who is alleged to be a debtor from parting with his property".[153] Normally a court will not grant an injunction to restrain a defendant from parting with his assets so that they may be preserved in case the plaintiff's claim succeeds.[154] In the *Mareva* case an injunction was granted to restrain a defendant out of the jurisdiction from removing property within the jurisdiction so as to prevent a plaintiff with a good arguable case for damages against the defendant which could properly be brought within the jurisdiction[155] from recovering the amount of any award he would obtain.[156] Jurisdiction to grant the order is based in Ireland on s 28(8) of the Supreme Court of Judicature Act (Ireland) 1877 which empowers a court to grant an injunction by interlocutory order in all cases in which it appears just or convenient to do so.[157] The case law shows that there must be a real risk of the removal of the defendant's assets, there must be a danger of default by the defendant, the plaintiff must show that he has a good arguable case and, weighing the considerations for and against the grant of an injunction, the balance of convenience must be in favour of granting it.[158]

This means, broadly speaking, that he must show the usual requirements for getting an interlocutory injunction as well as the special requirements for getting the *Mareva* injunction. It is not totally clear whether he must show anything more than "a fair question" to be tried. References to "a good arguable case" in some cases[159] might suggest

---

[149] The *Campus Oil* case at 96.

[150] *Capemel Ltd v Lister (No 2)* [1989] IR 323 at 325.

[151] *Ibid* at 326. Costello J called the situation "very unusual" at 324 and said at 326 that in normal circumstances the order would not be made. The related case is at [1989] IR 319. Appeals in both were dismissed save on a point about costs: see reporter's notes at the end of each report.

[152] *Mareva Compania Naviera SA v International Bulkcarriers SA* [1980] 1 All ER 213n; [1975] 2 Lloyd's Rep 509; 119 Sol J 660. *Cf Nippon Yusen Kaisha v Karageorgis* [1975] 3 All ER 282 decided a month before the *Mareva* case. Note that in England the jurisdiction has been confirmed by statute: s 37(3) of the Supreme Court Act 1981.

[153] *Fleming v Ranks (Ireland) Ltd* [1983] ILRM 541 at 545, McWilliam J citing *Lister v Stubbs* (1890) 45 Ch D 1.

[154] *Fleming's* case at 547.

[155] The plaintiffs in *Caudron v Air Zaire* [1985] IR 716 failed on this point.

[156] *Fleming's* case at 545.

[157] *Fleming's* case at 546. For a detailed and hostile Australian view of the *Mareva* doctrine and its consequences see Meagher Gummow Lehane *Equity Doctrine & Remedies* 3rd Ed (1992) at paras 2185-90. *Cf* Keane, *Equity and the Law of Trusts in the Republic of Ireland* (1988) at para 15.34-41 esp para 15.41. Of course s 28(8) is not confined to *Mareva* cases; note the views of Chatterton VC in *Cork Corporation v Rooney* (1881) 7 LRI 191 at 200.

[158] *Fleming's* case *ibid*.

[159] *Fleming's* case at 546 and the *Barclay-Johnson* case [1980] 3 All ER 190 at 195.

that a somewhat higher prospect of success might need to be shown but the judges were not laying that down as a principle and the most recent Irish case refers simply to "a stateable case".[160] Lynch J has said where a plaintiff had a stateable case against the defendant and the defendant had a stateable defence to the plaintiff's claim that it was not appropriate for the court to seek to establish anything more regarding the issue of liability on the hearing of an application for a *Mareva* injunction.[161] There has been similar variation in the language used by the courts in relation to applications for non-*Mareva* injunctions[162] so the better view seems to be that a plaintiff need not show anything stronger than a fair question. The granting of a *Mareva* injunction should be regarded as a limited exception to the principle just noted - ie, that "you cannot get an injunction to restrain a man who is alleged to be a debtor from parting with his property".[163]

[2.19] The granting of a *Mareva* injunction, like any other application for an interlocutory injunction,[164] is an ancillary or incidental relief in an action where a plaintiff has made a substantive claim. If he has not got a subsisting action within this jurisdiction he cannot get a *Mareva* injunction.[165] If he issues a writ showing a substantive cause of action but the courts hold that that is not triable within the jurisdiction he is left without any subsisting cause of action here.[166] He is not entitled to a *Mareva* injunction simply because he has instituted proceedings.[167] However, the jurisdiction is not confined to cases in which a defendant is resident outside the State[168] though the fact that a defendant has a foreign nationality, domicile or residence may be of importance in so far as it increases the risk of property being removed from the jurisdiction.[169] The plaintiff must show that the defendant intends to take his assets out of the jurisdiction or otherwise dispose of them so that any judgment obtained against him by the defendant will be useless.[170] That motive is important; the court will not restrain the disposal of assets merely for the purpose of carrying on as business or discharging lawful debts.[171] The *Mareva* prohibition on disposing of assets *within* the jurisdiction is a normal ancillary of the prohibition against removing the assets from the country.[172] If it did not prevent disposition within the jurisdiction a defendant could transfer them to a collaborator who would then remove them.[173]

---

[160] *Moloney v Laurib Investments Ltd* (HC) 20 July 1993, Lynch J, unrep at 2.
[161] *Moloney's* case at 2.
[162] See para **2.10** *supra*.
[163] *Fleming's* case at 546 citing *Lister v Stubbs* (1890) 45 Ch D 1.
[164] Note that *Mareva* interim injunctions are also granted. The first two English cases, *Mareva* itself and (a month earlier) *Nippon Yusen Kaisha v Karageorgis* [1975] 3 All ER 282, were both *ex parte* applications to continue interim injunctions. Here *Moloney's* case, *Fleming's* case and the *Powerscourt Estates* case [1984] ILRM 123 were all applications on notice for interlocutory injunctions. In *Caudron's* case the High Court gave liberty to serve outside the jurisdiction together with an interim *Mareva* injunction; the Supreme Court set aside the order for service outside the jurisdiction and therefore the *Mareva* injunction also had to be set aside.
[165] *Caudron v Air Zaire* [1985] IR 716 at 724.
[166] As occurred in *Caudron's* case: p 724.
[167] *Larkins v NUM* [1985] IR 671 at 694.
[168] *Powerscourt Estates v Gallagher* [1984] ILRM 123 at 126; *Fleming v Ranks (Ireland) Ltd* [1983] ILRM 541 at 546.
[169] The *Powerscourt Estates* case at 126 considering the judgment of Megarry VC in *Barclay-Johnson v Yuill* [1980] 3 All ER 190 at 194-5; [1980] 1 WLR 1259 at 1265-6.
[170] The *Larkins* case at 694.
[171] *Fleming's* case at 546.
[172] The *Powerscourt Estates* case at 126.
[173] *Barclay-Johnson's* case at 194 (All ER); 1266 (WLR).

It seems likely that the *Mareva* jurisdiction may be exercised in specific performance cases. A *Mareva* injunction might be sought reasonably by a vendor wishing to enforce a contract for sale against a purchaser if there is a serious risk that the latter will remove funds from the jurisdiction in order to defeat the plaintiff's claim. In a modern English case[174] it was agreed by counsel that the court could make an order for specific performance and also grant a *Mareva* injunction freezing part of the purchase money to cover a claim for damages by a sub-purchaser rather than let the defendant vendor have unrestricted access to the whole.[175] The issue fought was whether there was jurisdiction to combine the two orders into one and Hoffmann J held that there was.[176]

[2.20] Matters which have been weighed by the Irish courts or mentioned as possible factors for consideration in deciding whether to grant a *Mareva* interlocutory injunction have included hardship to the defendants or their creditors entitled to be paid in the ordinary course of business,[177] prejudice to bona fide creditors of the defendant,[178] existing discussions which might lead to the disposal of the defendant's only asset and were not designed to be implemented for the purpose of defeating the plaintiff's claim,[179] that the grant of the injunction would cause very serious damage if the defendant eventually won its case,[180] the weakness of the plaintiff's undertaking as to damages even though this was without any fault on his part,[181] and doubt whether granting the *Mareva* interlocutory injunction would improve the plaintiff's prospects of recovering on foot of a judgment.[182] A reluctance on the part of the defendant to disclose his assets, and actual or proposed dispositions by him which might favour creditors other than the plaintiff may indicate that the defendant is mainly interested in depriving a plaintiff of the opportunity of recovering on foot of his judgment.[183] A defendant may contend that it is a company with no record of defaulting on its commitments, that the injunction sought will not turn the plaintiff into a secured creditor, that the injunction would prevent the disposal of perishable goods and that the conduct of the plaintiffs should be taken into account.[184] Inter-company debts between associated companies should be scrutinised by the court where there is a question about the assets of companies available for payment of their debts and an order for liberty to inspect a company's books may be appropriate.[185]

---

[174] *Seven Seas Properties Ltd v Al-Essa* [1989] 1 All ER 164.
[175] At p 266.
[176] *Ibid*. The money was left in the joint names of the parties' solicitors. The judge noted that that gave the plaintiff purchaser better protection against other creditors than under a normal *Mareva* order but no issue was raised about that.
[177] *Powerscourt Estates v Gallagher* [1984] ILRM 123 at 126.
[178] *Moloney v Laurib Investments Ltd* (HC) 20 July 1993, Lynch J, unrep at 4-5.
[179] *Ibid.*
[180] *Moloney's* case at 6.
[181] *Ibid; cf Fleming v Ranks (Ireland) Ltd* [1983] ILRM 541 at 546.
[182] *Moloney's* case at 6.
[183] *Powerscourt Estates v Gallagher* [1984] ILRM 123 at 126.
[184] *Fleming v Ranks (Ireland)* Ltd [1983] ILRM 541 at 545.
[185] *Fleming's* case at 546.

Chapter 3

Some Aspects Of Contract Law

NEED FOR CONTRACT

[3.01] The first essential for success in an action for specific performance is to show that there *is* a contract.[1] Without a contract there can be no specific performance. If, for example, there are issues both whether there is a complete contract at all and also on the Statute of Frauds[2] and a court finds that parties' negotiations have not "ripened into the fullness of an entire contract", the plaintiff will fail, not just for want of the evidence necessary to enforce a contract for the sale of land, but simply in default of the existence of any such contract.[3] Since there would be no contract there would be nothing to be specifically enforced. If the parties do not get as far as a concluded contract the question whether there was a note or memorandum does not arise since the note or memorandum is required only for the purpose of evidencing a contract.[4] Similarly no question of part performance[5] arises if there is no contract.[6] There is simply nothing to be part performed even though either or both parties may have thought that there was a contract. Of course, if there *is* a contract but not enough evidence to satisfy the Statute and no other good ground to defeat a plea of the Statute a plaintiff cannot enforce the contract *by action* though he may have other remedies.[7]

[3.02] There must be *consensus* in the contract claimed by the plaintiff. It is of the essence of an enforceable simple contract that there is a *consensus ad idem* expressed in an offer and acceptance.[8] Such a consensus cannot be said to exist unless there is a "correspondence" between the offer and the acceptance.[9] If an offer is accepted in a fundamentally different sense from that in which it was made, and the circumstances are such as objectively justify such an acceptance, there cannot be said to be the meeting of minds which is essential for an enforceable contract.[10] However, if a person makes a deal giving the other party the impression that he understands the nature and effect of the contract, the general rule is that he will not avoid liability later because he did not understand its import and effect when he made it.[11] When an offer is accepted by the other

---

[1] For full treatment of Irish law of contract see Clark on *Contract*, 3rd Ed (1992). See paras **1.14-27** *ante* on the types of contracts where the remedy of specific performance may be available.

[2] Discussed in Ch 5 *post*.

[3] Per Henchy J in *Lynch v O'Meara* (SC) 8 May 1975, unrep at pp 4, 6. See also *Silverwraith Ltd v Siuicre Eireann Cpt* (HC) 8 June 1989, Keane J, unrep at 8-9.

[4] *Lynch's* case at pp 9-10. In practice a court will often decide both issues. Keane J did so in the *Silverwraith* case even though it involved making assumptions which were "in the teeth of the evidence": p 9. See also the judgments in *Boyle v Lee* [1992] 1 IR 555; [1992] ILRM 65.

[5] On which see Ch 6 *post*.

[6] *McQuaid v Lynam* [1965] IR 564, 574.

[7] See para **5.04** *post*.

[8] *Mespil Ltd v Capaldi* [1986] ILRM 373 at 376.

[9] *Ibid*.

[10] *Ibid*.

[11] Earlier on the same page.

side in a fundamentally different sense from the intended meaning the offeror will still be bound if the accepting party's construction of the offer was reasonable and he did not know of the offeror's different intention.[12]

If one party to an agreement does not advert to some facet of it, that does not make the agreement unenforceable.[13] If he is careless about reading conditions of a contract he may expect trouble. There exists in the law of contract a principle that a person of full capacity who chooses to sign a contract without reading or having explained to him its contents does so at his own risk and is bound by the contract.[14] It is necessary, however, in order to bind him that the party signing should understand that what he signs is a contract final in its form containing conditions and clauses.[15] Where a party signs a document under a fundamental mistake as to its nature and character, which mistake is not due to negligence on his part, he is not bound on the ground that there is in reality no contract at all.[16] The mind of the party signing does not go with the act of signing and, if he succeeds in a defence based on that point, he does so on the ground of *non est factum*.[17] The essence of a contract is that both parties should understand the *facts* on the basis of which they are about to contract.[18] If parties make a mistake about the general law which results in their agreement operating differently from their intentions this does not mean lack of consensus.[19] These points about mistake must, of course, be distinguished from the types of error which may support a defence of mistake[20] raised in an action for specific performance or the relief of rectification.[21] The burden of proving a contract, if this is in issue, is on the plaintiff who must show a "complete consummated contract clearly understood between the parties".[22]

Protection in negotiations

[3.03] Parties in negotiation[23] and their advisers must keep a keen eye on whether they have reached a complete contract on the facts of the particular case.[24] There is often a conflict between ensuring that a client gets sufficient protection in the purchase or sale of land and trying to ensure also that he gets an enforceable contract when he wants one. A party's solicitor trying to get the best contract for his client may be very careful not to bind the client in correspondence but this can bring a risk that the other party feels that he is being messed about and calls an end to the affair.[25] If parties have got as far as

---

[12] *O'Neill v Ryan (No 3)* 166 at 186-91.
[13] *Per* McCarthy J in *Re McCairns (PMPA) Plc* [1992] ILRM 19 at 22.
[14] *Siebel v Kent* [1976/7] ILRM 127 at 135-6. He must understand, *eg,* that the relevant written or printed conditions are incorporated with whatever document he actually signs and form part of the contract witnessed by that document: *ibid.*
[15] *Siebel's* case at 136. The contract used was a standard Law Society contract with minor changes mainly to adapt it from auction conditions to private treaty: pp 131, 136.
[16] *Bank of Ireland v McManamy* [1916] 2 IR 161 at 173.
[17] *Ibid.*
[18] *Gardiner v Tate* (1876) IR 10 CL 460, per Fitzgerald J at p 475. *Cf* Whiteside CJ at p 467 ("I think it reasonable that the purchaser should have a fair chance of knowing what he was buying") and O'Brien J at p 470.
[19] *Jackson v Stopford* [1923] 2 IR 1 at 11-12.
[20] Paras **9.66-9** *post.*
[21] Paras **10.15-19** *post.*
[22] *Gradwell v Maguire* (1872) IR 6 Eq 477 at 489 per Lord O'Hagan LC who added another descriptive phrase "a confluence of two minds reaching the same conclusion."
[23] *Cf* other aspects of negotiations at paras **4.19-20** *post.*
[24] See discussion of the material terms at paras **3.08-18** *infra.*
[25] As in *Parkgrange Investments Ltd v Shandon Park Mills Ltd* (HC) 3 May 1991, unrep at p 9.

considering heads of agreement, a draft formal contract or an exchange of proposals in correspondence a solicitor or other agent seeking to protect his client may make amendments to something which could be treated as an offer. That will probably amount to a counter offer which will mean that the original offer is not accepted.[26] By not accepting a document as proffered the risk is run that the counter offer will not be accepted and there will be no contract at all.[27] In practice the correspondence and any drafts are often protected by "subject to contract" or similar words and in such cases almost certainly there will be no contract even where a document is accepted without amendment.[28] A case of amending something which is an offer capable of acceptance[29] when no contract yet exists may be contrasted with one in which there is already a complete contract and one party's solicitor sends back a document amended. Here also he makes a new offer but non-acceptance of that leaves the original contract intact.[30] In another variation parties may agree certain terms, reduce them to writing and sign them but then agree to other terms which are reduced to writing but not signed by the party to be charged. Here the plaintiff usually will not be able to get specific performance of the contract as altered.[31] Also what may appear to be a complete written contract may not in fact be a contract at all. It is always open to parties to show that notwithstanding the terms of a document there is, in fact, no contract.[32] And even a formal and apparently complete contract signed by the relevant party may not in fact be a complete contract because it may misstate[33] or omit[34] a material term or include a term which is disputed.[35] Parties may also stipulate that they will not be bound until a certain event occurs, eg, an exchange of contractsor a written contract being signed by both sides[36] or deposit paid[37] - and that type of arrangement is likely to be upheld by the courts. There will be no concluded contract unless the event occurs. Or they may agree that an offer may be accepted only in a particular way in which case the offer must be accepted in the prescribed way or in some other manner no less beneficial to the offeror.[38] A purchaser who ignores a time limit for accepting an offer runs the risk that the offer will lapse.[39]

---

[26] Eg, *Swan v Miller* [1919] 1 IR 151: offer at £4,750, purported acceptance at £4,750 plus ground rent of £50 pa.

[27] *Parkgrange Investments Ltd v Shandon Park Mills Ltd* (HC) 2 May 1991, Carroll J, unrep at p 9.

[28] Note the discussion by Keane J of the use of "subject to contract" by a solicitor in *Mulhall v Haren* [1981] IR 364, esp at pp 391-4 and his views on its use by solicitors and laymen of common sense and business experience in *Silver Wraith Ltd v Siuicre Eireann Cpt* (HC) unrep, pp 2-4. Estate agents also use the phrase frequently. On "subject to contract" see Ch 4 *post, esp* discussion of *Boyle v Lee* at paras **4.21-25** *post.*

[29] Perhaps a draft agreement where there was no oral contract and the draft is furnished unprotected by "subject to contract".

[30] *Guerin v Ryan* (HC) 28 April 1978, McWilliam J, unrep at p 8.

[31] *New Hart Builders v Brindley* [1975] Ch 342; [1975] 1 All ER 1007 considered by McWilliam J in the *Guerin* case at p 7.

[32] Per Ronan LJ in *Russell & Baird v Hoban* [1922] 2 IR 159 at 161-2. In *Parkgrange Investments Ltd v Shandon Park Mills Ltd* (HC) 2 May 1991, unrep, Carroll J held that intending vendors signed a formal contract only to facilitate getting a CGT clearance certificate in the event that the sale proceeded and with no intention of being bound until the contract was sent back: p 8-9. In *Minister for Education v North Star Ltd* (HC) 12 January 1987, unrep, Lynch J held at 6 that want of mutual understanding over vehicle access meant that there was never really a concluded contract. *Cf Dore v Stephenson* (HC) Cir App, 24 April 1980, Kenny J, unrep at pp 1-3, 10-11.

[33] Note the possibility of specific performance with rectification, para **10.23** *post.*

[34] A party can sometimes enforce a contract by submitting to a missing term, para **5.13** *post.*

[35] A term can sometimes be waived, para **5.14** *post.*

[36] *Kelly v Irish Nursery & Landscape Co Ltd* [1981] ILRM 433.

[37] *Barry v Buckley* [1981] IR 306 at 310.

[38] *Walker v Glass* [1979] NI 129 at pp 134, 136.

[39] The *Parkgrange Investments* case at 8-9.

Discharge of existing contract by new one

[3.04] It is important to note also that an existing contract may be discharged by a new one. In order to discharge the original contract it is not necessary that the new one should be performed.[40] Nor is it necessary that the second contract should itself be *enforceable by action* once an intention to rescind the earlier one, as distinct from varying it, is clear.[41] Thus, if negotiations have in fact ripened into a complete contract it is important to keep in mind that further negotiations, perhaps meant as just dotting of "i"s and crossing of "t"s, could result in bringing about a new contract which will discharge an earlier one.

Physical layout

[3.05] The physical layout of property may create special problems over and above the need for agreement on the identity of the property in sale or some means of ascertaining it.[42] There may be features of the property which make it essential that the parties should agree terms about them and this is particularly important when the parties have different assumptions about the position in relation to those features.[43] Parties may not have thought it necessary to cover those matters when they were dealing or they may not have realised the legal complications which might result. This type of case is not one of mistake: it is to be regarded as a case where there was never a consensus and so no enforceable contract results.[44] This is so even if the parties, particularly when acting without the benefit of legal advice, believed that they had made a contract.[45] Thus, if part of a building is sold but the parties do not reach agreement about ownership of and rights of way over a foyer giving access to both parts of the building, there is probably no consensus.[46] And if a vendor sells a strip of land for access believing that it would be one of three entrances but the purchaser buys it intending it to be the sole access and being unaware of the vendor's understanding consensus is unlikely.[47] The parties have never been ad idem despite the apparent written contract.[48]

CONSIDERATION

[3.06] A plaintiff seeking specific performance should show that there was consideration for his contract. Equity will not assist a volunteer. A gift is a gift and if an intending donor has not gone the whole way towards completion of a gift the expectant donee has no

---

[40] *Headfort v Brocket* [1966] IR 227 at 261.
[41] *Ibid*, Budd J approving the House of Lords decision in *Morris v Baron & Co* [1918] AC 1 where the second contract for the sale of goods was unenforceable by virtue of s 4 of the Sale of Goods Act 1893 due to lack of writing.
[42] This is an essential term. See para **3.09** *infra*.
[43] Per Kenny J in *Dore v Stephenson*, Cir App, 24 April 1980, unrep at p 1.
[44] *Dore's* case, p 2.
[45] *Ibid*.
[46] As in *Dore's* case. Kenny J suggested at 10 that the parties should have agreed that either the plaintiff would be owner of the foyer with a right for the defendant, his customers and occupiers of flats to pass over it or else the defendant would remain owner of the foyer with like rights for the plaintiff and his customers.
[47] *Minister for Education v North Star Ltd*, Cir App, 12 January 1987, Lynch J, unrep at p 6.
[48] *Ibid*. The serious underlying point was that if the entrance was one of three it would carry much less traffic and allow a margin for traffic from the vendor's retained lands if they were developed later: p 5 of the transcript.

equity to compel the completion of the gift.[49] The main exception to this rule is that a completely constituted trust will be enforced. As Lord O'Hagan LC explained,

> "But the gift must be complete and perfect. Nothing must be left undone to carry it into effect in the very act of its creation. It must not be needful to invoke the aid of a Court to make it effectual; and, if it be, that aid will not be lent and it will fail of operation. But, when the gift is complete, when the trust is declared *in praesenti*, so as to have effect at once, when there is no imperfection to be supplemented, and the whole beneficial interest is taken out of the donor, the transaction will be equitably enforceable, and cannot be undone."[50]

Thus, in the case of registered land, the execution of a voluntary transfer will not be a complete gift; it must be *delivered* to the intended beneficiary.[51] However, if the transfer has been handed to the intended donee so that the latter can then register it himself without any further act by the grantor, or if it is shown that the donor had handed the transfer to his solicitor directing him to complete the registration, a binding unregistered right is established.[52] It should be remembered that marriage is valuable consideration; indeed it has been described as the "best that can be" and the "highest known to the law".[53]

Adequacy of consideration

[3.07] While an intended voluntary gift between relatives will not be specifically enforced the courts will execute a contract between relatives for valuable consideration and "ought not to weigh in nice scales the consideration, when it is fairly and honourably reduced in consequence of relationship and affection".[54] The relationship of parties[55] may suffice to uphold a transaction based upon a consideration which, though valuable, is so inadequate that it might under other circumstances raise an inference of fraud.[56] The relationship seems to be material to the *quantum* of consideration, not to its existence.[57] This kind of principle, however, is unlikely to save a conveyance to a relative in order to hinder, delay or defraud creditors[58] unless the grantee is a purchaser in good faith.[59] Even in cases not involving relatives the courts are reluctant to interfere with the exercise of free will and judgment of the parties by inquiring into adequacy of consideration.[60] However, a grossly inadequate consideration is likely to suggest fraud.[61] And a plaintiff who agrees to pay the full market price for a property but whose immediate vendor's only interest in it is under a contract at a nominal price in fraud of creditors of the former vendor cannot force that former vendor to enter into any conveyance.[62] Generally

---

[49] *Re Wilson; Grove-White v Wilson* [1933] IR 729 at 739. See discussion of incompletely constituted trusts by Keane, *Equity and the Law of Trusts in the Republic of Ireland* at paras 8.07-11.
[50] *Miller v Harrison* (1871) IR 5 Eq 324 at 341.
[51] *Devoy v Hanlon* [1929] IR 246 at 264.
[52] *Ibid.*
[53] *Re Downes* [1898] 2 IR 635 at 636.
[54] *Moore v Crofton* (1846) 9 Ir Eq R 344 at 348.
[55] *Eg*, spouses, parent and child, family arrangement.
[56] *Mullins v Guilfoyle* (1878) 2 LRI 95 at 109.
[57] *Ibid.*
[58] *Re O'Neill, a bankrupt* [1989] IR 544 (conveyance to daughter by insolvent father).
[59] In *O'Neill's* case Hamilton P was satisfied on the evidence that the daughter must have known her father's financial position: p 553.
[60] *O'Neill v Murphy* [1936] NI 16 at 30; *Murray v Palmer* (1805) 2 Schoales and Lefroy 474 at 488.
[61] See the defence of fraud, paras **9.10-11** *post*.
[62] *Hoban v Bute Investments* (SC) 17 December 1982, unrep.

speaking consideration must flow from the plaintiff[63] and a person who is not a party to a contract will find difficulty in showing that he has the standing to enforce it.[64] His best prospect is likely to be the principle that parties to a contract can create a trust of contractual rights for the benefit of a third party and that party can enforce them if his trustee does not do so.[65]

THE MATERIAL TERMS

[3.08] As we have seen,[66] consensus is vital to the existence of a contract. This must be consensus on the material terms of the contract claimed. We will discuss later how the material terms must be evidenced to satisfy the Statute of Frauds.[67] It is important to bear in mind that through both statutes and judicial decisions the law will imply certain terms, eg terms relating to title, requisitions, possession and incumbrances.[68] With those a contract need not deal. An agreement to sell implies that the whole of the vendor's interest in the land is to be sold and, in the absence of anything to lead to a contrary view, the interest is implied by law to be a fee simple.[69] It is just as important, however, to remember that the courts will not make parties' contracts for them.[70] Apart from terms which the law implies the court cannot supply any term which has not been agreed. That would be to make, and not to execute, an agreement, a jurisdiction which the court can never assume.[71] For example, if parties agree on a method of fixing the price which cannot work the court cannot substitute a different method which would work.[72] And if a party fails to prove the terms of the agreement relied on the court will not assist him by directing an issue or inquiry to ascertain what the terms are.[73] If terms in conditions of sale are ambiguous they are likely to be interpreted in favour of the purchaser.[74] This is an example of the "contra proferentem" rule as contracts are almost always prepared by vendors. However, the courts are slow to resort to this rule and it applies only when there is a real ambiguity and, usually, other rules of construction fail. If an agreement or deed carries out the intention of *neither* party the court will not, in setting it aside, made the parties execute some other agreement.[75]

[3.09] The material terms may be very straightforward. If one person agrees to sell a property to another for a named sum and the matter stops there a court would have to hold that there was a parol open contract to sell the property.[76] Thus the material terms of

---

[63] *McCoubray v Thompson* (1868) IR 2 CL 226; *Clitheroe v Simpson* (1879) 4 LRI 59 at 61. But *cf Barry v Barry* (1891) 28 LRI 45.
[64] See discussion by Clark, *Contract Law in Ireland*, 3rd Ed (1992) at pp 383-8.
[65] *Cadbury Ireland Ltd v Kerry Co-operative Creameries Ltd* [1982] ILRM 77 at 79-80.
[66] Paras **3.02, 3.05** *supra*.
[67] Ch 5 *post*, esp paras **5.12-14, 5.17, 5.22-4** (joinder of documents) and **5.25-8** (signature).
[68] *Godley v Power* (1957) 96 ILTR 135 at 147.
[69] *Ibid* at 145.
[70] *Dore v Stephenson* (HC) Cir App, 24 April 1980, Kenny J, unrep at 10; *Neville v Slattery Estates Co* (HC) 15 February 1984, Barrington J, unrep at 16.
[71] *Ormond v Anderson* (1813) 2 Ball & Beatty 363 at 369.
[72] *Carr v Phelan* [1976/7] ILRM 149 at 154-5.
[73] *Savage v Carroll* (1814) 2 Ball & Beatty 444 at 451.
[74] *Allman v McDaniel* [1911] 1 IR 467 at 472.
[75] *Cummins v Boylan* (1901) 35 ILTR 197.
[76] *Lynch v O'Meara* (SC) unrep at p 6. This passage from Henchy J also mentioned a 25% deposit paid but there was no issue about that. However, see paras **3.11-14** *infra* on deposits in the light of *Boyle v Lee* [1992] ILRM 65.

a contract for the sale of land may be simply the parties, the property and the price.[77] The identity of the vendor is obviously material but the court may be able to look at documents mentioned in conditions of sale to identify him.[78] If a purported vendor of an entire interest in property owns only a share in it and lacks the authority of his co-owner for the sale of the remaining share the contract may be incomplete in the sense that the purchaser does not intend to pay the full price for just the share.[79] A memorandum of the alleged contract may be bad in any event for mistakenly naming the vendor as selling the entire interest when he has only a share.[80] Agreement on the property sold including its area[81] is also essential. As we will see,[82] there is some scope for the introduction of oral evidence to assist on questions of identity of property in considering the adequacy of a *memorandum*. In that type of situation there has been agreement on the property in sale and the issue is the sufficiency of the memorandum. The price or method of ascertaining it is essential too.[83] For example, there cannot be a sale at a stated amount plus some unknown sum to be paid in the future.[84] Other matters relating to price such as payment by instalments as houses are built[85] and a substantial downpayment in settlement of a dispute about development of an estate[86] are also likely to be material terms. But a "luck penny" may be collateral and therefore not part of the contract for sale.[87]

[3.10] Cases which come to court are rarely as simple as having only the parties, property and price as their material terms. Even if there appears to have been an uncomplicated contract with just agreement on parties, price and property careful examination of the facts may show that more was involved and the parties may have fallen short of complete agreement by reason of failure to agree on other material terms.[88] The question what is material or essential must be considered, at any rate primarily, from the point of view of the parties themselves.[89] The test to be applied is a subjective one and the court is required to consider terms as essential to a contract which were so regarded by the parties themselves.[90] A court may regard some terms of a contract as essential to the contract for sale, for example, terms as to payment of the purchase price by instalments and other terms as mainly incidental to the contract, for example, terms relating to details of the construction of a building to be erected the land.[91] The circumstances of each case must

---

[77] See paras **5.31-5** *post* for the degree of accuracy with which these must be indicated in a memorandum to satisfy the Statute of Frauds and bear in mind *Boyle v Lee* and deposits.

[78] *Hodgens v Keon* [1894] 2 IR 657 at 659.

[79] *Carthy v O'Neill* [1981] ILRM 443 at 446.

[80] *Ibid*. Depending on the facts the memorandum could be good and the purported vendor liable in damages. See discussion of identification of parties in a memorandum at paras **5.32-3** *post*.

[81] *Law v Murphy* (HC) 12 April 1978, McWilliam J, unrep at 1-2 (alleged agreement for lease). *Cf Conaty v Ulster Development Ltd* (HC) NI, Lowry J, unrep at pp 6-7.

[82] Para **5.34** *post*.

[83] *Carr v Phelan* [1976/7] ILRM 149 at 155.

[84] *Maguire v Conway* [1950] IR 44 at 48.

[85] *Kelly v Danaher* (HC) Teevan J, unrep at 1-2. *Cf Tweddle v Henderson* [1975] 2 All ER 1096.

[86] *Tattan v Cadogan* [1979] ILRM 61.

[87] *Stinson v Owens* (HC) NI, McDermott LJ, unrep at 3, 15.

[88] As in *Lynch v O'Meara* where Henchy J's analysis shows that conditions about title and giving possession remained to be agreed.

[89] *Per* Lord McDermott in *Stinson v Owen* (1973) (HC), NI, unrep at 16. What is material will vary from case to case: *per* Kenny J in *Delgado v Crean* (HC) 24 May 1978, unrep at 11.

[90] *Anom Engineering Ltd v Thornton*, 1 February 1983, Costello J, unrep at 5-6.

[91] Examples given by Costello J in the *Anom Engineering* case at 5, having considered *Tweddle v Henderson* [1975] 1 WLR 1496; 1975 2 All ER 1096.

be examined to see if any term other than those which are always material has been deemed material by the parties.[92] Physical features of property sold, especially if part is being retained by the vendor, may make it essential to agree on terms relating to those features; those terms are likely to be material and without agreement on them there will be no complete contract.[93] And indeed it may become impossible to say that the *property* in sale has been agreed when essential rights such as access to it have not been agreed.[94]

The deposit

[3.11] Until recently[95] one probably would have advised that agreement in relation to the payment or amount of a deposit was not a material term of a contract for the sale of land in most cases and that accordingly a contract could be complete and enforceable without any such agreement. There can be little doubt that the payment of a deposit is a most important matter in the sale of land, and everybody knows this.[96] Lord Macnaghten has explained the purposes of a deposit thus:

> "The deposit serves two purposes - if the purchase is carried out it goes against the purchase-money but its primary purpose is this, it is a guarantee that the purchaser means business; and if there is a case in which a deposit is rightly and properly forfeited it is, I think, when a man enters into a contract to buy real property without taking the trouble to consider whether he can pay for it or not."[97]

There is a well established principle in the law of contract and particularly in the law of the sale of land that

> "... if monies are paid by way of deposit on a purchase price then apart from an express agreement to that effect and in the absence of an express agreement to the contrary in the event of the purchaser failing to comply with his obligation to complete the purchase those monies shall be forfeited to the vendor."[98]

On paying a deposit in pursuance of the contract a purchaser gets an equitable estate or interest in the property to the extent that the deposit is paid as part of the purchase money and he is accorded a lien to follow that estate or interest.[99] The deposit is thus a very important matter for both sides. Despite this importance there have been judicial views that agreement on payment or amount of a deposit is not necessarily a material term. Payment of a deposit has been described as "merely an incident, but not a necessary incident, of a sale".[100] In *Barrett v Costelloe*[101] Kenny J rejected a submission that a

---

[92] Cheshire & Fifoot, *Law of Contract*, 8th Ed (1972) at 185 in a passage considered by Lord McDermott in *Stinson's* case at 13.
[93] *Dore v Stephenson* (HC) 24 April 1980, Kenny J, unrep at 1-3, 10-11.
[94] *Dore's* case at 11.
[95] Until *Boyle v Lee* [1992] 1 IR 555; [1992] ILRM 65. See paras **3.12-14** *infra*.
[96] *Per* McVeigh J in *Morrow v Carty* [1957] NI 174 at 177.
[97] *Soper v Arnold* (1899) 14, 429 at 435 quoted with approval by McVeigh J in *Morrow's* case at 177.
[98] *Per* Finlay P in *Siebel v Kent* [1976-7] ILRM 127 at 136. See also Hamilton J in *International Securities Ltd v Portmarnock Estates Ltd* (HC) 9 April 1975, unrep at 18-19.
[99] *Re Barrett Apartments Ltd* [1985] IR 350 at 357-8, 359-61. If the contract goes off due to the purchaser's default he loses the lien: *Hedworth v Jenwise Ltd* [1994] EGCS 133. Note that a purchaser does not get a lien in respect of a "booking deposit": *Re Barrett Apartments Ltd* [1985] IR 350. A "booking deposit" (payment of one is not recommended) may be paid before there is any contract and usually is returnable upon notification by either party. Since there is no contract the purchaser gets no equitable interest in the property and thus there is no basis in law for a lien: *ibid* at 357. Therefore insolvency of a builder or other person to whom a booking deposit is paid is likely to mean the loss of the money; *ibid* at 361. Cf *Desmond v Brophy* [1985] IR 449.
[100] *Holohan v Ardmayle Estates*, (SC) 1 May 1967, unrep at 5.
[101] (HC) 13 July 1973, unrep at 5-7.

contract was not a concluded one because it did not provide for a deposit. In *Black v Kavanagh* Gannon J held that neither party "attached any importance to the matter of the payment of a deposit or its amount" and concluded:[102]

> "The question of whether or not a deposit should be paid was not considered by the parties to be a material matter, and in my opinion it is not an essential term of such a contract."

And in *Stinson v Owens*,[103] Lord McDermott held that agreement about the amount of a deposit was part of the oral contract but that "neither party looked on the deposit or its amount as material matters." If formal conditions of sale do provide for payment of a deposit the obligation to pay it is more likely to be held to be "an essential term of the contract"[104] and a standard condition providing for forfeiture of the deposit and re-sale in default of compliance supports that view.[105] A vendor should think carefully before fixing a deposit greater than a customary percentage of the purchase price. If he does so the courts may treat the higher deposit as a penalty and order the repayment of the entire with interest even when the purchaser has defaulted.[106]

[3.12] In *Boyle v Lee*[107] Finlay CJ, noting that the trial judge had found both relevant witnesses to be honest and candid, concluded:[108]

> "His findings on the question as to whether an oral contract for sale had been made, and completely made, between the plaintiff and Mr McManus[109] is based not, therefore, on the acceptance of the truth of one witness and the rejection of the truth or accuracy of another, but rather on inferences which he drew from the evidence. In particular, his finding that the failure of the parties to reach any agreement on the question of a deposit was irrelevant since it was of no importance in the contract, is a mixed question of law and fact.
>
> In my view, this finding was in error. The amount of a deposit to be made, even if a purchaser is willing to make a deposit of the appropriate amount, or the usual amount then experienced in transactions in Dublin, is too important a part of a contract for the sale of land in the large sum of £90,000 to be omitted from a concluded and complete oral agreement unless the parties in such an agreement had agreed that no deposit would be paid. In this case the evidence irresistibly leads to the conclusion that both Mr Boyle and Mr McManus agreed that there had to be a deposit, but left it over to be agreed between the solicitors when the formal contract was being settled as to its amount and form. In my view that evidence, which was not in contest, must lead to a conclusion that there was not a complete contract made orally between Mr Boyle and Mr McManus before 8 July 1988."

McCarthy J summarised the trial judge's conclusion in relation to the deposit:[110]

---

[102] (1973) 108 ILTR 91 at 95, 96.
[103] (1973) (HC), NI, unrep at 3-4.
[104] *Morrow's* case at p 178.
[105] *Ibid.* McVeigh J was referring to a condition before him to that effect. Note that condition 31 of the Law Society's *General Conditions of Sale* (1991) Ed, provides that failure to pay the deposit in full is a breach of condition entitling the vendor to terminate the sale etc.
[106] *Workers Trust & Merchant Bank Ltd v Dojap Investments Ltd* [1993] 1 EGLR 203 at 205-6.
[107] [1992] 1 IR 555; [1992] ILRM 65.
[108] At IR 571; ILRM 74-5 (Hederman J concurring).
[109] Agent of (alleged) vendors.
[110] At IR 576; ILRM 78.

"the question of a deposit did not appear to have had any real significance in the particular sale; the purchaser was at all times prepared to pay a substantial deposit and there was no problem in relation to it."

The trial judge had said:

"And it appears to me that the reality of the situation is reflected by Mr McManus in his letters to his clients when he sent them a copy of this letter of 8 July 1988. He added that he expected that the sale would now proceed without undue delay, and it appears to me that that letter is consistent with a concluded sale having previously been arrived at. It does not mention the question of a deposit, or the requesting of a deposit. So the question of a deposit doesn't appear to have had any real significance in this particular sale. It is obvious that Mr Boyle was at all times prepared to pay a deposit, even a substantial deposit, had it been accepted from him, and there was no problem in relation to the deposit, we know that."[111]

The heading of the letter of 8th July 1988 gave the names of the vendors and the address of the property in sale. The letter was sent to the vendors' solicitors and its text read:

"We refer to the recent negotiations in connection with the above property. I now write to confirm that we have received instructions from the vendors to accept an offer of IR£90,000 subject to contract. I would be obliged if you would prepare, and forward the contract which should incorporate the following agreed terms.

Proposed Purchasers:	Eoin Boyle & Susan Boyle, 165 Rathgar Road, Dublin 6.
Proposed Purchase Price:	IR£90,000 subject to contract.
Proposed Purchaser's Solicitors:	Patrick Clyne, Martin E Marren & Co, 10 Northumberland Road, Dublin 4.
Contents:	Contents of the apartments are included in the sale price.
Tenants:	The property is being sold subject to, and with the benefit of the tenants.
Closing date:	As soon as legal formalities can be completed.

I am sending a copy of this letter to Mrs Lee and Mrs Goyns for their information. In the meantime, you will appreciate that this letter is for information purposes only, and does not by itself, constitute part of a binding contract. I trust that the sale will proceed smoothly and satisfactorily and if I can assist you further at this stage, please let me know."[112]

[3.13] The very important question arises: how has the decision in *Boyle v Lee* affected the position existing previously?[113] The Chief Justice held[114] that the amount of a deposit to be made was "too important" to be omitted from a "concluded and complete" oral agreement for the sale of land even if the purchaser is willing to make a deposit of the "appropriate" or "usual" amount. He exempts cases where the parties have agreed that no deposit would be paid. Of course, in that situation also the parties have addressed the

---

[111] The judgment was oral and that passage is set out by Finlay CJ at IR 566-7; ILRM 71.
[112] The text of this letter is set out in full again in para **4.21** in a discussion of "subject to contract".
[113] See para **3.11** *supra*.
[114] In extracts quoted in para **3.12** *supra*, Hederman J concurring.

point and reached agreement on it. Though the price in *Boyle v Lee* was well above average and there were serious problems in relation to the flats in the property[115] there does not seem to have been anything about the case to distinguish it in principle from other cases in to the deposit. The effect of the judgment seems to be that agreement in relation to the deposit and its amount is a material or essential term of a contract for the sale of land unless the parties agree otherwise.

[3.14] On the other hand, McCarthy J held[116] that the trial judge was entitled to conclude that the parties had done a deal[117], the formalities to be cleared up by the solicitors. That necessarily meant deciding that agreement on the amount of the deposit was not an essential or material term on the facts of the case. Egan J held[118] that the absence of specific agreement in relation to the payment of a deposit or the amount thereof did not negative the existence of an oral agreement. It was usual to have a deposit in the case of sales of land but it was not essential in law. He also held that the deposit did not have to be covered by the memorandum[119] though he held that it was insufficient because it did not cover the "more serious" matter of the tenancies. With two judges on each side on this point we look to O'Flaherty J:[120]

> "...it is necessary to go back to the rudiments of the law of contract and find out whether there was an offer and acceptance and an intention to create legal relations. That there was an agreement on price, offer and acceptance, there is no doubt. But beyond that, in my judgment, there was much to be sorted out. For a start, the matter of the tenancies was not resolved. It was easy for the first plaintiff to say at the trial that he was prepared to take the property subject to the tenancies whatever kind they were - but one of his answers suggested that he might have had to engage in litigation because of what he felt was a misrepresentation in relation to a tenant who had, in effect, a six-year tenancy. It is common case that Mr McManus left him under the impression that they were all short tenancies, meaning thereby not more than one year. Then, there was no closing date agreed. Mr McManus expressly declined to take a deposit believing that that was a matter proper to be put into the formal contract. So, it appears to me, that there was no *consensus ad idem*. There was, at the most, an agreement to agree."

That is a very clear finding that there was no complete oral agreement. The refusal to take a deposit was a factor in that finding though the flats may have been the main factor.[121] The judgment does not go so far as saying that agreement on a deposit and its amount was an essential term of the particular contract, still less that such agreement would be a material term of all or most contracts for the sale of land. The majority in the Court therefore should not be regarded as holding that agreement on the deposit and its amount was an essential term.

However, it has always been open to parties to treat such agreement as a material term. The consideration of the status of the deposit by the Supreme Court and especially the strong line taken by the Chief Justice may increase the chances that parties to particular

---

[115] Covered particularly by O'Flaherty J at IR 581; ILRM 83-4 and Egan J IR 595; ILRM 94.
[116] At IR 576; ILRM 79.
[117] He held at IR 578; ILRM 80 that a part of the deal between the parties was that the deal itself was subject to contract and, in that sense, the deal was incomplete.
[118] At IR 594; ILRM 93.
[119] At IR 594-5; ILRM 94 citing *Black v Kavanagh* (1973) 108 ILTR 91.
[120] At IR 581-2; ILRM 83.
[121] Note Egan J's views on the flats at IR 590. 595; ILRM 90, 94.

contracts will treat the deposit and its amount as essential matters and that a court will hold accordingly. If that happens, then, of course, an oral contract for the sale of land cannot be complete without agreement in relation to the deposit and a memorandum will not satisfy the Statute of Frauds unless it covers the agreement on the deposit. If a formal contract uses the Law Society's *General Conditions of Sale* (1991) Ed without modification condition 31 will provide that failure to pay the deposit in full is a breach of condition entitling the vendor to "terminate the sale", sue the purchaser for damages or do both.

Completion date and giving possession

[3.15] Many other matters are capable of being material terms. As we have seen,[122] these matters will vary from case to case, the test is subjective and the court will consider terms as essential to a contract which were so regarded by the parties themselves. This means that the same point can be decided differently in different cases without any question of judicial inconsistency. A good example is the date for giving possession or closing the sale. If parties agree that they will await a special condition about a date for possession and then fail to agree on such a date they probably have failed to agree on a material term.[123] And if they agree that the date for handing over possession remains to be agreed, that is more or less the same and will be a material term also.[124] A closing date is likely to be a material term in sales of licensed premises.[125] Where an intending developer is unlikely to be able to proceed with his project for about a year a term about giving possession in four or six weeks is unlikely to be material.[126] If parties are indifferent to the date of completion provided it takes place in a reasonable time it is not a material term.[127] The prima facie position in sales of land other than special cases such as licensed premises appears to be that agreement on a closing date or date for possession is not a material term.[128] The courts have continually held that time is not of the essence of the contract[129] in the ordinary case of the sale and purchase of land and for that reason they have tended to regard the time fixed for completion as a detail introduced for the sake of convenience and not as an essential part of the bargain.[130] However if the evidence shows that an agreed closing date is important to either party or to both that date is likely to be a material term.[131] But a vague assurance about ample time for giving possession is unlikely to be considered material, especially if the party seeking to enforce the contract has in fact allowed ample time before suing.[132] A vendor is bound on completion to give vacant possession which involves the right to actual unimpeded physical enjoyment.[133] The parties may vary that duty by agreement and, for example, provide that a vendor will

---

[122] Para **3.10** *supra*.
[123] *Lynch v O'Meara* (SC) 8 May 1975, unrep at 7-8.
[124] *Mulhall v Haren* [1981] IR 364 at 394.
[125] *Delgado v Crean* (HC) 24 May 1978, Kenny J, unrep at 11, 13. *Cf Carthy v O'Neill* [1981] ILRM 443 at 445-6. On time being of the essence in sales of licensed premises see para **8.31** *post*.
[126] *Guardian Builders Ltd v Kelly* [1981] ILRM 127 at 132.
[127] *Barrett v Costelloe* (HC) 13 July 1973, Kenny J, unrep at 6-7.
[128] *Nyland v Brennan* (HC) 19 December 1970, Pringle J, unrep at 16-17.
[129] See discussion of time of the essence at paras **8.29-37** *post*.
[130] *Gray v Smith* (1889) 43 Ch D 208 approved by Pringle J in the *Nyland* case.
[131] *Hawkins v Price* [1947] 1 All ER 689 considered by Finlay P in *Doherty v Gallagher* (HC) 9 June 1975, unrep at 9-13.
[132] *Doherty's* case at 13-15.
[133] *Cumberland Consolidated Holdings Ltd v Ireland* [1946] KB 264 at 270, approved by Griffin J in *Viscount Securities Ltd* (SC) 6 May 1986, unrep at 4-6. See also paras **11.26-8** *infra*.

retain possession of part of property for an agreed period.[134] Any such variation is likely to be a material term.

Agreements for lease

[3.16] Agreements for lease need further essential terms to be agreed. It is well settled law that the date of the commencement of the period for which a lease is to be granted is an essential term in a contract to grant a lease.[135] There cannot be a concluded agreement without it.[136] However, a commencement date may be shown inferentially[137] or from indications in correspondence[138]. The fact of an agreement for lease itself being dated is not enough on its own to provide the commencement date of an intended lease.[139] It may be ascertained referentially as, eg, from the expiry of the six months period for redemption which the current tenant had,[140] from the time of payment of a sum of money[141] or when planning permission is obtained.[142] Occasionally, a commencement date may be supplied by statute.[143] The normal rule is that:

> "... it is sufficient if it appears either in express terms, or by reference to some writing which would make it certain, or by reasonable inference from the language used, on what date the term was to commence."[144]

[3.17] The duration of a lease or tenancy is also a material term.[145] The rent must be agreed or, at least, be "capable of being reduced to a certainty".[146] If there is no agreement on rent there cannot be a concluded contract.[147] While the rent will normally be the main consideration for the grant of a lease or tenancy there will sometimes be fines or lump sum payments and there may also be lessees' covenants to spend money on the premises over and above normal repairing and maintenance covenants. Care will obviously be taken to avoid infringing the restrictions in the ground rents legislation on the creation of new ground rents.[148] Where there are fines or covenants to spend money on the premises these are likely to be material terms of the agreement but, if so, they may be capable of

[134] As in *Usitravel Ltd v Freyer* (HC) 29 October 1973, Finlay J, unrep.

[135] *Per* Kenny J in *O'Flaherty v Arvan Properties Ltd* (SC) 21 July 1977, unrep at 5; *Swan v Miller* [1919] 1 IR 151, *per* Campbell C at 168.

[136] *Kerns v Manning* [1935] IR 869 at 880; *McQuaid v Lynam* [1965] IR 564 at 574; *Wyse v Russell* (1882) 11 LRI 173 at 178; *Lowe v Swift* (1814) 2 Ball & Beatty 529 at 35 (only term and amount of the rent agreed); *Phelan v Tedcastle* (1884) 15 LRI 169 at 174, 177-8; *Erskine v Armstrong* (1887) 20 LRI 296 at 299. *Cf White v Spendlove* [1942] IR 224.

[137] *Silver Wraith Ltd v Siuicre Eireann Cpt* (HC) 8 June 1989, Keane J, unrep at p 5.

[138] *Biggs v Brennan* (1907) 41 ILTR 60.

[139] *Wyse v Russell* (1882) 11 LRI 173. *Cf McNally v Donnelly* (1893) 28 ILTR 85 where a date fixed for the payment of rent was taken as evidence of the intended commencement date of a tenancy.

[140] *Phelan v Tedcastle* (1885) 15 LRI 169 at 177-9 - lease was to commence when the 6-month redemption period of a tenant about to be evicted would expire.

[141] *Erskine v Armstrong* (1887) 20 LRI 296 - 21 year lease to run from payment of £20.

[142] Considered in the *Silver Wraith* case at 5-6: plaintiff lost on other grounds.

[143] *Haire-Foster v McIntee* (1889) 23 LRI 529 533- parties did enough to import a time provision from the Land Law (Ireland) Act 1881; the plaintiff was defeated by laches.

[144] *Per* Sir Edward Sullivan C in *Phelan's* case at p 176.

[145] *Clinan v Cooke* (1802) 1 Schoales & Lefroy 22 at 32-3; *Crane v Naughten* (1912) 2 IR 318 at 326.

[146] *Shannon v Bradstreet* (1803) 1 Schoales & Lefroy 52 at 73.

[147] *McQuaid v Lynam* [1965] IR 564 at 574. The parties agreed a sale in fee simple by oral agreement which was evidenced by a memorandum (in two documents). They discharged that by a later agreement for sale by a long lease. As they never agreed the rent or commencement date the second "agreement" was never complete.

[148] On this see Wylie, *Irish Landlord and Tenant Law, esp* his notes in Ch 35 on s 2 of the Landlord and Tenant (Ground Rents) Act 1978.

being waived though, of course, this rarely would be considered unless they were of small amount or value. They may also be collateral contracts.[149] For example,[150] a covenant to spend £1,500 on improvements[151] was held to be collateral to a contract for the renewal of a lease[152] but if that had been an indivisible term of the contract it would have needed to be evidenced by a memorandum.[153] As in cases of outright sales of land, the identity of the property is vital.[154]

Identification of the parties is also essential and the precise identity of the lessee may be considerably more important than that of a purchaser of land. A vendor normally gets his money in exchange for an assurance of the land and he will rarely be much concerned with the purchaser after that. A landlord, however, is very much concerned with who the tenant is and with his solvency.[155] Questions of personal guarantees are also likely to arise in cases of intended leases, especially at full market rents.[156] It has been held that assignees of a bankrupt were not entitled to specific execution of a contract for lease for the accommodation of the bankrupt[157] and that an intending tenant in poor circumstances who got a man of substance to "front" for him as a trustee was not entitled either.[158] While it would be wrong to suggest that questions of guarantees or evidence of financial strength *must be* essential terms of *every* agreement for lease they are likely to be material terms of particular contracts. In addition lessee's covenants are in general more likely to be material terms of an agreement, especially if there is a superior lease, than are purchaser's covenants.[159] In some cases property will be sold by creating a sublease with a large fine and small rent[160] in order that the vendor/lessor can keep a better degree of control.[161] The factors which produce the need for that degree of control mean that covenants are more likely to be material terms.[162]

Some other examples of material terms

[3.18] It may be of interest to mention here some terms which have been held to be material in Irish case law. This must be done with a strong word of warning. As the test of what is a material term is subjective and results depend primarily on how the parties to particular cases regarded particular matters a finding that some point was (or was not) a material term in a decided case cannot mean that a similar (or apparently similar) issue must go the same way in another case. However, looking at these decided cases may help as a kind of check list to give ideas or reduce the risk of points being overlooked. We have already seen that the price is an essential term in sales of land and other money

---

[149] Paras **5.14-15** *post.*
[150] *Scott v McCombe* (CA) NI, 2 June 1965, unrep.
[151] Nearly twice the yearly rent so it was a significant sum.
[152] At p 7 of the transcript.
[153] *Ibid.*
[154] *Conaty v Ulster Development Ltd* (HC) NI, 4 October 1965, Lowry J, unrep at 6-7.
[155] *Per* Keane J in *Silver Wraith Ltd v Siuicre Eireann Cpt* (HC) 8 June 1989, unrep at p 8. *Cf* the *Conaty* case at 7-8.
[156] The *Silver Wraith* case at p 8.
[157] *Flood v Finlay* (1811) 2 Ball & Beatty 9.
[158] *O'Herlihy v Hedges* (1803) 1 Schoales & Lefroy 123 at 127-8.
[159] The *Conaty* case at p 6.
[160] Watching the point about grounds rents.
[161] By the use of a forfeiture clause and the satisfactory provisions of s 12 of Deasy's Act in relation to covenants: see discussion of s 12 by Wylie, *Irish Landlord and Tenant Law*, paras 21.21-4.
[162] See discussion of covenants by Lowry J in *Conaty's* case at 6.

terms may be too.[163] The same applies to a waiver of a right to have another party pay certain stamp duty and fees.[164] In the case of a proposed lease a deposit and the provision of personal guarantees are likely to be material terms.[165] So is a point about who is to pay rates.[166] And if a tenancy already exists or one has been terminated by notice to quit and the parties agree on an increase in rent the effective date of the increase will be a material term.[167] The price to be paid for stock being taken over when a public house is sold may be an essential term of the contract being negotiated for the purchase of the land[168] but it may also be a *collateral* contract.[169] Allowing a vendor a right of residence for five months after signing the contract probably will be an essential term[170] and likewise an agreement allowing him to keep a store room for three months.[171] Agreement for a leaseback of a part of the property sold after the conveyance is likely to be material too.[172] So is a term giving protection against claims by persons who had paid deposits under earlier transactions.[173] Terms relating to the physical state of land may be important. Failure to settle on mutual rights over a foyer where only part of a building was sold has led to a contract being held to be incomplete.[174] It is "particularly necessary that there should be agreement about any exceptional features when the purchaser is buying part of a building and the vendor is retaining the remainder of it".[175] Provisions about access may be vital, especially if they have substantial effects on likely traffic volumes or the chances of developing retained lands.[176] Other terms capable of being essential are provisions for the discharge of clean effluent and storm water and those relating to the supply of water and power.[177] Similarly a grant of a wayleave for the connection of water and sewage.[178] In sales of shares very different terms are often necessary.[179] For example, terms about the availability of the value of tax losses and indemnities in support may be vital.[180]

CONDITIONAL CONTRACTS

[3.19] Fairly often issues about conditions arise in actions for specific performance. Such points will also govern related claims such as those for damages or for the forfeiture or

---

[163] Para **3.09** *supra.*

[164] *Hoon v Nolan* (1966) 101 ILTR 99 at 109.

[165] *Silver Wraith Ltd v Siuicre Eireann Cpt* (HC) Keane J, unrep at 7-8.

[166] *Williams v Kenneally* (1912) 46 ILTR 292 at 294.

[167] *Ormond v Anderson* (1813) 2 Ball & Beatty 363 at 368-9.

[168] *Carthy v O'Neill* (1981) ILRM 443 at 445-6.

[169] *Godley v Power* (1957) 95 ILTR 135 at 146.

[170] *Cunningham v Maher* (1982) 9 ILT 168 at 169.

[171] *Usitravel Ltd v Freyer* (HC) 29 October 1973, unrep, Finlay J described this as a "special date" at p 11.

[172] *Field v Boland* (1837) 1 Drury & Walsh 37 at 49-51.

[173] *Guardian Builders Ltd v Sleecon Ltd* (HC) Blayney J, unrep (the case turned mainly on tax losses).

[174] *Dore v Stephenson* (HC) 24 April 1980, Kenny J, unrep at 8-11.

[175] *Per* Kenny J in *Dore's* case at 2.

[176] *Minister for Education v North Star Ltd* (HC) 12 January 1987, Lynch J, unrep at 5-6. A failure to agree on access could mean that there was no concluded contract even where the purchaser has been in possession for almost 5 years and has paid in full: see discussion by Murray J in *Mawhinney v Reid* [1984] 9 NIJB at 48-9. And *cf Anom Engineering Ltd v Thornton* (HC) 1 February 1983, Costello J, unrep.

[177] The *Anom Engineering* case at pp 6-7.

[178] *O'Mullane v Riordan* [1978] ILRM 73 at 78.

[179] If a deal is in substance the purchase of a company or a large slice of it will usually be extensive warranties by the vendors.

[180] As in the *Guardian Builders* case. It is well worth reading the judgments in *Pernod Ricard & Comrie Plc v FII Fyffes Plc* (HC) 21 October 1988, Costello J, unrep; (SC) 11 November 1988, unrep, to see examples of the types of points that can arise.

return of a deposit. The central issue is likely to be whether there was a complete and enforceable contract at the relevant time. A court may have to decide whether the parties ever got as far as reaching a contract at all.

This may involve considering questions such as the use of the phrase "subject to contract",[181] express conditions that parties will not be bound until a specified event occurs,[182] "agreements to agree"[183] or whether the parties are still only in negotiation or may just possibly have some *duty* to negotiate.[184] In other cases there will be a written contract containing something very clearly expressed to be a condition[185] and questions will arise about the effect of that condition and noncompliance with it. This type of case we consider now. But first a word of warning. Conditional contracts often lead to trouble and may produce a situation that one party can enforce a contract against the other but not vice versa.[186] Conditions are more often than not for the benefit of purchasers; vendors and their advisers will try to minimise or avoid them while purchasers will need their protection in varying degrees and thus both sides will have good reason to negotiate with great care.

Conditions precedent and subsequent

[3.20] A distinction may be made between a condition which must be satisfied before any legally binding contract comes into operation (a condition precedent) and one which is part of a legally binding contract but which, if not fulfilled, can result in the contract ceasing to be binding (a condition subsequent).[187] In the case of a condition precedent the condition must be fulfilled before the relevant party can be legally bound.[188] This type of case is in no way similar to that of a purchaser who buys a property but safeguards himself by providing that he may avoid the bargain if, eg, he fails to obtain a loan or get planning permission.[189] A necessary Land Commission consent has been described as the "condition precedent to his becoming a purchaser with the benefit of an enforceable contract."[190] In practice the distinction may not be very important in many cases. Non-fulfilment of either type of condition leads to the same ultimate result - ie, absence of both liability to complete the deal and ability to force the other side to complete it. Perhaps for this reason judges have rarely addressed the distinction in specific performance cases. Its existence was accepted by Gannon J in *Gaelcrann Teo v Payne*[191] taking the view that upon non-compliance with a condition stated to be a condition precedent the obligations of the contract cannot be enforced by a party in default.[192] In England there is uncertainty whether the term that a purchaser should pay a deposit is a condition precedent failure to fulfil which prevents the contract from coming into

181 Discussed in Ch 4.
182 Para **4.15** *post.*
183 Paras **4.16-18**.
184 Paras **4.19-20**.
185 Normally in a "special condition" where standard Law Society contracts are used.
186 *Delgado v Crean* (HC) 24 May 1978, unrep at 6.
187 *Per* Costello J in *Dorene Ltd v Suedes (Ireland) Ltd* [1981] IR 312 at 324 approving a passage from Wylie, *Irish Conveyancing Law* (1978) at para 9.069.
188 As in the *Dorene* case, pp 324-5.
189 Example given by Costello J in the *Dorene* case at p 325. And see para **3.21** below.
190 By Henchy J in *State (Callaghan) v Irish Land Commission* [1978] ILRM 201 at 202. *Cf* McWilliam J in relation to planning permission in *Maloney v Elf Investments Ltd* [1979] ILRM 253 at 255.
191 (1985) ILRM 109 at 114-6 (an insurance case).
192 At p 115 approving the judgment of Fletcher Moulton LJ in *Re Coleman's Depositories Ltd* [1907] 2 KB 798.

existence or is a fundamental term of the contract breach of which entitles the vendor to treat the contract as at an end.[193] Here Clause 31 of the Law Society's Standard Conditions (1991) Ed provides that failure to pay the deposit is "a breach of condition entitling the vendor to terminate the sale..."

Planning matters

[3.21] A condition often relates to planning matters. In *Healy v Healy*[194] the contract was "subject to the purchaser obtaining full planning permission for residential development in respect of the property at a density of not less than seven houses to the acre within 17 months of the date of this contract". Kenny J did not find it necessary to decide whether the clause was a "condition" holding that in principle "when a clause in a contract (whether it is a condition or a term) is inserted solely for the benefit of one party..." it could be waived in certain circumstances.[195] In *McKillop v McMullan*[196] a contract was signed "subject to the purchaser obtaining planning permission for the construction of a road over the area coloured green..." Murray J held that the clause "created a condition precedent to the coming into existence of an effective and enforceable contract of sale".[197] In *Sepia Ltd v Hanlon Ltd*[198] a clause made the contract "subject to the purchaser obtaining planning permission to develop the property the subject matter of the sale..." Costello J held that if the plaintiffs had failed to obtain planning permission by the closing date and if that date was not extended by mutual agreement, the defendants were entitled to treat the contract as at an end if the plaintiffs refused to complete.[199] Note that they could have waived the clause and completed.[200] In *Maloney v Elf Investments Ltd*[201] a clause was added "Sale subject to purchaser getting full planning permission before 31 July 1978." McWilliam J held that the clause "can only mean that the contract is only to be enforceable if the permission is obtained by that date..."[202] which treats the clause as a condition precedent and, of course, meant that without planning permission there was no enforceable contract. In *Tiernan Homes Ltd v Sheridan*[203] the contract was subject to the purchasers "procuring Full Planning Permission from the planning authority for the development of the land by the erection of dwellinghouses thereon in accordance with Plans to be prepared by purchasers and lodged with the Planning Authority." Kenny J[204] referred to this as "the condition as to planning permission"[205] and "term".[206] In *Hughes v Carter*[207] a clause was inserted "Should it transpire that the extension at the rear is not an

---

[193] See review of authorities by Warner J in *Millichamp v Jones* [1983] 1 All ER 267 at 271-5. *Cf Myton Ltd v Schwab-Morris* [1974] 1 All ER 326; *Damon Cia Naviera SA v Hapag-Lloyd International SA* [1985] 1 All ER 475.
[194] (HC) 3 December 1973, unrep.
[195] At 6. Waiver is discussed at para **3.24** *infra*.
[196] [1979] NI 85.
[197] At 92.
[198] [1979] ILRM 11.
[199] At 24.
[200] As Costello J pointed out at 24. On waiver see para **3.24** *post*.
[201] [1979] ILRM 253.
[202] At 255.
[203] [1981] ILRM 191.
[204] With whose judgment the other two members of the court agreed.
[205] At 195.
[206] At 196.
[207] (HC) 23 February 1978, unrep.

exempted development, the vendor will undertake to obtain retention permission."[208] Hamilton J referred to the clause as "a fundamental term of the agreement".[209]

Consents

[3.22] Land Commission consent to sales or lettings often has been needed for the validity of the transaction.[210] A person who agreed to buy subject to a term that if the consent of the Land Commission was not forthcoming the sale and contract would be at an end has been described as "only a conditional or contingent purchaser"[211] and the consent of the Land Commission was described as the "condition precedent to his becoming a purchaser with the benefit of an enforceable contract."[212] In practice the courts have also treated this type of condition as a condition subsequent. It has been held that a purchaser in a contract with this type of condition was bound to make a bona fide application for Land Commission consent and only when such an application had been made and turned down could the provisions in the special conditions for the return of the deposit come into operation.[213] The practical situation was that if the consent of the Land Commission was refused the transaction had to be "completely and entirely cancelled".[214] If a provisional list was published by the Land Commission[215] land could not be sold, transferred, let, sublet or subdivided without the consent of the Land Commission before the termination of proceedings for the acquisition of the land by the Land Commission.[216] But if the Land Commission gave consent to the registration of a purchaser on the folio without prejudice to the acquisition proceedings the contract could be enforced.[217] Of course, if a disposition was made in breach of a provision of the Land Purchase Acts it was illegal and unenforceable and could not be saved by a plea of estoppel.[218] And if a person took a step designed to evade a higher stamp duty payable under the Land Purchase Acts he would have difficulty trying to unravel it later.[219]

[3.23] Another consent often needed is that of a landlord. At common law the lessee has an interest which he can freely dispose of as he pleases unless prevented or restrained by clear words; if he wishes to cut down the lessee's freedom the lessor must insist on clear words going into the lease.[220] Almost all commercial leases nowadays contain restrictions on assignment, subletting and parting with or sharing possession. They are also likely to

---

[208] To cater for a condition in the plaintiff's loan approval.

[209] At p 13.

[210] The Lands Acts restricted letting, subletting and subdivision of agricultural or pastoral holdings. Likewise sales in non-urban areas to anybody other than a "qualified person" unless the land was certified by the Land Commission as required for urban development. A transaction in breach of the controls would be void. Ch 8 of Wylie, *Irish Conveyancing Law* (1978) deals fully with Land Act consents.

[211] By Henchy J in *State (Callaghan) v Irish Land Commission* [1978] ILRM 201 at 202.

[212] *Ibid. Cf* the older cases of *Kelly v Enright* (1883) 11 LRI 379 and *Beauclerk v Hanna* (1888) 23 LRI 144 where specific performance was granted subject to sanction by the Land Commission.

[213] *Costelloe v KN Maharaj Krishna Properties (Ireland) Ltd* (HC) 10 July 1975, Finlay P, unrep at 14-15.

[214] Per Finlay P in *Siebel v Kent* [1976-7] ILRM 127 at 130.

[215] Pursuant to s 40(2) of the Land Act 1923.

[216] s 13(1) of the Land Act 1965.

[217] *Horgan v Deasy* [1979] ILRM 71 at 73-4. Note that when the contract in that case was made no notice of inspection had been served so the contract could not have been impugned then: p 73.

[218] *Dempsey O'Reilly* [1958] IJR 75; *O'Kane v Burns* [1897] 2 IR 591 (cases on sublettings). See Illegality at paras **9.48-55** *post*.

[219] *Parkes v Parkes* [1980] ILRM 137 at 144-5.

[220] *Northern Ireland Carriers Ltd v Larne Harbour Ltd* [1981] NI 171 at 174; *Royal Avenue Hotel Ltd v Richard Shops Properties Ltd* [1985] 6 NIJB 52 at 77.

contain restrictions on user and landlord's consent to a change of user will be needed. In some cases when leasehold properties are sold the real issue will be a proposed change of user as the proposed assignee will be respectable and financially sound and his intended user will be known or indeed may be obvious from his identity.[221] Although it has been held[222] that consent to change of user should be sought by the tenant who wishes to make the new use the modern trend is to deal with questions of consent to assignment and change of user in the same set of proceedings if a landlord withholds consent.[223] Note that a condition for landlord's consent to assignment has been treated in England as a matter of title arising within the sale.[224] The point was important because, as a matter of title, the consent did not have to be obtained by the named closing date.[225] However, a decision of that sort is likely to turn on the actual wording of the particular contract and on the matter at issue being one of title.[226] Even though a point may be wholly or partly a matter of title, if parties make it a special condition[227] and provide for what is to happen if the condition is not met, the court is likely to treat it as "a condition precedent to the operation of the contract as a contract for sale".[228]

[3.24] Consents of third parties to fulfil a role may also be conditions of a contract. Thus, where a proposal is made to take a tenancy and it is accepted on condition that a named person will be security that condition has to be met or there will be no enforceable agreement.[229] And if a contract is made subject to the approval of a party[230] or that of the board of a company[231] there probably will be no concluded contract until that approval is given.[232]

[3.25] Very often a purchaser will try to get agreement that the contract is "subject to loan". A typical clause would provide that the contract was subject to the purchaser receiving loan approval from a lender[233] within a specified period.[234] A vendor must bear in mind that if a bona fide application is made for the loan approval and it fails the purchaser is entitled to get out of the contract. If the vendor is committed to buying another property he may be relying on the proceeds from the one he is selling to enable him to complete his own purchase. Vendors should be slow to agree to "subject to loan" clauses and, if they do agree, they should insist that the condition relates to loan

---

[221] Eg, *OHS Ltd v Green Property Co* [1986] IR 39; [1986] ILRM 451 where a landlord successfully resisted the advent of a building society to a shopping centre.

[222] *Lloyd v Earl of Pembroke* (1954) 89 ILTR 40.

[223] See Wylie, *Irish Landlord and Tenant Law* para 18.16.

[224] *Property and Bloodstock Ltd v Emerton* [1967] 2 All ER 839 (affirmed [1967] 3 All ER 321) considered by Barrington J in *Crean v Drinan* [1983] ILRM 82 at 87.

[225] [1967] 2 All ER at 849. No date for getting consent was named. This point is dangerous; if the need for consent is treated as a condition precedent (unlike the English case) time would be likely to be "of the essence". On time for complying with conditions see para **3.28** *infra*.

[226] *Crean v Drinan* [1983] ILRM 82 at 87. The point was not landlord's consent but getting an assignment of possible outstanding interests.

[227] Which is normal practice.

[228] *Crean's* case at 87.

[229] *White v McMahon* (1886) 18 LRI 460 at 466.

[230] *Dyas v Stafford* (1882) 9 LRI 520.

[231] *Irish Mainport Holdings Ltd v Crosshaven Sailing Centre Ltd* (HC) Keane J, unrep at 13.

[232] We are close now to "subject to contract": see para **4.14** *post*.

[233] The name of the lender is often specified.

[234] The time is likely to be of the essence: see para **3.28** below.

approval, not to the actual payment of the loan. In *Rooney v Byrne*[235] the agreement was in the form of a proposal by the purchaser accepted by the vendor. The proposal ended:

> "This proposal is subject to me getting an advance on the property."

Clearly the parties contemplated that the purchaser would need an advance for the purpose of providing the purchase money. The object of the clause was to provide that, in the event of his failing to get such an advance, the contract also failed.[236] The clause did not impose a time limit, refer specifically to loan *approval*, mention the amount of the loan required or name the intended lender; while none of those points was material in the actual case the clause is not an ideal precedent. The name of the lender was probably not important. However, the purchaser might have been further protected by naming an amount and the vendor by inserting a shortish time limit and directing the clause to loan *approval*. A better clause is found in a later case. In *Draisey v Fitzpatrick*[237] the contract was made on 17th December 1979 and contained this condition:

> "The obligations of both parties under this contract are subject to the purchasers being approved for a loan by the Irish Permanent Building Society on the security of the premises in the amount of £25,000.00 on or before the 2nd January next. Should the said loan approval be not forthcoming on or before that date then this contract shall be at an end and all amounts furnished by the purchasers will be refunded without any interest or compensation..."[238]

Loan approval issued within the time limit but the purchasers claimed that conditions attaching to it were unreasonable. Ellis J held that the clause was subject to the implied terms that the conditions of the loan approval should be reasonable, that they should reasonably have been in the contemplation of the parties when the contract was made and that they should be to the satisfaction of the purchasers acting reasonably.[239] If a clause simply makes the contract subject to a "satisfactory" mortgage this is likely to be construed as meaning satisfactory to the purchaser acting reasonably.[240]

Duty to try to fulfil conditions

[3.26] There is likely to be an implied obligation on parties to make reasonable efforts to fulfil a condition of a contract. It has been said that where the words of an instrument show that its efficacy depends or is to depend on an act to be done by one party, there is a contract by that party that he will do all that lies in his power to bring about that act.[241] Thus, a purchaser with the benefit of a condition entitling him to get out of his contract if the Land Commission refused consent was bound to make a bona fide application for

---

[235] [1933] IR 609.
[236] *Per O'Byrne J* at 615.
[237] [1981] ILRM 219.
[238] Set out at 220. The clause continued with a strange statement that it was for the benefit of the *vendor* who alone would have the right of waiver.
[239] At 223.
[240] *Lee-Parker v Izzet* [1971] 3 All ER 1099 at 1105 approved by Ellis J in *Draisey v Fitzpatrick* [1981] ILRM 219 at 222-3. There is a risk of an imprecise condition making the whole contract void for uncertainty: *Lee-Parker v Izzet* (No 2) [1972] 2 All ER 800; *Re Rich's Will Trusts* (1962) 106 Sol J 75. Cf *Janmohamed v Hassam* (1976) 241 EG 609.
[241] Blackburn J in *Worthington v Sudlow* 2 B&S 521 approved by May CJ in *McConnell v Kilgallen* (1878) 2 LRI 119 at 123. *Cf Byrne v Limerick Steamship Co Ltd* [1946] IR 138 at 149.

that consent[242] and was certainly not entitled to make it in such a way as to achieve the defeat of the application.[243] The issue was the good faith of the application and it was not necessary to show that the mala fide elements in the application were the effective cause of the refusal of consent.[244] If a landlord says that he is willing to give a necessary consent the vendor clearly must get it.[245] A vendor is certainly not entitled to procure his own landlord to refuse consent.[246] Under a typical condition making a sale subject to landlord's consent and saying nothing about any obligation to take proceedings the vendor must use his best endeavours to obtain the landlord's consent but he is under no obligation to take proceedings to force the landlord's hand.[247] The fact that a landlord's refusal of consent is unreasonable seems to be immaterial.[248] A court would not order specific performance of a contract where landlord's consent was needed and there was doubt whether the consent was being withheld reasonably or unreasonably.[249] If an essential licence or permission is refused there may be an obligation to show that all reasonable steps have been taken to have the refusal withdrawn.[250] And an initial refusal of a necessary consent is unlikely to justify repudiation of a contract if the consent is given later before the agreed completion date.[251]

[3.27] Apart from any special duty to try to fulfil conditions, each party to a contract of sale has the right to expect that the other will be reasonable in taking such necessary steps as may be incidental to closing the sale.[252] There will normally be an implied undertaking that a party will not disable himself from carrying out his contract.[253] Also there is implied into every contract (provided the other terms do not repel the implication) a term that neither party shall prevent the other from performing it.[254] While a court of equity will not compel a person to do something which is impossible[255] it will have little sympathy for someone whose own neglect or default makes it impossible for him to perform his contract.[256]

---

[242] *Costelloe v KN Maharaj Krishna Properties (Ireland) Ltd* (HC) 10 July 1975, unrep at 13, Finlay P having quoted with approval a long passage from the judgment of O'Byrne J in *Rooney v Byrne* [1933] IR 609 at 615-6.

[243] The *Costelloe* case at 18.

[244] *Ibid* p 14.

[245] *Fisher v Coan* [1894] 1 IR 179 at 182.

[246] As in *Day v Singleton* [1899] 2 Ch 320 considered by O'Connor MR in *Kelly v Duffy* [1922] 1 IR 62 at 67-69.

[247] *Royal Avenue Hotel Ltd v Richard Shops Properties Ltd* [1985] 6 NIJB 52 at 78-82.

[248] *Bickel v Courtenay Investments (Nominees) Ltd* [1984] 1 All ER 657 considered by Murray J in the *Royal Avenue Hotel* case.

[249] *Curtis Moffat Ltd v Wheeler* [1929] 2 Ch 224 at 235-236. The position in Ireland was even clearer while the prohibition in s 10 of Deasy's Act was in force; despite its repeal (by s 35 of the Landlord and Tenant (Ground Rents) Act 1967 it is not clear yet here whether an unreasonable withholding of landlord's consent would entitle a tenant to assign: see Wylie, *Irish Landlord and Tenant Law*, para 21.12.

[250] *Byrne v Limerick Steamship Co Ltd* [1946] IR 138 at 149.

[251] *Smith v Butler* [1900] 1 QB 694; *Re Sandwell Park Colliery Co* [1929] 1 Ch 277; [1928] All ER Rep 651.

[252] *Per* Barrington J in *Neville v Slattery Estates Co Ltd* (HC) 15 February 1984, unrep at 16.

[253] *Per* Earl Loreburn in *King v David Allen & Sons, Billposting Ltd* [1916] 2 AC 54 at 62 (an Irish appeal to the House of Lords).

[254] *Massarella v Massarella* (HC) 10 July 1980, Keane J, unrep at 17.

[255] For the defence of impossibility see paras **9.56-8** *post*.

[256] *Sheppard v Murphy* (1868) IR 2 Eq 544 at 557-8; *Arterial Drainage Co v Rathangan Drainage Board* (1880) 6 LRI 513 at 525-7. *Cf McConnell v Kilgallen* (1878) 2 LRI 119.

[3.28] A distinction has been drawn by the courts between the flexibility which they will show in relation to the closing date in contracts for the sale of land and the rigidity which they have adopted toward dates fixed by conditions on which the existence of the contract depends.[257] As Maugham J explained:[258]

> "Courts of equity, in dealing with actions for specific performance relating to land, have been accustomed to give effect to the real intention, rather than to the precise words, fixing the date for completion. The effect is that a clause fixing a date for completion is equivalent to a clause stating that completion shall be on that date or within a reasonable time thereafter. But there is no ground for a similar construction in the case of a condition upon which the validity of the contract as one for sale depends. The distinction is obvious. In the first case both parties are bound and a moderate delay in completion is thought not to injure either. In the latter, the very existence of the mutual obligations is dependent upon the performance of the condition. The purchasers do not know in the first instance if their purchase money will ever be required. In general, and in the present case, there is no promise or undertaking by the vendor that the condition will be fulfilled. Equity has, I think, never applied its liberal views as to time to such a condition. If a date is mentioned, the condition must be exactly complied with. If a date is not mentioned, the condition must be fulfilled within a reasonable time; there is no difference between the views of law and equity in considering what is a reasonable time, and the uncertain position of purchasers must be borne in mind."[259]

Subject to the important rule that the meaning of a contract is to be found in the intention of the parties as expressed in, or to be implied from, the language they have used[260] the courts have adopted the following general principles of interpretation:

(i)   Where a conditional contract of sale fixes the date for the completion of the sale then the condition must be fulfilled by that date;

(ii) Where a conditional contract of sale fixes no date for completion of the sale, then the condition must be fulfilled within a reasonable time;

(iii) Where a conditional contract of sale fixes (whether specifically or by reference to the date fixed for completion) the date by which the condition is to be fulfilled, then the date so fixed must be strictly adhered to, and the time allowed is not to be extended by reference to equitable principles.[261]

The completion date or "closing date" will be interpreted for the purpose of applying those principles as the date fixed by the contract for completion and the fact that a court of equity might not enforce that date is a different matter which does not affect the interpretation.[262] The courts will reject an argument that a reasonable time ought to be allowed for meeting a condition by analogy with the principle that the time for completing a contract is regarded in equity as the date fixed for completion or a reasonable time thereafter.[263]

---

257   *Per* Barrington J in *Crean v Drinan* [1983] ILRM 82 at 85.
258   In *Re Sandwell Park Colliery Co* [1929] 1 Ch 277 at 282; [1928] All ER Rep 651 at 653.
259   This passage was approved by the Privy Council in *Aberfoyle Plantations Ltd v Cheng* [1960] AC 115; [1959] 3 All ER 910 at 915; and by Barrington J in *Crean v Drinan* [1983] ILRM 82 at 85.
260   Accepted by Barrington J in *Crean's* case at 85.
261   *Per* Barrington J in *Crean's* case having approved *Aberfoyle Plantations* case and the passage from Maugham J just quoted. The third point was applied by McWilliam J in *Maloney v Elf Investments Ltd* [1979] ILRM 253 at 255.
262   *Crean's* case at 86.
263   *Maloney's* case at 255.

Waiver

[3.29] A provision in a contract sometimes may be waived by the person for whose benefit it was inserted. As Kenny J explained:[264]

> "On principle it seems to me that when a clause in a contract (whether it is a condition or a term) is inserted solely for the benefit of one party and is severable from the other clauses and when the other party on completion will get everything that he contracted for, the party for whose benefit the clause was inserted may waive performance of the clause and insist on completion despite the non-performance of the condition or term."

The rule that the condition waived must be solely for the benefit of the person waiving it is strict. The fact that a term may be inserted "mainly" for the benefit of one party will not entitle him to waive it unilaterally.[265] Still less can a party waive a term which is there solely for the benefit of the other side.[266] It has been said that if it is not obvious on the face of the contract that the stipulation is for the exclusive benefit of the party claiming to eliminate it, it cannot be struck out unilaterally.[267] It is doubtful that a court can enquire outside the terms of the contract to see where the benefit of a condition lies.[268] However, it would seem reasonable that as long as oral evidence is not offered as an attempt to *construe* or *contradict* the parties' contract it would be admissible to see whether a condition is *solely* for the benefit of one party where that is not made clear by the contract. A "subject to planning permission" condition will obviously benefit one party, usually the purchaser, but it may not be clear from the terms of the contract whether the condition also benefits the other party.[269] If a vendor retains adjoining land a condition about planning is quite likely to benefit him also (though it must, of course, depend on the precise facts) but the contract will not necessarily indicate that he is keeping any land. Waiver of a condition may take place at any time up to the date for fulfilling the condition but not later.[270] Although in a number of actions for specific performance waiver of a term of the contract has been allowed as late as the hearing of the action this does not apply to a case where the term is expressed as a condition to be performed by a definite date.[271] A failure to fulfil a condition may itself be waived by, for example, insistence on performance of the contract after the time for fulfilling the condition has passed without the condition being met.[272] The right to insist on compliance with the condition is not lost, however, and a new date may be fixed for its fulfilment by giving reasonable notice.[273] If a party gives notice as soon as a deadline passes with the condition unfulfilled that he refuses to go ahead he avoids the risk of being found to have waived his right to get out

---

[264] *Healy v Healy* (HC) 3 December 1973, unrep at 6. See also *Gordon v Gordon* [1951] IR 301 at 306.
[265] *Maloney v Elf Investments Ltd* [1979] ILRM 253 at 256.
[266] *Tiernan Homes Ltd v Sheridan* [1981] ILRM 191 at 195.
[267] By Brightman J in *Heron Garage Properties Ltd v Moss* [1974] 1 All ER 421 at 426; [1974] 1 WLR 148 at 153, considered by Murray J in *McKillop v McMullan* [1979] NI 85 at 92 and Kenny J in the *Tiernan Homes* case at 196.
[268] Brightman J suggests in the *Heron Garage* case that the court should not do so, Murray J accepts that view in *McKillop's* case at p 92 and in the *Tiernan Homes* case Kenny J gave as his reason for holding the waiver ineffective the fact that "the terms of the contract provided for a benefit for Harry Sheridan which was involved in the grant of planning permission".
[269] In all three cases cited at fn 268 it was clear from the text of the contract that there was some benefit for the second party.
[270] *Maloney's* case at 256; *Crean v Drinan* [1983] ILRM 82 at 86.
[271] *Maloney's* case at 256.
[272] *McKillop's* case at 92.
[273] *Ibid*, p 93.

of the contract or to have "revived" it.[274] The waiver of a condition attached to a contract is a very different matter from a waiver of a term which is part of the contract but not evidenced by the memorandum relied on to satisfy the Statute of Frauds and the latter type of case will be considered later.[275]

[3.30] Possibilities of waiver are not confined to any particular type of condition or situation. There is nothing in the Statute of Frauds to prevent a plaintiff in an action on a contract waiving a stipulation exclusively for his own benefit which was part of the arrangement between him and the defendant although not embodied in any memorandum signed by or on behalf of the defendant.[276] And a condition attached to an acceptance of an offer may also be waived provided that it was introduced to protect the acceptor.[277] A contract *as a whole* may be waived only if the other party accepts the waiver.[278] This type of waiver is itself a contract and it may be made orally though a case of waiver must be clearly made out.[279] There must be as clear evidence of the waiver as of the existence of the contract.[280]

Attempts to impose conditions post-contract

[3.31] Occasionally a party may try to impose a new condition after a complete contract has come into being. This seems most likely to arise when parties are unsure whether negotiations have got as far as a concluded contract or when delays cause frustration after a binding contract has been made. The attempt is clearly wrong in principle; a party to a contract cannot make a new condition without the agreement or assent of the other party.[281] If a contract has been reached and a draft formal contract is sent out a requirement that it be signed and returned in seven days is unlikely to be upheld; a court exercising equitable jurisdiction could not allow a vendor to escape his obligations by an unreasonable and unilateral act.[282] And a court will not allow a vendor to impose a condition relating to time which would have the effect of getting around the rule that when time was not originally of the essence a party cannot make it of the essence unless the other party has been guilty of unreasonable delay.[283]

AGENCY

[3.32] Some aspects of the law of agency have been important in actions for specific performance. These have related mainly to the negotiation of contracts and satisfying the Statute of Frauds.[284] It is important to bear in mind that the two are very different matters.

---

[274] *Crean's* case at 87-8.
[275] Para **5.14** *post.*
[276] Per Kenny J in *Healy v Healy* (HC) 3 December 1973, unrep at 11.
[277] *Maconchy v Trower* [1894] 2 IR 663 at 670, 677.
[278] *Carolan v Brabazon* (1846) 9 Ir Eq R 224 at 228-9.
[279] *Cartan v Bury* (1860) 10 Ir Ch R 387 at 400.
[280] *Ibid.*
[281] *Moynihan v Crowley* [1958] IJR 21 at 24 (purchaser would close only if £52.10.0d damages were allowed for delay.
[282] *Kelly v Park Hall School Ltd* [1979] IR 340 at 352.
[283] *Healy Ballsbridge Ltd v Alliance Property Corporation Ltd* [1974] IR 441 at 447-8; *Holohan v Ardmayle Estates* (SC) 1 May 1967, unrep, noted in the *Healy Ballsbridge* case at 441-2, 447-8.
[284] The statute is considered in Ch 5 *post.*

Also, an agent with power to negotiate does not necessarily have power to make a contract.[285] If he has authority to do a deal on behalf of his principal that does not mean that he will also have authority to prepare a formal contract or put something into writing which will satisfy the statute. The reverse is also true. The fact that someone has the authority to prepare a formal contract or otherwise prepare some memorandum or record of an oral contract does not mean that he had the authority to conclude an oral contract in the first place. To take a simple example, an estate agent often makes a contract on behalf of his client and usually has the necessary authority to do so; but it does not follow that he will have[286] authority to prepare a formal contract, commit his client in writing or do anything to satisfy the Statute of Frauds. If he is given express directions to "hold everything" or the like he will not have authority to write a letter confirming a sale agreed by the parties.[287] Occasionally parties themselves may agree a deal and an estate agent may have authority to put something into writing which will be a sufficient note or memorandum to satisfy the statute.[288]

Many different inferences may arise as to the extent of an agent's authority in a particular case. Depending on the extent of that authority he may or may not have power to commit his client to a contract for the sale of land and all the facts in each particular case require careful examination.[289] If a question of an agent's authority becomes an issue the onus of proof is on the person alleging that the necessary authority existed.[290] The *extent* of an agent's authority is to be determined first by the express instructions given to him and second on such implications as may arise from the conduct or situation of the parties or from necessity.[291] The authority of an agent may also be *conditional*, eg, where the agent has power to commit his clients to a sale at a stipulated figure provided he secures suitable alternative premises for them.[292] An agent's authority to act may be oral[293] or implied[294] from the facts of a case though not simply from his status as an estate agent.[295] It may occasionally be "ostensible".[296] The fact that an agent has a normal practice of confirming the terms of an agreement to the parties and their solicitors normally will not give him authority to do so on behalf of his principal[297] though in particular circumstances the fact that his client knows of the practice and expects him to follow it could be evidence to support a finding that the agent had implied or ostensible authority. If the contract an agent is authorised to make needs writing in order to satisfy the Statute of Frauds it does not follow that the agent's authority to make it must also be

---

[285] Para **3.34** *post, esp* consideration of *Law v Roberts* [1964] IR 292.

[286] Save perhaps "subject to contract" which, of course, is not a binding commitment. See Ch 4 *post*.

[287] *Lynch v Bulbulia* (HC) 25 July 1980, Costello J, unrep at 5, 9-10.

[288] *Ballyowen Castle Homes Ltd v Collins* (HC) 26 June 1986, Keane J, unrep at 7-8; *Guardian Builders Ltd v Kelly* [1981] ILRM 127 at 131. And see para **5.29** *post*.

[289] *Park Hall School Ltd v Overend* [1987] IR 1 at 9.

[290] *Kerns v Manning* [1935] IR 869 at 881; *Law v Roberts* [1964] IR 292 at 302; *Kelly v Kineen* 29 April 1980, McWilliam J, unrep at 10; *Ballyowen Castle Homes Ltd v Collins* (HC) Keane J, unrep at 4.

[291] *Barclay's Bank v Breen* (1956) 106 ILTR 179 at 185.

[292] As in *Delgado v Crean* (HC) 24 May 1978, Kenny J, unrep at 4.

[293] *McCausland v Murphy* (1881) 9 LRI 9 at 15; *Callaghan v Pepper* (1840) 2 IR Eq R 399 at 401; *Clinan v Cooke* (1802) 1 Schoales & Lefroy 22 at 31.

[294] *Guardian Builders Ltd v Kelly* [1981] ILRM 127 at 131.

[295] *Law v Roberts* [1964] IR 292 at 302; *Ballyowen Castle Homes Ltd v Collins* (HC) 26 June 1986, Keane J, unrep at 8. But it may be within his function as agent to write to the parties setting out his understanding as agent of the vendor what had been agreed between them: the *Ballyowen Castle Homes* case at 8.

[296] On this see paras **3.42-4** *infra*.

[297] *Ahern v Gilmore* (HC) Hamilton J, unrep at 12-13.

in writing.[298] There was a well-marked distinction in the Statute of Frauds between s 1[299] and s 2. Under the former an agent who actually made a lease for his principal whereby an interest was intended to be passed had to be authorised in writing to do so but under s 2 the agent need not be authorised in writing.[300]

[3.33] The material just discussed may be viewed in the light of the fact that the first and probably most obvious duty of an agent to his principal is that the agent is bound to act in accordance with the terms of his contract and not exceed his authority.[301] An agent can be either a servant of the principal or an independent contractor.[302] The facts that an estate agent is not subject to his principal's control as to the manner in which he carries out his engagement and that he lacks authority to conclude a contract do not prevent him being the agent of the principal.[303] An agent who is employed to act in the course of his trade, profession or business has in general implied authority to do whatever is normally incidental in the ordinary course of that trade, profession or business to doing the task he has been given.[304] It is vital to bear in mind exactly what that task is and consider it in the light of the case law; it will have a major bearing on the extent of the implied authority. For example, the making of a contract is no part of an estate agent's business and, although, on the facts of an individual case, his principal may authorise him to make a contract, such an authorisation is not lightly to be inferred from vague or ambiguous language.[305] On the other hand, the "apparent" authority of counsel or his opponent's expectations of the authority of counsel negotiating on eg, a question of compensation may lend him authority to cover important collateral matters.[306] If an agent does exceed his authority, then, in the absence of ostensible authority,[307] ratification[308] or the type of estoppel which arose in *Worboys v Carter*[309] the principal is not bound. If the agent's conduct is fraudulent this will give a purchaser a good defence to a claim for specific performance and entitle him to recover compensation from the agent for loss suffered.[310] If the agent is not fraudulent though lacking authority he may be liable to the purchaser in damages for breach of warranty of authority.[311]

Effect on principal of knowledge gained by agent

[3.34] If any fact or circumstance material to a transaction in which an agent is employed comes to his knowledge in the course of his employment and is of such a nature that it is

---

[298] *McCausland v Murphy* (1881) 9 LRI 9 at 15; *Clinan v Cooke* (1802) 1 Schoales & Lefroy 22 at 27, 31; *Callaghan v Pepper* (1840) 2 Ir Eq R 399 at 401-2.

[299] Repealed by s 104 and Schedule (B) of Deasy's Act and replaced by s 4 of Deasy's Act in relation to actual leases.

[300] *McCausland's* case at 15; *Cf Clinan's* case at 27.

[301] *Farmer v Casey* (1898) 33 ILTR 144; Bowstead on Agency, 15th Ed (1985) at p 138; Mahon, *Auctioneering and Estate Agency Law in Ireland* at 30.

[302] *Somers v Nichol* [1955] IR 83 at 87.

[303] *Ibid.* The prime issue was whether the plaintiff needed a licence as a "house agent" under the Auctioneers and House Agents Act 1947.

[304] *Bowstead*, p 111.

[305] *Per* Lord Greene MR in *Wragg v Lovett* [1948] 2 All ER 968 at 969, approved by Kenny J in *Law v Roberts* [1964] IR 292 at 301-2.

[306] *Barrett v Lenehan & Co Ltd* [1981] ILRM 206 at 212. *Cf Gordon v Gordon* [1951] IR 301.

[307] On which see paras **3.42-4** *infra.*

[308] Para **3.41** *infra.*

[309] [1987] 2 EGLR 1. See para **3.43** *infra.*

[310] *Ingram v Gillen* (1910) 44 ILTR 103. The auctioneer pretended bogus bids were genuine; there is no suggestion in the report that the vendor knew of the deceit. *Cf Delaney v Keogh* [1905] 2 IR 267.

[311] As in *McDonnell v McGuinness* [1939] IR 223.

his duty to communicate it to his principal, the principal is deemed to have notice of it from the time he would have got notice if the agent had done his duty to communicate.[312] There will be exceptions to this rule if an agent is involved in fraud or misfeasance against his principal.[313] As Walsh J explained:

"In my view the case where an agent is a party or privy to the commission of a fraud or of an act of deceit upon his principal is different from one where the agent, though being neither a party nor privy to the commission of the fraud, is, nevertheless, aware of it but for the sake of his own interests does not reveal that situation to his principal. In the latter case the knowledge of the agent when he is under a duty to communicate such knowledge to his principal is deemed to be the knowledge of his principal even though in fact it has not been communicated to him. But in the former case I am of opinion that even when there is a similar duty on the part of the agent the fact that he is a party or privy to the commission of a fraud or misfeasance upon his principal precludes his knowledge from being imputed to his principal because his participation requires the suppression of his knowledge – a circumstance which is a negation of the basis of the general rule that the knowledge of the agent is to be imputed to his principal."[314]

Even though the principal may be deemed to be on notice of something which his agent should have communicated to him, it does not follow that the principal is deemed to assent to it or be bound by it.[315] This may be vital if a term related to the information which should have been communicated is omitted from a formal contract by unilateral mistake of the other side.[316] It is important to remember also that knowledge cannot be imputed to the principal which has never been in the mind of the agent.[317]

Agent contracting personally

[3.35] Questions may arise also whether an agent is contracting on his own behalf. An agent for a disclosed principal is not himself liable in contract.[318] Where an agent acting for an undisclosed principal is shown to have contracted merely as agent the true position and intention of the parties is recognised and the agent drops out of the transaction.[319] Save in certain particular cases the general rule of law is that no agent can maintain an action in his own name on any contract made by him as such, whether the principal be disclosed or undisclosed.[320] One of the particular cases when the agent can sue in his own name is where he contracts *personally*.[321] A difficult question can arise where a purchaser signs a contract "in trust" or "in trust for a client". Does this mean that since he is acting for a client he is acting as agent only? Or does it mean that he is the buyer but will hold what he buys in trust for another, that being a matter only affecting the rights *inter se* of

---

[312] Bowstead on *Agency*, 15th Ed, at p 412 approved by Keane J *in Irish Life Assurance Co Ltd v Dublin Land Securities Ltd* [1986] IR 253 at 264.
[313] *Ibid.*
[314] *Wall v New Ireland Assurance Co Ltd* [1965] IR 386 at 408: this passage was approved by Griffin J in *United Dominions Trust (Ireland) Ltd v Shannon Caravans Ltd* [1976] IR 225 at 230-1.
[315] The *Irish Life* case at 345-7.
[316] As in the *Irish Life* case.
[317] *Gordon v Gordon* [1951] IR 301 at 310.
[318] *McGuill v Aer Lingus Teo* (HC) 3 October 1983, McWilliam J, unrep at 10.
[319] *United Yeast Co Ltd v Cameo Investments Ltd* (1975) 111 ILTR 13 at 16.
[320] *Lavan v Walsh* [1964] IR 87 at 96.
[321] *Ibid.* Budd J reviewed case law extensively in the next few pages but found himself thrown back on general principles: p 100.

the purchaser and his client?[322] Condition 30 of the current Law Society, *General Conditions of Sale* (1991) Ed, imposes personal liability on a person who signs a memorandum "in Trust", "as Trustee", "as Agent" or similarly without specifying the identity of the principal or other party for whom he signs unless and until he discloses to the vendor the name of his principal or other such party. When there is a written agreement the question whether the agent has contracted personally depends on the intention of the parties as appearing from the terms of the written agreement as a whole.[323] If a person agrees to buy property intending to put it into the name of a company which does not exist when he contracts he is likely to be held to have contracted personally.[324]

But if the contract *purports* to be entered into by a company or by any person on its behalf prior to its formation and the company later ratifies the contract it will become bound by it and entitled to the benefit of it.[325]

[3.36] Two other points should be noted in cases where persons are claimed to have acted as agents for companies. Firstly, if the heads of a family who are also the principal shareholders in and managers of their family company make a contract to sell premises owned by it a judge is likely to find it "repugnant" to hold, in the absence of compelling authority, that they had not authority to enter into the contract on behalf of the company.[326] This may well apply to all contracts by effective beneficial owners of companies for the sale of land owned by the company. Secondly, the principle of ostensible authority[327] may be applied to the actions of persons acting on behalf of companies. For example, it has been applied to an agreement by a chairman of a company sued in ejectment to surrender premises in consideration of a payment into the account of another company.[328] But if a purported contract is *outside* a company's *powers* no ostensible authority of, or representations by, its officers can estop or prevent the company from denying the authority of the agent who committed the ultra vires act.[329] Where, however, an outsider dealing with a company is not aware that a transaction is an improper *exercise* of its powers and there are no circumstances which should have caused him to enquire whether it was improper it will bind the company.[330]

---

[322] Budd J leant toward the latter meaning in the *Lavan* case at pp 100-1 but did not have to decide on that alone. In the *United Yeast Co* case Butler J was satisfied at p 16 "that by common usage a solicitor who signs a contract to purchase in trust is clearly recognised as acting merely as agent and, in the absence of a clear stipulation to the contrary, incurs no personal liability". However, the vendors knew at all times that the solicitors were acting for the particular principal: p 14.

[323] *Per* Budd J in the *Lavan* case at 96 applied by Costello J in *Dublin Laundry Co Ltd v Clarke* [1989] ILRM 29 at 38-9.

[324] *Dublin Laundry Co Ltd v Clarke* [1989] ILRM 29 at 37-8; *Parkgrange Investments Ltd v Shandon Park Mills Ltd* (HC) 2 May 1991, Carroll J, unrep at pp 2-3.

[325] Section 37 of the Companies Act 1963. See Keane, *Company Law in the Republic of Ireland*, 2nd Ed (1990) at para 12.02.

[326] *Howlin v Thomas F Power (Dublin) Ltd* (HC) 5 May 1978, McWilliam J, unrep at 10.

[327] On which see paras **3.42-4** *infra*.

[328] *Kilgobbin Mink and Stud Farm Ltd v National Credit Co Ltd* [1980] IR 175 at 181-2. See discussion of this case by Keane, *Company Law in the Republic of Ireland* 2nd Ed (1991) at 12.14.

[329] *Williamson Ltd v Bailieboro Co-operative Agricultural Society Ltd* (HC) 31 July 1986, Costello J, unrep at 13-15.

[330] Keane, *op cit*, para 12.06.

Estate agents

[3.37] The authority of estate agents to do deals and agree terms so as to bind their clients has often been an important issue.[331] In *Law v Roberts* Kenny J concluded:[332]

> "These cases seem to justify the following propositions:
>
> 1   When a contract for sale is made between a purchaser and an estate agent retained by the owner, the onus of proving that the estate agent had authority to make the contract is on the purchaser.
>
> 2   An estate agent as such has no implied authority to conclude a contract for sale.
>
> 3   An owner who puts his property on the books of an estate agent and authorises him to find a purchaser and to negotiate a sale does not thereby authorise him to conclude a contract.
>
> 4   An owner who puts his property on the books of an estate agent and informs him of the lowest price he will accept does not thereby authorise him to conclude a contract.
>
> 5   An estate agent who is instructed to sell at a defined price has authority to conclude a contract for sale at that defined price if the contract is an open contract.
>
> 6   An estate agent may be expressly authorised to accept on behalf of the owner an offer made to the agent and, in that event, has authority to conclude a contract.
>
> 7   If an offer is made to an estate agent and if he communicates it to the owner and is authorised to accept it or if the owner states that he will accept it, the agent has authority to make an open contract with the purchaser."

It is important to remember that an estate agent as such has no implied or general authority to make any binding contract for sale; his duty is to find a purchaser or tenant and communicate his offer to his principal.[333] It is common practice to place houses or estates on the books of a number of agents at the same time and, if each had authority to conclude a contract for the owner, the result would be that he might become bound to let or sell the same premises to several different parties at the same instant. If there are negotiations towards a sale and an agent has been told that his principal will accept a certain sum that probably is still not enough to authorise him to conclude a contract.[334] An agent instructed to negotiate has no authority to sign a contract.[335] Authority to conduct a sale by auction will not amount to a general employment to sell.[336]

[3.38] The nature in practice of an estate agent's contract with his client is explained by Gannon J in *Morrissey & Sons Ltd v Nalty*:[337]

> "Under such a type of contract the nature of the skills of the agent sought to be availed of by the vendor is the benefit of his knowledge of the potential market with a view to eliciting offers for the purpose of introducing the potential purchaser to the vendors and

---

[331] Most of the cases on which para **3.32** above is based involved estate agents.

[332] [1964] IR 292 at 302 having reviewed case law extensively at 298-302. This decision was affirmed by the Supreme Court: p 305.

[333] *Wilde v Watson* (1878) 1 LRI 402 at 405. *Cf Mortal v Lyons* (1858) 8 Ir Ch R 112 at 114, 117.

[334] *Carney v Fair* (1920) 54 ILTR 61.

[335] *Rooney v Thomas* (1947) 81 ILTR 64.

[336] *Morrissey & Sons Ltd v Nalty* [1976-7] ILRM 269 at 274.

[337] [1976-7] ILRM 269 at 274. *Cf* Lord Denning on the duties of an estate agent, esp not to delegate to a sub-agent without authority at *John McCann & Co v Pow* [1975] 1 All ER 129 at 131-2.

for the purpose of negotiation by the agent between these parties. In such circumstances there might be more than one agent engaged and there might be no competition between potential purchasers but the only reward which the agent might obtain would be commission to be paid out of whatever purchase money might be obtained upon a sale brought about by the agent to a purchaser introduced by him but no remuneration if the property were otherwise disposed of or through another agency. In such type of engagement the agent has no power to make any contract binding on the parties and he has to use his own discretion as to what form and terms of advertising he might use and he is at risk that the vendor might not sell to any particular purchaser found by him in spite of his best endeavours at negotiation."

The risk to the estate agent is a financial one - ie, that he may expend considerable time and effort in trying to sell property but then find that it does not sell or is sold in circumstances which do not entitle him to either commission or payment based on *quantum meruit*. This may happen where he is engaged to conduct an auction but his client cancels the auction and later sells privately, even to someone who first made contact through the agent's efforts.[338] Contracts of agency may deal in many varied ways with the event in which the agent is entitled to commission.[339] However, we are concerned primarily with the manner in which he may bind his principal. As O'Connor LJ explained:[340]

"When a man employs another to carry out a transaction on his behalf, he is responsible for what the other necessarily does in the carrying out of the transaction. Let me apply that principle to the negotiation and completion of a contract of sale. A principal party gives an agent full authority to negotiate and complete such a contract. This involves the necessity of the agent making offers, representations and statements as to the property to intending purchasers. Such statements are as binding on the principal as if made by the principal himself, because they are obviously within the scope of the agent's authority to bind the principal thereby. But it is, in my opinion, equally obvious that many statements may be made by the agent with regard to the property or transaction which are not binding on the principal, as not being within the scope of the agent's authority to bind the principal. To test whether the statement binds the principal one has to consider the nature of the statement and the circumstances in which it is made, including, for example, the person to whom, and the time at which, the statement is made."

An important feature of agents' statements is that, in addition to possibly leading to deals between the parties, they may have legal effects as representations[341] or warranties[342] or as bringing about collateral contracts.[343]

Solicitors

[3.39] Another person sometimes alleged to have had power to conclude a contract on behalf of someone else is a solicitor. A *formal* contract is normally prepared by a solicitor

---

[338] As in *Morrissey & Sons Ltd v Nalty* [1976/7] ILRM 269.

[339] See discussion by Henchy J in *Murphy Buckley & Keogh Ltd v Pye (Ireland) Ltd* [1971] IR 57 at 64-7. Remember that even a *sole agency* is not the same as a *sole right to sell* and may not prevent a principal himself selling without incurring liability to pay the agent - as in the *Murphy Buckley & Keogh* case. Cf *Galvin (Estates) Ltd v Hedigan* [1985] ILRM 295. See also Mahon, *Auctioneering and Estate Agency Law in Ireland*, Ch 2.

[340] *Swan v Miller* [1919] 1 IR 151 at 182-3.

[341] See innocent misrepresentation at paras **9.16-22**, fraudulent misrepresentation at paras **9.12-15** and damages for negligent misrepresentation at **8.48-9** *post*.

[342] See damages for breach of warranty at **8.50-1** *post*.

[343] See paras **5.15-6** in the context of the Statute of Frauds and para **8.51** in relation to damages.

but usually he will have taken no part in negotiations which led to the deal and often he is instructed only after the parties have reached an oral contract. Of course it is no part of his function to alter the terms of an oral contract already made by his client[344] unless the parties agree that he should do so. Parties who have done a deal usually accept that legal formalities are necessary and that suitable procedures will be followed by their solicitors.[345] If a party has done a deal and then instructs his solicitor "to proceed with the sale" or "to prepare a draft contract and to carry the matter through in the ordinary way" the solicitor will have authority to sign a memorandum which satisfies the Statute of Frauds.[346] Again the distinction between concluding a contract and providing something in writing to satisfy the statute is important. Comparatively slight evidence would, in accordance with ordinary experience, be required to prove that a solicitor had authority to make a memorandum as the legal evidence of a concluded contract, but that a solicitor had authority to deal with the substance of a transaction in any manner which he thought fit, is a fact which should be clearly proved.[347] If an offer is made to a solicitor who communicates it to his client it will be a question of fact whether the client authorised the solicitor to accept the offer.[348]

Occasionally the facts of a case will show that a solicitor has a wide general authority entitling him to sell and extending even to receiving purchase money and giving a good discharge therefore.[349] Under the general law he would have no implied authority *as solicitor* to receive the purchase money but he has a sort of statutory authority to do so on production of a deed duly executed and containing a receipt for the consideration by the person entitled to it.[350] If a client wishes his solicitor to do a deal on his behalf he should give the solicitor a specific and direct authority and not leave him in the dubious area of a mere general or implied authority.[351] The solicitor should protect himself by ensuring that he has express authority and should advise the client to be sure not to make any binding contract himself or let any other agent do so.[352] The solicitor should also satisfy himself, if he can, that neither the client nor any other agent has already bound the client. If there is the slightest risk that the client is already bound by another contract, even an oral one which, as far as the solicitor knows yet, may not satisfy the Statute of Frauds, there is the strongest possible reason for marking all correspondence "subject to contract" or the like.[353]

---

[344] Per Keane J in *Mulhall v Haren* [1981] IR 364 at 392. *Cf* Gannon J in *Black v Kavanagh* (1973) 108 ILTR 91 at 95, 96.

[345] *Black's* case at 95.

[346] *Arnold v Veale* (HC) 28 July 1977, Costello J, unrep at 18. This case was reversed by the Supreme Court on new evidence which proved that the deal was "subject to contract": see para **4.12** below. On this point see also para **5.29** *post.*

[347] *Kerns v Manning* [1935] IR 869 at 881.

[348] Note the facts considered in *Roberts v O'Neill* [1981] ILRM 403 at 405 (an appeal to the Supreme Court was argued only on a question of hardship: on which see paras **9.38-41** *post.*) *Cf* the facts considered in *Guardian Builders Ltd v Kelly* [1981] ILRM 127 at 129-30.

[349] *Barclays Bank v Breen* (1956) 96 ILTR 179 at 185.

[350] The *Barclays Bank* case at 184; s 56 of the Conveyancing Act, 1881 protects a purchaser who pays the purchase money in exchange for such a deed. The deed is the "sufficient authority" for the payment.

[351] See discussion in *Godley v Power* (1957) 95 ILTR 135 at 144-5.

[352] To avoid having two contracts which is usually disastrous.

[353] On "subject to contract" see Ch 4 *post.* Marking the first letter in a chain of correspondence is probably enough (para **4.11**) but some overkill in avoiding the two contracts disaster is forgivable.

Counsel

[3.40] If you strip counsel - metaphorically - of his wig and gown you have still an ordinary person who is capable of being an agent and of binding his principal.[354] Some English case law goes far in support of the authority of counsel to settle without express authority from his client and even upholds a settlement by counsel against the instructions of his client where the limitation on his apparent authority had not been communicated to the other side.[355] The argument for this very broad authority seems stronger when the settlement is made during the actual hearing when a sudden shift may necessitate an immediate exercise of discretion by counsel.[356] Settlements will often be attempted "at the door of the court"[357] and in the limited time available on the morning of a hearing it may not be possible "to reduce the terms of settlement to full and unambiguous written expression"[358] This produces the risk of mutual mistake resulting in there being no real agreement and any alleged settlement being a nullity.[359] Counsel's apparent authority is not unbounded. Normally he may not, without express authority, effect a compromise which involves matters collateral to the action.[360] However, much will depend on the nature of the matter being settled and the authority to negotiate which counsel on each side would expect his opponent to have.[361] Thus, where a landlord relies on a scheme of development or the like to recover possession from his tenant and the latter's legal advisers are authorised to negotiate on the issue of compensation, they are likely to have power to negotiate on matters such as the date or dates on which the tenant is to receive the compensation and give up possession, waiver of arrears of rent and a surrender of a right of way.[362] Neither the involvement of counsel nor the fact that a court hearing may be imminent affects the application of the Statute of Frauds. As we shall see, a sufficient memorandum and signature will be necessary in appropriate circumstances[363] and counsel's pleadings can provide a sufficient memorandum.[364]

Ratification

[3.41] If an agent lacks authority when he does something that lack may be made good later by ratification. No statute governs ratification so we are left to the rules of common law as to the mode in which the agent is to receive his authority.[365] Thus the ratification may be oral[366] or by conduct.[367] The conditions necessary for ratification are, firstly, that

---

[354] *Gordon v Gordon* [1951] IR 301 at 309, Kingsmill Moore J considering an argument.
[355] *Gordon's* case at 306; see discussion of case law at 307-8.
[356] *Gordon's* case at 307. But note that Kingsmill Moore J could not read *Neale v Lady Gordon Lennox* as restricted to a compromise effected during the actual conduct of a case in court. See also *Gethings v Cloney* (1913) 48 ILTR 55 at 57.
[357] As occurred in *Mespil Ltd v Capaldi* [1986] ILRM 373.
[358] Per Henchy J in the *Mespil Ltd* case at 375-6.
[359] The *Mespil Ltd* case at 376-7.
[360] *Gordon v Gordon* [1951] IR 301 at 309.
[361] *Barrett v Lenehan & Co Ltd* [1981] ILRM 206 at 212.
[362] *Ibid.*
[363] See para **5.07** *post.* And quite apart from the Statute of Frauds terms of settlement may themselves contemplate that they must be signed by the parties: *Gethings v Cloney* 48 ILTR 55 at 57-8.
[364] Para **5.20** *post.*
[365] Per O Dalaigh CJ giving the judgment of the Supreme Court in *Sheridan v Higgins* [1971] IR 291 at 301 approving a passage from the judgment of Best CJ in *Maclean v Dunn* (1828) 4 Bing 722
[366] *Callaghan v Pepper* (1840) 2 Ir Eq R 399 at 401; *Dyas v Cruise* (1845) 8 Ir Eq R 407 at 423-4 (ratification by informal letter, adoption of a lease and orally).
[367] *Barclays Bank v Breen* (1956) 96 ILTR 179 at 186 (allowing the agent to receive money on the bank's behalf); see the *Dyas* case at *note* 366 *supra.*

the relevant act was done in purported exercise of an authority from the principal and, secondly, that at the time of ratification the principal has full knowledge of all the material circumstances in which the act was done unless he intended to ratify the act and take the risk whatever the circumstances may have been.[368] It is not necessary that he should appreciate the legal effect of the act or of collateral circumstances affecting its nature.[369] Passive acquiescence in a contract for a length of time longer than that reasonably to be allowed for the expression of dissent may suffice.[370] When ratification does occur it operates retrospectively.[371] The relevant contract or act becomes that of the principal just as if he had authorised it at the time. The reason why a principal must be aware of all the material facts when he ratifies is that it would be unfair to hold a person bound by the obligations of a contract made on his behalf if he was debarred by lack of factual information from being able to assess what a ratification would let him in for.[372] If a contract for sale is made by an estate agent purportedly on behalf of the vendor the latter should not be held to ratify unless he is made aware of all facts in the knowledge of the estate agent which, in the particular circumstances and without the benefit of hindsight, could objectively be said to have been necessary to enable the vendor to decide if he should assent to the sale.[373] Not every single possible fact can be material. The mere fact that someone has made an enquiry about the terms on which a property might be sold is unlikely on its own to be held to be a consideration which might be expected to affect a decision to assent to an otherwise acceptable offer.[374] The contract or act to be ratified must be of substance and the principle of ratification will not apply to something which was in itself a nullity.[375]

Ostensible authority

[3.42] In the law of agency a distinction is drawn between actual (or real) authority and ostensible (or apparent) authority. Actual authority exists when it is based on an actual agreement between the principal and the agent. The nature of ostensible authority is stated succinctly by Henchy J:[376]

"Ostensible authority on the other hand derives not from any consensual arrangement between the principal and the agent but is founded on a representation made by the principal to the third party which is intended to convey and does convey to the third party that the arrangement entered into under the apparent authority of the agent will be binding on the principal."

It is vital to remember that the representation must be made by the principal himself or by some person having actual authority to manage the business of the principal either generally or in respect of those matters to which the contract relates.[377] The agent cannot

[368] *Barclays Bank v Breen* (1956) 96 ILTR 179 at 186.
[369] *Ibid.*
[370] From a passage in the 6th Ed of Fry, *Specific Performance* approved by O Dalaigh CJ in *Sheridan v Higgins* [1971 IR 291 at 301.
[371] *Brennan v O'Connell* [1980] IR 13 at 15; *Sheridan v Higgins* [1971] IR 291 at 303.
[372] *Per* Henchy J giving the judgment of the Supreme Court in *Brennan's* case at p 16.
[373] *Ibid.* And note Henchy J's rejection of a subjective test at p 17.
[374] As occurred in the *Brennan* case: pp 17-18.
[375] *Holmes v Trench* [1898] 1 IR 319 at 334. The relevant act could not occur until a certain prescribed condition was met and that had not happened.
[376] *Kett v Shannon* [1987] ILRM 364 at 366.
[377] *Nesbit & Co Ltd v McClure* (HC) NI, Gibson J, at 6; *Essfood Eksportlagtiernes Sallgsforening v Crown Shipping (Ireland) Ltd* [1991] ILRM 97 at 107-8.

enlarge his authority by his own representations[378] though if the principal knows that the purported agent is holding himself out as such and does not try to stop it he may become liable. The representation which creates ostensible authority may take a variety of forms but the most common is a representation by conduct by permitting the agent to act in some way in the conduct of the principal's business with other persons and thereby representing that the agent has the authority which an agent so acting in the conduct of his principal's business usually has.[379] Simply allowing a person to appear as agent when he is not may be enough.[380] The rationale of liability on the ground of ostensible authority is that the principal is estopped from denying the apparent authority.[381] The estoppel prevents him resisting an inference which a reasonable person would draw from his words or conduct.[382] Many cases show that it is enough to raise estoppel in the case of apparent authority that the plaintiff entered the contract in reliance on the representation without having to show any detriment as a result of doing so.[383] As the basis of liability is estoppel the principle will not operate in the case of a company if the relevant deal or act is outside the company's *powers* though it can be invoked in a case of improper *exercise* of those powers.[384]

[3.43] Modern Irish examples of ostensible authority are a trustee of property formerly in the name of a small family company letting a member of the family continue dealing with the property as if he was in control of it,[385] a bank permitting its branch manager to advise a customer and promise loans,[386] a liquidator allowing the directors to negotiate with prospective buyers of assets[387] and the chairman of a company sued in ejectment being allowed to make a settlement for a surrender of the premises in consideration *inter alia* of a payment of money into the account of an associated company which had been trading in the premises.[388] In another recent case an accountancy partnership was held liable for investment advice to a client company given by a senior partner who was also a director of that company.[389] The case for ostensible authority may be stronger when the alleged agency arises between partners. When one partner is put into a position of trust with a client that alone may be a representation that the partnership trusts that partner and will stand over whatever he does.[390] In England an estate agent who sold goods at auction below the reserve was held to have bound his principal.[391] However the result was otherwise when conditions of sale provided that each lot was offered subject to a reserve price; in that case the auctioneer who sold below the reserve did not bind his principal.[392]

---

[378] *Ibid* (both cases).
[379] *Armagas Ltd v Mundogas SA* [1985] 3 All ER 795 at 804 approved by Henchy J in *Kett's* case at 366.
[380] *Bank of Ireland v Fitzmaurice* [1989] ILRM 452 at 458.
[381] The *Nesbitt* case at 7; the *Bank of Ireland* case at 458.
[382] The *Essfood* case at 107.
[383] The *Nesbitt* case at 8.
[384] See para **3.35** above.
[385] *Bank of Ireland v Fitzmaurice* [1989] ILRM 452 at 457-8.
[386] *Allied Irish Banks v Murnane* (HC) 21 December 1988, Barron J, unrep.
[387] *Nesbitt & Co Ltd v McClure* (HC) (NI), Gibson J, unrep at 7.
[388] *Kilgobbin Mink and Stud Farm Ltd v National Credit Co Ltd* [1980] IR 175 at 180-182.
[389] *Allied Pharmaceutical Distributors Ltd v Walsh* [1991] 2 IR 8. The partnership audited the company's accounts and the absence of any comment about the transactions was a sufficient representation by conduct that the partner had the defendant's authority.
[390] The *Allied Pharmaceutical Distributors* case at 17.
[391] *Rainbow v Howkins* [1904] 2 KB 322.
[392] *McManus v Fortescue* [1907] 2 KB 1; [1904-7] All ER Rep 707. He discovered the error promptly and refused to sign a memorandum.

The reason for the different result was that the express condition about a reserve made each bid a conditional offer the condition being that the bid was up to the reserve price. Where auctioneers sold a house below the reserve price due to a misapprehension in their instructions[393] and signed a memorandum their principal was still not bound but the auctioneers were liable to the purchaser for breach of warranty of authority.[394] There could be no question of ostensible authority in the auctioneers. Such ostensible authority could only exist if the vendor or his duly authorised solicitors had placed the auctioneers in a position where the purchaser would reasonably suppose them to have authority to sell at the price at which they did.[395]

In an interesting recent case in England *Worboys v Carter*,[396] a land agent mistakenly thought that a document signed by his client, the defendant, authorised him to sell land which he did, the defendant later dealt with the purchaser without denying the agent's authority to act and the purchaser sold his own land in the belief, which he made clear that he held, that he had a binding contract to buy the defendant's land. The Court of Appeal held that an estoppel arose which prevented the defendant denying that there was a contract. He knew of the plaintiff's assumptions and the action taken pursuant to them; he was therefore under a duty to disclose the true position about the agent's lack of authority.[397] This was *not* a case of ostensible authority because the defendant had not made any representation to the purchaser at the time of the contract that the land agent had authority to act. The court also preferred not to deal with it as a case of ratification since Woolf LJ had reservations in his mind "as to whether a party can be said to have ratified a contract when it is clear on the material before the court that at all material times the one matter that he did not wish to be bound by was the contract in question."[398]

[3.44] Parties and their agents must be careful that the parties do not get caught by the principle of ostensible authority or the type of estoppel exemplified by the *Worboys* case.[399] The type of points discussed in the last two paragraphs and the propositions of law applying to estate agents identified by Kenny J in *Law v Roberts*[400] in general will minimise the risk of getting caught. It has been said that examples of instances where estate agents might have apparent authority are difficult to imagine.[401] However one must remember that ostensible authority probably can be created if, eg, the vendor or his duly authorised solicitors place estate agents or auctioneers in a position where the purchaser would reasonably suppose them to have authority for what they actually do.[402] And if an estate agent or auctioneer has sold property while lacking authority, actual, implied or ostensible, to do so and the intending purchaser shows that he believes he has an enforceable contract and may alter his position on that basis it is essential to correct that belief at once.[403] It is important to remember also that a *purchaser* may act by an agent

---

[393] From solicitors whose clerk did not know the limit the vendor wanted.
[394] *Fay v Miller, Wilkins & Co* [1941] 2 All ER 18 at 22, 27.
[395] *Fay's* case at 23, 26.
[396] [1987] 2 EGLR 1. *Cf Spiro v Lintern* [1973] 3 All ER 319.
[397] At p 5.
[398] *Ibid.*
[399] Considered in para **3.43** above.
[400] (1964) IR 292. See para **3.37** *supra*.
[401] Mahon, *Auctioneering and Estate Agency Law in Ireland*. The low incidence of trouble in the case law supports that view.
[402] *Fay v Miller, Wilkins & Co* [1948] 2 All ER 18 at 22-23, 27.
[403] Otherwise the owner may find himself in a position similar to that of the defendant in *Worboys v Carter* [1987] 2 EGLR 1.

and when that occurs it will be in the best interests of both the purchaser and his agent to understand clearly what authority, if any, is given and to avoid any risk of ostensible authority or estoppel.

AUCTIONS

[3.45] Traditionally conditions of sale at auction have contained a statement that the highest bidder shall be the purchaser.[404] If a dispute arises as to any bidding the traditional course has been to put the property up for sale again at the last undisputed bid.[405] A clause to the effect that the highest bidder is to be the purchaser is an offer which can be accepted by bidding at the auction and can constitute a contract between the vendor and highest bidder.[406] When property is put up for sale and is sold and a memorandum is signed there is an enforceable contract for the sale of the property to the person who has signed the memorandum; the clauses in the conditions which relate to what may happen before the purchaser signs the memorandum are capable of being an offer in connection with a different contract which may be accepted by bidding at the auction.[407] A contract is concluded when the property is "knocked down" by using the traditional "hammer" or giving some other indication to the public attending the auction that the property is sold.[408] If the vendor refuses to let the highest bidder, to whom the property has been "knocked down", sign a contract he will be liable in damages unless he can justify the refusal.[409] An auctioneer who puts property up for sale without a reserve pledges himself that the sale will be made without reserve and makes a contract to that effect with the highest bidder; if he breaks that contract he is liable in damages.[410]

[3.46] Most property is sold subject to a reserve price and with a right for the vendor to bid up to the reserve price.[411] In that situation each bid is a conditional offer, the condition being that the bid is up to the reserve price.[412] If property is sold without a reserve neither the vendor nor anyone on his behalf may bid and the property will be sold to the highest bidder whether the sum bid is equivalent to the real value or not.[413] In this situation it is unlawful for the vendor to employ any person to bid at the sale or for the auctioneer to take knowingly any bidding from any such person.[414] A bidder of this sort is often described as a "puffer" and that word probably comes from s 3 of the Sale of Land by Auction Act 1867 which defines "puffer" as "a person appointed to bid on the part of the owner".[415] A breach of this provision will make the sale illegal[416] and therefore

---

[404] The current Law Society standard conditions refer to the highest "accepted" bidder and give the auctioneer the right to refuse any bid: General Condition 4(*b*).
[405] The Auctioneer may now determine the dispute himself.
[406] *Tully v Irish Land Commission* (1961) 107 ILTR 174 at 176-8.
[407] *Ibid.*
[408] *Tully's* case at 179; *Dyas v Stafford* (1882) 9 LRI 520 at 523.
[409] *Johnston v Boyes* [1899] 2 Ch considered by Kenny J in *Tully v Irish Land Commission* (1961) 97 ILTR 174 at 178. In *Johnston's* case the refusal was upheld on the ground that the vendor was entitled to insist on payment of the deposit in cash. *Cf Morrow v Carty* [1957] NI 174.
[410] *Warlow v Harrison* 19 LJQB 14; 1 LT 211, [1843-607] All ER Rep 620 considered by Kenny J in the *Tully* case at 177.
[411] As in clause 4(*b*) and (*c*) of the Law Society, *General Conditions* (1991) Ed.
[412] *McManus v Fortescue* [1907] 2 KB 1; [1904] All ER Rep 707.
[413] See review of cases by Kenny J in the *Tully* case at 176-8.
[414] Section 5 of the Sale of Land by Auction Act 1867.
[415] See discussion of "puffer" in *Jones v Quinn* (1878) 2 LRI 516 at 518-9.
[416] See defence of illegality at paras **9.48-55** *post*. See also Wylie, *Irish Conveyancing Law* (1978) at paras 3.021-3.

unenforceable against an unwilling purchaser.[417] It is important to note that properties may be sold at first subject to a reserve but the reserve may be lifted later (or may have been exceeded) and the property "put on the market".[418] The 1867 Act will apply after the reserve ceases to operate and a subsequent bid by a puffer will make the sale invalid.[419] While individual purchasers seem to be the persons on whom improper or unfair practices are attempted most often the courts will also protect the public in general, other bidders and incumbrancers from fraud and will not enforce contracts tainted with such fraud.[420] In general the 1867 Act does not apply to court sales but the court may still re-open the biddings on the ground of fraud or improper conduct in the management of the sale.[421]

[3.47] It is vital to bear in mind the power of an auctioneer to sign a memorandum on behalf of the purchaser and - if necessary - on behalf of the vendor also.[422] The authority arises as soon as the contract is concluded and is irrevocable.[423] At auction the auctioneer is the agent of both parties and is authorised by them to affix their names to the contract; his signature binds both parties and is a compliance with the Statute of Frauds.[424] The basis on which he gets authority from the two parties is different and his authority on behalf of the vendor lasts longer. Ross J explained:[425]

> "The auctioneer is the agent for both the vendor and the purchaser. The authority of the vendor is given when he appoints the auctioneer to conduct the sale. In the case of the purchaser the agency is conferred by the acceptance of his bidding which is considered to imply an offer of such authority.
>
> I think from the very nature of the case the authority of the auctioneer as agent for the vendor is of a more permanent character than his authority as agent for the purchaser. There is some support for this proposition in the words of Pollock CB in *Mews v Carr*:[426] 'No doubt an auctioneer at the sale is agent for both seller and buyer; but the moment the sale is over the same principle does not apply and the auctioneer is no longer the agent of both parties but of the seller only'.
>
> The real test is whether the memorandum was made in substance at the time and as part of the transaction of sale. The circumstances of the case must be considered and common sense applied."[427]

If an auctioneer signs *as a witness* that nevertheless may bind the parties; it may still be taken to authenticate the contract contained in the paper that he has signed.[428] Of course there must *be* a concluded contract before the auctioneer can bind the parties. If for

---

[417] *Airlie v Fallon* [1976/73] ILRM 1 at 12-13.

[418] An announcement is made to that effect, often after a short chat between auctioneer, solicitor and vendor.

[419] As in *Airlie's* case at 12-13.

[420] *Re Ashe* (1855) 4 Ir Ch R 594 at 601, 602.

[421] Section 7 and 8; see further paras **3.60-1** *infra*.

[422] *Morrissey & Sons Ltd v Nalty* [1976/7] ILRM 269 at 273; *Tully v Irish Land Commission* (1961) 97 ILTR 174 at 179.

[423] *Tully's* case at 179 approving a passage from *Philips v Butler* 1945 Ch 358.

[424] *Gardiner v Tate* (1876) IR 10 CL 460 at 464, 468 and 473-4.

[425] *McMeekin v Stevenson* [1917] 1 IR 348 at 354.

[426] 1 H & N 484 at 488.

[427] In *McMeekin's* case the auctioneer signed on behalf of the vendor the morning after a sale which "lasted long into the winter evening". The vendor was bound. In *Carrigy v Brock* (1871) IR 5 CL 501 the auctioneer signed on the same day and the vendor was bound: p 504. *Cf Cherry v Anderson* (1876) IR 10 CL 204 at 209.

[428] *Wallace v Roe* [1903] 1 IR 32 at 35.

example the minds of both parties did not assent to the subject-matter of the apparent contract that may involve a lack of consensus which means that there was no real contract[429] and no auctioneer's signature can turn it into a binding contract.

[3.48] The courts seem slow generally to reach decisions which would have the effect of extending auctioneers, authority or contractual rights. Auctioneers engaged to offer premises for sale by public auction are unlikely to have authority to sell them by another method.[430] If a contract has been lawfully terminated the court will require evidence that the auctioneers acting in the matter had authority to revive the former contract or make a new one.[431] The courts are reluctant to accept that a trade usage or custom can be added to an already complete contract between client and auctioneer.[432] To be accepted as adding an implied term to a contract the alleged usage or custom must be "reasonable, definite, certain, notorious and uniformly acted upon by implication".[433]

[3.49] When a sale is by public auction the conditions will provide for a deposit and the stakeholder will be nominated by the vendor who drafts the conditions of sale and the vendor is therefore liable for his default.[434] The main reason for this is probably that the deposit paid by a purchaser, though primarily a guarantee that the purchaser means business, is also a part payment of the purchase money[435] and when a sale cannot be completed in circumstances under which the purchaser becomes entitled to recover the deposit from the stakeholder the vendor should be liable for any default of the stakeholder.[436]

Steps by intending purchasers

[3.50] An intending *purchaser* must also watch what he says and does at auction. He will be concerned both to try to protect himself in the possible purchase and to avoid incurring liability himself as a result of anything he says. He should not seek to deter other bidders by disparaging the property.[437] If he does so he risks liability under the tort of injurious falsehood, the essence of which is deceiving third parties so as to cause loss to the plaintiff.[438] And a misrepresentation by a *purchaser* about the property which reduces the

---

[429] As in *Gardiner's case*; also *Megaw v Molloy* (1878) 2 LRI 530 at 540-1. See discussion of consensus at paras **3.02-3** *supra*.

[430] *Morrissey & Sons Ltd v Nalty* [1976/7] ILRM 269 at 273-4.

[431] *Culhane v Hewson* [1979] IR 8 at 14.

[432] *Judd v Donegal Tweed Co Ltd* (1935) 69 ILTR 117 at 121-3. The alleged usage was that after an abortive auction the auctioneer remained as sole agent for a reasonable time, claimed as 3 months, and in the event of a sale within that period privately or through another agency the plaintiff was entitled to 5% commission.

[433] *Ibid* at 121.

[434] *Leemac Ltd v Harvey* [1973] IR 160 at 165. It is probably different when money is paid to an estate agent as a *pre-contract* deposit unless on the facts of the particular case the estate agent has express or implied authority to receive it on the vendor's behalf (*Sorrell v Finch* [1977] AC; [1976] 2 All ER 371 at 381) or, as in the *Leemac* case, it is taken pre-contract but *as* stakeholder. *Cf* Wylie, *Irish Conveyancing Law* (1978) at paras 3.079-81. Relief may be available in certain cases under the Auctioneers and House Agents Acts: see Wylie, *op cit*, paras 3.009, 3.079; Mahon, *Auctioneering and Estate Agency Law in Ireland* (1990) at 9-12. A purchaser's *solicitor* must take care about the basis on which he pays a pre-contract deposit to his opposite number: *Desmond v Brophy* [1985] IR 449 at 454-7.

[435] See para **3.11** *supra*.

[436] The *Leemac Ltd* case at 167-8.

[437] *Mayer v Pluck* (1971) 223 EG 33, 219: intending bidder asked if the auctioneer knew the house was built over an underground stream and had a flooded cellar; that made the property unsaleable and the bidder was liable in damages for malicious falsehood.

[438] See McMahon & Binchy, *Irish Law of Torts*, 2nd Ed at 673-4.

sale price can entitle the *vendor* to rescind a contract.[439] However these considerations must not inhibit bona fide enquiries at auction. An essential element of injurious falsehood is that the statement is made maliciously - ie without just cause or excuse.[440] No bona fide enquiry will have that characteristic and, if an enquiry does not contain within itself some incorrect statement or inference about the property, it cannot amount to a misrepresentation. The conditions of sale at auction are almost always prepared by the vendor's solicitor and it is very important that an intending purchaser should be advised by his own solicitor about those conditions before bidding.[441] Depending on the particular property it may be vital also to be advised by valuers or engineers about the nature and condition of the property, planning matters and building regulations.[442] Armed with such advice the intending purchaser or the agent who may bid for him[443] is in a much better position to raise queries about those matters; having read the conditions he can also address matters of title or restrictions in the contract. An intending purchaser's solicitor, even if he is instructed in good time may have little or no input into the conditions[444] but he may still be able to get some protection for the client by contacting his opposite number before auction or raising carefully chosen queries at the auction. The answers to those queries are capable of being representations,[445] or warranties[446] or even of leading to collateral contracts[447] and a purchaser may get valuable rights as a result.

[3.51] There is nothing wrong with two prospective purchasers deciding that only one of them will bid or negotiate for property and that they will divide it up later in an agreed manner.[448] A subsequent attempt by the one who buys to keep the entire for himself will be a fraud and a breach of trust and he will not be entitled to rely on the Statute of Frauds if there is no written evidence of the agreement between the two purchasers.[449] The vendor's protection against this sort of practice is simply to fix a suitable reserve price and keep the right to bid and to withdraw the property.[450]

Auctioneers' duty of care

[3.52] An auctioneer is bound by implied contract to exercise due diligence in carrying out the auction according to the conditions of sale.[451] As a person who holds himself out as qualified to do a particular kind of work he owes his client a duty to exercise reasonable care and skill as well as diligence. Dowse B explained:[452]

---

[439] *Goldsmith v Rodger* [1962] 2 Lloyds Rep 249. The case concerned a boat but the principle could apply to sales of "land".

[440] *Per* Lord Davey in *Royal Baking Powder Co v Wright Crossley & Co*: see McMahon & Binchy, *op cit* at 674.

[441] Note the warnings in Wylie, *Irish Conveyancing Law* (1978) at para 3.005 and discussion at paras 3.061-2.

[442] See Wylie, *op cit*, para 3.004.

[443] Typically the solicitor.

[444] For the reasons given by Wylie, *op cit* at paras 3.061-2.

[445] See innocent misrepresentation at paras **9.16-22** *post*, fraudulent misrepresentation at **9.12-15** and damages for negligent misrepresentation at **8.48-9** *post*.

[446] See damages for breach of warranty at paras **8.50-1** *post*.

[447] See paras **5.15-6** in the context of the Statute of Frauds and para **8.51** in relation to damages.

[448] *Gilmurray v Corr* [1978] NI 99 at 103-4; *McGillycuddy v Joy* [1959] IR 189 at 212-4; *Devine v Fields* (1920) 54 ILTR 101; *Re Davitt's Estate* (1935) 70 ILTR 53 at 55. *Cf Du Boulay v Raggett* [1989] 1 EGLR 229. An arrangement between a bidder and the vendor or auctioneer to try to prevent a property selling at full value is a different matter; a resulting sale may not be enforced: *Re Ashe* (1855) 4 Ir Ch R 594.

[449] The *Gilmurray, McGillycuddy, Devine* and *Davitt Estates* cases.

[450] *Per* Templeman J in *Harrop v Thompson* [1975] 2 All ER 94 at 98.

[451] *Farmer v Casey* (1899) 33 ILTR 144 at 146.

[452] *Kavanagh v Cuthbert* (1874) IR 9 CL 136 at 139-40.

"An auctioneer differs in no respect from any other person who holds himself out to the world as ready to undertake any work which he may be employed to do.

He impliedly, by undertaking a work, undertakes to bring reasonable care, skill and diligence to the doing of it. An important part of an auctioneer's work, when he sells real estate, on the very lowest estimate of his legal obligation to his employer, is to use reasonable care to have a binding contract under the Statute of Frauds, entered into by the person who purchases the property at the auction. It may be he does not undertake without any qualification to make a binding contract. It cannot be seriously disputed that he undertakes to bring the same amount of care to this part of his work that he undertakes to bring to other parts of it."[453]

The auctioneer also gives his client the benefit of his reputation and experience.[454] He does not guarantee that there will be a contract[455] and indeed any such guarantee would run contrary to the advice which would normally be given - *ie* that the vendor should protect himself with a reserve price and by retaining the right to bid or to withdraw the property.[456]

[3.53] An auctioneer may be liable in the tort of negligence to any person who is injured while attending a sale conducted by the auctioneer.[457] Perhaps of more frequent concern to us is whether the auctioneer can be liable to a bidder or intending bidder in respect of something said by him at the auction or prior to it. In *Bank of Ireland v Smith*[458] Kenny J rejected the very broad proposition that an auctioneer acting for a vendor should anticipate that any statements made by him about the property will be relied on by the purchaser and he therefore owes a duty of care to the purchaser and is liable in damages to him if the statement was incorrect and was made carelessly. That submission was based on *Hedley Byrne & Co Ltd v Heller & Partners Ltd*[459] but Kenny J summarised that case's effect thus:

"It decides that, if a person seeks information from another in circumstances in which a reasonable man would know that his judgment is being relied on, the person giving the information must use reasonable care to ensure that his answer is correct and if he does not do so, he is liable in damages: but the relationship between the person seeking the information and the person giving it, if not fiduciary or arising out of a contract for consideration, must be to use the words of Lord Devlin, 'equivalent to contract' before any liability can arise."

This may be a slightly restrictive view[460] and it seems well arguable that an auctioneer or estate agent is liable for negligently misinforming potential bidders or purchasers about

---

[453] See Fitzgerald B at 143-4 and Palles CB at 146. *Cf* Lord Denning on duties of an estate agent in *McCann v Pow* [1975] 1 All ER 129 at 131-2.
[454] *Morrissey & Sons Ltd v Nalty* [1976/7] ILRM 269 at 273.
[455] *Kavanagh's* case at 140, 141-2, 143-4.
[456] See discussion of a reserve at paras **3.45-6** *supra*.
[457] *Walker v Crabbe* [1916] WN 433 - sale of horses on property of the owner who was not liable as auctioneer was not his servant. Visitors injured on auctioneers' property may succeed on occupier's liability: see McMahon & Binchy, *Irish Law of Torts*, 2nd Ed (1990), Ch 12.
[458] [1964] IR 646 at 659-60.
[459] [1964] AC 465. *Hedley Byrne* was also approved in *Securities Trust Ltd v Hugh Moore & Alexander Ltd* [1964] IR 417 at 421-2 and applied in *McAnarney v Hanrahan* [1993] 3 IR 492 at 496-7; [1994] 1 ILRM at 213-4.
[460] Note discussion by O'Hanlon J in *TE Potterton Ltd v Northern Bank Ltd* [1993] 1 IR 413 at 420-23. *Cf McAnarney's* case at 496-7 (IR); 213-4 (ILRM). See also Wylie, *Irish Conveyancing Law* at paras 6.74-5, Mahon, *Auctioneering and Estate Agency Law in Ireland* (1990) at 83 and Murdoch, *The Law of Estate Agency & Auctions*, 2nd Ed (1984) at 230-2 (estate agents) and 431-2 (auctioneers).

the acreage of a property or such physical characteristics as its boundaries, sewerage and soundproofing, the size of an existing mortgage, the use to which the property could be put and what income and expenditure might result from that use.[461] Those are matters on which the enquirer could be expected to rely on the auctioneer's judgment. Likewise a query to the vendor's solicitor at or before auction about title or about the type of drink licence attaching to premises[462] would suggest likely reliance on the answer. In a recent case[463] Costello J held that a special relationship arose between the auctioneer for the vendor of a leasehold interest and an intending bidder which left the auctioneer liable in damages for giving the bidder his opinion about the likely cost of acquiring the fee simple without taking care to check what price the landlord would accept.[464]

COURT SALES

[3.54] A court sale, as usually understood, is one by order of the court and controlled by it but the court is *not* the vendor.[465] In fact there is not even a *concluded contract* until the sale is confirmed by the court.[466] The party who seeks a sale by order of the court and usually gets carriage of that sale is the vendor.[467] That party is typically a plaintiff in a mortgagee suit[468] and the first reliefs sought are usually a "well charged" declaration and the primary order for sale.[469] The plaintiff may have considered whether it would be best to sell without recourse to the court. A decision may depend on the amount of co-operation he is likely to get from the mortgagor or on the precise power of sale and prospects of getting possession the mortgagee has.[470] The court sale sought by a mortgagee is a way of enforcing his security and not one of implementing any existing contract for the sale of the land. Of course, the sale normally arises out of the arrangement which gave the security[471] and the failure of the mortgagor to meet his commitments. The primary order will direct a sale in default of payment, usually allowing a period of three months.[472] Carriage of sale is usually given to the plaintiff but may be given to a defendant owner[473]; carriage of proceedings may be transferred from one party to another.[474]

---

[461] As in some Commonwealth cases cited by Murdoch at 232-1.

[462] A hotel licence has given trouble which might have been avoided by that kind of enquiry: *Kelly v Crowley* [1985] IR 212; *Taylor v Ryan* (HC) 10 March 1983, Finlay P, unrep.

[463] *McAnarney v Hanrahan* [1993] 3 IR 492 at 496-7; [1994] 1 ILRM at 213-4.

[464] See paras **8.48-9** *post* on damages for negligent misrepresentation.

[465] *Bank of Ireland v Waldron* [1944] IR 303 at 306; *Bank of Ireland v Smith* [1966] IR 646 at 656.

[466] *Per* O'Brien C in *Re Longvale Brick and Lime Works Ltd* [1917] 1 IR 321 at 330. *Cf Vesey v Elwood* (1842) 3 Drury & Warren 74 at 79-80. Of course, there usually is a contract which is *conditional on* court approval.

[467] *Bank of Ireland v Waldron* [1944] IR 303 at 306.

[468] Under Order 51, Rule 1 of The Rules of the Superior Courts the court may order sales "in any case or matter relating to any real estate or chattel real" where it appears "necessary or expedient to do so". In an action for administration of an estate or execution of the trusts of a written instrument carriage is normally given to the executor, administrator or trustee: Order 50, Rule 11.

[469] On which see Wylie, *Irish Land Law*, 2nd Ed, para 13.040-1.

[470] See Wylie, *op cit*, para 13.013-047.

[471] Or, of course, a new or further advance on an existing security (see discussion of this by Barron J and the Supreme Court in *Bank of Ireland v Purcell* [1989] IR 327, 332); or a judgment mortgage (which is a process of execution).

[472] As in *Bank of Ireland v Smith* [1966] IR 646; *Bank of Ireland v Waldron* [1944] IR 303.

[473] Eg, in *Re Longvale Brick and Lime Works Ltd* [1917] 1 IR 321.

[474] As in *Bank of Ireland v Smith* [1966] IR 646. New defendants were joined and carriage transferred to them by consent. They were held to be the vendors and their solicitors and auctioneers were their agents for the sale: per Kenny J at 656.

Conduct of vendors in court sales

[3.55] The court expects exemplary conduct on the part of vendors selling under its order and will see that purchasers are fairly dealt with in every respect.[475] As Lord Macnaghten said:[476]

> "It has been laid down again and again that, in sales under the direction of the Court, it is incumbent on the Court to be scrupulous in the extreme, and very careful to see that no taint or touch of fraud or deceit or misrepresentation is found in the conduct of its ministers. The Court, it is said, must at any rate not fall below the standard of honesty which it exacts from those on whom it has to pass judgment. The slightest suspicion of trickery or unfairness must affect the honour of the Court and impair its usefulness."[477]

It has been said that if it would be unjust to compel a purchaser to carry out a contract in a case of specific performance it would be "doubly improper to compel him to do so in the case of a sale under the Court"[478] That does not mean that an issue will be decided in favour of a purchaser in a court sale more readily than it would have been in a specific performance suit on the same facts[479] but it does underline the courts' strong concern to deal fairly with the purchaser if an issue arises which could cause injustice to him.

[3.56] At times it may seem that the court expects higher standards of conduct from vendors and their agents in court sales than from others. A review of case law in a judgment[480] led to the sentence "*Quaere* whether the position in a Court sale differs from that in a sale outside Court" in the headnote. The cases reviewed[481] do certainly stress the courts' anxiety that purchasers always get a fair deal and that court sales are conducted in a manner above suspicion but it does not necessarily follow[482] that higher standards are required of persons in charge of court sales.[483] As Meredith MR put it in *Re Lewis deceased*:[484]

> "... while I must admit that there is no law rendering it obligatory for the parties having a sale in Court to be more superlatively honest than others with a purchaser, it is at least desirable for a purchaser buying in Court to know that the Court will see that right and justice will be done..."

Porter MR felt in *Manifold v Johnston*[485] that a question about a misleading condition in a court sale was very much the same as it would be in a specific performance suit but, when the purchaser succeeded on that issue, it would be "doubly improper" to compel him to carry out the contract. The position of a *trustee* as an officer of the court has been summarised thus:[486]

---

[475] Overend J in *Bank of Ireland v Waldron* [1944] IR 303 at 307.
[476] *Mahomed Kala Mea v AV Harperink* (1908) 25 TLR 180.
[477] Approved by Kenny J in *Bank of Ireland v Smith* [1966] IR 646 at 656-7.
[478] By Porter MR in *Manifold v Johnston* [1902] 1 IR 7 at 13.
[479] In the *Manifold* case the issue was a misleading condition and Porter MR said at p 11 "the question is very much the same as it would be if there was a suit for specific performance".
[480] By Kenny J in *Bank of Ireland v Smith* [1966] IR 646 at 656-7.
[481] The *Mahomed Kala Mea* and *Manifold* cases. See para **3.14** *supra*.
[482] And Kenny J did not say or imply in *Bank of Ireland v Smith*.
[483] Or that *lower* standards are accepted in sales outside court.
[484] (1908) 42 ILTR 210 at 211.
[485] [1902] 1 IR 7.
[486] Williams on *Bankruptcy*, (18th Ed) at p 275.

"Generally, the trustee will be ordered, as an officer of the Court, to do the fullest equity and in certain cases, an even higher standard of conduct is imposed on him. It is not easy to define the exact bounds of a principle based upon the control exercised by the Court over its officers, which, since it operates in a field not covered by the established rules of law and equity, is incapable of reduction to an exact formula, and must in its application be governed in part by ethical considerations."[487]

[3.57] Occasionally a reported case may suggest that an issue was decided more favourably to a purchaser in a court sale than it might have been in a sale outside court. However, other factors usually have existed which could explain the results. Thus, in *Connolly v Keating (No 2)*,[488] Porter MR said about an issue of dilapidation:[489]

"In the case of a private sale out of court, in the absence of warranty or fraud, I think he should be held to his bargain- obtaining the estate as it stood when the hammer fell. But in the case of a sale under the court, particularly where there is a receiver, I think that the purchaser is entitled to expect that he will get that which the court ordered to be sold; that is, that the fabric at least will be preserved as it stood, allowing for wear and tear and inevitable accident. I believe that he bought in that expectation and belief; and that apart from his having taken his conveyance and its operation as a waiver of claim,[490] that good faith which always attends sales by the court would entitle him to be compensated."

The result in that case could be explained also by a breach of a vendor's duty to take reasonable care of the property after contract while still in possession.[491] In *Smyth v Smyth*[492] a purchaser was allowed compensation for storm damage occurring two days after he bought at auction but one day before the chief clerk's certificate was filed.[493] However, the basis may have been that the property was still at vendor's risk because there was no complete contract before confirmation.[494] In *National Bank v Beirne*[495] an auctioneer settled "descriptive particulars" without any reference to the solicitors having carriage of sale[496] and a change made in those particulars took out a store attached to the lot which the purchaser bought: Porter MR awarded her compensation although, "as a juror" he was of opinion that the purchaser "knew perfectly well that she was not buying the store."[497] A court will be slow to approve of amendments made at the time of sale and, if any important amendment is allowed, it will be on terms that full notice of it is given, so as to reach the bidder.[498] If knowledge is not brought home to the purchaser and he acts bona fide on the original version he might not be held to his purchase on the basis of the

---

[487] Quoted by Murray J in *In re Brook Cottage Ltd* [1976] NI 78 at 106.
[488] [1903] 1 IR 356.
[489] At 361.
[490] He held later that there was no waiver: p 362.
[491] On which see paras **11.14-5** *post*.
[492] (1903) 37 ILTR 82.
[493] Under the general law (though not the modern Law Society conditions) risk passes to the purchaser at the time of contract: see paras **11.18-20** *post*.
[494] This view is supported by *Ex parte Minor* (1805) 11 Ves Junior 559 which was opened in argument in the *Smyth* case.
[495] (1900) 35 ILTR 9.
[496] It is the solicitors' duty to see that the particulars are in order: *ibid*.
[497] He had regard to her evidence that the auctioneer did not announce that a change had been made. The store was in the printed rental but not in the "descriptive particulars". Possibly his opinion that the purchaser knew she was not intended to get the store was really only suspicion. This case may be the strongest in support of a view that an issue might be decided in a purchaser's favour more easily in a court sale than in one outside court.
[498] *Re Trustees of Dargan's Estate* (1870) IR 4 Eq 323 at 324 (a Landed Estates Court sale).

amendment.[499] It is always an important principle in court sales that a purchaser should not be prejudiced by conditions which might mislead him.[500]

Keeping faith with purchasers

[3.58] Normally the court must keep faith with a purchaser in the sense of seeing that an agreement for sale is honoured. Once the court approves a sale it will uphold that sale against a later higher offer.[501] People will not make proposals to the court for the purchase of property if they cannot rely on the court keeping faith with them.[502] There is no general rule of law to support a contention that the highest bidder, no matter when or where the bid is made, must be declared to be the purchaser.[503] The position is the same when a court sale is carried through by private treaty.[504] And in a case of a sale by an official liquidator under the control of the court, if the court has already approved a sale when a higher offer is received, the court will consider itself bound, if not in law certainly in honour, to let the approved sale proceed.[505] The choice is between going on with the bargain it has approved and repudiating it for a better one.[506] But if a liquidator is not yet bound by an enforceable contract he seems free, and perhaps under an obligation, to accept a later, better offer.[507] At the least, he will be open to criticism if he does not investigate the new, higher bid.[508] A third party contracting with a liquidator in a compulsory winding up has to remember that the liquidator is under the control of the court and, in order to be absolutely sure of his ground, should stipulate for the approval of the contract by the court being obtained by the liquidator.[509] In the absence of that approval a later higher bid is likely to be accepted even though a contract at the earlier lower figure would have been perfectly proper.[510] If a sale is conditional on court approval the court will consider the matter as it stands at the time of the application for the approval[511] and will have regard to the primary duty of both court and liquidator to get the maximum price for the assets.[512] There is a vital difference between a situation where it is sought to discharge a court order approving a sale because a higher bid is received later and one where the higher bid comes in before the court's sanction has been given.[513] When no contract has yet been approved there is no purchaser to whom a duty of keeping faith is owed and a system which required acceptance of a lower bid[514] would bring the court into well-deserved

---

499 *Ibid.*
500 *Hibernian Bank v Cassidy* (1902) 36 ILTR 156.
501 *Van Hool McArdle v Rohan Industrial Estates* [1980] IR 237 at 242.
502 *Bank of Ireland v Farris* [1944] IR 150 at 153; *Munster and Leinster Bank v Munster Motor Co Ltd* [1922] 1 IR 15 at 19.
503 *Per* Haugh J in *Provincial Bank v Farris* [1944] IR 150 at 153.
504 *Munster & Leinster Bank v Munster Motor Co Ltd* [1922] 1 IR 15 at 19, approving *Re Bartlett* (1880) 16 Ch D 561.
505 *Re Hibernian Transport Co's Ltd* [1972] IR 190 at 203. The approved purchaser had altered its position court's approval but this may not have been essential to the decision.
506 *Ibid,* p 202.
507 See discussion by Murray J in *In Re Brook Cottage Ltd* [1976] NI 78 at 106-7.
508 *Ibid,* p 114-5.
509 *Ibid* at 117.
510 *Van Hool McArdle v Rohan Industrial Estates* [1980] IR 237 at 242.
511 *Per* O'Higgins CJ in the *Van Hool McArdle* case at 240-1.
512 *Per* Kenny J in the *Van Hool McArdle* case at 242-3. *Cf* in *Re Brook Cottage Ltd* [1976] NI 78 at 114, 115-6; *Holohan v Friends Provident and Century Life Office* [1966] IR 1 at 9, 20-21, 25.
513 See discussion by Kenny J in the *Van Hool McArdle* case at 242.
514 Because, *eg,* a contract at the earlier lower figure would have been bona fide and in due discharge of the liquidator's duty.

ridicule.[515] A liquidator has statutory power to sell property of the company without going to the court.[516] If he does so and his action is subsequently questioned, the court is only concerned to see whether he acted bona fide and in due discharge of his duties as liquidator.[517] However, the usual practice is to seek court approval for sales of assets of any significant value.[518]

[3.59] It is interesting to note the position of a mortgagee selling out of court who contracts to sell property at a price which was the best available at the time but then gets a higher offer; he is not discharged from his contract at the lower, agreed price.[519] The mortgagee selling out of court has not the same freedom to dispose of the mortgagor's property as if it were his own[520] but must act as a reasonable man in selling the property and this will include bearing in mind the interest of the mortgagor and any second or other mortgagees.[521] For example, he must be prepared to examine the possibilities of a better price and, if he will not do so, he risks an injunction to restrain the completion of the sale[522] and an order setting aside the concluded contract.[523] However, the receipt of even a much higher offer after a contract was made does not necessarily show that the lower price agreed was not the best that could be got at the time of the contract.[524]

Re-opening the biddings

[3.60] Before the passing of the Sale of Land by Auction Act 1867[525] the mere circumstance that someone had offered a higher sum would have been sufficient to cause "the biddings to be opened".[526] If, prior to confirmation of the report[527] a real advance in price was offered over and above the highest bid, the biddings would be re-opened by the court.[528] That practice has been described as "most pernicious", "unfair to the purchasers" and "prejudicial to the vendors".[529] It was in many cases a hardship on an innocent purchaser who had bid up to and beyond the reserve price; it had a prejudicial effect on court sales and discouraged purchasers.[530] As we have seen,[531] the modern courts are fully alive to the need that purchasers can rely on the court keeping faith with them. That approach is assisted by s 7 of the 1867 Act under which the biddings will no longer be

---

[515] The *Van Hool McArdle* case at 243.
[516] Section 231(2)(*a*) of the Companies Act 1963. See Keane, *Company Law in the Republic of Ireland*, 2nd Ed, paras 38.57, 40.15. See also the discussion of the statutory power by Kenny J in *Re Hibernian Transport Co's Ltd* [1972] IR 190 at 200-1 and by Murray J in *In Re Brook Cottage Ltd* [1976] NI 78 at 107-11.
[517] *Per* O'Higgins CJ in the *Van Hool McArdle* case at p 240.
[518] Keane, *op cit*, paras 38.57, 38.61.
[519] *Casey v Irish Intercontinental Bank* [1979] IR 364 at 371.
[520] *Holohan v Friends Provident and Century Life Office* [1966] IR 1 at 25.
[521] *Ibid* at p 21.
[522] As occurred in the *Holohan* case. Note the conditional order restraining completion of the contract made by Murray J in *In Re Brook Cottage Ltd* [1976] NI 78 at 117.
[523] See the review of authorities by Murray J in the *Brook Cottage* case at 103-7 and his conclusion and proposed order at 115-7.
[524] *Casey v Irish Intercontinental Bank* [1979] IR 364 at 371.
[525] Effective from 1 August 1867. We have considered puffers at paras **3.45-6** *supra*.
[526] *Per* Powell J in *Munster and Leinster Bank v Munster Motor Co Ltd* [1922] 1 IR 15 at 19.
[527] *Ie*, the report or certificate of the result of the sale.
[528] *Per* O'Brien LC in *Re Longvale Brick and Lime Works Ltd* [1917] 1 IR 321 at 328.
[529] *Re Bartlett* (1880) 16 Ch D 561 approved in *Munster & Leinster Bank v Munster Motor Co Ltd* [1922] 1 IR 15 at 19.
[530] *Re Longvale Brick and Lime Works Ltd* [1917] 1 IR 321 at 328.
[531] Para **3.61** *supra*.

opened simply to accommodate a new, higher bid. They may still be re-opened on the ground of fraud or[532] improper conduct in the management of the sale.[533] The words "improper conduct" do not mean only something bordering on fraud[534] but may include a mistaken statement affecting the value of the property offered for sale[535] or, perhaps, conditions of sale which are "depreciatory".[536]

[3.61] The 1867 Act does not affect the general jurisdiction of a court of equity to refuse, on proper grounds, to sanction the completion of a sale which has taken place under its control.[537] Circumstances might arise such that, if the sale were one out of court, specific performance would not be decreed by a court of equity or one of the parties might be entitled to rescind.[538] The Act only affects the court of equity opening biddings on the ground of undervalue; all other objections to sales can still be made.[539] It was not intended to have, and does not have, the effect of requiring a court to confirm a sale knowing that an error made by a person conducting the sale would thereby inflict a serious wrong on a litigant who has invoked the aid of the court.[540] The conduct of the purchaser may be taken into account; as Holmes LJ said in *Woods v Brown*:

> "But still here we have to consider the case of a purchaser who has not been guilty of any fraud, who has been perfectly honest throughout the whole transaction and who has bid a larger price than that fixed by a careful valuer. It would be very injurious to purchasers if under these circumstances, for some imaginary idea that a larger price might be obtained, we were to reopen the biddings and set aside the sale."[541]

The likelihood of a higher price being obtainable if a mistake were corrected is relevant. The facts that the reserve price is reached and there is no fraud or anything in the nature of fraud does not necessarily entitle a purchaser to hold on to his bargain despite injury to another party due to a mistake.[542] Any person interested in the land may apply for relief before the certificate of the result of the sale becomes binding and the court may hold a bidder bound by his bid or discharge him from being the purchaser and order the land to be resold.[543]

Protection of vendors and others

[3.62] While the reported cases largely concern the position of purchasers it is important to remember that the court will also protect vendors and others having an interest in the property sold. The court and any auctioneer appointed by it owe a duty to the persons interested in the purchase-money as well as to purchasers.[544] The duty of the auctioneer is to carry out a properly conducted sale and the duty of the court is to see that such a sale

[532] The disjunctive "or" is noted by Ronan LJ in the *Longvale Brick and Lime Works* case at p 331.
[533] Section 7 of the 1867 Act.
[534] *Per* Ronan LJ in *Re Longvale Brick and Lime Works Ltd* [1917] 1 IR 321 at 331. See also discussion by *O'Brien LC* at pp 327-8.
[535] As in the *Longvale Brick and Lime Works* case.
[536] This point failed in *Woods v Brown* [1915] 1 IR 29.
[537] *Re Longvale Brick and Lime Works Ltd* [1917] 1 IR 321 at 329.
[538] *Ibid.*
[539] See Palles CB in *Woods v Brown* [1915] 1 IR 29 at 36-7.
[540] The *Longvale Brick & Lime Works* case at 329.
[541] At p 38. See also *O'Brien LC* at 35.
[542] The *Longvale Brick & Lime Works* case at 326-7.
[543] Section 7 considered by Palles CB in *Woods v Brown* [1915] 1 IR 29 at 36-7.
[544] *Per* Ronan LJ in *Re Longvale Brick and Lime Works Ltd* [1917] 1 IR 321 at 330.

is carried out.[545] If the court sells a property it has a duty to see that it is sold at the best price that can be got[546] and this duty is written into the Rules of the Superior Courts.[547] As we have seen,[548] if an auctioneer handling a court sale makes a significant mistake which is likely to result in lower bids the court will probably refuse to confirm the sale on the ground of improper conduct in the management of the sale.[549] Also it has been said that an "unrealistic"[550] rate of interest should not be adopted in court sales.[551]

[3.63] Having carriage of sale imposes certain duties on the vendor and his agents. A party with carriage stands in a fiduciary position to all parties and incumbrancers in the cause.[552] His solicitor is responsible for the truth and accuracy of the particulars and should not delegate the duty of stating them to an auctioneer.[553] He should see that the conditions are not such as to deter parties from bidding.[554] The conditions may be settled by court counsel[555] and may go to the court for approval.[556] If they are settled by counsel he will be regarded as the agent of the vendor[557] who will have to accept responsibility for a statement which the court holds to be misleading.[558] It is the duty of the vendor to be able to give clear possession on the date fixed for completion and, in case of doubt, application can be made to the court in good time for an order for possession with a view to sale.[559] This can be done by a motion for possession[560] or with the initial application for the order for sale.[561] When an order for sale is made the court has the fullest power to order possession where it is in the interests of the parties to get possession from a mortgagor before the sale.[562] This is an *inherent* jurisdiction which the Court of Chancery has always possessed.[563] Formerly the courts may have been slow to grant orders for possession before sale[564] However, an order for possession would be made if a sale is being impeded by interference by a mortgagor or his family,[565] to prevent forfeiture of a licence,[566] to facilitate a sale even when there is no interference[567] or to enhance the likely

---

[545] *Ibid.*

[546] *Van Hool McArdle v Rohan Industrial Estates* [1980] IR 237 at 242-3; *In Re Brook Cottage Ltd* [1976] NI 78 at 114, 115-6; *Cf Holohan v Friends Provident & Century Life Office* [1966] IR 1 at 9, 20-21, 25.

[547] Order 51 Rule 5.

[548] Para **3.61** *supra.*

[549] *Re: Longvale Brick & Lime Works Ltd* [1917] 1 IR 321.

[550] In the context meaning "too low".

[551] *Per* Kenny J in *Law v Roberts (No 2)* [1964] IR 306 at 307. He was dealing with a specific performance case but included court sales in his statement.

[552] *Popham v Exham* (1860) 10 Ir Ch R 440 at 451.

[553] *National Bank v Beirne* (1900) 35 ILTR 9.

[554] *Per* Smith MR in *Popham v Exham* (1860) 10 IR Ch R 440 at 451. Note the consideration of depreciatory conditions by the Court of Appeal in *Woods v Brown* [1915] 1 IR 29 at 35, 36 and 38.

[555] RSC, Order 51, Rule 4.

[556] As in *Belfast Bank v Callan* [1910] 1 IR 38: see p 43. The conditions were settled by court counsel and submitted to Meredith MR personally for approval.

[557] *In re Banister, Broad v Munton* 12 Ch D 131 and *Union Bank v Munster* 37 Ch D 51, both approved by Overend J in *Bank of Ireland v* Waldron [1944] IR 303 at 306-7.

[558] *Ibid.*

[559] *Bank of Ireland v Waldron* [1944] IR 303 at 307; *Re O'Neill* [1967] NI 129 at 132-5.

[560] As in *Bank of Ireland v Smith* [1966] IR 646 at 652-3.

[561] Suggested by Lowry J in *Re O'Neill* [1967] NI 129 at 136.

[562] *Bank of Ireland v Slattery* [1911] 1 IR 33 at 40; *Bunyan v Bunyan* [1916] 1 IR 70 at 73.

[563] *Re O'Neill* [1967] NI 129 at 133, 135. Note discussion at 132-3 in *Bank of Ireland v Slattery*. Cf *Bunyan v Bunyan* [1916] 1 IR 70.

[564] *Re O'Neill* [1967] NI 129 at 132; *Irish Permanent Building Society v Ryan* [1950] IR 12 at 13.

[565] *Bank of Ireland v Slattery* [1911] 1 IR 33.

[566] *Doran v Hannin* (1906) 40 ILTR 186.

[567] *Bunyan v Bunyan* [1916] 1 IR 70.

price.[568] It has been suggested that applications for possession should be encouraged in suitable cases in view of the saving in costs for the defendant.[569] The plaintiff in his capacity as vendor[570] has a duty to sell at the best price that can be obtained.[571] It is also the duty of the party having carriage to make any necessary application to the court to perfect the purchaser's title and the costs of that application will ordinarily be treated as part of the costs of sale.[572] If it becomes necessary to seek the exercise of any of the court's other powers to advance sales[573] the person having carriage is the most appropriate to do so and not the purchaser[574] though there is jurisdiction to make an order on the application of the purchaser.[575]

[3.64] Another important point to note is that a party to a case in which the court directs a sale should not bid without the leave of the court.[576] This practice is adopted to prevent sales being so conducted as not to produce a fair value.[577] It is the duty of a party selling to produce a high price and the interest of a purchaser to give a low price; and if a party (especially one conducting the sale) intends to purchase, his interest may conflict with his duty.[578] However, the court has a discretion to confirm a sale despite an irregularity in this area.[579]

Does the Statute of Frauds apply?

[3.65] When the court directs a sale of "land" there may be no need to comply with the Statute of Frauds. Some old English case law[580] supports that view. The basis seems to be that in sales by the court there is no risk of the frauds and perjuries which the statute was intended to prevent.[581] However, the statute may be regarded also as protection against uncertainty in oral agreements or simply as meeting the need to prevent the mischief that could arise from proof by oral evidence of the contract or its terms.[582] We have already noted[583] the courts' strong concern to deal fairly with purchasers. In practice there is almost always a written contract in court sales and a contract is unlikely to be *concluded* until it has been approved by the court. Therefore an issue whether the statute has to be satisfied would rarely arise but a proposition that it *never* had to be satisfied in court sales may be viewed with some caution. The English courts declined an invitation to go one step further and hold that it was unnecessary to satisfy the statute in sales by auction.[584] As Grant MR said:

[568] *Irish Permanent Building Society v Ryan* [1950] IR 12 at 14.
[569] By Gavan Duffy P in *Irish Permanent Building Society v Ryan* [1950] IR 12 at 13-14. Note Lowry J's statement of the practice in Northern Ireland in *Re O'Neill* [1967] NI 129 at 132.
[570] He usually has another role, eg, mortgagee enforcing his security.
[571] *Popham v Exham* (1860) 10 Ir Ch R 440 at 451.
[572] *Kidd v O'Neill* [1931] IR 664 at 669-70.
[573] See paras **8.25-8** *post.*
[574] *Moorhead v Kirkwood* [1919] 1 IR 225.
[575] O'Connor MR did in the *Moorehead* case despite his reservation.
[576] *Shimmin v Bellew* (1867) IR 1 Eq 289 at 291; *Byrne v Lafferty* (1845) 8 Ir Eq R 47.
[577] *Shimmin's* case at 291.
[578] *Ibid.*
[579] *Shimmin's* case: cf *Byrne's* case where Blackburne MR would have needed "some special circumstances" to approve the sale.
[580] *AG v Day* (1749) 1 Ves Senior 466 at 472; *Blagden v Bradbear* (1806) 12 Ves 466 at 472; *Re Goren* (1838) 3 Deac 242 at 267.
[581] See discussion by Harwicke LC in *AG v Day*, at 220-1 and Grant MR in *Blagden's* case at 472.
[582] See para **5.03** and fns13 and 14 *ante.*
[583] Paras **3.56-8** *supra.*
[584] *Blagden's* case at 472.

"The words of the Statute are large enough to comprehend every Contract, by whatsoever preliminary means, whether verbal communication, or bidding at an Auction, it may have been brought about; and it is not clear to me that Sales by Auction are out of the Mischief, against which the Statute meant to guard. From the public nature of a Sale by Auction it does not follow, that what passes there must be a matter of certainty: so far from it, that I never saw more contradictory swearing than in these Cases, where attempts were made to introduce Evidence of what was said or done during the course of the Sale."[585]

While the risk of frauds and perjuries must be smaller when the courts control sales it may go a bit far to say that there is no risk of something happening which would render it just for a party to have the protection of being able to plead the Statute. The point is open in the Irish courts.

COMPULSORY PURCHASE

[3.66] Statutory contracts differ in important ways from contracts made between parties in the normal course. An obvious example is that consensus is not required and, indeed, the main need for compulsory acquisition powers is that acquiring authorities may not be able to buy all the property they need by agreement. The pre-requisites to the exercise of compulsory acquisition powers are, firstly, that such powers are vested by statute in the acquiring authority and, secondly, that the particular authority is charged by statute with the duty or function for which the property in question is required.[586] It is also necessary to show that the acquisition powers have been exercised in accordance with and within the confines of the statute.[587] The price may be fixed under machinery set up by the relevant Acts if the parties cannot agree. In a typical compulsory purchase situation the service of a notice to treat does not pass any estate or interest in the land to the acquiring authority nor does it constitute a contract; but it creates a relationship which ripens into an enforceable contract when the compensation has been agreed by the parties or assessed on arbitration.[588] In general service of notice to treat confers on an acquiring authority the right to get the land on payment of proper compensation and gives the landowner the right to have compensation assessed and paid.[589] A person entitled to buy the fee simple under the ground rents legislation brings about a statutory contract by serving notice of intention to acquire,[590] the price being fixed by arbitration in default of agreement.[591] If a party to the contract finds a need to enforce it relevant Acts usually contain the necessary means. However, the equitable jurisdiction to grant decrees of specific performance is not taken away simply by providing new statutory remedies.[592] A failure to use statutory mechanisms could affect questions of costs.[593] Thus an action for

---

[585] *Ibid.*

[586] McDermott and Woulfe, *Compulsory Purchase and Compensation: Law and Practice in Ireland*, (1992) p 49.

[587] *McDermott and Woulfe*, p 5.

[588] *In re Greendale Building Co* [1977] IR 256 at 265.

[589] *Ibid.* Notices to treat are considered in detail by McDermott and Woulfe, *op cit* at p 80-85 and Ch 7 and by Keane, *Law of Local Government in the Republic of Ireland* at 247-53.

[590] Under s 4 of the Landlord and Tenant (Ground Rents) Act 1967.

[591] *Smiths (Harcourt St) Ltd v Hardwicke Ltd* (HC) 30 July 1971, O'Keeffe P, at p 10.

[592] Not always equally available to both sides. However, McDermott and Woulfe note, *op cit* at p 84, that the steps which a claimant takes to have an arbitrator appointed are simple, speedy and cheap. See also *Re Cary-Elwes' Contract* [1906] 2 Ch 143 at 148.

[593] *The Regents Canal Co v Ware* (1857) 23 Beav 575 at 589. Note reference to specific performance by Lord Morris in *Birmingham Corporation v West Midland Baptist Trust Assoc* [1969] 3 All ER 172 at 180. *Cf Jersey (Earl) v Briton Ferry Floating Dock Co* (1869) LR 7 Eq 409.

specific performance might not be advisable but a party may apply to the courts where necessary to interpret the rights of parties under an award.[594] Under the Constitution the High Court has full original jurisdiction in all matters civil and criminal[595] and parliament would clearly try to avoid constitutional problems[596] if it tried to remove the power to decree specific performance in compulsory acquisition cases. Also, if an Act sought to oust that jurisdiction it would need to use clear language.[597]

[3.67] The normal law of vendor and purchaser applies largely to compulsory purchase situations subject, of course, to the relevant statute law.[598] Although the parties are usually brought together by a power for the compulsory purchase of the relevant land their basic legal positions are vendor and purchaser. For example, the vendor[599] will be entitled to interest once the acquiring authority goes into possession unless a statute provides to the contrary.[600] The transfer of title is normally done by deed of assurance in exchange for the compensation though acquiring authorities have back-up powers in certain situations of executing deed polls to themselves after lodging the compensation in court or making a vesting order.[601] An acquiring authority which serves a notice to treat pursuant to a CPO is under a duty to proceed to acquire the land and pay the compensation within a reasonable time and, if that is not done, the right to enforce the CPO may be lost.[602] The delay involved may have to be such that allowing the acquiring authority to continue to enforce its rights under the CPO would be in some real sense against good conscience.[603] In 1868[604] Lord Romilly MR set out some of the prejudice to a landowner caused by a 10-year delay:[605]

> "The injury to him would be very great. During the whole of the ten years he would have had but a qualified ownership or enjoyment of his own property. If land, he could not improve it or build on it; if a house, he could not rebuild or repair it, however urgent the necessity of doing so might be, without the strong probability of getting no return for the money laid out if the company ultimately took over the land..."[606]

An acquiring authority should serve a notice to treat within three years after a CPO becomes operative. This is the normal period in which a power of compulsory purchase must be "exercised"[607] and the service of a notice to treat may be a sufficient exercise of

---

[594] As occurred in the *Smiths (Harcourt St)* case where O'Keeffe P rejected an argument that when difficulty arose over a party's rights under an award of the County Registrar under the ground rents legislation the plaintiff should have gone to another arbitration: p 14 of the transcript.

[595] *Ibid* at 14.

[596] See discussion by Kelly, *The Irish Constitution*, 3rd Ed (1994) at 408-20.

[597] *Kelly v Enright* (1883) 11 LRI 379 at 385, 386 and 387.

[598] *Rafter v Dublin Corporation* [1953] IR 36 at 38. See also McDermott and Woulfe, *Compulsory Purchase and Compensation in Ireland: Law and Practice* at 86-90.

[599] *ie*, the person whose land is being acquired.

[600] Per Casey J in *Rafter's* case at 38 approving *Re Pigott & The Great Western Railway Co* (1881) 18 Ch D 146.

[601] McDermot and Woulfe, *op cit* at 85-89; Wylie, *Irish Conveyancing* Law, paras **9.112-5**; Keane, *Law of Local Government in the Republic of Ireland*, p 261-2.

[602] *Van Nierop v Commissioners of Public Works in Ireland* [1990] 2 IR 189 at 198.

[603] *Simpson's Motor Sales (London) Ltd v Hendon Corporation* [1963] 2 All ER 484 at 494.

[604] *Richmond v North London Railway Co* (1868) LR 5 Eq 352 at 258-9.

[605] The 10 years were an assumed period. In the *Van Nierop* case actual delay was over 9 years, nearly 13 if time was measured from an earlier notice of intention to enter and take possession.

[606] Quoted with approval by O'Hanlon J in the *Van Nierop* case at 197.

[607] Section 123 of the Lands Clauses Consolidation Act 1845.

the power to meet that time limit.[608] That is not necessarily so always and much depends on the particular statutory provisions and sometimes on what happens on foot of the notice to treat.[609]

[3.68] Other legal rights will arise in compulsory purchase cases just as they do in normal sales of land. Thus a vendor's lien will arise and cover unpaid compensation[610] in the absence of agreement to the contrary. The equitable doctrine of conversion will apply when compensation is ascertained because then there is an enforceable contract.[611]

[3.69] Property the subject of a CPO may still be bought and sold but, obviously, an intending purchaser should think carefully as the eventual loss of the land, even on payment of compensation, may be very inconvenient. He should also check that nothing has occurred which would leave the compensation he gets lower than the price he has paid. It is long established that when notice to treat is served a landowner can no longer deal with the land so as to increase the burden on the acquiring authority.[612] Article 2(1) in the Third Schedule to the Housing Act 1966 extended that principle back to the date when notice of a CPO being made is published.[613] Thus the property arbitrator in assessing compensation must leave out of account any interest in land created after that date.[614] He must also disregard any building erected or improvement or alteration made after that date if in his opinion the work was not reasonably necessary and[615] was carried out with a view to obtaining or increasing compensation.[616] If a CPO has not yet been confirmed by the relevant Minister a court may feel that little regard should be paid to it.[617] When one is confirmed it still does not affect the freedom to deal with the affected land. As we have seen,[618] even the next step, *ie,* the service of notice to treat, does not bring about a contract either. It does determine one important element of a contract, namely, the thing to be taken, but the price remains to be determined.[619]

Accordingly, when a landowner contracts to sell his land after a CPO has been confirmed and a notice to treat served, but before compensation is agreed or assessed, he still has the legal and equitable estate in the land.[620] Normally no money will have been paid yet by the acquiring authority so the position is consistent with the principle that a purchaser owns land in equity only to the extent to which he has paid for it.[621] In *Irish Life*

---

[608] Keane, *op cit* at 246; McDermott and Woulfe, *op cit* at 174.
[609] See discussion by Henchy J in *In re Green Dale Building Co* [1977] IR 256 at 264-5 and 266.
[610] *Walker v Ware, Hadham & Buntingford Rly Co* (1865) LR 1 Eq 195; *Wing v Tottenham & Hampstead Junction Rly Co* (1868) 3 Ch App 740.
[611] *Harding v Metropolitan Rly Co* (1872) 7 Ch App 154.
[612] *Cardiff Corporation v Cook* [1923] 2 Ch 115; *Mercer v Liverpool, St Helens & South Lancashire Rly* [1904] AC 461. See *Keane*, p 252-3; *McDermott and Woulfe*, pp 176-7.
[613] *McDermott & Woulfe* at 176-7.
[614] Article 2(1)(i).
[615] Note the conjunctive "and".
[616] Article 2(1)(ii).
[617] *O'Sullivan v Cork County Council* (HC) 18 December 1969, Teevan J, unrep at 13-14. The CPO was made after action brought and, for all the court knew, the Minister might refuse to confirm it.
[618] Para **3.66** above.
[619] *Blount v GW & W Rly Co* (1851) 2 Ir Ch R 40 at 47. *Cf Eaton v Midland Great Western Railway Co* (1847) 10 Ir LR 310 at 314.
[620] *Irish Life Assurance Co Ltd v Dublin Land Securities Ltd* [1986] IR 332 at 354, affirmed by the Supreme Court, (1989) IR 253.
[621] *Tempany v Hynes* [1976] IR 101 discussed at paras **11.02-13** *post.* Of course, he can normally insist on specific performance also.

Assurance Co Ltd v Dublin Land Securities Ltd[622] two CPOs affected the disputed land.[623] One had been confirmed by the Minister and a notice to treat had been served before the agreement between the parties but the second was not confirmed by the Minister until after the contract. Keane J rejected a submission that the plaintiff had ceased to own the land comprised in the first CPO and accordingly it would be impossible[624] for it to comply with an order for specific performance.[625] If a CPO is confirmed and a notice to treat served before completion of the sale the duty of the vendor is to convey the property to the purchaser subject to the notice to treat.[626] The notice to treat does not require the vendor to convey the land to the acquiring authority and there is no frustration[627] of the contract.[628] The purchaser is entitled in equity to the land or to any compensation which may be paid by the acquiring authority[629] and, if that authority gets the title vested in itself[630] before the contract between vendor and purchaser is completed, the purchaser is entitled to the compensation.[631]

[3.70] An important final point about compulsory purchase is that the Statute of Frauds does not have to be observed in relation to statutory contracts. Once a notice to treat has been served and the price is known[632] a binding obligation is created which is equivalent to a contract between the parties.[633] It is not an ordinary contract and oral evidence of its terms may therefore be admitted.[634]

---

[622] [1986] IR 332, affirmed [1989] IR 253.

[623] There was also some land outside both CPOs.

[624] For the defence of impossibility see paras **9.56-8** *post*.

[625] At [1986] IR 354.

[626] *Hillingdon Estates v Stonefield Estates* [1952] Ch 627; [1952] All ER 853 at 857 cited by Keane J in the *Irish Life* case at 354.

[627] On this defence see paras **9.59-65** *post*.

[628] The *Hillingdon Estates* case.

[629] Per Keane J in the *Irish Life* case. That assumes, of course, that the contract price is paid.

[630] *Eg*, by deed poll or vesting order - see para **3.67** *supra*.

[631] But he must pay the vendor any balance of the price.

[632] It may be fixed by the arbitrator and in such cases there is unlikely to be any need for oral evidence of the terms.

[633] *Per* Lord Denning in *Munton v Greater London Council* [1976] 2 All ER 815 at 818.

[634] *Pollard v Middlesex County Council* (1906) 95 LT 870 at 871 approved by Denning MR in *Munton's* case at 818.

Chapter 4

Subject to Contract

The phrase

[4.01]

"In modern times, probably the most important legal transaction a great number of people make in their lifetimes is the purchase or sale of their home. The avoidance of doubt and, therefore, the avoidance of litigation concerning such a transaction must be a well worthwhile social objective, as far as the law is concerned. To that end certainty in the question of what is or is not a sufficient note or memorandum is a desirable aim. In my view, the very definite statement that a note or memorandum of a contract made orally is not sufficient to satisfy the Statute of Frauds unless it directly or by very necessary implication recognises, not only the terms to be enforced, but also the existence of a concluded contract between the parties, and the corresponding principle that no such note or memorandum which contains any term or expression, such as 'subject to contract' can be sufficient, even if it can be established by oral evidence that such a term or expression did not form part of the originally orally concluded agreement, achieves that certainty."

Thus Finlay CJ in *Boyle v Lee*[1], Hederman J concurring. The existence of such a rule would not allow for the "exceptional cases" mentioned by Keane J in *Mulhall v Haren*.[2] Earlier in his judgment in *Boyle's* case Finlay CJ, alluding to the obligation of the courts in the implementation of a plain statutory provision, said that it did not seem that it could be justified to introduce into the interpretation of s 2 of the Statute of Frauds clauses or provisos which were not consistent with its plain meaning.[3] A feeling of duty to implement statute law in accordance with its clear meaning and concern to achieve a desirable social objective thus led in the same direction.

[4.02] In this chapter we look at "subject to contract" and some other matters which may occur before a concluded contract is reached. The plaintiff in *Boyle v Lee* lost on "subject to contract" in the view of all members of the Supreme Court. The effect of the case in relation to the need for agreement on a deposit in a contract for sale of land is less clear.[4] We return to it at the end of this chapter to see whether the passage quoted from the Chief Justice in para **4.01** above is clearly the law of the land[5] with special interest in whether there can now be any exceptions to the *prima facie* position that "subject to contract" means that there is no enforceable contract.

[4.03] The phrase "subject to contract" has given a lot of trouble in both Ireland and England in recent times. In the late 1970s the legal position of parties, once an estate

---

[1] [1992] 1 IR 555 at 574; [1992] ILRM 65 at 77, Hederman J concurring.
[2] [1981] IR 364.
[3] At 573 (IR); 76 (ILRM).
[4] Paras **3.12-14** *ante*.
[5] This would need the assent of one other member of the court.

agent had written to say that he had concluded a contract for the sale of land between them and setting out terms of sale, was fraught with uncertainty.[6] The phrase is often used by solicitors and others as well.[7] In many cases a deal will be done by estate agents, the matter will then go to solicitors and both professions will use the phrase. The doubt may well have been increased rather than reduced by any references to a formal contract to come into being later. In England the Court of Appeal had given two conflicting decisions[8] on the same topic and the Irish courts were free to follow whichever of those diverging paths seemed appropriate to them.[9] There has recently been a major change in English law in that contracts for the sale or other disposition of an interest in land made after 26 September 1989 must be in writing and be signed by or on behalf of each party.[10]

[4.04] The law was largely clarified in Ireland by four important decisions.[11] It became clear that normally the words "subject to contract" would mean that what had been agreed was subject to a full contract being agreed.[12] In other words, there was no binding agreement yet although the parties may have intended to reach one. It has been said that in the ordinary course of events an agreement for sale subject to contract meant nothing more than an agreement to enter into a contract which, as such, is not enforceable.[13] The words "subject to contract", it became clear, were normally inconsistent with the existence of a concluded contract.[14] Save in exceptional circumstances[15] they would be construed as postponing the incidence of liability until a formal document has been executed.[16] However, the words still cannot be regarded as a magic formula whose presence in a document amounts to a guarantee that no binding agreement has been reached.[17]

---

[6] As noted by O'Hanlon J in *Park Hall School Ltd v Overend* [1987] IR 1 at 10. This negligence action failed largely because the judge accepted that solicitors then faced a very uncertain state of the law. The solicitors took counsel's advice at every successive stage of the proceedings. *Boyle v Lee* means that the solicitors were not only free of negligence but *right*.

[7] Note discussion by Keane J of its use by a solicitor in *Mulhall v Haren* [1981] IR 364, esp at 391-4 and his views on its use by solicitors and laymen of common sense and business experience in *Silver Wraith Ltd v Siuicre Eireann Cpt*, (HC) 1987 No 6178P, unrep, p 2-4.

[8] *Law v Jones* [1974] Ch 112; [1973] 2 All ER 437 and *Tiverton Estates Ltd v Wearwell Ltd* [1975] Ch 146; [1974] 1 All ER 209. Finlay CJ described the views in the two cases as "diametrically contradictory" in *Boyle's* case at 571 (IR); 74 (ILRM). Keane J in *Mulhall's* case at 385 regarded the "forceful" judgments of Lord Denning and Stamp LJ in the *Tiverton Estates* case as the view of the law generally held in England. See Clark's two-part comparison of the English and Irish case law in *The Conveyancer* (1984) p 173 and 251.

[9] *Park Hall School Ltd v Overend* [1987] IR 1 at 11.

[10] Section 2 of the Law of Property (Miscellaneous Provisions) Act 1989, repealing s 40 of the Law of Property Act 1925 which had replaced s 4 of the English Statute of Frauds. See para **6.09** *post*. Note O'Flaherty J's views in *Boyle v Lee* [1992] 1 IR 555 at 589; [1992] ILRM 65 at 89-90.

[11] *Devlin v Northern Ireland Housing Executive* [1982] NI 377, *Kelly v Park Hall School Ltd* [1979] IR 340, *Carthy v O'Neill* [1981] ILRM 443 and *Mulhall v Haren* [1981] IR 364. The Supreme Court has refused to follow *Kelly's* case: para **4.24** below.

[12] *Per* Henchy J in *Carthy's* case at 446.

[13] Walsh J in *Re Hibernian Transport Co's Ltd* [1972] IR 190 at 202, considered by Keane J in *Mulhall's* case at 377.

[14] See Keane J's analysis of authorities in *Mulhall's* case at 391.

[15] We discuss later whether there can be *any* exceptions: paras **4.24-5**.

[16] *Per* Keane J in *Irish Mainport Holdings Ltd v Crosshaven Sailing Centre Ltd*, (HC) 16 May 1980, unrep at 16. *Cf* O'Flaherty J in *Boyle's* case at 587-8 (IR); 88-9 (ILRM).

[17] *Park Hall School Ltd v Overend* [1986] IR 1 at 10. In *Boyle's* case O'Flaherty J said at 581 (IR); 83 (ILRM) "This incantation has no talismanic property".

[4.05] Let us look at two statements of principle. The first is by Jessel MR in *Winn v Bull*:[18]

"Where you have a proposal or agreement made in writing expressed to be subject to a formal contract being prepared, it means what it says, it is subject to and is dependent upon a formal contract being prepared. When it is not expressly stated to be subject to a formal contract, it becomes a question of construction whether the parties intended that the terms agreed should merely be put into form, or whether they should be subject to a new agreement, the terms of which are not expressed in detail."

The second statement is by Gibson J in *Thompson v The King*[19]:

"Where an offer and acceptance are made subject to a subsequent formal contract, if such contract is a condition or term which until performed keeps the agreement in suspense, the offer and acceptance have no contractual force. On the other hand, if all the terms are agreed on, and a formal contract is only contemplated as putting the terms in legal shape, the agreement is effectual before and irrespective of such formal contract."

When we see the phrase "subject to contract" or any similar form of words, we are immediately alerted to the "overwhelming likelihood" that the agreement is in the first of Gibson J's two categories.[20] The phrase is *prima facie* a strong declaration that a concluded contract does not exist.[21] The fact that the words "offer" and "acceptance" may be used does not help the claimant; the accepted offer is conditional - it is "subject to contract".[22] In this situation the doctrine of part performance will not assist a claim. That doctrine has been described as a mode of evidencing the existence of a contract as an alternative to a note or memorandum but it is of no help if a concluded contract has not been made.[23] It cannot help the claimant because the contract which he says has been partly performed is not a complete contract but only a conditional one. Apart from any question of "subject to contract", if negotiations do not ripen into an entire contract a claim for specific performance will fail anyway, not just for want of evidence necessary for enforcement, but simply in default of the existence of any contract.[24]

Possible exceptional cases

[4.06] As we have seen,[25] it became clear that the normal meaning of "subject to contract" was that what had been agreed was subject to a full contract being agreed. Exceptions could occur[26] where words such as "we have agreed terms, subject to contract"[27] could be held to mean that a contract was made, subject to its being formalised in writing. The document had to contain not only all the essential terms of the contract but also a

---

[18] (1877) 7 Ch D 29 at 32, approved by Lowry LCJ in *Devlin v Northern Ireland Housing Executive* [1982] NI 377 at 387. O'Flaherty J approved a longer passage from the same judgment in *Boyle's* case at 586 (IR); 87-8 (ILRM).

[19] [1920] 2 IR 365, 386, quoted by Lowry LCJ in *Devlin's* case at 387. The decision in *Thompson* was affirmed by the CA: [1921] 2 IR 438.

[20] *Devlin's* case at p 387.

[21] *Per* O'Flaherty J in *Boyle's* case at 588 (IR); 88-9 (ILRM).

[22] *Devlin's* case at 387.

[23] By Lowry LCJ in *Devlin's* case at 386. Part performance is considered in Ch 6 *post*.

[24] *Lynch v O'Meara* (SC) 8 May 1975, unrep at 4. The High Court held that the agreement was not subject to contract; that was not an issue before the Supreme Court.

[25] Para **4.04** *supra*.

[26] This is subject to the point whether exceptions can still exist after *Boyle's* case: paras **4.24-5** *infra*.

[27] The phrase in the letter in *Kelly v Park Hall School Ltd* [1979] IR 340. This case was not followed in *Boyle's* case.

recognition that a contract had been made.[28] For a plaintiff to succeed there had to be a finding of fact that the parties had reached a completed agreement in the sense that nothing further was left to be negotiated.[29] All "necessary terms" had to be agreed.[30] In that type of situation it may have been fair to describe "subject to contract" as an "empty formula"[31] but it could also mean that the parties intended to execute a formal contract though not as a condition precedent to any contractual liability arising. If the document alleged to be a sufficient memorandum shows that essential parts of what was expected to become a contract remain to be negotiated the plaintiff cannot succeed.[32]

[4.07] A plaintiff trying to bring a case within that kind of exception always had a difficult task. The situation in *Kelly v Park Hall School*[33] illustrates the type of evidence likely to be needed:

> "...where the memorandum relied on recited, and the trial judge found, that all the terms of a completed oral contract had been agreed on, where the parties were each familiar with the title, where the vendor was willing to give and the purchaser was willing to accept that title,[34] where nothing further remained to be negotiated, so that in the exceptional and special circumstances of that case the court could not avoid holding that 'subject to contract' meant no more than a proviso that what had been comprehensively but orally agreed on should be given the form of a written contract."[35]

The words "exceptional and special circumstances" may be stressed; they and the extensive progress of the parties set out in that passage show that the court fully *intended* the decision in *Kelly's* case to be exceptional. The words fit well with Lord Lowry's "overwhelming likelihood"[36], O'Flaherty J's *"prima facie...*strong declaration"[37] and the description of *Kelly's* case by Keane J as "a special one decided on particular facts".[38] It is not surprising that Henchy J felt able later to describe the use of "subject to contract" in *Kelly's* case as an "empty formula".[39]

[4.08] Making an exception may have seemed more reasonable if an oral agreement contained no term that the deal was subject to contract. A later attempt to introduce "subject to contract" would fail to avoid liability, it would be argued. In *McInerney*

---

[28] *Per* Henchy J in *Kelly's* case at 352. This is consistent with the passage quoted from Finlay CJ in para **4.01** *supra*.

[29] *Ibid*.

[30] *Ibid* at 351.

[31] Henchy J so described the phrase as used in *Kelly's* case in his judgment in *Carthy v O'Neill* [1981] ILRM 443 at 445. Keane J described it as "being of no effect" in *Mulhall v Haren* [1981 IR 364 at 391.

[32] *Per* Henchy J in *Carthy's* case at 445. The letters showed that date of completion had to be agreed (the property was a pub), title on offer had to be submitted to the plaintiff's solicitors for approval and no agreement had been reached on the price of the stock.

[33] [1979] IR 340.

[34] The nature of the title is not always an essential term of a contract. It *may be* an essential term and often is when land is bought for development. However, in *Guardian Builders v Kelly* [1981] ILRM 127, land being bought for development, Costello J held at 132 that there were no material terms in respect of title or a right of way. In *Kelly v Park Hall School* [1979] IR 340 the parties were already familiar with the title: p 351.

[35] *Per* Henchy J in *Carthy v O'Neill* [1981] ILRM 443 at 445.

[36] See para **4.05** *supra*. The "overwhelming likelihood" was that there was no concluded contract.

[37] *Boyle v Lee* [1992] 1 IR 555 at 588; [1992] ILRM 65 at 88-9.

[38] *Mulhall v Haren* [1981] IR 364 at 389.

[39] In *Carthy's* case at 445. The phrase "could not avoid holding" shows no anxiety to increase the number of exceptional cases.

Properties v Roper[40] Hamilton J noted[41] that the judgment of Henchy J in *Kelly v Park Hall School*[42] did not consider that the phrase "subject to contract" prevented a document from being a sufficient note or memorandum to satisfy the Statute of Frauds if the contract had been made subject to being formalised in writing and the document contained an admission or recognition that a contract was made. Hamilton J held that the oral agreement was not subject to contract but was final and concluded.[43]

On the language of the letter before him he held that it recognised the existence of a contract despite being headed "subject to contract"[44]. In *Boyle v Lee*[45] Finlay CJ described this type of argument as one:

"...that a party to an orally concluded agreement which is complete and intended to be complete, should not be permitted by the unilateral insertion into a note or memorandum in writing which he makes of the terms of that agreement, of a denial of it, or of a provision such as the phrase "subject to contract" which is inconsistent with it, to escape on his own behalf or on behalf of his principal, from the enforcement of the contract."

Acknowledging that the argument was "attractive", he then made this powerful point against it:[46]

"...in my view, it necessarily involves the precise mischief which the Statute of Frauds, 1695, was intended to avoid, and that is that it invites the court to amend by deletion, or by ignoring one of its terms, the note or memorandum relied upon by the plaintiff and signed by the defendant, such amendment or deletion depending on the finding by the court on oral evidence as to what was the agreement between the parties."

McCarthy J said:[47]

"If the letter to the solicitors is to be held to provide the required compliance with s 2 of the Statute of Frauds, 1695, it means that the note itself has to be disregarded wherever it conflicts with the findings of fact made in respect of the oral agreement, and yet be used as the necessary evidence to support an action to enforce that agreement. In short, it means that the words 'subject to contract' do not mean what they say."

In *Casey v Irish Intercontinental Bank*[48] an auctioneer concluded an oral agreement without using the words "subject to contract" or the like.[49] A couple of days later he prepared a document which said, contrary to the fact, that the agreement had been made "subject to contract and title". The Supreme Court held[50] that even if the reference to contract and title were regarded as being incorporated in the contract it did not make the execution of a contract a term of the agreement or a condition precedent to any contractual liability arising. It seems now, however, that the fact that an oral contract has

---

[40] [1979] ILRM 119.
[41] At 133.
[42] [1979] IR 340.
[43] At 127.
[44] He analyses the letter (of 23 March 1978) at 133. *cf Alpenstow Ltd v Regalian Properties plc* [1985] 2 All ER 545; *Michael Richards Properties v St Saviour's Parish* [1975] 3 All ER 416.
[45] [1992] 1 IR 555 at 573; [1992] ILRM 65 at 76.
[46] *Ibid.*
[47] *Boyle's* case at 577 (IR); 80 (ILRM).
[48] [1979] IR 364.
[49] See judgment of Kenny J at 367.
[50] At 368. At 369 Kenny J held that the document was a sufficient note or memorandum.

no "subject to contract" element is much less likely to lead to exceptions being held to exist.[51]

[4.09] In other cases parties' oral agreements also had no "subject to contract" element but the words appeared in the document set up as a note or memorandum of an oral contract and were held to prevent it satisfying the Statute. The main issue was often[52] whether the document recognised that a contract existed. The presence of "subject to contract" in the document relied on did not *necessarily* prevent it being sufficient to satisfy the Statute.[53] However, the wording of s 2[54] envisaged something in writing which was evidence of a contract made by the party sued and this was not met by a document which used language inconsistent with the existence of a concluded contract.[55] Thus, for a plaintiff to succeed on foot of an alleged note containing the words "subject to contract" the court had to be satisfied that on the fair construction of the document in the special circumstances of the case it recognised the existence of a contract. That meaning could be given only if "subject to contract" could be fairly construed to (i) refer only to formalisation of the deal in a written contract, (ii) be of no effect, or (iii) be meaningless.[56] A plaintiff faced with "subject to contract" in the note relied on to satisfy the Statute thus had a difficult task and the difficulty increased as the exceptional nature of the decisions in *Kelly's* case[57] and *Casey's* case[58] came to be better appreciated.

Use of the words in correspondence

[4.10] Before the doubts referred to in para **4.03** above arose, a series of decisions had established beyond serious doubt that an oral agreement for the sale of land which was stated to be subject to contract was unenforceable.[59] It was certainly the law for a long time that the use of those words in any purported note of a contract left that contract unenforceable by action.[60] As a result solicitors, auctioneers and estate agents developed the habit of heading letters and other documents "subject to contract". They knew the danger of committing their clients to an "open" contract for the sale of land by writing a letter which would satisfy the Statute of Frauds. Also disputes might arise as to the terms of the bargain which could lead to expensive litigation. The phrase is also used in confirming details and asking the solicitor on the other side to forward the contract.[61]

[4.11] It is not necessary in order to get the protection of "subject to contract" to put the phrase in every letter in a chain of correspondence. There is certainly nothing wrong with doing so and caution may suggest that no room be left for doubt. The first letter should be "subject to contract" and the context should not suggest that the phrase is meaningless

---

[51] See further discussion of *Boyle's* case, paras **4.22-5** *infra*.

[52] Remember that we are still discussing the position prior to *Boyle's* case.

[53] The existence of exceptional decisions in both Ireland and England shows that. See paras **4.07-8** *supra*.

[54] Set out at para **5.01** *post*.

[55] *Mulhall v Haren* [1981] IR 364 at 386.

[56] The phrase could be meaningless if, for example, it appeared in a letter accepting tender conditions so complete that nothing could remain to be negotiated: *Michael Richards Properties v St. Saviour's Parish* [1975] 3 All ER 416, approved by Keane J in the *Mulhall* case at 385-6 and 391. Cf *Alpenstow Ltd v Regalian Properties plc* [1985] 2 All ER 545.

[57] [1979] IR 340.

[58] [1979] IR 364.

[59] See judgment of Keane J in *Mulhall v Haren* [1981] IR 364 at 375.

[60] *Per* Keane J in *Ballyowen Castle Homes Ltd v Collins* (HC) 26 June 1986, unrep at 3.

[61] On these points see *Mulhall's* case at p 375; the *Ballyowen Castle Homes Ltd* case at 3.

or an empty formula. It does not matter whether the writing relied on itself contains the words "subject to contract" or is part of a chain of correspondence initiated by a letter which makes it clear that any oral agreement already reached is subject to contract.[62] In England the subject to contract formula has been called an "umbrella" for parties starting negotiations.[63] It has also become clear that the umbrella does not disappear too readily. The test is whether the parties have expressly agreed that subject to contract qualifications should be expunged or that such an agreement should necessarily be implied.[64] It does not seem to matter whether a solicitor has *authority* to use such words. He usually will have that authority in the interest of protecting his client from the "traps and pitfalls" that beset the completion of sale of land.[65] Even if he has not got that authority the words should still destroy any recognition of a concluded contract.[66]

[4.12] The use of "subject to contract" in correspondence may also lead a court to conclude that what might otherwise have seemed to be a complete oral contract was not one in fact. Thus, in *Arnold v Veale* the High Court[67] found that there was a complete oral agreement which did not contain any term to the effect that it was subject to contract. Prior to the hearing of the appeal the defendant discovered a letter from the plaintiff which stated:

"I wish to confirm my offer of £10,000 subject to the following conditions: 1. Subject to contract. 2. Subject to..."

By oral judgments[68] the Supreme Court allowed the appeal on the ground of the absence of any concluded agreement between the parties. A similar approach appears in the judgment of McCarthy J in *Boyle v Lee*[69]. He held that the parties had done a deal which, though "highly informal", contained all the terms they regarded as essential.[70] However, having considered the "subject to contract" point, he held also that the parties' deal was incomplete in the sense that it was subject to contract.[71] We have already seen a different situation where a concluded oral agreement may be unenforceable because the document set up as a sufficient note or memorandum is marked "subject to contract".[72] That may not prove that there was no agreement but it normally means that an alleged note or memorandum is insufficient as it does not recognise the existence of a concluded agreement.[73] The use of "subject to contract" may thus lead either to a finding that there was no concluded contract at all or to a decision that a concluded contract is unenforceable by action because nothing in writing recognises its existence. In the

---

[62] *Mulhall v Haren* [1981] IR 364 at 375.
[63] By Brightman J in *Tevanan v Norman Brett (Builders) Ltd* [1972] 223 EG 1945 at 1947, approved by Templeman LJ in *Sherbrooke v Dipple* (1980) 41 P & CR 173 at 176; [1980] EGD 888 at 893 and by Cumming-Bruce LJ in *Cohen v Nessdale Ltd* [1982] 2 All ER 97 at 103-4.
[64] *Tevanan's* case, *per* Brightman J at p 1947, approved by Templeman LJ in *Sherbrooke's* case at 176 (P & CR); 893 (EGD) and Cumming-Bruce LJ in *Cohen's* case at 104.
[65] *Mulhall's* case at 392-3.
[66] *Ibid* at 392.
[67] 28 July 1977, unrep, Costello J.
[68] [1979] IR 342n at 343n.
[69] [1992] 1 IR 555; [1992] ILRM 65.
[70] The trial judge was entitled to come to that conclusion: p 576 (IR); 79 (ILRM).
[71] Page 578 (IR); 80 (ILRM).
[72] Para **4.09** *supra*.
[73] *Ballyowen Castle Homes Ltd v Collins* (HC) 26 June 1986, Keane J, unrep, at 2-3. See also *Cunningham v Maher* (1982) 9 ILT 168, 169.

former case there was no contract at all; in the latter the plaintiff fails an evidentiary test. The result will be the same unless, in the latter case only, something else defeats a plea of the Statute.[74]

Variations on the theme

[4.13] No particular wording is necessary. In the normal way there will be no difference between a writing which (i) denies that there was any contract; (ii) does not admit that there was any contract; (iii) says that the parties are in negotiation; or (iv) says that there was an agreement subject to contract.[75] A minor oddity in the phrasing does not matter once the intention is clear.[76]

[4.14] An *offer* subject to contract cannot be accepted so as to produce a binding contract.[77] An acceptance "in principle" may well be an enforceable contract as the words "in principle" cannot be equated to "subject to contract" and have not the same force in law.[78] An agreement or acceptance "subject to his approval" is unlikely to be either a concluded contract or a sufficient note or memorandum of a contract.[79] A "provisional agreement until a fully legalised agreement ... is signed" can be held to be binding from the outset[80]. A form containing the words "subject to a proper contract" and a reference to "such conditions as the Executive's Solicitors may consider necessary" is not likely to be more than a preliminary agreement which might lead to the formation of a contract.[81] The phrase "subject to title" will rarely prevent an agreement being binding. A vendor will have to show title in accordance with his contract so completion of a purchase is always subject to title in the broad sense of the words. If a title is dubious or complicated the words "subject to title" or "subject to contract and title" may increase the already strong probability that a "subject to contract" element has prevented an enforceable contract coming into being but usually "subject to title" should have no effect.[82] In negotiations for a lease, language like "subject to full lease being agreed" has no significant difference from "subject to contract".[83] Words such as "kindly let me have agreement for sale" will be considered later under the heading "Agreements to agree".[84]

---

[74] Eg part performance, on which see Ch 6 *post*.
[75] *Per* Lord Denning MR in *Tiverton Estates Ltd v Wearwell Ltd* [1975] Ch 146; [1974] 1 All ER 209, approved by Keane J in *Mulhall v Haren* [1981] IR 364 at 383.
[76] In *Thompson v The King* [1920] 2 IR 365 the phrase was "subject contract" in a telegram offering to sell. Other documents said "subject to its being in a form which is satisfactory and to a formal contract to be approved by the Chief Crown Solicitor" as well as "subject to contract".
[77] *Arnold v Veale* [1979] IR 342n.
[78] *Irish Mainport Holdings Ltd v Crosshaven Sailing Centre Ltd* (HC) 16 May 1980, Keane J, unrep at 14-17.
[79] *Dyas v Stafford* (1882) 9 LRI 520 at 524, 529. "His" referred to the vendor.
[80] *Branca v Cobarro* [1947] KB 854; [1947] 2 All ER 101, approved by Keane J in the *Irish Mainport Holdings Ltd* case at 16-17.
[81] *Devlin v Northern Ireland Housing Executive* [1982] NI 377 at 386-389. If there had been a concluded contract there would have been a sufficient note: 386.
[82] In the *Irish Mainport Holdings Ltd* case Keane J noted at 13 that it was not suggested that words "subject to title to the property being in clear and good order" were sufficient to prevent a binding and enforceable contract coming into being. The phrase "subject to contract and title" occurred in *Casey v Irish Intercontinental Bank* [1979] IR 364 but nothing turned on the reference to title.
[83] *Silver Wraith Ltd v Siuicre Eireann Cpt* (HC) 8 June 1989, Keane J, unrep at 9 (he held that there was no concluded contract but then also considered the sufficiency of the memorandum on an assumption "in the teeth of the evidence" that there was such an agreement). At pp 3-5 he discusses differences between the phrase used and the normal use of "subject to contract".
[84] Para **4.18** *infra*.

[4.15] Sometimes parties include express conditions that they will not be bound until a specified event occurs. Thus, a letter from solicitors enclosing formal contracts and title documents may say something like this:

> "Our client is prepared to sell the premises to your client provided contracts are exchanged within ten days from the date hereof. In default, our clients shall make alternative arrangements.
>
> It must be understood that no agreement enforceable at law is created or intended to be created until exchange of contracts has taken place."[85]

If no exchange of contracts occurs there will be no enforceable contract. The reason is that the parties have agreed that enforceability depends on an exchange.[86] Under the general law - ie, without any special stipulation being agreed - it is not necessary in Ireland to have an exchange of contracts to make an agreement enforceable at law.[87] If a vendor's solicitor makes it clear in his first letter that there will be no binding contract until the written contract has been signed by both parties and a deposit paid that stipulation is likely to be upheld. If the relevant events do not happen there is no concluded contract which can be specifically enforced.[88] Parties may also prescribe the manner in which an offer may be accepted. In that event the offer must be accepted in the prescribed mode or in a way which is as beneficial to the offeror.[89]

Agreements to agree

[4.16] In many cases where "subject to contract" is an issue there will also be a question whether, apart from the use of that phrase, it was a condition of any agreement reached between parties that a further contract must be executed before they are bound. That question may also arise in cases where neither "subject to contract" nor any similar phrase is used. As Parker J said in *Von Hatzfeldt-Wildenburg v Alexander:*[90]

> "It appears to be well settled by the authorities that if the documents or letters relied on as constituting a contract contemplate the execution of a further contract between the parties, it is a question of construction whether the execution of the further contract is a condition or term of the bargain or whether it is a mere expression of the desire of the parties as to the manner in which the transaction already agreed will in fact go through. In the former case there is no enforceable contract either because the condition is unfulfilled or because the law does not recognise a contract to enter into a contract. In the latter case there is a binding contract and the reference to the more formal contract may be ignored."[91]

The enquiry which the court must undertake in a case of this sort is to ascertain from the evidence what was the intention of the parties and, in particular, what significance arises

---

[85] *Kelly v Irish Nursery & Landscape Co Ltd* [1981] ILRM 433. The text of the letter is set out by Kenny J at 436.

[86] *Per* Walsh J at 435 and Kenny J at 439, O'Higgins CJ concurring with both.

[87] *Per* Kenny J at 438, O'Higgins CJ concurring.

[88] *Barry v Buckley* [1981] IR 306 at 310. The defendant's case was very powerful with "subject to contract" widespread.

[89] *Walker v Glass* [1979] NI 129 at 134, 136.

[90] [1912] 1 Ch 284 at 288.

[91] Approved in *Law v Roberts* [1964] IR 292 at 303 by Kenny J, affirmed by the Supreme Court (p 305); also approved by Kingsmill Moore J giving the majority judgment of the Supreme Court in *Godley v Power* (1957) 95 ILTR 135 at 147 and by Molony CJ in *Thompson v The King* [1920] 2 IR 365 at 383-4. Note discussion of 19th century case law by O'Flaherty J in *Boyle v Lee* [1992] 1 IR 555 at 585-7; [1992] ILRM 65 at 86-8.

from the fact that they contemplated the execution of a formal agreement.[92] It must consider whether the parties had come to a concluded agreement in the course of their discussions and whether the reference to the drawing up of a formal contract was merely the expression of a desire as to the manner in which the contract would be drawn up.[93] If an oral contract does not mention a further contract a reference in a subsequent letter to a future or formal contract cannot introduce any term in relation to the execution of such a contract.[94] It is, of course, possible for the parties to agree in their negotiations that their agreement is not to be enforceable until a written contract has come into existence.[95]

[4.17] The position is clear if parties execute a complete agreement containing their actual contract. This will be specifically enforced even though by its terms it contemplates some more formal contract being entered into.[96] The position is less clear if the terms are to a greater or less extent contained in a duly signed writing but expressed in that writing to be liable to be modified or added to by a future contract. If there are sufficient terms in writing which amount to a concluded contract, however bald the contract may be as to the method of carrying it out, the contract will be enforced.[97] In another type of situation parties may agree that their deal will be subject to such other covenants and conditions as one of them may reasonably require. In this case there is a contract and the courts have power to determine whether a term is reasonably required although there may also be an issue whether a party has repudiated the contract by refusing to accept a term required by the other.[98] There is nothing to prevent an intending vendor making any stipulations he thinks fit subject to the general law as to the property he is selling; if he gets agreement to them they usually will be upheld. This applies also to terms which the law will import if they are not expressed and which are therefore *prima facie* not essential; the parties may agree, however, that they are to be essential.[99] If a court concludes that parties "had agreed up to a point but were not fully agreed" and that expression of their full agreement was to be embodied in a formal document there is no contract which can be enforced.[100]

[4.18] A number of phrases have required consideration along these lines. Typical is "subject to the preparation of a formal contract to be prepared" by the vendor's solicitor.[101] Similar is "the vendor's solicitors to prepare title and conditions of sale".[102] Weaker is "No doubt you will be kind enough to prepare and forward draft contracts...to my Solicitor".[103]

---

[92] *Arnold v Veale* (HC) 28 July 1977, Costello J, unrep at 11. This was not a "subject to contract" case in the High Court but became one on new evidence in the Supreme Court: see [1979] IR 342n. See also *Mulhall v Haren* [1981] IR 364 at 375.
[93] *Arnold's* case at p 13 of the transcript.
[94] *Law v Roberts* [1964] IR 292 at 303.
[95] *Hoon v Nolan* (1966) 101 ILTR 99 at 102. The decision was reversed by the Supreme Court on the ground that the alleged memorandum omitted a material term: p 109.
[96] *Brien v Swainson* (1877) 1 LRI 135 at 139.
[97] *Brien's* case at 140.
[98] *Sweet & Maxwell Ltd v Universal News Services Ltd* [1964] 3 All ER 30 (agreement for lease where the parties had agreed the lease would contain "such other covenants and conditions as shall be reasonably required by" the intending lessor - the point is less appropriate in cases of outright sales).
[99] *Godley v Power* (1957) 95 ILTR 135 at 147; *Brien v Swainson* (1877) 1 LRI 135 at 140.
[100] *Lowis v Wilson* [1949] IR 347 at 350.
[101] *Lowis's* case - no concluded contract.
[102] *Donnelly v O'Connell* (1924) 58 ILTR 164 - no binding contract.
[103] *Arnold v Veale* (HC) 28 July 1977, Costello J, unrep - enforceable contract but this was reversed by the Supreme Court (noted at [1979] IR 342n) on new evidence which turned the case into one of "subject to contract".

In a telegram in 1877 the words were "subject to letter and agreement to be sent to your solicitor".[104] The simple "Kindly let me have agreement for sale" is likely to be consistent with a claim that there is a concluded agreement.[105] A more elaborate version was:

> "I understand your solicitors are R... and that you are instructing them to prepare a contract, the terms and conditions of which are to be agreed between the solicitors."[106]

While it is often useful to study a reported case which features a similar phrase it is vital to remember that much will depend on the precise context in which words appear and on the special facts of each case. The contexts from which the foregoing phrases are drawn vary widely. In one of those cases the judge laid stress on the facts that the defendant wrote "I confirm our agreement for the sale..." and that the terms of that agreement were set out "carefully and fully" in the letter.[107]

Negotiations

[4.19] Whenever there is an issue whether parties have reached a concluded agreement, a common alternative is that they are still in negotiation. If verbal negotiations take place between parties who intend to have a formal document drawn up by a solicitor it can be difficult to say whether they have concluded an agreement.[108] Lay persons may prepare documents and intend that the deal will be handed over to professionals to be dealt with in the normal way. It is then a question of construction whether they intended to undertake immediate, if temporary, obligations or whether they were suspending all liability until the conclusion of formalities.[109] There is no concluded contract if parties merely agree to certain terms which are contemplated as providing the basis for agreement to be negotiated in the future but the mere fact that both parties recognise that the agreement which they have reached is not to be the final form of the contract does not negative the existence of a binding contract.[110] The critical question is whether the parties regard themselves as merely in negotiation upon other material terms or whether the subsequent document is contemplated as ancillary to the earlier agreement in the sense of providing it with due form.[111] As Lord Blackburn put it in *Rossiter v Miller*:

> "But the mere fact that the parties have expressly stipulated that there shall afterwards be a formal agreement prepared, embodying the terms, which shall be signed by the parties does not, by itself, show that they continue merely in negotiation. It is a matter to be taken into account in construing the evidence and determining whether the parties have really come to a final agreement or not. But as soon as the fact is established of the final mutual assent of the parties so that those who draw up the formal agreement have not the power to vary the terms already settled, I think the contract is completed."[112]

In considering whether parties have reached a concluded agreement, the courts often have to give a detailed examination to the document set up as a memorandum. They will

---

[104] *Brien v Swainson* (1877) 1 LRI 135 - no concluded contract.
[105] *Godley v Power* (1957) 95 ILTR 135 at 147 - enforceable contract. The rest of the relevant letter was fairly strong in favour of a concluded contract.
[106] *Usitravel Ltd v Freyer*, Cir App, 29 May 1973, Finlay J - enforceable contract.
[107] The *Usitravel* case at 10.
[108] Murnaghan J described it as a "question of nicety" in *Kerns v Manning* [1935] IR 869 at 879.
[109] *Per* Murray J in *Mawhinney v Reid* [1984] 9 NIJB at 48, approving a passage from the 10th Ed of Cheshire & Fifoot, *Law of Contract*.
[110] *City of Glasgow Friendly Society Trustee Ltd v Gilpin Ltd,* NIJB, December 1970 at 5.
[111] *Ibid.*
[112] 3 App Cas 1124 at p 1151; [1874-80] All ER Rep 465 at p 475, approved by Kenny J in *Law v Roberts* [1964] IR 292 at 303 and applied by Finlay J in the *Usitravel Ltd* case at 8-9.

consider both whether the document recognises what the parties have done and whether it shows that what they have done is a concluded contract or just ongoing negotiations.[113] If one finds in correspondence, not an unqualified acceptance of a contract, but an acceptance subject to a condition that an agreement is to be prepared and agreed upon between the parties and until that condition is fulfilled no contract is to arise, there is no concluded contract.[114]

[4.20] Occasionally it is suggested that parties have a duty to negotiate or to seek a mutually acceptable conclusion. A possible argument of this sort was admitted by Murphy J at an interlocutory stage in *Bula Ltd v Tara Mines Ltd (No. 2)*[115] saying that consideration should be given to the observations (albeit *obiter*) of Lord Wright in *Hillas & Co Ltd v Arcos Ltd*:[116]

> "There is then no bargain except to negotiate, and negotiations may be fruitless and end without any contract ensuing; yet even then, in strict theory, there is a contract (if there is good consideration) to negotiate, though in the event of repudiation by one party the damages may be nominal, unless a jury think that the opportunity to negotiate was of some appreciable value to the injured party."[117]

He noted that this view was rejected by the Court of Appeal in *Courtney & Fairbairn Ltd v Tolaini Bros (Hotels) Ltd*[118] but felt that it offered "the bones of an argument" for the full hearing. While the point may be open in Ireland it does not look very convincing. Its chances are not helped by the fact that in another case an Irish court had held a clause to be unenforceable because, at best, it involved a commitment to enter into honest negotiations.[119] Nor are they helped in relation to sales of land by the general tone of the Supreme Court decision in *Boyle v Lee* to which we now return.

Boyle v Lee

[4.21] In *Boyle v Lee*,[120] three issues were decided by the High Court and the defendants appealed. The issues were:

(*a*) Whether prior to 8 July 1988 there was a concluded oral agreement between the parties for the sale of No 32 Elgin Road, Dublin at the price of £90,000.

(*b*) If so, what were the other terms thereof ?

(*c*) If there was a concluded oral agreement, whether a letter of 8 July 1988 from the vendor's estate agents to his solicitors satisfied the Statute of Frauds.

---

[113] Note, eg, the detailed consideration of letters by Morris J in *Aga Khan v Firestone* [1992] ILRM 31 at 43-4 and Keane J in *Silver Wraith Ltd v Siuicre Eireann Cpt* (HC) 8 June 1989, unrep, at 1-9.
[114] *Per* Lord Cairns in *Rossiter v Miller* (1878) 3 App Cas 1124, 1139; [1874-80] All ER Rep 465, 471 considering a judgment of Lord Westbury and approved by O'Flaherty J in *Boyle v Lee* [1992] 1 IR 555 at 587; [1992] ILRM 65 at 88.
[115] [1987] IR 95.
[116] (1932) 147 LT 503 at p 515.
[117] Quoted by Murphy J in the *Bula Ltd* case at 102.
[118] [1975] 1 WLR 297; [1975] 1 All ER 716.
[119] *Cadbury Ireland Ltd v Kerry Co-Operative Creameries Ltd* [1982] ILRM 77 at 85, Barrington J, considered by Murphy J in the *Bula Ltd* case at 102. Delay of seven years and changes in the dairying industry were factors in Barrington J's decision.
[120] [1992] 1 IR 555; [1992] ILRM 65.

The High Court answered issues (*a*) and (*c*) "Yes" and issue (*b*) by setting out seven terms[121] which need not concern us. The heading of the letter of 8 July 1988 gave the names of the vendors and the address of the property in sale. The letter was sent by the vendor's auctioneer to the vendors' solicitors and its text read:

> "We refer to the recent negotiations in connection with the above property. I now write to confirm that we have received instructions from the vendors to accept an offer of IR£90,000 subject to contract. I would be obliged if you would prepare, and forward the contract which should incorporate the following agreed terms.

Proposed Purchasers:	Eoin Boyle & Susan Boyle, 165 Rathgar Road, Dublin 6
Proposed Purchase Price:	IR£90,000 subject to contract.
Proposed Purchaser's Solicitors:	Patrick Clyne, Martin E. Marren & Co, 10 Northumberland Road, Dublin 4.
Contents:	Contents of the apartments are included in the sale price.
Tenants:	The property is being sold subject to, and with the benefits of the tenants.
Closing date:	As soon as legal formalities can be completed.

> I am sending a copy of this letter to Mrs Lee and Mrs Goynes for their information. In the meantime, you will appreciate that this letter is for information purposes only, and does not by itself, constitute part of a binding contract. I trust that the sale will proceed smoothly and satisfactorily and if I can assist you further at this stage, please let me know."

On the issue of whether there was a concluded oral contract Finlay CJ held (Hederman J concurring) that the parties had agreed that there had to be a deposit[122] but left it over to be agreed between the solicitors when the formal contract was being settled as to its amount and form.[123] That had to lead to the conclusion that there was not a complete contract made orally.[124] O'Flaherty J also held that there was no concluded contract. There was, at the most, an agreement to agree.[125] McCarthy J held that the parties had done a deal.[126] He accepted that it may have been a highly informal deal and may have omitted a variety of details that would be high in a lawyer's list of priorities; also that the estate agent may well have thought that there was no enforceable deal. However, there was a

---

[121] See out in full by Finlay CJ at 562 (IR); 67 (ILRM).
[122] On deposits see para **3.11-14** *ante*.
[123] Page 571 (IR); 75 (ILRM).
[124] *Ibid.*
[125] At 581-2 (IR); 83 (ILRM).
[126] Or that the trial judge was entitled to come to the conclusion that they had: p 576 (IR); 79 (ILRM). He was considering the question of a concluded oral contract independently of "subject to contract": at p 578 (IR); 80 (ILRM) he makes it clear that due to the "subject to contract" element the parties' deal was incomplete.

deal that contained "all that the parties deemed essential".[127] Egan J held that the trial judge was justified in holding that there had been a concluded oral agreement.[128]

[4.22] All five judges held that the "subject to contract" element was fatal to the plaintiffs' claim. Finlay CJ pointed out[129] that where a document which contains a recital of certain terms obviously relevant to a purchase and sale of land purports to deny the existence of a completed or concluded contract, or makes use of expressions specially adapted to exclude the existence of a complete or concluded contract, it did not seem that "as a matter of first principle" the terms of s 2 of the Act of 1695 could be complied with. In broad terms, it is the clearest possible purpose of the Statute of Frauds 1695 to put the written evidence as dominant and superseding any oral evidence.[130] He then approved the principle that no note or memorandum which contains any term or expression such as "subject to contract" can be sufficient even if it is established by oral evidence that the term or expression was not part of the originally orally concluded agreement.[131] That principle would not, in his view, allow for the "exceptional cases" mentioned by Keane J in *Mulhall v Haren*.[132]

[4.23] McCarthy J noted[133] that as a result of the Statute of Frauds some genuine bargains could not be enforced because of the absence of the required note or memorandum or some inadequacy[134] in it. He then continued:

> "The section came to be construed as liberally as possible - seeking to "find" the necessary evidence once the bargain was proved until, as appears to me to be the case, a note or memorandum which necessarily denied the existence of a bargain became itself evidence to support its enforcement. In my judgment, that is what happened here."[135]

O'Flaherty J noted[136] in the letter of 8 July 1988[137] the words "subject to contract" twice and drew attention also to the second last sentence of the letter. He said:

> "I cannot conceive of any language that could more clearly express the denial of the existence of a binding contract short of saying: "Existence of contract denied.""[138]

Even if an oral contract is concluded[139] and it is not itself made "subject to contract" or the like, nevertheless, if the initiating correspondence thereafter contains that or a similar

---

[127] *Ibid.*

[128] At 594 (IR); 93 (ILRM). He rejected the submission that certain terms remained outstanding including the closing date, the deposit and "final details in relation to the tenancies": that submission is noted at 593 (IR); 93 (ILRM) where he also emphasised that he was then dealing only with the question whether or not there was a concluded oral agreement.

[129] At 572-3 (IR); 76 (ILRM), Hederman J concurring

[130] Page 573 (IR); 76 (ILRM).

[131] Page 574 (IR); 77 (ILRM). See the discussion of the purpose of the Statute of Frauds at para **5.03** *post.*

[132] [1981] IR 364.

[133] At 578 (IR); 80 (ILRM).

[134] A good example of this is given by the judgment of Egan J in the *Boyle* case; he held at 595 (IR); 94 (ILRM) that the parties had covered the matter of the tenancies sufficiently in the oral agreement but the letter of 8 July 1988 did not cover it adequately. The missing factor was something to exonerate the vendors from liability if a problem arose over breach of planning law. For another example of exemption from a possible liability being a material term needed in the alleged note see *Hoon v Nolan* (1966) 101 ILTR 99 at 109.

[135] At 577 (IR): 79 (ILRM). Note also the passage quoted from him in para **4.08** *supra.*

[136] At 584 (IR); 85 (ILRM).

[137] Quoted in para **4.21** *supra.*

[138] At 584 (IR); 85 (ILRM). Note his conclusion on the point at 588 (IR); 88-9 (ILRM).

[139] Contrary to his actual finding.

phrase, it follows that there is no recognition, express or implied of the existence of an oral agreement in the sense of one meant to be a binding contract.[140] Egan J approved[141] the view of Keane J in *Mulhall v Haren*[142] that a letter which expressly states that a transaction is "subject to contract" cannot be a sufficient note or memorandum, since the use of those words is normally inconsistent with the existence of a concluded contract.

[4.24] Two other important questions need consideration. Firstly, has *Boyle v Lee*[143] overruled *Kelly v Park Hall School*[144] and *Casey v Irish Intercontinental Bank*?[145] And, if so, can there be any exceptions to the general rule that a document marked "subject to contract" cannot be said to recognise the existence of a contract? Finlay CJ said:[146]

> "The decision in *Kelly v Park Hall School*,[147]...in so far as it appears to amend by deletion the note or memorandum in writing signed on behalf of the vendor by reference to the evidence of the oral agreements which had previously been arrived at between the parties, with great reluctance, is not a decision which I think this court can and should follow."

He then said that it seemed to him that similar considerations might apply to *Casey v Irish Intercontinental Bank*.[148] We have already noted his view[149] that the principle that no note or memorandum which contains any term or expression such as "subject to contract" can be sufficient even if it is established by oral evidence that no such term or expression was part of the originally orally concluded agreement does not allow for the "exceptional cases" mentioned by Keane J in *Mulhall v Haren*. McCarthy J held that no particular set of facts surrounding the making of the contract itself can relieve a plaintiff from giving the necessary evidence in writing[150]. He considered that *Casey's* case held that the words "subject to contract" did not mean what they said[151] and he held that neither case should be followed.[152] O'Flaherty J would have accepted *Kelly's* case and *Casey's* case but regarded them as "exceptional and confined to the peculiar facts found in each case and as properly confined to the era in which they were decided".[153] Egan J also accepted *Kelly's* case and *Casey's* case. He expressly approved *Mulhall's* case[154] having noted Keane J's view that only in certain rare and exceptional circumstances such as in *Kelly's* case and *Michael Richards Properties v St Saviour's Parish*[155] could the words "subject to

---

[140] At 588 (IR); 89 (ILRM).
[141] At 596 (IR); 95 (ILRM).
[142] [1981] IR 364.
[143] [1992] 1 IR 555; [1992] ILRM 65.
[144] [1979] IR 340.
[145] [1979] IR 364.
[146] At 574 (IR); 77 (ILRM), Hederman J concurring.
[147] [1979] IR 340
[148] At 574 (IR); 77 (ILRM). He adds "though a decision on the validity of the concept of oral waiver of a suspensory condition in the writings which were part of the formation of the contract, is not a question at issue in this case."
[149] See para **4.22** *supra*
[150] At 578 (IR); 80 (ILRM). There was no issue about part performance or anything else which might have taken the case out of the Statute.
[151] *Ibid.* A "gremlin" may have stuck a surplus negative into the reports but hopefully our text represents the judge's view correctly.
[152] *Ibid.*
[153] At 588 (IR); 89 (ILRM).
[154] At 596 (IR); 95 (ILRM).
[155] [1975] 3 All ER 416.

contract" be treated as of no effect. He also noted[156] Henchy J's implied approval in *Carthy v O'Neill*[157] of the *Mulhall* decision.

[4.25] It seems clear that by a majority of 3 to 2 the Supreme Court has overruled *Kelly's* case. Finlay CJ is less definite about *Casey's* case but, as he has also taken the line that there should be no exceptions, he probably should be taken as holding that it also should not be followed[158]. On the other hand, McCarthy J has not gone as far as to say that there can be no exceptions.[159] Perhaps the best view is that the judgments in the *Boyle* case by a 3 to 2 majority still just allow the possibility of exceptions but those exceptions will be very difficult indeed to establish now with neither *Kelly's* case nor (probably) *Casey's* case available any longer as precedents in favour of making exceptions.[160] Argument is open on the validity of the concept of oral waiver of a suspensory condition in the writings which were part of the formation of the contract[161] and perhaps on the question of waiver of the "subject to contract" element in an alleged note or memorandum.[162]

---

[156] At 596 (IR); 95 (ILRM).

[157] [1981] ILRM 443.

[158] Hederman J concurring and with the support of McCarthy J.

[159] Though his view is clear that neither *Kelly's* case nor *Casey's* case should have been treated as an exception.

[160] At 588 (IR); 88-9 (ILRM) O'Flaherty J admits the possibility that on "cogent evidence of a contrary intention" the phrase "subject to contract" can be "put to one side". On the other hand McCarthy J's judgment may have the effect that an exception could be made if *but only if* the court can hold on cogent evidence that the words "subject to contract" in the particular document do not mean what they say.

[161] Note Finlay CJ at 574 (IR); 77 (ILRM).

[162] See the points from English law about the "umbrella" and its possible removal at para **4.11** *supra*.

Chapter 5

The Statute of Frauds

EFFECT AND PURPOSE

[5.01]

> "No action shall be brought whereby... to charge any person... upon any contract or sale of lands, tenements, or hereditaments, or any interest in or concerning them, or upon any agreement that is not to be performed within the space of one year from the making thereof, unless the agreement upon which such action shall be brought, or some memorandum or note thereof, shall be in writing and signed by the party to be charged therewith, or some other person thereunto by him lawfully authorised."

So run the parts of s 2 of the Statute of Frauds 1695 which concern us.[1] In some of the judgments "contract or sale" appears as "contract of sale" and in s 40(1) of the (English) Law of Property Act 1925 (superseded by the Law of Property (Miscellaneous Provisions) Act 1989 save in respect of contracts made before 27 September 1989) the phrase was "contract for sale". However, it does not seem that any such variations have made any difference in any decided case. The preamble to the Statute shows that it was passed for "prevention of many fraudulent practices which are commonly endeavoured to be upheld by perjury and subornation of perjury". Areas affected by those practices included sales of land. The sanction in s 2 is to make such contracts unenforceable *by action* if not evidenced sufficiently in writing. As we shall see later, the contract remains valid and may be enforced in other ways[2] where appropriate so the penalty imposed by the Statute of Frauds is different from, *eg*, the "sanction of voidness" for failure to comply with the Family Home Protection Act 1976.[3]

[5.02] The courts soon found that s 2 could give rise to serious injustice and this gave rise to the doctrine of part performance which we discuss in the next chapter. It also bred in modern times the practice of "gazumping", a practice by which the owner of a property agrees to sell it by means of an agreement which is unenforceable by action for want of writing and then, on receipt of a higher offer, resiles from his bargain and sells to the new purchaser.[4]

---

[1] The text of the section is set out in some modern judgments with minor variations in punctuation or spelling. See, *eg, Mulhall v Haren* [1981] IR 364 at 373-4, *Re Good deceased* (HC) Probate, 14 July 1986, Hamilton P, unrep at 3-4. A shorter version like that quoted is in *Stinson v Owens* (HC) NI, unrep at 10 (noted 107 ILTSJ 239).

[2] Para **5.04** *infra*.

[3] Considered in paras **7.17-18** *post*. See the defence of the Statute at paras **9.06-7** and the Statute *as* fraud at para **9.08-9**.

[4] As described by Costello J in *O'Connor v McCarthy* [1982] IR 161 at 169-70. The word includes cases where a gazumper forces a higher bid from the first purchaser by using a new offer from another: see definition at p 84 of *The Glossary of Property Terms* compiled in 1989 by Jones Lang Wootton in association with the Estates Gazette and South Bank Polytechnic.

"The gazumper is concerned with his own commercial advantage and not with any inconvenience, distress or loss which his actions may cause to the first purchaser or with any moral obligations that may have arisen from the first bargain."[5]

Sometimes a gazumper gets it wrong and finds himself in the disastrous plight of having two purchasers with enforceable contracts. Both cannot get specific performance[6] but the first probably will and the second is likely to get damages and there may be a heavy liability in costs to both.[7] In a falling market we may find the phenomenon of "reverse gazumping"[8] when a *purchaser* breaks his word and may try to negotiate an enforceable contract at a lower price or simply purchase elsewhere.

[5.03] Most cases in which the Statute is pleaded are claims that lands have been sold and in this chapter we look at it mainly in that context.[9] It has been said simply that the 2nd section of the Irish Statute of Frauds provides that no action shall be brought upon a contract for the sale of lands unless the agreement or some memorandum or note thereof is in writing and signed by the party to be charged or his authorised agent.[10] And

"The Irish Statute of Frauds 7 William III c 12 s 2 requires that upon any contract or sale of lands there shall be a memorandum or note in writing of the contract signed by the person to be charged therewith or some other person thereunto by him lawfully authorised."[11]

The purpose of the section has been stated neatly: "It provides, in order to guard against frauds, for a definite kind of proof before the agreement can be enforced against a party resisting its enforcement."[12] It has also been said, putting it mildly, that there can be uncertainty in oral agreements and that is why the Statute of Frauds is there in the case of the sale of land.[13] And that the object of the Statute is to prevent the mischief arising or likely to arise from proof by oral evidence of the contract or its terms.[14] At the same time the courts are alert to the fact that there can be a greater danger of permitting injustice and in that sense encouraging a fraud by a strict application of the Statute than by a liberal application.[15] On the other hand, in a much older case Lord Redesdale noted that the Statute was made "for the purpose of preventing perjuries and frauds" and commented that if the Statute had been rigorously observed there would probably have been fewer instances of parol agreements; agreements would be reduced to writing "from the necessity of the case".[16] It is vital to remember that before considering whether the

---

[5] *Ibid*, p 170. Note the views of Farrand, *Contract and Conveyance*, 4th Ed (1983) at 17 quoted by O'Flaherty J in the spirit of examining anything that may be said in defence of gazumping: *Boyle v Lee* [1992] 1 IR 555 at 584-5; [1992] ILRM 65 at 85-6.

[6] *Dunville Investments Ltd v Kelly* (HC) 27 April 1979, Costello J, unrep at p 3; *O'Connor's* case at 178.

[7] The disaster of having two purchasers is illustrated by *Roberts v O'Neill* [1983] IR 47. The first purchaser lost in the Supreme Court (*Carthy v O'Neill* [1981] ILRM 443) but till then the sale to the second could not proceed. The defendants suffered heavily by reason of the delay and a big increase in value which they could not get but failed in a defence of hardship. See defence of hardship at para **9.38-41** *post*.

[8] The term appears at p 158 of *The Glossary of Property Terms*.

[9] See discussion of different types of contract within the scope of the Statute at para **5.08-12** *infra*.

[10] *Bellew's (Lord) Estate* [1921] IR 174 at 176.

[11] *Godley v Power* (1957) 95 ILTR 135 at 144.

[12] *Bellew's* case at 176.

[13] By Keane J in *Ballyowen Castle Homes Ltd v Collins* (HC) 26 June 1986, unrep at p 3.

[14] Per Finlay P in *Doherty v Gallagher* (HC) 9 June 1975, Finlay P, unrep at 14.

[15] *Doherty's* case at 13.

[16] *Lindsay v Lynch* (1804) 2 Schoales & Lefroy 1 at p 5. The Lord Chancellor was concerned about opening a new door to fraud "under pretence of part-execution".

Statute has been satisfied in a particular case the first question of all is whether there is a contract. If there is no concluded contract the question whether there is a sufficient note or memorandum does not arise as there is nothing which requires to be evidenced to satisfy the Statute.[17] There is little or no analogy between the Statute of Frauds and any other legislation[18] so case law under other Acts is unlikely to help much in specific performance cases.

"NO ACTION SHALL BE BROUGHT WHEREBY ...TO CHARGE ANY PERSON..."

[5.04] The sanction imposed by s 2 is a prohibition on bringing an action to enforce a contract which is caught by the section. The contract's validity is not affected. To take an example, there is a well established principle in the law of the sale of land that if money is paid as a deposit on a purchase price, then, in the absence of an express agreement to the contrary, the vendor may forfeit the deposit if the purchaser fails to complete.[19] Accordingly, if there is a valid contract, though not enforceable by action - *eg*, if there is nothing in writing at all or any memorandum drawn up fails to satisfy the Statute - a deposit paid may be forfeited if the purchaser defaults.[20] It is vital that the money be paid *as a deposit*. Money paid as part payment of the purchase money but not as a deposit is likely to be recovered by the purchaser.[21] It has been held in England that where there was an oral contract for the purchase of a house and the purchaser gave a cheque for about half the agreed price but later stopped it the vendor was entitled to succeed in an action on foot of the cheque.[22] Of course, if parties do not get as far as having a concluded oral contract money paid as a deposit in relation to any intended contract is recoverable on the ground of being paid without consideration.[23]

A compromise of proceedings which is itself left unenforceable by action by reason of failure to satisfy the Statute is likely to remain a bar on the claims compromised.[24] So, if a settlement includes an agreement for a conveyance of land from one party to another and there is no sufficient memorandum, the settlement cannot be enforced by action. It remains a valid contract unless rescinded for any other reason and, as such, will continue to bar the settled claims.[25]

A vendor's lien is also unaffected by the lack of writing. This right is given by equity for the protection of vendors independently of any contract between the parties.[26] The position in relation to a purchaser's lien when his contract is caught by s 2 is unclear. The

---

[17] *Lynch v O'Meara* (SC) 8 May 1975, Henchy J, unrep at 4 and 10.

[18] In *British Wagon Credit Co Ltd v Henebry* (1962) 97 ILTR 123 at 125 Murnaghan J warned that there was no analogy between the Hire-Purchase Act 1946 and the Statute of Frauds. It had been argued that it was sufficient for the purposes of the 1946 Act that the note or memorandum was made at any time before action brought. *Cf Henry Forde & Son Finance Ltd v Forde* (HC) 13 June 1986, Carroll J, unrep at 3-4.

[19] *Siebel v Kent* [1976-7] ILRM 127 at 136. On deposits see para **3.11-15** above.

[20] *Monnickendam v Leanse* (1923) 39 TLR 445.

[21] *Mayson v Clouet* [1924] AC 980 where the purchaser had paid most of the purchase money by instalments but got back the entire save the part which had been paid as a deposit.

[22] *Low v Fry* (1935) 51 TLR 322.

[23] *Lowis v Wilson* [1949] IR 347. *Cf* judgments of Murnaghan J in *White v Spendlove* [1942] IR 224 at 239 and Meredith J at p 244-5.

[24] *O'Mahony v Gaffney* [1986] IR 36 at 38.

[25] *Ibid.*

[26] *Munster and Leinster Bank Ltd v McGlashan* [1937] IR 525 at 528, Meredith J, affirmed by Supreme Court (see note at bottom of p 531). See also *Re Aluminium Shop Fronts Ltd* [1987] IR 419 at 422.

rationale behind allowing a purchaser a lien on the purchased property in respect of the deposit paid to the vendor is that, by paying the deposit pursuant to the contract, the purchaser acquires an equitable estate or interest in the property[27] and should be allowed to follow that estate by being accorded a lien on it[28]. This is a lien in a secondary sense which does not depend on possession but arises by virtue of a duty or intention attributed in equity to the owner of the property to make it available to answer the particular claim.[29] It is clear that if he has an enforceable contract the purchaser has a lien and if there is no contract at all there cannot be a purchaser's lien.[30] In that case he is entitled to recover the deposit but problems can arise if the person to whom he paid the deposit becomes insolvent. The recent Irish decisions did not consider the position where there was a valid contract which was unenforceable by action by virtue of s 2[31] but the better view is probably that the purchaser's lien does exist in that situation and is not affected by the fact that the contract cannot be enforced by action.

[5.05] We are presently discussing the effect of the Statute on contracts without regard to any question whether specific performance would be an appropriate relief in particular cases.[32] Certain types of case will get outside the Statute anyway even though they relate to sales of land or interests in land; they may be regarded as exceptions to the application of the Statute and a common thread is prevention of fraud. Foremost are the doctrine of part performance[33] and the refusal of courts to allow use of the Statute to prevent evidence proving the existence of trusts.[34] In court sales also there probably is no need for writing.[35] The jurisdiction to order rectification is outside the prohibition of the Statute.[36] A statutory contract such as comes into being in a compulsory purchase situation is outside the Statute.[37] Generally speaking, the service of a notice to treat does not amount to a contract or pass any estate to the acquiring authority; but it creates a relationship which ripens into an enforceable contract when the compensation has been agreed by the parties or assessed by the arbitrator.[38]

"... UPON ANY CONTRACT OR SALE OF LANDS, TENEMENTS, OR HEREDITAMENTS..."

Contracts for the sale of land

[5.06] Contracts for the sale of land are within the Statute. Contracts leading to conveyances in fee simple or assignments of leasehold estates and tenancies are clearly

---

[27] *Tempany v Hynes* [1976] IR 101.
[28] *Re Barrett Apartments Ltd* [1985] IR 350 at 357, Henchy J.
[29] *Ibid.*
[30] *Re Barrett Apartments Ltd* [1985] IR 350 where intending purchasers paid "booking deposits" but had no contracts; they lost their claim for purchasers' liens. The "booking deposits" were not true deposits and it would not be just to advance those purchasers towards the head of the queue of creditors. *Cf Desmond v Brophy* [1985] IR 449.
[31] For the very good reason that the situation did not arise.
[32] See para **1.14-27** *ante* on where the remedy is available.
[33] See Ch 6.
[34] Discussed at para **9.09** *post*.
[35] See para **3.65** *ante*.
[36] *Monaghan County Council v Vaughan* [1948] IR 306 at 316, Dixon J approving a passage from the judgment of Lord Birkenhead in *United States v Motor Trucks Ltd* [1924] AC 196 at 200-1.
[37] *Munton v Greater London Council* [1976] 2 All ER 815; [1976] 1 WLR 649. See also Keane, *The Law of Local Government in the Republic of Ireland* p 249.
[38] *Re Green Dale Building Co. Ltd.*[1977] IR 256 at 265.

covered. The words "lands, tenements, or hereditaments" are broad and so is the word "sale". Extra breadth is given by the word "interest" and an interest which *concerns* lands, tenements or hereditaments without necessarily being "in" them is within the Statute. A contract to grant a mortgage or charge is clearly one for an interest in land and thus within the Statute. Even an informal mortgage by deposit of title deeds creates an interest in land and when further money is lent on the security the interest changes.[39] A contract relating to an incorporeal hereditament such as a letting of fishery rights is within s 2.[40] It would be only consistent with this that easements such as rights of way or of light and profits a prendre should be within the Statute. Some English case law supports the view that they are.[41] However, not everything which is done to or happens on land is an "interest" in or concerning it. For example, a contract submitting the assessment of a claimant's right to compensation for damage by a road being made through his land is not a contract about an interest in lands, tenements or hereditaments.[42] Nor is a contract for the erection of buildings on land.[43] A contract is none the less one for an interest in land if the immediate document sued on is an arbitrator's award.[44]

Compromises of proceedings

[5.07] A claim based on a compromise of proceedings has no special status in relation to the Statute. Where proceedings between parties are settled by a compromise that agreement is a new and independent contract between them and supersedes their original rights and causes of action.[45] If it involves a sale or transfer of an interest in land there must be a sufficient memorandum to enable either party to enforce the settlement if the other reneges.[46] As the contract contained in the settlement is valid despite being unenforceable by action the original claims of the parties are likely to remain barred unless the contract forming the settlement is rescinded.[47] Sometimes there may be a sufficient memorandum to enable one side to enforce the settlement but not the other.[48] Occasionally there will be enough material to enable both sides to sue but doubt about the terms so that a court has to construe the settlement between two parties who each want specific performance but mean different things.[49] A compromise which involves a sale or transfer of land as well as other matters is not likely to be severable. On this point it is helpful to consider whether the severance of an agreement to sell land could be

---

[39] *Bank of Ireland v Purcell* [1989] IR 333, considering the broad definition of "interest" in the Family Home Protection Act 1976. An equitable deposit is not within the Statute of Frauds: Wylie, *Irish Land Law* 2nd Ed (1986) at para 12.43. However, a contract to *assign* the equitable interest thereby created would be within the Statute.

[40] *Bayley v Marquis of Conyngham* (1865) 15 ICLR 406 at 411 and 418.

[41] *McManus v Cooke* (1887) 35 Ch D 681 (agreement for easement of light), *Cory v Davies* [1923] 2 Ch 95 (agreements for vehicular access), *Webber v Lee* (1882) 9 QBD 315 (profit à prendre). See also Gale, *The Law of Easements*, 15th Ed (1986), p 76-78.

[42] *Gillanders v Lord Rossmore* (1835) Jones 504.

[43] *Foley v Connolly* 5 Ir Jur NS 312.

[44] *Johnston v McAllister* (1835) Jones 499.

[45] *Per* Lardner J in *Taylor v Smyth* [1990] ILRM 377, 389.

[46] See judgment of Lynch J in *O'Mahony v Gaffney* [1986] IR 36 where he refers on p 37 to specific performance proceedings which failed due to lack of a memorandum. Cf. *Murphy v Quality Homes*, (HC) 22 June 1976, McWilliam J, where at p 2 he notes the order for specific performance which had been made.

[47] *O'Mahony's* case at 38.

[48] As occurred in the *O'Mahony* case: see p 37. There was enough in correspondence to enable one party to enforce but not the other.

[49] As occurred in *Alpine Investments Ltd v Elliott* (HC) 26 November 1980, Carroll J, unrep at 21-22 (noted at [1981] ILRM 377).

effected without altering the general character of the contract or whether the removal of that part would require the agreement to be remodelled, something the court cannot do.[50]

Contracts for leases

[5.08] A contract for the grant of a lease or tenancy is within the Statute as a contract creating an interest in land.[51] Even contracts for the grant of the types of short-term leases[52] which would come within s 4 of Deasy's Act are covered[53]. Although s 104 of Deasy's Act and Schedule (B) repealed s 1 of the Statute of Frauds[54] s 2 was left unaffected. There is no implied repeal of s 2.[55] An actual grant of a tenancy for six months is within s 4 of Deasy's Act and thus does not need writing under that Act.[56] Since it is within s 4 of Deasy's Act the Statute of Frauds does not apply.[57] A letting of meadowing, if this is a tenancy[58], would require evidence in writing under s 2 of the Statute but could be saved by the Sale of Goods Act 1893.[59] Agistment and conacre "lettings" will usually be licences.[60] However, they may be tenancies. As Murnaghan J explained in *Re Moore's Estates*:[61]

> "There has been, for a very long time, a clear distinction between two forms of agreement:
>
> (a)	where land was let by the owner to another person in such a manner that the possession of the land passed from the owner to that other person, and
>
> (b)	where the owner retained possession, but granted the grazing or some other form of user of the land, to the other party. In each of these cases a contractual relationship existed between the parties; the former was a contract of tenancy, the latter merely a contract, not of tenancy, but for grazing or other purposes."[62]

It has been held that a contract for the sale of growing timber is one for the sale of an interest in land and thus requires writing.[63] Trees constitute a portion of the soil itself as much as grass.[64] An agreement for the surrender of a tenancy is clearly within the Statute[65]

---

[50] *Per* Lardner J in *Taylor v Smyth* [1990] ILRM 377 at 387.
[51] *Bentham v Hardy* (1843) 6 ILR 179, 183, Pennefather CJ using the phrase "passing an interest in land".
[52] On s 4 tenancies see Wylie, *Irish Landlord and Tenant Law*, paras 5.02, 5.25-28.
[53] There being a vital distinction between a contract to make a letting and an actual letting.
[54] Which had provided inter alia that leases for more than three years must be in writing and an agent had to be authorised in writing.
[55] Judgment of Christian J in *Bayley v Conyngham* (1863) 15 ICLR 406 at 416-7. See also *McCausland v Murphy* (1881) 9 LRI 9 at 15. *Cf Leitrim v Geelan* (1873) IR 8 CL 122.
[56] *Crane v Naughten* [1912] 2 IR 318 at 326.
[57] *Ibid.* If the Statute applied the memorandum would be inadequate.
[58] If there is anything more than a licence.
[59] *Scully v Corboy* [1950] IR 140. The point was that the definition of "goods" included things forming part of or attached to the land which were agreed to be severed under the contract.
[60] *Collins v O'Brien* [1981] ILRM 328.
[61] [1944] IR 295.
[62] At p 299. Exclusive possession is no longer a *decisive* factor in deciding whether there is a tenancy or a licence: *per* Lord Denning MR in *Shell-Mex v Manchester Garages* [1971] 1 WLR 612 at 615; [1971] 1 All ER 841 at 843, approved by Griffin J in *Irish Shell and BP Ltd v John Costello Ltd* [1981] ILRM 66 at p 70. However, Murnaghan J's distinction is still important. See also the discussion by Budd J in *Carson v Jeffers* [1961] IR 44 at p 50-51.
[63] *Kennedy v Robinson* (1841) 2 Crawford & Dix 113.
[64] *Per* Pigot CB in *Rhodes v Baker* (1851) 1 ICLR 488 at 492.
[65] *Ronayne v Sherrard* (1877) IR 11 CL 146 at 149.

and it makes no difference whether the interest in the land moves to or from the claimant[66]. A contract for an assignment of a leasehold estate or a tenancy is obviously a sale of land and thus within the Statute.

Licences

[5.09] Property lawyers come across licences frequently in two situations. One is licence as distinct from tenancy[67] and the other is a licence relating to alcoholic drink. A licence in each of these contexts allows the licensee to do something which would otherwise be unlawful. A typical contractual licence to make a specified use of property passes no interest in the property.[68] It will confer a personal privilege without any interest in the land.[69] As there is no interest in the land it is outside the Statute. There may, of course, be a "licence coupled with an interest"[70] and then the question whether the Statute applies will depend on the nature of the interest.

An intoxicating liquor licence is inalienable and also must be attached to the relevant premises.[71] It has been said of the licensee that "He only had a permission or authority, in connection with, or attached to, the premises to do something which would otherwise have been unlawful."[72] It follows that there cannot be a sale of a licence on its own. It may not be sold as an item of property with a viable existence separate from the premises.[73] When a licence is sold with premises the purchaser will be entitled to "whatever benefit may result from the premises having been hitherto licensed".[74] In that event the Statute will apply but the reason, of course, is the premises, not the licence. There may be a kind of "sale" of a licence in that the holder may agree to its extinguishment[75] and in such cases, since no interest in "land" passes, the Statute will not apply.

Purchases of shares

[5.10] Sales of shares in companies are outside the Statute of Frauds[76]. This is so even if the only substantial asset of the company is land.[77] It seems to be otherwise if the company is a partnership so that a purchaser of shares will get an actual interest in the lands of the partnership.[78]

---

[66] *Ronayne's* case at 152.
[67] The practical point being often that a *genuine* licence is not protected by the Landlord and Tenant (Amendment) Act 1980: see Wylie, *Irish Landlord and Tenant Law* at para 37.816n.
[68] *Allen & Sons v King* [1915] 2 IR 448, *per* O'Brien LC at p 455, Ronan LJ at p 468 and Moloney LJ at p 479. This decision was upheld by the House of Lords [1916] 2 AC 54.
[69] *Per* O'Higgins CJ in *Bellew v Bellew* [1982] IR 447 at 458, 459.
[70] See Wylie, *Irish Landlord and Tenant Law* at para 3.04.
[71] *Per* Griffin J in *Macklin v Graecen & Co* [1983] IR 61 at 66.
[72] *Irish Industrial Building Society v O'Brien* [1941] IR 1 at 11.
[73] *Re Sherry-Brennan, a Bankrupt* [1979] ILRM 113 at 118. This Supreme Court judgment was given on 26 July 1983 and the point made by Henchy J is based on case law including *Macklin's* case.
[74] *Per* Murnaghan J in the *Irish Industrial Building Society* case at 7, Geoghegan and O'Byrne JJ concurring. It seems non-essential to cover the licence in a contract: *White v McCooey* [1976/7] ILRM at 78.
[75] Noted by Griffin J in *Macklin's* case at 66 where he outlines the kind of terms likely to be found in such a contract.
[76] *Per* Blayney J in *Guardian Buildings Ltd v Sleecon Ltd* (HC) 18 August 1988, unrep at p 14-15.
[77] *Ibid*, Blayney J rejecting a submission that the sale was really a sale of land and thus within s 2.
[78] *Boyce v Greene* (1826) Batty 608 considered by Blayney J in the *Guardian Builders* case.

"...OR UPON ANY AGREEMENT THAT IS NOT TO BE PERFORMED WITHIN THE SPACE OF ONE YEAR FROM THE MAKING THEREOF..."

[5.11] The test whether a contract comes within this passage from s 2 is whether the parties' arrangement is one which, by its nature, precluded performance within the year. One should look at the situation prevailing at the time the agreement was made and at the intention of the parties.[79] What the parties contemplated when they made their agreement is vital. Thus an oral agreement for four years' employment after a 3 month training period is a contract contemplated to extend over 4 years and 3 months and within the Statute.[80] As Palles CB put it in *Dublin Corporation v Blackrock Commissioners*:[81]

> "It has always been considered that the only mode in which you can test whether a contract is one not to be performed within the year is by ascertaining what are the obligations of the parties. If the obligations of the parties respectively are such that they may be reasonably intended to endure beyond the year, then, and not till then, the contract is within the statute."[82]

A parol contract to maintain a child of about five years of age until she was able to "do for herself" has been held to be one which was not to be performed within the year.[83] In modern times an agreement that on the death of one spouse in a marriage where both spouses had children by previous marriages everything brought into the new marriage by the spouse who died would go back to that spouse's children[84] and an agreement involving substantial works of construction[85] to be done over a period of time have been held to be agreements not to be performed within the year.

"...UNLESS THE AGREEMENT UPON WHICH SUCH ACTION SHALL BE BROUGHT OR SOME MEMORANDUM OF NOTE THEREOF SHALL BE IN WRITING..."

[5.12] The Statute refers to both an agreement in writing and a memorandum or note thereof. These are two very different things and the Statute clearly is intended to cover an oral agreement and require it to be supported by an adequate memorandum in order to be enforceable by action. If there is a formal agreement, especially if it is in a standard Law Society form, there will rarely be questions under the Statute. In cases of concluded oral contracts which cannot be taken outside the Statute for some other reason the issue frequently arises whether there is a sufficient memorandum. Questions may arise whether every term agreed by the parties must be in that memorandum. The case law makes it clear that some terms are always "essential" or "material" in contracts for the sale of land. These are the parties, the property and the consideration so these must be ascertainable from the memorandum relied on.[86] Terms which the general law would imply need not be shown in a memorandum.[87] For example, an agreement to sell implies

---

79   *Per* Barrington J in *Hynes v Hynes* (HC) 21 December 1984, unrep at p 27-8 of the transcript.
80   *Naughton v Limestone Land Co Ltd* [1952] IJR 18.
81   (1882) 16 ILTR 111.
82   At 113.
83   *Farrington v Donohoe* (1866) IR 1 CL 675; but *cf Murphy v O'Sullivan* (1866) 11 Ir Jur NS 111.
84   *Re Good deceased* (HC) Probate, 14 July 1986, Hamilton P, unrep.
85   *Hynes v Hynes* (HC) 21 December 1984, Barrington J, unrep.
86   *Godley v Power* (1957) 95 ILTR 135 at 145; *Black v Grealy* (HC) 10 November 1977, Costello J, unrep at 19; *Scott v Bradley* [1971] Ch 850; [1971] 1 All ER 583, approved by Costello J in *Black's* case at 22-24. The degree or accuracy of description needed is discussed at para **5.31-37** *infra*.
87   *Godley v Power* (1957) 95 ILTR 135 at 145.

114

that the whole of the vendor's interest in the land is to be sold though if the purchaser has notice that the vendor has only a leasehold title the contract will apply only to that title.[88] What other terms need to be set out? It is unlikely that the legislature intended that a memorandum of an oral agreement which omits a *material* or *essential* term could be enough to satisfy the Statute but it also seems unlikely that the intention was that the memorandum should reflect each and every term irrespective of its nature, weight or importance for the parties or any of them.[89] The best view would seem to be that when a memorandum is intended to be worked out by a more formal document it is not necessary that the memorandum sets out every stipulation which would be in the more formal document but the memorandum must contain all the *essential* or material terms of the agreement.[90] In *Stinson v Owens* Lord McDermott LCJ concluded:

> "... that a memorandum may satisfy the requirements of the Statute without mentioning every term that has been agreed between the parties, but that to be good it must mention all the terms which are essential or material. And I am further of the opinion that for the purposes of this requirement what is material or essential must be considered, at any rate primarily, from the point of view of the parties themselves."[91]

The test to be applied is a subjective one and, apart from the terms which are always essential[92], the courts will consider those terms essential to a contract which the parties themselves regarded as essential.[93] It follows that the *only* terms which must appear in the memorandum are the terms which are always essential and those other terms regarded by the parties as being material in each particular case.[94]

[5.13] In general a memorandum of a contract which includes terms purporting to be terms of that contract but which in fact are not agreed terms will not satisfy the Statute.[95] To hold the contrary would tend to aggravate the mischief the Statute was meant to prevent and to increase rather than diminish the uncertainties.[96] When parties to a contract reduce it to writing it speaks for itself and is "final and conclusive"[97] but a document needed to satisfy the Statute may be different. It is a memorandum of what the contract is[98] and, if it is not in accordance with the true contract, it is a bad memorandum.[99] Similarly a subsidiary memorandum which supplies a missing term will be ineffective if it also introduces new terms not agreed between the parties.[100] And if parties get as far as, *eg*, a draft tenancy agreement they may have to look to the correspondence to get a sufficient memorandum as the draft tenancy agreement will usually contains terms which

---

[88] *Ibid.*
[89] See the judgment of Lord McDermott LCJ in *Stinson v Owens* (HC) NI noted 107 ILTSJ 239.
[90] *Per* Cotton LJ in *Gray v Smith* (1889) 43 Ch D 208 at 219, approved by Lord McDermott LCJ in *Stinson's* case at 14.
[91] *Stinson's* case at 15. See also judgment of Kenny J in *Delgado v Crean* (HC) 24 May 1978, unrep at 11.
[92] The parties, the property and the consideration must always be ascertainable from the memorandum: *Godley v Power* (1957) 95 ILTR 135 at 145.
[93] *Per* Costello J in *Anom Engineering Ltd v Thornton* (HC) 1 February 1983, unrep at p 5-6.
[94] *Black v Grealy* (HC) 10 November 1977, Costello J, unrep at 19-20. In *Delgado v Crean* (HC) 24 May 1978, unrep, Kenny J pointed out at p 11 that "what is material will vary from case to case."
[95] *Stinson's* case at p 11 of the transcript.
[96] *Ibid.*
[97] *Crane v Naughten* [1912] 2 IR 318 at 324.
[98] *Ibid.*
[99] *Ibid.*
[100] A passage at p 563 of the 3rd Ed (1966) of Megarry and Wade, *The Law of Real Property* approved by Lord McDermott LCJ in *Stinson's* case at p 11.

have not been agreed by the parties.[101] The additional terms are often reasonable and, in the example given, may have been put into a draft tenancy agreement by the landlord's solicitor to protect his client; they are nevertheless terms which have not yet been agreed.

Waiver of terms or submission to terms

[5.14] A claimant can sometimes waive a term or submit to one in order to get his decree of specific performance. If parties make an oral contract which contains a term wholly for the benefit of one of them and there is a memorandum which does not contain any reference to that term, the party for whose benefit the term was inserted may waive it and sue successfully on the contract of which there is a memorandum.[102] The note or memorandum for the purposes of the Statute must be of the contract sued on, not necessarily the contract made.[103] Waiver in this context may be distinguished from the case in which there is a written contract containing a term which can be waived by a party for whose sole benefit the term was included[104] though the underlying principle that a party who solely benefits from a term may waive it is the same.

The converse also applies. If a stipulation is for the benefit of one party only and is omitted from the memorandum the other party in seeking to enforce the agreement may submit to be bound by the missing term and get his decree. Thus if a written contract for a lease omits an agreed term that the tenant is to pay a premium he may agree to pay that sum and as a result get a decree for specific performance.[105] If a party agrees to pay half the other party's costs of a sale but that term is omitted from the memorandum the first party can agree to pay the money and get his decree.[106] Where parties agree that a memorandum may treat the balance after payment of a deposit as the purchase price the purchaser may agree to waive the possible advantage, pay the full agreed purchase price and get his decree.[107] And a purchaser may also be able to waive a right to receive or get credit for a "luck penny" of £100.[108] Similarly a stipulation in an oral agreement entitling a purchaser to connect for water and power supply and/or effluent and storm water discharge at agreed points on the defendant's land may be waived.[109] However, in another case the Supreme Court may have held that

---

[101] *Scott v McCombe*, CA (NI), 2 June 1965, unrep at p 7.

[102] See *Barrett v Costelloe* (HC) 13 July 1973, Kenny J, unrep at 7, applied by Costello J in *Anom Engineering Ltd v Thornton* (HC) 1 February 1983, unrep at p 9.

[103] *Ibid*, included in the passage quoted and applied by Costello J. Remember that this is in the context of waiver and thus an exception to the position stated in para **5.13** above. Gannon J said in *White v McCooey* [1976/7] ILRM 72 at 79 that in the case of an oral agreement the inclusion in, or omission from, the note or memorandum of an alleged term of the agreement does not alter the contract.

[104] See para **3.29-30** above.

[105] *Martin v Pycroft* (1852) 2 De GM & G 785, approved by Costello J in *Black v Grealy* (HC) 10 November 1977, unrep at 23; also approved by Kenny J in *Healy v Healy* (HC) 3 December 1973, unrep at 10-11. *Healy's* case was one of a formal agreement with terms which could be waived by the party for whose benefit they existed.

[106] *Scott v Bradley* [1971] Ch. 850; [1971] 1 All ER 583, approved by Costello J in *Black's* case at 24.

[107] *Black's* case at p 25. Costello J rejected a plea of illegality at 12-13, 18. He held that because the price was misstated the memorandum did not satisfy the Statute but that it would be a fraudulent use of the Statute if the court let the defendant avoid liability on the ground that the memorandum, which was prepared in accordance with his wishes, treated the balance as the purchase price: p 21. See defence of illegality at para **9.48-55** below.

[108] *Stinson v Owens* (HC) NI noted 107 ILTSJ 239, at 15-16. Lord McDermott LCJ held that the luck penny was collateral: p 3.

[109] *Anom Engineering Ltd v Thornton* (HC) 1 February 1983, Costello J, unrep at p 9.

"the unusual clause"[110] that a *vendor* would pay stamp duty and certain legal fees could not be waived.[111]

Collateral contracts

[5.15] Parties may sometimes agree on a term or condition which is *collateral* to their main contract and which would not be itself a contract needing to be evidenced in writing in order to satisfy the Statute. If so, that term or condition does not have to be mentioned in the memorandum.[112] On the other hand, if it is part and parcel of the bargain for sale *and* a material or essential part of that bargain it must be evidenced by a memorandum.[113] If an additional term can fairly be described as a new contract which relates to the same deal but does not in itself concern the lands the Statute does not apply to it.[114] A collateral contract is likely to be dependent on the main contract being carried out and in some cases can fairly be described as "subsidiary". Kingsmill Moore J deals with an example in a sale of a public house and its stock:

> "If it could be shown clearly that the agreement for the taking over of the stock was part of the consideration for the sale of the lands then the memorandum would be defective, because it did not fully set out the consideration. But it seems more likely that any such agreement was a collateral and subsidiary contract. Its execution, indeed, depended on the completion of the contract for the sale of the lands, for it was only on completion that the stock could be ascertained and its value discovered; but it appears to me to be a reversal of probability to suggest that the sale of the lands was in any way contingent on the disposal of the residue of the stock."[115]

[5.16] Though a collateral contract may be "subsidiary" it is likely to affect the rights of the parties under the main contract. Thus a vendor who fails in his obligation under a collateral contract may find that the failure prevents him using a rescission clause in the main contract.[116] A separate cause of action may arise out of a collateral contract. A vendor of a leasehold term who agrees to pay a sum needed to get landlord's consent and fails to do so may be decreed for the amount.[117] Cases of collateral contracts must be distinguished from those where there is just one contract which includes matter which would have to be evidenced in writing and also matter which does not. In that situation the contract is indivisible and there must be a note in writing for the whole.[118] If part of

---

[110] The description used by Fitzgerald J. The clause was more or less the reverse of the normal situation.

[111] *Hoon v Nolan* (1967) 101 ILTR 99 at 109. Kenny J had held (p 106) that the purchaser could waive the term but the SC held that the "ultimate contract" was verbal and as the memorandum did not refer to Mrs Nolan's right to be released from the obligation to pay the stamp duty and legal fees it did not fulfill the Statute.

[112] *Anom Engineering Ltd v Thornton* (HC) 1 February 1983, Costello J, unrep at p 7; *Scott v McCombe* CA, NI, 2 June 1965, unrep at p 7.

[113] *Anom Engineering's* case at 7.

[114] *Scott v Anderson* (1857) 2 Ir Jur NS 422 at 423.

[115] *Godley v Power* (1957) 95 ILTR 135 at p 146. By clear implication the passage accepts that if the purchase of the stock had been a term of the contract for the sale of the land it would have been a *material* term. In *Carthy v O'Neill* [1981] ILRM 443 the price of the stock was one of the "essential parts of what was expected to become a contract" which "remained to be negotiated": *per* Henchy J at p 445. The parties there had not dealt with stock at all. See also *Greyhill Property Co Ltd v Whitechap Inn Ltd* (HC) 5 October 1993, Barr J, unrep at 30: representations about the fire officer's requirements amounted to a collateral contract the consideration for which was the purchase of the property.

[116] *Kennedy v Wrenne* [1981] ILRM 81 at 82. The vendor agreed by collateral contract to get a release of a mortgage but failed.

[117] *Carrigy v Brock* (1871) IR 5CL 501. Note that this case was decided before s 3 of the Conveyancing Act 1892 became law but note also that parties can contract out of s 3!

[118] *Bentham v Hardy* (1843) 6 ILR 179, 183.

an indivisible contract is within the Statute "you must have a note in writing for the whole; for the contract being entire, you cannot sever it".[119] This, of course, is subject to the normal rule that only the essential terms of the whole contract need be evidenced in writing and also subject to the principles of waiver or submission to an omitted term just discussed.

Essential terms and recognition

[5.17] The memorandum or note must be "of" the contract sued on[120] and must be in writing. The section does not specify any type of writing so informal documents will suffice. The document relied on must contain all the essential terms of the contract and a recognition that a contract has been reached.[121] How precisely it does those things is not important. A cheque with the following written low down on its face has been held sufficient:

> "£500 deposit on land comprising all that known locally as the Rath Liath, the Flat, the Clagan and adjoining fields agreed full purchase price £3,500."[122]

And in another modern case[123] this was held sufficient:

> ## "O'KEEFFE & O'SULLIVAN LIMITED
> Auctioneers - Valuers - Estate Agents
>
> I, Patrick Casey, Gurrane House, Donoughmore, agree to purchase Park House and lands for £110,000 subject to contract and title.[124] I agree to pay £25,250 as deposit.
>
> Patrick Casey.
>
> Directors: AB O'Keeffe   JL O'Sullivan"

Where a solicitor put the names of parties into his instructions book as the names of the parties who gave the instructions which followed and then set out the terms of the contract made between them there was a good memorandum.[125] A letter from a company's estate agent to its financial adviser setting out an agreement reached was sufficient.[126] And a note in an auctioneer's book with particulars from the conditions of sale, a statement that the lands were sold to the plaintiff for £2,100 and the auctioneer's signature was a sufficient memorandum taken with the conditions of sale.[127] A receipt referring to "£800 being the deposit on No 1 Kinvara Road" taken with an application to a building society was held to be a good memorandum.[128] It is important to remember that where parties

---

[119] *Bentham's* case at p 184.

[120] Note the word *"thereof"*.

[121] *Per* Henchy J in *Kelly v Park Hall School Ltd* [1979] IR 340 at 352.

[122] *Doherty v Gallagher* (HC) 9 June 1975, Finlay P, unrep. The defendant was the named payee and on cashing it he signed his name on the back.

[123] *Casey v Irish Intercontinental Bank Ltd* [1979] IR 364 at 366-9.

[124] Note that the "subject to contract" element did not prevent there being a contract - see para **4.07-08**, *supra*. We mention this case again on the subject of signature at para **5.27** fn 206, *infra*.

[125] *Murphy v Harrington* [1927] IR 339, 342-3. Both parties had instructed the solicitor.

[126] *Kelly v Park Hall School Ltd* [1979] IR 340. The letter is set out at 346-7 and Henchy J's view of it appears at 352.

[127] *McMeekin v Stevenson* [1917] 1 IR 348.

[128] *McQuaid v Lynam* [1965] IR 564 at 569-72; plaintiff lost as his oral agreement was varied by later agreement, itself incomplete: 574.

make a concluded oral agreement the memorandum or note of that agreement does not *become* the contract.[129] The section envisages a writing which is evidence of a contract made by the party being charged.[130] The note in writing has been described as "the requisite legal evidence" under the Statute.[131] It provides for a definite kind of proof before the agreement can be enforced against a party refusing to proceed.[132] However the same document may be used both to show the terms of an oral contract and as a memorandum sufficient to meet the Statute.[133]

[5.18] Very often a document relied on successfully as a memorandum satisfying the Statute comes into being with no intention that it will have that role. Kenny J said in *McQuaid v Lynam*:[134]

"It is settled law that the memorandum or note required by the Statute of Frauds may consist of a document which was not intended to be such a note or memorandum but it must however be signed by the party to be charged and the signature must have been intended to authenticate the whole document of which it forms a part."[135]

An important distinction has been made by O'Connor LJ in *Cloncurry v Laffan*:[136]

"It is sometimes said that an agent - in the absence of express authority to do so - has no power to bind his principal by signing a note or memorandum of a verbal contract already entered into by his principal. The proposition thus stated is in my opinion too wide. There is no doubt but that the signature by such an agent of a note or memorandum affixed merely for the sake of constituting such a note or memorandum will not bind the principal. The reason of course is obvious - namely that [the agent has no express authority to sign such note or memorandum for the mere purpose of binding his principal, nor is it within the scope of his implied authority to do so. But it may be that the agent has implied authority to sign something which if signed by the principal would be a note or memorandum within the Statute of Frauds - to sign it, not for the purpose of binding his principal (which is not within the scope of the agent's authority) but for other purposes which are within the scope of the agent's authority. Such a case may - and I think frequently does - arise where a solicitor is employed in reference to a contract for sale or purchase of land.][137] The solicitor has no authority for the sake of binding his principal to sign a note or memorandum of the contract. But if in the course of the transaction for which he is employed and in pursuance of the authority entrusted to him the solicitor has to sign something which if signed by the client would be a note or memorandum within the Statute of Frauds then the client is as much bound by the solicitor's signature as if it were his own."

---

[129] *McQuaid's* case at 573.
[130] *Per* Keane J in *Mulhall v Haren* [1979] IR 364 at 386.
[131] *Kerns v Manning* [1935] IR 869 at 879.
[132] *Per* Finlay P in *Doherty v Gallagher* (HC) 9 June 1975, Finlay P, unrep at 14.
[133] *Godley v Power* (1957) 95 ILTR 135: Kingsmill Moore J treated a letter as proving the terms of the oral contract (146) saying that it was a *confirmation* of an agreement already made and held it to be a good memorandum. At 148 Martin Maguire J said :"I think this letter, confirming the verbal agreement, affords a sufficient memorandum in writing to satisfy the Statute of Frauds".
[134] [1965] IR 564.
[135] At p 569.
[136] *Cloncurry v Laffan* [1924] 1 IR 78 at p 84. See also Kingsmill Moore J in *Godley v Power* (1957) 95 ILTR 135 at 145.
[137] The portion in square brackets was cited with approval by Ronan LJ at p 88-9. He dissented on how he would apply the principles.

[5.19] The central distinction made in that passage is between deliberately binding the client as an end in itself and doing something while processing the contract for the client which has the effect of satisfying the Statute and thus making the contract enforceable against the client. Instructing a solicitor to carry out a client's contract for him involves an authority to do everything that is necessary for the protection of his client's interests.[138] If a suggestion of limiting the title to be shown is made a purchaser's solicitor may rightly make the point that the parties have already agreed an "open" contract.[139] This is why in the *Cloncurry* case "he was lawfully authorised by his client to make the statement of the contract and to sign it."[140] Where clients have made their own agreement solicitors will not take upon themselves authority to negotiate or make a contract for the clients.[141] That does not mean that the solicitors lack authority to confirm and communicate terms of agreement made orally[142]; if they do so without using an effective "subject to contract" formula their letters risk being memoranda which satisfy the Statute. It is therefore vital that when commencing to act on behalf of a client in a purchase of land a solicitor will satisfy himself whether a contract has been reached and if so whether it is already evidenced in writing or could be outside the Statute for some other reason. If a vendor is already bound by a contract enforceable by action the solicitor should still try to reach agreement on the title which must be shown but of course he may be met with the retort that the parties have already made an "open" contract. If the client is not yet bound then unless the client is very anxious to maximise the chances of getting an enforceable contract as quickly as possible the solicitor will avoid providing a sufficient memorandum until he has agreed on satisfactory protection in relation to title and any other matters. There may indeed be cases where a solicitor feels that it is positively advantageous to his client to commit him to an open contract.[143] But in everyday cases of sales of property where parties have shaken hands on price they will still trust their solicitors to do everything necessary to protect them against the traps and pitfalls that beset the completion of sales of real property.[144] The solicitor may also warn his client of the risk that for some time there could be a sufficient memorandum to let the other party enforce a contract against him but not vice versa.[145]

[5.20] The circumstances in which a memorandum comes into being without any intention of satisfying the Statute are wide and varied. A letter or telex meant to cancel or repudiate a contract may be a sufficient memorandum of it.[146] Letters by estate agents and solicitors may be the most likely to provide an unintended memorandum. While a

---

[138] *Per* Molony CJ in *Cloncurry's* case at 81 quoting with agreement from the judgment of O'Connor MR. Note, however, that if a solicitor is instructed to prepare a formal agreement he is not likely to have authority to sign an informal memorandum: *Smith v Webster* (1876) 3 Ch D 49 approved by Molony CJ in the *Cloncurry* case at p 81 and 83.

[139] 40 years' title beginning with a good root of title must be shown under an "open" contract. See Wylie, *Irish Conveyancing Law* at para. 3.073 and his warning in a context of the Statute of Frauds at 10.051.

[140] *Per* Molony CJ in the *Cloncurry* case at 82.

[141] *Black v Kavanagh* (1973) 108 ILTR 91 at 96, Gannon J.

[142] *Black's* case at p 96.

[143] As noted by Keane J in *Mulhall v Haren* [1981] IR 364 at 392.

[144] *Ibid.* See the detailed consideration by Gannon J of parties' expectations of their solicitors in *Black v Kavanagh* (1974) 108 ILTR 91 at pp 94, 95 and 96.

[145] See para **5.25** *infra.*

[146] *Tradax (Ireland) Ltd v Irish Grain Board Ltd* [1984] ILRM 471 *per* O'Higgins CJ at 473, Henchy J at 484 and Griffin J at 486 (a case under s 4 of the Sale of Goods Act 1893).

solicitor is more likely than an estate agent to get into a situation that he provides a memorandum of a contract *already made* by his client it can happen to an estate agent too.[147] The solicitor will rarely have authority to *make* a contract and in many cases there will be a concluded contract often oral before the case comes to him at all. An estate agent reporting to his client's financial adviser is most unlikely to intend to provide a memorandum to satisfy the Statute but he may have that effect.[148] An agent's letter may be a good memorandum even if it is not shown to have reached his principal.[149] A client writing informally to her own solicitor may also provide a memorandum.[150] A telegram, a recital in a will, a letter written to a third party and a letter written to repudiate liabilities have been accepted by the courts as sufficient.[151] A signature of a chairman of a company affixed to a minute book to verify the accuracy of an entry was sufficient even though it was quite clear that he had no such intention.[152] If a person furnishes a statement to help another to defeat a claim by a third party that statement could be used against him as a memorandum of his own contract by the very person for whose assistance it was given.[153]

English case law illustrates some traps for lawyers. It has been held that a letter signed by a lessee's solicitor purporting to enclose an engrossed lease was a good memorandum.[154] And a note "16/5/58 [the purchaser] phoned and confirmed above" written on the back of a letter to the purchaser dealing with the completion date was sufficient.[155] Pleadings of counsel can also form an unintended memorandum.[156] A letter from a client to his own solicitor may be a good memorandum and, unless written for the purpose of getting advice, will not be protected from discovery by privilege.[157] The danger of bringing a memorandum into being unintentionally must always be watched carefully. It takes comparatively slight evidence to establish a solicitor's authority to make a note which may become unintended evidence of a concluded contract.[158] Solicitors might do well to advise their clients to put nothing in writing and to instruct

---

[147] As in *Ballyowen Castle Homes Ltd v Collins* (HC) 26 June 1986, Keane J, unrep at p 7-8. *Cf Lynch v Bulbulia* (HC) 25 July 1980 where Costello J held that the auctioneer wrote his letter confirming terms after being told by his client to hold everything: pp 5, 7, 10.

[148] As in *Kelly v Park Hall School Ltd* [1979] IR 340. Henchy J deals with the letter at 352.

[149] *Hudson v O Connor* [1947] IJR 21.

[150] *Waldron v Jacob* (1870) IR 5 Eq 131 at 136-7 The letter's adequacy as a memorandum was attacked mainly on the grounds that it did not sufficiently describe the property or specify the estate which was being sold.

[151] *Per* Hamilton J in *Kelly v Park Hall School Ltd* [1979] IR 340 at 350, quoting with approval from Cheshire & Fifoot, *The Law of Contract*, 4th Ed at 157.

[152] *Jones v The Victoria Graving Dock Co* 2 QBD 314, approved by Molony CJ in *Cloncurry v Laffan* [1924] 1 IR 78 at 82.

[153] *Daniels v Trefusis* [1914] 1 Ch 788 discussed by O Connor MR in *Cloncurry v Laffan* [1923] 1 IR 127 at 133-4. He described it at p 134-5 as "a very striking example of the general principle that no matter what the purpose for which a memorandum was signed it may be a memorandum within the Statute of Frauds...." His judgment was upheld on appeal by a majority, [1924] 1 IR 78.

[154] *Horner v Walker* [1923] 2 Ch 218.

[155] *Gavaghan v Edwards* [1961] 2 QB 220; [1961] 2 All ER 477 a case on special facts. The deal was agreed save for the possession date and one solicitor was acting for both parties; when they agreed that date there was nothing contradictory in the position of the solicitor to stop him creating an additional memorandum recording the final term so as to bind either or both his clients.

[156] *Grindell v Bass* [1920] 2 Ch 487; [1920] All ER Rep 219. Counsel was pleading a contract with a third party as a defence to the plaintiff's claim for specific performance. The plea was held a good memorandum in favour of the third party made before he was a party to the action. Note the suggestion by Murnaghan J in *White v Spendlove* [1942] IR 224, 236 that a defence plea could give the commencement date of a proposed lease.

[157] *Smith-Bird v Blower* [1939] 2 All ER 406 at 410.

[158] *Kerns v Manning* [1935] IR 869 at 881. Murnaghan J was *not* saying that a solicitor had authority to make the memorandum *for the purpose of* binding the client: note the important distinction by O'Connor LJ in *Cloncurry v Laffan* 1924 in the passage quoted at para **5.18** above.

estate agents likewise. They might also keep a close eye on their own notes and attendances to guard against those becoming unwanted memoranda.

[5.21] Normally the memorandum cannot be made before the alleged oral contract. Before any note or memorandum of a contract can be made, there must *be* a contract complete and concluded, which, but for the Statute of Frauds, would bind and be enforced against the party to be charged.[159] There seems to be an exception to this where an offer or counter-offer is capable of verbal acceptance whereupon the document making the offer or counter-offer may become a good memorandum of the contract which results from the acceptance.[160] To get within this exception a claimant must show that the document relied on is an offer which states all the terms and shows an intention to contract.[161] When the offer is accepted the document becomes a sufficient memorandum even though the contract is later in date than the document. The "written offer accepted orally" position is anomalous but may be explained by the fact that once there is an oral acceptance of a written offer the contract comes into existence at that moment and therefore the note or memorandum becomes relevant.[162]

Reverting to the normal situation where the memorandum does not pre-date the contract there is no need for the contract and memorandum to be made at or around the same time. A document may be a sufficient memorandum of an oral contract made much earlier.[163] The document relied on as a memorandum must exist before action brought though if it does not a later action based on the document which comes into being may be open.[164]

Joinder of documents

[5.22] A memorandum will sometimes be found in more than one document. The courts' approach to this has been described by Kenny J as "progressively liberal"[165] and he summarised the position:[166]

> "I think that the modern cases establish that a number of documents may together constitute a note or memorandum in writing if they have come into existence in connection with the same transaction or if they contain internal references which connect them with each other. But as the memorandum or note considered as a whole must be signed, it would seem to follow that the document which is signed must be the last of the documents in point of time, for it would be absurd to hold that a person who signed a document could be regarded as having signed another document which was not in existence when he signed the first."

---

[159] *Per* FitzGibbon LJ in *Dyas v Stafford* 9 LRI 520 at 529.

[160] *Boyle v Lee* [1992] 1 IR 555 at 588; [1992] ILRM 65 at 89, *per* O'Flaherty J; *Mulhall v Haren* [1981] IR at 383. *Cf Swan v Miller* [1919] 1 IR 151 at 168-9, 173, a dissenting judgment of Campbell C. The majority, Ronan and O'Connor LJJ, do not seem to reject the point and perhaps the judgment of O'Connor LJ at 180-1 accepts the principle while holding that it could not be applied in the case.

[161] *Parker v Clark* [1960] 1 All ER 93 at 102-3; [1960] 1 WLR 286; see also *Reuss v Pickley* (1866) LR 1 Exch 342.

[162] *Per* O'Flaherty J in *Boyle's* case, *ibid*.

[163] *Powell v Dillon* (1814) 2 Ball & Beatty 416. The letter relied on successfully was 24 years later than the agreement.

[164] As in *Lindsay v Lynch* (1804) 2 Schoales & Lefroy 1 where the plaintiff failed on the agreement he alleged but amended his bill to add an alternative claim based on a version the defendant admitted. Lord Redesdale dismissed the bill but without prejudice to any later attempt to rely on the defendant's version. See also *Grindell v Bass* at fn 156 above.

[165] *McQuaid v Lynam* [1965] IR 564 at 570.

[166] *Ibid*, citing *Long v Millar* (1879) 4 CPD 450, *Stokes v Whicher* [1920] 1 Ch 411 and *Timmins v Moreland Street Property Co* [1957] 3 All ER 265.

The point about the signature and the order in which documents are made is not applied too stringently. Thus:

> "If however on the same occasion and as part of one and the same transaction - for example as here the payment of a deposit under an oral agreement for sale - a vendor and purchaser sit down at a table and respectively write out a receipt and a cheque then assuming that these documents between them sufficiently evidence the terms of the bargain, it would be going too far to say that the vendor could not rely on them as constituting a memorandum if the purchaser signed his cheque a few seconds before the vendor signed the receipt. I think it is enough to say that the documents relied on were brought into being more or less contemporaneously for the purpose of furthering a bargain which the party had made."[167]

If one document and part of the second are contemporaneous but the other part of the second is completed some time later the two may still be taken together.[168] A reference from a signed document to the other may span a substantial period of time. An agreement which identified land only by reference to a poster used for an abortive auction three years earlier sufficed.[169] There must be an express or implied reference to the second document.[170] Thus, if an auctioneer sells a six month tenancy but does not refer to a poster which alone states the term it will be difficult to link in the poster.[171] Sometimes laying documents side by side will lead to the conclusion as a matter of *res ipsa loquitur* that the two are connected.[172] A mention of eg "the contract already in existence signed at £55,000" is a clear reference and likely to result in a good memorandum.[173] A solicitor's letter and accompanying draft are likely to be read together[174] assuming of course that no other precautions such as "subject to contract" are taken though, as we have seen,[175] a draft document which contains terms additional to those actually agreed may not be a good memorandum. Where a link is sought to be made between two documents which are both signed it will not matter if one is signed by a principal and the other by an agent.[176]

[5.23] If two documents are placed side by side no parol evidence is necessary to connect one with the other and they clearly relate on their faces to the same transaction they are a sufficient memorandum.[177] However, if there is no reference *at all* in one document to the other, oral evidence is not admissible to link them.[178] The borderline may be difficult

---

[167] *Per* Romer LJ in the *Timmins* case at 278 approved by Kenny J in the *McQuaid* case at 571.

[168] As in the *McQuaid* case where the gap was 23 days: pp 571-2.

[169] *Davis v Gallagher* [1933] L J Ir 2.

[170] *Waldron v Jacob* (1870) IR 5 Eq 131, 137; *Clinan v Cooke* (1802) 1 Schoales & Lefroy 22 at 33 - no reference to an advertisement in either case.

[171] *Crane v Naughten* [1912] 2 IR 318 at 326.

[172] *Per* Jenkins LJ in the *Timmins* case approved by Kenny J in *McQuaid's* case at 572 and McWilliam J in *Kelly v Kineen* (HC) 29 April 1980, unrep at p 7-8.

[173] *Delgado v Crean* (HC) 24 May 1978, Kenny J, unrep at p 11.

[174] *Craig v Elliott* (1885) 15 LRI 257 at 262-4; *Arnold v Veale* (HC) 28 July 1977, unrep at 18 (this became a "subject to contract" case on appeal); *Guerin v Ryan* (HC) 28 April 1978, McWilliam J, unrep at 7-8. The point was accepted in *Anom Engineering Ltd v Thornton* (HC) 1 February 1983, Costello J.

[175] Para **5.13**, *supra*.

[176] *Saunders v Cramer* (1842) 3 Drury & Warren 87, 101.

[177] *Burgess v Cox* [1950] 2 All ER 1212 approved by McWilliam J in *Howlin v Power (Dublin) Ltd* (HC) 5 May 1978, unrep at 5 (but not applied to the facts of the case before him).

[178] *Howlin's* case at 5; *White v Spendlove* [1942] IR 224, 233-4, Sullivan CJ; *Crane v Naughton* [1912] 2 IR 318, 326; *Clinan v Cooke* (1802) 1 Schoales & Lefroy 22, 33; *Boyce v Green* (1826) Batty 608.

to draw between allowing and keeping out oral evidence. The linking reference may be implied and the test would seem to be whether "any such reference can be spelt out of the document so signed" and if so parol evidence may be given to identify the other document referred to explain the other transaction and identify any document relating to it.[179] When there is a sufficient reference parol evidence may be received not only to identify a particular writing referred to but to prove that such a writing existed and must have been referred to by the writing which has been signed.[180] If by this process a document is brought to light which contains in writing all the terms of the bargain so far as not contained in the document signed by the party to be charged the two may be read together.[181]

[5.24] Older cases which suggest the need for a clearer link should now be treated with caution. Thus it would probably overstate the present state of the law to suggest that documents relied on as constituting the memorandum "must refer to each other in such a way as to dispense with parol evidence of connection."[182] A change towards easier admittance of oral evidence has probably taken place and this may be the reason for Kenny J's "progressively liberal" remark.[183] The change would be consistent with the concern of the modern courts that a strict application of the Statute of Frauds can risk permitting injustice and in that sense encouraging fraud.[184] Similarly to cases of creating a memorandum from a single document the necessary link between two or more documents can be made without any intention of satisfying the Statute. Thus where the signed document which identified the other document was the defendant's affidavit of discovery in which he made the case that the other document was privileged he hardly intended to make a memorandum to satisfy the Statute.[185] And where a memorandum of agreement and conditions of sale were not a sufficient memorandum because they did not name the vendor but the purchaser served a completion notice naming the vendor he created a sufficient memorandum.[186] The document which makes the link must be consistent with the other. If the second document says that the parties' contract was subject to conditions not contained in the first there is no sufficient memorandum.[187] That could produce the result that the second document refers to a different contract from that set up by the plaintiff and thus does not recognise the plaintiff's version so he cannot succeed on foot of an alleged memorandum in the two documents.[188] If a second document should be said to vary from the first in a material respect, it cannot form a sufficient memorandum with it.[189]

---

[179] *Per* Jenkins LJ in the *Timmins* case approved by Kenny J in *McQuaid's* case at p 572 and McWilliam J in *Kelly v Kineen* (HC) 29 April 1980, unrep at 7-8.

[180] *Per* Chatterton VC in *Craig's* case at 263.

[181] *Ibid.*

[182] As Gibson J may have done in *Crane v Naughton* [1912] 2 IR 318 at p 326-7. Note, however, that a case mentioned by him referred to a *contract*, not a memorandum.

[183] See para **5.22** and fn 164 above.

[184] As voiced by Finlay P in *Doherty v Gallagher* (HC) 9 June 1975, unrep at 13.

[185] *Murphy v Harrington* [1935] IR 339.

[186] *Irvine v Dane* (1850) 2 Ir Jur 209.

[187] *Haughton v Morton* (1855) 5 ICLR 329, *per* Moore J at p 340-2 (Perrin J concurring) and Crampton J at p 342-3.

[188] See the case law discussed by Moore J in *Haughton's* case at p 340.

[189] *Boyce v Greene* (1826) Batty 608 at 618.

"...AND SIGNED BY THE PARTY TO BE CHARGED THEREWITH OR SOME OTHER PERSON THEREUNTO BY HIM AUTHORISED."

[5.25] A signature is needed. It must be the signature of the person against whom it is sought to enforce a contract or of that person's agent. It does not have to be signed by or on behalf of the enforcing party and in practice often will not be in cases where there is an issue about the adequacy of a memorandum. If the non-signing party sues he makes himself liable to perform the contract. The reason is that by filing his proceedings he submits to having to perform his own part of the contract.[190] After some hesitation[191] it became settled that where only one party has signed an agreement or memorandum there is nothing in the Statute of Frauds to prevent specific performance at the instance of the other party[192] though the courts may not assist a party who has been trying to get some undue advantage or "has been playing what is called fast and loose".[193] If there are co-owners both must sign[194] or be named in the document[195] and have it signed by an agent for both[196] if they are to be bound.

[5.26] The purpose of the signature is to authenticate the document.[197] As Lord Westbury explained in 1867:[198]

"It must show that every part of the instrument emanates from the individual so signing and that the signature was intended to have that effect. It follows therefore that if a signature be found in an instrument incidentally only or having relation and reference only to a portion of the instrument the signature cannot have that legal effect and force which it must have in order to comply with the statute and to give authenticity to the whole of the memorandum."

It is vital to bear in mind that the thing which a signature must authenticate is the document of which it is part. It does not have to authenticate a contract which that document may evidence. As AL Smith LJ said in *John Griffiths Cycle Corporation Ltd v Humber & Co Ltd*:[199]

"It is undoubted law that the party to the contract himself may by signing a document subsequent to that containing the terms of the contract recognise the contract in the way required by s 4[200] of the Statute of Frauds. It is also undoubted law that a signature to a document which contains the terms of a contract is available for the purpose of satisfying

---

[190] *Fennelly v Anderson* (1851) 1 Ir Ch R 706 at 711.

[191] Note the judgment of Lord Redesdale in *Lawrenson v Butler* (1802) 1 Schoales & Lefroy 13.

[192] *Lord Ormond v Anderson* (1813) 2 Ball & Beatty 363 at 370-1, *per* Lord Manners. He acknowledges that "a doubt has been entertained by a judge in this court of very high authority".

[193] *Lord Ormond's* case at 371.

[194] *Re Hayes's Estate* [1920] 1 IR 207.

[195] *Carthy v O'Neill* [1981] ILRM 443 at 446. One reason why the memorandum was inadequate was that it failed to name a wife who was joint owner.

[196] *Mulhall v Haren* [1981] IR 364 at 372-3 (rejecting a plea under the Family Home Protection Act 1976 that a second consent was needed).

[197] *Per* Murnaghan J in *Kerns v Manning* [1935] IR 869 at 882 and Kenny J in *McQuaid v Lynam* [1965] IR 564 at 569.

[198] In *Caton v Caton* (1867) LR 2 (HL) 127 in a passage quoted by Kenny J in *McQuaid v Lynam* [1965] IR 564 at 569. Lord Westbury was himself referring to earlier English decisions.

[199] [1899] 2 QB 414. The passage quoted is at p 417 and was approved by Molony CJ in *Cloncurry v Laffan* [1924] 1 IR 78 at p 82.

[200] AL Smith LJ is referring to the (English) Statute of Frauds passed in 1677; s 4 of that corresponded with s 2 of the Irish Statute.

s 4 of the statute though put alio intuitu and not in order to attest or verify the contract: *Jones v The Victoria Graving Dock Co.*"[201]

Of the confusion which can arise on this point O'Connor LJ said in *Halley v O'Brien*:[202]

> "Not always, I think, is it sufficiently remembered that the statute does not require the signature to be to the contract itself; it is sufficient if there is a signed note or memorandum of the contract."[203]

The position of the signature is not crucial. It may be anywhere in the document as long as the person signing intended it to authenticate the document as a whole.[204]

[5.27] Neither does the signature have to be handwritten in the normal way. As O'Connor LJ explained in *Halley v O'Brien*:[205]

> "When we speak of 'signing' or 'signature' we usually think of the person's name signed by himself in the form he generally uses as a clue to or mark of his identity. That is the meaning of the term when we ask 'Is that Mr. H's signature?' Further, we usually associate 'signed' and 'signature' with a name subscribed or put at the end of a document. But these are not the sole meanings of 'signature' at all. One of the meanings, and for the purpose of this case, the appropriate meaning is 'the name of a person or something used as representing his name, affixed or appended to a writing or the like, either by himself or his deputy as a verification, authentication or assent': Century Dictionary."

A printed name may thus suffice. So if the party to be charged has written or dictated a document on or on to paper which has his name printed on it he should be regarded as having adopted the printed name as his signature and so should be regarded as having signed the document.[206] If an intending vendor sends a document containing his name in print to a purchaser but in such a way that the sender recognises his own name as such and the document contains the terms of a contract it is likely to satisfy the Statute.[207] The insertion of a party's name into a document by that person or his authorised agent as being a party to an agreement and the presentation of that document to the other party for signature may create a sufficient memorandum against the first party even though neither he nor his agent has actually signed it.[208] Although a high degree of informality may be accepted by the courts there must still be an intention that the thing relied on as a signature performed that role. Thus in *Casey v Irish Intercontinental Bank*[209] Kenny J laid

---

[201] (1877) 2 QBD 314. Both the *Jones* case and the *John Griffiths* case (which was reversed by the House of Lords on different grounds - see judgment of O'Connor MR in the *Cloncurry* case, [1923] 1 IR 127 at 134) were approved by Molony CJ in the *Cloncurry* case, [1924] 1 IR 78 at 82 and by Meredith J in *Murphy v Harrington* [1927] IR 339 at 342.

[202] [1920] 1 IR 330.

[203] At p 340.

[204] See case law discussed by Deasy LJ in *Dyas v Stafford* (1882) 9 LRI 520 at p 525-6; also Law C at p 524; also discussion by Powell J in *Halley v O'Brien* [1920] 1 IR 149 at 157-8 and on appeal by O'Connor LJ at [1920] 1 IR 338-9; also Meredith J in *Murphy v Harrington* [1927] IR 339 at 342.

[205] [1920] 1 IR 330 at p 339.

[206] *Casey v Irish Intercontinental Bank Ltd* [1979] IR 364 at 368. The note is set out in para **5.16** *supra*.

[207] *Tourret v Cripps* (1879) 48 LJ Ch 567 where the sheet of paper had the printed words "From Richard L Cripps". Part of the judgment of Hall VC in that case was quoted with approval by Kenny J in *Casey's* case at 369 and by Deasy LJ in the *Dyas* case at 527.

[208] *Evans v Hoare* [1892] 1 QB 593, approved by Powell J in *Halley v O'Brien* [1920] 1 IR 149 at 156-7 (which decision was affirmed on appeal, [1920] 1 IR 330).

weight on the fact that the auctioneer had "insisted" on his secretary typing the document on company notepaper and not plain paper.

[5.28] The *form* of a signature is not crucial either. As we have seen in para **5.24** above, a printed name may be a sufficient signature. So may a stamp.[210] Reviewing case law O'Connor LJ said in *Halley v O'Brien*:[211]

> "Accordingly the signature may - as has been decided in many cases under this statute - take any one of a great variety of forms. It may be typewritten; commercial contracts are, of course, frequently entered into by means of an offer or acceptance where the names of the persons making the offer or accepting it are typewritten. So also it may be lithographed or printed; there is no greater magic about typewriting than about print; and many cases have been decided in which print was held to be a good signature within the statute: ...Initials will do: ... for why should not one man sign a memorandum of a contract with his initials when a painter can 'sign' his picture or an architect his plans, in that fashion? So also the signature may consist of the name in the third person; 'Mr. John Jones accepts the offer" is quite as effectual as 'I John Jones accept the offer' or 'I accept the offer, John Jones'...."

In order to be signed, a document must have a signature or mark which identifies it as an act of the relevant party but this does not prevent a signature or mark being affixed by some mechanical means other than a pen.[212] It is important to realise that although informal signatures *may* be effective it does not follow that they *must* be. A likely reason for inadequacy to satisfy the Statute is an absence of the necessary intention that the alleged signature was to authenticate the document or failure to refer to another document so as to allow the two to be read together. Thus a solicitor's initials on an attendance docket have been held not to be acceptable as a signature.[213] And the writing by a solicitor of his client's name in a draft contract was also held insufficient.[214] A solicitor who signs a document as a witness or intended witness is unlikely to be held to sign a contract or a memorandum of a contract.[215] On the other hand, signature by the vendor's auctioneer as "witness" on a private sale after an abortive auction may bind the vendor.[216] The writing of the name of a party on a document is not necessarily a signature of the party nor necessarily intended to give authenticity to the document.[217]

---

[209] [1979] IR 364 at 368.

[210] *Hudson v O'Connor* [1947] IJR 21; the agent used a stamp embossed with "Higgins & Co."

[211] [1920] IR 330 at 339.

[212] *Henry Forde & Son Finance Ltd v Forde* (HC) 13 June 1981, Carroll J, unrep at p 3 (dealing with signature as required under the Hire-Purchase Act 1946).

[213] *Kelly v Kineen* (HC) 29 April 1980, McWilliam J, unrep at 8.

[214] *Fitzgerald v Alexander* (HC) 8 May 1990, Blayney J, oral judgment. *Cf Munday v Asprey* (1880) 13 Ch D 855, 857; Fry J held that an engrossment of a conveyance containing a recital that the vendor had agreed with the purchaser for the sale to him of land at a certain price, accompanied by a signed letter referring to the engrossment and payment of the price, was not a memorandum. The basis seems to have been that it was not shown that there was a concluded agreement and indeed the contract seems not to have been proved outside the documents.

[215] *Kerns v Manning* [1935] IR 869 at p 882-3. Murnaghan J analysed the draft contract in detail and held that there could not have been an intention of bringing about a binding contract. *Cf Welford v Beazley* (1747) 3 Atk 503 approved by Murnaghan J in the *Kerns* case at p 882.

[216] *Wallace v Roe* [1903] 1 IR 32 at 35. On the facts Chatterton VC held the use of the word "witness" was "unmeaning".

[217] *McQuaid v Lynam* [1965] IR 564 at 569. The writing of the name on the document (an application form directed to a building society) was only intended to give information to the society.

Signature of memorandum by an agent

[5.29] No formality is required to give an agent authority to sign a memorandum. It follows that oral authority is enough.[218] The authority may also be implied. Thus at a sale by auction[219] the auctioneer has authority to sign a memorandum on behalf of both the purchaser[220] and the vendor.[221] It may also be implied from circumstances or from instructions given. Perhaps the classic case is the solicitor who is instructed to process to completion a contract which his client or the client's agent has already made.[222] For example a vendor's solicitor will have authority to answer requisitions and then the requisitions and replies would be likely to incorporate by reference the contract.[223] Although it is usually difficult to show that an estate agent or auctioneer has implied authority to make a contract away from auction conditions[224] he may be held to have authority as agent of one party to record his understanding of what the parties felt they had agreed and the record may be a good memorandum.[225] There may be implied authority arising from the particular relationship between client and agent[226] or from the fact that an oral deal being made, the agent says he will write a letter to the client's solicitor asking him to prepare a contract and nobody says otherwise.[227] If an unsigned contract receives later recognition by a notice given by an agent specifying the unsigned contract the agent needs no more than oral authority.[228] The onus of proving that an agent has authority to sign a memorandum is on the person alleging it though comparatively slight evidence will suffice in some cases.[229]

Ratification

[5.30] If an agent lacks authority when he signs a document that lack may be made good later by ratification. The Statute does not require that either the ratification or the authority of an agent should be in writing. It only requires some note or memorandum in writing to be signed by the party to be charged or "his agent thereunto lawfully authorised" thus leaving us to the rules of common law, as to the mode in which the agent receives his authority.[230] So the ratification may be oral[231] or by conduct.[232] The principles applying to ratification have been discussed earlier.[233]

---

[218] *McCausland v Murphy* (1881) 9 LRI 9 at 15; *Callaghan v Pepper* (1840) 2 Ir Eq R 399 at 401; *Clinan v Cooke* (1802) 1 Schoales & Lefroy 22 at 31.

[219] On auctions see para **3.45-53** *supra*.

[220] *Gardiner v Tate* (1876) IR 10 CL 460, *per* Whiteside CJ at p 464, O'Brien J at p 468 and Fitzgerald J at p 474.

[221] *McMeekin v Stevenson* [1917] 1 IR 348; *Carrigy v Brock* (1871) IR 5 CL 501 at 504.

[222] See passage quoted at para **5.17** above from O'Connor LJ in *Cloncurry v Laffan* [1924] 1 IR 78 at 84. See also *Black v Kavanagh* (1973) 108 ILTR 91 at 96.

[223] *Sheridan v Higgins* [1971] IR 291 at 300.

[224] The leading modern case is *Law v Roberts* [1964] IR 292 where seven important propositions extracted by Kenny J from the the case law are set out in the headnote. See para **3.37** *ante*.

[225] *Ballyowen Castle Homes Ltd v Collins* (HC) 26 June 1986, Keane J, unrep, at p 8.

[226] *Guardian Builders Ltd v Kelly* [1981] ILRM 127 at 131. Note that an estate agent *as such* has no implied authority to conclude a contract; this is the second of the seven principles in *Law v Roberts* (see para **3.37** above). *Cf Mortal v Lyons* (1858) 8 Ir Ch R 112 at 117.

[227] The *Guardian Builders* case at 131.

[228] *Norris v Cooke* (1857) 7 ICLR 37 at 43 at 45.

[229] As in *Kerns v Manning* [1935] IR 869 at 881.

[230] *Per* O'Dalaigh CJ giving the judgment of the Supreme Court in *Sheridan v Higgins* [1971] IR 291 at p 301 approving a passage from the judgment of Best CJ in *Maclean v Dunn* (1828) 4 Bing 722.

[231] *Callaghan v Pepper* (1840) 2 Ir Eq R 399 at 401; *Dyas v Cruise* (1845) 8 Ir Eq R 407 at 423-4 (ratification by informal letter, adoption of a lease and orally).

[232] *Barclays Bank v Breen* (1956) 96 ILTR 179 at 186 (allowing the agent to receive money on the bank's behalf); see *Dyas's* case at fn 231 *supra*.

[233] Para **3.41** above.

ACCURACY OF DESCRIPTION

[5.31] We have seen that in every contract for the sale of land or memorandum thereof some terms are always "essential" or "material" and that other terms which the parties consider essential in a particular contract will be treated as such by the courts.[234] In the most common other form of contract within the Statute of Frauds - i.e. agreements for leases - certain further terms are essential and must therefore appear in the contract or memorandum. We look now at the degree of accuracy of description of those essential matters which the courts require of a memorandum to satisfy the Statute.

[5.32] The memorandum relied on ideally should give the names of both buyer and seller.[235] However the names do not have to be actually stated if they can be ascertained from other material. Thus where a vendor was described as "selling as the executrix of the assignee of the lessee" the court could look at the lease, an assignment and a grant of probate.[236] If there is reference in a document to something *dehors* it is settled law that that something is capable of proof.[237] After some early doubt[238] the principle became clearly established that:-

> "... it is not necessary that the actual names of the parties should appear in the memorandum but if the parties are sufficiently described or indicated or referred to so that there is no real doubt as to their identity the statute is satisfied."[239]

And the result was that:

> "The application of this principle has led to considerable variety of judicial decision, and we have had cases in which the words 'proprietor', or 'owner' or 'mortgagee' has been held a sufficient description; while in other cases the words 'vendor', 'my client' and 'landlord' have been held insufficient ... I am satisfied that in all the cases the court did travel outside the four corners of the memorandum and looked at the surrounding facts and circumstances under which the document was signed and if it was thereby possible, beyond doubt,[240] to identify the person described, indicated or referred to in the memorandum, the latter was held sufficient."[241]

So in the case of a guarantee "I hereby guarantee you against any loss of any money by Mr H while in your employment to the amount of £40" it was held that the plaintiff was sufficiently identified by the words "you" and "in your employment".[242]

[5.33] The memorandum of a contract required by the Statute should not be held to be defective because one or two words in the name of a company are omitted.[243] Similarly

---

[234] Para **5.12** *ante*.

[235] *Boyce v Greene* (1826) Batty 608 at 618.

[236] *Hodgens v Keon* [1894] 2 IR 657 at 659, *per* Palles CB.

[237] *Massereene v Finlay* (1850) 13 ILR 496.

[238] See judgment in *Williams v Lake* (1859) 29 LJQB 1 (considered by Kenny J in *Bacon & Co Ltd v Kavanagh* (1908) 42 ILTR 120 at 12).

[239] *Per* Kenny J in *Bacon's* case at 121.

[240] It is unlikely that Kenny J intended to import the criminal standard of proof of being satisfied beyond reasonable doubt.

[241] *Bacon's* case, *ibid.*

[242] Kenny J placed particular weight on *Carr v Lynch* [1900] 1 Ch 613, where Farwell J held that "you" and "you having paid me £50" were a sufficient description so that the identity of the person intended could not be fairly disputed.

[243] *Law v Roberts* [1964] IR 292, 304, *per* Kenny J. See also *Guardian Builders Ltd v Kelly* [1981] ILRM 127, 132; *Irvine v Dane* (1850) 2 Ir Jur 209.

an individual and a company controlled by him may be sufficiently covered by the reference to the individual alone on the ground that the parties can be readily identified.[244] It is important to remember that a purchaser is normally entitled[245] to take his conveyance in any name or names he wishes and this is frequently done.[246] In such cases there is no valid objection on the ground that the names put forward are not covered by the memorandum.

[5.34] The property need not be stated with complete accuracy. The test is that it should be "readily identifiable".[247] Thus, if a letter is headed "The Nurseries Park Avenue" and it states that a sale had been concluded of "half of the above site" and that the site area had been agreed, oral evidence can be let in to identify the property exactly.[248] A description of the property sold as "this place" in a letter written by the vendor let in oral evidence of where the letter was written and thus became a sufficient description.[249] When a description of this sort is used without qualification *prima facie* it will cover the entire of the relevant property.[250]

[5.35] The price of property sold is of the essence of a contract for sale.[251] Until the purchase price has been ascertained there is no contract between the parties which the court can specifically enforce.[252] If the purchase price is misstated by a document offered as a memorandum the Statute is not satisfied.[253] This is so even where a misstatement is made by agreement and does not involve illegality.[254] Arrangements relating to the manner of payment of purchase money may be material terms and thus need to be evidenced by the memorandum. These could include items such as an immediate large down payment[255] or payment of the price by instalments as houses are completed.[256]

Parties may agree that a price will be fixed by valuation or arbitration and if so the fact that the price is to be fixed by such a method must appear from the memorandum. It

---

[244] The *Guardian Builders* case at 131-2. But *cf Carthy v O'Neill* [1981] ILRM 443 where the letters relied on were inadequate because they did not identify a wife who was joint owner. *Cf Dublin Laundry Co Ltd v Clarke* [1989] ILRM 29, 37-8 where a person dealt with the intention that the obligations and benefits of his contract would be taken over by a company to be formed.

[245] *Ie* in the absence of a provision to the contrary in any contract. In a case where there is an issue about the adequacy of a memorandum this will rarely arise. However, there is no reason why parties should not agree that the precise identity of the purchaser is to be a material term. The identity of an intended *lessee* is more likely to be material: see *Silver Wraith Ltd v Siuicre Eireann Cpt* (HC) 8 June 1989, Keane J, unrep at p 7-8.

[246] *Guerin v Ryan* (HC) 28 April 1978, McWilliam J, unrep at 9.

[247] *Guardian Builders Ltd v Kelly* [1981] ILRM 127 at 131. Of course, if the documents do not refer to the property at all there cannot be a good memorandum: *Law v Murphy* (HC) 12 April 1978. McWilliam J at p 2 (no reference to area to be leased).

[248] *Ibid*. The oral evidence produced a map which had been agreed between the parties.

[249] *Waldron v Jacob* (1870) IR 5 Eq 131 at 136. Chatterton VC applied the maxim *id certum est quod certum reddi potest* - ie, that is certain which can be rendered certain.

[250] *Waldron's* case at p 137.

[251] *Carr v Phelan* [1976-7] ILRM 149 at 153.

[252] *Ibid*.

[253] *Black v Greally* (HC) Costello J, 10 November 1977, unrep at 20-21.

[254] As in *Black's* case. The document gave the balance after payment of the deposit as the purchase price. Costello J said at p 21: "It is not apt to describe the resultant written document as a memorandum 'of' the parties' oral agreement (as it does not properly state the full consideration for the sale); rather it is a memorandum which is 'in accordance with' one of the stipulations of the oral agreement which is not quite the same thing." However, the defendant was not let rely on the point to escape liability; that would have been fraudulent use of the Statute: p 21.

[255] As in *Tattan v Cadogan* [1979] ILRM 61.

[256] *Kelly v Danaher* (HC) 12 June 1970, Teevan J, unrep at pp 1-2.

remains to be seen how far the Irish courts will approve the decision of the House of Lords in *Sudbrook Trading Estate Ltd v Eggleton*[257] and hold that if machinery agreed by the parties for ascertainment of the price breaks down, then, providing that it is subsidiary and non-essential to the main part of an agreement, the courts may substitute other machinery to ascertain the price in order to ensure that the agreement is carried out. The Court of Appeal[258] had analysed extensive case law since 1807[259] and deduced and applied the consistent judicial opinion that if one term such as price is left to be determined either by agreement of the parties, which is not forthcoming, or by determination of some other person,and the procedure designated fails or the persons designated fail to reach a conclusion, the agreement is not enforceable.[260] The majority of the House of Lords held that though the machinery for fixing the price had proved inoperable it was in the circumstances of the case to be disregarded, thus enabling the court to give effect to the intention of the parties which was that the sale should be carried out at a fair and reasonable price.[261] The basis of the House of Lords decision is that the earlier decisions had erred in invariably treating the machinery for ascertaining the price as an essential part of the agreement. The proper method for determining in any case whether the agreed machinery could be abandoned was whether the mode of ascertaining the price was an essential term of the contract or whether, though indicated in the contract, it is subsidiary and non-essential.[262] In any event the courts have no power to go so far as substituting a completely different mode of ascertaining the purchase price to that envisaged or intended by the parties.[263]

Agreements for lease

[5.36] We have seen that the date of commencement of a lease or tenancy or the means of ascertaining it is an essential term of an agreement for lease.[264] It follows that a document relied on as a memorandum to satisfy the Statute must cover the commencement date of the term.[265] It must appear reasonably clearly and if a court is left in doubt which of two or more dates is intended the memorandum is bad.[266] The duration of a lease or tenancy is another essential term[267] and must be ascertainable from the memorandum.[268] Likewise the rent must be ascertainable from the memorandum.[269] As in cases of outright sales identification of the parties and the property is vital and must be evidenced in writing.[270] Where there are fines or covenants to spend money on premises

---

[257] [1983] 1 AC 444; [1982] 3 All ER 1. See further Clark, *Contract Law in Ireland*, 3rd Ed (1992) at 29-31.

[258] Reported at [1981] 3 All ER 105.

[259] Including *Milnes v Gery* 14 Ves 400; [1803-1813] All ER Rep 369 which was approved by Hamilton J in *Carr's* case at 155.

[260] Per Gibson LJ in *Lonergan v McCartney* [1983] NI 129, 131. He distinguished the *Sudbrook* case for reasons given at 133-5. *Lonergan's* case, *Carr's* case and the *Sudbrook* case all involved actual contracts, not memoranda.

[261] *Per* Gibson LJ, *ibid.*

[262] As analysed by Gibson LJ in the *Lonergan* case at 133.

[263] *Carr v Phelan* [1976/7] ILRM 149 at 155.

[264] Para **3.16** *supra*.

[265] *Law v Murphy* (HC) 12 April 1978, McWilliam J, unrep at 2; *Conaty v Ulster Developments Ltd* (HC) 4 October 1965, Lowry J, unrep at 6; *Biggs v Brennan* (1907) 41 ILTR 60; *White v McMahon* (1886) 18 LRI 460 at 465-6.

[266] *Williams v Kenneally* (1912) 46 ILTR 292 at 294.

[267] See para **3.17** above.

[268] *Clinan v Cooke* (1802) 1 Schoales & Lefroy 22 at 32-3; *Crane v Naughten* [1912] 2 IR 318 at 326.

[269] *Shannon v Bradstreet* (1803) 1 Schoales & Lefroy 52 at 73.

[270] *Conaty v Ulster Developments Ltd* (HC) 4 October 1965, Lowry J, unrep at 4-5.

these are likely to be material terms of particular contracts needing to be covered by the memorandum though in some cases they are capable of being waived or may be collateral.[271] At least *some* lessee's covenants are likely to be material terms especially if the intending landlord already holds under a lease himself.[272] Questions of personal guarantees are likely to be material particularly if proposed lettings are at market rents.[273]

---

[271] *Scott v McCombe,* CA (NI) 2 June 1965, unrep, esp at p 7 of the transcript. See also para **3.17** *ante*.
[272] *Conaty's* case at 6.
[273] *Silver Wraith Ltd v Siucre Eireann Cpt* (HC) 8 June 1989, Keane J, unrep at 7-8. See also para **3.17** *ante*.

Chapter 6

Part Performance

[6.01] The principle underlying the doctrine of part performance is that the court will not allow a statute which was passed to prevent fraud to be made itself an instrument of fraud.[1] To prevent that happening the court disregards the absence of that formality which the statute requires when insistence upon it would render it a means of effecting, instead of averting, fraud.[2] A party who has permitted another to perform acts on the faith of an agreement is not allowed to insist that the agreement is bad and that he is entitled to treat those acts as if the agreement never existed.[3] So where the party seeking relief has taken some step in pursuance of his contract which has left him in such a position that it would amount to a fraud or be inequitable for the other party to rely on the fact that there was no sufficient memorandum of the contract, the case is taken out of the Statute of Frauds and the courts will enforce the contract.[4]

The modern English approach has been similar. As Lord Reid explained in *Steadman v Steadman:*[5]

> "If one party to an agreement stands by and lets the other party incur expense or prejudice his position on the faith of the agreement being valid he will not then be allowed to turn round and assert that the agreement is unenforceable. Using fraud in its older and less precise sense, that would be fraudulent on his part and it has become proverbial that courts of equity will not permit the statute to be made an instrument of fraud.
>
> It must be remembered that this legislation did not and does not make oral contracts relating to land void; it only makes them unenforceable. And the statutory provision must be pleaded; otherwise the court does not apply it. So it is in keeping with equitable principles that in proper circumstances a person will not be allowed 'fraudulently' to take advantage of a defence of this kind."[6]

If in reliance on a contract a plaintiff conveys land to a third party, enters into occupation of premises agreed to be let or sold to him, ejects tenants at the request of the other party or begins to carry on business in partnership[7] he may rely on part performance.[8] If he has taken some "conclusive", "irrevocable" or "prejudicial" step[9] in pursuance of the contract that step is likely to be a sufficient act of part performance. The doctrine is applicable in any case in which a court of equity would decree specific performance.[10] The Irish courts

---

[1] *Per* Andrews LJ in *Lowry v Reid* [1927] NI 142 at 154.

[2] *Ibid.*

[3] See judgment of Palles CB in *Crowley v O'Sullivan* [1900] 2 IR 478, at p 491 quoting from the judgment of Kay J in *McManus v Cooke* (1887) 35 Ch D 681 (Kay J himself quoting from an earlier case).

[4] *Howlin v Thomas F. Power (Dublin) Ltd* (HC) 5 May 1978, McWilliam J, unrep at 6.

[5] [1976] AC 536 at p 540; [1974] 2 All ER 977 at p 980-1. But note the major change in English law mentioned in para **6.09** *infra*.

[6] See also Lord Simon at [1976] AC 558, [1974] 2 All ER 996 and Lord Salmon at [1976] AC 566, [1974] 2 All ER 1003.

[7] Note that in a case involving partnership, *Crowley v O'Sullivan* [1900] 2 IR 478, a sale of land was involved but at pp 489-92 Palles CB concludes that the doctrine is not confined to cases of sales of "land". *Cf Bagnell v Edwards* (1876) 10 IR Eq 215. On partnership see paras **1.13, 1.25** *ante*.

[8] These three examples given by McWilliam J in *Howlin's* case at 6-7 from the case law considered by him.

[9] *Ibid*, McWilliam J's adjectives in relation to his examples.

[10] *Crowley v O'Sullivan* [1900] 2 IR 478 at 489-492, *per* Palles CB.

have rejected arguments that it can apply only in cases of sales of land.[11] The position was less clear-cut in England but the better modern view seems to have been similar to the Irish one.[12]

[6.02] The doctrine has been described as "engrafted" on the Statute.[13] At first impression it might be thought to actually *overrule* or *contradict* the words of the Statute[14] and occasionally an older judgment shows regret that the cases have taken agreements out of the Statute.[15] The doctrine's compatibility with the Statute may perhaps be supported by the thought that when the Statute says that no action is to be brought to charge any person upon a contract concerning land it has in view the simple case in which he is charged upon the contract only and not that in which there are equities arising from *res gestae* subsequent to and arising out of the contract.[16] It has been said also that the right to relief rests not so much on the contract as on what has been done in pursuance to or in execution of it.[17] And that in a suit based on part performance the defendant is really "charged" upon the equities resulting from the acts done in the execution of the contract and not (within the meaning of the Statute) upon the contract itself.[18]

Operating on conscience

[6.03] The doctrine works by operating on the *conscience* of the person charged. As Lord Redesdale explained in 1802:[19]

> "The Statute of Frauds says that no action or suit shall be maintained on an agreement relating to lands which is not in writing signed by the party to be charged with it; and yet the court is in the daily habit of relieving, where the party seeking relief has been put into a situation which makes it against conscience in the other party to insist on the want of writing so signed, as a bar to his relief."[20]

The question in each case is whether the plaintiff has an equity arising from part performance which is so "affixed to the conscience" of the defendant that it would amount to fraud on his part to take advantage of the absence of writing.[21] Under the doctrine of part performance the equity must be possessed not by the person to be charged but by the plaintiff - the person who seeks relief; and this equity arises from his

---

[11] *Lowry's* case at 157; *Crowley's* case at 489-492.

[12] Jones & Goodhart, *Specific Performance* at 101, published in 1986 before a major change in English law in 1989 noted in para **6.09** *infra*.

[13] By Chatterton VC in *Hope v Cloncurry* (1874) IR 8 Eq 555 at 557.

[14] For the wording see para **5.01** *ante*.

[15] *Eg*, Lord Manners LC in *Savage v Carroll* (1814) 2 Ball & Beatty 444 at 456. *Cf Toole v Medlicott* (1810) 1 Ball & Beatty 393 at 404. Note Lord Redesdale's reservations about carrying the doctrine of part performance too far: *Lindsay v Lynch* (1804) 2 Schoales & Lefroy 1 at 5.

[16] *Per* Flanagan J in *Lanyon v Martin* (1884) 13 LRI 297 at 302 quoting a passage from Lord Selborne in *Maddison v Alderson* 8 App Cas 467.

[17] By Andrews LJ in *Lowry v Reid* [1927] NI 142 at 155.

[18] Lord Selborne in *Maddison v Alderson* 8 App Cas 467, 475 approved by Palles CB in *Crowley v O'Sullivan* 478 at 489.

[19] In *Bond v Hopkins* (1802) 1 Schoales & Lefroy 413 at 433. The passage quoted is followed by a review of case law and is approved by Andrews LJ in *Lowry v Reid* [1927] NI 142 at 154.

[20] Note Lord Redesdale's reservations about carrying the doctrine of part performance too far in *Lindsay v Lynch* (1804) 2 Schoales & Lefroy 1 at 5. Sugden LC had no intention of "going beyond the authorities": *Brennan v Bolton* (1842) 2 Drury & Warren 349 at 356.

[21] *Per* Andrews LJ in *Lowry v Reid* [1927] NI 142 at 154-5.

part performance of the contract.[22] However, an event may be an act by *both* sides. For example, where an intending purchaser or tenant gets possession that is both an act of taking possession by him and one of giving possession by the intending vendor or landlord. Where parties agree on a reduced rent the tenant part performs by availing of the reduction tendering at the reduced rate and accepting a receipt; the landlord part performs by accepting the reduced rent and letting the tenant remain in possession.[23] It has been said that "nothing is considered as part performance which does not put the party into a situation that it is a fraud upon him unless the agreement is performed".[24] If the act relied on as part performance can be undone the fraud or equity which gives the right to rely on part performance to get over the lack of writing may possibly be removed.[25] If there is no fraud on the part of the person sued the doctrine cannot be used with success. Thus a remainderman who knows nothing of the agreement and has not acquiesced in the acts of part performance normally will not be bound.[26] If the remainderman does acquiesce he is likely to be bound.[27] And if a lease is agreed by a tenant for life within his leasing powers the remainderman normally will be bound.[28]

[6.04] This approach based on conscience is not confined to claims for specific performance or to cases involving the Statute of Frauds and conscience may be bound even where the person affected has, for example, got a court conveyance which on its face gives him absolute title.[29] The doctrine of part performance also applies to claims for specific performance where contracts are invalid or irregular for reasons unconnected with the Statute as, for example, where a contract by a corporation should have been made under the corporate seal.[30] In such a case it does not matter whether the body pleading the lack of proper execution of the contract is plaintiff or defendant.[31]

Need for a concluded contract

[6.05] For a plaintiff to get as far as relying on part performance there must be a concluded contract. If there is no valid contract the question of part performance does not arise.[32] The plaintiff must be able to show what the material terms of his claimed contract are. If a court believes that there was a complete and binding agreement between the parties but the plaintiff fails to satisfy it of the certainty of its terms specific performance cannot be decreed.[33] It has been said in older cases involving questions of part

---

[22]   *Ibid*, p 155. He makes the important distinction that under the Statute a note or memorandum must be signed by the party to be charged but under the doctrine of part performance the equity must be possessed by the person seeking relief.

[23]   *Beauclerk v Hanna* (1888) 23 LRI 144 at 150.

[24]   *Clinan v Cooke* (1802) 1 Schoales & Lefroy 22 at 41.

[25]   *Howlin v Thomas F Power (Dublin) Ltd* (HC) 5 May 1978, McWilliam J, unrep at 9 - tender of repayment of money paid. See money paid as part performance in paras **6.13-15** *infra*.

[26]   *Hope v Cloncurry* (1874) IR 8 Eq 555 at 557. *Cf O'Fay v Burke* (1858) 8 Ir Ch R 511.

[27]   *Shannon v Bradstreet* (1803) 1 Schoales & Lefroy 52 at 73-4. *Cf Lowe v Swift* (1814) 2 Ball & Beatty 529.

[28]   *Shannon's* case at 59-62. *Cf Lowe's* case at 535.

[29]   *O'Hanlon v Murdock* [1901] 1 IR 122 where the defendant tried to work a fraud by sheltering under a Landed Estates Court Conveyance.

[30]   As in *Steeven's Hospital v Dyas* (1864) 15 Ir Ch R 405 at 420-1. The plaintiff had power under statute to make leases. *Cf Dublin Corporation v Blackrock Commissioners* (1882) 16 ILTR 111 where the defendants had already got all they were entitled to under the contract: p 112, Palles CB.

[31]   *Donovan v South Dublin Guardians* 5 NIJR 106.

[32]   *McQuaid v Lynam* [1965] IR 564 at 574.

[33]   *Williams v Kenneally* (1912) 46 ILTR 292 at 294. *Cf Harnett v Yielding* (1805) 2 Schoales & Lefroy 549.

performance that "the terms of the contract must be made out satisfactorily to the court".[34] And that the terms of the agreement alleged to be part performed must be shown "plainly and distinctly".[35] There are also indications that evidence of the part performance by plaintiffs seeking specific performance against estates of deceased persons should be treated with great caution.[36] The point has been made

> "...when no such written instrument exists I do think that the utmost caution must be observed in fastening on a man in his grave a contract binding his estate..."[37]

A plaintiff may expect that his evidence will be "rigorously scrutinised" if the other party to the alleged agreement is dead.[38] However the onus of proof remains the balance of probability.[39] If there is a concluded contract it will not matter that instead of being entirely oral it is partly in writing and partly oral; the doctrine of part performance may be invoked.[40]

Reference to a contract

[6.06] The acts of part performance relied on must be referable to a contract. The modern view is that they do not have to be referable to any particular contract. The true principle seems to be that the operation of the doctrine of part performance requires only that the acts in question be such that they must be referred to some contract and may be referred to the alleged one; that they prove the existence of some contract and are consistent with the contract alleged.[41] Keane J has said that the acts should be "unequivocally referable" to the "type of" contract alleged.[42] That is a different matter from having to unequivocally refer to the particular contract alleged. The same judge writing in *Equity and the Law of Trusts in the Republic of Ireland*[43] has suggested that the current of modern authority favours the less strict view - ie that acts will suffice if they are unequivocally referable to a contract of the nature alleged and are at least not inconsistent with the existence of the particular contract. That view ties in well with the approach of Andrews LJ in *Lowry v Reid*[44] and with a general modern view that a strict application of the Statute may carry more risk of permitting injustice and in that sense encouraging a fraud than a liberal application would do.[45] It is also consistent with the mainstream of recent English authority. As Lord Simon explained in *Steadman v Steadman*:[46]

---

[34] *Mortal v Lyons* (1858) 8 Ir Ch R 112 at 118.
[35] *Lanyon v Martin* (1884) 13 LRI 297 at 301.
[36] *Hope v Cloncurry* (1874) IR 8 Eq 555 (court not satisfied that defendant tenant in tail stood by with knowledge of an alleged oral agreement with his father while the plaintiff expended money); *Howe v Hall* (1870) IR 4 Eq 242: (plaintiff trying to rely on increased rent, draining and planting).
[37] *Howe's* case at 252.
[38] *Steadman v Steadman* [1976] AC 536 at 566; [1974] 2 All ER 977 at 1002.
[39] *Ibid. Cf* rectification at para **10.22** below.
[40] *Lanyon v Martin* (1884) 13 LRI 297 at 301.
[41] *Per* Andrews LJ in *Lowry v Reid*. [1927] NI 142 at 159-60. Moore LCJ refers at 151 to defence counsel arguing that acts of part performance must "unequivocally establish" the existence of "some such contract".
[42] Words used by Keane J in *Silver Wraith Ltd v Siuicre Eireann Cpt* (HC) 8 June 1989, unrep at 12. The plaintiff fell at the first hurdle by failing to prove a concluded contract and Keane J dealt with part performance out of deference to arguments of counsel.
[43] At para 16.14.
[44] On which the third sentence in this para is based.
[45] As voiced by Finlay P in *Doherty v Gallagher* (HC) 9 June 1975, unrep at p 13 (on the adequacy of a memorandum).
[46] [1976] AC 536 at p 562; [1974] 2 All ER 977 at p 999.

"If the plaintiff proves that he carried out acts in part performance of *some contract* to which the defendant was a party while the latter stood by, it becomes inequitable that the latter should be allowed to plead, in exoneration of reciprocal obligations, that *any such contract* was unenforceable by reason of the statute - particularly when it is borne in mind that few acts of performance point exclusively to a particular contract, least of all a particular multi-term contract. But 'some such contract' must be a contract with the defendant - otherwise no equity arises against him to preclude his pleading the statute."[47]

Lord Morris, Viscount Dilhorne and Lord Salmon all approved this passage from the 6th Ed (1921) of Fry on *Specific Performance*:

"The true principle however of the operation of acts of part performance seems only to require that the acts in question be such as must be referred to some contract and may be referred to the alleged one; that they prove the existence of some contract, and are consistent with the contract alleged."[48]

While the language used by judges sometimes suggests a need for a higher standard of proof than the normal one in civil proceedings of proof on the balance of probabilities, the modern view is that that normal civil standard of proof does apply though the evidence will be more jealously scrutinised where the other party to the alleged contract is dead.[49] It is sufficient to show that it was more likely than not that the acts proved were in part performance of some contract to which the defendant was a party.[50]

[6.07] Some older Irish case law may have tended towards a more exacting requirement that the acts of part performance must be referable to the particular contract alleged. However the cases need a careful look because, although they do use phrases which could suggest that view, they do not necessarily decide that nothing less would do. Some in fact are close to the modern view. Thus Lord Manners LC said in *Savage v Carroll*:[51]

"Now whether the Possession be an unequivocal Act, amounting to Part Performance, must depend upon the Transaction itself, whether it be so circumstanced that it can refer only to a Contract of Sale; if it be so, the Party may go into Evidence of the Terms of that Contract."

And a few lines later:

"Here I think it is such a Delivery of Possession, accompanied by the other Circumstances, as refers to a Contract of Sale, and would render it a Fraud in either Party to recede: the Evidence then of the Terms of the Contract is in my Opinion admissible."

In both passages the *indefinite* article in the phrase "a Contract of Sale" should be noted. In *Toole v Medlicott*[52] he said of the acts set up:

"...Delivery of Possession and Expenditure of Money, in the permanent Improvement of the Land, are strong marked Circumstances and naturally imply the Existence of an Agreement for a Lease, and then Parol Evidence is admitted to prove the Terms."

---

[47] The italics are Lord Simon's.
[48] At p 278 of Fry, quoted by Lord Morris at [1976] AC 546; [1974] 2 All ER 986; by Viscount Dilhorne at [1976] AC 553; [1974] 2 All ER 992; and by Lord Salmon at [1976] AC 569; [1974] 2 All ER 1004.
[49] See discussion by Lord Simon in *Steadman's* case at [1976] AC 563-4; [1974] 2 All ER 1000-1. *Cf* Lord Reid at [1976] AC 541; [1974] 2 All ER 981. See also para **6.05** *ante*.
[50] *Steadman's* case at [1976] AC 564; [1974] 2 All ER 1001.
[51] (1810) 1 Ball & Beatty 265 at p 282.
[52] (1810) 1 Ball & Beatty 393 at 404.

Neither the use of the words "naturally imply" nor the indefinite article in "an Agreement for a Lease" suggests a very strict approach. In *Humphreys v Green*[53] Baggallay LJ said:

"The fact of the plaintiff being in possession of the property was not a sufficient part performance of the parol agreement, for it was equally consistent with his continuing in possession under his previous tenancy, as of his possession being due to some agreement between himself and his landlord. Moreover Lord Cranworth[54] declined to treat a proved expenditure of money upon the property as a part performance; but he held that there was a clear part performance by payment and acceptance of the Michaelmas rent at the increased rate, being of opinion that the payment of the increased amount could be referable only to some agreement; and upon that ground, and upon that ground alone, he made a decree for specific performance."

The word "some" before "agreement" near the end of that passage may be noted. In *Conner v Fitzgerald*[55] Chatterton VC said of the relevant acts that they "can only be referred to that agreement" but as he had just approved the above passage from the judgment of Baggallay LJ and he also approved the judgment in *Nunn v Fabian*[56] he clearly meant that the acts did refer to the particular agreement, not that they necessarily had to.

[6.08] Language used in other Irish cases does seem to support the view that acts of part performance must be referable to the actual. contract. In *Kine v Balfe*[57] Lord Manners LC said of the act claimed:

"If it be distinctly referable to the Contract alleged in the Pleadings, I think no case has denied that it is a Part-performance"

and then, having described the taking of possession,[58] asked "How is it possible to refer this Possession to any other Title?" In *Moore v Crofton*[59] the continuance in possession could "only be referred to the contract". In *Beauclerk v Hanna*[60] Chatterton VC described the acts as "referable to the very agreement relied on by the plaintiff". In *Howe v Hall*[61] Sullivan MR said that the court ought not to be deterred from giving effect to a "clearly proved verbal contract" when part performance is "plainly referable to it". In all four cases the particular agreement alleged was pleaded as would be normal practice. In the first three the courts held that there were concluded agreements and the acts of part performance were clearly referable to them but in *Howe's* case the court was not satisfied that there had been a concluded agreement. There is no clear inconsistency between these cases and the modern view.[62] In the first three the claimant would obviously have also

---

[53] 10 QBD 148, cited with approval by Chatterton VC in *Conner v Fitzgerald* (1883) 11 LRI 106 at 115.

[54] A reference to Lord Cranworth's decision in *Nunn v Fabian* LR 1 Ch 35 which Chatterton VC. also approved in *Conner's* case at 114-5. The tenant in *Nunn's* case already had a tenancy; entry into possession and expenditure on the property by a person who has agreed to take one will normally be sufficient part performance: see para. **6.10** *infra*.

[55] (1883) 11 LRI 106 at 115.

[56] L R 1 Ch 35. It was also approved by Christian J in *Archbold v Lord Howth* (1866) IR 1 CL 608, 621 and by Sullivan MR in *Howe v Hall* IR 4 Eq 242 at 252.

[57] (1813) 2 Ball & Beatty 343 at p 348.

[58] The plaintiff signed the agreement and "the defendant immediately took it up, carried it off, went into possession and has ever since paid rent according to the Terms of the Agreement": p 348.

[59] (1846) 9 Ir Eq R 344 at p 349.

[60] (1888) 23 LRI 144 at 150.

[61] (1870) IR 4 Eq 242 at 252.

[62] Discussed at para **6.06** *supra*.

succeeded if the modern view had been expressly applied but there is nothing in the judgments which clearly shows that the claimants *had to* tie in the acts of part performance with their contracts by a test as exacting as being unequivocally referable to the particular contracts. In *Howe's* case the claimant had to fail anyway when he failed to prove a concluded contract.

Major change in English law

[6.09] There has been a major change in English law by the Law of Property (Miscellaneous Provisions) Act 1989 which repealed s 40[63] of the Law of Property Act 1925 save in relation to contracts made before 27 September 1989.[64] The new position may be summarised thus[65]:

> "In the first place a contract for the sale or other disposition of an interest in land can now only be made in writing: this goes beyond the old requirement that there be written evidence of a contract (which could have been made orally). All the terms which the parties have expressly agreed must be incorporated in one document or, where contracts are exchanged, in each. Secondly, the contract or, where exchange takes place, one copy (but not necessarily the same one) must be signed by or on behalf of each party: this goes further than s 40 which merely required signature by or on behalf of the party to be charged."

There are no exceptions in respect of sales by the court or part performance.[66] The doctrine of part performance thus disappears from the field of equity in England after two and a half centuries.[67] The intention of the 1989 Act is to prevent disputes over whether the parties had entered into a binding agreement or over what terms they had agreed.[68] It will be interesting to see whether the 1989 cure turns out any better than the Statute of Frauds disease. The new Act may assist gazumpers.[69] Certainly they will have latitude from the phrase "all the terms which the parties have expressly agreed".[70] It is unclear that the courts will be able to confine that provision to "material" or "essential" terms; so parties whose express agreement includes some terms which are less than "material" or "essential" may not have a contract at all.[71]

Examples of part performance

[6.10] The classic example of a sufficient act of part performance is the giving and taking of possession. An intending vendor or landlord gives it and the intending purchaser or tenant takes it. As we have seen,[72] this is normally a part performance by each side so both will be enabled to enforce the oral contract. The situation must be distinguished from one

---

[63] Which was similar to s 2 of the Irish Statute of Frauds.
[64] Section 2 of the 1989 Act replaced s 40 of the 1925 Act.
[65] Snell's, *Equity*, 29th Ed (1990) p 601.
[66] *Ibid*. There *are* exceptions in relation to contracts made in the course of a public auction and contracts to grant a lease to take effect in possession for a term not exceeding 3 years at the best rent reasonably obtainable: Snell, *ibid*. There appears to be a growth in England of "lock-out" agreements by which A agrees not to negotiate with anyone except B in relation to the sale of a property for a specified period: *Pitt v PHH Asset Management Ltd* [1993] 4 All ER 961; [1993] 2 EGLR 217.
[67] Snell, *op cit*, p 601-2.
[68] *Per* Hoffmann J in *Spiro v Glencrown Properties Ltd* [1991] 1 All ER 600 at 602.
[69] This breed is discussed at para **5.02** *ante*.
[70] The words appear in s 2(1); the contract can be made "only by incorporating" all those terms.
[71] See para **5.12** *ante* on the extent to which terms have to appear in a note or memorandum to satisfy the Statute of Frauds.
[72] Para **6.03** *supra*.

where the claimant is already in possession.[73] Often other acts will accompany the taking of possession and these are likely to strengthen the case further. Thus, entry and demolition of buildings will suffice.[74] Entry and use of the property for the plaintiff's business with both parties contributing to the cost of improvements will be enough.[75] Entry on premises coupled with expenditure on the property should do.[76] In cases of agreements for a lease or tenancy the simple facts of entry into possession and payment of rent are sufficient acts of part performance.[77]

[6.11] Mere continuance of a tenant in possession will not normally suffice as part performance of an oral agreement for a new tenancy. As Lord Sugden LC explained in 1842:[78]

"...the rule is perfectly clear, that if a man is in possession of land as tenant, a mere parol agreement cannot have any operation in law[79] for the Statute of Frauds is in the way, and there is nothing, but the subsisting tenancy to which this court can refer any act, which may have been done, where it is consistent with his character as tenant. His remaining in possession is a mere continuance of the character, which he all along filled, and any act which may be thus referred to a title distinct from the agreement cannot be considered as operating to take the case out of the Statute. I cannot, therefore, refer any act of the tenant after his possession as tenant, to a new tenancy under a parol agreement."

There may be doubt about cases where tenants stay in possession at a reduced rent as the decrease may be explainable as an abatement or voluntary reduction by the landlord[80] as well as by a new parol agreement.[81] The evidence in the particular case is likely to be vital.[82] Monroe J warned in *Haire-Foster v McIntee*[83] that clear and specific proof should be given to satisfy the court that increased or decreased rent was referable to an alleged parol agreement and that it could not reasonably be attributable to anything else. However, we have noted earlier[84] the view of Lord Cranworth that payment of an increased amount could be referable only to some agreement and that that view was approved by Chatterton VC so the warning of Monroe J may be best directed to cases of reduced rents.[85] One thing *not* usually expected of a tenant whose established tenancy continues is payment of an increased rent[86] and for that reason the view of Lord

---

[73] Usually under an existing lease or tenancy. See para **6.11** *infra*.
[74] *Starling Securities Ltd v Woods* (HC) 24 May 1977, McWilliam J, unrep at p 6.
[75] *McCarter & Co Ltd v Roughan* [1986] ILRM 447 at 449-50.
[76] *In re Sullivan's Estate* (1889) 23 LRI 255 at 256; *Hope v Cloncurry* (1874) IR 8 Eq 555 at 557; *Toole v Medlicott* (1810) 1 Ball & Beatty 393 at 404; *Shannon v Bradstreet* (1803) 1 Schoales & Lefroy 52 at 73-4. *Cf O'Fay v Burke* (1858) 8 Ir Ch R 511.
[77] *Kine v Balfe* (1813) 2 Ball & Beatty 343 at 348. *Cf Clinan v Cook* (1802) 1 Schoales & Lefroy 22.
[78] *Brennan v Bolton* 2 Drury & Warren 349 at p 354.
[79] The distinction between a *contract for* and a *grant of* a tenancy is discussed by Wylie in *Irish Landlord and Tenant Law* at paras 5.01-03. Note also that Lord Sugden's judgment predated Deasy's Act.
[80] See abatement of rent, Wylie, *op cit*, para 10.10-11.
[81] Chatterton VC could have had difficulty about this point in *Beauclerk v Hanna* (1888) 23 LRI 144 at 149.
[82] As in *Beauclerk's* case where at p 150 Chatterton VC relied on an admission by the tenant that the reduced rent of £24 was a "judicial rent" which was "quite conclusive of the existence of the parol agreement alleged by the plaintiff, and that the reduced rent was accepted on the faith of it." In *Foster v McIntee* (1889) 23 LRI 529 the evidence was insufficient.
[83] (1889) 23 LRI 528, 534.
[84] Para **6.07** *supra*.
[85] As in the case before him.
[86] Unless the lease or tenancy provides for a specific increase or contains a rent review clause or a statute allows an increase to be obtained. Wylie discusses rent review in Ch 11 of *Irish Landlord and Tenant Law* and the fixing of rents under the Housing (Private Rented Dwellings) Acts 1982 and 1983 in paras 29.31-32. On the latter see also de Blacam, *Private Rented Dwellings*, 2nd Ed (1992) at 41-4.

Cranworth and its approval by Chatterton VC seem well rooted in common sense. If a tenant's term has expired and the tenant has no title when an oral agreement is made the facts that he is permitted to remain in possession and pays rent will be sufficient part performance.[87] Of course if the tenant has statutory rights his continuation in possession may be referable to those rights.[88] Some tenancies may provide for a fixed term followed by a tenancy from month to month or other period[89] and other tenancies may have clauses to the effect that if the agreed term shall continue beyond its expiry date the tenancy is deemed to be one terminable by specified notice to quit.[90] And if a tenant simply continues in possession after the expiry of a term and pays rent which is accepted without there being any new agreement a new periodic tenancy is likely to be held to have arisen.[91]

[6.12] Things which would normally be expected to be done by a tenant will not usually be sufficient acts of part performance. So alleged improvements and expenditure by a farm tenant may be no more than what takes place in the ordinary course of husbandry.[92] And improvements of "no substantial value" done by a tenant may not be enough to persuade a judge that they were made in reliance on a promise of a lease.[93] The fact that rents of a landlord's other tenants have been increased at the same time as the plaintiff's may weigh against a higher rent paid by him being sufficient.[94]

Money payments as part performance

[6.13] Before *Steadman v Steadman*[95] it was thought that the mere payment of money could never be a sufficient act of part performance.[96] Lord Redesdale pointed out:-[97]

> "Payment of money is not part-performance for it may be repaid; and then the parties will be just as they were before especially if repaid with interest."

In *Steadman's* case four of the five Law Lords and two of the three Judges of the Court of Appeal refused to accept the proposition that the mere payment of money could not constitute a sufficient act of part performance.[98] As Lord Salmon explained:

> "Although I accept the authorities which show that acts of part performance if they are to take a parol contract out of the statute must be acts from which the nature of the contract can be deduced, I do not accept the line of authority which ...laid down that payment can never constitute such an act because it is impossible to deduce from payment the nature of the contract in respect of which the payment is made. It is no doubt true that often it is impossible to deduce even the existence of any contract from

---

[87] *Lanyon v Martin* (1884) 13 LRI 297 at p 301.
[88] See *Baumann v Elgin Contractors Ltd* [1973] IR 169 in relation to the Landlord and Tenant Act 1931 and *McCombe v Sheehan* [1954] IR 183 in relation to the former Rent Restrictions Acts.
[89] As in *Esso Teo v Wong* [1975] IR 416.
[90] *Forte v Wright* (1908) 42 ILTR 264.
[91] Wylie, *Irish Landlord and Tenant Law* para 4.13. The position may be different if, *eg*, a tenant has statutory rights (see the cases in fn 88) or negotiations occur.
[92] *Brennan v Bolton* (1842) 2 Drury & Warren 349 at 355.
[93] *Howe v Hall* (1870) IR 4 Eq 242 at 251.
[94] *Howe's* case at p 254.
[95] [1976] AC 536; [1974] 2 All ER 977.
[96] *Clinan v Cooke* (1802) 1 Schoales & Lefroy 22 at 40-42. This case is cited by Jones & Goodhart, *Specific Performance* (1986) as authority for this proposition at 104.
[97] *Clinan's* case at 41.
[98] As noted by McWilliam J in *Howlin v Power (Dublin) Ltd* (HC) 5 May 1978, unrep at p 8.

payment. For example a payment by a parent to his child or a husband to his wife is in general no evidence of a contract; indeed the presumption[99] is to the contrary. Nevertheless the circumstances surrounding a payment may be such that the payment becomes evidence not only of the existence of the contract under which it was made but also of the nature of that contract. What the payment proves in the light of its surrounding circumstances is not a matter of law but a matter of fact. There is no rule of law which excludes evidence of the relevant circumstances surrounding the payment - save parol evidence of the contract on behalf of the person seeking to enforce the contract under which the payment is alleged to have been made."

Thus if property is sold, the price is paid and there is reason to believe that the vendor cannot repay the money that payment is likely to be sufficient evidence of both the existence of the contract under which it was made and also of the nature of that contract.[100] Once a party to a parol contract admits that he has received a benefit under it which he is unable or unwilling to restore the mischief aimed at by the Statute disappears.[101]

[6.14] In *Howlin v Power (Dublin) Ltd*[102] McWilliam J said of the *Steadman* case:

"I cannot disagree with the reasoning of the majority of the judges in that case but, accepting that the decision is correct on the question of the mere payment of money constituting an act of part performance sufficient to take the case out of the statute, I must keep before my mind that the statute does provide that a contract for the sale of land shall not be enforceable unless there is a sufficient note or memorandum thereof in writing and that the application of the doctrine of part performance is still confined to cases in which it would be fraudulent or inequitable for a defendant to rely on the statute because a plaintiff has prejudiced himself in some way by reason of the contract."

He found that there was no prejudice to the plaintiff[103] and said that the following passage from the judgment of Lord Reid in *Steadman's* case appeared relevant:

"Normally the consideration for the purchase of land is a sum of money and there are statements that a sum of money can never be treated as part performance. Such statements would be reasonable if the person pleading the statute tendered repayment of any part of the price which he had received and was able thus to make restitutio in integrum. That would remove any fraud or any equity on which the purchaser could properly rely. But to make a general rule that payment of money can never be part performance would seem to me to defeat the whole purpose of the doctrine and I do not think that we are compelled to do that."[104]

In the *Steadman* case the wife had retained a sum of £100 paid to her (the husband relied on other acts of part performance as we shall see in the next paragraph) and Viscount Dilhorne felt that to let her resile from the agreement and retain the £100 would be to allow s 40 of the Law of Property Act 1925 to be an instrument of injustice.[105] Lord

---

[99] The concept of *advancement* which is discussed by Wylie, *Irish Land Law*, 2nd Ed (1986), para 9.044 (money), 9.047, (land) and by Keane, *Equity and the Law of Trusts in the Republic of Ireland* para 12.03A-05.
[100] This is the thrust of two examples given by Lord Salmon in the *Steadman* case at [1976] AC 570-1; [1974] 2 All ER 1006-7. See also Lord Simon at [1976] AC 565; [1974] 2 All ER 1002. When the price is paid in full the purchaser is likely to have taken possession which is normally sufficient part performance anyway.
[101] Lord Salmon in *Steadman's* case at [1976] AC 571; [1974] 2 All ER 1007.
[102] (HC) 5 May 1978, unrep at 8-9.
[103] At p 8-9 of the transcript.
[104] The sum paid as part of the purchase price had been tendered in repayment to the plaintiff: p 10.
[105] At [1976] AC 541; [1977] 2 All ER 981, quoted by McWilliam J at p 9-10 in the *Howlin* case.

Salmon noted that she had never repaid or offered to repay the £100 and held that the payment barred her from relying on the statute.[106] Those views support the passage quoted by McWilliam J from Lord Reid. The retention of the £100 was thus a significant element in the *Steadman* decision which supports McWilliam J in the importance he gave to the tender of repayment in the *Howlin* case.

[6.15] It is vital to note that the plaintiff relied on other acts of part performance in the *Steadman* case, ie, getting his solicitor to consent to an order by justices which placed him under a continuing legal obligation, asking his solicitor not to seek more advantageous orders from the justices and incurring the cost of preparing a conveyance for execution by the wife.[107] The payment of the £100 on its own probably would not have been held to be a sufficient act of part performance.[108] Lord Morris (dissenting) held that it did not prove that there had been some contract, still less one concerning land. Viscount Dilhorne felt that the £100 did suffice taking it in the context of what had preceded it and the announcement made to the magistrates.[109] Lord Simon distinguished[110] between the acts of part performance which "specifically indicated the land in question"[111] and those which proved that there had been *some* contract with the wife though without specifically indicating the terms which concerned the house.[112] Later he tied the two strands together pointing out that what was said (ie done) in the magistrates' court in part performance of the agreement made it plain that the payment of the £100 was also in part performance of the agreement and not a spontaneous act of generosity, discharge of a legal obligation or attributable to any other hypothesis.[113] Lord Salmon made the vital distinction that the payment of the £100 - looked at without regard to its surrounding circumstances - would not be evidence of any contract,[114] let alone of a contract concerning land but looked at in the light of its surrounding circumstances was plainly made in part performance of a parol contract concerning land.[115] Lord Reid said that the payment of the £100 to the wife was, taking the words in their ordinary sense, in part performance of the agreement but this was in the context that he had just said that the oral agreement of 2 March 1972 was indivisible and not severable.[116]

[6.16] The *Steadman* case may have destroyed any theory that the payment of money on its own can never be a sufficient act of part performance but it has certainly left intact the principle that the doctrine of part performance is still confined to cases where it would be a fraud or inequitable on the part of the defendant to plead the Statute. As we have seen,[117] it is clearly established that acts of part performance suffice if "they prove the

---

[106] At [1976] AC 555; [1974] 2 All ER 993.
[107] At [1976] AC 573; [1974] 2 All ER 1008.
[108] *Per* Lord Simon at [1976] AC 566; [1974] 2 All ER 1002. *Cf* Lord Reid at [1976] AC 540; [1974] 2 All ER 980, Viscount Dilhorne at [1976] AC 552; [1974] 2 All ER 991 and Lord Salmon at [1976] AC 572-3; [1974] 2 All ER 1008.
[109] At [1976] AC 548; [1974] 2 All ER 987.
[110] At 555 (AC); 993 (All ER).
[111] At [1976] AC 563; [1974] 2 All ER 1000.
[112] Procuring his solicitor to inform the justices of the entire bargain and inviting them to implement those terms which they could deal with and getting the solicitor to prepare the conveyance.
[113] The consent to the justices' orders and the £100. These were "only reasonably intelligible on the hypothesis that the issues raised by the cross-summonses in the magistrates' court had been settled by agreement."
[114] At [1976] AC 565; [1974] 2 All ER 1002.
[115] At 571-2 (AC): 1007-8 (All ER).
[116] At [1976] AC 540; [1974] 2 All ER 980.
[117] Para **6.06** *supra*.

existence of some contract and are consistent with the contract alleged" and it "becomes inequitable" that the defendant should plead the Statute. The payment of the £100 *on its own*[118] in the *Steadman* case probably would not have met that test.[119] The change in English law in 1989[120] means that no volume of English case law can build up now to show how far the *Steadman* case extended the previous law of part performance in relation to payments of money. In *Daulia Ltd v Four Millbank Nominees Ltd*[121] the Court of Appeal refused to accept that obtaining a bank draft for the deposit and signing a formal contract in terms already orally agreed were sufficient acts.[122] But in *Cohen v Nessdale Ltd* payment of £50 intended as payment of a ground rent under an agreed new lease was sufficient.[123] In those two cases the issue of the payments turned on whether they referred sufficiently to a contract, not on whether the offer or making of payment made it a fraud or inequitable for the defendant to rely on the Statute. It may be that if any money paid as part of a purchase price is repaid or tendered, especially if interest is also offered, the part payment of the price will not be a sufficient act of part performance. This view would fit in with the general thrust of the speeches in the *Steadman* case, what McWilliam J said about it in the *Howlin* case, his actual decision in that case and the view of Lord Redesdale in *Clinan v Cooke*.[124] In one other modern Irish case[125] a lump sum payment for goodwill was one of the acts of part performance held to be sufficient, the others being the defendant going into possession and the payment and acceptance of rent.[126] If money is merely offered as, *eg*, a cheque sent as a deposit, but not accepted even temporarily it is difficult to see how a sufficient equity could arise for a plaintiff to succeed on the doctrine of part performance.

Third parties

[6.17] Although many acts of part performance held to be sufficient are acts by the plaintiff which benefit the defendant this does not have to be the case. Acts involving third parties may suffice if they are done in reliance on the contract alleged. Thus a plaintiff who gave up his own property to his brother on the faith of his mother's promises was entitled to specific performance.[127] And a consent to the grant of a lease to a third party may be a sufficient act.[128] So may a surrender of a lease on the faith of the lessor's promise to grant a new lease to a third party.[129] And the taking of possession *by*

---

[118] *ie*, without even being linked to the alleged oral contract by admissible evidence.

[119] See para **6.15** *ante*.

[120] See para **6.09**.

[121] [1978] Ch 231; [1978] 2 All ER 557.

[122] The Judges held that one could not look at the acts in the light of the oral contract alleged: Goff LJ at 564-5 and Buckley LJ at 570.

[123] [1981] 3 All ER 118. The plaintiff was a statutory tenant under the Rent Acts and alleged an oral agreement for a sale by way of a 99-year lease at a ground rent. He lost on a "subject to contract" point and an appeal was dismissed on that point: [1982] 2 All ER 97.

[124] (1802) 1 Schoales & Lefroy 22 at 40-42. Of course, in so far as he accepted that payment of money could *never* be sufficient part performance the modern view differs.

[125] *Clinton v Finnegan* (HC) Cir App, 13 April 1973, Pringle J, unrep. He said at p 3 that it was "hardly likely" that the defendant would pay £350 for the goodwill if the tenancy was only weekly. So it was likely that the payment was made pursuant to a contract such as that claimed - ie, an agreement for a 10-year term at the weekly rent of £4.

[126] Page 2-3 of the transcript. Pringle J held that there was a good memorandum anyway: p 2.

[127] *Lowry v Reid* [1927] NI 142 *per* Moore LCJ at p 152-3 and Andrews LJ at pp 160-1.

[128] *Kelly v Walsh* (1878) 1 LRI 275 at 283.

[129] *In re Cooke's Trustee's Estate* (1880) 5 LRI 99 at 102.

third parties may be an act of part performance if the contract has been made for their benefit.[130]

Looking at the contract

[6.18] There is controversy whether one can properly consider the terms of the alleged oral contract to see whether the acts of part performance are sufficient. In *Lowry v Reid*[131] Moore LCJ rejected an argument that evidence of the parol contract cannot be admitted unless it is first established that the alleged acts of part performance unequivocally establish the existence of some such contract, describing it as "an inversion of the principle which should obtain." His opinion was that the court must at some stage consider the contract and its effect before it was in a position to judge whether or not the acts relied on to take the case out of the Statute were acts of part performance of the contract. Andrews LJ said in the same case:[132]

> "I would add that I can find no authority to support Mr. McGonigal's contention that it is not permissible even to consider the terms of the parol agreement until it is clearly established that the acts of part performance refer unequivocally to the contract relied upon and to that alone. Indeed it would be in my opinion impossible to apply the proposition as so stated in practice; for how, I ask, could it be said that the acts of part performance referred unequivocally to an agreement the terms of which were ex hypothesi not known, unless, indeed, they were acts of such a clear, cogent and conclusive character that they embodied and themselves proved the actual terms of the agreement, in which case it would be wholly unnecessary for the plaintiff to make any reference to or rely in any way upon the parol agreement."[133]

Note that the judges dealt with somewhat different points. Moore LCJ rejected an argument that the acts of part performance had to show the existence of "some such contract" and Andrews LJ a submission that the acts must point to the *particular* contract. Their views are mutually consistent and the difference should not matter on this question of admissibility of evidence.

[6.19] A more conservative view is that acts of part performance have to prove the existence of a contract before the terms of the alleged oral contract could be proved.[134] The majority of the Law Lords in *Steadman v Steadman*[135] took that view. Thus Lord Reid said:

> "You must not first look at the oral contract and then see whether the alleged acts of part performance are consistent with it. You must first look at the alleged acts of part performance to see whether they prove that there must have been a contract and it is only if they do so prove that you can bring in the oral contract."[136]

---

[130] *Hohler v Aston* [1920] 2 Ch 420 at 425. See Jones and Goodhart, *Specific Performance* (1986) at 98.

[131] [1927] NI 142 at 151.

[132] At p 157.

[133] Best LJ agreed with both judgments.

[134] This is reflected in the judgments of Lord Manners LC in *Savage v Carroll* (1810) 1 Ball & Beatty 265 at 282 and *Toole v Medlicott* (1810) 1 Ball & Beatty 393 at 401-2, 404. He does not so hold expressly but the judgments proceed on that basis.

[135] [1976] AC 536; [1974] 2 All ER 977.

[136] At [1976] AC 541; [1974] 2 All ER 981. This passage was applied by the Court of Appeal in *Daulia Ltd v Four Millbank Nominees Ltd* [1978] Ch 231; [1978] 2 All ER 557.

Lord Morris of Borth-y-Gest said that when examining the alleged acts of part performance the evidence, if already given, of the terms of the oral contract which it is sought to enforce must be disregarded.[137] Lord Simon explained:

> "But what was in origin a rule of substantive law[138] designed to vindicate conscientious dealing seems to have come in time sometimes to have been considered somewhat as a rule of evidence. It is easy to appreciate how this happened. Part performance could be viewed as a way of proving an agreement falling within s 4[139] notwithstanding the absence of writing. Seen as such it was no doubt considered necessary to frame stringent requirements to prevent the doctrine from carting a sedan chair through the provisions of the statute. If part performance was to be evidence of a contract which could not otherwise and directly be proved, the acts of part performance should themselves intrinsically be capable of proving some such contract as that alleged. Oral evidence was not admissible to connect them with the alleged contract: otherwise it was held the statutory object would be defeated by allowing an interest in land to pass on mere oral testimony."[140]

A few lines later Lord Simon questioned whether it was direct respect for the Statute which led to such confinement of the doctrine or whether it was not rather because part performance seems sometimes to have been regarded as an alternative way of proving an oral agreement.

[6.20] Viscount Dilhorne's views in the *Steadman's* case were consistent with the judgments of the Northern Ireland Court of Appeal in *Lowry's* case. He said:

> "As to the fourth condition stated in *Fry*, that there must be proper parol evidence of the contract which is let in by the acts of part performance, there was here proper parol evidence of the contract. I think that in the statement of this condition the use of the words 'let in' was a little unfortunate for it lends some support to the argument advanced by Mr. Morland that acts of part performance are the key which opens the door to the contract. I do not think that that is so. They are the key to rendering the contract enforceable. But as Lord Selborne said, at p 475,[141] a court is not estopped from inquiring into and taking notice of the truth of the facts. The contract is not a nullity. The acts of part performance must be of part performance of that contract and whether they are or not cannot be determined without regard to the contract. The party seeking to rely on such a contract has to prove it and to prove such acts. But at a trial the matters are not dealt with separately. Such a party does not first have to prove such acts and the court has first to decide whether they can be so regarded and then, if the court holds that they can, the party does not have to produce evidence of the contract and the court to determine whether or not there is any contract. The court is not required to operate in blinkers. If the contract is proved, it does not prevent the court from considering and deciding whether the alleged acts of part performance are unequivocally and of their own nature referable to a contract of the character alleged."[142]

Lowry's case does not seem to have been cited to the House of Lords in *Steadman*. The notion of part performance as a rule of evidence does indeed have support in the English

---

[137] At [1976] AC 547; [1974] 2 All ER 986.
[138] *Ie*, the doctrine of part performance.
[139] Equivalent to s 2 of the Irish Statute.
[140] At [1976] AC 559; [1974] 2 All ER 996. *Cf* Lord Salmon at [1976] AC 566; [1974] 2 All ER 1003.
[141] In *Maddison v Alderson* (1883) 8 App Cas 467.
[142] At [1976] AC 556; [1974] 2 All ER 994.

case law as indicated in the passages quoted above from Lord Simon and Viscount Dilhorne.[143] It does not have that kind of support from Irish case law. The point remains open in the Republic but the views of the Northern Ireland Court of Appeal and Viscount Dilhorne seem the more attractive and practical and no convincing point of principle stands against them.

Raising the statute

[6.21] It is important to bear in mind that the doctrine of part performance does not enable a claimant to defeat any defences other than "raising the Statute" - ie pleading that the Statute applies and the lack of writing sufficient to satisfy it. Thus a plaintiff may prove an oral contract and take it out of the Statute by proving acts of part performance but may still fall foul of another defence or a ground for refusing to exercise discretion in favour of a claimant. For example, a defence of illegality may still prevail.[144] So may a plea of laches[145] or a submission that the plaintiff had so misconducted himself that equity would not assist him.[146] And acts which appear at first impression to be part performance of a contract may turn out to be done only preparatory to or in contemplation of entry into a contract[147] or pursuant to conditions attached to a unilateral offer by one party which might lead to a concluded contract.[148] Steps taken to deal with problems emerging in the course of negotiations do not establish that a concluded bargain was reached.[149] We have noted that before any question of part performance can arise there must be a concluded contract.[150] A plaintiff who can prove a suitable act of part performance may fail to discharge the onus of showing the terms of the contract satisfactorily.[151] And a court may decide to consider an issue of part performance even though it has held that the plaintiff fell at the first fence by failing to prove a concluded contract.[152] Expenditure of money on doing work to a house, which is obviously capable of being a sufficient act of part performance of a concluded contract, will fail to assist a claimant where a "subject to contract" element means that there has been no concluded contract, even an oral one.[153] In that type of situation questions may arise of estoppel and possible equitable rights of the person who spent the money[154] but the expenditure cannot be part performance of a contract.

---

[143] *Cf* Lord Reid at [1976] AC 542; [1974] 2 All ER 982 where he refers to "an idea, never clearly defined, to the effect that the law of part performance is a rule of evidence rather than an application of an equitable principle" and then calls that idea "a fundamental departure from the true doctrine of part performance". See also Jones & Goodhart, *Specific Performance* (1986) at p. 97.

[144] As occurred in *Starling Securities Ltd v Woods* (HC) 24 May 1977, McWilliam J, unrep at p 6.

[145] *Haire-Foster v McIntee* (1889) 23 LRI 529 at 535. *Cf Archbold v Lord Howth* (1866) IR 1 CL 608 at 621.

[146] *O'Herlihy v Hedges* (1803) 1 Schoales & Lefroy 123 at 129-30 (an insolvent intending tenant deceiving the landlord into thinking that a solvent trustee was the real tenant).

[147] *Daulia Ltd v Four Millbank Nominees Ltd* [1978] 2 All ER 557 at 564, 570.

[148] As in the *Daulia Ltd* case.

[149] *Barry v Buckley* [1981] IR 306 at 311.

[150] Para **6.05** *supra*.

[151] As in *Mortal v Lyons* (1858) 8 Ir Ch R 112, 118-9 and *Howe v Hall* (1870) IR 4 Eq 242 at 253-4.

[152] Keane J did so "in deference to the arguments of counsel" in *Silver Wraith Ltd v Siuicre Eireann Cpt* (HC) 8 June 1989, unrep at p 10-12.

[153] *Devlin v Northern Ireland Housing Executive* [1982] NI 377. If there had been a concluded oral contract the expenditure probably would have taken the case out of the Statute.

[154] See discussion by Lord Lowry LCJ in *Devlin's* case at p 389-92. *Cf* Murray J in *Mawhinney v Reid* [1984] 9 NIJB at p 49 of the transcript.

Chapter 7

The Family Home Protection Act 1976

[7.01] To get an order for specific performance a claimant must show first and foremost that there is a valid contract. The Family Home Protection Act 1976 may have the effect that in the case of a "family home", as defined by that Act, an alleged contract is void. A successful plea of the Act is therefore a good defence to a claim for specific performance. The main sanction of the Act is in s 3(1):

> Where a spouse, without the prior consent in writing of the other spouse, purports to convey[1] any interest[2] in the family home[3] to any person except the other spouse, then, subject to sub-sections (2) and (3) and section 4,[4] the purported conveyance shall be void.[5]

The sanction is not confined to contracts *in writing*. Thus, an oral contract for sale which could be taken out of the Statute of Frauds by the doctrine of part performance[6] may be caught by the 1976 Act. In this chapter we will consider among other things the purpose[7] of the Act, its likely interpretation,[8] the nature of the non-owning spouse's right[9] and the enquiries which a purchaser should make.[10] A brief look will also be taken on other rights of a family nature in a broad sense[11] since such rights can arise in some cases where the 1976 Act does not apply.

The Purpose of the 1976 Act

[7.02] The long title to the 1976 Act reads "AN ACT TO PROVIDE FOR THE PROTECTION OF THE FAMILY HOME AND FOR RELATED MATTERS". The main purpose of the Act is to ensure that the family home, or any interest in it, cannot be sold or in any way disposed of by the owner over the head of his spouse.[12] Although the Act applies to both spouses and, therefore, protects the husband where the wife is the legal owner, the Act is largely designed to protect the wife and dependent children.[13] The purpose has been said to be to prevent voluntary alienation of an interest in the family home by one spouse to the prejudice of the other or their dependent children.[14] The Act must be used primarily to secure the protection of the family in the family home and all

---

[1] "Conveyance" and "convey" are considered in para **7.14** *infra*.

[2] On "interest" see para **7.14** *infra*.

[3] The definition of "family home" is set out and considered in para **7.10** *infra*.

[4] On exceptions see paras **7.20-23** *infra*.

[5] See paras **7.17-18** *infra* on the sanction of voidness.

[6] See Ch 6 *ante*. "Conveyance" includes a *contract* for sale or for various other forms of disposition: para **7.14** *infra*.

[7] Para **7.02-4** *infra*.

[8] Paras **7.05-6** and **7.08**. Retrospection is considered in para **7.09** *infra*.

[9] Para **7.19** *infra*.

[10] Paras **7.22-5** and **7.38-9** *infra*.

[11] Paras **7.29-39** *infra*.

[12] *Somers v W* [1979] IR 94, *per* Griffin J at p 112.

[13] Griffin J said (*ibid*) that "for all practical purposes the Act is designed to protect the wife and the dependent children (as defined in s 1 of the Act) of the family, since in Ireland the legal title to a house is rarely vested in the wife alone."

[14] *O'N v O'N* (HC) 6 October 1989, Barron J, unrep at 5.

other claims to the property must remain secondary.[15] Henchy J explains the protection given by s 3(1) in *Nestor v Murphy*:[16]

> "The basic purpose of the sub-section is to protect the family home by giving a right of avoidance[17] to the spouse who was not a party to the transaction. It ensures that protection by requiring, for the validity of the contract to dispose and of the actual disposition, that the non-disposing spouse should have given a prior consent in writing. The point and purpose of imposing the sanction of voidness is to enforce the right of the non-disposing spouse to veto the disposition by the other spouse of an interest in the family home."

[7.03] Before the Act was passed the owning spouse was largely[18] free to dispose of the family home. Now he normally cannot convey any interest in it to any third party without the prior consent of his spouse. An attempt to do so is void unless it comes within the exceptions in s 3[19], there is an order pursuant to s 4 dispensing with the consent or, of course, it can be shown that the Act does not apply. Prior to the Act:

> ... the spouse who owned the family home could effectively put the other spouse out on the street by selling it or mortgaging it. This was sometimes done out of vindictiveness and the other spouse had no redress. Most frequently the victimised spouse was the wife. She and her children could be left to fend for themselves so far as accommodation was concerned. It was to secure the position of such a spouse the Act of 1976 was passed.[20]

The right given to the non-owning spouse has been described as a "right to veto the disposition to a third party of any legal or equitable interest in the family home"[21] and as the "right of avoidance given when the non-participating spouse has not consented in writing to the alienation of any interest in the family home".[22]

[7.04] The courts are alert to the constitutional duty which led to the Act being passed. Henchy J put it thus in *Hamilton v Hamilton*:[23]

> "The Act of 1976 provides for the protection of the family home, presumably as an implication of the constitutional duty that falls on the State to protect the family and to guard with special care the institution of marriage."

And McCarthy J said in *W v Somers*:[24]

> "I draw attention to the wide range of powers granted to the courts in s 5[25] as indicative of the concern of the legislature, in enacting the Act of 1976, to fulfil the function of the legislative branch of the State as set out in Article 41, s 1, of the Constitution of Ireland

---

[15] *W v Somers* [1983] IR 122 at 126, *per* McCarthy J.

[16] [1979] IR 326 at 328.

[17] As the rest of the quoted passage makes clear, Henchy J has not in mind a right to apply to have a contract or conveyance set aside. See also paras **7.18** *infra*.

[18] The non-owning spouse may have rights outside the Act in equity or the law of trusts. Issues of notice could arise between that spouse and a purchaser from the owning spouse. See paras **7.29-39** *infra*.

[19] The *Somers* case at p 112-3. The exceptions are discussed at paras **7.20-25** *infra*.

[20] *Per* Walsh J in *Bank of Ireland v Purcell* [1989] IR 327 at 333.

[21] *Hamilton v Hamilton* [1982] IR 466 at 486, Henchy J

[22] Hamilton P in *Barclays Bank Ireland v Carroll* (HC) (Bankruptcy), 10 September 1986, unrep at p 8-9 (considering *Nestor v Murphy* [1979] IR 326).

[23] [1982] IR 466 at p 485.

[24] [1983] IR 122 at 126.

[25] Section 5 deals with cases where the family home or any interest is being risked or has been lost by the conduct of a spouse. McCarthy J emphasised that orders of the court can be directed not only to the spouse at fault but also to "any other person".

1937. In my view, the Act of 1976 must be used primarily to secure the protection of the family in the family home, and all other claims to the premises that constitute such home must remain secondary to it. The judicial branch of government of the State must also recognise its duty under Article 41 and seek to achieve the objectives as set out in that Article."[26]

There has been judicial controversy over the effect of Article 41 on property rights between husband and wife.[27] The Supreme Court recently resolved this in a manner which shows that the courts are alert to their constitutional duty but also careful not to trespass on the legislative function of the Oireachtas.[28]

Interpretation

[7.05] It is important to bear in mind that the changes made by the 1976 Act are more than procedural. This is made clear by Henchy J in *Hamilton v Hamilton*[29] where he disowns any suggestion that the change in the law effected by the 1976 Act is procedural only and says "It amounts to a novel and profound change in substantive land law and, consequently, in the law of conveyancing." O'Higgins CJ put it very clearly when he said of the Act:

> "It is not an Act dealing merely with form or procedure. It is an Act which declares to be unenforceable and void certain transactions which were previously regarded in law as binding and valid - if the transactions are not carried out in accordance with the provisions of s 3."[30]

The Act has been described as a "remedial social statute".[31] It is not to be construed as if it were a conveyancing statute[32] but it certainly has added a new dimension to the practice of conveyancing.[33] The new dimension requires a purchaser to investigate matters which previously were not title matters at all. He must ascertain whether the property, because of its present or past use, is a family home within the 1976 Act. If it is, he must ascertain whether the sale is by a spouse and, if so, whether the conveyance[34] should be preceded by the consent in writing of the other spouse so as to prevent it being rendered void under s 3. If that spouse omits or refuses to consent he must consider asking the vendor to seek an order dispensing with the consent.[35] If a dispensing order under s 4 is needed it must be obtained *before conveyance*.[36]

[7.06] The courts are likely to interpret the 1976 Act broadly though not to the extent of permitting absurd results. Their alertness to the principles of Article 41 of the

---

[26] Note also discussion by Finlay CJ (Hederman J concurring) of Art. 41.2.1° and 2° in *BL v ML* [1992] 2 IR 77 at 105-9.

[27] See Duncan & Scully, *Marriage Breakdown in Ireland* paras 10.042-9.

[28] *BL v ML,* see para **7.32** *infra*.

[29] [1982] IR 466 at p 484.

[30] *Hamilton v Hamilton* [1982] IR 466 at 473.

[31] *Bank of Ireland v Purcell* [1989] IR 327 at 333.

[32] *Ibid.*

[33] *Somers v W* [1979] IR 94 at 111.

[34] Remember that "conveyance" is defined by s 1(1) to include a *contract*. We are primarily concerned here with the purchase deed but spouse's prior consent in writing is normally needed for an enforceable contract. A second consent to the purchase deed is not needed: see paras **7.06-7** *infra*. See paras **7.24-5** on pre-contract enquiries.

[35] On these points see *Somers v W* [1979] IR 94 at 111.

[36] *Somers'* case, *per* Henchy J at 112 and Griffin J at 114.

Constitution points to a broad approach. The unwillingness to permit absurd results became clear when a question of construction arose in *Nestor v Murphy.*[37] The defendants, a married couple, signed a contract for the sale of their family home to the plaintiff. They argued that the contract was void because the wife had not given her prior written consent to it. Henchy J agreed that a "surface" or "literal" appraisal of s 3(1) might be thought to give support to that point. However, if both spouses join in a contract for sale (which is a "conveyance" within the meaning of the Act) there is no question of a unilateral alienation of the home by one spouse. Henchy J summed up the position:

> "To construe the sub-section in the way proposed on behalf of the defendants would lead to a pointless absurdity. As is conceded by counsel for the defendants, if their construction of s 3(1) is correct then either the husband or the wife could have the contract declared void because the other did not give a prior consent in writing. Such an avoidance of an otherwise enforceable obligation would not be required for the protection of the family home when both spouses have entered into a contract to sell it. Therefore, it would be outside the spirit and purpose of the Act."[38]

The defendants' argument would have the effect that contracts could be unfairly or dishonestly repudiated by parties who entered into them freely, willingly and with full knowledge. Henchy J therefore held that the spouse whose "conveyance" is made void by s 3(1) is an owning spouse who has purported to "convey" unilaterally (i.e. without the other spouse joining) and without the prior consent in writing of the other spouse.[39] It is only by thus confining the reach of s 3(1) that its operation can be kept within the legislative intent.[40]

[7.07] When the non-owning spouse gives prior consent in writing to a contract for sale a further consent is not needed for the conveyance pursuant to that contract.[41] In practice the second consent is often obtained so that it will be readily available in the future as part of the title documents.[42] If an agent with the necessary authority concludes a contract for sale on behalf of both spouses no further consent of either is needed for the conveyance.[43]

The courts take a practical approach to the requirement of prior written consent. Where, for example, one spouse buys a property so that it will be the couple's home and executes a mortgage to secure a loan made to assist the purchase this may be regarded as a "joint conveyancing transaction" by which the purchasing spouse acquires an equity of redemption in the property; it would be inconsistent with the purposes and provisions of the 1976 Act if the consent of the non-owning spouse to the mortgage was required.[44]

---

[37] [1979] IR 326.

[38] At p 329.

[39] Remember that this word includes a contract for sale.

[40] *Nestor's* case at p 329-30. This approach was applied by Hamilton P in *Barclays Bank Ireland v Carroll* (HC) (Bankruptcy), 10 September 1986, unrep at p 8-9. The wife of a transferor of registered land did not wish to challenge the validity of the transfer some years later.

[41] *Kyne v Tiernan* (HC) 15 July 1980, McWilliam J, unrep. He agreed at p 9 that on a strict interpretation of s 3 one could say that there must be consent to both contract and conveyance but said "I cannot imagine that it could have been the intention of the legislature to require two consents for the completion of one transaction, namely, the sale of one house..."

[42] *Eg*, by endorsing it on the purchase deed.

[43] *Mulhall v Haren* [1981] IR 364 at 372-3 applying *Nestor v Murphy.*

[44] *National Irish Bank Ltd v Graham* [1994] 2 ILRM 109 at 104.

Different considerations would arise if the property was purchased by conveyance, perhaps with the help of a bridging loan, and then mortgaged even after a short time.[45] A mortgage by equitable deposit by leaving a title document with a lender is void if the attempt is complete before the non-owning spouse gives the "prior consent in writing".[46] But a court may find in the particular circumstances of a case that there was an implied agreement that the lender would hold the title document as a mere custodian until the non-owning spouse signed the necessary consent whereupon the basis on which the document was held would change.[47] In particular circumstances also a deed of charge could be considered pending receipt of a consent in writing as signed and sealed but not yet delivered or, alternatively, as having been delivered as an escrow.[48]

[7.08] In *Bank of Ireland v Purcell*[49] Walsh J said that, as had been frequently pointed out, remedial statutes are to be construed "as widely and liberally as can fairly be done".[50] The first consideration in construing s 3 is to ascertain the purpose of the section.[51] Walsh J was satisfied that the Act never contemplated the position whereby a family home could be endangered by encumbrances created by advances made after the commencement of the 1976 Act by an equitable mortgage made before the Act.[52] At first sight there might seem to be inconsistency between the confining approach in *Nestor v Murphy* and the wide and liberal approach in *Bank of Ireland v Purcell*. However, there is common ground in that both judgments put the purpose of the section first. There is no disagreement between them on what that purpose is. Thus, while it was open to the court to approve the interpretation requiring two consents in *Nestor v Murphy* and such a construction would have been "wide" and "liberal", it could hardly be said to be "fairly ...done".[53] The confining interpretation was therefore made in the interest of fairness. If there is any inconsistency between the two cases the older decision is surely preferable. It was necessary there to go into the question of interpretation with great care whereas in the later case there was no need to consider interpretation at all.[54] Also, the later judgment does not mention the earlier one and it is unlikely that the court intended in *obiter* remarks to explain or disapprove a statement of law without mentioning the case in which it was made. Recently the court rejected a submission based on *Bank of Ireland v Purcell* that it should give a liberal interpretation to the definition of "family home" in order to bring within that definition a home which a married couple was about to occupy for the first time.[55]

---

[45] *Ibid.*
[46] *Bank of Ireland v Hanrahan* (HC) 10 February 1987, O'Hanlon J, unrep at 3.
[47] *Ibid.* The gap in time was about two hours.
[48] *Bank of Ireland v Smyth* [1993] 2 IR 102 at 107.
[49] [1989] IR 327.
[50] At 333.
[51] *Ibid.*
[52] *Bank of Ireland v Purcell* [1989] IR 327 at 334.
[53] The degree of protection it would give is not needed and it would enable contracts to be unfairly or dishonestly repudiated by parties who entered into them freely, willingly and with full knowledge: *per* Henchy J in *Nestor v Murphy* [1979] IR 326 at 329.
[54] Walsh J agreed with the trial judge that a mortgage by deposit of deeds could be a "conveyance" within the Act and each time a further advance was made the interest in the property was altered. This hardly needed a wide or liberal interpretation.
[55] *National Irish Bank v Graham* [1994] 2 ILRM 109 at 113.

Whether retrospective effect

[7.09] The 1976 Act as a whole had no retrospective effect. Retrospective legislation, since it necessarily affects vested rights, has always been regarded as being prima facie unjust.[56] This is even more strongly the case if proceedings have already been brought based on the earlier legal position. When an Act changes the substantive, as distinct from procedural, law then, regardless of whether the Act is otherwise prospective or retrospective in its operation, it is not deemed to affect proceedings brought under the previous law unless the new Act expressly or by necessary intendment provides to the contrary.[57] A retrospective intent on the part of the Oireachtas in enacting the 1976 Act would have indicated a "lack of concern for contractual rights acquired before the requirement of the other spouse's consent became necessary".[58] If the Act had the result that a purchaser with a valid pre-Act contract could not insist on completion of his purchase after the Act commenced, it was retrospective in substance. If the pre-Act contract could not be brought to fruition in a deed of conveyance there would necessarily be a retrospective depreciation of its legal effect.[59] As we shall see, however[60], there is an element of retrospection in the 1976 Act in that a spouse who left the family home prior to the commencement of the Act may be protected in certain circumstances. There is a distinction between applying a new law to past events and taking past events into account. To do the latter is not to apply the Act retrospectively.[61]

Definition of "family home"

[7.10] Section 2 of the 1976 Act provides:

(1)   In this Act "family home" means, primarily, a dwelling in which a married couple ordinarily reside. The expression comprises, in addition, a dwelling in which a spouse whose protection is in issue ordinarily resides or, if that spouse has left the other spouse, ordinarily resided before so leaving.

(2)   In sub-subsection (1) "dwelling" means -

(*a*)   any building, or

(*b*)   any structure, vehicle or vessel (whether mobile or not),

or part thereof, occupied as a separate dwelling and includes any garden or portion of ground attached to and usually occupied with the dwelling or otherwise required for the amenity or convenience of the dwelling.

---

[56] O'Higgins CJ covers this fully in *Hamilton v Hamilton* [1982] IR 466 at p 474-5 with express support of Henchy J at 484.

[57] *Per* Henchy J *ibid* at 480-3. He made it clear at 487 that he would allow the appeal both on the special ground that the appellant was pursuing a valid claim for specific performance when the Act was passed and on the more general ground that the avoidance of conveyances by s 3 applied only to agreements to convey and instruments of conveyance which came into existence after the Act was passed. Griffin and Hederman JJ made the same point at 488.

[58] *Per* O'Higgins CJ, *ibid* at 477. He found no evidence or indication of such lack of concern; indeed there were indications to the contrary as he explains on the same page.

[59] *Per* Henchy J in the *Hamilton* case at 484.

[60] *Per* **7.11** *infra*.

[61] In *O'H v O'H.* [1991] ILRM 108 at 112 Barron J quotes with approval from Craies on *Statute Law* "but a statute is not properly called a retrospective statute because a part of the requisites for its action is drawn from a time antecedent to its passing".

The necessity for the word "primarily" becomes clear when one considers the second sentence in s 2(1).[62] That sentence contains an additional or subsidiary definition. Both are expressed in complete terms and leave no room for the addition of any other subsidiary definition by judicial interpretation.[63]

The meaning of "dwelling" is not confined to a "house". A flat or bedsitter can be a "structure" and probably a "building" although one might refer to it more naturally as part of a building. Subsection (2) expressly includes a range of possible abodes. However, the dwelling must remain habitable[64] as otherwise it would be difficult to contend that the couple ordinarily reside there. It is essential to the definition that a "married couple" are present. They must be *in* occupation; an intention to take up occupation shortly is unlikely to be enough.[65] The reference to a "married couple" probably means a couple having a valid marriage under the law for the time being in force.[66] That construction would be consistent with the duty of the State under Article 41 of the Constitution to protect the family.[67] The dwelling has to be occupied as a "separate" one. It is arguable that the word "separate" and the phrase "in which a married couple ordinarily reside" (with "couple" in the singular[68]) have the result that a dwelling occupied or used by two or more married couples each having some title, right or permission to do so[69] might not be protected by the Act.[70] However, as the singular normally includes the plural and *vice versa* in an Act of the Oireachtas[71] and the word "separate" seems to relate more closely to "dwelling" in the subsection than to "occupied" the better view probably is that the occupation or use of a dwelling by more than one couple does not prejudice the protection of the Act.[72] It says nothing about the title of occupying couples and this suggests that once the fact of occupation exists the precise nature of any right or title to occupy does not matter.

In cases where a family home is owned by a company it seems likely that a couple occupying only by leave or licence are covered by the Act.[73] In this type of case the 1976 Act would prima facie apply only to the licence or other interest of the married couple which would be of little attraction to a purchaser.[74] The estate of the company would not be affected. However, there must be some danger, especially if the arrangements made

[62] The meaning and effect of "primarily" are considered by Finlay CJ in *National Irish Bank Ltd v Graham* [1994] 2 ILRM 109 at 113.
[63] *Ibid.*
[64] *Carrigan v Carrigan* (HC) 12 May 1983, O'Hanlon J, unrep at p 8.
[65] *National Irish Bank Ltd v Graham* [1994] 2 ILRM 109 at 113-4.
[66] *The State (Nicolaou) v An Bord Uchtala* [1966] IR 567 at 643-4.
[67] *O'B v S.* [1984] IR 316 at 333-335. This case involved the Succession Act 1965 much of which is also aimed at protecting and improving the position of the family.
[68] By s 11(*a*) of the Interpretation Act 1937 singular imports plural and vice versa if there is no contrary intention.
[69] *Eg*, under licences, tenancies or by some informal arrangements.
[70] *Cf* the concept of "separate dwelling" under the Housing (Private Rented Dwellings) Acts 1982 and 1983 and the former Rent Acts: see Wylie, *Irish Landlord and Tenant Law*, para 29.08; de Blacam, *Private Rented Dwellings*, 2nd Ed (1992) at 15-16.
[71] Interpretation Act 1937 s 11(*a*).
[72] It would not apply to a couple other than the couple which includes the disposing spouse.
[73] *Walpoles (Ireland) Ltd v Jay* (HC) 20 November 1980, McWilliam J, unrep; *Carrigan v Carrigan* (HC) 2 May 1983, O Hanlon J, unrep. Neither case does more than give an impression that occupation by leave or licence probably would be covered.
[74] A true licence is a personal privilege: *per* Denning MR in *Shell-Mex v Manchester Garages* [1971] 1 WLR 612 at 615; [1971] 1 All ER 841 at 843, approved by Griffin J in *Irish Shell & BP Ltd v John Costello Ltd* [1981] ILRM 66 at 70. It is very doubtful that a personal privilege is capable of being assigned. See Wylie, *op cit*, para 3.09.

are found to be a device to try to defeat the purposes of the 1976 Act[75], that a court would "pierce the corporate veil" or hold on suitable facts that the company was trustee for a spouse who was the real owner of the home. Then the Act could apply in the normal way between that "real owner" and the non-owning spouse even though the home is in the name of the company. The courts may not be too reluctant to defeat devices aimed at getting around the Act.

[7.11] The second sentence in s 2(1) covers the common situation in which one spouse has left the home and the other remains there. Under the first part of the sentence the spouse whose "protection is in issue" - ie, the non-owning spouse - is the one who stays in the home. The language used lets in cases where the owning spouse left before the commencement of the Act. The latter part of the sentence covers the situation where the non-owning spouse has left the home. In this case the spouse who has left is the one whose "protection is in issue". The text of the subsection does not use the word "desertion" and desertion would not remove the need for the prior consent.[76] The text here also admits cases where the spouse who left did so before the commencement of the Act.[77] That spouse must have ordinarily resided there before leaving.[78]

[7.12] The 1976 Act has no provision for apportionment. This means that a conveyance without the necessary consent is void in relation to its entire parcel if it includes any property which comes within the definition of "family home". It might be suggested that the voidness under s 3(1) would only make the conveyance void in so far as it related to the "family home" as defined in the Act but the deed would be valid in relation to the rest of the parcel. That would strain the meaning of the words "the purported conveyance shall be void" in s 3(1) which contemplate a single conveyance which will be either wholly valid or wholly void. It would also leave an impossible situation for the parties as nobody would be likely to be satisfied with the splitting of the property and there is no provision for any adjustment of a purchase price. The legislature can hardly have intended such a result. The point was considered in the minority judgment of Costello J in *Hamilton v Hamilton*[79] where it was pleaded that if s 3 of the Act applied to the proposed conveyance it applied only to that part of the property which came within the definition of "dwelling". It was accepted that the house and garden were a "family home". Costello J concluded:

> "But once this concession is made, as indeed it had to be made, it seems to me that Mr. Dunne's argument must fail. The effect of the proposed conveyance will be to convey this family home, even though there will be conveyed with the family home additional land which may not form part of it. Once a proposed conveyance includes a family home then, it seems to me, the provisions of s 3, subs 1, of the Act of 1976 apply to it and the written consent mentioned in the sub-section is required - unless the transaction falls within one of the four exceptions set out in the section."[80]

---

[75] O'Hanlon J referred to the possibility of a subterfuge in the *Carrigan* case at p 8 but he did not have to decide the point because the property was no longer habitable and a favourable finding would not benefit the wife.

[76] *H & L v S* [1979] ILRM 105 at p 108.

[77] *Hegarty v Morgan* (HC) 15 March 1979, McWilliam J, unrep at p 7; *H & L v S* [1979] ILRM 105 at p 107.

[78] *Per* Griffin J in *Somers v W* [1979] IR 94 at p 114. In that case the wife left about three years before the commencement of the Act.

[79] [1982] IR 466. The majority judgments did not need to consider this point since they held that the Act did not apply retrospectively.

[80] At p 490.

He then noted that no arguments were advanced to support the alternative plea that the court should sever the property and decided that written consent was required to a conveyance of the portion of the property comprising the family home but that no such consent was required to a conveyance of the remainder of the property. He did not think that such a contention was sustainable; the court was concerned with "a proposal to convey a family home within the meaning of the Act of 1976".[81]

[7.13] Note that the definition of "dwelling" in s 2(2) "includes any garden or portion of ground attached to and usually occupied with the dwelling or otherwise required for the amenity or convenience of the dwelling." The words "portion of ground" are broader than "garden". The nature of the use made of and access from the home to a portion of ground are likely to be major factors in deciding whether it is "attached to" the home. The nature of the use should be the major factor in deciding whether it was "usually occupied with the dwelling".[82] If a vendor has a large area of land with a family home on it he may be able to sell most of the land separately from the family home without having to get his spouse's consent but he must be careful to exclude any garden or portion of land which could come within the extension to the definition of a dwelling.

Interests affected

[7.14] The sanction of s 3(1)[83] is aimed at a purported conveyance of any "interest" in a family home. "Interest" is defined broadly to mean "any estate, right, title or other interest, legal or equitable".[84] Section 1(1) defines "conveyance" thus:

"conveyance" includes a mortgage, lease, assent, transfer, disclaimer, release and any other disposition of property[85] otherwise than by a will or a *donatio mortis causa* and also includes an enforceable agreement (whether conditional[86] or unconditional) to make any such conveyance, and "convey" shall be construed accordingly;

The definition of "mortgage"[87] includes "an equitable mortgage, a charge on registered land and a chattel mortgage" and cognate words are to be construed accordingly. Gifts by will are presumably omitted because the Succession Act 1965 was felt to give adequate protection. That Act also gives some redress against a *donatio mortis causa* by bringing it within the scope of s 121 which deals with dispositions for the purpose of disinheriting a spouse or children.[88] This breadth of scope in the 1976 Act has been noted by the courts.

---

[81] *Ibid.*
[82] On the points just discussed see *Hamilton v Armstrong* [1984] ILRM 306, 308-9. O'Hanlon J warned that no help is to be derived from observing how similar terms have been construed in other statutes. The case before him concerned s 56(14) of the Succession Act 1965 and, despite his very proper warning, it seems reasonable to seek help from that case. The words used are the same and a major element in the Act of protecting spouse and family is similar to the 1976 Act.
[83] Set out and discussed at para **7.17** *infra*.
[84] In s 1(1).
[85] The word "property" is very broad and catches things which would not be covered by land as defined by the Interpretation Act 1937. Thus a "vehicle or vessel (whether mobile or not)" is within the meaning of "dwelling" in s 2(2) of the 1976 Act, would often not be "land" within the 1937 Act but is caught by the word "property". Section 9 of the 1976 Act makes special provisions for "household chattels" but that fact probably does not prevent them being also covered by the word "property" in so far as they can be alienated by a "conveyance".
[86] The notion of an agreement which is both "enforceable" and "conditional" may seem a little odd. Perhaps the idea is to make clear that a contract cannot escape the Act by being conditional on some other factor. Conditional contracts are discussed at paras **3.19-28** *ante* and subject to contract in Ch 4.
[87] Also in s 1(1).
[88] See McGuire, *The Succession Act 1965*, 2nd Ed by Pearce, p 297-8.

The prohibition "covers every conceivable type of disposition of the family home by the defendant's husband".[89] The word "interest" is defined "more widely than a reference to an estate" and every time further money is advanced on foot of a mortgage "the interest of the mortgagor in those lands is altered" so that these further advances are "the conveyance of an interest" for the purposes of the 1976 Act.[90] The word "right" in the definition of "interest" is very broad and presumably will cover matters which would not normally be regarded as an "estate" or a "title". It seems broad enough to include profits, rights of residence and licences.

[7.15] Despite the broad coverage there is a limit. A judgment mortgage is not affected by the 1976 Act[91] in the absence of fraud or connivance. A judgment mortgage is a process of execution under the Judgment Mortgage (Ireland) Act 1850, as amended by the Judgment Mortgage (Ireland) Act 1858.[92] Physically it is the affidavit made on behalf of the judgment creditor for the purpose of registering a judgment as a mortgage.[93] If registered against a family home it is a unilateral act by the creditor: it is not a disposition by a spouse and therefore it cannot be a disposition by a spouse purporting to convey an interest in the home.[94] For that reason s 3(1) cannot get its teeth into a judgment mortgage. This may explain a careful choice of word when the purpose of the 1976 Act has been described as to prevent "voluntary" alienation of an interest in the family home by one spouse to the prejudice of the other or their dependent children.[95] However, if there is fraud or connivance leading to the creation of a judgment mortgage there is a substantial risk that the 1976 Act may be held to apply.[96] In this kind of situation the judgment mortgage probably would not be a wholly unilateral act by the judgment creditor but would be partly a voluntary act of the indebted spouse. The mere fact that a man has irresponsibly let himself get into debt or allowed a judgment to be obtained against him so that his creditor registers a judgment mortgage against his interest in the family home would hardly justify a court in saying that he has conveyed or purported to convey his interest in the family home to the judgment mortgagee.[97] However, if there is collusion between an owning spouse and his creditor,[98] there must be a risk of a court holding that the collusive judgment mortgage was a "disposition of property" within s 1(1) of the 1976 Act. It would be argued that the expressions "purports" and "purported conveyance" in s 3(1) cover not only *direct* participation in the "conveyance" but also the *indirect* causing of the creditor to effect the judgment mortgage. The risk of such an outcome must be increased by the courts' views of the purpose of the Act[99] and the fact

---

[89] *Per* Griffin J in *Somers v W* [1979] IR 94 at p 113 in the course of what he described over-modestly as a "few observations" of his own.

[90] *Per* Barron J in *Bank of Ireland v Purcell* [1989] IR 327 at 330-331, approved by the Supreme Court (Walsh J) at 333.

[91] *Containercare (Ireland) Ltd v Wycherley* [1982] IR 143; *Murray v Diamond* [1982] ILRM 113. These two reserved judgments were delivered only 12 days apart and neither was available when the other case was argued. For this reason neither judgment refers to the other.

[92] *Per* Carroll J in the *Containercare* case at 149.

[93] *Per* Barrington J in *Murray's* case at 114.

[94] As explained by Carroll J in the *Containercare* case at 150 and Barrington J in *Murray's* case at 115.

[95] By Barron J in *O'N v O'N* (HC) CA, 6 October 1989, unrep at p 5 of the transcript.

[96] There is a strong inference of this possibility in the judgment of Barrington J in *Murray v Diamond* [1982] ILRM 113 at p 115. Note also the careful abstinence of Walsh J in *Bank of Ireland v Purcell* [1989] IR 327 at 334 from expressing any view on the situation if a judgment mortgage came into being later.

[97] *Per* Barrington J in *Murray's* case at 115.

[98] *Eg*, if that spouse fails to resist judgment in a claim which clearly should have been defended.

[99] See para **7.02** *supra*.

that as a remedial statute it should be construed as widely and liberally as can fairly be done.[100]

[7.16] There is a partial exception in cases of registered land. This arises from the conclusive character of the register.[101] On a sale of registered land enquiries relating to the 1976 Act should be made in relation to the particular contract of sale and the intended transfer to an intending purchaser but beyond that the intending purchaser need not and should not go.[102] Section 31(1)[103] of the Registration of Title Act 1964 affords sufficient protection of the vendor and the intending purchaser in relation to all prior transactions affecting the registered ownership as appearing on title.[104] The duty of ensuring that any instrument of transfer is valid and effective so as to enable the purchaser to be registered as owner falls on the registrar at the time of registration.[105] It follows that if the registrar registered a purchaser as owner having taken a mistaken view that a transfer was valid and effective the purchaser could still rely on the conclusiveness of the register. A transfer could in fact be void for infringing s 3 of the 1976 Act but the spouse's right under the section could be unwittingly circumvented by registration of the purchaser as owner.[106] Of course, if fraud exists there is no such safety for the new registered owner but, in the absence of fraud, the register is conclusive evidence of the validity of the title.[107] Unlike cases of registered land it is necessary in unregistered conveyancing to check that no conveyance since the commencement of the Act has been made void by s 3. If title to unregistered land is shown to be freehold the fact that a deed over 12 years old was made void by s 3 may be alleviated by adverse possession so as to produce an acceptable title but a "squatter's title" against a leasehold title is not marketable.[108] At the time of writing a proposal is pending in the Oireachtas which, broadly speaking, would deem a conveyance to be valid unless steps are taken against it within six years.[109]

The sanction of voidness

[7.17] Section 3(1) of the 1976 Act provides:

> Where a spouse, without the prior consent in writing of the other spouse, purports to convey any interest in the family home to any person except the other spouse, then,

---

[100] *Per* Walsh J in *Bank of Ireland v Purcell* [1989] IR 327 at p 333.
[101] For discussion of this see Wylie, *Irish Land Law*, 2nd Ed para 21.03; Fitzgerald, *Land Registry Practice* (1989) at p 10-13.
[102] *Guckian v Brennan* [1981] IR 478 at p 488-9, Gannon J. See also *Barclays Bank Ireland v Carroll* (HC) (Bankruptcy), 10 September 1986, Hamilton P, unrep where the bankrupt had been registered on foot of a transfer made without the prior consent in writing of the transferor's wife (she knew of the sale and consented, though not in writing).
[103] Which provides for the conclusiveness of the register.
[104] *Guckian s* case at p 489.
[105] *Ibid.*
[106] Something of the sort may have happened in *Barclays Bank Ireland v Carroll* (HC) (Bankruptcy), Hamilton P, unrep where at least part of the relevant land was a "family home" but the wife had not given prior consent in writing: see pp 6-7 of the transcript.
[107] *Guckian s* case at 489.
[108] In *Perry v Woodfarm Homes Ltd* [1975] IR 104 the Supreme Court held that there is no "parliamentary conveyance" of a true owner's title to a squatter and only the lowest title is barred by squatting. Superior titles are not affected before the end of the term created by the barred lease as the next superior owner is not entitled to possession until then. Only when the lowest estate terminates anyway (a different matter from *title to it* being barred) does time begin to run against the next superior estate which is not barred until after a further 12 years of adverse possession. See Wylie *Irish Landlord and Tenant Law* paras 28.07; Wylie, *Irish Land Law*, 2nd Ed (1986), paras 23.15-19.
[109] Section 48(1) of the Family Law Bill 1994.

subject to sub-sections (2) and (3) and section 4, the purported conveyance shall be void.[110]

We have already considered the meaning of "family home"[111], "interest" and "conveyance"[112] and offered the view that the 1976 Act applies only to couples who have a marriage valid under the laws of the State.[113] The consent should be "prior"[114] and written. One of the elements in the new dimension imported into conveyancing by the 1976 Act is that in the event of a sale of a "family home" by a "spouse" the purchaser must find out "whether the conveyance should be preceded by the consent in writing of the other spouse".[115] If a husband intends to sell the family home "he cannot do so without first discussing the matter with (his wife) and obtaining her prior consent in writing".[116] If he intends to raise money on the property by a deposit of title deeds he must ensure that his wife's consent in writing is given before the equitable deposit is complete.[117] A spouse may agree with his bank that it will retain title documents *as a mere custodian* until the other spouse comes in to sign the necessary consent whereupon the bank is to be entitled to retain the documents as equitable mortgagee.[118] The effect of such an agreement is that the equitable deposit is made only when the consent has been furnished.

It is vital as the law stands now to ensure that the spouse's consent given is a consent to a particular transaction. A blanket consent to the owning spouse disposing of the family home as he or she may choose at any time in the future or within a stated period is unlikely to satisfy s 3(1).[119] The fact such a consent was given, perhaps as part of an otherwise beneficial settlement, probably could be taken into account later in deciding whether a necessary consent was being withheld unreasonably. That would arise in an application for an order under s 4 of the 1976 Act dispensing with the consent of the non-owning spouse and seeking that order would recognise that the blanket consent did not satisfy s 3(1). The circumstances of both spouses are likely to change from time to time and the more they do change the less weight a blanket consent would have on a s 4 application.

[7.18] Another vital feature of s 3(1) is the phrase "shall be void". The word "void" is sometimes interpreted as "voidable", eg, in s 10 of the Conveyancing Act (Ireland) 1634 which protects creditors.[120] The question therefore arises which is the correct interpretation of s 3(1) of the 1976 Act. There is no express finding on the point in a reported case but there is a clear general thrust in favour of the view that in s 3(1) "void" means "void" and not just "voidable". In *Somers v W*[121] the judgments of Henchy and

---

[110] Set out also in para **3.01** *ante*, repeated here for convenience.
[111] At paras **7.10-13** *supra*.
[112] Paras **7.14-15** *supra*.
[113] Paras **7.10** *supra*.
[114] See also paras **7.07** *supra*.
[115] *Per* Henchy J in *Somers v W* [1979] IR 94 at p 111. Note the use of "preceded by".
[116] *Per* Griffin J in *Somers'* case at 113. He clearly contemplates that the discussion and the consent must precede the contract for sale (which is a "conveyance" under the Act).
[117] *Bank of Ireland v Hanrahan* (HC) 10 February 1987, unrep at 3. O'Hanlon J found implied agreements. *Cf Bank of Ireland v Smyth* [1993] 2 IR 102 at 106-7.
[118] *The Bank of Ireland* case at 4. This conclusion was in the "particular circumstances" of the case. See also para **7.07** *supra*.
[119] Section 48(1)(ii) of the Family Law Bill 1994 proposes to authorise a "general consent in writing to any future conveyance" and make that a sufficient consent for the purposes of s 3(1) of the 1976 Act.
[120] See Wylie, *Irish Land Law*, 2nd Ed (1986), para 9.076.
[121] [1979] IR 94.

Griffin JJ strongly suggest that the relevant conveyance would be void.[122] In *Nestor v Murphy*[123] Henchy J speaks both of a "right of avoidance" and "sanction of voidness".[124] The latter clearly means that the conveyance is void. The former would let in "voidable". However, at p 329 Henchy J in one long sentence equates the "right of avoidance" with enabling a spouse, who was not a party to a "conveyance" and did not give a prior consent to it, to "have it declared void" and then, still in the same sentence, speaks of the spouse whose "conveyance" is "avoided" by s 3(1). This surely indicates that he is regarding a conveyance in breach of s 3(1) as void, not merely voidable. This view gets further support when in *W v Somers*[125] McCarthy J referred to the conveyance[126] as having been "rendered void" and to the Supreme Court as having so held in *Somers v W.*[127] In *Bank of Ireland v Purcell*[128] Walsh J said that any interest of the type under consideration was created without the consent of the defendant's wife "and therefore was void as a mortgage". The clearest passage of all comes from the judgment of Henchy J in *Hamilton v Hamilton*[129] when, having spoken of the 1976 Act as being presumably an implementation of the State's constitutional duty to protect the family, he says:

> "To this end, the Act of 1976 (as I have pointed out) created a new right whereby (save in excepted cases) the non-disposing spouse is given a right to veto the disposition to a third party of any legal or equitable interest in the family home. But the Act goes further than giving such a power of veto. Even in cases where the non-disposing spouse does not profess to exercise the right to veto (because, for example, he or she does not know of such a right), or where such spouse is willing to refrain from exercising the right to veto and has expressed such willingness orally, nevertheless, if the prior consent in writing has not been given by the non-disposing spouse, the purported conveyance (save in the excepted cases) is rendered void by s 3 of the Act of 1976. This, to my mind, shows that the legislature, in order to preserve inviolate the dual and interlocking rights of the spouses in the family home, intended the penalty of voidness to apply in order to prevent either a legal or an equitable right in the family home being disposed of to a third party by the unilateral action of one of the spouses."[130]

It must be acknowledged that in *Barclays Bank Ireland v Carroll*[131], Hamilton P applies the judgment in *Nestor v Murphy* in a manner which suggests that he took it as favouring the "voidable" interpretation.[132] However, the thrust of the extracts from Supreme Court judgments is strongly to the effect that "void" in s 3(1) means void and not voidable.

---

[122] At 108 Henchy J speaks of an exception allowing a conveyance to "escape being void under that section" (not "voidable") and at 113 Griffin J says that a purported conveyance "is void unless it is within the exceptions in s 3" (again, not "voidable").

[123] [1979] IR 326.

[124] At 328. At 329 "right of avoidance" appears again but he also speaks of the "spouse whose 'conveyance' is avoided".

[125] [1983] IR 122.

[126] The same deed was at the centre of *Somers v W* and *W v Somers*.

[127] At pp 125-6.

[128] [1989] IR 327 at 334.

[129] [1982] IR 466.

[130] At 485-6.

[131] (HC) (Bankruptcy), 10 September 1986, Hamilton P, unrep at 8-9.

[132] Counsel for the former vendor's wife told the Court that she did not wish to avail of the right of avoidance as she knew of the sale at all times and consented though not in writing: pp 8-9. The ratio is that, as she would not challenge the transfer, the new purchaser, bankrupt and Official Assignee could not do so either. The decision can be supported anyway by the conclusiveness of the register.

[7.19] Although the right given to the non-owning spouse by s 3 of the 1976 Act is important and valuable, it does not amount to an estate or interest in the property. A feature which sharply distinguishes the s 3 right from estates or interests in property is that the circumstances which give rise to the right do not relate to title, ownership or conveyancing practice and may arise in relation to some periods of ownership but not others.[133] Thus a house can only be a "family home" if and while a married couple ordinarily reside in it.[134] If a couple cease to ordinarily reside there the house ceases to be a "family home" and the s 3 right disappears. The protection is likely to cease if the family home is damaged to the extent of becoming uninhabitable[135] or if a couple move house but retain the former home as an investment.[136] The right of veto affects the instrument of conveyance and not the existing title. If the instrument is invalid there is no transmission of ownership. However the spouse for whose benefit the conveyance is rendered ineffective obtains no estate or interest which can affect the ownership or title to the property purported to be conveyed.[137] Nor does the 1976 Act give the non-owning spouse any right affecting land or property which could fall within any of the classes of burden within s 72[138] of the Registration of Title Act 1964.[139] One result of the right under s 3(1) not being a property right of the kind contemplated by the Registration of Title Act 1964 is that a judgment mortgagee takes free of the right.[140] The 1976 Act does not limit in any way the estate or interest of the owning spouse and his estate will vest automatically in the judgment mortgagee on the creation of a judgment mortgage against his estate.[141] The fact of marriage to a person having an interest in property or land may be registered in the Registry of Deeds or the Land Registry under s 12(1) of the 1976 Act and the registration of such a notice may prevent or delay a sale.[142] However, if a court is satisfied that the relevant property is not a family home or that the spouse against whom the notice is registered has no interest in the property it may direct the removal of the notice from the folio.[143]

Exceptions to the sanction

[7.20] There are four exceptions to the right of veto. It does not apply to a conveyance made by a spouse in pursuance of an enforceable agreement made before the marriage of the spouses.[144] The exemption covers both agreements made between the spouses and also agreements between one spouse or both spouses and third parties. This exception is essential as otherwise parties could get out of contracts by marrying and thus turning the property in sale into a "family home". It is called in aid by O'Higgins CJ in *Hamilton v*

---

133 *Per* Gannon J in *Guckian v Brennan* [1981] IR 478 at 486.
134 *Ibid.*
135 *Carrigan v Carrigan* (HC) 12 May 1983, O'Hanlon J, unrep at p 8. The case was decided on the point that the husband was not shown to have had any interest in the property.
136 In *FG v PG* [1982] ILRM 155 a couple moved to the US in 1966 retaining their Dublin home. The wife established a 30% beneficial interest by virtue of her contributions to the "general family pool".
137 On these points see *Guckian v Brennan* [1981] IR 478 at 485, approved in *Containercare (Ireland) Ltd v Wycherley* [1982] IR 143 at 153 and *Murray v Diamond* [1982] ILRM 113 at 116; see also *Lloyd v Sulllvan* (HC) 6 March 1981, McWilliam J, unrep at 2.
138 Burdens which affect registered land without registration.
139 *Guckian's* case at 485.
140 *Murray v Diamond* [1982] ILRM 113 at 116. See discussion of judgment mortgages at para **7.15** *supra.*
141 *Containercare (Ireland) Ltd v Wycherley* [1982] IR 143 at 153.
142 *Carrigan v Carrigan* (HC) 12 May 1983, O'Hanlon J, unrep at p 2-3, 6. There was also a *lis pendens.*
143 *Carrigan's* case at 9. Vacation of the *lis pendens* was directed.
144 Section 3(2).

Hamilton[145] as an indication of the concern of the legislature for contractual rights acquired before the other spouse's consent became necessary and thus as a pointer against an intention that the Act was retrospective:

> "It would be strange indeed that a legislature which showed this concern for contractual rights acquired prior to the marriage of the conveying spouse (but after the commencement of the Act of 1976) should have intended to affect and impair similar contractual rights acquired before the Act came into operation."

Another exception is in favour of a purchaser for full value and we look at this very important matter in the next paragraph. The third exempts a conveyance by a person other than the spouse making the purported conveyance referred to in s 3(1) which is made to a purchaser for value.[146] This may have been inserted for the removal of doubt as it is difficult to see that s 3(1) would have caught such conveyances. Finally conveyances are exempted if their validity depends on the validity of a conveyance which comes within any of the other three exceptions.[147] The burden of proof is on the person claiming that a conveyance is valid by reason of coming within any of the exceptions if the question arises in any proceedings.[148]

[7.21] The most important exception is that in favour of a purchaser for full value. This is also called in aid by O'Higgins CJ in *Hamilton v Hamilton* on the retrospection point:

> "Further an exclusion from the avoidance provisions is made in favour of a purchaser in good faith who acquires an interest in the property for full value ...The legislature is indicating a concern for the contractual rights of persons who buy property in good faith after the Act of 1976 became law and that in my view is completely inconsistent with an intention to disregard callously similar rights of persons who bona fide agreed to purchase before the enactment went on the statute book and before they could have known of the necessity for the other spouse's consent."[149]

As might be expected in the case of a major exception to a very important protection, it is carefully confined by the legislature. As we have seen the onus of proof is on a purchaser trying to enforce his contract by relying on the exception.[150] The purchaser must be one for "full value" and this is defined as "such value as amounts or approximates to the value of that for which it is given".[151] The definition of "purchaser" includes the requirement of "good faith".[152] Finally the words "as such" are deleted from s 3 of the Conveyancing Act 1882 in so far as it is to apply to the material in s 3 of the 1976 Act.[153] Under s 3(1)(i) of the 1882 Act a purchaser is fixed with notice of any instrument, fact or thing which is within his own knowledge or would have come to his knowledge if he made such inquiries and inspections as he ought reasonably to have made. Under s

---

[145] [1982] IR 466 at 477.
[146] Section 3(3)(*b*).
[147] Section 3 (3)(*c*).
[148] Section 3(4).
[149] [1982] IR 466 at p 477.
[150] Section 3(4).
[151] Section 3(5).
[152] Section 3(6).
[153] Section 3(7). The effect is that the purchaser is fixed with notice of information which his solicitor has got in any capacity in the same transaction, not just as the solicitor for the purchaser.

3(1)(ii) of the 1882 Act he is also prejudicially affected with notice of any instrument fact or thing if:

> In the same transaction with respect to which a question of notice to the purchaser arises, it has come to the knowledge of his counsel, [as such,] or of his solicitor, or other agent, [as such,] or would have come to the knowledge of his solicitor, or other agent, [as such,] if such inquiries and inspections had been made as ought reasonably to have been made by the solicitor or other agent.

The words in square brackets are deleted from the 1882 Act for the purposes of s 3 of the 1976 Act. The result is an extension of the doctrine of constructive notice. Thus, if, for example, the same solicitor acts for both parties it will not matter in which capacity he got information.[154]

[7.22] The question whether a purchaser has acted in good faith necessarily depends on the extent of his knowledge of the relevant circumstances. In earlier times the tendency was to judge a purchaser solely by the facts that had actually come to his knowledge. This became unacceptable as Henchy J explains in *Somers v W*:[155]

> "In the course of time it came to be held that it would be unconscionable for the purchaser to take his stand on the facts that had come to his notice to the exclusion of those which ordinary prudence or circumspection or skill should have called to his attention. When the facts at his command beckoned him to look and inquire further and he refrained from doing so equity fixed him with constructive notice of what he would have ascertained if he had pursued the proper investigation which a person of reasonable care and skill would have felt proper to make in the circumstances. He would not be allowed to say 'I acted in good faith in ignorance of those facts of which I learned only after I took the conveyance' if those facts were such as a reasonable man in the circumstances would have brought within his knowledge."[156]

What type of enquiries should a purchaser make having regard to the changes made by the 1976 Act? If there is a dispute whether there is a binding contract at all there is not likely to be co-operation from an alleged vendor. The purchaser trying to prove and enforce a contract will have to maintain a suit for specific performance while at all times trying to get as much information as he can from enquiries, pleadings, requests for particulars, discovery of documents and any other steps open to him. He will bear in mind that if he launches or perseveres with a suit for specific performance without reasonable cause he may be held guilty of malice and have to pay damages for abuse of the processes of the court.[157] Thus, persevering with a claim after it becomes clear that a defence plea of s 3(1) of the 1976 Act must succeed is likely to get him into that type of trouble.

---

[154] *H & L v S* [1979] ILRM 105 at 108.

[155] [1979] IR 94 at p 108.

[156] This passage was approved by Gannon J in *Guckian v Brennan* [1981] IR 478 at 487 but he was dealing with registered property and, as he pointed out at 488, the purpose of registration of title is to avoid the application of the equitable doctrine of constructive or imputed notice in the absence of fraud. He held that the title was good but this was based on the conclusiveness of the register.

[157] *Dorene Ltd v Suedes (Ireland) Ltd* [1981] IR 312.

[7.23] In the happier situation where parties are negotiating towards a contract in a normal way or a contract is already in place enquiries will usually get a reasonable reaction. Henchy J offers this guidance to a purchaser:[158]

> "He must ascertain if the property, because of its present and past use, is a family home within the meaning of the Act of 1976. If it is, he must find out if it is a sale by a spouse and if so whether the conveyance should be preceded by the consent in writing of the other spouse so as to prevent its being rendered void under section 3. If that other spouse omits or refuses to consent the purchaser should require the vendor to apply to the court for an order under s 4 of the Act of 1976 dispensing with the consent...
>
> If ...the purchasers's case is that the wife's prior consent did not arise because he was a purchaser for full value without notice, he must show that the consideration amounted or approximated to the full value of the property and also that he, or his agent, made such inquiries or inspections as ought reasonably to have been made."[159]

If a purchaser takes a conveyance of a family home without spouse's consent, he carries the onus of showing that he comes within one of the exceptions in sub-ss 2 and 3. He cannot benefit from making inadequate enquiries. If proper inquiries or inspections have not been made but would, if made, have shown that a spouse's consent or an order dispensing with consent was needed, his conveyance will be every bit as bad as if he actually knew the position.

Whether property is a "family home"

[7.24] A purchaser of a dwelling must check before taking a conveyance whether the property[160] is a "family home" within the meaning of the 1976 Act. If it is, he will ask for spouse's consent and make normal enquiries to satisfy himself that the property is indeed the family home of that particular couple and cannot be the family home of one of them arising out of some other relationship or the family home of any other couple. In many cases the vendor and spouse will offer evidence on statutory declaration that they have each been married once only, *ie* to each other. If the vendor was married before[161] and the former partner is alive evidence may be offered - *eg* that the former spouse never lived in the house being sold - to show that the property could not be the "family home" of the vendor and former spouse. There will usually be nothing to throw doubt on that evidence so the purchaser should normally accept it.[162] The evidence would remove the risk that there is a different spouse under Irish law whose consent might be needed. If the spouse's consent in writing is given a subsequent dispute between vendor and spouse - *eg* as to the disposition of the purchase price - will not vitiate the consent.[163] If a property is a "family

---

[158] *Somers v W* [1979] IR 94 at p 111. The Supreme Court's decision is noted by McWilliam J in *Walpoles (Ireland) Ltd v Jay* (HC) 20 November 1980, unrep at p 3-4 as showing that a purchaser of a family home must make all proper inquiries into the position and must be satisfied that the facts disclosed do not give any rights to the spouse. In *Crowley v Flynn* [1983] ILRM 513 Barron J said that it held that the definition of "purchaser" as somebody who acquired in good faith put such person on notice of all matters which would have come to his solicitor's knowledge if such enquiries had been made as ought reasonably to have been made in the particular sale.

[159] These passages are set out in fuller form and applied by McWilliam J in *H & L v S* [1979] ILRM 105 at p 108.

[160] See para **7.14** and fn 85 *supra* on the use of the word "property" in s 3(1).

[161] For practical reasons most solicitors will treat both the present marriage of a vendor and any former marriage as valid and ensure that there can be no breach of s 3 in relation to either marriage. That avoids having to go into the area of marriage law.

[162] Note the approach of Costello J in *Reynolds v Waters* [1982] ILRM 335 at 338. *Cf Martin v Irish Permanent Building Society* (HC) McWilliam J, 30 July 1980, unrep.

[163] *Kyne v Tiernan* (HC) 15 July 1980, McWilliam J, unrep at 9.

home" and spouse's consent is not available the purchaser will often look for an order dispensing with consent and he will remember that he must have the consent in writing *before* conveyance.[164] Even if spouse's consent to the conveyance is not necessary[165] a solicitor may still prefer to get the consent for the conveyance in order to head off queries in the future. If spouse's consent to a conveyance is really needed it was probably needed also for the contract which would be void without that consent.[166] A solicitor may therefore make his inquiries with some discretion but if there must be a choice between risking the loss of the contract[167] and the client getting a void conveyance he will tell his client that the former risk is the less serious.

[7.25] If the purchaser's solicitor is told in reply to proper inquiries (which would normally include the use of the Law Society's standard requisitions[168]) that the property is not a "family home" within the 1976 Act he will require reasonable evidence to support the statement. If he gets that evidence he will not insist on getting either a consent or an order dispensing with it. He should expect to be told facts which if true establish that the dwelling is not a family home and to get agreement that those facts will be put on statutory declaration at closing.[169] A satisfactory declaration may be accepted without further corroboration unless there is some reason for doubt.[170] There is no general principle to the effect that a prudent purchaser should not accept the uncorroborated statutory declaration of a vendor merely because the vendor is gaining financially from the transaction.[171] On the other hand the purchaser's solicitor will not accept declaration evidence which is "a wild and inaccurate leap in the dark".[172] Nor will he recklessly let the vendor make a solemn statutory declaration which is untrue and can readily be so discovered.[173] The declaration should of course set out the facts relied on and they should be sufficient to establish that the property is not a family home.[174] It ought to be handed over duly completed when the sale is closed although, if a party refuses to complete, the fact that the declaration was not finalised by the agreed closing date is not necessarily a good defence to an action for specific performance.[175]

[7.26] If a formal contract exists and a dispute arises over any of these matters a typical issue being whether there is sufficient evidence that a property is not a family home

---

[164] *Somers v W* [1979] IR 94, Henchy J at 112 and Griffin J at 114.

[165] Note the points at para **7.07** *supra*.

[166] *H & L v S* [1979] ILRM 105 at 109. Note the *Pre-Contract* Check List issued by the Law Society with the July/August 1990 Gazette; item 14 asks whether the property is a "family home" within the 1976 Act.

[167] If, *eg*, the enquiries get a reaction of refusal to proceed with the contract claiming it was void due to lack of spouse's prior consent in writing.

[168] Item 14 of the Law Society's 1990 Purchaser's Solicitor's *Pre-Contract* Check List on the acquisition of private dwellinghouses draws attention to the possibility that property sold or part of it may be a "family home" within the 1976 Act. This looks like a move nearer pre-contract requisitions though the Check List is not framed as such. A note on it says that it is not designed for use as pre-contract requisitions.

[169] *Reynolds v Waters* [1982] ILRM 335 at p 338.

[170] *Ibid.* If he does not accept the declaration he may be held guilty of "default" and become liable to pay interest. Note too the view of McWilliam J in *Martin v Irish Permanent Building Society* (HC) 30 July 1980, unrep at p 4 that it is reasonable to assume that stated facts are true unless contradicted.

[171] *Reynolds's* case at 338.

[172] A phrase used by Henchy J in *Somers v W* [1979] IR 94 at 107 to describe a statement in a declaration that by virtue of a separation agreement a wife now had no interest in the property sold. The solicitor had never seen the separation agreement!

[173] McCarthy J's comment on the same events in *W v Somers* [1983] IR 122 at 127.

[174] *Hegarty v Morgan* (HC) 15 March 1979, McWilliam J, unrep at 8-9.

[175] *Dublin Laundry Co Ltd v Clarke* [1989] ILRM 29 at 36.

within the 1976 Act, the best vehicle for testing the matter is usually a Vendor and Purchaser summons.[176] The 1976 Act has in practice given rise to many conveyancing problems and purchasers' solicitors have not only to satisfy themselves that their clients can safely take their purchase deeds but they must also try to guard against difficulties which may arise when the property is re-sold.[177] The Vendor and Purchaser Act 1874 provides a comparatively simple procedure for resolving disputes between vendors and purchasers.[178] The procedure cannot be used to get declarations that statements of fact made on affidavit or declaration are true although it is reasonable to assume that they are true unless contradicted. A judge might be willing to make a declaration that facts shown in a declaration, if true, establish that a property is not a family home within the meaning of the 1976 Act.[179] Once the facts of a case have been established or the vendor has failed to make disclosure and the parties have joined issue over the legal effect of the facts or the failure to furnish information, it is then for the court to decide what is the legal position - whether good title has been shown or whether the vendor was bound to furnish further or better evidence of title.[180]

The consent and dispensing with it

[7.27] The 1976 Act does not require any particular formality for the consent and a letter from the spouse is fine.[181] Although a consent may be informal other steps may also be needed and care should be taken that everything required is covered. Thus if a married couple are joint owners and *eg* the husband is selling or mortgaging his share in the family home his wife must consent to that under s 3(1). Where the wife's share is also intended to be sold or mortgaged she must give a conveyance or mortgage of her share as well as her consent in writing to the disposition of her husband's share.[182] Of course, if the couple convey or mortgage the home *jointly*, as is the usual situation, there is no need for each to consent to the disposal by the other.[183]

An issue may arise whether the consenting spouse fully understood the effect of the consent and had any independent advice that might be necessary. This seems most likely to arise in cases where a wife gives consent to a security created by the husband on the family home and in this area Irish law is unclear.[184] One view is that in most cases there is no special relationship or position on the part of a lender which requires the giving of independent legal advice.[185] Another is that the husband and wife relationship has a "consequent inherent likelihood of influence and reliance" and a lender seeking the

---

[176] On Vendor and Purchaser summonses see paras **8.53-9** *post*.
[177] As noted by Costello J in *Reynolds v Waters* [1982] ILRM 335 at 338. The solicitor may also have to "certify" title for a lender.
[178] *Per* McWilliam J in *Martin v Irish Permanent Building Society* (HC) 30 July 1980, unrep.
[179] As McWilliam J did in *Martin's* case a bit reluctantly and with reservations about the approach of the parties to the case.
[180] *Mulligan v Dillon* (HC) 7 November 1980, McWilliam J, unrep at 3-4.
[181] *Kyne v Tiernan* (HC) 15 July 1980, McWilliam J, unrep at 9. Many solicitors have it endorsed on a purchase deed.
[182] *Re White, a Bankrupt*, Hamilton P, 4 December 1990, reported as a courts news item, *Irish Times*, 5 December 1990.
[183] *Nestor v Murphy* [1979] IR 326 at 328-9.
[184] The cases mentioned in the next two footnotes are both under appeal. See also Doyle, *Husband and Wives - Undue Influence in Banking Law*, Law Society Gazette, June 1994 at 187-190. *Cf Allied Irish Banks Plc v English* (1992) 11 LT 208.
[185] *Bank of Nova Scotia v Hogan*, 21 December 1992, Keane J, unrep at 14-15. *Cf CIBC Mortgages v Pitt* [1993] 4 All ER 433.

wife's consent pursuant to the 1976 Act is under extensive duties to explain the position and recommend independent advice.[186] If the consent is obtained by ,*eg*, misrepresentation and the lender has notice of the relevant facts the consent is likely to be held invalid.[187] In the normal case of a *sale* of a house no special relationship will exist between the parties and the purchaser usually will be unaware of any irregularity concerning the consent of the vendor's spouse.

Under s 4 of the 1976 Act the court has power to dispense with the consent of a spouse whose consent is required but who omits or refuses to give it. The need for a dispensing order and the fact that one has been made are the matters which concern parties to actions for specific performance.[188] Section 3(1) of the 1976 Act is expressed to be subject to s 4 so when a dispensing order is made under s 4 the sanction of voidness under s 3 cannot arise.

Disability

[7.28] The court has power to give a consent on behalf of a spouse who is incapable of consenting by reason of unsoundness of mind or other mental disability or one who cannot be found after reasonable inquiries.[189] Formerly a valid consent which could be repudiated on attaining majority could not be obtained from a spouse who was an infant[190] and the omission of reference to infants in s 4(4) could not be construed as meaning that the legislature considered that a minor spouse was able to give the necessary consent without any court approval.[191] However s 10(1) of the Family Law Act 1981 validated consents by spouses who had not attained the age of majority.[192] The Age of Majority Act 1985 reduced the age of majority from 21 to 18 and provides that a person attains full age on marrying under the age of 18 after the commencement of the Act.[193] This reference to marrying presumably has in mind a valid marriage according to the law for the time being and this probably means that there is still a difficulty over a purported consent by a person under 18 who is in a relationship short of a valid marriage.

Other family rights

[7.29] In most cases careful enquiries aimed at the 1976 Act will produce information which will dispose of other possible family rights.[194] However, this is not always so and a careful eye must be kept on other possibilities. At this stage in the chapter we use the word "family" in a flexible sense and there may be rights between an unmarried couple in equity or under an implied trust.[195] Rights may also arise from the fact that a woman is a mother even if she is not married.[196] A judicial effort has been made to extend or develop

---

[186] *Bank of Ireland v Smyth* [1993] IR 102 at 108-11.
[187] *Barclays Bank plc v O'Brien* [1993] 4 All ER 416.
[188] A detailed discussion of the approach of the courts to dispensation with consent may be found at paras 11.024-31 of Duncan & Scully, *Marriage Breakdown in Ireland* (1990).
[189] Section 4 (4).
[190] *Lloyd v Sullivan* (HC) 6 March 1981, McWilliam J, unrep at p 3.
[191] *Lloyd's* case at 3.
[192] The validation includes consents given before the passing of the 1981 Act. Subsection (2) validated consents by guardians prior to the passing of the 1981 Act.
[193] Section 2(1)(*b*).
[194] Parke J in *Northern Bank Ltd v Henry* [1981] IR 1 at p 22.
[195] The law was considered fully by Gannon J in *McGill v LS* [1979] IR 283; he held that the facts were insufficient to enable the woman to establish a beneficial interest in the house in the man's name. See also para **7.35** *infra*.
[196] See para **7.34** *infra*.

the law so that by carrying out the "constitutionally endorsed activities of a wife and mother within the home"[197] a woman should get certain property rights but the Supreme Court felt that taking that road would usurp the function of the legislature.[198] The obligation on the State to endeavour to ensure that mothers shall not be obliged by economic necessity to engage in labour outside the home to the neglect of their duties applies also to the Judiciary as one of the organs of the State.[199] However, that duty does not grant jurisdiction to the courts to award to a wife and mother any particular interest in the family home.[200] As this is *not* a book on family law[201] or on equity generally,[202] we will cover this ground briefly.

[7.30] The development of the law applying to a situation where a wife has contributed to the purchase of the family home was noted by Henchy J in *McC v McC*:[203]

> "Since the decision of Kenny J in *C v C* (1976) IR 254,[204] it has been judicially accepted that where the matrimonial home has been purchased in the name of the husband and the wife has, either directly or indirectly, made contributions towards the purchase price or towards the discharge of mortgage instalments the husband will be held to be a trustee for the wife of a share in the house roughly corresponding with the proportion of the purchase money represented by the wife's total contribution. Such a trust will be inferred when the wife's contribution is of such a size and kind as will justify the conclusion that the acquisition of the house was achieved by the joint efforts of the spouses.
>
> When the wife's contribution has been indirect (such as by contributing by means of her earnings to a general family fund) the courts will, in the absence of any express or implied agreement to the contrary, infer a trust in favour of the wife, on the ground that she has to that extent relieved the husband of the financial burden he incurred in purchasing the house."[205]

If there is an agreement between spouses as to the ownership of the family home the court will enforce it.[206] Usually there is no agreement. An express agreement is rarely made. Trying to infer an implied agreement when payments are made or expenses paid by a wife may be futile because when the spouses are living happily together, they are not likely to think of stipulating that payments by one of them are made to acquire a share in the home.[207] However, in view of the particular features of dealings between husband and wife in an amicable marriage, a trust may arise from the indirect contributions by the provision through earnings of money for the family pool.[208] A direct contribution by a wife makes the position easier to assess. Where she makes a money contribution to the purchase of a property by her husband in his sole name, then, in the absence of evidence

---

[197] The phrase used by Finlay CJ in *L v L* [1992] 2 IR 77 at 108, Hederman J concurring. See also para **7.32** *infra*.
[198] *Ibid* at 107.
[199] *Ibid*, p 108.
[200] *Ibid*. See discussion at para **7.32** *infra*.
[201] Duncan & Scully on *Marriage Breakdown in Ireland* (1990) discuss many property issues in a family context in Chapters 10, 12 and 13.
[202] See Keane, *Equity and the Law of Trusts in the Republic of Ireland* (1988), Ch 12, esp paras 12.12 to 12.16.
[203] [1986] ILRM 1 at 2.
[204] See also *Heavey v Heavey* (1974) 111 ILTR 1.
[205] Almost the entire of that passage is quoted with approval by Egan J in *L v L* [1992] IR 77 at 113-4.
[206] *C v C* [1976] IR 254 at 257.
[207] *Ibid*, p 258. And see *Heavey v Heavey* (1974) 111 ILTR 1.
[208] Finlay CJ in *L v L* at 107-8, Hederman J concurring.

of some inconsistent agreement or arrangement, she is entitled to an equitable interest in the property roughly proportionate to the extent of her contribution as against the value of the property when she made the contribution.[209]

The reverse does not usually work. If a husband makes a contribution to the purchase of property in his wife's sole name he is presumed by a rebuttable presumption to have intended to *advance* his wife and will have no claim to an equitable estate in the property unless he rebuts that presumption.[210] The equitable doctrine of advancement as applied to transactions between husband and wife has the effect that when a husband buys property and has it conveyed to himself and his wife jointly there is a presumption that the wife's paper title does give her a beneficial estate or interest in the property.[211] The estate or interest is treated in law as an advancement, *ie,* a material benefit given in anticipation of the performance by the husband of his duty to provide for the wife.[212] To rebut the presumption the husband must show by reference to acts or statements before or around the transaction or from subsequent acts or statements by the wife that a beneficial interest was not intended to be conveyed.[213] If the relevant circumstances show that the paper result produced by a conveyance conceals the real intention and that the benefit contended for by the wife was not intended the court will hold that the presumption of advancement has been rebutted.[214]

A spouse, usually the wife, who is entitled to a beneficial share in property in the sole name of the other spouse should beware of leading others to believe that the owning spouse is in fact sole beneficial owner. Doing so may estop her from asserting her claim in priority to the misled person. Thus a wife who represents by conduct to an intending lender that her husband is sole beneficial owner of the property, she is consenting to him mortgaging it and she has no beneficial interest in it will not be able to assert her claim against the lender.[215] The estoppel does not destroy the claim but does postpone it to the rights of the lender.[216]

[7.31] The redemption of any form of charge or mortgage on property is an acquisition by the owner or mortgagor of an estate in the property with which he had parted when he created the mortgage or charge.[217] There can be no distinction in principle between a wife's contribution made to the discharge of a mortgage or charge and one made to an original purchase.[218] If there is no inconsistent agreement or arrangement she also becomes entitled to an equitable interest in the property by contributing to the payment of mortgage *instalments* directly or indirectly.[219] In principle it would seem that there is a change in the extent of a mortgagor's and a mortgagee's estates in property when any part of the sum secured is repaid. This is consistent with the fact that whenever a *further*

---

[209] *W v W* [1981] ILRM 202 at 204.
[210] *Ibid.*
[211] *RF v MF* (SC) 24 October 1985, unrep, *per* Henchy J at 6.
[212] *Ibid,* p 7.
[213] *Ibid.*
[214] *Ibid,* p 8.
[215] *Doherty v Doherty* [1991] 2 IR 458 at 463; *Hibernian Life Association Ltd v Gibbs* (HC) 23 July 1993, 5 Costello J, unrep at 5; *Ulster Bank Ltd v Shanks* [1982] NI 143 at 148-50.
[216] *Doherty s* case at 463.
[217] *EN v RN* [1992] 2 IR 116 at 123 quoting from his judgment in *W v W* [1981] ILRM 202. He is giving the judgment of a court of five.
[218] *Ibid.*
[219] *McC v McC* [1986] ILRM 1 at 2; *W v W* [1981] ILRM 202 at 203.

advance is made on the security of property the interest of the mortgagor in the property charged is altered.[220] Where both spouses have contributed to the purchase of a house and payment of the mortgage but one spouse ceases to do so it is likely that the shares of the spouses in the property will be fixed as they stood when the spouse ceased to contribute.[221] If the house is mortgaged the value to be shared is the difference between the market value and the debt due to the mortgagee, that difference being expressed as a percentage of the market value.[222] Apparently a contribution, even a direct one in money's worth, to *improvement* of the family home in the sole name of the husband would not entitle the wife to a beneficial interest in it under the pre-1989 law[223] in the absence of an express or readily implied agreement.[224] Even if a right to recompense were established either by expressed agreement or from circumstances showing that the wife making the contribution was led to believe that she would have such a right she would only have a right to payment of money, not a share in the property.[225] Nor would a contribution to the acquisition of furniture lead to a share in the house though it could, of course, confer an interest in the furniture itself.[226] No matter how desirable it may be that a wife who is also a mother should, if possible, work in the family home and carry out the duties involved, in particular, in rearing children there if she did not wish to be employed outside[227] it seemed impossible to infer any form of resulting or constructive trust in her favour from that conduct.[228] This was so even though she might save a probable expenditure from her husband's earnings on a housekeeper or nanny.[229] However, work done which is different from the work of a wife and mother could qualify her for a beneficial interest in the house.[230] It is important to bear in mind that the points noted here are subject, where a decree of judicial separation is granted, to the 1989 changes in the law considered later.[231]

[7.32] It is "the constitutionally preferred option that a wife who is also a mother should remain at home and devote herself entirely to the family after the marriage". Thus a submission on behalf of the wife in *L v L*.[232] It was contended that Article 41 gave the courts jurisdiction to declare that the wife was entitled to a share in the beneficial ownership of the family home, not because of any financial contribution direct or indirect to the acquisition of the home, but on the basis that the Constitution warranted the

---

[220] *Bank of Ireland v Purcell* [1989] IR 327 at 331 at 333.

[221] As Finlay P did in *L v L*, Cir App, 27 February 1984, unrep.

[222] *L's* case at p 6. Finlay P gave a "simple example": if the amount outstanding on the mortgage at the relevant time was 10% of the market value, then the wife, whom he held entitled to 50% of the equity of redemption, would be entitled to 45% of the value of the house.

[223] The position is probably different now under the Judicial Separation and Family Law Reform Act 1989 which came into force on 19 October 1989.

[224] *EN v RN* [1992] 2 IR 116 at 122. *Cf* where a husband borrows money to make improvements to a house in his wife's name let in flats; she may not be let retain the rents without letting the husband's debt be paid out of them: *Heavey v Heavey* (1974) 111 ILTR 1.

[225] *W v W* [1981] ILRM 202 at 205.

[226] *McC v McC* [1986] ILRM 1 at 2.

[227] Finlay CJ referred to this as the "constitutionally preferred course of conduct" in *EN v RN* [1992] 2 IR 116 at 122.

[228] *Ibid.*

[229] *Ibid.* But see now s 20(2)(f) of the Judicial Separation and Family Law Reform Act 1989 discussed in para **7.33** *nfra*.

[230] *EN's* case at 123-4. The wife totally managed bedsitter apartments in the house, collected the rents and did the general care and maintenance.

[231] Para **7.33** *infra*. The High Court has dismissed a constitutional attack on this Act but an appeal is pending at the time of writing. Note that the Family Law Bill 1994 is going through the Oireachtas.

[232] [1992] 2 IR 77 at 103.

declaration of such a share.[233] The Supreme Court was sympathetic to the submissions.[234] It accepted that there is an inconsistency between the position of a wife who does paid work outside the home and contributes directly or indirectly in money terms and the less advantageous position with regard to ownership of an interest in the family home of the wife who follows the constitutionally preferred activity of staying at home to look after the family.[235] However, it could not accept that the courts had jurisdiction, by reason of the provisions of Article 41 of the Constitution, or by reason of any general principle to be derived from them, to make specific declarations concerning ownership of the family home which were derived from a principle of reward or implied benefit not known to the existing doctrines of resulting or constructive trust.[236] To grant the right sought would be to identify a brand new right and secure it to the plaintiff, not development of any known principle of the common law.[237] Unless that new right is something clearly and unambiguously warranted by the Constitution or made necessary for the protection of a specified or unspecified right under it, granting the right would be legislation by the courts and thus a usurpation of the function of the legislature.[238] It would be making a quantum leap in constitutional law to hold that by her life within the home the mother acquires a beneficial interest in it.[239] It is interesting to note, however, that one member of the court left open the possibility that in another case circumstances might arise whereby on the true interpretation of the relevant Article it would prove necessary to accord to the mother some proprietary interest in the home.[240]

[7.33] The legislature may, of course, confer jurisdiction on the courts to deal with property rights between spouses. It has done so by virtue of Part II of the Judicial Separation and Family Law Reform Act 1989 as part of the general jurisdiction on the granting of a judicial separation. In deciding whether to exercise its powers the court has the primary aim of seeking to ensure that provision is made for any spouse and dependent children which "is adequate and reasonable having regard to all the circumstances of the case".[241] The courts will exercise these powers in obedience to and furtherance of Article 41.2.2 of the Constitution.[242] Section 20 (2)(*f*) of the 1989 Act now requires the court in exercising its powers under ss 13, 14, 15 or 16(*a*) or (*b*) of the Act to have regard to

> the contributions which each of the spouses has made or is likely in the foreseeable future to make to the welfare of the family, including the contribution made by each spouse to the income earning capacity, property and financial resources of the other and any contribution by looking after the home or caring for the family.

Section 15(1) of the 1989 Act confers wide powers to make property adjustment orders on granting a decree of judicial separation.[243] A claim for a property adjustment order will

---

[233] See Finlay CJ at 103-7.
[234] See the approach of Finlay CJ at 106-7, Hederman J concurring.
[235] *Ibid*, at 106, Hederman J concurring.
[236] *EN v RN* [1992] 2 IR 116 at 122 referring to the reasoning in his judgment in *L's* case. In *L's* case McCarthy J left open the possibility that circumstances might arise whereby, on the true interpretation of the relevant Article, it would prove necessary to accord to the mother some proprietary interest in the home: p 110.
[237] Finlay CJ in *L v L* [1992] 2 IR 77 at 107, Hederman J concurring.
[238] *Ibid.*
[239] McCarthy J in *L's* case at 111.
[240] *Ibid.*
[241] Section 20(1) of the 1989 Act.
[242] *Per* Finlay CJ in *L's* case at 109, Hederman J concurring. He had in mind Article 41.2.2.
[243] See discussion at paras 13.010-015 of Duncan & Scully, *Marriage Breakdown in Ireland* (1990).

usually justify the registration of a *lis pendens*.[244] Under s 16(*a*) the court may give either spouse a right to occupy the family home to the exclusion of the other and s 16(*b*) gives power to order a sale of the family home subject to such conditions as the court considers proper.[245] The broad wording of s 20(2)(*f*) of the 1989 Act entitles the courts to place a money or property value on the work done by one spouse, usually the wife in looking after the family and the home and in giving the other spouse back-up which contributes to his success in his work outside the home. It may also allow the courts to hold a spouse to be entitled to a share in the family home because of contributions[246] to *improvement* of the home or provision of furniture and fittings. The primary element is now contributions by the spouses to family welfare.[247]

However, the Oireachtas must take care in its amending legislation not to encroach too far on the authority of the family. The courts accept the advantages of encouraging by any appropriate means joint ownership in family homes as being conducive to the dignity, reassurance and independence of each of the spouses and the partnership concept of marriage which is fundamental to it.[248] However, the potentially indiscriminate alteration by a new law of many joint decisions validly made within the authority of the family concerning the ownership of the family home cannot reasonably be justified even by such an important aspect of the common good.[249]

[7.34] It is interesting to note that rights under Article 41.2.2 may not be confined to *married* mothers.[250] Article 41.2. reads:

1°   In particular the State recognises that by her life within the home, woman gives to the State a support without which the common good cannot be achieved.

2°   The State shall, therefore[251], endeavour to ensure that mothers shall not be obliged by economic necessity to engage in labour to the neglect of their duties in the home.

Section 2 of the Article is clearly referring to "mothers" only: not wives nor wives and mothers, but mothers.[252] It requires the State to endeavour to ensure that mothers with children to rear or to be cared for are given economic aid by the State though it would be open to the State to say that it was doing its best having regard to its overall budgetary situation.[253]

[7.35] To a large extent the basic principles of law applying between husband and wife are the same as between strangers. In *McFarlane v McFarlane*[254] Lowry J summarised the effect of recent decisions as follows:

"In my opinion the recent cases in the House of Lords clearly show that the rights acquired by a wife in property which at law belongs to her husband depend not on her

---

[244] *AS v GS* [1994] 2 ILRM 68 at 73.
[245] Duncan & Scully, *op cit*, paras 13.016-018.
[246] Such contributions probably come within s 20(2)(*f*) of the 1989 Act.
[247] The wording of s (20)(2)(*f*) has "the welfare of the family" as its primary element.
[248] *In re Article 26 and the Matrimonial Home Bill 1993* [1994] 1 ILRM 241 at 254.
[249] *Ibid.*
[250] See McCarthy J in *L v L* [1992] 2 IR 77 at 111; O'Flaherty J at 112.
[251] McCarthy J on "therefore" in *L's* case at 111; Egan J at 115.
[252] *Per* O'Flaherty J in *L's* case at 112.
[253] *Ibid.*
[254] [1972] NI 59.

deserts as a wife but on legal principles which are equally applicable between strangers: a direct contribution to the purchase price will, in the absence of a contrary intention, attract an equitable interest; an indirect contribution accompanied by an agreement will, and unaccompanied by an agreement will not, give the contributor an equitable interest. Two modifications apply between spouses, first that an arrangement is as good as an agreement, and second that the doctrine of advancement *may* operate against a husband contributor."[255]

Thus, in the case of two persons who are not spouses, evidence of a consensus derived from words or conduct and intended to have legal consequences would support a trust expressed or implied or constructive.[256] But whether the party having the legal estate and the party claiming an equitable interest be spouses or not, the court will not impute a relationship of trustee and cestui que trust from the facts of a couple living together in (or seemingly in) the married state and sharing expenses without any more cogent evidence.[257] However, when an unmarried couple live together both may make substantial *direct* contributions to the purchase of the relevant property though it is put into the name of just one of them.[258] The direct contributions by the non-owning party will attract an equitable interest in the absence of agreement to the contrary. The court also may be entitled to take into account contributions towards living expenses which affect the amount of contributions the other party can make towards acquisition of the house.[259] It would often seem reasonable to infer a consensus that indirect contributions of the sort would be treated as going in part towards acquisition of the house.[260]

[7.36] A party wishing to claim any of the family type rights just discussed[261] against a purchaser of land registered in the Land Registry may have to move fast. On completing his contract and getting a valid transfer and possession a purchaser will seek registration as owner in the Registry. If the claimant has not registered a caution or inhibition the purchaser is likely to get himself duly registered[262] and will then be able to rely on the conclusiveness of the register in the absence of fraud.[263] Cautions and inhibitions are in effect restrictions on dealings with registered land without notice to or consent of parties who claim some unregistered right or interest.[264] A caution may be registered by "any person entitled to any right in, to, or over registered land or a registered charge".[265] It has the primary effect that "no dealing with the land or charge is to be had on the part of the registered owner until notice has been served on the cautioner".[266] An inhibition can be

---

[255] At 78. The passage is quoted with approval by Gannon J in *McGill v S* [1979] IR 283 at 288-9.
[256] *Per* Gannon J in *McGill v S* [1979] IR 283 at 289.
[257] *Ibid.*
[258] As in *Power v Conroy* [1980] ILRM 31. The position was thus significantly different from that in *McGill s* case.
[259] *Power's* case at 32.
[260] *McGill's* case was not opened in *Power's* case. The two are consistent. Gannon J was satisfied in *McGill* that a "consensus" would support a trust (at 289) but the woman made no significant direct contributions (291-2). In *Power* contributions by the woman to living expenses affected the mortgage payments the man could make.
[261] Paras **7.29-35** *supra.*
[262] Depending on the circumstances the claimant may already be too late if the purchaser gets an enforceable contract without notice of the claim.
[263] On conclusiveness in relation to the 1976 Act see para **7.16** *supra*. Section 29(4) of the 1979 Act deals with bona fide purchasers but does not affect the conclusiveness of the register.
[264] See discussion in Ch 10 of Fitzgerald, *Land Registry Practice* (1989); para 21.51 of Wylie, *Irish Land Law*, 2nd Ed (1986) and para 5.11 of Keane, *Equity and the Law of Trusts in the Republic of Ireland* (1988).
[265] Section 97(1) of the Registration of Title Act 1964.
[266] *Ibid.*

registered on the application of "any person interested in any registered land or charge".[267] It has the effect of "inhibiting for a time, or until the occurrence of an event to be named in the order or entry, or except with the consent of or after notice to some specified person or generally until further order or entry, any dealing with any registered land or registered charge".[268]

[7.37] We have already discussed the exception in favour of a bona fide purchaser for full value from the sanction of voidness under the Family Home Protection Act 1976.[269] Section 29(2) of the Judicial Separation and Family Law Reform Act 1989 empowers the courts in certain circumstances to restrain an intended disposition or set aside one already made. A disposition in this context does not include a provision by will or codicil but, with that exception, includes any conveyance, assurance or gift of property of any description, whether made by an instrument or otherwise.[270] However, the 1989 Act excepts a disposition made for valuable consideration (other than marriage) to a person who, at the time of the disposition, acted in relation to it in good faith and without notice of any intention on the part of the disponor to defeat an applicant's claim for financial relief.[271] The expression "financial relief"[272] includes property adjustment orders pursuant to s 15 of the 1989 Act and orders pursuant to s 16(*a*) giving a spouse the right to occupy the family home to the exclusion of the other spouse or pursuant to s 16(*b*) for the sale of the family home. If it is ever held that under some Article of the Constitution or some principle deriving from any such Article it is right to confer some proprietary interest in a home on a mother[273] it is unlikely that the courts would give that interest priority over the claim of a bona fide purchaser for value without notice of the relevant facts.[274] There are three main types of notice, actual, constructive and imputed. Actual notice may be something less than spelling out exactly what the relevant matter is but must consist of information on which a reasonable man or an ordinary man of business would act and by which he would regulate his conduct.[275] The information would need to be a clear indication from a reliable source.[276] If an inference is relied on to fix a person with actual notice he must be shown to have known facts from which he *must* have inferred the relevant matter.[277] Simply failing to accept[278] information available or failing to make normal inquiries are criteria of constructive notice, not actual notice.[279] A failure to

---

[267] Section 98(1) of the 1964 Act.

[268] *Ibid.*

[269] Paras **7.21-25** *supra*.

[270] Section 29(6) of the 1989 Act.

[271] Section 29(4).

[272] Defined in s 29(1).

[273] Remember that in *L v L* [1992] 2 IR 77 McCarthy J referred to this kind of possibility: see para **7.32** and fn 236 *supra*.

[274] Probably the normal test of notice under s 3 of the Conveyancing Act 1881 would apply without the special deletion for the purposes of the 1976 Act: on this see para **7.21** *supra*.

[275] See judgment of Lord Cairns in *Lloyd v Banks* (1863) 3 Ch App 488 at 491 approved by Costello J in *O Connor v McCarthy* [1982] IR 161 at p 175.

[276] *O'Connor's* case at 175.

[277] *Bank of Ireland v Rockfield Ltd* [1979] IR 21 at 37.

[278] The word "accept" had been used in the High Court judgment at p 28; neither court used it to mean refusing to believe something which had been clearly communicated. The High Court may have meant "act on" or "make enquiries because of" and the Supreme Court felt that the High Court had blurred the distinction between actual notice and constructive notice: p 38.

[279] *Ibid*, p 38. The allegation was that the bank should have known that the money lent would be used for the purchase of shares in the borrower. Kenny J held at p 38 that the bank knew enough to be fixed with *constructive* notice but that was not the test.

inspect documents may well be an omission to do something which should have been done but it is not normally actual notice.[280] Imputed notice is the actual or constructive notice of an agent employed in the transaction in question.[281] It must, however, be knowledge which the agent was under a duty to communicate to his principal.[282]

[7.38] The type of notice most likely to need consideration in practice is *constructive* notice. Under s 3(1) of the Conveyancing Act 1882 a purchaser is not prejudicially affected with notice of any instrument, fact or thing unless:

(i)   It is within his own knowledge, or would have come to his knowledge if such inquiries and inspections had been made as ought reasonably to have been made by him; or

(ii)   In the same transaction with respect to which a question of notice to the purchaser arises, it has come to the knowledge of his counsel, as such, or of his solicitor, or other agent, as such, or would have come to the knowledge of his solicitor, or other agent, as such, if such inquiries and inspections had been made as ought reasonably to have been made by the solicitor or other agent.[283]

That text did not amount to the imposition of any novel or unfair duty of investigation of title on purchasers.[284] Well before the Act of 1882 the Chancery judges had evolved the same test for determining whether a purchaser or mortgagee should have constructive notice attributed to him.[285] As Henchy J explained, s 3(1) of the 1882 Act:[286]

"... gave statutory stress to the existing judicial insistence that constructive notice could be found only when the lack of knowledge was due to such careless inactivity as would not be expected in the circumstances from a reasonable man. The default of a reasonable man is to be distinguished from the default of a prudent man. The prudence of the worldly wise may justifiably persuade a purchaser that it would be unbusinesslike to stop and look more deeply into certain aspects of the title. But the reasonable man in the eyes of the law will be expected to look beyond the impact of his decisions on his own affairs and to consider whether they may unfairly and prejudicially affect his 'neighbour' in the sense in which that word has been given juristic currency by Lord Atkin in *Donoghue v Stevenson*.[287]"

The test of what inquiries and inspections ought reasonably to be made is an objective test which depends not on what the particular purchaser thought proper to do in the particular circumstances but on what a purchaser of the particular property ought reasonably to have done in order to acquire title to it.[288] A person who abstains from enquiry when enquiry ought to have been made cannot be allowed to rely on his

---

[280] *Ibid* p 39. It would have led to a finding of constructive notice if that had been the test.
[281] Wylie, *Irish Land Law*, 2nd Ed (1986), para 3.073.
[282] *Re Burmester* (1858) 9 Ir Ch R 513; Snell's *Equity*, 29th Ed (1990), p 55.
[283] This has been considered at para **7.21** *supra* in the context of the 1976 Act with the special deletion of "as such".
[284] *Per* Henchy J in *Northern Bank v Henry* [1981] IR 1 at 11.
[285] *Ibid*. Note that the definition of "purchaser" in s 1(4)(iii) of the 1882 Act includes "a lessee or mortgagee, or an intending purchaser, lessee, or mortgagee, or other person who, for valuable consideration, takes or deals for property".
[286] *Ibid*, pp 11-12.
[287] [1932] AC 562.
[288] *Northern Bank Ltd v Henry* [1981] IR 1 at 9.

ignorance.[289] The plea of purchaser for value without notice is a single plea to be proved by the person pleading it; it is not to be regarded as a plea of purchaser for value to be met by a reply of notice.[290] Thus a person who makes no enquiries *at all* cannot discharge the onus of proof on him.[291] Nor is it likely to suffice to have a "title looked at summarily".[292]

[7.39] Anyone who is offered a title to what is or includes a home by one spouse or partner should be alert to the possibility that the second person may have a claim which would be upheld by the courts to at least a share in the beneficial interest in the property.[293] For many years the so called "working wife", who brings a regular pay packet into the home, has been a familiar figure on the domestic scene; and since the working wife's own money often finds its way in whole or in part, and directly or indirectly, into the purchase of the matrimonial home,[294] the existence in a working wife of a proprietary interest in the matrimonial home is a familiar feature in cases coming before the courts nowadays.[295] If the property is in the sole name of the husband it may still be wholly owned beneficially by the wife.[296] And if the house is in the joint names it may also be solely owned beneficially by the wife, *eg* if there is a resulting trust of the husband's apparent share.[297] More rarely[298] a house in the joint names can turn out to be wholly owned beneficially by the husband.[299] All of these possibilities exist also where there is some form of partnership or association other than marriage.

Wholly apart from family type claims a purchaser's knowledge that persons are in occupation is likely to be held to be notice of their tenancies and all rights attaching to those tenancies.[300] The fact that a wife is in occupation of a house may be material to the question whether a purchaser or mortgagee is on constructive notice of any claims she may have.[301] It has been said that a prospective purchaser or mortgagee must at his peril take steps to investigate the rights (if any) of a person in occupation of the property in question other than the prospective vendor or mortgagor with whom he is dealing.[302] It is important to remember that more than one person can be in occupation of a property at any given time and a prospective purchaser or mortgagee must act accordingly.[303] Family type rights of the sort we have been discussing[304] do not depend on occupation by the

---

[289] *Per* Ross J in *Bunbury v Hibernian Bank Ltd* [1908] 1 IR 261 at 268 approving a passage from Kerr on *Fraud*. *Cf Waldron v Jacob* (1870) IR 5 Eq 131 at 138-9.

[290] *Per* Farwell J in *Re Nisbet and Potts' Contract* [1905] 1 Ch 391 at 402 approved by Meredith and O'Byrne JJ in *Heneghan v Davitt* [1933] IR 375 at p 377 and 379; and Kenny J in *Northern Bank Ltd v Henry* [1981] IR 1 at 19.

[291] *Allied Irish Banks Ltd v McWilliams* [1982] NI 156 at 161.

[292] Henchy J's phrase in *Northern Bank Ltd v Henry* [1981] IR 1 at 8.

[293] The *Northern Bank* case at 21 (Parke J). Cf Henchy J at 10.

[294] See paras **7.30-31** *supra*.

[295] *Per* Murray J in *Ulster Bank Ltd v Shanks* [1982] NI 143, 146. See also Henchy J in the *Northern Bank* case at 10 and Parke J at 21.

[296] As occurred in the *Northern Bank* case.

[297] As in *Allied Irish Banks Ltd v McWilliams* [1982] NI 156.

[298] Because he will have to prove a resulting trust and rebut the presumption of advancement.

[299] As in *RF v MF* (SC) 24 October 1985, unrep.

[300] *Healy v Farragher* (SC) 21 December 1972, unrep at 8-12; *Carroll v Keayes* (1873) IR 8 Eq 97. *Cf Clements v Conroy* [1911] 2 IR 500.

[301] *Northern Bank Ltd v Henry* [1981] IR 1, *per* Henchy J at p 9-10 and Parke J at p 21 (Kenny J said at p 19 that a mortgagee was not bound to inspect the property on which he is taking a mortgage).

[302] By Murray J in *Ulster Bank Ltd v Shanks* [1982] NI 143 at 150.

[303] *Ibid*, p 147.

[304] From paras **7.29** to **7.39**.

claimant but the fact that a claimant does occupy is at least consistent with having a right to do so. If an intending purchaser or mortgagee suspects that such a right may exist how should he deal with it? Let us adopt the words of Parke J:[305]

> "Having been alerted to the possible existence of such a claim, it is the duty of those investigating the title to dispose of it. It would not be right for me to attempt to suggest how this should have been done, because different conditions may apply to different cases. In the present case the standard requisition as to threatened litigation would have been sufficient because the wife had already threatened proceedings; in other cases it might not. In some cases it might appear to the investigator that it was desirable to obtain evidence of the consent of the other spouse to a sale.[306] A requisition requiring vacant possession (on a sale) or evidence that there was no person in possession on any claim of right (on a mortgage) would have sufficed in the present case because the wife was in possession; but a spouse's claim to an interest in the matrimonial home does not depend upon occupation, so this requisition might be ineffectual."

Of course, in a claim for specific performance the first issue is often whether there is a complete and binding contract at all; the parties usually will not get down to the civilities of raising requisitions and replying to them. The party claiming specific performance must still keep alert for possible family type claims usually, but not always, from a spouse.

---

[305] The *Northern Bank* case at 21-2.
[306] Remember that the relevant facts in this case occurred before the commencement of the 1976 Act.

Chapter 8

The Plaintiff's Case

[8.01] A person thinking of suing for specific performance and his legal advisers will consider first of all whether there is a contract.[1] They will expect problems if there was no consideration or any consideration given was very small.[2] If there was a contract and normal valuable consideration for it, was it a kind of contract which would be enforced by specific performance?[3] Are any circumstances known which, having regard to the discretionary nature[4] of the remedy, might lead to the relief being withheld? Does the Statute of Frauds apply and, if so, can the plaintiff show that it was satisfied when the defendant puts this in issue?[5] If there is not enough in writing to satisfy the statute is there anything to take the case out of the statute?[6] The plaintiff will also consider whether the Family Home Protection Act 1976 applies and, if it does, what steps, if any, can and should be taken.[7] He will try to foresee likely defences and how he will deal with them.[8] In addition the plaintiff and his advisers will consider with care the various matters about to be discussed in this chapter.[9]

JURISDICTION

The High Court

[8.02] Under Article 34.2.3.1. of the Constitution the High Court is invested with full original jurisdiction in and power to determine all matters and questions whether of law or fact, civil or criminal.[10] This jurisdiction has been described as a universal original jurisdiction in all matters of fact and of law in addition to all other jurisdictions which have been transferred to it[11] by statute.[12] The fact that a former court had no jurisdiction

---

[1] See discussion of consensus in paras **3.01-05**, the material terms at paras **3.08-18**, conditional contracts at paras **3.19-28** and "subject to contract" in Ch 4.

[2] See paras **3.06-7** *post*.

[3] Paras **1.14-27** *ante*.

[4] On the discretion see paras **1.06-9** *ante*.

[5] The statute is considered in Ch 5.

[6] Usually part performance which is discussed in Ch 6.

[7] See Ch 7.

[8] Defences are discussed in Ch 9 below.

[9] We consider jurisdiction in paras **8.02-11**, parties in paras **8.12-20**, pleadings in paras **8.12-4**, possible court orders in paras **8.25-8**, time in paras **8.29-40**, "ready, willing and able" at paras **8.41-3**, interest in paras **8.44-7**, damages in certain circumstances at paras **8.48-52** and vendor and purchaser summonses at paras **8.53-9**. Aspects of relationships between damages and the relief of specific performance were discussed at paras **1.01, 1.05, 1.08, 1.10** and **1.28-31** *ante*. Ch 11 covers other matters such as a vendor's duties to a purchaser after a contract is made (paras **11.14-17**), risk (paras **11.18-20**), and the right of a purchaser to clear possession on completion (paras **11.26-8**). This list is not exhaustive; many other matters will arise in individual cases.

[10] See Kelly, *The Irish Constitution*, 3rd Ed (1994) at 408-20. See also O'Keeffe P *in Smiths (Harcourt St) Ltd v Hardwicke Ltd* (HC) 30 July 1971, unrep at 14. The modern courts were established by the Courts (Establishment and Constitution) Act 1961 and regulated by the Courts (Supplemental Provisions) Act 1961 as amended: see coverage of the Acts by Delaney, *The Courts Acts 1924-1991* (1994).

[11] *Ie*, The High Court.

[12] *RD Cox Ltd v Owners of MV Fritz Raabe* (SC) 1 August 1974, per Walsh J at 12, Griffin J concurring. *Cf The People (AG) v Bell* [1969] IR 24 at 43-4.

in certain types of cases[13] does not in any way restrict the jurisdiction of the High Court to adjudicate in any justifiable controversy.[14] While the High Court undoubtedly has this "full original jurisdiction" Article 34.2.3.1. must be read in conjunction with Article 34.3.4. which provides that the courts of first instance shall also include courts of local and limited jurisdiction with a right of appeal as determined by law. An example of this is the Circuit Court jurisdiction based on rateable valuation in many areas including actions for specific performance.[15] Clearly the Constitution contemplates the establishment of other courts of first instance and courts with appellate jurisdictions from those courts.[16] Accordingly the Oireachtas can set up, *eg*, appellate and consultative jurisdiction in the High Court, consultative jurisdiction in the Supreme Court and appellate jurisdiction in that court from courts other than the High Court.[17] On the other hand, the fact that under Article 34.4.1 the Supreme Court is the court of final appeal does not mean that all appellants can get as far as that court; the Oireachtas may, *eg*, exclude a right of further appeal to the Supreme Court against a decision of the High Court in a Circuit Court Appeal.[18]

[8.03] Article 36 enables laws to be made for the distribution of jurisdiction and business among all the courts which may be established under the Constitution including courts of first instance other than the High Court.[19] Thus business which falls within the full original jurisdiction of the High Court may be assigned to some other court. It may be so assigned *to the exclusion of* the High Court, at least in certain instances, for the allocation of jurisdiction would otherwise be overlapping and unworkable.[20] It also follows that the Oireachtas may enact laws empowering the High Court to remit actions to the Circuit Court which are within the jurisdiction of that court.[21] In dealing with an application of this sort the courts will keep in mind the policy of the Oireachtas that for the convenience of litigants, and indeed in mercy to the parties, the ordinary every-day actions, those not involving very large sums of money or raising exceptional questions for determination, should be tried in the ordinary course in the local venue by the Circuit Court.[22]

> "Broadly speaking, all actions within the jurisdiction of the Circuit Court are fit to be tried in that court, and, if not commenced in it, they ought to be transferred, unless some circumstances appear in the case by which it becomes apparent that the action is more fit

---

[13] Such as the former Admiralty Court considered in the *Cox* case.

[14] The *Cox* case at 13. Henchy J took the opposite view holding at Article 34.3.1. was "investitive of jurisdiction, not creative of jurisdiction": pp 7-8. *Cf* the position in relation to the Circuit Court: para **8.06-9** *post*.

[15] Paras **8.07-9** *infra*.

[16] *The People (AG) v Conmey* [1975] IR 341 at 349.

[17] Examples given by Walsh J in *State (Browne) v Feran* [1967] IR 147 at 157.

[18] *Eamonn Andrews Productions Ltd v Gaiety Theatre Enterprises Ltd* [1973] IR 295.

[19] *Ward v Kinehan Electrical Ltd* [1984] IR 292 at 295. *Cf Connor v O'Brien* [1925] 2 IR 24 at 27-8.

[20] *Tormey v Ireland* [1985] IR 289 at 295. However the High Court's full jurisdiction may be invoked, if necessary, in proceedings such as habeas corpus, certiorari, prohibition, mandamus, quo warranto, injunction or a declaratory action: *ibid* at 296-7.

[21] *Ward's* case at 295 holding that s 25 of the Courts of Justice Act 1924 as amended by s 11 of the Courts of Justice Act 1936 was consistent with the Constitution. In *Neary v McDonnell* (1971) 105 ILTR 121 a specific performance action was remitted to the Circuit Court. See further Delaney, *The Courts Acts 1924-1991* (1994) at 4-9.

[22] *Hosie v Lawless* [1927] IR 464 at 471, decided before s 11(2)(*a*) of the Courts of Justice Act 1936 became law.

to be tried in the High Court; for example a serious question of law for decision or some special reason for a direct appeal to this court."[23]

An action should be retained in the High Court where the court is satisfied that, having regard to all the circumstances, it was reasonable that it should have been commenced in the High Court even though it could have been commenced in the Circuit Court.[24] Section 11(2)(*a*) of the Courts of Justice Act 1936 has been described as removing from the High Court "the obligation to transfer an action simply because the subject matter of the action fell within the jurisdiction of the Circuit Court."[25]

An application for remittal or transfer of an action may be made at any time before the commencement of the trial.[26] But where no cause of action is disclosed the proper course is to dismiss or strike out the action rather than remitting it to the Circuit Court.[27] On the other hand, a defendant cannot avail of the power to remit a claim for a liquidated sum to the Circuit Court unless he can show a "good" defence to the action or some part thereof or discloses facts which in the opinion of the High Court are sufficient to entitle him to defend such action.[28] There is no similar statutory requirement to show a defence to claims for specific performance or other equitable reliefs but, since the power to remit is a discretionary one, a court may feel that it should not remit a claim if the defendant does not show a defence.[29] A plaintiff cannot avoid the power to remit by including a wholly unsustainable claim which would bring the property affected above the rateable valuation limit for the Circuit Court.[30] Any deficiency which might exist in the rules of procedure or forms of the receiving court is not sufficient reason for refusing to remit a case; if necessary the judge of the receiving court will himself mould a convenient form of procedure.[31] In a rare case there may be some good reason why an action could not have been commenced in the Circuit Court at the time proceedings were issued and, if so, the case should not be transferred to that court later.[32] If the legislature were minded to remove the jurisdiction to order specific performance from the courts generally it would need to use clear language[33] and to consider carefully the constitutional points which could arise.

[8.04] Actions for specific performance in the High Court should be commenced by plenary summons because in such cases procedure by summary summons or by special summons is not required or authorised by the Rules of the Superior Courts.[34] Admittedly, the parties may proceed by summary summons by consent[35] but there seems to be little

---

[23] *Per* Kennedy CJ in *Hosie's* case at 471-472. *Cf* Hanna J in *Lloyd v Dunne* [1937] IR 514 at 519.

[24] Section 11(2)(*a*) of the Courts of Justice Act 1936 described by O Dalaigh CJ in *Ronayne v Ronayne* [1970] IR 15 at 23 as favouring the retention in the High Court of actions which might otherwise have been commenced in the Circuit Court.

[25] *O'Shea v Mallow UDC* [1993] ILRM 884 at 886.

[26] Section 15(3), the Courts Act 1991.

[27] *Bond v Holton* [1959] IR 302 at at 308, 311, 312 (no contract pleaded).

[28] Section 11(2)(*b*) of the Courts of Justice Act 1936. See *United Drug & Chemical Co Ltd v McSweeney* [1959] IR 149.

[29] *McDonald v Byrne* (1902) 3 NIJR 37.

[30] *Byrne v Hughes* [1925] 1 IR 126 at 131. The unsustainable part was struck out. *Cf Hickey v Donovan* (1896) 30 ILTR 536.

[31] *Byrne's* case at 130-1.

[32] Eg, where the Circuit Court had not been set up when the writ was issued: *Moore v O'Reilly* [1925] 1 IR 133; *McCollum v Tease* [1925] 2 IR 33.

[33] *Kelly v Enright* (1883) 11 LRI 379 at 385, 386 and 387. *Cf Smiths (Harcourt St) Ltd v Hardwicke Ltd* (HC) 30 July 1971, O'Keeffe P, unrep at 14-15.

[34] Order 1, rule 6.

[35] Order 2, rule 2.

point in doing this, even if consent is available; the conflicts of evidence likely in specific performance actions would make most cases unsuitable for hearing on affidavit[36] so a case commenced by summary summons would be likely to go to plenary hearing anyway.[37] Some pleadings are normally desirable[38] so the parties usually would ask the Master of the High Court for directions as to pleadings.[39] Of course, some other matters which may need consideration in cases of possible claims for specific performance may be covered in other ways. Thus, a claim for interest or one for the return of a deposit on the basis that the parties did not reach full agreement and therefore the deposit was paid without consideration[40] may be brought by summary summons.[41] The High Court has a special jurisdiction to determine questions under s 9 of the Vendor and Purchaser Act 1874[42] and proceedings of this sort are commenced by special summons.[43] Often a vendor and purchaser summons may be a practical alternative to an action for specific performance and its quicker and less expensive procedure by special summons is a major factor in its favour.[44]

[8.05] It is important to remember the penalties in costs under the Courts Act 1991[45] for proceeding in a higher court than necessary. This will often need consideration because, as we shall see, the jurisdiction of the Circuit Court based on rateable valuation is very extensive indeed.[46] Where an order is made by a court in favour of a plaintiff or applicant and the court is not the lowest one having jurisdiction to grant the relevant relief the plaintiff[47] is not entitled to recover more costs than he would have been entitled to recover if the proceedings had been commenced and determined in the lowest court which had jurisdiction.[48] This principle is modified in relation to claims for damages.[49] The new provisions are tougher than the 1981 equivalent which allowed the judge hearing an action[50] to grant a "special certificate" that it was reasonable in the interests of justice generally, owing to the exceptional nature of the proceedings or of any question of law contained therein, to commence the proceedings in the court in which they were in fact commenced.[51] That type of provision has been around for a long time and the limitation of the right to costs without a special certificate has been described as emphasising the desire of the legislature to keep smaller cases in the Circuit Court and District Court.[52]

---

[36] *Cf* paras **8.53-9** *infra* in relation to vendor and purchaser summonses.
[37] Pursuant to Order 37, rule 6.
[38] See paras **8.21-4** *infra*.
[39] Order 37, rule 6.
[40] As in *Lowis v Wilson* [1949] IR 347.
[41] These would be within Order 2, rule 2(1)(*a*).
[42] Discussed in paras **8.53-9** *infra*.
[43] Order 3, item (12).
[44] In England a practice direction of 1967 providing a specially expedited procedure for the hearing of vendor and purchaser summonses was cancelled in 1970, there being too few cases to justify it: see [1967] 1 All ER 656 and [1970] 1 All ER 672. The use of such summonses has declined in England, probably because the spread of registration of title and the conveyancing reforms introduced in and since 1925 have greatly reduced the number of cases in which serious title problems arise: Jones & Goodhart, *Specific Performance* (1986) at 209.
[45] Section 17 of the Courts Act 1981 inserted by s 14 of the 1991 Act.
[46] Paras **8.06-9** *infra*.
[47] Or "applicant", presumably.
[48] Section 17(1) of the 1981 Act, inserted by s 14 of the 1991 Act.
[49] Section 17(2) and (3) inserted by s 14 of the 1991 Act.
[50] Save claims for liquidated sums covered by s 17(2) and (3).
[51] Section 17(5).
[52] *Per* Hanna J in *Lloyd v Brown* [1937] IR 514 at 519.

Under the 1991 Act, however, as well as suffering a likely penalty in failing to recover part of his own party and party costs, a plaintiff who succeeds in any proceedings (not being an appeal) in a court which is not the lowest one having the appropriate jurisdiction may be ordered to pay an amount to the defendant.[53] The order may be made by the judge concerned if in all the circumstances he thinks it appropriate to do so. The amount may not exceed the additional party and party costs to which the defendant or respondent has been put by being sued in the higher court.[54] The defendant or respondent is given an express right to set off costs awarded to him against costs which he must pay the successful party in the proceedings.[55]

The Circuit Court

[8.06] It was once suggested [56] that the Circuit Court set up under the Courts of Justice Act 1924 simply had the old equity jurisdiction of the former County Court subject to modifications made in 1924. However, the correct view was that the 1924 Act set up an entirely new court in the Circuit Court which was *not* the old County Court continued with extended jurisdiction.[57] The only limitations on the jurisdiction of that Circuit Court were those expressed or implied in the 1924 Act and, subject to those limitations, the Circuit Court had within its locality all the jurisdiction of the High Court.[58] The present Circuit Court was set up by the Courts (Establishment and Constitution Act) 1961.[59] Its jurisdiction is now governed mainly[60] by s 22 of the Courts (Supplemental Provisions) Act 1961 as amended by s 21 of the Courts Act 1981[61] and further amended by s 2 of the Courts Act 1991.[62] Section 22 of the 1961 Act operates primarily by reference to the Third Schedule to that Act[63] and to numerous older statutory jurisdictions mentioned in the Fourth and Fifth Schedules The latter rarely would be relevant to parties in specific performance proceedings or considering other types of relief for breach of contract. The Court's jurisdiction has been described as "an almost universal jurisdiction in subject matter, that is to say, qualitatively but limited quantitatively."[64] There is no reference in s 22 or any of the Schedules to s 9 of the Vendor and Purchaser Act 1874 and accordingly the Circuit Court has no jurisdiction in vendor and purchaser summonses.[65]

[8.07] The main amendment of interest to us is the increase of the rateable valuation limit of jurisdiction in proceedings for specific performance of contracts relating to land from £60 in 1961 to £100 in 1971 and then to £200 in 1981.[66] Section 22(1)(*a*) of the 1961 Act provides:

---

[53] Section 17(5) of the 1981 Act inserted by s 14 of the 1991 Act.
[54] Note the detailed provisions of s 17(5)(*a*)(i) and (ii).
[55] Section 17(5)(*b*) as inserted.
[56] *Argue v Henry* [1926] IR 99 at 101. The personalty limit was increased from £500 to £1,000 and RV limit from £30 to £60. The former limits were in s 33(*d*) of the County Officers and Courts (Ireland) Act 1877. Cf *Miller v Hatrick* [1907] 1 IR 82. Note that the former RV limit of £30 in relation to land did not apply to suits for specific performance which were governed by the purchase money.
[57] *Per* Kennedy CJ in *Sligo Corporation v Gilbride* [1929] IR 351 at 361, 363. *Cf* Murnaghan J at 370.
[58] *Per* Fitzgibbon J in the *Sligo Corporation* case at 368.
[59] Section 4.
[60] Including proceedings for specific performance.
[61] Noted by O'Hanlon J in *Parsons v Kavanagh* [1990] ILRM 560 at 567. The 1981 Act set the present RV limit of £200.
[62] The 1991 Act did not change the RV limit in relation to specific performance or most other claims.
[63] There are numerous references to that Schedule in s 22(1).
[64] By O Dalaigh CJ in *Ronayne v Ronayne* [1970] IR 15 at 23.
[65] Vendor and purchaser summonses are considered in paras **8.53-9** *post*.
[66] The Courts Act 1971, then s 2(1)(*d*) of the Courts Act 1981.

"Subject to paras (*b*) and (*c*) of this subsection, the Circuit Court shall, concurrently with the High Court, have all the jurisdiction of the High Court to hear and determine any proceedings of the kind mentioned in column (2) of the Third Schedule to this Act at any reference number."

Paragraphs (*b*) and (*c*) have the effect that the Circuit Court has no jurisdiction in excess of the limits set out in column (3) of the Third Schedule[67] unless the necessary parties to the proceedings in a cause sign the form of consent prescribed by rules of court either before or at any time during the hearing. The jurisdiction in proceedings for specific performance is set out in the Third Schedule at reference number 22. The quantitative exclusion of jurisdiction (except by consent of necessary parties) is in the following terms:[68]

"Where the subject matter:

(*a*)   in so far as it consists of personalty, exceeds in amount or value £2,000,[69] or[70]

(*b*)   in so far as it consists of land,[71] exceeds the rateable valuation of £60."[72]

Where the subject matter of the proceedings consists entirely of personalty the jurisdiction is exercised by the judge of the circuit where the defendant or one of the defendants resides or carries on business.[73] If it consists in whole or in part of land the plaintiff has the option of suing either (*a*) in the circuit where the defendant or one of the defendants resides or carries on business or (*b*) the circuit where the land or any part of it is situate.[74] Where an incorporeal hereditament[75] is involved in proceedings the situation of the land to which that hereditament belongs will decide which circuit has jurisdiction.[76] If a plaintiff chooses not to seek specific performance but sues only for damages or some liquidated sum the limit of Circuit Court jurisdiction is £30,000. There is now statutory jurisdiction to remit actions from the Circuit Court to the District Court if the Circuit Court judge does not consider the action fit to be prosecuted in the Circuit Court.[77] A judge of the Circuit Court is empowered to hear and determine outside his circuit any application which he has power to hear and determine within it and which in his opinion should be dealt with as a matter of urgency.[78] He may make out of court orders which he may deem to be urgent.[79] All powers ancillary to any jurisdiction, including power to appoint a receiver, are expressly conferred on the court.[80]

---

[67]   As amended from time to time.

[68]   Column (3).

[69]   Now £30,000 under s 2(1)(*a*) of the Courts Act 1991.

[70]   As we shall see in para **8.09** *infra*, the disjunctive "or" is important.

[71]   Defined by s 15 to include incorporeal hereditaments. Section 12 of the Interpretation Act 1937 and Item 14 in that Schedule provide "the work 'land' includes messuages, tenements, hereditaments, houses and buildings, of any tenure". Section 15 of the 1961 Act is probably not a sufficient "contrary intention" to stop the 1937 definition applying but modifies it to ensure that incorporeal hereditaments are included.

[72]   Now £200 under s 2(1)(*d*) of the Courts Act 1981.

[73]   Courts (Supplemental Provisions) Act 1961, Third Schedule, reference no 22, column (4).

[74]   *Ibid.*

[75]   Eg, a right of way.

[76]   Section 22(1)(*e*) of the 1961 Act.

[77]   Section 15 of the Courts Act 1991. Remember that the District Court has no jurisdiction in proceedings for specific performance: see para **8.10** *infra* on its jurisdiction.

[78]   Section 22(11) of the 1961 Act.

[79]   Section 22(14).

[80]   Section 22(7).

[8.08] Any party to an action commenced and pending in the Circuit Court may apply at any time to the judge before whom it is pending to have the action forwarded to the High Court.[81] The judge may send it forward to the High Court if it is one fit to be tried in the High Court and that court appears to be the more appropriate tribunal in the circumstances.[82] Possibly this jurisdiction can be exercised even if the Circuit Court has no jurisdiction to hear and determine the case.[83] Maybe a party can submit by conduct to the jurisdiction of the Circuit Court and thus lose the right to have a point about jurisdiction decided in his favour.[84] It would seem arguable, however, that the exclusion of jurisdiction (except by consent of necessary parties) in column (3) of the Third Schedule to the Courts (Supplemental Provisions) Act 1961, as amended, has the effect that the Circuit Court could not make any order at all except to strike out proceedings for specific performance of a contract for the sale of land if the rateable valuation exceeds £200.[85]

[8.09] It is important to note the disjunctive 'or' in reference number 22 in the Third Schedule to the 1961 Act. As a result, if the rateable valuation of the relevant land does not exceed £200, the Circuit Court has jurisdiction in claims for specific performance even when the purchase price would exceed the personalty limit if that were the criterion.[86] This means that the court has jurisdiction in claims for specific performance over properties the value of which is far greater than the general monetary limit of £30,000 in contract and tort. But if a claim in that court is one to which the personalty limit applies continuing interest which brings it over that limit will bring it outside the Circuit Court jurisdiction.[87] The question whether the Circuit Court has jurisdiction within a rateable valuation limit is one of fact. Section 22 and the Third Schedule to the 1961 Act (as amended) do not require formal proof. As O'Hanlon J explained:[88]

> "The applicants claim that formal proof of the rateable valuation of the lands was necessary in order to give the respondent[89] jurisdiction to entertain the claim, but I do not construe the provisions of the Courts (Supplemental Provisions) Act 1961 s 22 and the Third Schedule to the Act (as amended) in this manner. It appears to me that proof should be given in every case to show that the matter is within the jurisdiction of the court, but that if it is not given and the case is allowed to proceed a situation arises in which the court may or may not have jurisdiction to deal with the dispute which is being litigated before it. If it proceeds to judgment and it transpires that the matter was not within the proper jurisdiction of the Circuit Court, then the court has made an order without having jurisdiction to do so and that order should, in the normal course of events be set aside, *ex debito justitiae*, on the application of a party who is affected by the making of the order."

---

[81] Section 22(8) of the Courts (Supplemental Provisions) Act 1961.
[82] *Ibid.*
[83] In *Parsons v Kavanagh* [1990] ILRM 560 O'Hanlon J said at 567 that if the jurisdictional point had been taken before the Circuit Court judge he could have transferred the action to the High Court. But *cf Knipe v Lyons* (1885) 15 LRI 507 at 509-10.
[84] *Parson's* case at 567.
[85] Or the value of personalty exceeds £30,000.
[86] *Neary v McDonnell* (1971) 105 ILTR 121.
[87] *National Bank Ltd v McManmon* [1926] IR 393 at 396.
[88] *Harrington v Murphy* [1989] IR 207 at 208-9.
[89] The Circuit Court judge.

A court will often allow an amendment dealing with a matter of jurisdiction if necessary[90] but this must never be taken for granted. If a parcel is not separately valued and as a result it cannot be definitely stated to fall within or without the Circuit Court limit a claim is properly brought in the High Court.[91]

The District Court

[8.10] The District Court was also established by the Courts (Establishment and Constitution) Act 1961.[92] Its jurisdiction is conferred mainly by s 33 of the Courts (Supplemental Provisions) Act 1961 as amended.[93] The District Court has no jurisdiction in claims for specific performance. Questions of title also have limited its jurisdiction historically. Formerly its jurisdiction in criminal matters was ousted when a bona fide question of title to real property arose.[94] Under the Courts of Justice Act 1924, which set up the former District Court, the civil jurisdiction given in cases of tort was qualified by a proviso[95] which ousted jurisdiction in cases where a bona fide question of title to land with a rateable valuation exceeding £10 was in issue. Another proviso[96] saved the jurisdiction when land of a lesser RV was involved but provided that a decision of the court was not to operate as an estoppel in or bar to a suit in relation to such land. The present position is that the District Court has civil jurisdiction in contract, breach of contract and important areas of tort subject only to a proviso that the decision of the District Court in a case in which a question of title to land is in issue shall not operate as an estoppel in or bar to a suit in any other court in relation to such land.[97] The monetary limit of jurisdiction is now £5,000.[98] As we have seen,[99] there is now power to remit actions from the Circuit Court to the District Court and, if this occurs, the jurisdiction of the District Court in a remitted action claiming unliquidated damages is £10,000.[100] If a party decides not to claim specific performance and seeks damages, interest[101] or a liquidated sum the District Court appears to have jurisdiction up to a claim of £5,000 even though the relevant contract involves consideration outside its jurisdiction; the plaintiff must beware of possible penalties in costs if he sues in a higher court.[102] Litigating a question such as entitlement to interest in the District Court may be a practical alternative to a vendor and purchaser summons.[103]

---

[90] *O'Brien v Coyne* (1903) 37 ILTR 98; *Doherty v McDonnell* (1904) 38 ILTR 209. But *cf Hickey v O'Donovan* (1896) 30 ILTR 536.
[91] *Mulvey v Flanaghan* [1936] IJR 40.
[92] Section 5.
[93] Mainly by the Courts Act 1971, the Courts Act 1981 and latterly by s 4 of the Courts Act 1991.
[94] Crotty, *Practice and Procedure in the District Court* (1959), pp 139-41; see also the very detailed discussion by Kennedy CJ in *R (Moore) v Hanrahan* [1927] IR 406 at 414-9. *Cf* Palles CB in *Lord Talbot de Malahide v Dunne* [1914] 2 IR 125 at 131-4.
[95] Section 77A(ii) noted by Kennedy CJ in *R (Moore)* at 416.
[96] Also noted by Kennedy CJ at 416.
[97] Section 77A(i) of the 1924 Act inserted by s 4(*a*) of the 1991 Act.
[98] *Ibid.*
[99] Para **8.07** supra.
[100] Sections 15(1) and (2) of the 1991 Act.
[101] In *Greene v Quinn* (1940) 75 ILTR 107 interest was recovered in a District Court appeal.
[102] On which see para **8.05** *supra.*
[103] In *Greene's* case the parties agreed to litigate such a dispute in the District Court to avoid the expense of a vendor and purchaser summons: p 108.

Foisting jurisdiction

[8.11] It is not permissible to foist or "confer" jurisdiction which does not exist otherwise. Thus, if a lease does not qualify to buy the fee simple under the ground rents legislation, parties cannot provide validly for a county registrar to determine the price of the fee simple "as if the rent reserved by the said lease was a ground rent within the meaning of that Act".[104] Nor should parties provide that a liquidator's sale is subject to the consent of a chief clerk who has no statutory function in relation to such sales.[105] While no Irish case has considered an attempt to confer or impose jurisdiction on a court which otherwise it has not got there would seem to be a strong argument based on public policy that the courts should not be available for such purposes. Of course the parties can cover most matters[106] by a properly drafted agreement for arbitration or decision by an independent expert.

PARTIES

[8.12] A party seeking specific performance is usually the plaintiff. If the other side gets in first with proceedings he may be able to counterclaim for specific performance in those proceedings, depending on their nature.[107] An alternative may be to bring a cross-action for specific performance but this may result in a successful party not recovering full party and party costs if the court feels that the parties should have been able to agree on a form of determination which would allow all the issues arising for determination to be resolved in a single set of proceedings.[108] In principle a contract, if it is a binding one, can be enforced against any party to it in whom is vested the legal and beneficial interest in the relevant property.[109] On the other hand, an action on a contract against a defendant who is a stranger to that contract must fail[110] unless, perhaps, the defendant and a party to the deed can be connected through some trust.[111] A party may of course be sued in a representative capacity in certain cases.[112] In general an order obtained without joining persons whose rights would be affected is of no effect against them.[113] Sometimes a person who is a party to a contract should be joined in proceedings for the sake of conformity.[114] This usually is not necessary in the case of a person who may have an interest in a deal but is not party to the contract. If, for example, it turns out that a plaintiff was in fact buying for himself and someone else, that does not cause a problem; a purchaser is normally entitled to take his conveyance in any names he wishes and this is

---

[104] *Carr v Phelan* [1976/7] ILRM 149 at 154-5. Obviously, if the lease does qualify there is no need for any such agrement.

[105] *Re Brook Cottage Ltd* [1976] NI 78 at 115.

[106] As, eg, the object of the exercise in *Carr v Phelan*.

[107] *Eg*, where one party wants specific performance of a written contract as it stands and the other wants specific performance with rectification (on which see para **10.23** *post*).

[108] *Bradley v Donegal County Council* (HC) Cir App, 14 November 1989, O'Hanlon J, unrep at 8. Of course if there are two sets of proceedings they may be consolidated if they are in the same court.

[109] *Sanders v Cramer* (1842) 3 Drury & Warren 87 at 99.

[110] *Clitheroe v Simpson* (1879) 4 LRI 59 at 61. Cf *Macklin v Graecen & Co Ltd* [1983] IR 61 at 67.

[111] *Clitheroe's* case, *ibid*.

[112] Most often on a death; see para **8.14** *infra*. Cf the position in *Holohan's* case noted at fn 114 below.

[113] *Giffard v Hort* (1803) 1 Schoales & Lefroy 386.

[114] *Holohan v Ardmayle Estates* (SC) 1 May 1967, unrep at 6. The contract was signed by the first plaintiff in trust and it was later claimed that the second plaintiff was his principal. The statement of claim alleged that the contract for sale was to both plaintiffs and the defense expressly admitted that: p 1-2.

frequently done.[115] In actions for specific performance of contracts relating to registered land or charges there is express statutory power for the court to cause all parties who have registered rights in the land or charge, or have entered cautions or inhibitions against the same, to appear in the action and show cause why the contract should not be specifically performed.[116] The courts have been reluctant in vendor and purchaser summonses[117] to join persons who have not been parties to the relevant contracts[118] but occasionally it has been done.[119]

[8.13] A plaintiff who has a contract for the purchase of lands but has not yet got a conveyance has sufficient standing to seek an injunction restraining his vendor from selling to a third person or demolishing buildings on the land in sale.[120] The fact that land may be vested in a third party is not a bar to a claim for specific performance if that party can be compelled to convey. Thus, if A agrees to sell an unencumbered fee simple in Blackacre to B, and the fee simple is then outstanding in C, this is no obstacle whatever to A successfully suing B for specific performance if on the date on which the court directs completion of the sale A is in a position to compel C to convey the unencumbered fee simple to B.[121] When a person agrees to do something which he can himself do, or has the means of procuring others to do, the court requires him to do it or get it done unless the circumstances of the case make it highly unreasonable to do so.[122] However, the court will not compel a purchaser to accept a vendor with whom he did not contract at all.[123]

Occasionally a vendor conveys to a third party despite having an enforceable agreement with an earlier purchaser. In that event the first purchaser is likely to sue both vendor and third party and get an order for specific performance against the third party unless the latter discharges the onus of proving that he was a purchaser for value without notice of the prior contract.[124] Notice in this context does not have to be actual notice; it may be *constructive*.[125] A third party who purchases for value without notice of a prior contract will not have it enforced against him.[126] If the third party registers his contract in the Registry of Deeds in accordance with the Registration of Deeds Act 1707 before an earlier contract he gets priority over it subject to the doctrine of notice; to deprive him of this statutory priority he must be shown to have had *actual* notice.[127] If there are two different contracts for the sale of the same land by different vendors - *eg*, by a mortgagor and his mortgagee[128] - to the same purchaser the latter may sue both vendors but in this

---

[115] *Guerin v Ryan* (HC) 28 April 1978, McWilliam J, unrep at 9.
[116] Registration of Title Act 1964 s 22.
[117] Vendor and purchaser summonses are discussed at paras **8.53-9** *infra*.
[118] *Re Brown and Mitchell's Contract* (1902) 2 NIJR 106; *Re Carolan & Scott's Contract* [1899] 1 IR 4.
[119] Eg, in *Re Antrim County Land, Building & Investment Co Ltd & Dobbin's Contract* (1909) 43 ILTR 120 - landlord whose consent was needed. See also para **8.55** *infra*.
[120] *O'Hara v Flint* [1979] ILRM 156 at 159.
[121] *Northern Bank Ltd v Wilson* [1984] 16 NIJB at 16. *Cf Sidebottom Ltd v Leonard* (HC) 18 May 1973, unrep at 2-3.
[122] *Costigan v Hastler* (1804) 2 Schoales & Lefroy 160 at 166.
[123] *Re McLoughlin & McGrath's Contract* (1914) 48 ILTR 87 at 89.
[124] *Henegan v Davitt* [1933] IR 375 AT 377, 379.
[125] *Henegan's* case at 379; *Waldron v Jacob* (1870) IR 5 Eq 131 at 138-9. *Cf Crofton v Ormsby* (1806) 2 Schoales & Lefroy 583 at 598-601.
[126] *Archbold v Lord Howth* (1866) IR 1 CL 608 at 628.
[127] *O'Connor v McCarthy* [1982] IR 161 at 171-5, summons for directions in a liquidation served on two contending purchasers. The parties agreed that all issues should be determined in the one court: pp 170-1. *Cf Bank of Ireland v Rockfield Ltd* [1979] IR 21 at 37.
[128] As in *Casey v Irish Intercontinental Bank Ltd* [1979] IR 364.

type of case, while both contracts may be valid, specific performance would be ordered only against one defendant as there cannot be two orders for specific performance against different defendants.[129]

[8.14] In the event of the death of a party to a contract for the sale of land it normally can be enforced by or against his personal representative.[130] It is the duty of the personal representative to perform the contracts of his testator or intestate which can be enforced against him and he is certainly *entitled* to carry them out.[131] If there are clear words or a necessary implication to the contrary, the contract is not enforceable by or against the estate[132] but any such words or implication would be very unusual in contracts relating to land. The estate of a person who dies intestate or who is testate but leaves no executor surviving him vests in the President of the High Court until administration is granted[133] but the President should not be joined as a party in proceedings.[134] The vesting provision in s 13 of the Succession Act 1965 is "a mere matter of necessary convenience and protection".[135] An intending plaintiff is not left without remedy and can, for example, apply for a special grant limited to the defence of proceedings.[136] The real and personal estate of a deceased person vests on his death in his personal representatives[137] and they hold the estate as trustees for the persons entitled thereto.[138] Their rights and liabilities on foot of any contracts of the deceased are therefore as trustees.

Insolvency

[8.15] Insolvency of a party between contract and completion can cause complications. A contract is not terminated by bankruptcy; in fact it is novated by operation of law[139] subject to the Official Assignee's right of disclaimer.[140] Nor can the fact of a bankruptcy change the terms of a contract. There is nothing in the principles of the law of bankruptcy which could conceivably support what would be a unique operation whereby the terms of a contract entered into by the bankrupt and another person could be altered and new and different terms substituted for them.[141] It has been thought that when a purchaser or intending lessee became bankrupt before completion his assigns in bankruptcy were not entitled to specific performance of the agreement for sale or lease, primarily because he was no longer able to perform his part of the bargain, but the modern view is that the Official Assignee becomes entitled to the contractual rights and obligations of the

---

[129] *Casey's* case at 371. The Supreme Court approved the High Court decision not to order specific performance of the second contract "at present". *Cf Field v Boland* (1837) 1 Drury & Walsh 37 at 51-2.

[130] *Nyland v Brennan* (HC) 19 december 1970, Pringle J, unrep at 12-13; *Drimmie v Davies* [1899] 1 IR 176 at 187. *Cf Dowdall v McCartan* (1880) 5 LRI 642; *White v Beck* (1871) IR 6 Eq 63.

[131] *Per* Budd J in *Re O'Leary* [1961] IJR 45 at 48. Note s 60(4) of the Succession Act 1965.

[132] *Nyland's* case at 13. *Cf Drimmie's* case at 186-7.

[133] Section 13, Succession Act 1965. See McGuire, *The Succession Act 1965*, 2nd Ed (1986) by Pearce, pp 43-5; Brady, *Succession Law in Ireland* (1989), pp 233-6.

[134] *Flack v The President of the High Court* (HC) 29 November 1983, Costello J, unrep at 3, 5.

[135] *Re Deans* [1954] 1 All ER 496 at 498 quoted by Costello J in *Flack's* case at 5.

[136] Section 27(1) and (4) of the 1965 Act, noted in *Flack's* case at 5.

[137] Section 10(1) of the Succession Act 1965.

[138] Section 10(3).

[139] *Re Casey* [1991] 2 IR 146 at 158. This case dealt with the pre-1988 law but there has been no relevant change on this point or the next.

[140] Which is discussed at para **8.17** *infra*.

[141] *Re Casey* at 159.

bankrupt under the contract unless he disclaims it.[142] Of course contracts may contain express provision for the effect of bankruptcy. Typical is a clause in a lease for forfeiture on the tenant becoming bankrupt but this is now void against the Official Assignee.[143]

Also a party to a contract had to be very careful if on notice of an act of bankruptcy committed by the other party. A purchaser who had committed an available act of bankruptcy of which the vendor knew could not enforce the contract because he could not pay the purchase money to the vendor so that the latter could be certain of retaining it against the trustee if bankruptcy occurred within the relevant period.[144] A purchaser dealing with a vendor who had committed an available act of bankruptcy had to be very careful in the intermediate period between that act and an adjudication of bankruptcy because the Official Assignee's title would relate back to an act of bankruptcy committed up to six months before the filing of the petition for bankruptcy.[145] This position also has been modified by the Bankruptcy Act 1988 but there is still need for caution as possibilities of setting aside fraudulent preferences and certain other transactions and settlements have been retained.[146]

[8.16] When a person is adjudicated bankrupt now his property vests in the Official Assignee on the date of adjudication for the benefit of the creditors.[147] This is an automatic vesting in the Official Assignee and there is no question of any election save in respect of "after-acquired" property.[148] His title to the property of the bankrupt does not commence any earlier than the date of adjudication.[149] It seems well arguable that when a purchaser of land becomes bankrupt the "property" which vests in the Official Assignee includes the beneficial estate of a purchaser who has paid part of the purchase price,[150] his right to have the contract completed and the right to sue for specific performance of it, if necessary and appropriate.[151] Another argument could lead to the same result. The property which vests in him includes all powers vested in the bankrupt which he might have legally exercised in relation to any property immediately before the date of adjudication.[152] Those "powers", the argument would run, include a right to have a contract completed and a right to sue for specific performance if necessary and appropriate. Accordingly, on the basis of one argument or the other, the Official Assignee would have the right to specific performance of a contract made by the bankrupt if the latter had that right before he was adjudicated, provided, of course, that the Official

---

[142] *Re Casey* at 158. On the former view see *Flood v Finlay* (1811) 2 Ball & Beatty 9 at 14-15, not deciding the "abstract question" whether assignees of a bankrupt were ever entitled to specific performance. *Cf* Forde, *Bankruptcy Law in Ireland*, p 84; Jones & Goodhart, *Specific Performance* (1986) at 118, 172. See also para **8.16** *infra*.

[143] Section 49 of the Bankruptcy Act 1988. See Wylie, *Irish Landlord and Tenant Law*, paras 24.08, 24.11; Forde, *op cit*, at 81, 83; Sanfey & Holohan, *Bankruptcy Law & Practice in Ireland*, para 7.02 and fn 6.

[144] *Dyster v Randall & Sons* [1926] Ch 932 at 941.

[145] Wylie, *op cit*, para 11.22, Sanfey & Holohan, *op cit*, para 6.3.

[146] Sections 57, 58 and 59: see para **8.18** *infra*.

[147] Section 44(1) of the Bankruptcy Act 1988.

[148] Which is covered by s 44(5).

[149] Section 44(2). If s 44(1) and (2) stood on their own that would be the abolition of the doctrine of relation back.

[150] On which see paras **11.01-13** *post*.

[151] In view of the very broad definition of "property" in s 3.

[152] Section 44(3)(*a*).

Assignee was willing and able to perform the remaining obligations of the bankrupt under the contract.[153]

[8.17] The Official Assignee has power to disclaim onerous property with the leave of the court[154] except after-acquired property.[155] Onerous property[156] comprises land of any tenure burdened with onerous covenants, shares or stock in companies, unprofitable contracts and any other property which is unsaleable or not readily saleable by reason of its binding the possessor thereof to perform an onerous act or pay a sum of money.[157] The Official Assignee has 12 months from adjudication to disclaim[158] or, if the relevant property does not come to his knowledge within one month after adjudication, 12 months from the time he becomes aware of It.[159] In either case the court may allow an extended period. If he does not decide quickly his hand can be forced. Any persons interested in the relevant property may apply in writing to him requiring him to decide whether or not to disclaim and, if he does not give notice to the applicant within 28 days[160] of receipt of the application that he intends to apply for leave to disclaim, he may not disclaim thereafter.[161] In the case of a contract, if the Official Assignee does not disclaim it within the 28 days, or such extended period as the court allows, he is deemed to have adopted it.[162]

The solvent party to a contract has a further option. Instead of waiting for the Official Assignee to decide whether to disclaim or trying to force his hand as just discussed, the solvent party may apply to the court for an order rescinding the contract.[163] The court has power to do so on such terms as it thinks just, including payment by or to either party of damages for the non-performance of the contract.[164] The valid exercise of the right of disclaimer or a rescinding order by the court would, of course, bring to an end any right to an order against the Official Assignee for specific performance of the contract. On the other hand, if the Official Assignee adopts a contract, or is deemed to do so, there seems to be no reason why the solvent party should not get a decree of specific performance against him if he could have got one against the bankrupt prior to adjudication. The position is more doubtful if neither party takes any steps in relation to disclaimer as there is no provision in the 1988 Act that the Official Assignee, if he simply runs out of time for disclaiming, is deemed to have adopted the contract.[165] Thus the solvent party, if he wishes to get an order for specific performance against the Official Assignee, should

---

[153] Note the view of Forde, *Bankruptcy Law in Ireland* at 84 that, with "relation back" having been repealed, the bankrupt normally would be entitled to insist on land being conveyed if he tendered the purchase price: if this is so, then the assignee can also insist on specific performance. For the English position see Jones & Goodhart, *Specific Performance* (1986) at 171-3.

[154] Section 56(1).

[155] Which does not vest automatically.

[156] See discussion of what is onerous property by Forde, *op cit*, at 106-7 and Sanfey & Holohan, *Bankruptcy Law and Practice in Ireland* at 107-10.

[157] Section 56(1).

[158] *Ibid.*

[159] Section 56(2).

[160] The court may also extend this period.

[161] Section 56(5).

[162] *Ibid.*

[163] Section 56(6). The application may be made by "any person who is, as against the Official Assignee, entitled to the benefit or subject to the burden of a contract made with the bankrupt.

[164] *Ibid.*

[165] Note the view of Jones & Goodhart, *Specific Performance* (1986) at 173 that in the similar English position the solvent party probably would not get an order for specific performance.

make a written application pursuant to s 56(5) as soon as convenient. One final, vital point about disclaimer should be noted. If a vendor of land becomes bankrupt and an equitable estate has already passed to the purchaser[166] the Official Assignee cannot disclaim the contract for sale.[167] A disclaimer in that situation would not have the effect of relieving the bankrupt of onerous property but would deprive the purchaser of an equitable estate and the right to insist on a conveyance in exchange for any balance of the purchase money.

[8.18] The 1988 changes in the law on relation back are "subject to the provisions of this Act" which qualification lets in the avoidance of certain fraudulent preferences occurring within six months before adjudication.[168] Also avoided under the 1988 Act are sales of any property which in the opinion of the court are substantially below market value and transactions which have the effect of substantially reducing the sum available for distribution to creditors occurring in each case in the period of three months between the debtor committing an act of bankruptcy and being adjudicated bankrupt.[169] This does not apply to a transaction *bona fide* entered into where the other party had not at the time notice of any prior act of bankruptcy committed by the bankrupt.[170] Nor does it affect the rights of any person making title in good faith and for valuable consideration through or under a person (other than the bankrupt) who was a party to such a transaction.[171] These provisions may be described as a "limited statutory form" of the doctrine of relation back.[172] Thirdly, the new Act avoids certain settlements[173] if the settlor is adjudicated bankrupt within two years after the date of the settlement[174] or within five years of it unless the parties claiming under the settlement prove that when it was made the settlor was able to pay all his debts without recourse to the particular property *and* that the interest of the settlor did pass to the trustee of the settlement on its execution.[175] Settlements made before and in consideration of marriage[176] are excluded from this sanction and so are settlements made in favour of a purchaser or incumbrancer in good faith[177] and for valuable consideration. It suffices that the purchaser or incumbrancer acted in good faith and it is not necessary that both parties did so[178] - *ie,* that the future bankrupt also acted in good faith.

[8.19] In the last four paragraphs we have considered circumstances in which the Official Assignee ought to be a party to proceedings for specific performance or in which some step likely to involve him should be taken under the Bankruptcy Act 1988. Quite similar

---

[166] As when he has paid all or some of the purchase money: see paras **11.01-13** *post.*

[167] *Pearce v Bastable's Trustee* [1901] 2 Ch 122; *Re Bastable* [1901] 2 KB 518, approved by Flood J *in Re Abbeyford Estates Ltd* (HC) 29 October 1993, unrep at 5-7; *Re Scheibler* (1874) 9 Ch App 722.

[168] Section 57. A person making title in good faith and for valuable consideration through or under a creditor of the bankrupt is not affected.

[169] Section 58(1) of the 1988 Act.

[170] Ibid.

[171] Section 58(2).

[172] See note on the section in Sweet & Maxwell, *Irish Current Law Statutes Annotated.*

[173] Section 59(4) defines "settlement" to include any conveyance or transfer of property; "property" is defined very widely in s 3.

[174] Section 59(1)(*a*).

[175] Section 59(1)(*b*). The period under earlier legislation was 10 years.

[176] There are detailed provisions about this in s 59(2) and (3).

[177] See discussion of "good faith" by Hamilton P in *Re Thomas O'Neill* [1989] IR 544 at 551-3.

[178] *Mackintosh v Pogose* [1895] 1 Ch 505 at 509, approved by Hamilton P in *O'Neill's* case at 551.

matters may arise when a company goes into liquidation. However, the property of a company does not become vested in the liquidator unless an order is made pursuant to s 230 of the Companies Act 1963.[179] It follows that normally the liquidator will not be a party himself. If issues arise about rights to specific performance they may be dealt with on a summons or motion for directions.[180] It is important to note that a court normally will not allow a liquidator to disclaim a contract for sale which a *bona fide* purchaser wishes to enforce.[181]

Joinder of parties

[8.20] In the High Court all persons may be joined in one action as plaintiffs in whom any right to relief is alleged to exist in respect of or arising out of the same transaction or series of transactions; likewise all persons may be joined as defendants against whom the right to any relief is alleged to exist.[182] In each case the relief may be sought jointly, severally or in the alternative. No matter should be defeated by reason of the misjoinder or non-joinder of parties. The court may at any stage in proceedings, upon or without the application of a party, strike out the names of any parties improperly joined or add the names of any parties, whether plaintiffs or defendants, who ought to have been joined or whose presence before it may be necessary to enable the court effectually and completely to adjudicate upon and settle all questions involved.[183] Any application to add, strike out or substitute a plaintiff or defendant may be made to the court at any time before trial by motion or at the trial in a summary manner.[184] Of course, natural justice must be observed and a party joined at a trial should be given prior notice and an opportunity to plead or be heard.[185]

PLEADINGS

[8.21] As we have noted frequently, the first essential in a claim for specific performance is a contract. A party who makes a claim of a sort normally made on foot of a contract but fails to plead one risks having his claim dismissed or struck out for disclosing no cause of action.[186] The court would consider an application for an amendment.[187] A former view of the need in pleading a claim for specific performance was that when a party was plaintiff it was incumbent on him to state in his bill the agreement of which he called on the court to decree performance and to prove that agreement as stated.[188] If a person came into court for the specific performance of an agreement he should accurately state the

---

[179] See Keane, *Company Law in the Republic of Ireland*, 2nd Ed (1991) at 38.54; Forde, *Company Law in Ireland* (1985) at 15.19.
[180] As in *O'Connor v McCarthy* [1982] IR 161 where Costello J dealt with claims for specific performance by two purchasers. That was a voluntary liquidation. The manner in which the dispute reached the court appears at pp 170-1.
[181] *Re Abbeyford Estates Ltd* 29 October 1993, Flood J, unrep at 8. The liquidator sought an order under s 290 of the Companies Act 1963.
[182] Rules of the Superior Courts, order 15, rule 1 and 4.
[183] Order 15, rule 13.
[184] Order 15, rule 14. An application to be joined in a specific performance action failed in *O'Hara v Flint* [1976] ILRM 156 at 159.
[185] *Carthy v O'Neill* [1981] ILRM 443 at 445.
[186] *Bond v Holton* [1959] IR 302 at 308, 310-11.
[187] *Bond's* case at 308, 312: the plaintiff did not seek an amendment. *Cf Sun Fat Chan v Osseous Ltd* [1992] 1 IR 425 at 428.
[188] *Savage v Carroll* (1815) 2 Ball & Beatty 444 at 451.

terms of the agreement he sought to have executed and prove the case he stated on the record.[189] A reference or issue would not be granted to ascertain the terms of a contract.[190] The modern view is perhaps less demanding and the pleadings in a basic claim for specific performance are simple. It may suffice in most cases to plead the contract and claim specific performance and other appropriate reliefs.[191] Walsh J has said:[192]

> "It was also submitted on behalf of the defendants that the statement of claim should have pleaded that some part of the purchase money had been paid. It is quite true that in former years when pleadings gave considerably more information than they now give it was customary to plead all the relevant facts such as the making of the contract, the payment of the deposit, the ability and willingness of the plaintiff to complete and the refusal or failure of the defendant to complete. A great deal of information is now left to be sought by means of notice for particulars. In the present case no notice for particulars was served by the defendants and, of course, the defendants were well aware that part of the purchase money had been paid as the defendants had received it."

However, the supremacy of the simple approach is not clear-cut. There is a modern suggestion that a defendant's failure or refusal to carry out the contract should be pleaded.[193] In Northern Ireland it has been said to be necessary for the plaintiff to plead that he is ready and willing to carry out the contract.[194] Occasionally further facts must be pleaded in a claim for specific performance. If allegations of misrepresentation, fraud, breach of trust, wilful default or undue influence are made particulars must be set out in the pleadings.[195] A condition precedent, the performance or occurrence of which is intended to be contested, should be distinctly specified in his pleading by the plaintiff or defendant and, subject thereto, an averment of the performance or occurrence of all conditions precedent necessary for the case of that party is implied in his pleading.[196] In addition other claims may be joined with a claim for specific performance and the pleader must consider what is needed in respect of those.

[8.22] Under the current Rules of the Superior Courts a statement of claim should state specifically the relief which the plaintiff claims, either simply or in the alternative, and it is not necessary to ask for general or other relief which may always be given, as the court may think just, to the same extent as if it had been asked for; the same applies to any counterclaim or relief sought in a defence.[197] A party may apply by letter for a further and better statement of the nature of the claim or defence or further and better particulars of any manner stated in any pleading, notice or written proceeding requiring particulars; if this is not done satisfactorily the court may make an appropriate order upon such terms

---

[189] *Ormond v Anderson* (1813) 2 Ball & Beatty 363 at 369.
[190] *Savage v Carroll* (1810) 1 Ball & Beatty 265 at 283-4.
[191] But see paras **8.22-3** below.
[192] *Holohan v Ardmayle Estates* (SC) 1 May 1967, unrep at 4-5, said in the context of the Rules of the Superior Courts made in 1962 and effective from 1 January 1963. The present rules came into force on 1 October 1986. There is no change relevant to Walsh J's views.
[193] By Kenny J in *Hoon v Nolan* (1966) 101 ILTR 99 at 101. However, the absence was made good by some defence pleas.
[194] *Morrow v Carty* [1957] NI 174 at 178. A modern English view is that it does not: Jones v Goodhart, *Specific Performance* (1986) at 187.
[195] Order 19, rule 5(2).
[196] Order 19, rule 14.
[197] Order 20, rule 7, same as Order 20, rule 7 at the time of *Holohan's* case.

as to costs and otherwise as may be just.[198] The court will not order delivery of particulars before defence or reply, as the case may be, unless they are necessary or desirable to enable the defendant or plaintiff to plead or ought to be delivered for any other special reason.[199] Though not strictly necessary, there is much to be said for pleading the matters which Walsh J recorded[200] as having been customarily pleaded and perhaps also such matters as a document relied on as satisfying the Statute of Frauds, an act of part performance relied on as taking the case out of the statute or the authority of an agent.[201] If this is done the defendant must cover those points in his defence. He must deal specifically with each allegation of fact in a statement of claim except damages.[202] The plaintiff will thus get ample notice of any defence which is more than a traverse[203] and have the opportunity of seeking particulars. Of course, pleadings must not be too extensive. The statements contained in them should be as brief as the nature of the case will admit and the Taxing Master may inquire into any unnecessary prolixity and order the costs caused by it to be borne by the party responsible.[204]

[8.23] How pleadings deal with a deposit or a part payment of the price may depend on whether specific performance is sought. It has been said that a decree for specific performance does not depend upon the fact of whether or not a deposit has been paid.[205] When a contract is treated as being at an end or where it is alleged that it never took effect the purchaser would expressly claim the return of the deposit paid because then he would claim it on the basis of money had or received to his use or perhaps money paid for a consideration which had failed.[206] If specific performance is decreed the deposit will play its role of part payment of the purchase price.[207] When the facts of the case are such that the trial judge considers that he could make an order for specific performance but in his discretion does not do so[208] but awards damages in lieu thereof, he must take into account in assessing the damages not merely such items as the loss of bargain and other loss which flows from the breach[209] but the out of pocket expenses and any other money laid out by the plaintiff which would naturally include any part of the purchase money already paid.[210] In the latter situation the purchaser would not claim the return of the deposit in his pleadings. Doing so would be inconsistent with seeking to enforce the contract. However, if the purchaser claims that the parties did not reach any contract he will expressly claim the return of the deposit and should use the summary summons procedure if the sum involved exceeds the Circuit Court jurisdiction.[211]

---

[198] Order 19, rule 7(1) and (2). Again the wording is identical to Order 19, rule 6(1) and (2) of the previous rules.

[199] Order 19, rule 7(3), previously Order 19, rule 6(3).

[200] In the passage quoted at para **8.31**. Note the cases cited at fnn 193 and 194 above.

[201] On which *Mortal v Lyons* (1858) 8 Ir Ch R 112 at 117-8.

[202] Order 19, rule 17. See *Jones v Quinn* (1878) 2 LRI 516 at 519 on the "much abused general issue".

[203] Save matters which the defendant does not have to plead - eg, illegality, on which see paras **9.48-55** *infra*. But note Order 19, rule 15.

[204] Order 19, rule 1.

[205] *Per* Walsh J in *Holohan v Ardmayle Estates* (SC) 1 May 1967, unrep at 5. But now see discussion of the position of the deposit at paras **3.11-14** *ante*.

[206] *Holohan's* case at 4.

[207] See para **3.11** *ante*.

[208] On this see paras **1.06-9** *ante*.

[209] In a context, of course, of breach of contract, the rule in *Bain v Fothergill* not applying.

[210] *Holohan's* case at 4.

[211] As in *Lowis v Wilson* [1949] IR 347 where the purchaser's summary summons claimed on precisely the two alternative bases suggested by Walsh J in the passage quoted.

[8.24] In an Equity suit in the Circuit Court claiming specific performance of a contract for the sale of land the plaintiff should 'show jurisdiction'.[212] There should be sufficient description of the property to show that it is located within the particular circuit.[213] Traditionally an Equity Civil Bill has contained a statement that the rateable valuation of the subject property does not exceed £200.[214] However, it is a question of fact whether the court has jurisdiction. If a matter is within the jurisdiction of the court the failure of the parties to prove it or the failure of the judge to insist on proper proof being adduced to establish his jurisdiction does not have the effect of depriving him of jurisdiction or invalidating any order made by him.[215] Despite this, "proof should be given in every case to show that the matter is within the jurisdiction of the court".[216] In some cases, obviously, rateable valuations will be close to the Circuit Court limit. Occasionally a property is not separately rated so that it is impossible to say whether it is within the jurisdiction or not and then it is proper to bring the proceedings in the High Court.[217]

Possible court orders

[8.25] In many cases a plaintiff's target is simply an order for specific performance. However, sometimes he should consider other possible orders the court can make. These may assist towards getting an order for specific performance, they may avoid the need for it or they may give further relief to the plaintiff after he has got an order for specific performance but less than satisfactory compliance with it.

[8.26] The court has important powers which can help a purchaser to enforce or implement contracts for the sale of land if the vendor fails, refuses or becomes unable to complete the deal and execute a conveyance or if certain other difficulties occur. Where judgment is given for the specific performance of a contract concerning any land the court may declare that any of the parties to the action are trustees of the land or any part thereof within the meaning of the Trustee Act 1893.[218] This power can give ancillary relief when a suit for specific performance has been brought.[219] But that does not limit the power of the court to act under s 26(vi) of the 1893 Act in cases where a suit for specific performance is unnecessary - eg, if the only result of it would be to make costs.[220] Where a trustee jointly or solely entitled to or possessed of any land has been required to convey the land to a person entitled to such a conveyance and wilfully refuses to do so the court may make a "vesting order" vesting the land in any such person as it may direct.[221] A trustee in this context includes a constructive or implied trustee.[222] A party who has no defence to an action for specific performance of a contract for the sale of land is a trustee within the scope of this jurisdiction[223] but if a defence to an action for specific

---

[212] Order 5, rule 2 of the Rules of the Circuit Court 1950 requires the Civic Bill in every equity suit to be headed "Equity Civil Bill" and to "state such facts as may be necessary to show the jurisdiction of the court".
[213] On this aspect of jurisdiction see para **8.07** *supra*.
[214] Or whatever lower limit applied formerly.
[215] *Harrington v Murphy* [1989] IR 207 at 209.
[216] *Ibid*.
[217] *Mulvey v Flanagan* [1936] IJR 40.
[218] Section 31 of the 1893 Act.
[219] Per FitzGibbon LJ in *Re Ruthven's Trusts* [1906] 1 IR 236 at 246.
[220] *Ibid*.
[221] The 1893 Act s 26(vi) which allows 28 days for compliance.
[222] *Re Ruthven's Trusts* [1906] 1 IR 236 per Walker C at p 241 and Holmes LJ at p 246. Note the definition of "trustee" in s 50 of the 1893 Act.
[223] *Re Ruthven's Trusts* [1906] 1 IR 236.

performance can be put forward the court will not act summarily under the Trustee Act.[224] Any *arguable* defence would probably suffice to fend off an order under this jurisdiction. To justify a vesting order the court should feel that specific performance would be ordered as a matter of course[225] or that the case for specific performance is "plain and clear".[226] A vesting order may also be made where a trustee entitled to or possessed of any land or entitled to a contingent right therein, either solely or jointly with any other person, is a minor,[227] is outside the jurisdiction[228] or cannot be found.[229] Likewise if a vendor becomes *non compos mentis* after signing the contract[230] or dies leaving an infant successor in title[231] In the latter instance the contract was made by the deceased vendor while *sui juris* so the situation is very different from that of a minor who does a deal and may raise a defence of incapacity later.[232] The provision relating to a trustee who cannot be found may cover a situation where the legal estate in the relevant property was vested in a company which has been dissolved.[233] The powers of the court cover cases where trustees are already in place, eg, have already been appointed by deed.[234] A vesting order has the same effect as if all proper conveyances[235] are executed for such estate as the court directs.[236] In all cases where a vesting order can be made the court may, if it is more convenient, appoint a person to convey the land[237] and a conveyance pursuant to the order has the same effect as a vesting order under the appropriate provision.[238]

[8.27] The courts have further powers outside the Trustee Act 1893 by which they can assist the completion of contracts for the sale of land. Thus, if a tenant for life sells land and then refuses to appoint trustees of the settlement to receive the purchase money[239] though having power to do so, he can be ordered to appoint them.[240] And if he still fails to make the appointment the purchaser may be given liberty to apply in the vendor's name, and also the purchaser's own name, for the appointment of the necessary trustees by the court under s 38 of the Settled Land Act 1882.[241] In a case of the death of a person interested in the relevant matter where there is no personal representative the court may proceed in the absence of any person representing the estate of the deceased or may

---

[224] *Re Ruthven's Trusts* [1906] 1 IR 236 at 244.
[225] Walker C in the *Ruthven* case at 243 and Fitzgibbon LJ at 244.
[226] *Per* Holmes LJ in the *Ruthven* case at 247.
[227] Section 26(ii)(*a*) ("infant" in the 1893 Act).
[228] Section 26(ii)(*b*).
[229] Section 26(ii)(*c*).
[230] *Re Pagani* [1892] 1 Ch 236 where the order was made under a similar section in the Lunacy Act 1890: see discussion by Walker C and Fitzgibbon LJ in *Re Ruthven's Trusts* [1906] 1 IR 236 at 242-3, 244-5. *Cf Cross v Cross* (1897) 33 ILTR 50 where the court directed a sale in a partition action and a person entitled to a share was of unsound mind not so found.
[231] *Re Beaufort's Will* (1898) WN 148 cited by Walker C in the *Ruthven* case at p 243 and by FitzGibbon LJ at p 245.
[232] Considered under "Want of mutuality" in para **9.73** post.
[233] *Application of Kavanagh* (HC) 23 November 1984, Costello J, unrep. The State did not claim the legal estate as bona vacantia. See his discussion of conflicting English judgments at pp 3-4.
[234] *Re Kenny's Trusts* [1906] 1 IR 531.
[235] Note the broad defnition of "convey" and "conveyance" in s 50 of the Trustee Act 1893.
[236] Section 32 of the 1893 Act.
[237] Section 33 of the 1893 Act. Contingent rights may be released too.
[238] *Ibid*. See *Beale v Bragg* [1902] 1 IR 99.
[239] A receipt by the trustees or the court is essential for the purchaser to get good title: see Wylie, *Irish Land Law*, 2nd Ed, para 8.094; Wylie, *Irish Conveyancing Law*, para 16.047.
[240] *Hennessy v Kiernan* (1904) 38 ILTR 250.
[241] *Hennessy v Kiernan* (1905) 39 ILTR 145.

appoint some person to represent his estate for the purposes of the proceedings.[242] There is power also under s 27 of the Succession Act 1965 to make a grant of representation limited to the defence of proceedings.[243] As we have seen, however,[244] it would be wrong to join the President of the High Court as a party[245] even though the property of a deceased person vests in him until administration is granted where the deceased was intestate or left a will but no surviving executor.[246]

[8.28] In a *vendor's* action for specific performance a defendant who does not comply with a decree may be ordered to pay the purchase money into court within a limited time. If he does not comply the court may direct the plaintiff to execute a conveyance as an escrow[247] and the defendant to pay the purchase money to the plaintiff and, if necessary, issue a writ of fieri facias to enforce payment of the money.[248] Of course, the vendor is not bound to continue with his claim for specific performance. He may instead apply to the court to dissolve the order for specific performance and put an end to the contract.[249] The court will deal with such an application in accordance with general equitable principles[250] and will allow a defaulting purchaser to complete the sale on appropriate terms if it would be unjust in the circumstances to dissolve the contract.[251] If the contract is dissolved the normal remedies of forfeiture of the deposit[252] and damages[253] are likely to be available. The date on which damages will be assessed is likely to be that of the application to dissolve the order for specific performance on the basis that the vendors have acted reasonably in pursuing the remedy of specific performance.[254] The date at which that remedy became aborted (not by the vendor's fault) should logically be fixed as the date on which damages should be assessed.[255] An order could also be made which caters for both the possibility of the contract proceeding and that of it being rescinded. Thus, when a purchaser has failed to comply with an initial decree of specific performance the court may order him to obey it within a specified period in default of which the contract will be rescinded and the vendor may have an inquiry as to damages.[256]

---

[242] Rules of the Superior Courts, Order 15, rule 37. Costello J felt that an application under the corresponding former rule could have been brought in *Solomon v Estates Management & Development Agency Ltd*, 14 April 1980, unrep at p 7.

[243] *Flack v The President of the High Court* (HC) 29 November 1983, Costello J, unrep at p 5. See discussion by McGuire, *The Succession Act 1965*, 2nd Ed (by Pearce) at p 45.

[244] In para **8.14** *supra*.

[245] *Flack's* case at p 3-5.

[246] Succession Act 1965 s 13.

[247] To be delivered on payment of purchase-money, interest etc.

[248] *Jessop v Smyth* [1895] 1 IR 508.

[249] *Johnson v Agnew* [1980] AC 367; [1979] 2 WLR 487 at 493, approved by McWilliam J *in Vandeleur v Dargan* [1981] ILRM 75 at 77 and by Costello J in *Solomon v Estates Management and Development Agency Ltd* (HC) 14 July 1980, unrep at p 4.

[250] *Solomon's* case at pp 5-7. Note *Bourke v Grimes* (1929) 63 ILTR 53 where the Supreme Court held that a plaintiff who had got an order for specific performance had to furnish an abstract to the purchaser and show that the latter could not complete.

[251] As occurred in the *Solomon* case.

[252] *McGuire v Conwell* (1932) 66 ILTR 213 at 214. Note the dual role of the deposit: para **3.11** above.

[253] *Johnson v Agnew* [1980] AC 367; [1979] 2 WLR 487 at 493, approved by McWilliam J in *Vandeleur v Dargan* [1981] ILRM 75 at 77.

[254] *Vandeleur's* case at 77,

[255] *Johnson v Agnew* [1980] AC 367; [1979] 2 WLR 487 at 493, approved by McWilliam J in *Vandeleur v Dargan* [1981] ILRM 75 at 77.

[256] *Abbot v Ryan* (1901) 1 NIJR 75.

CONTRACTUAL TIME LIMITS

When time is of the essence

[8.29] A plaintiff must take great care about questions involving time limits. Most contracts will have some time limit even if only an agreed closing date. The first point for consideration usually is whether time is of the essence in a particular case. If it is not already of the essence but a party is considering making it so[257] he should bear in mind that doing that could backfire unless he is satisfied that he can fulfil all his own obligations.[258] The present position about when time is of the essence has been put thus:

> "The modern law, in the case of contracts of all types, may be summarised as follows. Time will not be considered to be of the essence unless: (1) the parties expressly stipulate that conditions as to time must be strictly complied with; or (2) the nature of the subject matter of the contract or the surrounding circumstances show that time should be considered to be of the essence; or (3) a party who has been subjected to unreasonable delay gives notice to the party in default making time of the essence."[259]

There had been a difference of approach between the common-law and equitable rules. However, the Supreme Court of Judicature (Ireland) Act 1877 provided that stipulations in contracts, as to time or otherwise, were to receive in all courts the same construction and effect as they had received in equity till then.[260] Kenny J has noted the former distinction:

> "In the common-law courts, when a contract provided that certain things were to be done within a certain time or on a specified date, the party who sought to sue on the contract had to plead and prove that he had complied with the stipulation as to time and was ready and willing to perform any other parts of the contract which remained unperformed ... In the courts of equity (where the ideas summarised in the maxim 'equity looks to the intent, not to the form' were applied and developed) relief would be given against failure to comply with a stipulation as to time in a contract, unless time was of the essence of the contract. A plaintiff or defendant who had not complied with a stipulation as to time in a contract could succeed on his claim or defence unless it was established that time was of the essence of the contract."[261]

At law time was always of the essence of the contract. When any time was fixed for its completion it had to be completed on the day specified or an action would lie for the breach of it.[262] Courts of equity, which would not countenance fraud or assist unfair dealings, would relieve against breach of a time limit unless time was of the essence and order specific performance even though the party seeking relief could not succeed in an action at law.[263] They would not allow a party to make unfair use of the letter of his

---

[257] See paras **8.32-7** *infra*.

[258] See para **8.41** *infra* ("Ready, willing and able").

[259] Halsbury's *Laws of England*, 4th Ed, Vol 9, para 481 approved by McWilliam J in *Hynes Ltd v Independent Newspapers Ltd* [1980] IR 204 at 209. The first two principles were approved by O'Higgins CJ at 215, the third not being relevant in that case.

[260] Section 28(7).

[261] The *Hynes Ltd* case at 218-9. See also *Cartan v Bury* (1860) 10 Ir Ch R 387 at 394-5 and *Lennon v Napper* (1802) 2 Schoales & Lefroy 682 at 684-5; *cf Dyas v Rooney* (1890) 27 LRI 4.

[262] *Cartan's* case at 394.

[263] *Jessop v King* (1812) 2 Ball & Beatty 81 at 94.

contract in relation to the completion date.[264] As long ago as 1802 Lord Redesdale noted that the courts were in the constant habit of relieving against the lapse of time where the time element was not essential to the substance of the contract.[265]

[8.30] An express stipulation by parties that time is to be of the essence for completion will be upheld.[266] Even in equity stipulations as to time may not always be disregarded and one case in which such a stipulation cannot be disregarded is where the parties themselves have provided that it should be essential.[267] There has been controversy in other jurisdictions whether equity can give relief by reinstating a contract after its rescission and the forfeiture of a deposit[268] for failure to complete thus restoring the purchaser's equitable interest in the property[269] and enabling him to get specific performance when otherwise appropriate.[270] If such jurisdiction exists its exercise probably will be exceptional. The Privy Council has recently ruled that there is jurisdiction to give relief against the forfeiture of a deposit which is higher than the sum which would be fixed as a "reasonable amount of earnest".[271] That, if approved in Ireland, will remove one element of injustice which might seem to support the need for power to order the reinstatement of contracts.

Issues may arise about other time limits where the time is stated to be of the essence. One which arises fairly often is a clause making a purchaser state any objections and raise his requisitions within a fixed time in default of which they are deemed to be waived, time being made of the essence for the purposes of the clause. A vendor cannot bind his purchaser by this kind of time condition if an objection "goes to the root of the title".[272] When a defect in title turns up the vendor usually should be given a reasonable time to cure it.[273] The current Law Society conditions acknowledge the general law by applying only to "Any Objection or Requisition ... not going to the root of the title ..."[274] In the absence of such a condition it seems that requisitions may be delivered within a reasonable time[275] so it is not surprising that time limits are imposed.

---

[264] A modern example is *Maye v Merriman* (HC) 13 February 1980, unrep. The vendor's claim for damages for a 2-week delay in closing failed. Hamilton J pointed out at 19 that, though the claim was one at common law for damages for breach of contract, he had to approach it including the time stipulation on the same basis as if it were a claim for equitable relief. Note the 4:1 decision of the House of Lords in *Raineri v Miles* [1981] AC 1050; [1980] 2 All ER 145 holding a party liable in damages for a month's delay in completing a sale of a house even though time was not of the essence. The dissenting speech of Viscount Dilhorne is consistent with Hamilton J's decision. In *Raineri's* case the sale was part of a "chain" of two sales.

[265] *Lennon v Napper* (1802) 2 Schoales & Lefroy 682 at 684-5.

[266] Point (1) in the passage from Halsbury approved in *Hynes Ltd v Independent Newspapers Ltd* [1980] IR 204 by McWilliam J at 209 and, on appeal, by O'Higgins CJ at 215. Note also the passage from Fry on *Specific Performance* approved by Kenny J at 219. Parke J agreed with both judgments.

[267] *United Yeast Co Ltd v Cameo Investments Ltd* (1975) 111 ILTR 13 at 16-7.

[268] On which see paras **3.11** *ante* and **11.12** *post*.

[269] See paras **11.01-13** *post*.

[270] See Jones & Goodhart, *Specific Performance* (1986) at 43-8; Meagher Gummow Lehane, *Equity Doctrine & Remedies*, 3rd Ed (1992) at paras 18.27-9 discussing the important Australian decisions in *Legione v Hately* (1983) 152 CLR 406; 46 ALR 1 and *Stern v McArthur* (1988) 165 CLR 489 (neither unanimous).

[271] *Worker's Trust & Merchant Bank Ltd v Dojap Investments Ltd* [1993] 1 EGLR 203 at 205.

[272] *Re Carrige & McDonnell's Contract* [1895] 1 IR 288 at 296.

[273] *Clegg v Wright* (1920) 54 ILTR 69 at 71-2. And see para **9.77** *post*.

[274] General Condition 17 (1991) Ed. See discussion of the time for requisitions by Wylie, *Irish Conveyancing Law* (1978) at paras 14.20-22.

[275] *Re Todd & McFadden's Contract* [1908] 1 IR 213 at 220.

[8.31] The general rule in cases of the sale and purchase of land is that time is not of the essence of the contract.[276] The courts of equity have regarded the time fixed for completion as a detail introduced for the sake of convenience to indicate when the parties should come together.[277] However, there may be implications from the nature of the subject matter or the circumstances of a case which lead to the conclusion that the parties intended time to be of the essence even though they did not say so. Cases where the courts are likely to treat time as being of the essence without this being stated expressly include purchases of licensed premises,[278] a residential property known to the parties to be required for immediate and urgent occupation by the purchaser,[279] a grazing letting for the season,[280] possibly farms in some circumstances although this may depend on seasonal factors[281] and a lease dependent on lives.[282] In the case of licensed premises the courts will have regard to the needs of the purchaser in relation to getting possession and commencing trading and also the needs of the vendor to know when his obligations in relation to staff, suppliers and the licensing laws will cease and perhaps to make alternative arrangements in relation to his own occupation or business.[283]

The conclusion that time is of the essence in such cases even though not expressed to be so is a *prima facie* position. Therefore it can be displaced by other matters, eg, a provision that if the purchaser is not completed on the agreed date the purchaser shall pay interest or a step taken by the vendor's solicitor after the agreed completion date towards getting the contract closed.[284] That allows room for some uncertainty. It may be wise to provide expressly that time is or is not of the essence of the contract in sales where the courts might hold otherwise that time was of the essence though not expressed to be so.

Making time of the essence

[8.32] This heading may be a misdescription[285] though the phrase is very widely used.[286] To suggest that by writing a letter one party can make time of the essence when it was not so before has been said to be a convenient but inaccurate way of putting it.[287] Kenny J has protested against the commonly held view that one party to a contract in which time is not of the essence can make it of the essence by serving a notice:[288]

> "The true position is that when time is not of the essence and the vendor or the purchaser has been guilty of unreasonable delay, the other party may by notice limit a reasonable time within which the contract must be completed if the party on whom the notice is served is not to lose the remedy of specific performance and have the contract terminated against him."

[276] *Nyland v Brennan* (HC) 19 February 1970, Pringle J, unrep at 16; *Hynes Ltd v Independent Newpapers Ltd* [1980] IR 204 at 218-9 (Kenny J stating the position in equity).
[277] *Nyland's* case at 17 approving a passage from *Gray v Smith* (1889) 43 Ch D 208 at 214.
[278] *O'Brien v Seaview Enterprises Ltd* (HC) 31 May 1976, Finlay P, unrep at 14-15 (facts considered at 15-16 showed an intent that time was not of the essence in that case); *cf* Kenny J in *Delgado v Crean* (HC) 24 May 1978, unrep at 11 on the importance of the closing date in sales of licensed premises.
[279] *Webb v Hughes* (1870) LR 10 Eq 281 noted by Finlay P in *O'Brien's* case at 16.
[280] *Dyas v Rooney* (1890) 27 LRI 4 at 9.
[281] See discussion in *Guerin v Heffernan* [1925] 1 IR 57 at 67-8.
[282] *Ormond v Anderson* (1813) 2 Ball & Beatty 363 at 370.
[283] *O'Brien's* case at 14-15.
[284] *O'Brien's* case at 15-16; *Webb's* case.
[285] O'Caoimh P's word in *Sidebottom Ltd v Leonard* (HC) 18 May 1973, unrep at 4.
[286] But see Kenny J's reference to *Fry* quoted later in this para.
[287] *Smith v Hamilton* [1951] Ch 174 at 181; [1950] 2 All ER 928 at 933, cited by Kenny J in *Healy v Ballsbridge Ltd v Alliance Property Corporation Ltd* [1974] IR 441 at 447.
[288] 6th Ed, para 1092.

He then refers to Fry on *Specific Performance of Contracts*:[289]

> "... the statement appears that where time was not originally of the essence of the contract, but one party has been guilt of gross, vexatious, unreasonable or unnecessary delay or default in relation to it, the other party becomes entitled to limit a reasonable time within which the contract should be perfected by the other. The author then adds that it is only when such default or delay has happened that this right occurs and that there is no general right to either party to limit a time."[290]

Another long respected textbook was quoted by an Irish Judge in 1930:

> "Where time is not made of the essence of a contract by the contract itself, although a day for performing it is named, of course neither party can strictly make it so after the contract; but if either party is guilty of delay, a distinct notice written by the other that he shall consider the contract at an end if it be not completed within a reasonable time to be named, would be treated in equity as binding on the party to whom it is given."[291]

O'Caoimh P has explained the effect of a notice "making time of the essence":[292]

> "What the notice can do is give to the other party notice that his failure to complete within a reasonable time specified in the notice will be treated by the other party as a refusal on his part to carry out the contract and that is what normally is meant by making time of the essence in a contract such as this..."

[8.33] There may not be very much difference in substance in any of the material just mentioned. It is crystal clear that when time is not originally of the essence in a contract neither party has any right to make it so[293] simply because time has passed without the contract being completed. On the other hand, if there has been a sufficient degree of delay or default[294] by one side the innocent party may stipulate a reasonable time[295] within which he requires the non-complying party to perform the contract. In this way he "makes time of the essence" in the broad meaning of the phrase and, when the stipulated time has passed without compliance, removes any possible doubt about the right to sue for specific performance[296] and gains the right to treat continued non-performance as a refusal to carry out the contract. A formal contract may provide that if a party fails to comply with a completion notice within the relevant period or any agreed extension he is deemed to fail to comply with the conditions "in a material respect" and the innocent party may, without further notice, enforce such rights and remedies as may be available to him at law or in equity.[297]

---

[289] *Holohan v Ardmayle Estates* (HC) 5 March 1966, unrep, approved by (SC) 1 May 1967, unrep at 8, qutoed by Kenny J in the *Healy Ballsbridge* case at 447, affirmed *ex tempore* by (SC) 18 December 1973.

[290] *Holohan's* case approved by (SC), *ibid*, quoted by Kenny J in the *Healy Ballsbridge* case at 448, affirmed by (SC) 18 December 1973.

[291] Sugden's, *Vendors and Purchasers* (13th Ec), at 227 approved by Johnston J in *Hopkins v Geoghegan* [1931] IR 135 at 139-40.

[292] *Sidebottom Ltd v Leonard* (HC) 18 May 1973, unrep at 5.

[293] To avoid doubt, the meaning just given by O'Caoimh P to the notice is intended here. *Cf* the modern Law Society condition noted in the next para.

[294] On which see the next para below.

[295] On this see para **8.36** *infra*.

[296] See para **8.29** *supra* on time being of the essence.

[297] Eg, the Law Society's, *General Conditions of Sale* (1991) Ed, condition 40(*d*) (purchaser in default - forfeiture of deposit and re-sale under condition 41 are expressly imported) and (*e*) (vendor in default).

[8.34] The courts do not specify what amount of delay or default will entitle the innocent party to make time of the essence. Obviously this must depend on the facts of each case. It has been described as "unreasonable delay",[298] "such default as to entitle the vendor to rescind the contract subject to its being done by reasonable notice",[299] "serious delay in fulfilling their obligations under the contract"[300] and "gross, vexatious, unreasonable or unnecessary delay or default".[301] It has also been said simply that it must "be reasonable to serve the notice".[302] A court will be slow to hold that there has been sufficiently improper conduct merely because of a genuine dispute based on a misinterpretation of the contract.[303] It will also take into account the fact that there has been delay on both sides[304] or that the delay on one side was not "a source of great annoyance or upset" to the other.[305] A vendor and purchaser summons[306] served while a completion notice is running will have the effect of staying the operation of the notice.[307] A court would not, where a purchaser has issued a vendor and purchaser summons to have a dispute about some matter connected with the contract decided, allow a vendor to make time of the essence so that, if he were successful in the summons, he could rescind the contract and forfeit the deposit.[308]

It is important to note that the modern Law Society *General Conditions of Sale* remove the need to show delay or default and any possible arguments whether a 28-day period of notice is reasonable. If time is not of the essence originally then, if the sale be not completed on or before the agreed closing date, either party may on or after that date (unless the sale shall first have been rescinded or become void) give to the other party notice to complete.[309] There is no requirement here to show any delay or default; the simple fact that the completion date has passed without completion is what matters. Subject to the modifications to be noted shortly[310] the party giving the notice must himself "then" either be "able, ready and willing" to complete the sale or be not so able, ready or willing by reason of the default or misconduct of the other party. The party served must complete the sale within 28 days after getting the notice without prejudice to any intermediate right of rescission by either party.[311] He must give the server "reasonable advice of his readiness to complete."[312] Time is made of the essence of the contract and there is no need to show that the 28-day period is reasonable. In normal circumstances

---

[298] *Holohan v Ardmayle Estates* (HC) 7 March 1966, Kenny J, unrep, affirmed by (SC) 1 May 1967, unrep at 8, quoted by Kenny J in *Healy Ballsbridge Ltd v Alliance Property Corporation Ltd* [1974] IR 441 at 447 affirmed by (SC) at 449. *Cf* "unnecessary delay" in *Hopkins v Geoghegan* [1931] IR 135 at 140.
[299] *International Securities Ltd v Portmarnock Estates Ltd* (HC) 9 April 1975, Hamilton P, unrep at 14.
[300] The *International Securities Ltd* case at 16.
[301] A passage from Fry, *Specific Performance*, 6th Ed, para 1092, cited by Kenny J in *Holohan's* case and quoted in [1974] IR at 448.
[302] *Hickey v Keating* (HC) 25 January 1980, McWilliam J, unrep at 4.
[303] The *International Securities Ltd case* at 15.
[304] *Gibson v Butler* (1964) 99 ILTR 116.
[305] *Commane v Walsh* (HC) 2 May 1983, O'Hanlon J, unrep at 6.
[306] Discussed in paras **8.53-9** *infra*.
[307] *Hickey v Keating* (HC) 25 January 1980, McWilliams, unrep at 3-4. See also para **8.59** *infra*.
[308] *Ibid*. It may be otherwise if the dispute is not *bona fide*.
[309] General condition 40(*a*).
[310] Para **8.35** *infra*.
[311] General condition 40(*b*).
[312] General condition 40(*c*).

clauses of this sort are likely to be upheld by the courts and they have in fact been upheld in England.[313]

[8.35] Normally it is essential also that the party giving the notice is himself able to complete the contract when he serves notice making time of the essence.[314] This broad proposition is modified by the Law Society's *General Conditions of Sale* (1991) Ed so that a vendor is not deemed to be other than ready, willing and able to complete a sale by the fact that the subject property has been mortgaged or charged so long as the property can be discharged out of the sale price.[315] He is protected similarly where he cannot fulfil a duty to give vacant possession when he serves the notice but can give it on completion if given reasonable advice of the defaulter's intention to close.[316] Under the general law a party cannot serve a valid completion notice if at the time of service he has not shown title in accordance with contract[317] or cannot give vacant possession.[318]

[8.36] The notice making time of the essence must allow a reasonable time.[319] In deciding what is and what is not a reasonable time the court must take all the circumstances into consideration.[320] A vital factor in deciding what is reasonable is what remains to be done when notice is served. If a party wishes to show that the time given for completion for a sale is unreasonable because of what remained to be done in order to be ready to complete the onus is on him to show what remained to be done.[321] The nature of the property sold is likely to be of considerable importance. Thus, the fact that the property comprises licensed premises sold as a going concern is material even if on the facts of a case that does not result in time being of the essence in the contract.[322] Finlay P has set out factors likely to be material:[323]

> "The circumstances and factors which I am satisfied on the authorities are relevant to the question of reasonableness of this time are firstly any problems of an unusual nature which might arise in regard to the conveyancing aspects of the completion. Secondly the time which had elapsed since the original date fixed for completion which is relevant by reason of the fact that it is the time during which the purchaser and his legal adviser have been aware of what required to be done and of the fact that a contract for sale had been concluded and must now be completed. Thirdly I take the view that a factor with regard to the reasonableness of time was the nature of the premises under sale and the importance from the point of view of the vendor as well as of the purchaser of a

---

[313] *Hooker v Wyle* [1973] 3 All ER 707; *Cumberland Court (Brighton) Ltd v Taylor* [1963] 2 All ER 536; *Innisfail Laundry Ltd* (1963) 107 SJ 437.
[314] *Viscount Securities Ltd v Kennedy* (SC) 6 May 1986, unrep, per Walsh J at 13-14 and Griffin J at 6-8; *Holohan v Ardmayle Securities* (SC) 1 May 1967, Walsh J, unrep at 8; *Healy Ballsbridge Ltd v Alliance Property Corporation Ltd* [1974] IR 441 at 448.
[315] Condition 40(*g*)(i).
[316] Condition 40(*g*)(ii).
[317] *Holohan v Ardmayle Estates* (SC) 1 May 1967, Walsh J, unrep at 8; *Healy Ballsbridge Ltd v Alliance Property Corporation Ltd* [1974] IR 441 at 448,. Questions of title are discussed at paras **9.74-83** *post*.
[318] As in *Viscount Securities Ltd* case; *cf United Yeast Co Ltd v Cameo Investments Ltd* (1975) 111 ILTR 13 (where time was expressly of the essence under the contract). On the purchaser's right to possession see paras **11.26-8** *post*.
[319] But note the modern *Law Society* condition: see para **8.34** *supra*.
[320] *International Securities Ltd v Portmarnock Estates Ltd* (HC) 9 April 1975, Hamilton J, unrep at 16; *Commane v Walsh* (HC) 2 May 1983, O'Hanlon J, unrep at 6.
[321] The *International Securities Ltd* case at 17-8.
[322] *O'Brien v Seaview Enterprises Ltd* (HC) 31 May 1976, Finlay P, unrep.
[323] *O'Brien's* case at 20-21.

completion as close as possible to the date originally fixed. Fourthly I am satisfied in this context any communication on behalf of the purchaser to the vendor indicating the difficulty or difficulties which had arisen in his completion of the contract and putting the vendor at least in the position of being aware of his genuine intention of closing and of reasons which might appear to be valid while such closing might be delayed would be material."

A purchaser's difficulties in raising finance may be relevant if they are known to the vendor at the time of the contract, especially if the vendor himself has a role in the relevant dealings.[324] They probably are not material if they are unknown to the vendor[325] and certainly not if the delay is caused by attempts to get finance in the cheapest possible way.[326]

[8.37] It is important to note that both a clause in a contract making time of the essence and a valid completion notice doing the same will be *mutually* binding.[327] Time is made of the essence of the contract as a whole and in respect of both parties.[328] The giver of the notice is equally bound because completion of the deal is an activity in which both parties necessarily cooperate.[329] It follows that a person making time of the essence must feel quite sure that he can comply with his own obligations as otherwise he may lose the benefit of the contract himself.[330]

Suing early

[8.38] A plaintiff seems to be entitled to sue for specific performance once the agreed completion date has passed without making time of the essence.[331] He must make time of the essence if he seeks to enforce a right to forfeit the deposit[332] but not if he is simply calling upon the defendant to "do what he has engaged to do".[333] English case law indicates that he may sue before the completion date. The right of action for specific performance should not be equated with a cause of action at law; in equity all that is required is to show circumstances which will justify the intervention of a court of equity.[334] In a case where the court should award damages in lieu of specific performance, *eg*, where the parties complete the relevant contract after the issue in good faith of a writ for specific performance and damages in addition to or in lieu of specific performance so that the only matter for decision at the hearing is damages for delay, the facts that the writ was issued before the completion date and that an action for damages alone begun on the same day would have been premature do not prevent the plaintiff getting damages.[335]

---

[324] *Re Barr's Contract* [1956] 2 All ER 853 at 857-8 considered by Finlay P in *O'Brien's* case at 22.
[325] Finlay P did not have to consider this in the *O'Brien* case. *Cf Raineri v Miles* (HL) [1981] AC 1050; [1980] 2 All ER 145.
[326] *O'Brien's* case at 23.
[327] *United Yeast Co Ltd v Cameo Investments Ltd* (1975) 111 ILTR 13 at 16; *Viscount Securities Ltd v Kennedy* (SC) 6 May 1986, Griffin J, unrep at 7.
[328] *Quadrangle Development and Construction Co Ltd v Jennr* [1974] 1 All ER 729 at 732-3 approved in the *United Yeast Co Ltd* case at 17-18.
[329] Per Russell LJ in the *Quadrangle Development* case at 732 approved by Griffin J *in Viscount Securities Ltd v Kennedy* (SC) 6 May 1986, unrep at 6-7.
[330] See Wylie, *Irish Conveyancing Law* (1978) at para 12.12. The author describes making time of the essence as a "two-edged sword".
[331] *Sidebottom Ltd v Leonard* (HC) 18 May 1973, O'Caoimh P, unrep at 4-5.
[332] The *Sidebottom Ltd* case at 4.
[333] *Ibid* at 5.
[334] *Hasham v Zenab* [1960] AC 316 at 329 (Privy Council).
[335] *Oakacre Ltd v Claire Cleaners (Holdings) Ltd* [1981] 3 All ER 667.

Equity is willing to deal with "the whole case" and in doing so the courts will deal with any damages sustained after the institution of the specific performance claim.[336] It has been suggested that issuing a writ for specific performance before an actual breach of contract was to enable a purchaser, if he thought right, to register his action as a *lis pendens*.[337] An action may be commenced justifiably if the other party has indicated an intention not to perform the contract[338] or when the vendor has delayed significantly after an agreed completion date even though time has not been made of the essence.[339] A party probably is not entitled to seek specific performance when a transaction is proceeding smoothly without any reason to expect this to change. Since something must justify the intervention of equity he probably needs to show some kind of breach or reason to expect one.

Waiver of a time limit

[8.39] Where time is of the essence the relevant time limit may be waived. That may be done by conduct. A vendor who fails to comply with a time limit for sending an abstract of title or the title documents agreed to be sent[340] is likely to lose the right to insist on the purchaser raising his objections or requisitions within the time limited for that purpose.[341] If the delay is serious it may even amount to waiver of a clause in the contract making time of the essence for completion of a sale.[342] Once a stipulation that time is of the essence has been waived neither party is entitled to insist upon mere delay as a ground for treating the contract as at an end until he has fixed a reasonable time by notice requiring the other side to complete the contract and that time has expired.[343] An agreement by parties simply to extend the time for completion to a substituted date is likely to be a waiver of the former date but only to the extent of allowing the extra time so no further completion notice will be needed.[344] If, however, the former completion date is waived without fixing a later one a new completion date still can be fixed but principles of equity will require reasonable notice to be given.[345]

Getting contract signed quickly

[8.40] Sometimes a party is anxious to compel the other side to sign a contract speedily. A vendor who wants a contract signed quickly by his purchaser should present the draft contract quickly and then, if the purchaser delays, serve a notice making time of the essence after a short specified period.[346] In practice, of course, a vendor's solicitor often will protect his client by a "subject to contract" clause[347] or by a letter or clause to the

---

[336] *Oakacre Ltd's* case at 670.

[337] *Marks v Lilley* [1959] 2 All ER 647 at 648. *Lites Pendentes* are covered at paras **10.10-14** *post*.

[338] *Hasham's* case.

[339] *Marks v Lilley* [1959] 2 All ER 647.

[340] The latter is the normal modern practice.

[341] *Cellulose Processors Ltd v Flynn & O'Flaherty Ltd* (HC) 28 April 1986, Finlay P, unrep at 11-12; *Re Todd & McFadden's Contract* [1908] 1 IR 213 at 220-1.

[342] *Mills v Healy* [1937] IR 437 at 444 - documents to vouch title not furnished till after completion date.

[343] *Mill's* case at 446.

[344] *Barclay v Messenger* (1874) 43 LJ Eq 449 noted by Murray J in *McKillop v McMullan* [1979] NI 85 at 92-3.

[345] *McKillop's* case at 93.

[346] *Kelly v Park Hall School Ltd* [1979] IR 340 at 352.

[347] On which see Ch 4.

effect that the vendor is not bound until an exchange of contracts has taken place.[348] There may be an implied term that a written contract would be signed by a purchaser without delay but, by his own delay in sending out the written contract, the vendor may waive[349] that term to the extent, at least, that he may insist only on reasonable compliance with the requirement of promptitude.[350] However, the courts will not let a vendor impose unilaterally an unreasonably short period for the purchaser to sign a formal contract where no such term had been agreed in the parties' oral agreement[351] It appears that a purchaser signing a contract which provides for a normal or short period for completion is entitled to expect the vendor to execute it promptly in turn.[352]

READY, WILLING AND ABLE

[8.41] A person seeking specific performance must show that he is ready, willing and able to perform the contract at the material time or times. He probably does not have to plead this[353] but it is customary to do so and this may be useful. The fact may not be denied; if it is denied by anything more than a traverse the plaintiff will have a better idea of the likely arguments against his case and may be able to seek particulars. The parties' obligations will depend on the terms of their contracts but the main ones are fairly obvious. A vendor normally must be in a position at the material times to show good title and give vacant possession[354] unless the particular contract puts some limits on those obligations. A purchaser normally should present a conveyance for execution and offer the balance of the purchase money.[355] He must have the necessary money or be able to get it in time[356] though a vendor and his solicitor must beware of assuming too readily that the purchaser cannot do so.[357] If a vendor disputes the purchaser's readiness he may have to show that the purchaser could not have obtained a sufficient loan on the security of the property if he was given good title to it.[358] An intending lessee should be able to show that he was ready or offered to accept a lease in accordance with the agreement.[359] Even a repudiation of a contract by a defendant may not absolve the plaintiff from showing performance or readiness to perform at the material time.[360]

[8.42] It is vital to bear in mind that the completion date, either one agreed originally or one brought about by time being made of the essence or in some other way, often is not the only date on which a party must be ready, willing and able. Under a typical clause

---

[348] *Kelly v Irish Nursery & Landscape Co Ltd* [1981] ILRM 433. The text of the letter is set out at 436. See para **4.15** *ante.*

[349] On waiver of time limits see para **8.39** *supra.*

[350] *Kelly v Park Hall School Ltd* [1979] IR 340 at 352-3.

[351] *Ibid* at 352.

[352] *Cellulose Processors Ltd v Flynn & O'Flaherty Ltd* (HC) 28 April 1986, Finlay P, unrep at 13.

[353] *Holohan v Ardmayle Estates* (SC) 1 May 1967, unrep at 5. *Cf Morrow v Carty* [1957] NI 174 at 178; *Dolan v McTernan* (1846) 9 ILR 175 at 178. And see para 8.21 ante.

[354] *Viscount Securities Ltd v Kennedy* (SC) 6 May 1986, unrep, *per* Walsh J at 13-14 and Griffin J (on possession) at 4-8.

[355] *Jackson v Veich* (1858) 3 Ir Jur NS 201.

[356] *Morrow v Carty* [1957] NI 174 at 178-9 (could not pay deposit in cash).

[357] *Mills v Healy* [1937] IR at 444-5; *cf Holohan v Ardmayle Estates* (SC) 1 May 1967, unrep at 7-8.

[358] *Bourke v Grimes* (1929) 63 ILTR 53 at 54, per FitzGibbon J.

[359] *Dolan v McTernan* (1846) 9 ILR 175 at 178.

[360] *Morrow's* case at 178.

used in standard conditions considered in the case law a person serving the notice making time of the essence must be able to complete the deal when he serves the notice and at all times while the notice is running.[361] This has been modified to an extent by the Law Society's *General Conditions of Sale* (1991) Ed[362] but considerable care is still needed. The point is that when time is of the essence it is so mutually.[363] There is no question of one party being bound by time being of the essence while the other has the benefit of the equitable rule permitting a reasonable extension.[364] It is "really ludicrous to think of an obligation on the one party to complete the contract time being of the essence without there being necessarily on the other side of the coin a similar obligation on the party giving the notice to fulfil his own outstanding obligations under the contract."[365] The danger for a party in making time of the essence without being able to complete himself is that the other side will have the chance to get out of the contract because, if the party giving the notice or relying on an original agreement making time of the essence slips up, he will not be entitled to an extension of time.[366] Taking this one step further, a vendor who relies wrongly on time being of the essence and purports to rescind the contract and forfeit the deposit may find that his conduct is treated as a wrongful repudiation of the contract by the purchaser who can thus get out of all liability under the contract and get his deposit back.[367]

[8.43] A plaintiff who has committed a breach of an essential term of a contract cannot obtain specific performance but this principle does not extend to non-essential or trivial breaches.[368] A defendant is not entitled to repudiate the contract unless the plaintiff's breaches deprive him of substantially the whole benefit of the contract.[369] But though a plaintiff's breaches may not be serious enough to justify the defendant repudiating the contract it does not necessarily follow that the plaintiff must get specific performance. His breaches may cause the remedy to be withheld as an exercise of the court's discretion[370] or may help some defence to succeed.[371] On the other hand, his breaches may be waived by the other side.[372] The defendant cannot rely on breaches by the plaintiff which were caused by the defendant's default.[373] An invalid attempt by one side to treat a contract as at an end may give the other side a chance to mend his hand in relation to a breach before time is validly made of the essence of the contract.[374]

A vendor who has already got an order for specific performance but wishes to have the order dissolved and the contract rescinded[375] must still show that he is prepared to

---

[361] *Viscount Securities Ltd v Kennedy* (SC) 6 May 1986, Griffin J, unrep at 6-8.
[362] See para **8.35** *supra.*
[363] See para **8.37** *supra.*
[364] *United Yeast Co Ltd v Cameo Investments Ltd* (1975) 111 ILTR 13 at 16-17.
[365] *Per* Russell LJ in *Quadrangle Development and Construction Co Ltd v Jenner* [1974] 1 All ER 729 at 732 approved by Butler J in the *United Yeast Co Ltd* case at 17.
[366] As occurred in the *United Yeast Co Ltd* case. See further Wylie, *Irish Conveyancing Law* (1978) at para 12.12.
[367] *Mills v Healy* [1937] IR 437 at 446, 447-8.
[368] *Dyster v Randall* [1926] Ch 932; [1926] All ER 150 at 156.
[369] *Taylor v Smyth* [1991] 1 IR 142 at 155-6, 171.
[370] On which see paras **1.06-9** *ante.*
[371] *Eg,* laches on which see paras **9.42-7** *post.*
[372] As in *Holohan v Ardmayle Estates* (SC) 1 May 1967, unrep at 7.
[373] *Johnson v Agnew* [1979] 1 All ER 883 at 895.
[374] *Mills v Healy* [1937] IR 437 at 447-8 - purchaser took chance to rescind.
[375] See para **8.28** *supra.*

perform the contract and that his purchaser is unwilling or unable to complete.[376] On this basis he asks the court to let him accept the defendant's repudiation and to award him damages.[377]

INTEREST

[8.44] A vendor often has occasion to claim interest on the unpaid balance of the purchase price. This may be joined with a claim for specific performance or advanced as a separate claim. The latter is a suitable course, for example, when a sale has been completed save that an issue remaining is liability for interest; the District Court may have jurisdiction.[378] Normally a contract for sale contains a clause[379] entitling the vendor to interest if completion is delayed in certain circumstances. The reason for an interest clause is to protect a vendor from dilatoriness on the part of the purchaser.[380] Where a contract does not fix a rate of interest the court will do so; it is not confined to any "court rate" but will have regard to prevailing yields on securities and the rates of interest fixed in private sales generally.[381] The courts of equity have regularly awarded simple interest as ancillary relief in respect of equitable remedies such as specific performance, rescission and the taking of an account.[382] The court will bear in mind that a purchaser liable for interest at too low a rate will find it in his interest to delay completion.[383] On the other hand a vendor who thinks he could enforce a high contract rate of interest might be tempted to hold up completion; so when the vendor is in default and the purchaser opts to take the rents and profits he may be entitled to pay interest at a lower rate than that fixed by the contract.[384]

[8.45] Wording frequently used in the past[385] in formal contracts for the sale of land obliged the purchaser to pay interest at a stated rate if from any cause whatever the purchase was not completed by the agreed completion date. The courts have held that the words "other than the wilful default of the vendor" should be read into the condition.[386] That principle has been embodied in other conditions which have provided that if, from any cause whatsoever other than the wilful default of the vendor, the purchase was not completed by the agreed completion date the purchaser must pay interest at the contract rate. The reason for the reference to the vendor's wilful default was that the vendor normally fixed the date for completion and he knew the material facts and the difficulties he might face; if no limit were placed on interest clauses, either by construction[387] or by

---

[376] *Bourke v Grimes* (1929) 63 ILTR 53; plaintiff failed to deal with objection raised by court counsel.
[377] *Vandeleur v Dargan* [1981] ILRM 75 at 77.
[378] As in *Green v Quinn* (1940) 75 ILTR 107. See also para **8.10** *supra*.
[379] We consider examples in the next two paras. See also Wylie, *Irish Conveyancing Law* (1978) paras 10.074, 18.09-10.
[380] *Re Postmaster-General & Colgan's Contract* (1906) 1 IR 287 at 298.
[381] *Law v Roberts (No 2)* [1964] IR 306; at the time the yields and the usual rates of interest in contracts were both around 6%.
[382] *Per* Lord Brandon in *President of India v La Pintada Cia* [1984] 2 All ER 773 at 779.
[383] *Law's* case at 307. See also para **11.24** *post*.
[384] *Manton v Mannion* [1958] IR 324 at 325.
[385] See next para for typical modern clause.
[386] *Sheridan v Higgins* [1971] IR 291 at 303; *cf Re Kissock & Taylor's Contract* [1916] 1 IR 393 at 399. The modern Law Society condition, *General Condition* 25, (1991) Ed, makes interest payable if delay in completion is "by reason of any default on the part of the purchaser".
[387] As in the type of condition noted earlier in this para.

their own wording, to prevent vendors taking advantage of their own wrong, the clauses would be very oppressive.[388]

Even that qualification may not be enough to treat the purchaser with complete fairness. A vendor can be in breach of his contract and yet free of wilful default. Default involves "either not doing what you ought or doing what you ought not, having regard to your relations with the other parties concerned in the transaction; in other words, it involves the breach of some duty you owe to another or others".[389] The adjective "wilful" in the law of vendor and purchaser does not carry any overtones of "moral obliquity".[390] It means simply that the person of whose action or default the word is used knows what he is doing, intends to do it and is a free agent.[391] Just as a purchaser owes a duty to his vendor in the course of the implementation of a contract for sale so too does a vendor owe a duty to the purchaser; the nature and extent of that duty is likely to be different as the sale progresses.[392] It has been held that a vendor who moved with due diligence to remove a defect in title was free of wilful default and therefore entitled to interest at the contract rate.[393] A vendor who refuses to close on reasonable terms suggested by the purchaser risks losing the right to interest in respect of the period of delay caused by that stance.[394] In general it might be thought fair that the risks in relation to interest should be borne by the vendor rather than the purchaser when neither has been in default and the vendor retains possession.

[8.46] The typical modern interest clause entitles the vendor to interest only when the delay is caused "by reason of any default on the part of the purchaser".[395] The interest may be expressed to run from the later of (*a*) the agreed closing date, or (*b*) the later date when delay in completing has ceased to be due to default on the part of the vendor.[396] Under this type of clause the vendor must show that there has been default by the purchaser and may have to face a claim that he has been in default himself. Thus the claim for interest will fail if the vendor does not deliver copies of title documents which he is bound to furnish[397] or fails to answer a proper requisition.[398] A purchaser who raises unreasonable requirements is likely to be in default and thus liable to pay interest at the contract rate.[399] So is a purchaser who still fails to complete after defects in the property sold have been put right.[400] In some cases a plaintiff may recover interest for part but not all of the disputed period. If there is default by the purchaser which results in the sale not being closed on the day agreed interest is payable by him and further interest will run against

---

[388] *Re Postmaster-General & Colgan's Contract* [1906] 1 IR 287 at 298-9 approving a passage from *Re Woods & Lewis's Contract* [1898] 2 Ch 211 at 213; *cf Kissock's* case at 398-9.

[389] Per Parker J in *Re Bayley-Worthington & Cohen's Contract* [1909] 1 Ch 648 in a long passage approved by Costello J in *Northern Bank Ltd v Duffy* [1981] ILRM 308 at 309-10.

[390] Ibid at 314.

[391] *Re Young & Harston's Contract* (1885) 31 Ch D 168 at 174, approved by Costello J in the *Northern Bank* case at 314.

[392] The *Northern Bank* case at 313-5.

[393] *Lappen v Purcell* [1965] IJR 1 at 3.

[394] The *Northern Bank* case at 313-5.

[395] *General Condition* 25 of the Law Society's conditions, (1991) Ed; the vendor may elect to take the rents and profits less outgoings.

[396] As in *General Condition* 25.

[397] *Cellulose Processors Ltd v Flynn & O'Flaherty Ltd* (HC)28 April 1986, Finlay P, unrep at 11-14.

[398] *Meagher v Blount* [1984] ILRM 671 at 676, 678.

[399] *Reynolds v Waters* [1982] ILRM 335 at 339.

[400] *Treacy v Dwyer Nolan Developments Ltd* [1979] ILRM 163 at 164-5.

him if more delay arises which is not his fault but arises from the ordinary problems of investigating a title.[401] But if default by the vendor supervenes and causes further delay in completion interest is not payable in respect of the period attributable to the vendor's default.[402]

[8.47] A few other points about interest should be noted. Of course giving the purchaser possession prior to completion makes a major difference; we discuss that later.[403] In certain cases a purchaser entitled to damages for the vendor's breach of contract may have to set off the amount of the interest, which he has "saved" by not having to complete on time.[404] Regard should be had to the fact that a purchaser deprived of possession by the wilful default of the vendor normally has the use of the unpaid purchase money.[405] In other situations payment of interest is likely to be a term on which a defaulting purchaser may be given a chance to complete his deal.[406] A party may seek liberty to pay money into court to stop interest running against him.[407] He may also be entitled to place the money on deposit in which event the vendor only gets the interest earned.[408] In any event a purchaser having disputes with his vendor should consider trying to arrange that he gets possession in exchange for placing the unpaid balance on deposit with the interest going to the vendor on completion. This may help to narrow the issues between the parties and reduce the costs incurred but obviously it depends on the purchaser having the money and to that end the property in sale may be needed as security. In a case where specific performance is ordered but the plaintiff vendor later gets an order dissolving the order and an award of damages[409] the latter are likely to include the agreed rate of interest on the balance of the purchase price from the date fixed for completion by the contract until the date for completion under the order for specific performance.[410] Finally, it is important to ensure that a rate of interest fixed is not invalid as a penalty. A rate of 22% has been upheld having regard to prevailing rates of interest and bank overdraft rates.[411]

DAMAGES FOR NEGLIGENT MISREPRESENTATION OF BREACH OF A WARRANTY OR COLLATERAL CONTRACT

[8.48] We are in general not concerned with damages but have noted that the inadequacy of damages as a remedy is one of the most important elements in a decision to grant specific performance.[412] We have also considered the jurisdiction to award damages in

---

[401] *Northern Bank Ltd v Duffy* [1981] ILRM 308 at 313.
[402] *Ibid* at 314.
[403] Paras **11.23-5** *post.*
[404] *O'Brien v White-Spunner* [1979] ILRM 240.
[405] *Sheidan v Higgins* [1971] IR 291 at 304.
[406] *Solomon v Estates Management & Development Agency Ltd* (HC) 14 July 1980, Costello J, unrep at 8-10. See para **8.28** *supra.*
[407] *Soloman's* case at 8-9.
[408] *Treacy v Dwyer Nolan Developments Ltd* [1979] ILRM 163 at 165. See Wylie, *Irish Conveyancing Law* (1978) paras 10.074, 18.09-10 and English cases cited; Jones & Goodhart, *Specific Performance* (1986) at 215. An express right to do this sometimes appears in conditions of sale. The purchaser may have to prove a right of this sort and that he is not in default himself.
[409] On ths see para **8.28** *supra.*
[410] *Vandeleur v Dargan* [1981] ILRM 75 at 77-8. No argument was addressed to McWilliam J about the position from then until the order dissolving the decree for specific performance.
[411] *Taylor v Smyth* [1991] 1 IR 142 at 158, affirmed at 172.
[412] Para **1.10** *ante.*

lieu of or in addition to specific performance.[413] Another type of situation where a good claim for damages can arise may be of interest. Occasionally something happens in negotiations or appears in an advertisement, brochure or other material attracting a person to a property which induces him to make a deal and causes him loss. We will now look at the possibility of recovering damages for this kind of event.

Normally damages cannot be recovered for statements which are only innocent misrepresentation[414] but there are important exceptions. One is *negligent* misrepresentation. The speeches in the House of Lords in *Hedley Byrne & Co Ltd v Heller*[415] establish that in some cases a negligent misrepresentation to anyone who, to the knowledge of the speaker or writer, will rely on it and will be damaged if it is incorrect, gives a right to damages: they do not establish that *every* innocent misrepresentation gives such a right.[416] Circumstances may create a relationship between two parties in which, if one seeks information from the other and is given it, that other is under a duty of reasonable care to ensure that the information given is correct.[417] Negligent misrepresentation where the breach of the duty of care is less than reckless[418] remains innocent as distinct from fraudulent and thus can be a defence to a claim for specific performance only when innocent misrepresentation in general would be a good defence.[419] We will see later two important distinctions between innocent and fraudulent misrepresentation. Firstly, when a sale is completed by conveyance equity will not set it aside unless there has been fraud or misrepresentation amounting to fraud; secondly, there is no right to rescission of a contract prior to completion for innocent misrepresentation unless there is a "complete difference in substance" between what was supposed to be taken and what is actually taken.[420]

[8.49] A right of action for damages for negligent misrepresentation or "negligent misstatement"[421] may be very important to a purchaser who becomes aware of the relevant facts only after taking a conveyance.[422] Purchasers have recovered damages under this head where an auctioneer assured them before they signed a contract to buy a leasehold estate with a short unexpired residue that the freehold could be bought at a certain price without having taken care to see what price the landlords would require for their interest.[423] The information concerning the purchase of the freehold "materially induced" the decision to purchase at a price higher than that which they originally were prepared to bid.[424] However, a claim is likely to fail where an error is "one which could be made

---

[413] Paras **1.28-31** *ante.*
[414] Clark, *Contract Law in Ireland*, 3rd Ed (1992) at 237.
[415] (1964) AC 465 considered in *Bank of Ireland v Smith* [1966] IR 646 at 657, 659-60; *Securities Trust Ltd v Hugh Moore & Alexander Ltd* [1964] IR 417 at 421; *Stafford v Mahony* [1980] ILRM 53 at 61-4. See also Clark, *op cit*, at 236-9.
[416] *Per* Kenny J in *Bank of Ireland v Smith* [1966] IR 646 at 657.
[417] *Securities Trust Ltd v Hugh Moore & Alexander Ltd* [1964] IR 417 at 421. See now *TE Potterton Ltd v Northern Bank Ltd* [1993] 1 IR 413 at 420-4; *McAnarney v Hanrahan* [1993] 3 IR 492 at 496-7; [1994] ILRM 210 at 213-4. *Cf Stafford v Mahony* [1980] ILRM at 61-4.
[418] If it is reckless it is fraudulent in law: para **9.12** *post.*
[419] On which see paras **9.16-22** *post.*
[420] See para **9.22** on these distinctions.
[421] Words used in *McAnarney v Hanrahan* [1993] 3 IR 492 at 496; [1994] ILRM 210 at 213-4. The expression "negligent misrepresentation" was also used.
[422] In *McAnarney's* case the purchasers ascertained the relevant facts about two years after taking their conveyance. They sued an individual auctioneer and his employer but did not sue the vendor.
[423] *McAnarney's* case at 496-7 (IR); 213-4 (ILRM).
[424] *Ibid* at 497 (IR); 213 (ILRM).

by the most careful of auctioneers".[425] If the misleading information or advice is not given to the plaintiff directly it must at least be given to someone who is likely to pass it on to him.[426] And, of course, the plaintiff must prove that a duty of care exists and that it is owed to him.[427] He will establish a "special relationship" but there is no magic in that phrase; "it means no more than a relationship the nature of which is such that one party, for a variety of possible reasons, will be regarded by the law as under a duty of care to the other".[428]

This type of claim may be useful in other situations. A lessee who finds after taking his lease that he was misled may be able to show a right to damages for negligent misrepresentation or misstatement without trying to set aside the lease.[429] If a sale breaks down with, *eg*, the purchaser refusing to complete without compensation and the vendor selling elsewhere and trying to keep the deposit, the purchaser may be able to rely on negligent misrepresentation to recover the deposit and appropriate damages.[430]

[8.50] Damages are also recoverable when a statement which may be a representation can be shown to be a *warranty* or a *collateral contract* and there has been a breach of that warranty or contract. A representation is not necessarily a warranty; it may be "only an inducement".[431] The rule that an innocent misrepresentation causing loss does not entitle a person to recover damages produces injustice in many cases[432] when completion has taken place and thus the possible remedies of rescission of a contract[433] or abatement of the purchase price[434] for innocent misrepresentation are not available. The modern cases show a welcome tendency to treat a representation made in connection with a sale as being a warranty unless the person who made it can show that he was innocent of fault in connection with it.[435] If a representation is made in the course of dealings for a contract for the very purpose of inducing the other party to act on it, and it actually induces him to act on it by entering into a contract, that is *prima facie* ground for inferring that the representation was intended as a warranty; it is not necessary to speak of it as being collateral.[436] Suffice it to say that the representation was intended to be acted upon and was in fact acted on; but the maker of the representation can rebut the inference of a

---

[425] *Bank of Ireland v Smith* [1966] IR 646 at 660; the plaintiff succeeded on breach of warranty. Note the discussion of that case by O'Hanlon J in *TE Potterton Ltd v Northern Bank Ltd* [1993] 1 IR 413 at 420-3. He considered (p 423) that "significant developments" had taken place in the law of negligent misrepresentation or misstatement since *Hedley Byrne* was interpreted by Kenny J in *Bank of Ireland v Smith*. The *Bank of Ireland* case was also distinguished in the *McAnarney* case at 497 (IR); 214 (ILRM).

[426] *Stafford v Mahony* [1980] ILRM 53 at 63.

[427] *Securities Trust Ltd v Hugh Moore & Alexander Ltd* [1964] IR 417 at 421-2; duty owed to members of a company was not owed also to a member as agent for another company. *Cf McAnarney's* case at 496-7 (IR); 213-4 (ILRM).

[428] *Per* Ormrod LJ in *Esso Petroleum Co Ltd v Mardon* [1976] 2 All ER 5 at 22, approved by Barr J in *Greyhill Property Co Ltd v Whitechap Inn Ltd* (HC) 5 October 1993, unrep at 23.

[429] In *Connswater Properties Ltd v Wilson* (HC) NI, 8 July 1986, MacDermott J thought at p 6 that a case of negligent misstatement could be made out (he held that the real cause of action was breach of contract: *ibid.*) *Cf Donnellan v Dungoyne Ltd* (HC) Cir App, 15 August 1994, O'Hanlon J, unrep at 10: negligent misrepresentation and warranty that all units in a shopping centre would be trading by Christmas or New Year.

[430] The *Greyhill Property Co* case at 22-30.

[431] *Lecky v Walter* [1914] 1 IR 378 at 389.

[432] *Per* Kenny J in *Bank of Ireland v Smith* [1966] IR 646 at 659.

[433] On which see paras **9.17-8**, **9.23** *post*.

[434] *Connor v Potts* [1897] 1 IR 534; *cf Keating v Bank of Ireland* [1983] ILRM 295.

[435] *Bank of Ireland v Smith* [1966] IR 646 at 659.

[436] *Per* Denning LJ in *Dick Bentley Productions Ltd v Smith (Motors)* Ltd [1965] 2 All ER 65 in a passage approved by Kenny J in *Bank of Ireland v Smith* [1966] IR 646 at 659.

warranty if he shows that it was innocent and that it would not be reasonable in the circumstances for him to be bound by it.[437] A statement that a house is dry and free from damp is likely to be a warranty breach of which will give rise to a claim for damages even though the statement was made with an honest belief in its truth.[438] A promise to a person about to return to Ireland from abroad that a house would be ready on a certain date is likely to be a warranty.[439] Telling an intending lessee that he alone would provide "sit-down" restaurant facilities in a shopping centre has been held to be a collateral contract and also to amount to a warranty.[440] The large damages awarded in that instance are a striking example of the possible grave consequences of incorrect statements which induce a person to take a lease of commercial premises with subsequent poor trading.[441] A statement made to an intending lessee that the other tenants occupying stalls or units in a development would be of high class quality retail type may be a representation[442] and also would seem capable of being a warranty.[443]

[8.51] A collateral contract is a contract the consideration for which is the making of some other contract. Both contracts have an independent existence and the full character and status of a contract.[444] A collateral contract may perhaps be regarded as something of a device but "the purpose of the device usually is to enforce a promise given prior to the main contract and but for which this main contract would not have been made".[445] It is important to note that breach of a collateral contract may also affect a party's right to rely on provisions of the "main" contract[446] in addition to giving rise to a claim for damages for breach of the collateral contract itself.[447]

Promising an intending lessee a substantial promotion by advertising of the shopping complex which includes his unit may be a collateral contract.[448] Telling him that he alone will provide "sit-down" restaurant facilities in a shopping centre has been held to be a collateral contract and also a warranty.[449] In a sale of land there may be a collateral contract by the vendor to get a release of a mortgage.[450] A verbal agreement by a vendor at an auction to pay a sum which a landlord required for his consent to assignment was held to be a collateral contract breach of which entitled the purchaser to judgment against

---

[437] *Ibid.*

[438] *Carbin v Somerville* [1933] IR 276 and 291. It was not necessary to decide the point because the Supreme Court held for the plaintiff on fraudulent misrepresentation.

[439] *O'Donoghue and Co Ltd v Collins* (HC) 10 March 1972, Kenny J, unrep at 13.

[440] *Connswater Properties Ltd v Wilson* (HC) NI, 8 July 1986, MacDermott J, unrep at 5-7.

[441] The defendants were denied the opportunity to produce good figures; p 12. The award was £217,560 including future loss: p 16.

[442] *Grafton Court Ltd v Wadson Sales Ltd* (HC) 17 February 1975, unrep at 12. Finlay P held that the lessee knew the true position when he executed the lease and did not rely on the statement.

[443] The words do not seem to have been alleged to be a warranty in the *Grafton Court Ltd* case. *Cf Donnellan v Dungoyne Ltd* (HC) Cir App, 15 August 1994, O'Hanlon J, unrep at 10: negligent misrepresentation and warranty that all units in a shopping centre would be trading by Christmas or New Year.

[444] *Bank of Ireland v Smith* [1966] IR 646 at 658, Kenny J quoting from Lord Moulton in *Heilbut, Symons & Co v Buckleton* [1913] AC 30. See also paras **5.15-6** *ante*.

[445] From a passage in the 9th Ed of Cheshire & Fifoot, *Law of Contract* at 58 approved by MacDermott J in the *Connswater Properties Ltd* case at 7. *Cf Fitzpatrick v Harty* (HC) 25 February 1983, O'Hanlon J, unrep.

[446] *Kennedy v Wrenne* [1981] ILRM 81. On collateral contracts see further paras **5.15-6** above; Clark, *Contract Law in Ireland* 3rd Ed (1992) at 111-3.

[447] See discussion of damages at Ch 19 of Clark, *op cit.*

[448] *Grafton Court Ltd v Wadson Sales Ltd* (HC) NI, 8 July 1986, MacDermott J, unrep at 5-7.

[449] *Connswater Properties Ltd v Wilson* (HC) NI, 8 July 1986, MacDermott J, unrep at 15.

[450] *Kennedy v Wrenne* [1981] ILRM 81 at 81-2.

the vendor for the sum which the purchaser in fact had to pay the landlord.[451] Depending on the circumstances the sale of the stock of a business may be a collateral contract or an essential term of the contract for sale.[452] Payment of a "luck penny" on a sale may also be a collateral agreement[453] and so may an agreement to carry out improvements in relation to a renewal of a lease.[454]

[8.52] The court will expect a party claiming damages[455] to lay before it facts to support the claim made; it is not acceptable practice for a court to be faced with a paucity of facts or an abundance of sometimes conflicting data.[456] It is not the function of a court to supply the deficiencies in the evidence of either party or to have to guess in the assessment of damages which are susceptible of reasonably precise calculation by adducing appropriate evidence.[457] However, a court should not be deterred from assessing compensation by difficulty in proof as distinct from failure to adduce available evidence.[458] In that context the court should be both alert and ingenious in assessing a general sum for damages even though it may involve some element of speculation.[459] If someone deliberately breaks his contract with the intention of making a gain or profit which he would not otherwise achieve and has in that way acted *mala fide*, it seems that the court should, in assessing damages, look to the profit or gain unjustly obtained by the breach of contract as well as at the loss suffered by the injured party.[460]

VENDOR AND PURCHASER SUMMONSES

[8.53] This jurisdiction was created by s 9 of the Vendor and Purchaser Act 1874. The Act recites that it is "expedient to facilitate the transfer of land by means of certain amendments in the law of vendor and purchaser". The jurisdiction has been described as "a comparatively simple procedure for resolving disputes between vendors and purchasers".[461] However, it is no function of the court to take over the duties of conveyancing counsel or solicitors on an investigation of title.[462] Thus, in relation to a point about title, once the facts have been established or the vendor has failed to make disclosure and the parties have joined issue as to the legal effect of the facts or the failure of the vendor to disclose information, it is then for the court to decide the legal position - whether good title has been shown or whether the vendor was bound to furnish further

---

[451] *Carrigy v Brock* (1871) IR 5 CL 501 at 505. That case was decided before s 3 of the Conveyancing Act 1892 became law; note that parties can contract out of s 3.
[452] *Godley v Power* (1957) 95 ILTR 135 at 146 (collateral); *Carthy v O'Neill* [1981] ILRM 443 at 445 (essential part of contract remaining to be negotiated); cf *Aga Khan v Firestone* [1992] ILRM 31 at 45-6.
[453] *Stinson v Owens* (HC) NI, MacDermott LCJ, unrep at 3, 15-16 (noted at 107 ILTSJ 239).
[454] *Scott v McCombe* (CA) NI, 2 June 1965, Curran LJ, unrep at 7.
[455] As in the *Grafton Court Ltd* and *Connswater Properties Ltd* cases.
[456] The *Connswater Properties Ltd* case at 7-8.
[457] *McKenna v Meighan* [1966] IR 285 at 294 (a personal injury case, Walsh J considering scanty evidence on plaintiff's economic future).
[458] *Hickey & Co Ltd v Roches Stores (Dublin) Ltd* (HC) 14 July 1976, Finlay P, unrep at 23; the *Connswater Properties* case at 7.
[459] *Hickey & Co's* case at 23. Cf *Grafton Court Ltd v Wadson Sales Ltd* (HC) 17 February 1975, Finlay P, unrep at 21-2.
[460] *Hickey & Co's* case at 21-2. See further Clark, *op cit* at 446.
[461] By McWilliam J in *Martin v Irish Permanent building Society* (HC) 30 July 1980, unrep at 3. See discussion of the relief by Wylie, *Irish Conveyancing Law* (1978) p 208-10 (dealing with the similar s 49(1) of the Law of Property Act, 1925).
[462] *Mulligan v Dillon* (HC) 7 November 1980, McWilliam J, unrep at 3; cf *Martin's* case at 3-4.

or better evidence of title.[463] The use of vendor and purchaser summonses in England has declined in recent years, probably because the spread of registration of title and the conveyancing reforms introduced in and since 1925 have greatly reduced the number of cases in which serious title problems arise.[464] Little such progress has been made in Ireland and the jurisdiction remains very useful here. Sometimes it will be practicable to take out a vendor and purchaser summons in lieu of an action for specific performance.[465] That cannot always be done[466] and in the next few paragraphs we will look at situations where the jurisdiction can be used.

[8.54] The first part of s 9 of the 1874 Act deals with the English jurisdiction. It provides:

> "A vendor or purchaser of real or leasehold estate in England, or their representatives respectively, may at any time or times and from time to time apply in a summary way to a judge of the Court of Chancery in England in chambers, in respect of any requisitions or objections, or any claim for compensation, or any other question arising out of or connected with the contract, (not being a question affecting the existence or validity of the contract) and the judge shall make such order upon the application as to him shall appear just, and shall order how and by whom all or any of the costs of and incident to the application shall be borne and paid."[467]

The section continues by providing for the Irish jurisdiction:

> "A vendor or purchaser of real or leasehold estate in Ireland, or their representatives respectively, may in like manner and for the same purpose apply to a judge of the Court of Chancery in Ireland, and the judge shall make such order upon the application as to him shall appear just, and shall order how and by whom all or any of the costs of and incident to the application shall be borne and paid."

The latter part of the section has no reference to chambers. An early Irish decision did hold that the proper mode of commencing vendor and purchaser proceedings was "by summons at Chambers".[468] In another early Irish case a judge did not see why the authority of the court to direct service out of the jurisdiction in cases of administration summonses and summary petitions should not extend to vendor and purchaser summonses.[469] Nowadays the application may be brought by special summons in the High Court[470] and the case is heard in open court in the normal way. Save in so far as the court orders otherwise proceedings commenced by special summons are heard on affidavit though there is a right to cross-examine deponents on their affidavits.[471] Pleadings are not allowed except by order of the court, which order may be made in any case where the delivery of a statement of claim or other pleading "appears to be requisite".[472] Where it

---

[463] *Mulligan's* case at 3-4.
[464] Jones and Goodhart, *Specific Performance* (1986), p 209.
[465] *Re Clibborn and Horan's Contract* [1921] 1 IR 93 at 97.
[466] O'Connor MR made no such suggestion in *Clibborn's* case.
[467] The entire section may be found, eg, at p 14 of Wolstenholme's *Conveyancing and Settled Land Acts*, 10th Ed (1913) and *Lyons v Thomas* (1966) IR 666 at 668. See discussion by Wylie, *Irish Conveyancing Law* (1978) at paras 12.25-8.
[468] *Re Vian and Gaffney's Contract* (1877) 11 IR Eq 521.
[469] *Draper Co v McCann* (1878) 1 LRI 13 at 14.
[470] Rules of the Superior Courts, Order 3, item (12).
[471] Order 38, rule 3.
[472] Order 20, rule 1.

appears that determination of some question or questions of fact is necessary for the proper decision or ruling as to relief to be granted in proceedings begun by special summons or as to any matter arising therein the trial of issues may be directed and evidence may be given either orally or on affidavit or partly in each way as the court thinks proper in the circumstances.[473] A case may also be adjourned for plenary hearing as if it had commenced by plenary summons and appropriate directions may be given as to pleadings, discovery or issues.[474] The greater the complexity of fact and conflict of evidence the stronger the case for an adjournment to plenary hearing and for pleadings, particulars and perhaps discovery of documents. Even in this type of situation the court may have regard to the parties' wish for an expeditious procedure and deal with the issues as best possible on a mixture of affidavits and oral evidence.[475]

[8.55] The jurisdiction under s 9 clearly covers the normal sale of land. It is not dependent on there being a right to specific performance.[476] The s 9 jurisdiction may be used even though the result may let one party exercise a contractual right to rescind the contract[477] or one party is also claiming a right to rescind for misrepresentation.[478] It also extends to questions between intending lessors and lessees[479] and contracts for fee farm grants.[480] If the parties cannot agree on particular covenants the court can decide the issues on a vendor and purchaser summons.[481] In a modern Irish case a vendor and purchaser summons was issued between a purchaser and his building society with the "loan approval" put forward as the contract for the purposes of s 9 of the 1874 Act; the court did assist the parties but seemed unhappy about that point and other aspects of the case.[482] In a suitable case the court will try a specific performance action and a vendor and purchaser summons together[483] but then the parties are likely to lose the benefit of the relatively quick and inexpensive character of the summons.

The courts are reluctant to decide the rights of third parties on a vendor and purchaser summons. A summons between a vendor selling as administrator of an estate and the purchaser has been described as "not a proceeding to decide adverse claims to the estate".[484] The court has also refused to decide a question on a vendor and purchaser summons which might affect the rights of third parties under a will who were not represented.[485] And if a vendor's title depends on a difficult question of construction of a will so that a purchaser would run a risk of future litigation the court may decline to decide that point on a vendor and purchaser summons.[486] The court may offer to allow the

---

[473] Order 38, rule 8.

[474] Order 38, rule 9.

[475] As in *McCambridge v Winters* (HC) 28 May 1984, Murphy J, unrep (noted 1985 ILRM at 700).

[476] *Re Lander and Bagley's Contract* [1892] 3 Ch 41.

[477] *Re Jackson and Woodburn's Contract* (1887) 37 Ch D 44.

[478] *Re Hughes and Ashley's Contract* [1900] 2 Ch 595.

[479] *Re Lecky and Aiken's Contract* (1905) 40 ILTR 65.

[480] *Colhoun v Trustees of Foyle College* [1898] 1 IR 233.

[481] *Lecky's* case (insuring); *Colhoun's* case (quiet enjoyment).

[482] *Martin v Irish Permanent Building Society* (HC) 30 July 1980, McWilliam J, unrep.

[483] As in *Lyons v Murphy* [1986] IR 666; a vital issue in each was whether the vendor was justified in rescinding the contract.;

[484] *Re Carolan & Scott's Contract* [1899] 1 IR 1 at 5.

[485] *Re Brown & Mitchell's Contract* (1902) 2 NIJR 106.

[486] *Re Hogan & Marnell's Contract* [1919] 1 IR 422 at 428-9 applying *Re Nicholl & Von Joel's Contract* [1910] 1 CH 43. Note that the court did decide a question of construction of a will in a V & P Summons in *Re Bishop & Richardson's Contract* [1899] 1 IR 71. The decision was against the vendor and there would have been little point in giving him the chance to issue a construction summons.

vendor and purchaser application to stand over to allow the parties take out a construction summons which would bind everybody.[487] However, when there can be only one reasonable construction of such a document, the legal effect of that construction is clear and the result is that the vendor has good title the court will not hesitate so to decide on a vendor and purchaser summons.[488] A third party may be joined if a judge feels that he could not decide the case in that person's absence.[489] It has been said also that the 1874 Act cannot be used to make a declaration of title to bind future purchasers of property where no opportunity is given to persons who may be interested to dispute that title.[490]

[8.56] Issues of title usually are well suited for determination on vendor and purchaser summonses. Normally it is not necessary to embark on an action for a declaration of title[491] or to issue specific performance proceedings to deal with matters of title. Of course a court may deal with such matters in an action for specific performance if necessary[492] but the relatively quick and inexpensive vendor and purchaser summons is a very attractive vehicle. A vendor who feels that he has dealt sufficiently with points raised by the purchaser is likely to seek a declaration that he has answered a requisition sufficiently and that good title has been shown.[493] Typical questions covered on such summonses have been whether words of limitation could be read into a habendum so as to pass the fee simple,[494] the effect on a deed of appointment of the absence of words of limitation,[495] the reality and adequacy of an indemnity,[496] whether a personal representative must assent in writing to vesting in himself when he is also the person entitled,[497] the power of sale of vendors as executors and trustees of a will,[498] the possible effects on the power of sale of a personal representative of a long interval of time between the death and the sale,[499] doubts over the execution of a power of appointment,[500] issues under the Family Home Protection Act 1976,[501] the effect, if any, of a "name and arms" clause[502] and whether notices should have been disclosed.[503]

[8.57] Many other issues decided on vendor and purchaser summonses have been connected to a greater or lesser extent with title or have not been connected with title at

---

[487] *Hogan's* case at 429; *Nichols's* case at 46. *Cf* discussion in *Horton v Kurzke* [1971] 2 All ER 577 at 579-81.
[488] *Hogan's* case at 428. *Cf Re Murphy and Griffin's Contract* [1919] 1 IR 187 at 203-4.
[489] *Re Antrim County Land, Building and Investment Co Ltd & Dobbin's Contract* (1909) 43 ILTR 120 (joinder of landlord whose consent was needed).
[490] By McWilliam J in *Martin v Irish Permanent Building society* (HC) 30 July 1980, unrep at 3-4.
[491] *Re Murphy and Griffin's Contract* [1919] 1 IR 187 at 203.
[492] As in, eg, *Dublin Laundry Co Ltd v Clarke* [1989] ILRM 29; *O'Connor v McCarthy* [1982] IR 161. See further paras **9.80-81** *post.*
[493] As in *Guckian v Brennan* [1981] IR 478; *Shiels v Flynn* [1975] IR 296; *Kearns v Manresa Estates,* (HC) 25 July 1975, Kenny J; *Re Murphy & Griffin's Contract* [1919] 1 IR 187.
[494] *Re Ford & Ferguson's Contract* [1906] 1 IR 607.
[495] *Re Murphy and Griffin's Contract* [1919] 1 IR 187.
[496] *Manifold v Johnson* [1902] 1 IR 7 at 11-12.
[497] *Mohan v Roche* [1991] 1 IR 560 at 564-7.
[498] *Re McDonnell & Branigan's Contract* (1922) 56 ILTR 143.
[499] *Sheils v Flynn* [1975] IR 296; *Crowley v Flynn* [1983] ILRM 513; the position may vary depending on whether the title is registered in the Land Registry.
[500] *Re Walker & Elgee's Contract* (1918) 53 ILTR 22.
[501] *Reynolds v Waters* [1982] ILRM 335; *Guckian v Brennan* [1981] IR 478; *Walpoles (Ireland) Ltd v Jay* (HC) 20 November 1980, McWilliam J, unrep; *Lloyd v Sullivan* (HC) 6 March 1981, McWilliam J, unrep; *Martin v Irish Permanent Building Society* (HC) 30 July 1980, McWilliam J, unrep.
[502] *Kearns v Manresa Estates* (HC) 25 July 1975, Kenny J, unrep.
[503] *Re Flynn and Newman's Contract* [1948] IR 104. *Cf McCann v Valentine* (1900) 1 NIJR 28.

all. These include questions whether the vendor is bound to deliver an abstract of title[504] or affecting the form of a document. An example of the latter is whether a purchaser was entitled to have the vendor convey to him "as beneficial owner" without any words limiting the covenants thereby implied.[505] Another such issue has been the manner of dealing in an assignment of part of a leasehold parcel with apportionment of the rent payable.[506] Many of the decided cases concern the validity of attempts to rescind[507] a contract. The courts have considered whether, in the event of a vendor being unable or unwilling to comply with an objection or requisition as to title, the purchase deed or any other matter relating or incidental to the sale,[508] his use of a clause in a contract entitling him to rescind was valid.[509] They have also ruled on his use of such a clause to escape a liability for compensation for breach of his duty to maintain the property pending completion,[510] whether he was entitled to rescind the contract and forfeit the deposit for alleged default by the purchaser,[511] any effect on a vendor's second rescission notice of a defective notice served earlier,[512] whether a rescission by a purchaser on the ground of bad title[513] or delay[514] was valid, the validity of rescission by reason of nonfulfilment of a condition precedent,[515] the degree of clarity needed in a rescission notice,[516] a vendor's claim to interest[517] and matters relating to stamp duty.[518]

[8.58] Many other matters cannot be covered by a vendor and purchaser summons. The remedy of specific performance itself appears to be outside its scope.[519] So is the relief of rectification.[520] A claim for specific performance could hardly be an application "in respect of any requisitions or objections" within the meaning of s 9 of the 1874 Act[521] and is clearly not "any claim for compensation". Possibly the claim could be "any other question arising out of or connected with the contract" but it is not easy to believe that the legislature intended, in creating this useful "summary" jurisdiction, that a major equitable relief should be granted under it. No Irish court appears to have decreed specific performance or rectification on a vendor and purchaser summons.[522]

---

[504] *Re Priestley and Davidson's Contract* (1892) 31 LRI 122. The practice of delivering abstracts has more or less died out in Ireland. See Wylie, *Irish Conveyancing Law* (1978) paras 13.43-5.
[505] *Re Geraghty and Lyons' Contract* (1919) 53 ILTR 57 at 58-9.
[506] *Re Doherty's Contract* (1884) 15 LRI 247.
[507] Note that rescission has various meanings; see paras **10.25-6** *post*.
[508] Formal contracts usually have such a provision; it is clause 18 of the 1991 Ed of the Law Society's *General Conditions of Sale*.
[509] *Williams v Kennedy* (SC) Finlay CJ, unrep; *Lyons v Thomas* [1986] IR 666 at 677-82; *Kennedy v Wrenne* [1981] ILRM 81; *Re Commins and Hanafy's Contract* (1905) 5 NIJR 111; *Molphy v Coyne* (1919) 53 ILTR 177.
[510] *Lyons v Thomas* [1986] IR 666 at 680-82. The complaint was "incidental to the sale" within general condition 10 of the 1978 Ed of the Law Society's, *General Conditions of Sale*; p 680. Cf *Molphy v Coyne* (1919) 53 ILTR 177 where a vendor innocently failed to disclose the existence of a right of way and was entitled to use the clause.
[511] *Coyle v Central Trust Investment Society Ltd* [1978] ILRM 211; *Re Priestley and Davidson's Contract* (1892) 32 LRI 122.
[512] *McCambridge v Winters* (HC) 28 May 1984, Murphy J unrep at 10-13 (noted [1985] ILRM 700).
[513] *Re Clibborn and Horan's Contract* [1921] 1 IR 93 at 97-9.
[514] *Commane v Walsh* (HC) 2 May 1983, O'Hanlon J, unrep at 4, 6 (noted [1985] ILRM 166-7).
[515] *Maloney v Elf Investments Ltd* [1979] ILRM 253.
[516] *Commane's* case at 5-6
[517] *Reynolds v Waters* [1982] ILRM 335; *Northern Bank Ltd v Duffy* [1981] ILRM 308.
[518] *McCall v Bradish-Ellames* [1950] IJR 16 at 20.
[519] *Re Ford & Ferguson's Contract* [1906] 1 IR 607 at 609.
[520] *Ibid*. also *Re McDermott and Kellett's Contract* (1904) 4 NIJR 89 at 90. On rectification see paras **10.15-24** *post*.
[521] The text of s 9 is set out in para **8.54** *supra*.
[522] On compensation see para **8.59** *infra*.

The jurisdiction cannot be used to determine the validity of the contract[523] nor in substance to try to amend a contract which the parties have agreed.[524] However, the court can deal with the question whether a particular clause in a contract is a nullity.[525] Issues of fraud are generally outside its scope and are more properly tried in an action for specific performance.[526] It may be possible for a court to hold that requisitions have been answered properly and good title shown even though a threat has been made in the past to impeach a title document for fraud.[527] The court may also consider whether an element of fraud might prevent a vendor relying on a contractual right to rescind[528] or whether a condition is misleading[529] A question whether a contract may be avoided for innocent misrepresentation probably may not be decided on a vendor and purchaser summons.[530] Issues involving priorities and what notice was had by a purchaser may be unsuitable for determination on this kind of application[531] unless perhaps the position becomes clear from documentary evidence. It has been held on a vendor and purchaser summons that a court will not force a purchaser to accept a vendor with whom he did not contract.[532] That may be contrasted with a case in which a vendor does not own the property but can compel the person who owns it to convey to the purchaser.[533]

[8.59] Three final points may be noted. Firstly, a court will make orders ancillary to its decision. Thus, if it finds that a vendor has failed to show good title in accordance with the contract it is likely also to order him to return the deposit and pay the purchaser's costs of investigating title.[534] It may also declare those sums charged on the vendor's interest in the lands.[535]

Secondly, a dispute may occur in which one party serves a notice of a type which may lead to an attempt to rescind the contract and before the expiry of the time limited the other party brings a vendor and purchaser application to have the dispute decided. An issue may arise then whether the notice continues valid and effective so that, if the point in the vendor and purchaser summons is decided in favour of the defendant, he is entitled then to rescind the contract because of failure to comply with the notice. In this type of situation the party who has issued the summons is entitled to have the matter in issue between the parties decided without prejudice to his other rights under the contract.[536] The proper course for the defendant, if he gets judgment in his favour on the vendor and

---

[523] *Re Scott* (1879) 13 ICLR 139 at 140.

[524] *March Properties Ltd v Commissioners of Public Works in Ireland* (SC) 11 November 1993, unrep at 8-9.

[525] *Re Mitchell and McElhinney's Contract* [1902] 1 IR 84; the contract was not impeached on any ground going further than that; p 86.

[526] *Re Delaney & Deegan's Contract* [1905] 1 IR 602 at 605.

[527] *Ibid*, 605-6. An action attacking the deed had been discontinued.

[528] *Re Commins and Hanafy's Contact* (1905) 5 NIJR 111.

[529] *Re Turpin and Ahern's Contract* [1905] 1 IR 86 at 93, 103-4, 107.

[530] *Re Flynn and Newman's Contract* [1948] IR 104 at 113-4. *Cf* consideration of alleged representations by Murphy J in *McCambridge v Winters* (HC) 28 May 1984, unrep at 9, 11-12 (noted (1985) ILRM 700).

[531] *Re Kissock and Currie's Contract* [1916] 1 IR 376 at 388, 392.

[532] *Re McLoughlin and McGrath's Contract* (1914) 48 ILTR 87 at 89.

[533] On which see para **8.13** *supra*.

[534] *Re McDermott and Kellett's Contract* (1904) 4 NIJR 89 at 90.

[535] *Re Priestley and Davidson's Contract* (1892) 31 LRI 122.

[536] *Hickey v Keating* (HC) 25 January 1980, McWilliam J, unrep at 4. A court may not take the same view if there is no substance in the dispute and the summons has been issued only as a delaying tactic or an attempt to apply pressure. See also para **8.34** *supra*.

purchaser summons, is probably to serve a new notice making time of the essence and, depending on the circumstances, a very short time might properly be limited.[537]

Thirdly, although s 9 includes a claim for compensation this must arise out of or be connected with the contract. In principle this would cover a claim for a declaration that a purchaser is entitled to compensation or "an abatement of the purchase-money" by reason, *eg*, of the existence of a right of way[538] or a shortfall in the area of land sold.[539] For a very long time normal contracts have contained clauses likely to cover parties' rights in such circumstances[540] and modern contracts also may have relevant arbitration clauses.[541] If there is no normal contract there is a greater chance of an issue "affecting the existence or validity of the contract" which would be outside the scope of s 9. Some English case law has distinguished between compensation and damages, the latter being outside s 9.[542] For these reasons there does not seem to be very much opportunity in practice for the use of s 9 in relation to claims for compensation.

---

[537] *Ibid* at 405.

[538] *Molphy v Coyne* (1919) 53 ILTR 177.

[539] *Re Terry and White's Contract* (1886) 32 Ch D 14.

[540] *Molphy's* case and *Terry's* case are examples.

[541] Clause 51 of the Law Society's *General Conditions of Sale* (1991 Ed).

[542] *Re Wilson & Stevens' Contract* [1894] 3 Ch 546; *Re Hargreaves and Thompson's Contract* (1886) 32 Ch D 454. See Jones and Goodhart, *Specific Performance* (1986) at 210.

Chapter 9

Defences

[9.01] Three important points should be noted before dealing with some possible defences to an action for specific performance. Firstly, the fact that a number of defences are considered in a chapter headed "*Defences*" must not be taken as suggesting that cases where the remedy is refused fall into defined categories Black LJ said in *Conlon v Murray*:[1]

> "It was argued on behalf of the plaintiff that cases in which equity refuses the remedy of specific performance fall within one or other of certain defined categories. I cannot accept this view. Certainly equity acts on certain broad and ascertained principles, but it has always refused to be forced into rigid categories."

Secondly, the remedy of specific performance is discretionary as we have already seen.[2] The relief may be withheld as an exercise of that discretion even where a plaintiff proves a valid contract and no particular defence or ground for refusal is established. Once the plaintiff establishes a valid contract which is not defeated by any defence or ground the discretion arises as to what the form of relief will be: will it be specific performance, or is it one of the cases where the court of equity will say: "It is not fair to specifically perform this contract; we will award damages instead."[3] Equitable relief may be refused even though there has been no improper conduct on the part of the plaintiff - it is enough if the facts as a whole make it inequitable to grant the relief.[4] The discretion to grant or refuse the relief will be exercised in a manner which is neither arbitrary nor capricious but which has regard to the essential fairness of the transaction involved.[5] In ordinary cases where the remedy is available justice is better done by carrying out the contract than by awarding damages.[6] The normal rule is for the court to grant specific performance of a contract for the sale of land and in such a case the onus is on the defendant of establishing a ground or grounds upon which the relief should be refused.[7]

The third point to be noted is that in addition to the matters discussed in this chapter various other submissions may be made or grounds offered to the court to defeat a claim for specific performance. Thus, a defendant may submit successfully that the relief is not available in the type of case brought against him.[8] Infringement of the Family Home Protection Act 1976 makes a contract *void* and we have considered that in Chapter 7. Those and other successful submissions would be "defences" in the same broad meaning of the word as is intended in the rest of this chapter.

---

[1] [1958] NI 17 at 26.

[2] See discussion at paras **1.06-9** *ante*.

[3] *O'Neill v Ryan (No 3)* [1992] 1 IR 166 at 196. See also judgment of Costello J at 191 and defence of Unfairness at paras **9.39-41** *infra*.

[4] *Buckley v Irwin* [1960] NI 98 at 103.

[5] *Smelter Corporation v O'Driscoll* [1977] IR 305 at 310-11; *McCrystal v O'Kane* [1986] NI 123 at 131-2. Cf *Smyth v Lynn* [1951] NI 69 at 76, 78.

[6] *Patrick v Williams* (1897) 31 ILTR 166 at 167.

[7] *McCrystal v O'Kane* [1986] NI 123 at 132.

[8] Discussed in paras **1.14-27** *ante*.

NO CONTRACT

[9.02] As we have seen,[9] the first essential for a plaintiff is to prove that there was a contract. He must plead one. If he fails to do so his action may be struck out.[10] If he pleads one but his case is an abuse of the process of the court[11] the defendant may apply to have the claim struck out on that ground[12] and, if he suffers loss as a result, may get damages for the plaintiff's abuse of the court's processes.[13] An interesting point to note is that, applying similar logic, a defendant possibly may be denied the right to defend an action at a plenary hearing if the facts are clear and it is shown that the defence is unsustainable.[14]

[9.03] However, in the great majority of cases the plaintiff will plead a contract which may be disputed but his claim cannot be held to be an abuse of process. In such cases the defence will deny that the alleged or any contract was made and, if that defence succeeds, the plaintiff cannot get specific performance and must fail also on all other claims based on the contract he alleged but failed to prove. In addition to a simple denial of the contract pleaded the defendant may be advised to plead one or more of the particular reasons why he contends that there has been no contract in his case. There may be many such reasons. Negotiations may not have "ripened into the fullness of an entire contract".[15] There may not be the consensus which is essential to an enforceable contract.[16] A degree of consensus may have failed to cover all the material terms of an alleged contract.[17] An offer may not have been accepted or it may have been met by a counter-offer which rejected the offer and was not accepted itself.[18] A time limit may not have been met, a stipulated method of acceptance of an offer may not have been observed sufficiently or a step which is an agreed prerequisite to a binding contract may not have been taken.[19] For one reason or another an apparently complete written contract may not be in fact the complete agreement of the parties[20] although, if this is contested, the party claiming not to have agreed to what seems a fully agreed contract may have difficulty in satisfying a court, especially if he had competent advice when a document was prepared. A condition precedent may not have been fulfilled.[21] Parties may have agreed that their dealings were "subject to contract"[22] and any correspondence may be marked accordingly.[23] A separate point which may arise in that kind of situation is whether it was a condition of any agreement reached that a further contract must be executed before the

---

[9] Paras **3.01-3** *ante*. See also consideration of the material terms at paras **3.08-18** and conditional contracts at paras **3.19-28**.

[10] *Bond v Holton* [1959] IR 302 at 308, 310-11.

[11] This is considered in paras **10.01-09** *post*. See in particular *Sun Fat Chan v Osseous Ltd* [1992] 1 IR 425 at 428-9.

[12] See paras **10.01-09** *post* and *Sun Fat Chan's* case at 428-9.

[13] *Dorene Ltd v Suedes (Ireland) Ltd* [1981] IR 312 at 314-9. And see paras **10.06-9**.

[14] *Per* McCarthy J in *Sun Fat Chan's* case at 428.

[15] *Lynch v O'Meara* (SC) 8 May 1975 unrep at 4 6.

[16] See paras **3.02 3.05** and **3.08** *ante*.

[17] Which are discussed at paras **3.08-18** *ante*.

[18] Para **3.03** *ante*.

[19] *Ibid*. On formal exchange of contracts and the like see para **4.15** *ante*.

[20] Para **3.03** *ante*.

[21] See paras **3.19-28** *ante*.

[22] Discussed in Ch 4 *ante*.

[23] See paras **4.10-12** *ante*.

parties are bound. If this is the case, and it is a question of construction, there is nothing enforceable until the further contract is executed.[24]

[9.04] If a binding contract does come into being it may cease to be such for various reasons. It may be discharged by a later contract.[25] A condition subsequent may not be fulfilled.[26] The contract may have been validly rescinded pursuant to a rescission clause[27] or on grounds such as misrepresentation[28] or mistake.[29] Or it may have been discharged by impossibility of performance,[30] frustration[31] or accepted repudiation.[32] Grounds of defence such as these should be pleaded and may, of course, be pleaded as alternatives to a plea that there never was a contract at all.[33] It is wrong to simply plead the "general issue".[34]

LACK OF CONSIDERATION

[9.05] A plaintiff must show that there was consideration for his contract[35] and that it, or some of it, flowed from him.[36] Absence of consideration is a good defence to a claim for specific performance. A plaintiff relying on consideration given by a third person will fail even though both were parties to the agreement[37] and a person who is not a party to a contract or deed normally cannot sue on it.[38] Of course in most cases consideration will flow from more than one party.[39] An antecedent debt or "past consideration" will not suffice although forbearance to sue for an existing debt normally will.[40] The courts are generally reluctant to enquire into the *adequacy* of consideration[41] but gross inadequacy may suggest fraud.[42] A nominal consideration of 50p has been described as "a complete anachronism" which "does not constitute any consideration".[43] The case law draws a

---

[24] Paras **4.16** *ante*.
[25] Para **3.04** *ante*.
[26] Para **3.20** *ante*.
[27] On which see paras **10.34-42** *post*.
[28] Fraudulent misrepresentation is discussed at paras **9.12-15** and innocent misrepresentation at **9.16-21**. Two major distinctions between them are noted at para **9.22** *infra*.
[29] Rescission on the ground of mistake is discussed at paras **10.30-31** and the defence of mistake at paras **9.67-70**.
[30] Paras **9.57-9** *infra*.
[31] Paras **9.60-69** *infra*.
[32] *Mills v Healy* [1937] IR 437 at 446, 447-8.
[33] See para **9.03** *supra* .
[34] *Jones v Quinn* (1876) 2 LRI 516 at 519.
[35] Para **3.06-7** *ante*. See discussion of the doctrine of consideration in Ch 2 of Clark, *Contract Law in Ireland*, 3rd Ed (1992) esp pp 50-52.
[36] *McCoubray v Thompson* (1868) IR 2 CL 226 at 227-8; *Clitheroe v Simpson* (1879) 4 LRI 59 at 61. *Cf Barry v Barry* (1891) 28 LRI 45 where in fact there seems to have been consideration of forbearance to sue and consent to a devisee getting possession.
[37] *McCoubray v Thomson* (1868) IR 2 CL 226 at 227-8.
[38] *Clitheroe v Simpson* (1879) 4 LRI 59 at 61. *Cf Donohoe v Conrahy* (1845) 8 IR Eq R 679 at 684. Note s 5 of the Real Property Act 1845 by which a person may take the benefit of a "condition or covenant" in an "indenture" though not named a party to it: see Wylie, *Irish Land Law*, 2nd Ed (1986) at para 19.16.
[39] As in normal sales of land. Note the opinion of Monahan CJ in *McCoubray's* case at p 228 that in cases opened to him "something was done by the Plaintiff". *Cf Mullins's* case at 107-8.
[40] *Crofts v Feuge* (1854) 4 IR Ch R 316 at 317; *Barry v Barry* (1891) 28 LRI 45 at 50, 51.
[41] *O'Neill v Murphy* [1936] NI 16 at 30; *Mullins v Guilfoyle* (1878) 2 LRI 95 at 109; *Slator v Nolan* (1876) IR 11 Eq 367 at 392 (affirmed by CA: see note at 408); *Moore v Crofton* (1846) 9 IR Eq R 344 at 348; *Murray v Palmer*, (1805) 2 Schoales & Lefroy 474 at 488.
[42] The defence of fraud is discussed at paras **9.10-15** *infra*.
[43] By Lynch J in *Noonan v O'Connell* (HC) 10 April 1987, unrep at 8.

distinction between cases in which there is a substantial undervalue and those in which the undervalue is so gross as to be evidence itself of fraud.[44] If an agreement for sale is at so low a consideration that it is a fraud it must be struck down as being a nullity in the eyes of the law[45] and a sub-purchaser from that fraudulent purchaser is in no better position.[46] Oral evidence is not admissible in a claim for specific performance to prove that a contract within the Statute of Frauds which appears on its face to be voluntary was in fact made for consideration.[47] It has been said that where a contract is within the Statute the consideration must appear on its face.[48] One must bear in mind that the consideration or method of ascertaining it is an essential term of a note or memorandum relied on as satisfying the Statute.[49]

If a question of hindering, delaying or defrauding creditors arises, the purchaser must be one for valuable consideration in good faith.[50] Pleas such as unfairness,[51] improvidence[52] or undue influence[53] may necessitate the adequacy of the consideration being examined carefully in evidence. Thus a low consideration will not often be a defence in itself but may be strong evidence helping to establish other defences.

THE STATUTE OF FRAUDS

[9.06] A widely used defence to claims for specific performance is a plea of the Statute of Frauds. The defendant pleads that the alleged contract was not evidenced in writing so as to satisfy the statute. Of course the plea can only assist the defendant if the alleged contract is one where it is necessary to satisfy the statute[54] and the case has not been taken out of the statute for some reason, *eg,* part performance.[55] This plea is often coupled with a denial that there was any contract at all; if there is no contract there is nothing which needs to be evidenced to satisfy the statute.[56] If successful the plea of the Statute of Frauds will defeat a claim for specific performance or any other claim which has to be enforced *by action.* The reason is that the statute requires written evidence to allow the contract to be enforced by action[57] but does not render it void. That means that the statute will not defeat steps which can be taken without the need for an action.[58] Since we are dealing here with defences to actions which *have* been brought this qualification will not be directly relevant but it may still be borne in mind in advising a client, including when a

---

[44] *McCrystal v O'Kane* [1986] NI 123 at 133. *Cf Buckley v Irwin* [1960] NI 98.
[45] *Hoban v Bute Investments Ltd* (SC) unrep at 4.
[46] *Hoban's* case at 4-5.
[47] *Kelly v Walsh* (1878) 1 LRI 275 at 282-3; *Crofts v Feuge* (1854) 4 IR Ch R 316 at 317. In cases outside the statute consideration can be proved by oral evidence provided that it does not contradict any relevant instrument: *Kelly's* case at 283. There, part performance took the contract out of the statute. *Cf Mullins v Guilfoyle* (1877) 2 LRI 95 at 110; *Molloy v Egan* (1845) 7 IR Eq R 590 at 593.
[48] *Crofts v Feuge* (1854) 4 IR Ch R 316 at 317. The context was a letter agreeing to execute a legal mortgage in favour of the petitioner who already had a judgment binding the land.
[49] See para **5.35** *ante.*
[50] *Re O'Neill* [1989] IR 544 at 553. *Cf Mullins v Guilfoyle* (1878) 2 LRI 95.
[51] Considered at paras **9.36-7** *infra.*
[52] Paras **9.32-5** *infra.*
[53] Paras **9.24-31** *infra.*
[54] On this see paras **5.06-11** *ante.*
[55] Discussed in Ch 6. *Cf* The Statute *AS* Fraud in paras **9.08-09** *infra.*
[56] *Lynch v O'Meara* (SC) 8 May 1975, Henchy J, unrep at 4, 10.
[57] "No action shall be brought whereby ...." in s 2.
[58] On which see para **5.04** *ante.*

defence is being prepared, about all options open to the plaintiff whether pursued by action or otherwise.

The defence of the Statute of Frauds must be pleaded.[59] However, if it is not pleaded a court is unlikely to see difficulty under modern practice about allowing an amendment of the defence as a matter of discretion.[60] Although the court has power to allow an amendment of pleadings at any stage[61] one should be sought as promptly as possible and a very late application, eg, at the end of the plaintiff's evidence,[62] might run into deserved problems. If the defence does not plead the statute the court does not have to take notice of it so an oral contract can be enforced by action.[63] When that happens the usual rule of estoppel applies and a defendant who does not plead the statute on an issue in one action cannot rely on it on the same issue in a second action between the same parties.[64] Where a counterclaim is dismissed the defendant will not be allowed to litigate the same matter later in a separate claim against the same opponent.[65] Estoppel is merely a rule of evidence[66] and the application of that rule to questions involving the Statute of Frauds does not conflict with the true purpose of the statute which is to prevent fraud and perjury. When the contract has been proved orally to the satisfaction of the court without a plea of the statute a refusal to let it be sued on later would encourage dishonesty without any corresponding advantage to the public.[67]

[9.07] Sometimes a defence denies the plaintiff's version of an agreement and alleges a different version. The plaintiff may decide to persist with his version and seek an order of specific performance of the defendant's version in the alternative. In this situation the court may be concerned about opening a door to new frauds.[68] As Lord Redesdale noted:

> "It would be of dangerous consequence to permit this; for the Plaintiff would first take the chance of getting the witnesses to swear to the agreement as alleged by him; and, failing in that, he would then be sure to succeed upon the Defendant's admission."[69]

If it finds that the defendant's version was agreed the court may dismiss the plaintiff's claim but leave it open to sue for specific performance of the defendant's version.[70] But if a plaintiff insists unfairly on the literal construction of a written agreement knowing that it was not the true agreement his claim will be dismissed without leaving him a chance to enforce the true contract.[71] If his claim was put forward under a mistake or

---

[59] *James v Smith* [1891] 1 Ch 384; *Clarke v Callow* (1876) 46 LJQB 53. *Cf* submissions in *Clinan v Cooke* (1802) 1 Schoales & Lefroy 23 at 31.
[60] *Re Gonin decd* [1977] 2 All ER 720 at 730; the application was made at the hearing but the plaintiff was told by letter in advance: p 729.
[61] Rules of the Superior Courts, Order 28 r 1.
[62] As in *James v Smith* [1891] 1 Ch 384. See discussion in *Re Gonin* at 729-30 which covers the very different former practice. *Cf Broughton v Snook* [1938] 1 All ER 411 at 416-7.
[63] *Broughton's* case at 417-8; *cf* submissions in *Clinan's* case at 30-31.
[64] *Humphries v Humphries* [1908-10] All ER p 733 at 735; [1910] 2 KB 531. *Cf Irish Land Commission v Ryan* [1900] 2 IR 565 (estoppel in the context of a limitations point).
[65] *White v Spendlove* [1942] IR 224 at 233-4 (Sullivan CJ), 239 (Murnaghan J) and 255-7 (O'Byrne J). Meredith and Geoghegan JJ dissented holding that the matter in the second claim was not the same cause of action as in the dismissed counterclaim.
[66] Estoppel is discussed in Ch 12 of Fennell, *The Law of Evidence in Ireland* (1992).
[67] *Humphries's* case at 735.
[68] *Lindsay v Lynch* (1804) 2 Schoales & Lefroy 1 at 10.
[69] *Lindsay's* case at 10.
[70] *Lindsay's* case at 11; *Denniston v Little* (1803) noted at 2 Schoales & Lefroy 11-12.
[71] *Molloy v Egan* (1845) 7 IR Eq R 590 at 593-4.

misconception and he accepts the version put forward by the defendant and amends his pleadings accordingly he may be given specific performance.[72] The English courts have decreed specific performance where the defendant admits the contract in a varied form and the variation is immaterial.[73]

The Statute as Fraud

[9.08] A major restriction on the availability of this defence is that the courts will not allow the statute to be used as an instrument of fraud.[74] This consideration may affect the manner in which the courts apply the statute in some cases but in others it leads the courts to refuse to let a party rely on the statute at all. In some contexts where the statute is applied there may be a greater danger of permitting injustice and in that sense encouraging fraud by a strict application of the statute than by a liberal application.[75] That may lead to it being applied less strictly on a point in issue.[76] It has been said that a defendant cannot, in circumstances in which he admits an agreement with the plaintiff, invoke the statute simply to deprive the plaintiff of the benefit of the agreement as that would be a fraud of the converse nature to that which the statute is expressed to prevent.[77] Sometimes the action of a party in seeking to rely on the statute is itself a fraud and it is the duty of a court of equity to overcome all technicalities in order to defeat a fraud.[78] The court "disregards the absence of that formality which the statute requires when insistence upon it would render it a means of effecting, instead of a means of averting, fraud".[79]

The most common instance of this is the doctrine of part performance[80] and we shall look at another fairly common example soon - *ie*, cases where a trust exists.[81] However, the refusal of the courts to allow the statute to be used as fraud cannot be tied down into categories. The word "fraud" is used in this context in its older and less precise sense.[82] Conduct which is "inequitable"[83] will suffice to prevent reliance on the statute. Thus, a person who asks for a memorandum of a contract to be prepared showing as the consideration the amount which actually is the balance of the purchase price may not be allowed to use the discrepancy as a matter showing failure to satisfy the statute.[84] And a person who fraudulently prevents a memorandum coming into existence cannot rely

---

[72] Unnamed case considered by Lord Redesdale in *Lindsay's* case at 9.
[73] Jones & Goodhart, *Specific Performance* (1986), p 102 and cases cited at fn 6.
[74] *Black v Greally* (HC) 10 November 1977, Costello J, unrep at 21; *White v McCooey* (HC) 26 April 1976 Gannon J, unrep at 14; *Lowry v Reid* [1927] NI 142 at 154.
[75] *Per* Finlay P in *Doherty v Gallagher* (HC) 9 June 1975, unrep at 13.
[76] In *Doherty's* case it would have been an injustice to refuse an order for specific performance on the ground that what could only be considered a vague assurance relating to time was not set out in the note or memorandum.
[77] *White v McCooey* (HC) 26 June 1976, unrep at 15. Gannon J was dealing with the sufficiency of the note or memorandum.
[78] *Devine v Fields* (1920) 54 ILTR 101 at 103. The plaintiff lulled the defendant into not bidding and the court decided that he held in trust.
[79] *Per* Andrews LJ in *Lowry v Reid* [1927] NI 142 at 154.
[80] Considered in Ch 6 *ante*.
[81] Para **9.09** *infra*.
[82] *Per* Lord Reid in *Steadman v Steadman* [1976] AC 536 at 540; [1974] 2 All ER 977 at 980-1. *Cf* "unconscionable" used by Lord Salmon at 566 (AC); 1003 (AER). We discuss the breadth of fraud as a defence in para **9.10** *infra*.
[83] Used by McWilliam J as alternative to "fraudulent" in *Howlin v Thomas F Power (Dublin) Ltd*, (HC) 5 May 1978, unrep at 9.
[84] *Black v Greally* (HC) 10 November 1977, Costello J, unrep at 21. He held that the contract was not tainted with illegality: p 18.

successfully on the want of writing.[85] It seems that where there are two or more defendants fraud on the part of one which prevents him relying on the statute will not prevent another doing so if the latter did not know of the agreement or acquiesce in the relevant events which amounted to fraud on the part of the first defendant.[86] Where one person is prevented from relying on the statute another claiming through him or as a mortgagee of his interest is probably in no better position.[87]

[9.09] A trustee holding property in his name cannot rely on the Statute of Frauds to defeat a claim to it by the beneficiary.[88] As Lindley LJ explained:[89]

"It is further established by a series of cases, the propriety of which cannot now be questioned, that the Statute of Frauds does not prevent the proof of a fraud; and that it is a fraud on the part of a person to whom land is conveyed as a trustee, and who knows it was so conveyed, to deny the trust and claim the land himself. Consequently, notwithstanding the statute, it is competent for a person claiming land conveyed to another to prove by parol evidence that it was so conveyed upon trust for the claimant, and that the grantee, knowing the facts, is denying the trust and relying upon the form of the conveyance and the statute, in order to keep the land himself."

Oral evidence may be used to prove the trust and get a declaration that the grantee is a trustee.[90] There is no difference in principle between a case where a conveyance of land has been executed and one where events have only progressed to a contract made between a vendor and purchaser and that purchaser goes back on a prior agreement he made with another person about the land and denies the existence of a trust.[91] Thus if two persons each want part of property which is for sale and they agree that only one will bid and he will make over part of the property on agreed terms afterwards the court will hold that the bidder, if the property is sold to him, holds the relevant part of the property as trustee for the other person.[92] The purchaser/trustee will not be entitled to take advantage of the situation by, *eg*, negotiating a new restrictive covenant for his benefit.[93] If a consent of some third party, such as a consent to subdivision or a landlord's consent to assignment, is needed it is the duty of the purchaser/trustee to seek it[94] and it has been said that both parties are bound to take whatever steps are necessary to carry out the agreement.[95] If necessary, the court will protect the equitable right under the trust by granting an injunction.[96]

---

[85] *Maxwell v Lady Montacute* (1719) 1 Eq Cas Abr 19, cited in Osborne's *County Courts Practice in Equity in Ireland*, 2nd Ed (1910) by Babington at 159.

[86] *Hope v Lord Cloncurry* (1874) IR 8 Eq 555 at 557-8: remainderman not affected by part performance by intending tenant of the tenant for life. *Cf O'Fay v Burke* (1858) 8 IR Ch R 225; *Lowe v Swift* (1814) 2 Ball & Beatty 529.

[87] *Re Davitt's Estate*, (1935) 70 ILTR 53 at 55 approving *Davis v Whitehead* [1894] 2 Ch 133. In the *Davitt's Estate* case the beneficiary acquiesced in the bank's security and the money secured was held well charged on the land.

[88] *Re Davitt's Estate, ibid*, approving *Davis's* case.

[89] *Rochefoucauld v Boustead* [1897] 1 Ch 196 at 205 approved by Budd J ln *McGillycuddy v Joy* [1959] IR 189 at 212 and paraphrased with approval by Lowry LCJ in *Gilmurray v Corr* [1978] NI 99 at 104

[90] *Gilmurray v Corr* [1978] NI 99 at 104, affirmed - see note at 106

[91] *McGillycuddy v Joy* [1959] IR 189 at 212

[92] *Gilmurray's* case at 103; *McGillycuddy's* case at 213-4; *Devine v Fields* (1920) 54 ILTR 101 at 103.

[93] *Gilmurray's* case at 103-4.

[94] *Gilmurray's* case at 104-5; *McGillycuddy's* case at 207, 213-4; *O'Regan v White* [1919] 2 IR 339 at 385, 387, 391 *per* O'Connor LJ: *cf* Ronan LJ at 362, 368. On such consents see paras **3.22-4** *ante*.

[95] *McGillycuddy's* case at 207. *Cf O'Regan's* case at 386-7

[96] *O'Regan's* case at p 383, *per* Ronan LJ.

FRAUD

[9.10] The concept of fraud in equity is very broad.[97] The "fraud" which may enable a contract to be set aside includes "transactions in which the Court is of opinion that it is unconscientious for a person to avail himself of legal advantage which he has obtained."[98] The courts will refuse the order for specific performance if a bargain may be fairly considered as unethical or infringing the principles of fairness which a court of equity requires to be observed so that substantial justice would not be done unless the order is refused.[99] It has been pointed out that undue influence[100] is a form of fraud.[101] Knowingly taking advantage of the recklessness of another person in an unequal position may be fraud and result in a transaction being set aside.[102] Fraud is the key which defeats a defence that an incorrect statement was only an opinion.[103] It is also the essential ingredient for setting aside the contract of a lunatic who is apparently sane at the time of the contract.[104] And if a party to a contract is at a "serious disadvantage" and there is a "fundamental unfairness" in the transaction so that it would "create a hardship" and "be unjust to decree specific performance" we seem to be in the broad area of equitable fraud even though the word "fraud" is never mentioned in a judgment.[105]

If silence is asserted to be fraud it is essential to show that communication was a duty.[106] A duty to disclose may be clear from the circumstances and thus silence or non-disclosure will be fraudulent.[107] The fact that a person who says something does not know it is false will not necessarily prevent a defence of fraud succeeding; actual consciousness of falsehood is not required and knowledge of facts inconsistent with the statement will suffice.[108] And if a person having no knowledge whatever on the subject takes it upon himself to represent a certain state of facts to exist he does so at his peril.[109] It would seem that recklessness in, eg, publishing advertisements may constitute legal fraud.[110] There is no need in law for a person alleging fraud to establish a motive for it although the complete absence of any plausible motive could create a doubt about proof of the fraud alleged.[111]

---

[97] Sheridan, *Fraud in Equity* (1957).

[98] *Per* James LJ in *Torrance v Bolton* (1872) LR 8 Ch 118 at 125 approved by Hutton J in *Rooney v Conway* [1982] 5 NIJB at 22 and McVeigh J in *Buckley v Irwin* [1960] NI 98 at 105.

[99] *Buckley's* case at 104

[100] Discussed in paras **9.24-31** *infra*.

[101] *O'Neill v Murphy* [1936] NI 16 at 34.

[102] *Slator v Nolan* (1876) IR 11 Eq 367 at 387-92.

[103] *Bissett v Wilkinson* [1927] AC 177 at 181, approved by Curran J in *Smyth v Lynn* [1951] NI 69 at 72. See para **9.15** *infra*.

[104] *Hassard v Smith* (1872) IR 6 Eq 429 at 433-4; *Hart v O'Connor* [1985] AC 1000 considered by Murray J in *McCrystal v O'Kane* [1986] NI 123 at 133.

[105] *Smelter Corporation of Ireland Ltd v O'Driscoll* [1977] IR 305 at 311. Fraud does not seem to have been pleaded or argued either.

[106] *Archbold v Lord Howth* (1866) IR 1 CL 608 at 629. *Cf* representation by conduct, *eg*, in *Doherty v Doherty* [1991] 2 IR 458.

[107] As in *Northern Bank Finance Corp Ltd v Charlton* [1979] IR 149 at 166-7. The Supreme Court held that the findings of fraud by Finlay P were open to him; it was not the court's task to go further. See O'Higgins CJ at 181, Butler J concurring, Henchy J at 193-4 and Griffin J at 205-6, Parke J concurring at 212. O'Higgins CJ mentioned "non-disclosure or silence" at 176 and Henchy J "concealments" at 193

[108] *Phelps v White* (1881) 7 LRI 160 at 170-1, 172.

[109] *Ibid* at 170.

[110] *Smyth v Lynn* [1951] NI 69 at 76.

[111] *Northern Bank Finance Corp Ltd v Charlton* [1979] IR 149 at 168.

[9.11] Certain authorities have suggested that the onus of proof of fraud might be of higher standard than the norm in civil matters.[112] That norm is, of course, that the person on whom lies the onus of proving a particular averment is held to have discharged that onus if the court is satisfied on the balance of probabilities that the averment in question is correct.[113] The Supreme Court has examined the point in a recent case and has made it clear that the onus of proof is on the normal standard for civil matters:

> "If, as has been suggested, the degree of proof of fraud in civil cases is higher than the balance of probabilities but not as high as to be (as is required in criminal cases) beyond reasonable doubt, it is difficult to see how that higher degree of proof is to be gauged or expressed. To require some such intermediately high degree of probability would, in my opinion, introduce a vague and uncertain element, just as if, for example, negligence were required to be proved in certain cases to the level of gross negligence. Moreover, since in this jurisdiction many civil cases involving fraud are tried by juries,[114] it would be difficult for a trial judge to charge a jury as to this higher degree of proof without running the risk of confusing the jurors.
>
> In any event, it is difficult to put forward a rational and cogent reason for singling out civil cases of fraud for this higher degree of proof. It is of course to be said that a finding of fraud usually carries with it a high degree of moral condemnation which may have serious consequences for the person so condemned. But similar consequences may follow from a finding against a defendant in other types of civil proceedings."[115]

Henchy J was unable therefore to discern, in principle or practice, any rational or cogent reason why fraud in civil cases should require a higher degree of proof than is required for the proof of other issues in civil claims.

Fraudulent misrepresentation

[9.12] Fraudulent misrepresentation may establish a defence of fraud to a claim for specific performance and a right to rescind the contract or it may give rise to a separate cause of action for the person misled. To show a good cause of action based on fraudulent misrepresentation[116] there obviously must be proof of fraud and, equally clearly, fraud is proved when it is shown that the person making the representation knew it was false.[117] To prevent a false statement being fraudulent there must be an honest belief in its truth.[118] An untrue statement made recklessly, not caring whether it was true or false, is fraudulent representation even though the conduct may fall short of "actual fraud".[119] A person who may not intend anything dishonest but induces another to act on a supposition which he must know is untrue makes a fraudulent representation.[120] A statement made inadvertently but with knowledge that the contrary of the representation is the fact will be fraudulent in law even though the person who made the effective mistake may be considered free of

---

[112] Discussed by Hamilton P in *Banco Ambrosiano v Ansbacher & Co* [1987] ILRM 669 at 672-3

[113] *Per* Henchy J in the *Banco Ambrosiano* case at 700-701.

[114] Since that judgment the Courts Act 1988 abolished the right to jury in cases of personal injury or death due to negligence, nuisance and other causes but there is no effect on fraud cases. See the detailed General Notes in Sweet & Maxwell, *Irish Current Law Statutes Annotated* at 88/14-02 and 88/14-04.

[115] *Per* Henchy J in the *Banco Ambrosiano* case at 701, all other Judges concurring: note Finlay CJ at 691.

[116] Or a good defence to a claim for specific performance.

[117] *Delaney v Keogh* [1905] 2 IR 267 at 286.

[118] *Per* Lord Herschell in *Derry v Peek* 14 App Cas 374 approved by Holmes LJ in *Delaney's* case at 286.

[119] *Doyle v Youell* (1937) 72 ILTR 253 at 254. *Cf Greyhill Property Co Ltd v Whitechap Inn Ltd* (HC) 5 October 1993, Barr J, unrep at 19; *Airlie v Fallon* [1976-7] ILRM 1 at 12.

[120] *Costello v Martin* (1867) 1 IR Eq R 50 at 55-6.

moral culpability.[121] A person who represents that a certain state of facts exists may be said to take upon himself to warrant his own belief in the truth of what he asserts.[122]

[9.13] The precise circumstances in which something is said or done may be vital. Thus, the context of words may create liability. "Words may be used in such circumstances, and in such a connection, as to convey to the person to whom they are addressed a meaning or inference beyond what is expressed; and if it appears that the person employing them knew this, and also knew that such meaning or inference was false, there is sufficient proof of fraud."[123] The maker of a statement which can bear two meanings one of which he knows is false cannot escape liability by saying that the representee should have taken the other meaning.[124] If new information comes to hand which shows that a previous statement made honestly is incorrect there will be a duty to correct the false impression before others have acted on it[125] and, if the correction is not made, there is fraud. A person who makes a false statement and does not correct it cannot escape liability by saying that he was acting under the directions of another; in matters of truth and falsehood, of honesty and dishonesty, the law requires a person to judge for himself.[126]

[9.14] The misrepresentation must be an inducing cause of the purchase.[127] Usually it must be made before there is a contract but occasionally it may be made later, *eg*, in reply to a requisition or enquiry. In that kind of situation, in order to set up the defence of fraud in an action for specific performance, it probably would have to relate to or cover up something which would have enabled the purchaser to get out of the contract or, at the least, gain some benefit such as compensation or abatement of the price.[128] A fraudulent misrepresentation made between the time parties reach a "general agreement" which is "subject to contract" and the signing of a formal contract is one made prior to contract.[129] If a plaintiff is induced to buy a property by fraudulent misrepresentation he is entitled to repudiate the bargain provided this is done without undue delay.[130] It is enough to show a *fraudulent* misrepresentation as to *any* part of the matters which induced the misled party to enter into the contract which he seeks to rescind.[131]

[9.15] When an agent is acting[132] there may be fraud only on the part of either principal or agent, the other being innocent. It usually is not necessary for the misled person to

---

[121] *Phelps v White* (1881) 7 LRI 160 at 162-3

[122] *Per* Maule J in *Evans v Redmond* 13 CB 786 cited with approval by Deasy LJ in *Phelps's* case at 171.

[123] *Per* Holmes LJ in *Delaney's* case at 286-7.

[124] *Smith v Chadwick* 9 App Cas 201, approved by Holmes LJ in *Delaney's* case at 289.

[125] *Delaney's* case at 289.

[126] *Delaney's* case at 290. Note that where two persons provide wrong information one may do so fraudulently and the other may be liable in negligence if he believes the material to be true but does not check the accuracy of the facts presented: *O'Donoghue v LV Nolan Incorporated* (HC) 29 July 1993, Carroll J, unrep at 6-9.

[127] *Fenton v Schofield* (1965) 100 ILTR 69 at 77 (an appeal related only to damages); *Smyth v Lynn* [1951] NI 69 at 76-8.

[128] Usually a false reply to a requisition would not affect the purchaser's commitments; see Wylie, *Irish Conveyancing Law*, para 14.55

[129] *Fenton's* case at 77.

[130] *Carbin v Somerville* [1933] IR 276 at 289. Cf *Peilow v ffrench O'Carroll* (1969) 106 ILTR 29 at 54 and on affirmance at 52-4. There was no allegation of fraudulent misrepresentation at the appeal: p 44.

[131] *Kennedy v Panama, New Zealand & Australian Royal Mail Co* (1867) LR 2 QB 580 at 587, approved in *Carbin's* case at 288 and also approved by O'Connor MR in *Lecky v Walter* [1914]1 IR 378 at 386. See paras **9.16-22** *infra* in relation to *innocent* misrepresentation.

[132] Agency is considered at paras **3.32-43** *ante*.

show which was fraudulent. The two represent one person and if between them a fraudulent misrepresentation is made which induces a wrong, and that causes damage, "it matters not which is the person who makes the representation, or which is the person who had the guilty knowledge".[133] Thus a principal may be liable for the fraudulent misrepresentation of the agent even though it reached the third party through the innocent channel of the principal just as the principal would be if he fraudulently caused an innocent agent to communicate a misrepresentation to a third party.[134] However, in the absence of actual fraud or dishonesty on the part of a principal, knowledge by him of facts which render false a statement made innocently by his agent does not render the principal guilty of fraudulent misrepresentation.[135] Often it is clear who was fraudulent. Fraud on the part of a vendor's agent will give a purchaser a good defence to a claim by the innocent principal for specific performance and entitle him to compensation from the agent for loss suffered.[136] It is no answer that the agent who commits fraud may have been acting on the instructions of another agent also acting for the same principal.[137] False information given by a vendor to his agent who passes it on in good faith to an intending purchaser makes the vendor guilty of fraud even though the agent acted innocently.[138] It is interesting to compare this with the situation in *Smelter Corporation of Ireland Ltd v O'Driscoll*[139] where the managing director of a company knew the true facts, knew or should have known that an agent for the company had given inaccurate information to a potential vendor placing her at a serious disadvantage and allowed negotiations to continue without correcting the wrong impression given. Although the agent acted in good faith the incorrect information was a major factor in the decision that it would be unjust to decree specific performance. The case was decided on the basis of "a fundamental unfairness"[140] but an argument that the facts came within the broad meaning in equity of fraud[141] might have succeeded if fraudulent misrepresentation had been pleaded.[142]

INNOCENT MISREPRESENTATION

[9.16] Innocent misrepresentation will give rise to a right to rescind a contract and a good defence to an action for specific performance if a statement is made which is wrong, even though made in good faith and with no intention to mislead, the statement is material, it

---

[133] *Pearson v Dublin Corporation* [1907] 2 IR 537, *per* Lord Halsbury at 544; *cf* Loreburn LC at 539. The "guilty knowledge" was in the agent.
[134] *Anglo-Scottish Beet Sugar Corporation Ltd v Spalding UDC* [1937] 3 All ER 335 at 343 considering the *Pearson* case and approved by Romer LJ in *Armstrong v Strain* [1952] 1 All ER 139 at 144-5.
[135] *Armstrong's* case, headnote. The principal did not know that the statements were being made. They were made in negotiations for the sale of a bungalow; the claim was for damages after completion. No question arose how the discretion of the court might have been used if the vendor had been suing for specific performance.
[136] *Ingram v Gillen* (1910) 44 ILTR 103: auctioneer pretending bogus bids were genuine, no suggestion in the report that vendor knew of the fraud).
[137] *Delaney v Keogh* [1905] 2 IR 267 at 289-90; auctioneer did not correct error because he was under instructions from a solicitor.
[138] *Fenton v Schofield* (1965) 100 ILTR 69 at 75-6.
[139] [1977] IR 305 at 311. There seems to have been no plea or argument of fraud or fraudulent misrepresentation.
[140] Page 311: the main grounds of defence are noted by O'Higgins CJ at 308.
[141] On which see para **9.10** *supra*.
[142] The defendant may not have known of the managing director's knowledge in time to make the necessary case.

is made with the intention of inducing the representee to act on it and he does act or rely on it.[143] Of course, the purchaser does not have to rescind the contract. As an alternative he may opt to take the property so far as the vendor can assure it with compensation for any deficiency.[144] Modern standard conditions dealing with matters such as misdescription and sometimes providing for arbitration are likely to be read in the light of the traditional practice of equity in deducting any compensation payable to a purchaser from the purchase price prior to closing.[145] A condition in a written contract to the effect that any error, misstatement or omission in the particulars or conditions should not annul the sale or be a ground for any abatement or compensation will not enable a vendor to enforce a contract despite an innocent misrepresentation where the misstatement goes to the root of the contract.[146] If there is fraud a party cannot escape liability for his own fraudulent statement by inserting a clause in a contract that the other party shall not rely on it[147] though it is possible that an innocent principal might be able to guard himself by "apt and express clauses" from liability for the fraud of his own agents.[148]

[9.17] The test whether a statement is material is an objective one to be applied by the court.[149] The relevant representation does not have to be the sole cause of a transaction; it suffices if it is a material inducement or one of the factors inducing entry into the contract.[150] The fact that a representee could ascertain the truth makes no difference. A vendor who by his misrepresentation induces the purchaser to enter into a contract to purchase need not expect to have his misrepresentation excused or overlooked and the purchaser deprived of a right to rescind because he does not ignore the misrepresentation and pursue matters further so as to establish the truth of what was misrepresented.[151] Constructive notice does not affect a purchaser in cases of misrepresentation.[152]

[9.18] If both incorrect and correct statements are made there may still be liability for misrepresentation. Thus the reading of a lease at an auction may not excuse a misdescription of its terms in the particulars of sale.[153] Where a vendor wishes to sell property without an appurtenant right but has inadvertently described it in such a way that a draft contract includes the appurtenant right either expressly or by implication of law it is his duty to correct the conditions of sale so as to exclude that which he does not wish to sell or convey or is not able to sell or convey.[154] A representation may be made by

---

[143] *Gahan v Boland* (HC) 21 January 1983, Murphy J, unrep at 13-14; (SC) 20 January 1984, unrep at 2-3. The courts were dealing with a contract which had not been completed. The plaintiff got rescission; a cross action for specific performance failed: see p 18 of Murphy J's judgment. *Cf Peilow v ffrench O'Carroll* (1966) 106 ILTR 29 at 52. Note that the Sale of Goods and Supply of Services Act 1980 does not apply to land.

[144] *Connor v Potts* [1897] 2 IR 534 at 538-9; *Keating v Bank of* Ireland [1983]ILRM 295 at 299.

[145] *Keating's* case at 299.

[146] *Peilow v ffrench O'Carroll* (1969) 106 ILTR 29 at 52. *General Condition* 33 of the 1991 Ed of the Law Society's *General Conditions of Sale* is fairer and more sophisticated than the version in *Peilow's* case. It allows compensation for "error" which is defined to include misstatement and misrepresentation. See further para **9.86** *infra*. If need be, the parties can go to arbitration under *General Condition* 51.

[147] *Pearson v Dublin Corporation* [1907] 2 IR 537 at 539, 541, 545, 547.

[148] *Ibid*, p 539.

[149] *Per* Murphy J in *Gahan v Boland* (HC) 21 January 1983, unrep at 13.

[150] *Gahan's* case (SC) at 3; *Lecky v Walter* [1914] 1 IR 378 at 384.

[151] *Gahan's* case (SC) at 4. *Cf Phelps v White* (1881) 7 LRI 160 at 162.

[152] *Geoghegan v Connolly* (1859) 8 IR Ch R 598 at 609; *Cf Vaughan v Magill* (1849) 12 IR Eq R 207 at 212-3.

[153] *Per* Tyndal CJ in *Flight v Booth* 1 Bing NC, 370 approved in *Geoghegan v Connolly* (1859) 8 IR Ch R 598 at 608.

[154] *Peilow v ffrench O'Carroll* (1969) 106 ILTR 29 at 49.

implication, *eg,* by advertising a house for sale as having a back entrance, which may, depending on the circumstances including physical features, represent that there is a right of way by which that entrance may be used.[155] Issuing an advertisement or auctioneer's hand-out is likely to amount to or include a representation.[156] However, the law gives no special sanctity to statements in an advertisement for the sale of property. They may be made the subject of proceedings based on misrepresentation or may be relied on as grounds for rescission of a contract or in answer to a claim for specific performance - provided the necessary elements are present.[157] It is common knowledge that the purpose of such advertisements is to draw attention to the good points of the property and that one usually finds in such advertisements rather flourishing statements.[158] Exaggerated statements like "puffing" advertisements will not be taken into account but a wrong description in an advertisement may amount to a misrepresentation in a very material matter.[159] A suggestion that any information given by auctioneers should be taken as incorporated into a contract would go too far.[160] So would a suggestion that a vendor's auctioneer should anticipate that any statements made by him about the property will be relied on by the purchaser thus putting him under a duty of care.[161] There is an obvious risk in inaccuracy but it does not always give a good defence to a claim for specific performance. A statement of a party's intention is capable of amounting to a representation.[162] A representation is a statement of *fact*. The state of a person's mind is a matter of fact although it may be difficult to prove; accordingly a misrepresentation of the state of a person's mind is a mis-statement of fact.[163]

[9.19] As we saw in relation to fraudulent misrepresentation,[164] the circumstances of a case may produce a duty of disclosure and failure to make that disclosure may amount to a misrepresentation. Thus, if an intending purchaser of leasehold property states his object in buying and the seller is silent as to a covenant in his lease prohibiting or interfering with that object his silence may be equivalent to a representation that there was no such covenant whether or not the seller knew of the extent or operation of the covenant.[165] A vendor of a leasehold interest is bound to know what covenants are in his lease and to communicate such knowledge to an intending purchaser if the covenants can be reasonably interpreted as affecting the object which he is aware the purchaser has in view in buying the premises.[166] There is normally a duty not to suppress material information about title and misrepresentation may arise as much from suppression of material facts as from misstating them.[167] Even observations or an inquiry made by a

---

[155] *Peilow's case* at 48-9, 50-51. *Cf Re Flanigan & McGarvey & Thompson's Contract* [1945] NI 32 at 39; *Spunner v Walsh* (1847) 11 IR Eq R 597 at 599.

[156] *Peilow's* case at 52, 60

[157] *Smyth v Lynn* [1951] NI 69 at 76.

[158] *Per* Curran J in *Smyth's* case at 76-7.

[159] *Thomson v Guy* (1844) 7 IR L R 6 at 14, 15

[160] *Peilow's* case at 59.

[161] *Per* Kenny J in *Bank of Ireland v* [1966] IR 646 at 659-60. See consideration of *negligent misrepresentation* at paras **8.48-9** *ante.*

[162] See discussion by Pringle J in *Reg Armstrong Motors Ltd v Texaco (Ireland) Ltd* (HC) 21 December 1971, unrep at 13-17. The defendant failed to discharge the onus of proving that a statement of intention was made.

[163] *Edgington v Fitzmaurice* (1885) 29 Ch D 459 at 483. See discussion by Cheshire, Fifoot and Furmston's, *Law of Contract,* 11th Ed (1986) at 258-9. *Cf Smyth v Lynn* [1951] NI 69 at 73.

[164] Para **9.10** *supra.*

[165] *Power v Barrett* (1887) 19 LRI 450 at 457.

[166] *Power's* case at 457-8.

[167] *Geoghegan v Connolly* (1859) 8 IR Ch R 598 at 609.

vendor, depending on the circumstances, can amount to a misrepresentation by him to his intending purchaser.[168] A partial disclosure without actual misstatement but leading to an inference that a covenant is different from what it actually is may be a misrepresentation.[169]

However, in other cases information may be given to a purchaser which, though incomplete, puts him on enquiry. Thus, if he is told or is otherwise aware that property is subject to tenants or occupiers it is up to him to ascertain the extent of their rights.[170] In this type of situation the purchaser's notice of possession by the relevant persons supersedes the vendor's duty of disclosure and, if both remain silent, the purchaser takes subject to all existing rights.[171] A purchaser told that tenants hold at certain rents cannot complain if it turns out later that the tenure is greater than he assumed it to have been without any reason.[172] The general rule is that notice of the existence of a lease amounts in law to notice of its contents.[173] Where property is stated to be held under a lease it is the business of the purchaser to look at it and see whether there is any covenant which may materially influence his judgment as to the value.[174]

[9.20] It is important to distinguish between a representation and a statement of opinion. A statement of mere opinion by one party to a contract which is relied on by the other party and which induces the contract does not in general give any right to relief unless fraud is established.[175] "In an action for rescission, as in an action for specific performance of an executory contract, when misrepresentation is the alleged ground of relief of the party who repudiates the contract, it is, of course, essential to ascertain whether that which is relied upon is a representation of a specific fact, or a statement of opinion, since an erroneous opinion stated by the party affirming the contract, though it may have been relied upon and have induced the contract on the part of the party who seeks rescission, gives no right to relief without fraud."[176] In a case where the facts are equally well known to both parties what one says to the other is frequently nothing but an expression of opinion. However, if the facts are not equally well known to both sides, then a statement of opinion by the one who knows the facts best may involve a statement of material effect on the basis that he impliedly states that he knows facts which justify his opinion.[177]

[9.21] Of course, if a purchaser *does* know the truth about any matter on which a representation has been made he could not be said to have been induced to enter the contract by the representation.[178] The representor may show that the representee knew the

---

[168] *Power's* case at 458.

[169] *Flight v Booth* 1 Bing NC 370 considered in *Geoghegan's* case at 608

[170] *Healy v Farragher*, (SC) 21 December 1972, unrep at 8-11; *Carroll v Keayes* (1873) IR 8 Eq at 136, 138; *Clements v Conroy* (1911) 2 IR 500 at 524-5, 529-50.

[171] *Per* Christian LJ in *Carroll's* case at 136

[172] *Per* Holmes LJ in *Clements's* case at 530.

[173] *Power's* case at 456; *Vaughan v Magill* (1849) 12 IR Eq R 207 at 209. *Cf Geoghegan's* case at 608. Note, however, that an incorrect statement about the effect of a deed may entitle a purchaser to get out of his contract: *Manifold v Johnston* [1902] 1 IR 7.

[174] *Per* Brady LC in *Vaughan's* case at 209.

[175] *Smyth v Lynn* [1951] NI 69 at headnote.

[176] *Per* Lord Merivale in *Bissett v Wilkinson* [1927] AC 177 at 181, approved by Curran J in *Smyth v Lynn* [1951] NI 69 at 72.

[177] See discussion and cases cited in *Smyth's* case at 72-4.

[178] *Gahan's* case (HC) at 17; *McCambridge v Winters* (HC) 28 May 1984, Murphy J, unrep at 12 (*noted* at [1985] ILRM 700).

truth and thus remove his right to rely on any representation made. But he must have had complete knowledge; it is not enough to show that he had partial or fragmentary knowledge.[179] If a representation is made but by the time a party takes a critical step, such as executing a lease, he knows the extent to which the actual state of affairs falls short of the representation, he cannot be regarded as relying on the representations made to him.[180]

[9.22] Two major distinctions between cases of fraudulent and innocent misrepresentation may be noted. One arises when transactions have been completed. At that stage it is not "the principle of equity" that relief should be given later against a conveyance - *ie* that it should be set aside - unless there has been fraud or misrepresentation amounting to fraud by which the purchaser was deceived.[181] The second is relevant before or after completion. It is sufficient to show that there was a *fraudulent* misrepresentation as to *any part* of that which induced the party to enter into the contract which he seeks to rescind but where there has been an *innocent* misrepresentation there is no right to rescission unless there is a "complete difference in substance" between what was supposed to be taken and what was actually taken.[182] Fitzgibbon J gave an example:

> "To sell a leaky house or a leaky ship on a *fraudulent* misrepresentation that it is sound entitles the party defrauded to rescind the contract, but if the misrepresentation be innocent there is not that difference in the subject matter of the sale which would entitle the party to be relieved of his bargain on the ground of defect of substance when there is really only an inferiority of quality. Any remedy the purchaser may have in such a case would sound in damages only."[183]

In a much older Irish case in which an intending landlord made an innocent misrepresentation that no public right of way affected the property to be leased Manners LC approached the matter thus:[184]

> "Then arises the Question, whether under the Head of Fraud or Mistake, the Defendant is bound to make good the Injury the Plaintiff has sustained, by Reason of the Right of Way being established; and if he is; whether that is to be done by altogether rescinding the Contract, and cancelling the Leases, or by making Compensation by Way of Damages?
>
> If it were a wilful Misrepresentation, the Plaintiff might be entitled to Relief; but where the Parties have expressed their Meaning by a Lease, that has been, with due Deliberation, executed; and where there is no wilful Misrepresentation, nor any Mistake, in omitting to introduce a Covenant, respecting this Right of way into the Deed, it would be very dangerous to correct this Deed upon such slight Grounds."[185]

---

[179] *Peilow v ffrench O'Carroll* (1969) 106 ILTR 29 at 51.

[180] *Grafton Court Ltd v Wadson Sales Ltd* (HC) 17 February 1975, Finlay P, unrep at 12.

[181] *Per* Lord Selborne in *Brownlie v Campbell* 5 App Cas 925 at 937 approved by O'Connor MR in *Lecky v Walters* [1914] 1 IR 378 at 385-6.

[182] *Kennedy v Panama, New Zealand & Australian Royal Mail Co* (1867) LR 2 QB 580 at 587, approved in *Carbin's* case at 288 and in *Lecky's* case at 386. However, note the earlier reference in the passage to "a difference in substance" (omitting the word "complete").

[183] *Carbin's* case at p 288.

[184] *Legge v Croker* (1811) 1 Ball & Beatty 506 at 514.

[185] The right was only a foot-way, a carriage-way having been stopped by a Grand Jury presentment in 1772. It may not seem easy to make an *innocent* misrepresentation that no public right of way goes through a site but the representor's belief was understandable in *Legge's* case.

It is interesting to note that the plaintiff apparently would have had a remedy if a covenant had been included in the lease to the effect that there was no right of way.[186] The modern rule about defects in property, including rights of way, is that a purchaser must take it subject to any defects which are patent on inspection and not inconsistent with the description in a contract for sale.[187]

UNDUE INFLUENCE

[9.23] Undue influence is capable of lasting for a long period. Also a person exercising undue influence will rarely let himself get into a position where he must sue for specific performance to realise his benefit. If he does so, the party subject to the influence is much more likely than previously to get competent independent legal advice. These may be reasons why the Irish case law on undue influence consists mainly of attempts to overturn completed *inter vivos* transactions or wills. However, one can suggest with confidence that undue influence will be a good defence to a claim for specific performance[188] of a contract not yet completed as, to say the very least, it is unfair in the eyes of equity. It is reasonable to suggest that undue influence is within the meaning of fraud in its broad equitable sense[189] and fraud is clearly a good defence to a claim for specific performance. Undue influence has been described as "a form of fraud"[190] and "a plea similar to fraud".[191] The type of fraud which may amount to undue influence "does not here mean deceit or circumvention; it means an unconscientious use of the power arising out of these circumstances and conditions"[192] Lowry LCJ put it thus in *R (Proctor) v Hutton*:[193]

> "When relying on 'express undue influence' the plaintiff must prove that an unfair advantage has been gained by an unconscientious use of power in the form of some unfair and improper conduct, some coercion from outside,[194] some overreaching, some form of cheating."

Pleas of undue influence and fraud are "pleas of quite a serious nature and they would require strong and clear evidence to substantiate them".[195] Exercising or being presumed to have exercised undue influence may in certain cases be considered a "smear".[196]

---

[186] Manners LC returned to the point at 516.

[187] *Re Flanigan & McGarvey & Thompson's Contract* [1945] NI 32 at 38. The position also may be modified by other parts of a contract.

[188] This view is also stated by Hanbury & Maudsley, *Modern Equity*, 13th Ed (1989) at 679 citing *Fry v Lane* (1888) 40 Ch D 12; [1886-90] All ER 1084 which may have been based more on "unfair dealing". In *McCrystal v Kane* [1986] NI 123, a claim for specific performance, a defence of undue influence failed on the facts: p 131.

[189] On which see para **9.10** *supra*.

[190] *O'Neill v Murphy* [1936] NI 16 at 34.

[191] *In re Rutledge* [1981] ILRM 198 at 202. Note reference to "constructive fraud" in *Gregg v Kidd* [1956] IR 183 at 194.

[192] *Per* Lord Selborne LC in *Earl of Aylesford v Morris* (1873) 8 Ch App 484 at 490-1; [1861-73] All ER 300 at 303, approved by Black J in the *Provincial Bank* case at 479.

[193] *R. (Proctor) v Hutton* [1978] NI 139 at 146. See also *Mulligan v Stewart* (HC) 25 November 1977, McWilliam J, unrep at 8.

[194] Too high a test should not be set by the word "coercion" (which had appeared in older case law): see Costello J in *Re Kavanagh decd* (HC) 24 October 1978, unrep at 6.

[195] *Harris v Swordy* (HC) 21 December 1967, Henchy J, unrep at 18 (not a case where undue influence was presumed).

[196] *R (Proctor) v Hutton* (CA) NI, unrep at 9, affirming [1978] NI 139.

On the other hand, undue influence is usually short of "conscious fraud" and may be, *eg*, the result of "over-zeal" allied to some ignorance of the rules of equity.[197] It may be "unconscious" and even "well meant".[198] The courts have declined to define exactly what undue influence is.[199] However, if a party is a weak person, liable to be imposed on, the court will look at a gift with a very jealous eye and very strictly examine the conduct of the person in whose favour it is made and if it sees that the least speck of imposition is at the bottom the court will and ought to interpose.[200] If a party is not weak or likely to be imposed on and there is no relationship which raises a presumption of undue influence[201] a court would expect evidence that the person against whom undue influence is alleged exercised "an unfair, undue and unreasonable mental control" over the influenced party.[202]

[9.24] The equitable doctrine of undue influence is not intended to save people from their own folly but is intended to prevent victimisation.[203] It certainly never was developed to upset or avoid transactions in which there has been neither victimisation or folly.[204] A court of equity also should be solicitous to see, consistently with the case law, that an equitable doctrine such as undue influence is not used to work inequity.[205] The conduct of a party alleging undue influence may be examined carefully to see whether it is consistent with the claim of having acted under undue influence.[206] It is important to remember also that a person can make an irrevocable voluntary gift at his pleasure even though it may be unwise to do so. While cases of voluntary donations may be especially vulnerable to attack on grounds of undue influence[207] (they have been described as "analogous" to cases of undue influence[208]) the right to equitable relief is not confined to voluntary gifts. It may be given in "all other cases where influence, however acquired, has resulted in gain to the person possessing at the expense of the person subject to it".[209] The right has often been upheld in cases of purchases where the vendor was poor and ignorant and the purchase was at an undervalue or otherwise unconscionable.[210]

The doctrine of undue influence will also cover benefits obtained by third parties. A court of equity may take away from third persons the benefits which they have derived

---

[197] *McMackin v Hibernian Bank* [1905] 1 IR 296 at 303.

[198] *Provincial Bank of Ireland v McKeever* [1941] IR 471 at 485

[199] *O'Flanagan v Ray-Ger Ltd* (HC) Costello J, unrep at 20.

[200] *Ibid*, quoting a passage from *Huguenin v Basely* (1807) 14 Ves 273

[201] On which see paras **9.26-7** *infra*.

[202] *Harris v Swordy* (HC) 21 December 1967, Henchy J, unrep at 15. *Cf* the speech of Lord Scarman in *National Westminster Bank plc v Morgan* [1985] AC 686; [1985] 1 All ER 821 and discussion of that decision by Keane, *Equity & the Law of Trusts in the Republic of Ireland* (1988), para 29.05. In the *National Westminster Bank* case the bank manager had not crossed the line between on the one hand explaining an ordinary banking transaction in the course of a normal business relationship between banker and customer and on the other hand entering into a relationship in which he had a dominating influence (All ER headnote). Jones & Goodhart, *Specific Performance* (1986) cite it at 76 to support a view that inequality of bargaining power is not a ground for setting aside a contract or refusing specific performance where there has been no misconduct by the stronger party.

[203] *Allcard v Skinner* (1887) 36 Ch D 145 at 183; [1886-90] All ER 90 at 99, approved by Black J in the *Provincial Bank* case at 485, 491.

[204] *Provincial Bank of Ireland v McKeever* [1941] IR 471 at 491; *R (Proctor) v Hutton* [1978] NI 139 at 149-50, affirmed by CA.

[205] The *Provincial Bank* case at 491; *Proctor's* case at 150 and, on appeal, unrep, at pp 9-10 of the transcript.

[206] As in *RF v MF*, (SC) unrep at 3-4.

[207] See discussion by Budd J in *Gregg v Kidd* [1956] IR 183 at 193-4.

[208] By Lord Selborne LC in *Earl of Aylesford v Morris* (1873) 8 Ch App 484 at 490-1; [1861-73] All ER 300 at 303.

[209] *Ibid*.

[210] The *Provincial Bank* case at 478-9.

from the fraud, imposition or undue influence of others.[211] It is not essential that those third parties should "claim under" the person who applied the influence.[212] It does seem necessary, however, that the third party knew at the material time of the equitable right to relief or of the circumstances from which the court would infer the equity.[213]

[9.25] It seems that a party seeking a relief other than an equitable one can rely on undue influence continuing to hold him in its grasp until within six years before action brought in order to avoid being barred by a limitation period.[214] Of course the Statute of Limitations, 1957 does not apply to claims for specific performance, injunctions or other equitable relief.[215] However, the person seeking to set a transaction aside on the ground of undue influence must beware of the equitable doctrine of laches.[216] Once the influence ceases that person must commence his proceedings within a reasonable time or he or she will be taken to abide by the transaction and confirm it.[217] It has been felt legitimate to take subsequent conduct including acquiescence into account as an aid to judging what the mentality of a party was at the time of a transaction and whether it was unduly influenced.[218] Thus, allowing eight years to pass without making any complaint that a person's execution of a transfer was oppressive or unfair was "so tainted with delay as to be inconsistent with" a claim that the party had acted under undue influence.[219] The situation and mental capacity of a person said to have acquiesced will also be taken into account.[220]

[9.26] A presumption of undue influence may arise in two sorts of cases. In one type it depends on the relationship of the parties and in the other it emerges from careful consideration of the facts in the evidence. Costello J summarised the principles involved:

> "The cases where a plaintiff seeks to set aside a gift or other transaction on the ground that it was procured by undue influence have been divided into two classes; firstly, those in which it can be expressly proved that undue influence was exercised, in which circumstances the court intervenes on the principle that no one should be allowed to retain any benefit arising from his own fraud or wrongful act; secondly, those in which the relations between the donor and donee have at or shortly before the execution of a gift been such as to raise a presumption that the donor had influence over the donee. Then the court intervenes, not on the ground that any wrongful act has in fact been committed by the donee but on the ground of public policy[221] and to prevent the relations which existed between the parties and the influence arising therefrom being abused."[222]

---

[211] *Gregg v Kidd* [956] IR 183 at 195 approving a passage from Lord Eldon in *Huegenin v Baseley* 14 Ves 273.

[212] The *Provincial Bank* case at 482.

[213] *Ibid*; also *Gregg v Kidd* [11956] IR 183 at 195.

[214] *O'Neill v Murphy* [1936] NI 36 at 42-3; *cf Blennerhassett v Day* (1812) 2 Ball & Beatty 104.

[215] Section 11(9)(a) of the Statute; see *JH v WJH* (HC) 20 December 1979, Keane J, unrep at 33-4; also Brady & Kerr, *The Limitation of Actions*, 2nd Ed (1994) at 167-9.

[216] Considered as a defence at paras **9.42-7** *infra*.

[217] *RF v MF* (SC) 24 October 1985, unrep at 4; *JH v WJH* (HC) 20 December 1979, Keane J, unrep at 31, approving *Allcard v Skinner* (1887) 36 Ch D 145.

[218] *Provincial Bank of Ireland v McKeever* [1941] IR 471 at 498

[219] *RF v MF* (SC) 24 October 1985, unrep at 4.

[220] *Noonan v O'Connell* (HC) 10 April 1987, Lynch J, unrep at 10.

[221] A similar point on public policy is made by Andrews LJ in *O'Neill v Murphy* [1936] NI 16 at 36. See also *Provincial Bank of Ireland v McKeever* [1941] IR 471 at 485, 494.

[222] *O'Flanagan v Ray-Ger Ltd* (HC) 28 April 1983, unrep at 18-19.

Jones LJ explained:

> "Now the presumption of undue influence may arise in two sorts of cases. The evidence may show a particular relationship, for example that of solicitor and client, trustee and cestui que trust, doctor and patient or religious adviser and pupil. Those cases or some of them, depending on the facts, may of themselves raise the presumption. Such examples, as regards undue influence, have much in common with the doctrine of res ipsa loquitur in relation to negligence. But then there is the other sort of case, the precise range of which is indeterminate, in which the whole evidence, when meticulously considered, may disclose facts from which it should be inferred that a relationship is disclosed which justifies a finding that there is a presumption of undue influence. In other words the presumption enables a party to achieve justice by bridging a gap in the evidence, where there is a gap, because the evidence is difficult or impossible to come by."[223]

The courts have never confined the application of those principles to any stated forms of relationship. To do so would fetter that wide jurisdiction to relieve against all manner of constructive fraud which courts administering equitable principles have always exercised.[224] Lowry LCJ has pointed out that the undue influence which is *presumed* from a relationship is influence of the same kind as actual influence shown to have been expressly used: "the difference lies in not being able to prove its exercise but, by virtue of the presumption, undue influence is deemed to have been exercised until its exercise is negatived on a balance of probabilities by evidence."[225]

Since *presumed* undue influence conveys the notion that the influence which arises from the relationship was actually exercised, even if not proved, it must, in order to count, be capable of affecting the relevant transaction.[226] In a case where undue influence must be proved and may be raised into a presumption by the evidence[227] the undue influence must be shown to have brought about the transaction or, at least, to have affected it. Thus a person who alleges undue influence but has himself alone originated the relevant plan will fail in his claim for relief.[228]

[9.27] To raise the presumption in a "particular relationship"[229] case it is necessary to prove "the making of a substantial gift"[230] and, secondly, the existence of a relationship in which the donor has such confidence and trust in the donee as to place the donee in a position to exercise undue influence over the donor in making the gift.[231] The relationships which raise the presumption are left unlimited,[232] wide open on the facts and

---

[223] *R (Proctor) v Hutton* (CA) NI, Jones LJ, unrep at 7, affirming [1978] NI 139. See also p 5 where Jones LJ approves a passage from Hanbury & Maudsley, *Modern Equity*, which now appears in modified form but with little change of meaning at p 789-80 of the 13th Ed (1989).

[224] *Gregg v Kidd* p[1956] IR 183 at 194, *per* Budd J.

[225] *Per* Lord Lowry LCJ ln the *Proctor* case (HC) [1978] NI 139 at 146. See his broad discussion of undue influence at p 145-50.

[226] *Proctor's* case at 152.

[227] *Ie*, one where the relationship does not raise the presumption.

[228] *Grealish v Murphy* [1946] IR 35 at 49; *cf De Blaquiere v Daly* [1955-6] IJR 82 at 84.

[229] Jones LJ's words in the passage quoted in para **9.26** *infra*.

[230] *Per* Lowry LCJ in *R. (Proctor)'s* case at 147. This means something having a significant element of gift. Keane, *Equity & the Law of Trusts in the Republic of Ireland* (1988) says helpfully at 29.04 "one party must have derived a significant benefit from the transaction".

[231] *R (Proctor) v Hutton* [1978] NI 139 at 147, affirmed by CA

[232] Some of the best known examples are noted by Jones LJ in the passage quoted above. See also the passage quoted from Black J in para **9.29** below; *O'Flanagan v Ray-Ger Ltd* (HC) 28 April 1983, Costello J, unrep at 19 and discussion by Keane, *op cit* at para 29.06.

in all the circumstances of each particular case as it arises.[233] To confine the application of the principle to any stated forms of relationship would fetter that wide jurisdiction to relieve against all manner of constructive fraud which courts of equity have always exercised.[234] It is a common *but not necessary* feature of the relationship that the person on whose part undue influence is alleged assumed a responsibility for advising the donor or even managing his property.[235] But if a transaction similar to the one which eventually occurs is envisaged by the parties from the outset before any influence can be acquired it may be difficult to say that the deal done has been affected by undue influence.[236] The presumption does not arise in *every* case where any fiduciary relationship exists between donor and donee but it does apply to all the variety of relations by which domination may be exercised by one person over another.[237] It does not apply in *all* cases of close family relationship as blood relationship is not sufficient of itself to call the principle into play.[238] Cases without "particular relationships" will depend very much on their own facts and call for meticulous examination of the evidence. Subject to that cautionary note, factors which have helped to raise presumptions of undue influence have included the degree of improvidence involved,[239] absence of or inadequate independent advice,[240] the fact that a young person has only just attained majority,[241] a drink problem,[242] physical illness and financial pressures,[243] age and deteriorating mental capacity[244] or simply dependence on the kindness and assistance of another.[245]

[9.28] To rebut a presumption of undue influence it is necessary to show that the transaction "was the result of the free exercise of independent will" and that the person entering into it must have had "full appreciation of what he was doing".[246] Rebuttable presumptions are rules of evidence; they arise only when the facts are not sufficiently known and operate only until the facts become known.[247] When a presumption is raised the onus is on the benefiting party to prove that no influence was exercised in fact.[248] In a "particular relationship"[249] case where undue influence is presumed the onus of supporting the gift or transaction is on the donee or grantee.[250] If no such relationship

---

[233] *Proctor's* case at 147. *McGonigle v Black*, (HC) Cir App, 14 November 1988, unrep at 9.

[234] *Gregg v Kidd* [1956] IR 183 at 194.

[235] *Proctor's* case at 147; *McGonigle's* case at 9.

[236] *Grealish v Murphy* [1946] IR 35 at 48; *cf De Blaquiere v Daly* [1955-6] IJR 82 at 84.

[237] *Provincial Bank of Ireland v McKeever* [1941] IR 471 at 479.

[238] *Gregg's* case at 195. Note Budd J's discussion of family relationships at 194-5.

[239] Para **9.30** *infra*. On improvident transactions see paras **9.31-4**.

[240] *McMackin v Hibernian Bank* [1905] 1 IR 296 at 306; *Noonan v O'Connell* (HC) 10 April 1987, Lynch J, unrep at 7-8; *McGonigle v Black* (HC) Cir App, Barr J, 14 November 1988, unrep at 7-8, 10-11. *Cf* discussion of need for legal advice in *Conlon v Murray* [1958] NI 17 at 26 and *Buckley v Irwin* [1960] NI 98 at 104 (both decided on the discretion of a court of equity).

[241] *McMackin's* case; *Aylward v Kearney* (1814) 2 Ball & Beatty 463 at 477-8.

[242] *McGonigle's* case. But see *McCrystal v O'Kane* [1986] NI 123 at 132 where a plaintiff seeking specific performance was held not to have found the defendant affected by drink or to have taken any advantage of him. *Cf* also *White v McCooey* (HC) 26 April 1976, Gannon J, Unrep.

[243] *O'Flanagan v Ray-Ger Ltd* (HC) 28 April 1983, Costello J, unrep at 27-29.

[244] *Noonan's* case at 6-7. *Cf De Blaquiere v Daly* [1955-6] IJR 82. See also *Rooney v Conway* [1982] 5 NIJB at 20-22 (unconscionable bargain).

[245] *Per* Budd J in *Gregg v Kidd* [1956] IR 183 at 194-5.

[246] *Per* Black J in *Provincial Bank of Ireland v McKeever* [1941] IR 471 at 484 quoting Lord Hailsham LC in *Inche Noriah v Shaik Allie Bin Omar* [1929] AC 127.

[247] *R. (Proctor) v Hutton* [1978] NI 139 at 148, affirmed by CA

[248] *McGonigle v Black* (HC) Cir App, 14 November 1988, Barr J, unrep at 9-10 .

[249] Jones LJ's words in the passage quoted in para **9.30** *supra*.

[250] *O'Neill v Murphy* [1936] NI 16 at 32; *Gregg v Kidd* [1953] IR 183 at 196.

exists the onus is on the donor or grantor[251] but, if his evidence carefully considered raises a presumption of undue influence, he succeeds unless that presumption is rebutted.[252] One cannot expect absolute disproof of undue influence. It is enough to establish a reasonable probability of the exercise of independent will founded upon adequate understanding.[253] The most likely method of rebutting the presumption is by showing that the party concerned had independent *and adequate* legal advice and acted on it.[254] For practical purposes, proof that a donor had received full and well-informed advice will (in the absence of countervailing evidence) rebut the presumption.[255] Any such independent advice relied on to defeat the presumption must be a reality, not a sham; it must not be "a mere cloak to cover up the transaction".[256] The courts usually will expect that a donor or grantor who is in some way "infirm" has had a complete explanation of the nature and effect of the transaction from an adviser who himself knew all the relevant circumstances.[257] This is so even when the adviser was selected by the donor or grantor himself.[258]

[9.29] However, adequate independent advice is not the only way in which a presumption of undue influence may be rebutted and, if there has been such advice, it is not always necessary to show that it was acted upon.[259] For example, a donor may unwisely confer a benefit on his trustee contrary to the best independent advice duly given to him, yet he might do so with an independent will and with a full appreciation of what he was doing and in such a case the transaction will stand.[260] But even if full and well-informed advice is given the evidence may show that it was not sufficiently understood or that the influence prevented it being acted upon. Black J summed up the position regarding independent advice not accepted:[261]

> "Although independent advice is not a *sine qua non*, yet where it has been proved to have been given and rejected, there are indications in the decisions that proof of its having been given might alone be sufficient to rebut the presumption of undue influence. Nevertheless, the giving of such advice would not prove that the person to whom it was given fully understood it, and even if evidence were given (for instance of statements made by the advised person) showing that he did understand it, he might still have rejected it under the interested, or it might be, the well meant, perhaps even unconscious but none the less undue influence of his trustee, parent, physician, solicitor, or religious superior. One cannot expect absolute disproof of undue influence. It is enough to establish a reasonable probability of the exercise of independent will founded upon adequate understanding."

---

[251] *O'Neill's* case at 32.

[252] As in *McGonigle's* case; and *Gregg's* case (uncle/nephew cases where the blood relationship *alone* would not raise the presumption).

[253] *Provincial Bank of Ireland v McKeever* [1941] IR 471 at 485.

[254] *Gregg v Kidd* [1956] IR 183 at 196. *Cf McCormack v Bennett* (1973) 107 ILTR 127 at 129-30. The importance of this in unconscionable bargains is discussed at paras **9.36** and **9.38** *infra*.

[255] *Per* Lowry LCJ in *Proctor's* case, (HC) at 148. Note his reference at 151 to evidence of independent advice being often the only *effective* proof that undue influence has not been exercised. *Cf RF v MF* (SC) 24 October 1985, unrep at 3-4.

[256] *McMakin v Hibernian Bank* [1905] 1 IR 296 at 305.

[257] *Grealish v Murphy* [1946] IR 35 at 50.

[258] *Williams v Williams* [1937] 4 All ER 34 at 38 approved in *Grealish's* case at 50

[259] The *Provincial Bank* case at 484

[260] The *Provincial Bank* case at 485. In *Smyth v Smyth* (HC) 22 November 1978, Costello J, unrep a purchase by a trustee from his beneficiary survived attack.

[261] The *Provincial Bank* case at 485.

Complete absence of competent independent advice is likely to be a major factor in a finding that there has been undue influence.[262] A solicitor acting for both sides is unlikely to be accepted as an independent legal adviser.[263] If there is independent advice which is not adequate it probably will not defeat a presumption of undue influence.[264] However, the absence of independent professional advice does not *necessarily* make a transaction invalid for undue influence.[265] And the fact that independent advice may be flawed, *eg*, because the adviser did not know all the relevant circumstances, does not prevent the court holding on other evidence that a deed was an act entirely of the free will of the relevant person.[266]

[9.30] The *strength* of a presumption of undue influence will vary greatly with the circumstances of the case. In particular it may depend on the degree of improvidence.[267] As Black J explained:[268]

> "In nearly all the reported cases where transactions such as I am dealing with were avoided, there was an element of improvidence - often gross sacrifice. In these cases the presumption of undue influence would be very strong. The less improvident the transaction the less strong the presumption. If there is no improvidence at all, the presumption of undue influence may be very weak and the evidence required to rebut it proportionately slight for the simple reason that there is no natural improbability that a person would freely confer a benefit on another, if doing so was in every way prudent from his own point of view, merely because that other stood in a fiduciary relation towards him. In some cases the equitable presumption might dwindle almost to the insignificance of a technical scintilla."

The degree of the selfish interest in the transaction of the person against whom undue influence is alleged or presumed is highly relevant; the less that interest the less the incentive to exercise undue influence and the weaker the probability of its having been brought to bear.[269] If there are findings that a purchaser was not particularly eager and that he paid fair value it becomes much easier for him to stand over a deal.[270] A donee who discourages the giving of benefits to himself increases his chance of being acquitted of undue influence.[271] The simplicity or complexity of a transaction has to be considered in its bearing on the likelihood of its author having understood what he was doing. A full understanding may greatly weaken, although alone it may not rebut, the presumption of undue influence.[272]

---

[262] *McMakin v Hibernian Bank* [1905] 1 IR 296 at 306; *Noonan v O'Connell* (HC) 10 April 1987, Lynch J, unrep at 7-8

[263] *Noonan's* case at 8.

[264] *McGonigle v Black* (HC) Cir App, Barr J, 14 November 1988, unrep at 7-8, 10-11. *Cf Proctor's* case, (HC) at 148. On this point in relation to unconscionable bargains see *Rooney v Conway* [1982] 5 NIJB at 16-19; *Grealish v Murphy* [1946] IR 35 at 45-48

[265] *Smyth v Smyth* (HC) Costello J, unrep at 24

[266] *McCormack v Bennett* (1973) 107 ILTR 127 at 131; *Williams v Williams* [1937] 4 All ER 34 at 38.

[267] The other major factor in the case law is lack of *adequate* independent advice.

[268] *Provincial Bank of Ireland v McKeever* [1941] IR 471 at 486

[269] *Ibid.*

[270] *Smyth v Smyth* (HC) Costello J, unrep at 8 ("rather unwilling purchaser"), 14-15, 22 (value).

[271] *R (Proctor) v Hutton* [1978] NI 139 at 149; on appeal at 9. The courts held also that no presumption arose: p 150 and, on appeal, p 9

[272] The *Provincial Bank* case at 486

UNCONSCIONABLE BARGAINS/IMPROVIDENT TRANSACTIONS

[9.31] If two persons stand in such a relation to each other that one can take an undue advantage of the other, whether by reason of distress, or recklessness or wildness or want of care, and the facts show that such advantage has been taken, a transaction resting on such unconscionable dealing will not be allowed to stand.[273] Where the parties are not on equal terms, even if no confidential relationship exists, the party who gets a benefit cannot hold onto it without proving that everything has been right and fair and reasonable on his part.[274] The cardinal principle (from which exceptions are rare) is that equity comes to the rescue whenever the parties to a contract have not met on equal terms.[275] The corollary is that the court must inquire whether a grantor, shown to be unequal to protecting himself, has had the protection which was his due by reason of his infirmity, and that infirmity may take various forms.[276]

A court will be slower to undo a transaction for value than a voluntary one but the fundamental. principle to justify radical interference by the court is the same, whether value be shown or not.[277] Doubt has been expressed whether these principles could apply to a sale for full consideration.[278] While no judge seems to have given a concluded view on the point the Irish cases where fair value has been given have upheld impugned transactions.[279] The origin of equity's approach to unconscionable bargains appears to have been in protecting family property and expectant heirs who were under pressure[280] but the court extended its aid to all cases in which the parties to a contract have not met on equal terms.[281] Equity considers both parties' interests. If a transaction is set aside on the ground of being an unconscionable bargain it will be set aside on equitable terms.[282] Accordingly the court will order that a sum paid under the deal which is set aside or any appropriate balance of it should be repaid. Also the plaintiff may have to account to the defendant for the value of any improvements done by the latter while in possession although a set-off of an occupation rent is likely.[283]

[9.32] In practice a claim to have a transaction set aside on the ground that it was an unconscionable bargain is fairly similar to an attack on the deal based on undue influence. Often the facts of a case will make it reasonable to rely on both grounds as alternatives. The two elements may combine in the result of a case enabling a court to hold that, *eg*, a deal was "a grossly improvident transaction which was brought about by undue influence".[284] In both types of case the evidence is likely to disclose similar

---

[273] *Slator v Nolan* (1876) IR 11 Eq 367 at 386.
[274] *Slator's* case at 387. *Cf Rae v Joyce* (1892) 29 LRI 500 at 509, 520-1, 523.
[275] *Grealish v Murphy* [1946] IR 35 at 49; *O'Flanagan v Ray-Ger Ltd* (HC) 28 April 1983, Costello J, unrep at 21. The plaintiffs won on undue influence so the unconscionable bargain point was not decided: p 30
[276] *Grealish's* case at 49-50; *Haverty v Brooks* [1970] IR 214 at 219
[277] *Grealish's* case at 50.
[278] *Nyland v Brennan* (HC) 19 December 1970, Pringle J, unrep at 10.
[279] *Nyland's* case. In *Kelly v Morrisroe* (1919) 53 ILTR 145 the deal was fair on the facts known at the time and was upheld as "a fair and honest transaction": p 147. In *Smyth v Smyth* (HC) 22 April 1978, unrep Costello J held that the sale was not at an undervalue and not otherwise unconscionable.
[280] On which see *Rae v Joyce* (1892) 29 LRI 500 at 509, 520-1.
[281] *O'Rorke v Bolingbroke* (1877) 2 App Cas 814 at 823; from a dissenting (on facts) judgment of Lord Hatherley cited with approval in *Grealish's* case at 49 and *O'Flanagan's* case at 21.
[282] *Rooney v Conway* [1982] 5 NIJB at 22, Hutton J approving a statement in Halsbury.
[283] *Rooney's* case at 22
[284] *McGonigle v Black* (HC) Cir App, 14 November 1988, Barr J unrep at 11.

features, typically a poor price for a disposal, absence or inadequacy of independent advice and inability to understand the nature and effects of the transaction or of any advice given. However, the presence of those elements in the evidence does not necessarily show that a transaction is unconscionable. Thus, failure to make the best bargain possible does not mean that a transaction is improvident.[285] Nor does absence of legal advice conclude a point, especially if a party has had an opportunity to go to a solicitor but declined to do so.[286] Absence of independent advice is not of itself a defence to an action for specific performance but a party must not do anything to induce the other party not to get such advice.[287] The main difference between the two situations in practice is that it is not necessary when claiming that a bargain is unconscionable or improvident to show that the party who got the benefit behaved, or is presumed[288] to have behaved, in any improper manner. A submission that a transfer should not be set aside because there was nothing improper in the conduct of the defendant has been rejected.[289] A plaintiff seeking to set aside a deal may fail on undue influence because none was exercised and no presumption came into play but succeed on improvidence relying on the poor terms of the deal and his own mental weakness.[290]

[9.33] Examples of transactions set aside as being unconscionable or improvident include a disposition by an elderly lady without any advice and not fully understanding the effect of the disposition on her retained property,[291] a sale at a very low consideration by a man of weak mental capacity without adequate independent advice,[292] a sale for a price greatly below value by an elderly man of weak and eccentric disposition without a disinterested legal adviser,[293] a sale of his home farm for a "small fraction of its true value" by a bachelor without adequate legal advice who, because of a combination of bereavement, inability to cope, loneliness, alcoholism and ill-health was vulnerable to manipulation,[294] a sale by a reckless and improvident man at a "flagrantly inadequate" consideration to his brother-in-law who was well versed in business, the vendor getting legal advice only after the contract was made,[295] an exchange by a man over 60 years of age and mentally deficient of his absolute title for a life interest in consideration of personal covenants backed by no adequate sanctions where his solicitor did not know all the relevant facts,[296] a sale by a seriously ill 69 year old woman at an undervalue (not "gross") in haste late at night without independent legal advice[297] and a disposition for no real consideration by a

[285] *Mulligan v Stewart* (HC) 25 November 1977, McWilliam J, unrep at 7.
[286] *Mulligan's* case at 7-8.
[287] *Conlon v Murray* [1958] NI 17 at 26; *Guy v O'Hagan* (1904) 5 NIJR 172 at 176
[288] On the presumptions of undue influence see paras **9.26-30** *supra*.
[289] *Rooney v Conway* [1982] 5 NIJB at 19-22.
[290] *Grealish v Murphy* [1946] IR 35 at 49-51, 53.
[291] *McGuirk v Branigan* (HC) Cir App, 9 November 1992, Morris J, unrep at 2-3, 5-6.
[292] *Rooney v Conway* [1982] 5 NIJB, 8 March 1982, Hutton J, at 17.
[293] *Longmate v Ledger* (1860) 2 Giff 157; 66 ER 67 considered extensively and applied in *Rooney's* case.
[294] *McGonigle v Black*, (HC) Cir App, 14 November 1988, Barr J, unrep; undue influence was the primary basis of the decision but the findings at p 11 would also support setting aside on the basis of improvidence and unconscionable bargain.
[295] *Slator v Nolan* (1876) IR 11 Eq 367.
[296] *Grealish v Murphy* [1946] IR 35.
[297] *Conlon v Murray* [1958] NI 17. This case is of special interest to us being a claim for specific performance. It was dismissed on the basis of the court's discretion to grant or refuse a decree. Curran J held at first instance that the onus of proof was on the plaintiff to show that he had not taken "an undue advantage" and that he failed to discharge the onus of proving "that everything has been right and fair and reasonable on his part": p 18. He also found inequality of the parties; submissions at 19-20. The ingredients of an unconscionable bargain were thus present. *Cf Buckley v Irwin* [1960] NI 98.

73 year old bachelor of impaired mental capacity without fully informed and completely independent legal advice.[298] An agreement by a widow to "compromise my statutory rights" under the Succession Act 1965 on the death of her husband for modest sums without provision for upward review and without independent advice would have been set aside but for serious delay on the part of the widow.[299] The terms of an impugned deed will be taken into account by the court. Matters such as the absence of a revocation clause[300] or lack of adequate sanctions to back up personal covenants[301] may increase the risk of a transaction being set aside. The omissions tend to suggest improvidence and lack of adequate independent advice.

On the other hand, a sale at a fair price by a 76 year old woman who was capable, took a long time to make her mind and had "full and careful" advice from her solicitor was upheld.[302] So was a sale by an eccentric old woman in humble circumstances without legal advice but with the advice of her former employer and at a fair value on the facts at the time.[303] A sale by a 76-year-old man at a fair price who wanted to avoid disqualifying himself from receiving the old age pension was upheld even though the solicitor acted for both parties and did not have all the facts.[304] A trustee who bought from his beneficiary as a "rather unwilling purchaser" and at a fair price had his deal upheld.[305]

[9.34] A high standard of independent advice is usually needed in order to uphold a sale by a person of weak intellect for a very low consideration against attack on the ground that it was an unconscionable bargain.[306] The simple fact of an unequal relationship is likely to call for extra care to protect the weaker person by fully informed and totally independent legal advice.[307] It is highly important that the advisers should have a just appreciation of their client's mental debility and his special need of protection.[308]

UNFAIRNESS

[9.35] If a court applying equitable principles is truly to act as a court of conscience it must consider the conduct of the parties with particular regard to whether it is unjust or unfair[309] and it must consider the consequences and the justice of those consequences from both sides' points of view.[310] Every agreement ought to be certain, fair and just in all its parts and, if any of those ingredients is wanting, the court will not decree specific performance.[311] The court will not assist unfair dealings[312] or allow a party to profit by his

---

[298] *Noonan v O'Connell* (HC) 10 April 1987, Lynch J, unrep.
[299] *JH v WJH* (HC) 20 December 1979, Keane J, unrep at 32-38.
[300] *Lydon v Coyne* [1946] IJR 64 at 67-8; *Gregg v Kidd* [1956] IR 183 at 201, 206.
[301] *Grealish v Murphy* [1946] IR 35 at 45.
[302] *Nyland v Brennan* (HC) 19 December 1970, Pringle J unrep.
[303] *Kelly v Morrisroe* (1919) 53 ILTR 145 at 147.
[304] *Haverty v Brooks* [1970] IR 214.
[305] *Smyth v Smyth* (HC) Costello J, unrep at 8 ("rather unwilling purchaser"), 14-15, 22 (value).
[306] *Rooney v Conway* [1982] 5 NIJB at 17; *Grealish v Murphy* [1946] IR 35 at 45-8.
[307] *Noonan v O'Connell* (HC) 10 April 1987, Lynch J, unrep at 8.
[308] *Grealish's* case at 48. *Cf Gregg v Kidd* [1956] IR 183 at 201-3, 206. See also discussion of an independent solicitor's role in an expectant heir case, *Rae v Joyce* (1892) 29 LRI 500 at 521-2, 525-6.
[309] The words used by Finlay P were "wrong or wilful".
[310] *McMahon v Kerry County Council* [1981] ILRM 4i9 at 421.
[311] *Ellard v Lord Llandaff* (1810) 1 Ball & Beatty 241 at 250-1, citing Lord Hardwicke in *Buxton v Lyster* (1746) 3 Atk 383.
[312] *Jessop v King* (1811) 2 Ball & Beatty 81 at 94.

bad faith.[313] If the court is of opinion that the circumstances in which a contract was made were unfair, if they were in any way oppressive, if there was any advantage taken by one party of another, then the court may refuse to grant specific performance.[314] Thus, it is against the principles of equity to grant specific performance to a party who knowingly suppresses a material ingredient in an agreement.[315] The same applies where a vendor has framed conditions of sale which are calculated to throw a purchaser off his guard and to mislead him.[316] Even if there is no bad faith or misrepresentation a misleading condition may still make it unjust to decree specific performance.[317] In written contracts for the sale of land the most prominent instances of unfairness occur in connection with the statement in a contract of the nature of the vendor's title or the interest offered for sale or in conditions restricting the purchaser's right to investigate the title; if anything is unfairly stated or suppressed so as to mislead the purchaser he may resist specific performance.[318]

[9.36] Considerations of fairness will also guide the courts in dealing with the use parties seek to make of particular clauses in their contracts. This seems most likely to arise in practice in relation to time limits. The date fixed for completion in a contract for the sale of land is no less a part of the contract than any other clause but equity will grant relief where a party seeks to make an unfair use of the letter of his contract in this respect having regard to the state of the law relating to real property.[319] Of course, equity stipulated that the time fixed should be essential or where there was something in the nature of the property or the surrounding circumstances which would render it inequitable to treat a time stipulation as a non-essential term of the contract.[320] A vendor must himself comply with a time stipulation before he can hold the purchaser bound by a similar one. It has been described as "a monstrous injustice" that a person who has himself not complied with a time limit should by his own act alter the date from which time is to be calculated by the other side.[321] Thus, if a vendor fails to send the agreed list of documents vouching title within the time limit applying to him he cannot hold the purchaser to the agreed time for raising requisitions.[322] A purchaser's claim for damages based on a delay of two weeks in closing a sale where time was not of the essence has been held to be an unfair use of the letter of the contract and therefore failed.[323]

The maxims of equity

[9.37] Judges in specific performance actions sometimes refer to maxims of equity. These aphorisms have played an important role in the development of a number of

---

[313] *RF v MF* (SC) 24 October 1985, unrep at 9.

[314] *Hoon v Nolan* (1966) 101 ILTR 99 at 104, reversed on another point.

[315] *Ellard's* case at 251.

[316] *Boyd v Dickson* (1876) IR 10 Eq 239 at 255.

[317] *Manifold v Johnston* [1902] 1 IR 7 at 13.

[318] *Heffernan v Kavanagh* (HC) 14 November 1969, Pringle J, unrep at 14 approving a passage from the 3rd Ed of Williams, *Vendor and Purchaser* at 1061. On the facts the non-disclosure did not prevent the plaintiff getting specific performance: p 15.

[319] *Stickney v Keeble* [1915] AC 386 at 400; [1914-15] All ER 73 at 77, approved by Hamilton J in *Maye v Merriman* (HC) 13 February 1980, at 19.

[320] *Stickney's* case at 416 (AC), 81 (All ER,) approved by Hamilton J in *Maye's* case at 20.

[321] By James LJ in *Upperton v Nickolson* (1871) 6 Ch App 436 at 443 in a passage approved by Kenny J in *Re Todd & Mcfadden's Contract* [1908] 1 IR 213 at 221.

[322] *Cellulose Processors Ltd v Flynn & O'Flaherty Ltd* (HC) 28 April 1986, Finlay P, unrep at 12, 14-15 applying the *Todd* case.

[323] *Maye's* case at 22. Because the case involved a contract for the sale of land Hamilton J treated the case including the time stipulation as if it were a claim for equitable relief: p 19.

features of equitable jurisdiction.[324] Three of them deserve mention in the context of our present discussion of unfairness. One, "Delay defeats Equity", is highly relevant to the defence of laches.[325] It may be noted that laches essentially consists of a substantial lapse of time coupled with the existence of circumstances which make it inequitable to enforce the claim.[326] Another, "He who seeks equity must do equity", has been confirmed recently as "a fundamental principle of equity".[327] A purchaser who gives the vendor to understand that there would be three entrances to a development and then proposes to cut them down to the one over the vendor's retained lands leaving those subject to much greater traffic does not do equity.[328] Thirdly, a plaintiff must come into court "with clean hands"[329] and, if he fails to do so, equitable relief sought by him normally will be refused.[330] The obligation to come to court with clean hands relates only to matters affecting the parties and not to dealings with third parties.[331] Failure to have clean hands may jeopardise a person's position in many other areas. For example, a decision of an owner of an equitable interest in property to stay silent about it when a mortgage is being effected with the intention of asserting it later when the mortgagee sought to realise his security would be conduct of which a court administering equity could not possibly approve and could leave that owner open to a charge of coming to court with hands which were not clean.[332] A husband who puts land into his wife's name to avoid a substantial stamp duty will not be allowed to take advantage of his own dishonesty and succeed in a claim that she holds in trust for him.[333]

HARDSHIP

[9.38] The court, it is well established, will not enforce the specific performance of a contract the result of which would be to impose great hardship on either of the parties to it.[334] Refusal of specific performance on this ground has been described as "quite unusual and exceptional".[335] In *Roberts v O'Neill*[336] McCarthy J said, having cited the salient circumstances:

> "In my judgment, they fall far short of establishing the type of case in which the court should intervene to deny the ordinary remedy to one of the contracting parties in what was, at the time, a perfectly fair and proper transaction. There may be cases in which the court should intervene or, to put it more crudely, interfere with the express wording of a contract, and in which the duty to do justice may override strictly legal principles and the well-recognised procedures of the courts of equity."

---

[324] See discussion of them in Ch 3 of Keane, *Equity & the Law of Trusts in the Republic of Ireland* (1988).
[325] Paras **9.42-7** *infra*.
[326] Snell's *Principles of Equity*, 27th Ed, p 35 approved by Henchy J in *Murphy v The Attorney* General [1982] IR 241 at 318.
[327] By Lynch J in *Minister for Education v North Star Ltd* (HC) Cir App, 1669/1986, 12 January 1987, at 6.
[328] *Ibid* at 4-6: specific performance refused.
[329] *White v McCooey* (HC) 26 April 1976, Gannon J, unrep at 3; *Starling Securities Ltd v Woods* (HC) 24 May 1977, McWilliam J, unrep at 5-7; *Ardent Fisheries Ltd v Minister for Tourism, Fisheries & Forestry* [1987] ILRM 528 at 533 (an injunction case).
[330] Keane, *op cit*, notes three exceptions at para 3.09.
[331] *Starling Securities'* case at 7; otherwise with illegality.
[332] *Ulster Bank Ltd v Shanks* [1982] NI 143 at 150.
[333] *Parkes v Parkes* [1980] ILRM 137 at 144-5.
[334] *Lavan v Walsh* [1964] IR 87 at 102 approved by McCarthy J in *Roberts v O'Neill* [1983] IR 47 at 55.
[335] By Budd J in *Lavan's* case at 105.
[336] [1983] IR 47 at 57.

Another point further cuts down the instances where this defence will succeed. Save in exceptional cases only a matter of hardship existing at the date of the contract may be taken into consideration as a possible defence.[337] If a deal is reasonable and fair as matters appear at the time and the plaintiff has acted with complete propriety throughout it would be very rare for the defence of hardship to succeed.[338] It has been said, however, that hardship is permitted to defeat specific performance where an existing hardship was not known at the relevant time, being the date of the contract.[339] To permit, as an ordinary rule, a defence of subsequent hardship would be to add a further hazard to the already trouble-strewn area of the law of contracts for the sale of land.[340] Changes of circumstances taking place later, making a contract less beneficial to one party, are immaterial as a rule unless brought about by the action of the other party.[341] The principle is very long established that "subsequent events will not vary a contract fairly entered into".[342] Analogy has been drawn with the principle that if something happens between contract and conveyance to enhance or reduce the value of the property that gain or loss is the purchaser's.[343] A modern point made is that hardship which might persuade the court not to decree specific performance should not ordinarily include cases of hardship resulting from inflation alone.[344]

There will be a rare exception to the rule against allowing subsequent hardship to defeat a claim for specific performance. If it happens by lapse of time and change of circumstances that it would be harsh and unjust to require exact compliance with a contract equity may refuse specific performance unless the party seeking it agrees to a "conscientious modification".[345] If both parties to a contract have behaved properly a purchaser usually will have to complete even though there may be some element of hardship to him in doing so.[346] The fact that a party, or even the court, may consider a contract to be hard or a poor bargain is not, of course, a good defence to an action for specific performance.[347] Neither is a later, better offer after an enforceable contract is made even though creditors might benefit or workers keep their jobs if the later offer could be accepted.[348]

[9.39] Hardship which would be suffered by third parties may be taken into account. The fact that a vendor would be leaving her brother with nowhere to live was taken into account in the exercise of the court's discretion to refuse an order specific performance

---

[337] *Lavan's* case at 103. The point was conceded in *Lavan's* case but Budd J agreed and McCarthy J approved in *Roberts'* case at 56. Cf *Nesbitt & Co Ltd v McClure* (HC) NI, Gibson J, unrep at 9-10. Budd J accepted *Costigan v Hastler* (1804) 2 Schoales & Lefroy 160 as an exception though it seems more a case of intending lessors failing to make title. Cf *City of London v Nash* (1747) 3 Atk 512, also admitted by Budd J as an exception; see consideration by Goulding J in *Patel v Ali* [1984] 1 All ER 978 at 981. Laches was a factor.

[338] *Nesbitt & Co's* case at 10.

[339] Per McCarthy J in *Roberts'* case at 56.

[340] *Ibid.*

[341] *Lavan's* case at 102.

[342] *Revell v Hussey* (1813) 2 Ball & Beatty 280 at 287.

[343] *Ibid.*

[344] *Roberts'* case at 56.

[345] *Davis v Hone* (1805) 2 Schoales & Lefroy 341 at 348. See discussion of this case in *Revell's* case at 286. Cf *Evans v Walsh* (1805) 2 Schoales & Lefroy 519. It would seem that *Davis's* case depended very much on its special circumstances.

[346] *Smith v Lynn* [1951] NI 69 at 78 (wrong *opinion* about condition of house).

[347] *McCrystal v O'Kane* [1986] NI 123 at 134; *Cork Corporation v Rooney* (1881) 7 LRI 191 at 200.

[348] *Nesbitt & Co Ltd v McClure* (HC) NI, Gibson J, unrep at 9-10.

of a contract having regard to the conduct of the parties and all the circumstances of a case.[349] However, if the important normal test of the hardship having to exist at the date of the contract is not satisfied, and no other special circumstances exist[350] the hardship of third parties such as additional losses of creditors if a later, higher offer cannot be accepted or the loss of their jobs by workers if a company cannot be sold as a going concern will not prevent an order for specific performance being made.[351] Concern by a party about the welfare of, *eg,* an elderly mother will be considered by the court although, of course, the court will also have to be satisfied of the genuineness of the case made and will consider to what extent the position would be different if the contract were implemented.[352]

[9.40] In deciding whether a plaintiff should be left to a claim for damages rather than obtain an order that the contract be specifically enforced the court must balance against the defendant's hardship the hardship which the plaintiff would suffer if the contract was not · specifically enforced.[353] In approaching this question of balance it must be remembered that when a plaintiff is refused specific performance on the ground of hardship he will be entitled to damages instead. A successful defence of hardship would defeat only the right to specific performance; it would not affect the validity of the contract. The normal rule as to damages for breach of contract would apply and the measure of damages would be the difference between the value of the property at the time the sale should have been completed and its value at the time of judgment.[354] The rule in *Bain v Fothergill*[355] has nothing whatever to do with damages on the refusal of specific performance on the ground of hardship.[356] Where the alleged hardship relates only to the value of the property or related matters the hardship to defendants would be much the same whether they complete the contract at the prices agreed to keep the property and pay the difference in damages.[357] In that case there is little or nothing to go into the balance.

In a modern English case, *Patel v Ali*[358] the defence of hardship succeeded where the circumstances of a defendant changed disastrously. At the date of the contract she had one child and appeared to be in good health. Delays occurred through neither side's fault. In the interval she had two more children[359] and lost her right leg. If she had to complete she would also lose the support of friends and neighbours. Goulding J explained:[360]

---

[349] *Conlon v Murray* [1958] NI 17 at 25-6.

[350] Such as the general conduct of the parties, as in *Conlon's* case.

[351] *Nesbitt & Co Ltd v McClure* (HC) NI, Gibson J, unrep at 10.

[352] *Lavan v Walsh* [1964] IR 87 at 102-5. *Cf Patel v Ali* [1984] 1 All ER 978 - delay of several years through neither side's fault, disabled young mother with three young children: see para **9.40** *infra.*

[353] *O'Neill v Ryan (No 3)* [1992] 1 IR 166 at 192.

[354] *Per* McWilliam J in *Roberts v O'Neill* [1983] IR 47 at 50. McCarthy J, giving the judgment of the Supreme Court, did not dissent from the trial judge's observations on the balancing of hardship but preferred to rest his judgment on other matters: p 57. *Cf O'Neill v Ryan (No 3)* [1992] 1 IR 166 at 192 (the property was shares).

[355] On the rule see Wylie, *Irish Conveyancing Law* (1978) paras 12.78-83.

[356] *Per* McWilliam J in *Roberts'* case at 50.

[357] *Ibid.* McWilliam J of course dealt with the facts before him. The defence was that due to the delay caused by the events in *Carthy v O'Neill* [1981] ILRM 443, a huge increase in prices of pubs and inability to buy viable premises with the original purchase price it would cause excessive hardship to the defendants to have to complete.

[358] [1984] 1 All ER 978.

[359] The children were taken into account only as part of her own hardship: see end or this para.

[360] At 982.

"The important and true principle, in my view, is that only in extraordinary and persuasive circumstances can hardship supply an excuse for resisting performance of a contract for the sale of immovable property. A person of full capacity who sells or buys a house takes the risk of hardship to himself and his dependants, whether arising from existing facts or unexpectedly supervening in the interval before completion. This is where, to my mind, great importance attaches to the immense delay in the present case, not attributable to the defendant's conduct.[361] Even after issue of the writ, she could not complete, if she had wanted to, without the concurrence of the absent Mr. Ahmed. Thus, in a sense, she can say she is being asked to do what she never bargained for, namely to complete the sale after more than four years, after all the unforeseeable changes that such a period entails. I think that in this way she can fairly assert that specific performance would inflict on her 'a hardship amounting to injustice' to use the phrase employed by James LJ[362] in a different but comparable context, in *Tamplin v James*[363]

...Equitable relief may, in my view, be refused because of an unforeseen change of circumstances not amounting to legal frustration, just as it may on the ground of mistake insufficient to avoid a contract at law."

Goulding J did not take into account the welfare of the children except as part of the defendant's own personal hardship. He doubted that the interests of the children were material in their own right but quoted an Australian case suggesting that the interests of third persons so connected with the defendant that he owed them some legal or moral obligation could be properly weighed for the purpose of determining the discretion of the court.[364] In general his decision would seem consistent with the Irish cases[365] including the point in an old Irish case that a court ought not give specific performance in accordance with the letter of a covenant if that were unconscientious against the defendant due to change of circumstances.[366]

[9.41] Hardship may operate with other factors to produce a refusal of specific performance. The creation of a hardship may render it unjust to decree specific performance and be a major factor in a decision to withhold specific performance because a contract is not equal and fair.[367] Hardship may be considered with the conduct of the parties and the circumstances of a case.[368] The cases where a defendant has escaped from an order for specific performance of a contract on the ground of a mistake[369] not contributed to by the plaintiff have been for the most part cases where a hardship amounting to injustice would have been inflicted upon him by holding him to his bargain and it was unreasonable to hold him to it.[370] Where a plaintiff has delayed for a substantial

---

[361] It was not attributable to the plaintiff either: p 982f.

[362] In a passage approved by Costello J in *O'Neill v Ryan (No 3)* [1992] 1 IR 166 at 192.

[363] (1880) 15 Ch D 215 at 221, [1874-80] All ER, 560 at 562.

[364] *Gall v Mitchell* (1924) 35 CLR 22, at 230.

[365] Irish courts might be readier to take into account personal hardship of young children, elderly parents and the like. The judgment of Budd J in *Lavan v Walsh* [1946] IR 87 at 102-5 suggests that he would have taken into account the welfare of the elderly mother if the defendant proved the facts to his satisfaction and got over the normal rule that only hardship existing at the date of the contract is considered. In *Conlon v Murray* [1958] NI 17 having to evict her brother was hardship on the defendant and a factor in the exercise of the discretion not to decree specific performance: p. 25-6.

[366] *Davis v Hone* (1805) 2 Schoales & Lefroy 341 at 348.

[367] *Smelter Corporation of Ireland Ltd v O'Driscoll* [1977] IR 305 at 311.

[368] *Conlon v Murray* [1978] NI 17 at 25-6.

[369] For the defence of mistake see paras **9.66-69** *infra*.

[370] *Per* James LJ in *Tamplin v James* (1880) 15 Ch D 215 at 221; [1874-80] All ER 560 at 562, approved by Costello J in *O'Neill v Ryan* (No 3) [1992] 1 IR 166 at 191-2.

time and has acted in a manner suggesting that he does not intend to insist on his contract the hardship which a defendant would suffer by having to perform the contract in the end can be a major factor in establishing the defence of laches,[371] a subject to which we now turn.

LACHES

[9.42] "Laches essentially consists of a substantial lapse of time coupled with the existence of circumstances which make it inequitable to enforce the claim."[372] What is a "substantial lapse of time" must depend on the circumstances of the particular case.[373] A person who sleeps on his rights does not find favour in a Court of Equity.[374] The language of old cases indicates that a plaintiff must show himself to be "ready, prompt and eager" to carry out this contract.[375] A modern expression of that view is that in a court of equity a person is bound to prosecute his claim with reasonable diligence and without undue delay.[376] There is no discrepancy; as long ago as 1808 it was said that "due diligence" was necessary to call a Court of Equity into activity; that court "always discountenances laches and neglect".[377] The expectation of "due diligence" leaves some flexibility. A plaintiff who "has not shown that degree of diligence which entitles him to favour from the court" may still be held to be entitled to specific performance "on the whole".[378] Mere assertion of a claim is not sufficient diligence[379] although making it clear to the intended defendant that he is going to sue will help a plaintiff to defeat a defence of laches, at least where the subsequent delay is of no great significance.[380]

[9.43] The Statute of Limitations, 1957 does not apply to claims for specific performance.[381] However, there is no bar on the court applying by analogy any provision of s 11 of the 1957 Statute in like manner as it formerly applied corresponding repealed enactments.[382] The courts do not in fact apply limitation periods by analogy in specific performance cases. They are likely to hold that the periods will not operate as bars to equitable relief if the lapse of time, since the right to such relief accrued, would not prevent equitable relief.[383] That leaves open the risk that plaintiffs lacking in diligence will become barred by laches in a much shorter time than the limitation periods which normally would apply to claims in contract.[384]

---

[371] *Guerin v Heffernan* [1925] 1 IR 57 at 66, 68; *Burke v Lynch* (1814) 2 Ball & Beatty 426 at 433. *Cf JH v WJH* (HC) 20 December 1979, Keane J, unrep at 33-38.

[372] Snell's *Principle of Equity*, 27th Ed, p 35 approved by Henchy J in *Murphy v The Attorney General* [1982] IR 241 at 318 (an income tax/constitutional case). The same sentence is at p 35 of the 29th Ed (1990). *Cf* consideration of delay in a CPO situation in *Van Nierop v Commissioners of Public Works in Ireland* [1990] 2 IR 189.

[373] *Per* Henchy J in *Murphy's* case at 318 and O'Connor J in *Guerin v Heffernan* [1925] 1 IR 57 at 68.

[374] *Guerin v Heffernan* [1925] 1 IR 57 at 68.

[375] *Haire-Foster v McIntee* (1889) 23 LRI 529 at 535.

[376] *McCausland v Young* [1949] NI 49 at 89.

[377] *Moore v Blake* (1808) 1 Ball & Beatty 62 at 69.

[378] *Burke v Smyth* (1846) 9 IR Eq R 135 at 138: six months delay after the defendant tried to insist on an untenable term.

[379] *McCausland's* case at 89.

[380] *Guardian Builders v Kelly* [1981] ILRM 127 at 133.

[381] Section 11(9)(*a*). See discussion by Brady & Kerr, *The Limitations of Actions*, 2nd Ed (1994) at 167-9; *JH v WJH*, (HC) 20 December 1979, Keane J, unrep at 33-4.

[382] Section 11(9)(*b*).

[383] *Bond v Hopkins* (1802) 1 Schoales & Lefroy 413 at 434.

[384] On which see Brady & Kerr, *op cit* at 42-4.

[9.44] If delay is extreme the mere fact of a person being left in undisturbed and undisputed possession for many years dealing with a property as if free from any obligation may be enough to make out the defence of laches.[385] Thus, where a right accrued in 1853 to performance of a covenant for *toties quoties* renewal, little was done until 1875 when the claim was queried in a letter, no reply was sent to that letter and nothing at all was done until issuing a writ in 1897 the court concluded "If laches can, under any circumstances, defeat such a claim, I think it must do so here."[386] A clear repudiation of the contract by the person against whom the plaintiff wishes to enforce it seems to be a factor making the defence of laches more likely to succeed if the claimant does not move diligently.[387] This may apply, depending on the circumstances, even where the repudiating party has been taking the benefit of the alleged agreement.[388] If a court can conclude that the plaintiff had acquiesced in a repudiation even a shortish period of seven months is likely to be fatal.[389] An attempt by a party to insist on an unjustifiable term going into a lease may make it more important for the other party to proceed diligently.[390] If *both* sides are guilty of delay this will be taken into account in considering a plea of laches and may defeat it.[391] A court might feel that neither party deserved much sympathy as nothing had been done for so long.[392] Actions by both sides indicating that they believe the whole deal to be at an end will increase the chances of a finding of laches if either tries to enforce the contract later.[393] So will delay by a plaintiff coupled with acts which are only consistent with his acquiescence in a repudiation and his election to treat the contract as an end.[394] Acts or omissions by a party to suit his own interests in preference to performing his obligations may also increase the chances of a finding of laches.[395]

[9.45] The second vital ingredient in laches is that circumstances must exist which would make it inequitable to enforce the claim. It has long been accepted that where a party has slept upon his rights and thereby created difficulty and imposed hardship on another it would be an injustice to permit him to derive benefit from them.[396] Courts of equity ought to refuse specific performance where the delay would be very injurious to the party sought to be charged.[397] A court dealing with a plea of laches may expect evidence from which it could be asked to infer that the plaintiff intended to abandon his claim and that there was injurious effect on the defendant's position.[398] It will wish to ascertain whether the defendant has been placed in a worse position by reason of the delay which has taken place.[399] Delay will thus be fatal if it is evidence of an agreement by the plaintiff to

---

[385] *Coey v Pascoe* [1899] 1 IR 125 at 141.
[386] *Coey's* case at 141.
[387] *Connor v McCarthy* (1877) 12 ILTSJ 336 - 11-year delay after repudiation. *Cf Brophy v Connolly* (1857) 7 IR Ch R 173.
[388] *Haire-Foster v McIntee* (1889) 23 LRI 528 at 535.
[389] *Lydon v Lydon* (1874) 8 ILTR 85 at 87 *per* Lawson LC: Christian LJ rested his judgment on the simple, narrow point that seven months was too long: *ibid*.
[390] *Burke v Smyth* (1846) 9 Ir Eq R 135 - the plaintiff entitled to succeed "on the whole": p 138.
[391] *Gibson v Butler* (1964) 99 ILTR 116 at 117; *Macfarlane v Dunne* (1889) 24 ILTR 17 at 20.
[392] *Gibson's* case at 117. There was no evidence that either side had been prejudiced by the delay.
[393] *Guerin v Heffernan* [1925] 1 IR 57 at 66, 68-9.
[394] *Guerin's* case at 68.
[395] *Lark Developments Ltd v Dublin Corporation* (HC) 10 February 1993, Murphy J, unrep at 13-15: developer purchaser scaling down his building programme due to downturn in market.
[396] *Burke v Lynch* (1814) 2 Ball & Beatty 426 at 433.
[397] *Per* Lord Redesdale in *Crofton v Ormsby* (1806) 2 Schoales & Lefroy 583 at 604.
[398] *White v McCooey* (HC) 26 April 1976, Gannon J, unrep at 33.
[399] *Macfarlane v Dunne* (1889) 24 ILTR 17 at 19.

abandon or release his right or if the plaintiff has so acted as to induce the defendant to alter his position in the reasonable belief that the claim has been released or abandoned.[400] Likewise if the delay has resulted in the destruction or loss of evidence by which the claim might have been rebutted.[401] The court must therefore consider the circumstances in which the defendant will find himself if the claim is allowed despite the period of delay as contrasted with the circumstances in which he would have found himself if the plaintiff had proceeded with proper diligence.[402] A person who has worked a farm to the best of his ability and, in effect, invested ten years of his life's work in it has altered his position in a very real sense in the reasonable belief that the other party was not making a claim.[403] So has a defendant who releases a third party from a purchase of part of the defendant's own property acting under the belief that the plaintiff's claim against him has been abandoned.[404]

A rise in price or value may be accepted by the courts as a factor making it inequitable in cases of delay that specific performance should be ordered.[405] This is not inconsistent with the unwillingness of the courts to accept the results of inflation alone as enough to establish a defence of hardship.[406] The point which removes inconsistency is that the party in delay in a case of laches has been the sole or main cause of the problem. The conduct of both parties is relevant and if *both* have acted in a manner suggesting that they considered the whole transaction to be at an end it is likely to be inequitable to hold that the contract is a living one which either must perform.[407]

[9.46] Delay after proceedings have been instituted is less likely in practice to damage a plaintiff's case. A plea of laches may fail where proceedings have been in place for many years. In one case[408] a very long delay of 40 years failed to sustain the plea, the court taking into account questions of fraud and the fact that the defendant could have applied to dismiss the bill. However, it would be gravely mistaken to assume that the running of time and the effects of laches can be frozen by just issuing proceedings or that any such proceedings may be prosecuted at a leisurely pace. For one thing delay in bringing a case to trial attracts a risk of being refused specific performance and having to make do with an award of damages.[409] Of course, even when there is no evidence from which the court could be asked to infer that the plaintiff intended to abandon his claim and no evidence either of any injurious effect on the defendant's position from such delay as has occurred the court retains its jurisdiction to award damages in lieu of specific

---

[400] *JH v WJH* (HC) 20 December 1979, Keane J, unrep at 34 approving a passage from Snell which included the sentence approved by Henchy J in *Murphy's* case: see fn 75 *supra* .

[401] And see *Reimers v Druce* (1857) 23 Beav 145.

[402] *JH's* case at 35.

[403] *JH's* case at 37-8.

[404] *Guerin v Heffernan* [1925] 1 IR 57 at 66, 69.

[405] *JH's* case at 36. Note also the case of *Mr. Sparrow*, unrep, referred to by Lord Redesdale in *Crofton v Ormsby* (1806) 2 Schoales and Lefroy 583 at 603-4.

[406] *Roberts v O'Neill* [1983] IR 47 at 56: see para **9.38** *infra*.

[407] *Guerin v Heffernan* [1925] 1 IR 57 at 66, 68-9.

[408] *Giffard v Hort* (1804) 1 Schoales & Lefroy 386 at 405-7.

[409] *Murphy v Harrington* [1927] IR 339 at 345. Meredith J took into account a delay of three years (it is not clear how much was after proceedings brought) and the fact that both parties had "accommodated themselves to the position arising under the broken contract".

[410] As in *White v McCooey* (HC) 26 April 1986, Gannon J, unrep at 33-35. See paras **1.28** and **1.30-31** *ante* on the jurisdiction. *Cf Murphy's* case at 345.

performance.[410] If delays are substantial after proceedings are begun a court might conclude that laches are equally as strong against a plaintiff in not prosecuting a suit as in not commencing it.[411] Even after an order for specific performance has been made questions of laches may arise. Enforcement of the decree after a long lapse of time will be refused when there is insufficient explanation for the delay *and* the other party has suffered detriment as a result of it.[412] Those issues will depend on the whole facts of the particular case.[413]

[9.47] A plea of laches will not often succeed against an intending purchaser or lessee who has substantially completed the transaction, got possession and remains in possession.[414] Once he has reached that stage he usually is not acquiescing in anything to his detriment if delays occur in finalising the transaction.[415] It would be very strange if in this situation his behaviour gave the other party reason to believe that he was abandoning his rights under the contract.[416] This is all the more so if any delays are explained.[417] The type of laches which consists of the party in possession not clothing his equitable estate with a legal title will not prevail against the equitable title.[418] Apparently in the times of Lord Redesdale it was not unusual for parties to continue to hold property in this country under an equitable contract for 40 or 50 years without clothing it with the legal title.[419] However, the defence of laches may still succeed in certain cases. If a tenant is in possession and fails or refuses to execute a lease despite being called on to do so by the landlord he may become bound by laches.[420] A tenant already in possession under a periodic tenancy but whose landlord repudiates an alleged agreement for a 21-year lease must beware of the defence of laches.[421] The position is very different from "a clear case of enjoyment of the tenancy under the alleged agreement for a lease".[422] If the title which the party in possession asserts is disputed and he does nothing to enforce it for a long time this may be a clear case of laches.[423] A tenant in possession who agrees on a form of sale and leaseback but is *dispossessed*, then brings proceedings for specific performance after a decree in ejectment against him but before its execution, receives a defence denying his claim and then delays for 19 years "unaccounted for" has been bound by laches.[424]

---

[411] *Moore v Blake* (1808) 1 Ball & Beatty 62 at 69.
[412] *Easton v Browne* [1981] 3 All ER 278 at 283.
[413] *Ibid.* Cf discussion in *Bond v Hopkins* (1802) 1 Schoales & Lefroy 413 at 434-41 - earlier litigation and considerable delays.
[414] *Horgan v Deasy* [1979] ILRM 71 at 74; *Cartan v Bury* (1860) 10 IR Ch R 387 at 395-6; *Clarke v Moore* (1844) 7 IR Eq R 515 at 517; *Crofton v Ormsby* (1806) 2 Schoales & Lefroy 583 at 603-4. *Cf Barclay's Bank v Breen* (1956) 96 ILTR 179 at 182.
[415] *Horgan v Deasy* [1979] ILRM 71 at 74.
[416] But see examples given later in this para.
[417] *Horgan's* case at 74, noting that in *Wroth v Tyler* [1973] 2 WLR 405 Megarry J had referred to "unexplained delay" at 423.
[418] *Crofton v Ormsby* (1806) 2 Schoales & Lefroy 583 at 603
[419] *Ibid.* One would not recommend this as good practice!
[420] *Cartan v Bury* (1860) 10 IR Ch R 387 at 396.
[421] *Connor v McCarthy* 12 ILTSJ 336.
[422] *Per* Ball C, *ibid.*
[423] *Coey v Pascoe* [1899] 1 IR 125 at 140-1 - covenant for *toties quoties* renewal where the party in possession did nothing for 22 years since getting a letter querying his claim.
[424] *Moore v Blake* (1808) 1 Ball & Beatty 62 at 69, 71-2 (facts set out at 67) - laches as strong against plaintiff in not prosecuting, as in not commencing, his suit.

ILLEGALITY

[9.48] *Ex turpi causa non oritur actio* is an old and well-known legal maxim. No court ought to enforce an illegal contract or allow itself to be made the instrument of enforcing obligations alleged to arise out of a contract or transaction which is illegal.[425] It is an established principle that the court will not lend its aid in order to enforce a contract entered into with a view to carrying into effect anything which is prohibited by law.[426] In modern specific performance cases a type of illegality which seems to arise fairly often is attempted fraud on the revenue. The courts are not entitled to countenance such attempted frauds by enforcing the contracts at the instance of either party.[427] Typically parties might represent the purchase price as being less than the true price [428]as that might "save" some stamp duty for the purchaser and some capital gains tax for the vendor.[429] The fact that an illegal stamp duty saving would be insignificant may be considered in assessing the evidence to decide whether in fact there was any fraud on the revenue[430] but that is very different from any notion that the courts might allow parties to get away with a fraud as long as it was small. If a contract itself is proper when it is made but the parties are later tempted to try to complete it in such a way as to save stamp duty in an unlawful manner the contract itself will not be tainted by any illegality in the suggested method of completion.[431] There is a vital difference between a contract deliberately arranged for the purpose of defrauding the revenue and an ordinary one made without contemplating any such fraud.[432] If a deal is *completed* with a stamp duty fraud having been committed the whole transaction is tainted with illegality and a party to that fraud need not expect the court to apply its equitable principles in his favour later.[433]

Another type of illegality which sometimes arises in specific performance cases is an attempt to dispose of an intoxicating liquor licence *as such*. It is well established that there can be no property in a licence separate from the building to which it attaches[434] and in this area also it has been stated firmly that it is the duty of the court not to assist in a violation of the law.[435] The licence *per se* is inalienable and on that ground specific performance of an agreement for the *sale* of a licence cannot be enforced by the courts[436] though an agreement by the holder of a licence for its *extinguishment* is likely to be enforceable.[437] Further examples in the case law of possible illegality include alleged

---

[425] *Scott v Brown, Doering, McNab & Co* [1892] 2 QB 724; [1891-4] All ER 654 approved by Andrews J in *Furnivall v O'Neill* [1902] 2 IR 422 at 430 and O'Daly J in *McIlvenna v Ferris* [1955] IR 318 at 322.

[426] *Per* Le Blanc J in *Langton v Hughes* 1 M & S 593 at 597 approved by Murnaghan J in *Gavin Low Ltd v Field* [1942] IR 86 at 95. *Cf* O'Byrne J at 104-5 and Dixon J in *Fibretex v Beleir Ltd* (1949) 89 ILTR 141 at 143.

[427] *Starling Securities Ltd v Woods* (HC) 24 May 1977, McWilliam J, unrep at 6. *Cf Hayden v Sean Quinn Properties Ltd* (HC) 6 December 1993, Barron J, unrep at 13-14 (part of salary ascribed to expenses which, at best, were minimal).

[428] As in the *Starling Securities* case. *Cf Black v Grealy* (HC) 10 November 1977, Costello J, unrep at 7-8, 11-12; *Cork Shoe Co Ltd v Woods* (HC) 15 November 1971, Kenny J, unrep at 3.

[429] The purchaser might well be stuck with the lower, untrue price as the base for his own future CGT liability.

[430] *Black's case* at 12.

[431] *Guerin v Ryan* (HC) 28 May 1978, McWilliam J, unrep at 5-6. That does not mean that the courts would enforce a method of completion which involved an illegal "saving" of stamp duty.

[432] *Guerin's* case at 5-6 comparing it with *Starling Securities*.

[433] *Parkes v Parkes* [1980] ILRM 137 at 144-5.

[434] See para **5.09** *ante*.

[435] *Per* O'Brien LC in *James J Murphy & Co Ltd v Crean* [1915] 1 IR 111 at 140.

[436] *Macklin v Graecen & Co Ltd* [1983] IR 61 at 65-6.

[437] *Macklin's* case at 66.

breaches of land law statutes[438] and dispositions by tenants without necessary consents of their landlords.[439] Another example which occasionally needs consideration in specific performance cases is the involvement of a "puffer" after the reserve price at an auction has been reached.[440]

[9.49] The fact that a party does not realise that a clause in his contract breaks the law usually will not help him.[441] However, the parties' degrees of knowledge of and involvement in the illegal elements in cases may affect outcomes in certain ways. If the parties are not *in pari delicto* the courts may assist the one who is innocent or less at fault, especially if failure to do so would let the other keep a benefit of fraud or illegality. Thus a plaintiff who does not know of the facts which constitute the illegality may be able to enforce the contract if it is not expressly forbidden by statute.[442] A defendant purchaser who is not *particeps criminis* may get the assistance of the court by an order for the return of purchase money paid.[443] A party who enters into an illegal contract due to fraud, duress or undue influence on the part of the other is also likely to be allowed to recover his money paid.[444] In England a person who, acting without advice, unwittingly broke exchange control law in paying money under a "pretty swindle" worked against her was entitled to recover that money in an action for fraud.[445] And a money-lender induced by fraud to give a loan was allowed to recover the money even though the loan contravened the Moneylenders Act 1900 and was illegal.[446] English case law also indicates that where a party to an illegal executory contract repents before performance he may recover what he has transferred to the other party if he takes proceedings before the illegal purpose has been substantially performed.[447]

[9.50] A contract legal in itself but connected with an unlawful act or purpose in such a way that there is a unity of design and purpose between the two so that they may be regarded as one entire unlawful scheme will not be enforced by the courts.[448] The position is similar if there are two contracts and one is tainted by illegality but the other is innocent in itself. In that situation the innocent contract will not be enforced when the two contracts are connected by the facts of a case. Thus, forbearance to sue on a deed

---

[438] *Horgan v Deasy* [1979] ILRM 71; *The State (Callaghan) v Irish Land Commission* [1978] ILRM 201; *Tiernan v Feely* [1949] IR 381; *Dempsey v O'Reilly* [1958] IJR 75; *O'Kane v Burns* [1897] 2 IR 592; *Guy v O'Hagan* (1904) 5 NIJR 172; *Fogarty v Shanahan* [1896] 2 IR 273; *Canavan v Burton* [1900] 2 IR 359; *Murtagh v Allen* (1890) 27 LRI 118. Note detailed discussion of the need for Land Commission consent by Budd J in *McGillycuddy v Joy* [1959] IR 189 at 206-9. *Cf Kelly v Enright* (1883) 11 LRI 379; *Beauclerk v Hanna* (1888) 23 LRI 144; *Re Wakeham's Estate* [1924] 1 IR 53. See paras **3.20, 3.22** *ante* on conditions about Land Commission consent.

[439] *O'Toole v Lyons* [1948] IR 115. *Cf Fisher v Coan* [1894] 1 IR 179 Note that the statutory prohibitions in Deasy's Act on assignment and subletting in breach of covenant were repealed by s 35 of the Landlord and Tenant (Ground Rents) Act 1967. On landlord's consent see also para **3.23** *ante*.

[440] *Airlie v Fallon* [1976/7] ILRM 1 at 12. See para **3.45** *ante*.

[441] *Jackson v Stopford* [1923] 2 IR 1 at .11.

[442] *Marrinan v O'Haran* (HC) 17 June 1971, Pringle J, unrep at 4, 15. *Cf Wall v New Ireland Assurance Co Ltd* [1965] IR 386 at 405-6.

[443] *Guy v O'Hagan* (1904) 5 NIJR 172 at 176, 178.

[444] *Sumner v Sumner* (1935) 69 ILTR 101.

[445] *Shelley v Paddock* [1980] 1 All ER 1009, CA, Brandon LJ dubitante.

[446] *Dott v Brickwell* (1906) 23 TLR 61. *Cf* generally in relation to moneylending *Cripps Warburg Ltd v Cologne Investment Co Ltd* [1980] IR 455 at 475, 477-8; *Handelman v Davies* (1937) 71 ILTR 268.

[447] See discussion in Cheshire, Fifoot & Furmston's, *Law of Contract*, 11th Ed (1986) at 367-8. *Cf* Clark, *Contract Law in Ireland*, 3rd Ed (1992) at 319.

[448] *Gavin Low Ltd v Field* [1942] IR 86 at 94.

which the person forbearing knows is illegal cannot constitute consideration to support a separate promise to pay a balance due on that deed.[449] Money lent by a person who knows that it is to be used by the borrower for illegal gaming cannot be recovered even if it is not proved that it was used for that purpose.[450] A guarantee of the rent payable under a letting for an illegal purpose is itself unenforceable.[451] An option to buy the landlord's interest contained in a lease void for infringing a Land Act cannot be severed from the void lease and enforced separately.[452] A bond taken as a new security for a debt covered by a bankruptcy and a later discharge therefrom cannot be enforced where the consideration for the bond was an agreement by the plaintiff to discontinue proceedings to set aside the discharge on the ground that it was obtained by fraud.[453] And a publican who cannot sue for the price of drink supplied on credit cannot enforce a security given for payment of that money.[454] Estoppel will not assist a person trying to enforce a contract which is in breach of a statute.[455] Nor can the courts allow something to be done indirectly which would be in breach of the law if done directly.[456] It is possible that a contract partly legal and partly illegal, if the illegal part is not *malum in se* and rests in understanding only, may be specifically performed so far as legally capable of execution.[457] It is possible too, but likely to depend on the precise wording of the legislation, that a contract can be enforced with the exclusion of an illegal part of the consideration.[458] It may depend on whether the relevant Act, like the Statute of Frauds or the Statute of Limitations, bars a remedy without making the transaction void or is a prohibitory Act creating a crime or making the deal void.[459] A legal contract is not made unenforceable by a suggested method of completing it which does or may involve illegality[460] but, of course, this does not mean that the courts would enforce an illegal method of completion. The fact that a contract may be illegal under the law of another jurisdiction does not make it unenforceable here.[461]

[9.51] The manner in which it is intended at the time of forming a contract to carry it out has an important bearing on its legality. That may be distinguished from a situation in which an illegal method of carrying out a perfectly legal contract may be considered at a later stage.[462] A contract which, on the apparent intention of the parties at the time of its

---

[449] *Furnivall v O'Neill* [1902] 2 IR 422 at 430.

[450] *Anthony v Shea* (1951) 86 ILTR 29 at 30. *Cf Duff v The Racing Board*, (HC) Cir App, Pringle J, 19 November 1971, Pringle J, unrep at 3-5.

[451] *Devine v Scott* (1931) 66 ILTR 107.

[452] *Tiernan v Feely* [1949] IR 381 at 383.

[453] *Daly v Daly* (1871) IR 5 CL 108 at 114-5.

[454] *Sheehy v Sheehy* [1901] 1 IR 239 at 244, 247 - breach of the Tippling Acts. Apportionment was possible on the facts.

[455] *Dempsey v O'Reilly* [1958] IJR 75 at 77; *O'Kane v Burns* [1897] 2 IR 591. *Cf O'Dea & Co Ltd v Minister for Posts & Telegraphs* [1952] IJR 7.

[456] *O'Kane's* case at 594-7; *Namlooze Venootschap de Faam v The Dorset Manufacturing Co Ltd* [1949] IR 203 at 207 - contract not void but payment restricted by exchange control. *Cf Fibretex v Beleir Ltd* (1949) 89 ILTR 141; *Guy v O'Hagan* (1904) 5 NIJR 172.

[457] *Carolan v Brabazon* (1846) 9 IR Eq Rep at 231-2. The parties had completed their deal so the court did not have to decide the point.

[458] *Sheehy v Sheehy* [1901] 1 IR 238 at 243. But *cf* Palles CB in *Rourke v Mealy* (1879) 4 LRI 166 at 171-2.

[459] *Sheehy's* case at 243, *per* FitzGibbon LJ; *cf* Walker LJ at 245 and Holmes LJ at 246-7.

[460] *Guerin v Ryan*, (HC) 28 April 1978 McWilliam J, unrep at 5-6.

[461] *Stanhope v Hospitals Trust Ltd (No 2)* [1936] IJR 25. A similar point arises on public policy: *Fraser v Buckle* [1994] 1 IR 1 at 22-3.

[462] As in *Guerin's* case. See paras **9.48** and **9.50** *supra*.

formation, could be and would be carried out in a legal fashion is enforceable by the innocent party even though the other in reality intended to carry it out in an illegal fashion.[463] On the other hand, if the acknowledged and accepted intention of both parties at the time of the formation of the contract is that it would be carried out in an illegal manner, the contract is unenforceable and contrary to public policy and cannot be upheld by the court.[464] The date for determining the legality of a contract is the day it is made.[465] Its legality, cannot depend on matters subsequent although performance of a contract is occasionally made impossible by a change in the law or a change in the operation of the law by new facts supervening.[466] The legality of a contract and its enforceability in an action for specific performance are very different things[467] so the fact that a contract is legal does not necessarily mean that it will be enforceable by specific performance even if it is in an area where the remedy is available.[468]

[9.52] Once an illegal contract has been completed and the property comprised in it transferred that transfer is effective and remains so.[469] The transferor, having achieved his unworthy end, cannot be allowed to turn around and repudiate the means by which he did it.[470] The transferee, having obtained the property, can assert his title to it against all the world, not because he has any merit of his own but because there is no one who can assert a better title to it - the court does not confiscate the property because of the illegality.[471] A trustee seeking to acquire property in breach of trust will not get specific performance because the courts of equity will not give relief to a trustee acting in breach of trust[472] Likewise specific performance will not be granted to enforce an agreement for lease which would be a fraud on a power.[473] However, if the trustee manages to complete his deal his wrongful act does not make the transaction void; if he converts trust property into some other form the property into which it has been converted becomes subject to the trust.[474] And if the landlord simply has insufficient title to grant all that he agreed to give, there being no fraud, the court may order him to grant what he can give and pay compensation for any difference in value.[475] A landlord who has actually granted an illegal lease or tenancy will not get the assistance of the courts to enforce his rights under it. Rent cannot be recovered.[476] However, a landlord who has granted an illegal tenancy agreement is not prevented by that illegality from recovering possession in a claim based

[463] *Whitecross Potatoes (International) Ltd v Coyle* [1978] ILRM 31 at 33.
[464] The *Whitecross Potatoes* case at 33-4.
[465] *O'Regan v White* [1919] 2 IR 339 at 386; *McGillycuddy v Joy* [1959] IR 189 at 207.
[466] *Per* Costello J, dissenting, in *Hamilton v Hamilton* [1982] IR 466 at 502 approving a passage from the 23rd Ed of Anson's *Law of Contract* at 463.
[467] *O'Regan's* case at 387.
[468] On which see paras **1.14-27** *ante*.
[469] *Hortensius Ltd v Bishop* [1989] ILRM 294 at 302-3.
[470] *Belvoir Finance Co v Stapleton* [1971] 1 QB 210 at 219 approved by Costello J in the *Hortensius Ltd* case at 302.
[471] *Ibid. Cf Carolan v Brabazon* (1846) 9 IR Eq R 224 at 231-2.
[472] The *Hortensius Ltd* case at 301.
[473] *Ellard v Lord Llandaff* (1810) 1 Ball & Beatty 241 at 251; *Lawrenson v Butler* (1802) 1 Schoales & Lefroy 13 at 19-20; *Cruise* (1845) 8 IR Eq R 407 at 429-31.
[474] The *Hortensius Ltd* case at 301.
[475] *Leslie v Crommelin* (1867) IR 2 Eq 134 at 139-41.
[476] *Gray v Cathcart* (1898) 33 ILTR 35 (house condemned as insanitary); *Devine v Scott* (1931) 66 ILTR 107 at 108 (letting for illegal bookmaking - claim against guarantor also failed).

on his title.[477] The critical point here is that the landlord did not have to found his claim on the illegal contract or plead or depend on it in support of his claim.[478]

[9.53] The defence of illegality *should* be pleaded[479] like all other defences but, *unlike* most defences, once evidence of illegality has been properly introduced in respect of an issue in the case, the court cannot ignore it.[480] It makes no difference that the defendant does not plead illegality.[481] This is so even if the defendant does not wish the point of illegality to be taken by the court.[482] Parties may not call on the courts, even by agreement, to assist them to carry out an illegal transaction between themselves.[483] The onus of proving the illegality is on the person relying on it.[484]

Public policy

[9.54] Illegality is a very wide subject[485] and may often be closely linked with considerations of public policy. The courts have regard to public policy in deciding whether to grant the remedy of specific performance. They will not make an order which would have the effect, even indirectly, of compelling a person to do something which is prohibited by law for the time being as it would be improper and contrary to public policy to do so.[486] The fact that an arrangement would be a fraud upon the public taints a transaction with impropriety and specific performance will be refused.[487] Considerations of public policy may also affect the exercise of the discretion to grant the relief where the transaction is not prohibited by law. Specific performance of an agreement to surrender premises controlled by the Rent Restrictions Act 1946 was refused, having considered the policy of the Act, where the tenant's rights were not discussed at the time the agreement was signed.[488] Public policy is a major element in the presumption of undue influence in certain cases from the existence of a particular relationship.[489] Also on grounds of public policy a promise by a person to procure a sale by a sheriff otherwise than in accordance with his public duty cannot be enforced.[490] And agreements aimed at "stifling" a prosecution or inducing a person not to give evidence in a criminal or even a civil suit are illegal as being against public policy.[491] A bond as new security for a debt

---

[477] *Amar Singh v Kulubya* [1964] AC 142; [1963] 3 All ER 499 at 503.
[478] *Ibid* at 505 (All ER).
[479] *Starling Securities Ltd v Woods*, (HC) 24 May 1977 McWilliam J, unrep at 6.
[480] *Ibid.*
[481] *McIlvenna v Ferris* [1955] IR 318 at 322; *Conway v Smith* [1950] IJR 3 at 5; *Duff v The Racing Board*, (HC) Cir App 19 November 1971 Pringle J, unrep at 3.
[482] *Gedge v Royal Exchange Assurance Corporation* [1900] 2 QB 214 at 221;[1900-03] All ER 179 at 182 approved by O'Daly J in *McIlvenna's case* at 322. *Cf Marrinan v O'Haran*, (HC) 17 June 1971 Pringle J, unrep at 14.
[483] *Stanhope v Irish Hospitals Trust Ltd (No. 2)* 25 at 28.
[484] *Whitecross Potatoes (International) Ltd v Coyle* [1978] ILRM 31 at 32.
[485] Considered very fully by Clarke, *Contract Law in Ireland*, 3rd Ed (1992) in Ch 14.
[486] *Namlooze Venootschap de Faam v The Dorset Manufacturing Co Ltd* [1949] IR 203 at 207 - contract not void but payment restricted by exchange control. *Cf Fibretex v Beleir Ltd* (1949) 89 ILTR 141; *Westpac Banking Corporation v Dempsey* [1993] 3 IR 331. Note the discussion of public policy by Costello J in *Fraser v Buckle* [1994] 1 IR 1 at 19-21. The fact that agreements are contrary to public policy elsewhere does not thereby make them unenforceable in Ireland: *Fraser's* case at 22-3. The same applies to illegality: *Stanhope v Hospitals Trust Ltd (No 2)* [1936] IJR 25.
[487] *Guy v O'Hagan* (1904) 5 NIJR 172 at 175-6 - sham tenancy.
[488] *Traynor v Duffy* [1947] IJR 9 at 11.
[489] *O'Flanagan v Ray-Ger Ltd*, (HC) 28 April 1983 Costello J, unrep at 18-19; *O'Neill v Murphy* [1936] NI 16 at 36: *Provincial Bank of Ireland v McKeever* [1941] IR 471 at 485, 494. And see para **9.30** *ante*.
[490] *Moher v O'Grady* (1879) 4 LRI 54 at 57-8.
[491] Discussed by Palles CB in *Rourke v Mealy* (1879) 4 LRI 166 at 171-6.

covered by a bankruptcy and the discharge therefrom was not enforced where the consideration for the bond was an agreement by the plaintiff to discontinue proceedings to set aside the discharge on the ground that it was obtained by fraud.[492] The validity of the adjudication of discharge was not merely a question between the insolvent and the plaintiff. The plaintiff could not be allowed, consistently with public policy, to use such a proceeding as a means of procuring a money security for himself.[493] At common law the enforcement of certain contracts was regarded as being against public policy and such contracts were term "illegal". Illegal contracts included those which tend to injure the public service, pervert the course of justice, abuse the legal process, are contrary to good morals, restrain trade or cannot be performed without a breach of the criminal law.[494]

[9.55] To consider the effect of a statute on a contract distinctions may need to be made. As Costello J explained:[495]

> "Some statutes may expressly declare certain types of contract to be void and unenforceable (without declaring them to be illegal) as does s 18 of the Gaming Act 1845 which provides that all agreements by way of wagering shall be null and void and which prohibits any action brought to recover a sum alleged to have been won on a wager. Others may prohibit the making of certain contracts and impose penalties for doing so but remain silent as to the civil rights of the parties to them; it is then a question of the construction of the statute as to whether the contract between the parties is to be regarded as an illegal one."

In certain other cases the contract remains valid but some step to be taken under it is prohibited by statute, perhaps the vital act of paying the agreed price.[496] We have considered earlier the words "no action shall be brought" in s 2 of the Statute of Frauds and the word "void" in s 3(1) of the Family Home Protection Act 1976.[497] In the former case the contract remains valid though it may not be *enforced by action;* in the latter the better view is that the contract is *void*, not just *voidable*. In neither case is the affected contract *illegal*.

IMPOSSIBILITY

[9.56] It is a clear rule of equity that the court will not make a decree to compel a party to do that which he cannot.[498] It is equally clear that a party may not make something impossible for himself and then attempt to rely on that principle.[499] How can a purchaser who refuses to perform a duty resting on him rely on his own neglect or perverseness to come within that rule of equity?[500] Allowing that kind of conduct would be inconsistent

---

[492] *Daly v Daly* (1871) IR 5 CL 108 at 114-5.
[493] *Ibid.*
[494] *Hortensius Ltd v Bishop* [1989] ILRM 294 at 300-1.
[495] *Hortensius Ltd v Bishop* [1989] ILRM 294 at 301.
[496] Eg, under exchange control: *Fibretex Ltd v Beleir Ltd* (1949) 89 ILTR 141; *Westpac Banking Corporation v Dempsey* [1993] 3 IR 331; *Namlooze Venootsachap de Faam v Dorset Manufacturing Co Ltd* [1949] IR 203.
[497] Para **5.04** and **7.18** *ante* respectively.
[498] *Sheppard v Murphy* (1868) IR 2 Eq 544 at 557. cf *Neville & Sons Ltd v Guardian Builders Ltd* [1990] ILRM 601 at 616; *McConnell v Kilgallen* (1878) 2 LRI 119.
[499] *Sheppard's* case at 557-8; *Arterial Drainage Company v Rathangan Drainage Board* (1880) 6 LRI 513 at 525-7.
[500] *Sheppard's* case at 558.

with the willingness of the courts to find implied terms that parties to contracts will not disable themselves from carrying out the contracts or prevent the other parties from doing so and that each party may expect the other to be reasonable in taking steps incidental to closing a sale.[501]

[9.57] It appears to be impossible to confer (or "impose") jurisdiction on a court or office holder to decide cases when the relevant statute law does not give such jurisdiction.[502] It is also impossible to make provisions in relation to an intoxicating liquor licence which contravene the legal principle tying it to the relevant premises. Thus, apportionment of the purchase price of licensed premises after their sale into part of the price to be attributed to the premises and the remainder to be related to the licence was legally and factually impossible where all persons involved had agreed on the property being sold with the licence as a going concern.[503] Since a licence must be attached to the relevant premises it is impossible to sell it as a separate entity.[504] Title problems[505] may give rise to impossibility. Thus it is impossible to complete a disposition when it depends on steps to be taken by trustees and the latter are entitled to refuse to take those steps.[506] A purchaser whose vendor cannot make title because someone else who contracted to sell to that vendor can show that that contract is a nullity has no right to specific performance.[507] The remedy cannot be ordered against a person who has already disposed of the title necessary to enable him to fulfil his contract or other obligation.[508] Likewise a prior order of specific performance will prevent a court ordering specific performance of a second contract relating to the same land.[509] And where specific performance is sought against two different defendants - *eg*, a mortgagor and a mortgagee both of whom are claimed to have made enforceable contracts - an order for specific performance cannot be made against both at the same time.[510]

[9.58] Supervening events after the date of a contract or even subsequent to the commencement of an action for specific performance may result in impossibility. Thus a change in the law after the date of a contract or a change in the operation of the law by new facts supervening may make it legally impossible to perform a contract and in such a case specific performance must be refused.[511] A "provisional list" under the Land Acts made it impossible to get a valid transfer of land agreed to be sold before the publication of the list unless the consent of the Land Commission was given.[512] An order for the sale of land at the suit of a mortgagee after the commencement of an action for specific

---

[501] On such implied terms see paras **3.26-7** *ante*.

[502] *Carr v Phelan* [1976/7] ILRM 149 at 152; *Re Brook Cottage Ltd* [1976] NI 78 at 115.

[503] *Re Sherry-Brennan* (SC) 26 July 1983, unrep. *Cf Irish Industrial Building Society v O'Brien* [1941] IR 1 where a similar point was raised *before* sale.

[504] *Macklin v Graecen & Co Ltd* [1983] IR 61 at 65-6.

[505] See paras **9.74-84** *infra* in relation to title.

[506] *Gyles v Beausang* [1895] 2 IR 326 at 336-7.

[507] *Hoban v Bute Investments Ltd* (SC) unrep at 3.

[508] *Moffett v Greene* [1906] 1 IR 501 at 504. Barton J left open the question of the defendant's liability for damages.

[509] *Dunville Investments Ltd v Kelly* (HC) 27 April 1979, Costello J, unrep at 3 (damages left open).

[510] *Casey v Irish Intercontinental Bank Ltd* [1979] IR 364 at 371.

[511] *Per* Costello J in *Hamilton v Hamilton* [1982] IR 466 at 502 approving a passage from the 23rd Ed of Anson's *Law of Contract* at 463. The majority of the court held that the Family Home Protection Act 1976 was not retrospective (see paras **7.09**, **7.20-1** *ante*) and the contract should be performed.

[512] *Horgan v Deasy* [1979] ILRM 71 at 73-4.

performance of a contract for the sale of the same land by an intending purchaser against the vendor/mortgagor makes it impossible to order specific performance.[513] The grant of a new tenancy to a person who proves a right of renewal under the Landlord and Tenant (Amendment) Act 1980 will make it impossible for the landlord to carry out a contract for lease with someone else or to honour a lease actually granted.[514] Arguably that type of situation can be an example of *frustration*[515] and we turn to that subject now.

FRUSTRATION

[9.59] The doctrine of frustration has developed substantially since 1863[516] and doubts about it have been largely removed by a recent Supreme Court decision in a specific performance case.[517] The court approved the following passage from the speech of Lord Simon in *National Carriers v Panalpina Ltd*:[518]

> "Frustration of a contract takes place when there supervenes an event (without default of either party and for which the contract makes no sufficient provision) which so significantly changes the nature (not merely the expense or onerousness) of the outstanding contractual rights and/or obligations from what the parties could reasonably have contemplated at the time of its execution that it would be unjust to hold them to the literal sense of its stipulations in the new circumstances: in such case the law declares both parties to be discharged from further performance."[519]

Blayney J found this passage from Lord Roskill[520] virtually identical in its analysis:

> "There must have been by reason of some supervening event some such fundamental change of circumstances as to enable the Court to say, 'This was not the bargain which these parties made and their bargain must be treated as at an end', a view which Lord Radcliffe himself[521] tersely summarised in a quotation of five words from the Aeneid: 'non haec in foedera veni'."[522]

The Court found in the speech of Lord Wilberforce in the *National Carriers* case[523] a correct statement of the principles relating to the basis on which in the circumstances in which frustration occurs the court has power to declare that the contract is at an end:

> "Various theories have been expressed as to its justification in law (ie the doctrine of frustration):[524] as a device by which the rules as to absolute contracts are reconciled with a special exception which justice demands, as an implied term, as a matter of construction of the contract, as related to removal of the foundation of the contract, as a

---

[513] *McLoughlin v Alexander* (1910) 44 ILTR 253 at 255.
[514] *Irish Leisure Industries Ltd v Gaiety Theatre Enterprises Ltd* (HC) 12 February 1975, O'Higgins CJ, unrep at 2-5.
[515] *The Irish Leisure Industries Ltd* case at 1.
[516] Ie, since *Taylor v Caldwell* of which more in para **9.60** *infra*.
[517] *Neville & Sons Ltd v Guardian Builders Ltd,* Blayney J, 27 July 1994, unrep.
[518] [1981] AC 675 at 700; [1981] 1 All ER 161 at 175.
[519] Approved by Blayney J at 13.
[520] [1981] AC at 717; [1981] 1 All ER at 188.
[521] In *Davis Contractors Ltd v Fareham UDC* [1956] 2 All ER 145 at 160; he explained the quotation as "It was not this that I promised to do".
[522] Approved by Blayney J at 14.
[523] At 693 (AC); 170 (All ER).
[524] Passage in brackets supplied by Blayney J.

total failure of consideration. It is not necessary to attempt selection of any one of these as the true basis; my own view would be that they shade into one another and that a choice between them is a choice of what is most appropriate to the particular contract under consideration. One could see, in relation to the present contract, that it could provisionally be said to be appropriate to refer to an implied term, in view of the grant of the right of way, or to removal of the foundation of the contract, viz use as a warehouse. In any event, the doctrine can now be stated generally as part of the law of contract; as all judicially evolved doctrines it is, and ought to be, flexible and capable of new applications."[525]

The doctrine seems to have featured in one modern Irish case involving a lease[526] but that may not have been a true case of frustration as the defendant was held liable in damages for breach of contract.[527] A submission that the doctrine applies only at common law and not where equitable relief is sought has been rejected.[528]

[9.60] The Supreme Court has not disapproved of any earlier judgment in its decision in the *Neville & Sons Ltd* case.[529] Earlier cases[530] may therefore help to see how relevant principles shade into one another and how to apply them best to the particular contract being considered.[531] Accordingly we will look now at some case law in the development of the doctrine of frustration.[532]

The common law made a distinction between cases where *the law* created a duty or charge and those where a party did so *by his own contract*.[533] In the former case, if the relevant party was disabled from performing the duty or charge without default on his part and had no remedy over, the law would excuse him. "But when the party by his own contract creates a duty or charge upon himself he is bound to make it good, if he may, notwithstanding any accident by inevitable necessity because he might have provided against it by his contract."[534] This rule could be thought to operate harshly in certain cases.[535] In 1863 Blackburn J said:[536]

"There seems no doubt that, where there is a positive contract to do a thing not in itself unlawful, the contractor must perform it or pay damages for not doing it, although, in consequence of unforeseen accident, the performance of the contract has become unexpectedly burdensome, or even impossible."

---

[525] Approved at 15-16.
[526] *Irish Leisure Industries Ltd v Gaiety Theatre Enterprises Ltd* (HC) 12 February 1975, O'Higgins CJ, unrep on damages due to "the breach of contract involved in the frustration of the lease granted"; the decision on frustration seems to have been oral.
[527] See discussion by Wylie, *Irish Landlord & Tenant Law*, para 26.16; Clark, *Contract Law in Ireland*, 3rd Ed (1992) 435-6.
[528] *Neville & Sons Ltd's* case at 616.
[529] 351/89 and 27/90, 27 July 1994, Blayney J, unrep.
[530] Especially the more recent ones.
[531] Consistently with the passage quoted by Blayney J from Lord Wilberforce and set out in para **9.59** above.
[532] From here until the end of para **9.65**.
[533] *Paradine v Jane* (1647) Aleyn, 26; [1558-1774] All ER 172 at 173.
[534] *Ibid*. The rule was approved by Pigot CB in *Gamble v Accident Assurance Co Ltd* IR 4 CL 204 at 215. See also *Herman v Owners of the SS "Vicia"* [1942] IR 305 at 325.
[535] In *Gamble's* case at 214 Pigot CB held a term *not* unreasonable; cf *Leeson v North British Oil & Candle Ltd* (1874) 8 IRCl 309.
[536] *Taylor v Caldwell* (1863) 3 B & S 826; [1861-73] All ER 24 at 27.

He then pointed out that the rule was only applicable when the contract was "positive and absolute" and not subject to any condition, either express or implied. He then recognised this principle:[537]

> "...where, from the nature of the contract, it appears that the parties must from the beginning have known that it could not be fulfilled unless, when the time for the fulfilment of the contract arrived, some particular specified thing continued to exist, so that when entering into the contract they must have contemplated such continued existence as the foundation of what was to be done, there, in the absence of any expressed or implied warranty that the thing shall exist, the contract is not be construed as a positive contract, but as subject to an implied condition that the parties shall be excused in case, before breach, performance becomes impossible from the perishing of the thing without default of the contractor."

In that case a music hall was destroyed by fire just before the beginning of a four day letting. The hall was the "specified thing" which had not continued to exist. The principle applies also where the essential thing survives but "its condition has by some casualty been so changed as to be not available for the purposes of the contract".[538] Likewise where a building remains intact but the object of a contract for its use fails[539] or apparently where a mutual expectation fails to materialise thus defeating what is effectively the only means of performing the agreement short of requiring one or other party to do something which he had not agreed to do at all.[540] Of course the principle does not go so far as to let a party out of his contract just because subsequent circumstances have made it "very prejudicial" even though the remedy of specific performance is discretionary.[541] *Impossibility* of performance normally is necessary but impossibility of performing any substantial part of the consideration may suffice, especially if the consideration is indivisible.[542]

[9.61] In *Browne v Mulligan*[543] Kenny J noted that at least three possible bases for the doctrine of frustration of a contract have been suggested each of which could claim eminent judicial support. The first is that it depends on an implied term in the contract[544] or upon the "presumed common intention of the parties".[545] The second rejects wholly the implied term theory and rests the doctrine on the true construction of the contract read in the light of the nature of the contract and the relevant surrounding circumstances.[546] Perhaps it would be simpler to say that frustration occurs whenever the law recognises

---

[537] *Ibid.* Accepted in *Gamble's* case at 215 but distinguished; also accepted in *Cummings v Stewart* [1913] 1 IR 95 at 118.
[538] *Per* Lord Wright in *Constantine Line v Imperial Smelting Corporation* [1942] AC 154 in a passage approved by Kenny J in *Browne v Mulligan* [1976-7] ILRM 327 at 332.
[539] As in the Coronation cases considered by Murphy J in *Neville & Sons Ltd v Guardian Builders Ltd* [1990] ILRM 601 at 615.
[540] The *Neville & Sons Ltd* case at 615.
[541] *Revell v Hussey* (1813) 2 Ball & Beatty 280 at 288-9. See consideration of hardship in para **9.38** *supra*. Cf Clarke, *Contract Law in Ireland*, 3rd Ed (1992) at 425-6 on the *Suez Canal* cases.
[542] *Cummings v Stewart* [1913] 1 IR 95 at 119-20.
[543] [1976-7] ILRM at 332-3. All three bases would seem to fit within the material approved by the Supreme Court in *Neville & Sons Ltd v Guardian Builders Ltd*, 351/89 & 27/90, 27 July 1994 Blayney J, unrep at 13-16. See para **9.59** *supra*. Cf detailed discussion of frustration by Hanna J in *Herman v Owners of s SS "Vicia"* [1942] IR 305 at 321-5.
[544] Viscount Simon in *Constantine Line v Imperial Smelting Corporation* [1942] AC 154. This principle may be traced back to *Taylor v Caldwell* considered in para **9.60** *supra*.
[545] Viscount Maugham in the *Constantine Line* case.
[546] Lord Reid in *Davis Construction v Fareham UDC* [1956] AC 696 at 720.

that, without default of either party, a contractual obligation has become incapable of being performed because the circumstances in which performance is called for would render it a thing radically different from that which was undertaken by the contract.[547] O'Flaherty J has said:

> "Frustration occurs whenever the law recognises that without default of either party a contractual obligation has become incapable of being performed because of some intervening illegality or because the circumstances in which performance is called for would render it something radically different from that which was undertaken by the contract."[548]

The third theory noted by Kenny J is that where the dispute between the parties arises from an event which they never thought of, the court imposes the solution which is just and reasonable.[549] On the facts of *Browne's* case the doctrine could not apply in any event so it was not necessary to decide which basis to adopt. In *Neville & Sons Ltd v Guardian Builders*[550] Murphy J seems to prefer[551] the second theory noted by Kenny J and quotes this passage from Lord Radcliffe:[552]

> "The court must act upon a general impression of what its rule requires. It is for that reason that special importance is necessarily attached to the occurrence of any unexpected event that, as it were, changes the face of things. But, even so, it is not hardship or inconvenience or material loss itself which calls the principle of frustration into play. There must be as well such a change in the significance of the obligation that the thing undertaken would, if performed, be a different thing from that contracted for."

In *McGuill v Aer Lingus Teo*[553] McWilliam J identified the following principles from case law considered by him:

> "1. A party may bind himself by an absolute contract to perform something which subsequently becomes impossible.
> 2. Frustration occurs when, without default of either party, a contractual obligation has become incapable of being performed.
> 3. The circumstances alleged to occasion frustration should be strictly scrutinised and the doctrine is not to be lightly applied.
> 4. Where the circumstances alleged to cause the frustration have arisen from the act or default of one of the parties, that party cannot rely on the doctrine.
> 5. All the circumstances of the contract should also be strictly scrutinised.
> 6. The event must be an unexpected event.
> 7. If one party anticipated or should have anticipated the possibility of the event which is alleged to cause the frustration and did not incorporate a clause in the contract to deal with it, he should not be permitted to rely on the happening of the event as causing frustration."

---

[547] Lord Radcliffe in the *Davis Construction* case at 728 quoted by Kenny J in *Browne's* case at 332 and Murphy J in *Neville & Sons Ltd v Guardian Builders Ltd* [1990] ILRM 601 at 615.
[548] *Bates v Model Bakery Ltd* [1993] 1 IR 539 at 369.
[549] *Browne's* case at 333; Lord Wright's *Legal Essays & Addresses* at 258; *Denny Mott & Dickson Ltd v Fraser & Co Ltd* [1944] AC 265 at 275.
[550] [1990] ILRM 601.
[551] The headnote has him so holding but it is not certain that he did so or needed to do so for the purpose of his decision. For the decision on appeal see para **9.59** *supra* . See also detailed consideration of the theoretical basis of frustration by Clark, *Contract Law in Ireland*, 3rd Ed (1992) at 428-9.
[552] In the *Davis Contractors* case at 729 quoted by Murphy J at 615 in the *Neville & Sons Ltd* case.
[553] (HC) 3 October 1983, unrep at 13-14. The material seems compatible with the Supreme Court decision in the *Neville & Sons Ltd* case: see para **9.59** *supra*.

[9.62] A contract should not be held to be frustrated unless it is just and reasonable to do so.[554] Nor can the doctrine apply if the terms of the contract show that the parties contemplated the possibility of the event relied on as frustrating the contract.[555] The event relied on must be unanticipated by the parties and so not mentioned in the contract; if it was dealt with in the contract, then it was within the contemplation of the parties and the doctrine cannot apply.[556] If a party should have anticipated the possibility of the event but failed to do so and, due to that failure, did not deal with it in the contract it seems that normally he cannot rely on the doctrine.[557] That would fit in fairly comfortably with the view that a defence of frustration should not succeed unless it is just and reasonable for it to do so. However, the courts may feel difficulty in holding against the defence of frustration and decreeing specific performance of something radically different from what the parties agreed simply because they, or one of them, probably ought to have thought of the relevant event and covered it in their contract. If parties do cover the relevant event but a mutual expectation of how it will turn out is destroyed between the date of the contract and the date of completion the defence may succeed.[558] When frustration does occur it does not merely provide one party with a defence in an action brought by the other; it kills the contract itself and discharges both parties automatically.[559] The determination of the contract does not depend on the volition, or even the knowledge, of the parties.[560]

[9.63] The *entire* of the contract normally goes when frustration occurs.[561] Thus a judge has had difficulty with an argument that a lease as a whole still subsists but a party can escape from liability under a repairing covenant in it due to changed circumstances.[562] A right that comes into existence before frustration occurs - an "accrued right" - may survive in certain cases[563] but it would seem very difficult to argue that the normal right of a party to a contract to get specific performance is an accrued right which could survive the defence of frustration. Such an argument, if successful, would either destroy the defence in *all* cases or do so in those where the party seeking to enforce the contract is able to perform his own obligations under it. The argument might run that a party could insist on performance of a contract despite a defence of frustration in an appropriate case by waiving performance of the terms which cannot be performed or possibly by seeking compensation for their non-performance.[564] However, the idea of getting any

---

[554] *Herman v Owners of SS "Vicia"* [1942] IR 305 at 322.
[555] *Browne v Mulligan* [1976-7] ILRM 327 at 333.
[556] *Ibid.*
[557] Part of the 7th principle of McWilliam J in the *McGuill* case.
[558] In *Neville & Sons Ltd v Guardian Builders Ltd* [1990] ILRM 601, Murphy J found at 615 that both parties necessarily believed or assumed that Dublin County Council, owner of a crucial strip of land, would facilitate the intended development. The Supreme Court held that the defendant had sufficient agreement with the Council to fulfil its obligation to the plaintiff though that would be more onerous: so the defence of frustration failed. See Blayney J's analysis of the facts at p 16-24 of the transcript and his conclusions at 24-6.
[559] *Per* Viscount Simon in *Constantine Line v Imperial Smelting Corporation* [1942] AC 154 in a passage quoted by Hanna J in *Herman v Owners of s SS "Vicia"* [1942] IR 305 at 321. *Cf Kearney v Saorstat & Continental Shipping Co Ltd* [1943] IJR 8.
[560] *Byrne v Limerick s SS Co Ltd* [1946] IR 138 at 150.
[561] *Ibid.*
[562] *Groome v Fodhla Printing Co* [1946] IR 380 at 413-4.
[563] *Herman v Owners of s SS "Vicia"* [1942] IR 305 at 324-5, a seaman's case dealing with special rights (p 326-9) and thus very difficult to apply to a specific performance case.
[564] Considered in *Neville & Sons Ltd's* case at 616. Murphy J held that it was not an appropriate case but the Supreme Court held that the defence of frustration failed: see fn 558 and para **9.59** *supra*.

compensation at all would grate against the element in the doctrine of frustration that inability to perform has occurred without any default by the relevant party. The argument would be at its weakest where the party standing over the contract is not able to perform his own part of the bargain.[565] It would seem stronger, *eg,* in a purchaser's suit for specific performance where, due to facts which could support a defence of frustration, the vendor cannot perform all or part of his obligations but the purchaser still claims specific performance on the basis that he will pay the agreed price in full, perform any other obligations on him and not seek compensation for the elements the vendor cannot perform. He would contend that it was not just and reasonable then to hold that there had been frustration. However, he should expect difficulty with the points that frustration kills the contract and occurs without the volition or even the knowledge of the parties.

[9.64] A party may not rely on an alleged frustration which he has induced himself. He would then be in breach of the fourth principle found by McWilliam J in the *McGuill* case.[566] He could not get within any of the three possible bases of frustration considered by Kenny J in *Browne v Mulligan.*[567] As in cases of impossibility,[568] permitting that kind of stance would be inconsistent with the willingness of the courts to find implied terms such as that parties to contracts will not disable themselves from carrying out their contracts. Thus a party who aborts a contract by his own negligence or desire to save expense cannot rely on a defence of frustration.[569] If a contract needs a licence or permission a party must make reasonable efforts to get it or, if it is refused, take all reasonable steps to have the refusal withdrawn.[570]

[9.65] Another similarity to the defence of *impossibility*[571] is that a change in the law or a step taken pursuant to statutory authority may frustrate a contract. If a new Act makes it impossible for a person to perform his contract or makes it necessary for him to get a consent to such performance which in fact he cannot get the doctrine of frustration is likely to apply.[572] A compulsory purchase order after a contract has been made very much alters the situation but not to the degree which would justify a court in saying that the contract has been frustrated.[573] The purchaser will become entitled to either the land or any compensation payable for it.[574] As we have seen, the grant of a new tenancy under Part II of the Landlord and Tenant (Amendment) Act 1980 may frustrate a lease of the same property granted to another person.[575] A statute may give a form of option to a party. For example, s 40 of Deasy's Act gives a right to a tenant to surrender his lease, if it does not contain an express covenant to repair, when the "substantial matter" of the demise is

---

[565] As held at first instance in *Neville & Sons Ltd's* case: p 616.
[566] (HC) 3 October 1983, unrep at 13-14; para **9.61** *supra.*
[567] [1976-7] ILRM 327 at 332-3. See para **9.61** *supra.*
[568] See paras **9.56-8** *supra* . On implied terms see paras **3.26-7** *ante.*
[569] *Herman v Owners of SS "Vicia"* [1942] IR 305 at 330.
[570] *Byrne v Limerick SS Co Ltd* [1946] IR 138 at 149.
[571] On this see paras **9.56-8** *supra.*
[572] *Hamilton v Hamilton* [1982] IR 466 at 502, Costello J, dissenting. The majority held that the Family Home Protection Act 1976 was not retrospective and did not affect the contract: see paras **7.09**, **7.20-1** *ante.*
[573] *Hillingdon Estates Co v Stonefield Estates Ltd* [1952] 1 All ER 853 at 856.
[574] *Irish Life Assurance Co Ltd v Dublin Land Securities* Ltd [1986] IR 332 at 354.
[575] *Irish Leisure Industries Ltd v Gaiety Theatre Enterprises Ltd* (HC) 12 February 1975, O'Higgins CJ, unrep at 1. On that case see further para **9.59** *supra* and Wylie, *Irish Landlord & Tenant Law,* para 26.16; Clark *Contract Law in Ireland,* 3rd Ed (1992) 435-6.

destroyed or rendered substantially unusable by accidental fire or other inevitable accident without any default or neglect on the part of the tenant. This has been described as "similar to one possible cause of frustration"[576]

MISTAKE

[9.66] Mistake is often relevant in specific performance cases. It may prevent there being consensus and thus mean that no contract has been reached.[577] If there is no contract there is nothing of which specific performance can be decreed.[578] Mistake may give a right to rescission of a contract.[579] The equitable remedy of rectification may be invoked in a suitable case to cure a result of mistake[580] and the relevant mistake may be either mutual[581] or unilateral.[582] If a party is entitled to rectification the courts have power to decree specific performance with the appropriate rectification.[583] A right of rescission for mistake or, of course, for any other reason, means that specific performance of the contract will not be decreed. A party who is entitled to rectification, equally obviously, will not have the unrectified contract enforced against him.

[9.67] The court also has the very important discretionary power to withhold the relief of specific performance on the ground of mistake although the plaintiff has proved a valid and enforceable contract.[584] Even when plaintiffs have not contributed in any way to the making of mistakes the court has power to grant relief to defendants although this will be done rarely. Courts of Equity have at all times relieved against honest mistakes in contracts where the literal effect and specific performance of them would impose a burden not contemplated, and which it would be against all reason and justice to fix, upon a person who inadvertently committed an accidental mistake.[585] Similarly if the mistake would give an unconscionable advantage to either party.[586] Cases where defendants escape from the consequences of a mistake not contributed to by the plaintiff mostly will be cases where a hardship amounting to injustice would be inflicted on him by holding him to his bargain.[587] If the decree of specific performance is withheld in a case of this sort the plaintiff remains entitled to damages. The discretion being exercised is not as to whether *any* relief will be given to the party who has a binding contract at law but rather as to what the form of the relief will be.[588] In deciding how to exercise the discretion the court will take into account, not only the hardship which the defendant will suffer if

---

[576] Wylie, *op cit*, para 26.15.
[577] See para **3.02** *ante*.
[578] *Lynch v O'Meara* (SC) 8 May 1975, Henchy J, unrep at 4. See defence of No Contract at paras **9.02-4** above.
[579] Paras **10.30-31** *post*.
[580] Paras **10.15-24** *post*.
[581] Paras **10.15-17** *post*.
[582] Paras **10.18-19** *post*.
[583] Paras **10.23** *post*.
[584] On the discretion see paras **1.06-9** *supra*.
[585] *Burrow v Scammell* (1881) 19 Ch D 175 at 182 approved by Costello J in *O'Neill v Ryan (No 3)* [1992] 1 IR 166 at 191; note views of Finlay CJ and O'Flaherty J at 196.
[586] *Ibid*.
[587] *Tamplin v James* (1880) 15 Ch D 215 at 221; [1874-80] All ER 560 at 562 approved by Costello J in *O'Neill v Ryan (No 3)* [1992] 1 IR 166 at 191-2; note views of Finlay CJ and O'Flaherty J at 196. See defence of Hardship at paras **9.38-41** *supra*.
[588] *O'Neill's* case at 196 *per* Finlay CJ.

forced to perform, but also the hardship which the plaintiff will suffer if he does not get specific performance.[589]

[9.68] It is vital to remember in considering mistake as a ground for resisting specific performance of a valid and enforceable contract that the discretion to grant or withhold the relief must be exercised in a manner which is neither arbitrary nor capricious but which has regard to the essential fairness of the transaction.[590] Regard will be had to the conduct of both parties and all the circumstances of the case.[591] If the mistake has not been induced or contributed to by any act or omission on the part of the plaintiff specific performance is likely to be granted unless it is highly unreasonable to enforce the agreement specifically.[592] Where the plaintiff does contribute to the mistake, even innocently[593] and unaware that the defendant makes the mistake,[594] there is an increased chance that specific performance will be withheld. This may happen, *eg*, where the purchaser makes a mistake about the boundaries of the property due in part to a poor plan provided by the vendor[595] or there is an error about the quantity of land being sold.[596] But the defendant must have reasonable excuse for his mistake; there is no injustice in holding a man to a contract which specifically describes the property sold in a way not calculated to mislead.[597] It is within the court's discretion, if there is reasonable excuse for a defendant's mistake, to withhold specific performance unless the plaintiff agrees to take the contract as the defendant understood it.[598] Alternatively it may decree specific performance subject to a condition dealing with the mistake.[599] Evidence proving the mistake is admissible and is not affected by the Statute of Frauds.[600] But if the evidence is offered, not to prove fraud, mistake or surprise, but to contradict, explain or vary the written contract it is not admissible.[601] Finally on this topic, it should be noted that the courts are unwilling to try to define the cases in which specific performance will be refused on the ground of mistake.[602]

[9.69] The court may also *set aside* a contract on the ground of *shared common* mistake[603] even though it is not avoided by that mistake.[604] A contract is liable in equity to be set

---

[589] *Per* Costello J in *O'Neill's* case at 192 approved by Finlay CJ and O'Flaherty J at 196. See Hardship at paras **9.38-41** *infra*, *esp* the similar balancing at para **9.40**.
[590] *Smelter Corporation of Ireland Ltd v O'Driscoll* [1977] IR 305 at 310-1. See paras **1.06-9** *ante* on the discretionary nature of the remedy and paras **9.35-6** *supra* on the defence of unfairness.
[591] *Conlon v Murray* [1958] NI 17 at 25.
[592] *Stewart v Kennedy* (1890) 15 App Cas 75 at 105.
[593] If the contribution is not innocent the defendant may well have a defence of fraud (paras **9.10-15** *infra*). That may include fraudulent misrepresentation or a *reckless* statement: para **9.12** *infra*.
[594] If he knows that the defendant is making the mistake the latter may get rectification for unilateral mistake: *Irish Life Assurance Co Ltd v Dublin Land Securities Ltd* [1989] IR 253 at 260.1. And see paras **10.18-19** *post*. Rescission may also be appropriate: the *Irish Life* case at 260; paras **10.30-31** *post*.
[595] *Denny v Hancock* (1870) 6 Ch App 1.
[596] *Dyas v Stafford* (1881) 7 LRI 590, on appeal, 9 LRI 520 at 522-3.
[597] *Per* Cotton LJ in *Tamplin's* case: the plans used were fine.
[598] *Baskcomb v Beckwith* (1869) LR 8 Eq 100; *Preston v Luck* (1884) 27 Ch D 497; *McKenzie v Hesketh* (1877) 7 Ch D 675.
[599] *Baskcomb's* case: intention of vendor to retain small part of property free from mutual restrictive covenants not made clear enough.
[600] *Clinan v Cooke* (1802) 1 Schoales & Lefroy 22 at 38-9.
[601] *Clowes v Higginson* [1803-13] All ER 186 at 188-9. *Cf* para **9.05** *ante*.
[602] *Per* Cotton LJ in *Tamplin's* case; *cf* Brett LJ in that case.
[603] See the detailed consideration of mistake in Ch 10 of Clark, *Contract Law in Ireland*, 3rd Ed (1992), esp 204-13.
[604] *O'Neill v Ryan (No 3)* [1992] 1 IR 166 at 185.

aside if the parties were under a common misapprehension either as to facts or as to their relative and respective rights provided that the misapprehension was fundamental and the party seeking to set it aside was not himself at fault.[605] In the exercise of its discretion the court may refuse to make an order for *specific performance* in cases of common shared mistakes.[606] In exercising its power to refuse specific performance or to set aside a contract on the ground of common mistake the court may impose conditions, even one to enter into a new contract on appropriate terms.[607]

WANT OF MUTUALITY

[9.70] Generally speaking it would not be even-handed justice to compel specific performance against the one party, where the same remedy would not be available against the other party in respect of matters to be by him performed under the contract.[608] The nature of the defence of want of mutuality may not be entirely clear. One important question is at what time an issue of mutuality should be tested. It has been said by a leading author that a contract to be specifically enforced by the courts must as a general rule be mutual - *ie,* "such that it might, at the time it was entered into, have been enforced by either of the parties against the other of them".[609] The part of that statement which sets up the date of the contract as the proper one for testing mutuality has been criticised by judges and writers including an Irish judge.[610] However, the point has also received Irish judicial support.[611] It came for consideration in the English Court of Appeal in 1977.[612] The court held that the relevant date was that of the hearing.[613] The powerful point was made: "Surely the defence of want of mutuality should be governed by the state of affairs as seen at the hearing, since one is dealing not with a question affecting the initial validity of the contract, but with whether or not the discretionary remedy of specific performance should be granted".[614] The defence should be judged on the facts and circumstances as they exist at the hearing, albeit in the light of the whole conduct of the parties in relation to the subject-matter, and, in the absence of any other disqualifying circumstances, the court will grant specific performance if it can be done without injustice or unfairness to the defendant.[615] It is important to remember that want of mutuality is not an absolute bar to specific performance but is a factor which a court of equity may have to consider in deciding whether or not to grant the relief.[616]

[9.71] Another area of doubt was the interplay of the concept of mutuality with the Statute of Frauds.[617] It was suggested in that context that there is a want of mutuality fatal

---

[605] *Per* Denning LJ in *Solle v Butcher* [1950] 1 KB 671 at 693; [1949] 2 All ER 1107 at 1120 approved by Costello J in the *O'Neill* case at 185.
[606] *Ibid*, Costello J considering *Grist v Bailey* [1967] Ch 532.
[607] *Grist's* case at 543.
[608] *Per* O'Connor LJ in *O'Regan v White* [1919] 2 IR 339 at 393.
[609] Fry, *Specific Performance* 6th Ed (1921) at 219; *cf* discussion by Jones & Goodhart, *Specific Performance* (1986) at 22-7.
[610] O'Connor LJ in *O'Regan v White* [1919] IR 339 at 392-5.
[611] Meredith J in *Murphy v Harrington* [1927] IR 339 at 344.
[612] *Price v Strange* [1977] 3 All ER 371; [1978] Ch 337.
[613] *Per* Goff LJ at 383 (All ER) and Buckley LJ at 392, 395, Scarman LJ concurring with both.
[614] *Per* Goff LJ at 383. *Cf* Buckley LJ at 394.
[615] *Ibid. Cf* Buckley LJ at 392.
[616] *Lyus v Prowsa Developments Ltd* [1982] 2 All ER 953 at 961.
[617] Considered in Ch 5 *supra* .

to a right to specific performance where only one party to a contract is bound by a note or memorandum sufficient to satisfy the statute. Lord Redesdale was worried about this in 1802.[618] He had "heard it urged" that a construction enabling just one party to sue when only the other had signed a note or memorandum would "make the statute really a statute *of frauds*, for it would enable any person who had procured another to sign an agreement to make it depend on his own will and pleasure whether it should be an agreement or not."[619] It could be a suspicious circumstance that a plaintiff "should take so much pains to bind the defendant to an agreement to which, so far as the contract speaks for itself, he is not under the same obligation to perform".[620] However, around the same time it was the "daily practice" of the courts that a contract signed by one party would be enforced in equity against that party.[621] If the party not bound was trying to obtain some "undue advantage" or was playing "fast and loose" the court would not assist him[622] but that is a different matter. In 1851 Brady LC dealt firmly with the point:

> "That the objection of want of mutuality of remedy to enforce the contract does not in all cases prevail, is manifested in cases decided under the Statute of Frauds, where it has been held that the plaintiff may obtain a decree for specific performance of a contract signed by the defendant but not signed by the plaintiff. The reason of this doctrine is that the plaintiff by filing his bill submits to perform his part of the contract; and of the plaintiff's non-signature the other party is not allowed to avail himself, because although he could not have compelled the plaintiff to complete the contract, yet he (the defendant) has, by signing, thought proper to run the chance of the plaintiff performing his part, which, if he do not rely upon the Statute of Frauds, the Court will decree him to perform."[623]

It has been said that by filing his bill the plaintiff "has made the remedy mutual".[624] In practice, of course, proceedings issued by or on behalf of a plaintiff and stating the contract sought to be enforced will be signed by him or his solicitor and that signature will satisfy the statute.[625]

[9.72] What is the modern principle in the defence of want of mutuality in claims for specific performance? This statement seems attractive:

> "...the court will not compel a defendant to perform his obligations specifically if it cannot at the same time ensure that any unperformed obligations of the plaintiff will be specifically performed, unless, perhaps, damages would be an adequate remedy to the defendant for any default on the plaintiff's part."[626]

Having said that the doctrine of mutuality as generally stated needed some modification O'Connor LJ continued in *O'Regan v White*:[627]

---

[618] *Lawrenson v Butler* (1802) 1 Schoales & Lefroy 13 at 20-21.
[619] *Lawrenson's* case at 20; Lord Redesdale's emphasis.
[620] *O'Rourke v Perceval* (1811) 2 Ball & Beatty 58 at 62-3.
[621] *Ormond v Anderson* (1813) 2 Ball & Beatty 363 at 371.
[622] *Ibid*. Nothing of the sort was done in that case.
[623] *Fennelly v Anderson* (1851) 1 IR Ch R 706 at 711.
[624] *Flight v Bollard* [1824-34] All ER 372 at 373.
[625] If a plenary summons does not state the contract sufficiently the Statement of Claim will do so; otherwise the proceedings may be struck out: *Bond v Holton* [1959] IR 302 at 308, 310-11 (dealing with a summary summons). See paras **8.21-4** *ante* on pleadings.
[626] *Per* Buckley LJ in *Price v Strange* [1977] 3 All ER 371 at 392.
[627] [1919] 2 IR 339 at 395.

"...it seems to me that there is a great deal of force in the observations of the learned writer[628] in 19 *Law Quarterly Review*, July, 1903, at p 341 (cited in Fry,[629] p 235, *n* 2), that the exceptions to the doctrine of mutuality 'are all referable to one and the same general principle, viz, that the defence of want of mutuality will not avail to prevent the Court from exercising its beneficial jurisdiction where the contract can be properly enforced without any possible injustice to the defendant, provided a corresponding equitable remedy' (he might have said 'if necessary') 'becomes available against the plaintiff on or before his institution of the action.'

[9.73] In practice the defence of lack of mutuality seems most likely to arise where there are title difficulties.[630] Even here the defence will not succeed very often. Lack of mutuality is only of significance where the defendant from whom specific performance is sought can show that at whatever may be the relevant date the plaintiff cannot be, or (if a past date is relevant) could not have been, ordered to perform his unperformed obligations specifically.[631] A vendor's normal obligation is to show good title in accordance with the contract by the agreed completion date but showing it even later usually suffices if time has not been made of the essence.[632]

Another situation where mutuality may need consideration is in contracts of minors. A minor cannot sue for specific performance because a similar decree could not be made against him[633] though possibly he can succeed if he has already performed his side of the deal. The act of filing the bill by his next friend while he was a minor could not bind him.[634] Once he reaches his majority a claim by him for specific performance probably cannot be defeated by a defence of lack of mutuality.[635] In this case there is mutuality at the date of the hearing of the former minor's suit for specific performance though there was not while he was still under age. On the other hand, if a contract for the sale or purchase of land by a minor is *voidable* and not void,[636] a claim against him for specific performance after he is 18 may succeed if he does not repudiate the contract within a reasonable time after attaining his majority.[637] Another area in which questions of mutuality could crop up in less enlightened times was that of contracts for the sale of the real estate of married women.[638]

In certain other cases consideration given by one party may be matters such as rendering services or doing works which the court would not order to be specifically performed;[639] but if those things are done the court will order specific performance of the other party's obligations if those are of a sort where the remedy is available.[640] Indeed

---

[628] Deriving from Mutuality in Specific Performance published in the *Columbia Law Review* for January 1903 and reprinted in Ames's, *Lectures on Legal History*, p 370. Another extract is cited by Keane, *Equity and the Law of Trusts in the Republic of Ireland* (1988) at 16.07.

[629] The 5th Ed.

[630] Considered in the remainder of this chapter; note the cases cited by Buckley LJ in *Price's* case at 389.

[631] *Per* Buckley LJ in *Price's* case at 390.

[632] *McGirr v Devine* [1925] NI 94 at 97. See also para **9.76** *post*.

[633] *Flight v Bollard* [1824-34] All ER 372. *Cf Lumley v Ravenscroft* [1895] 1 QB 863 where one of two intending lessors was an infant.

[634] *Flight's* case at 373.

[635] *Clayton v Ashdown* (1714) 9 Vin Abr 393.

[636] There seems to be no direct authority on this difficult point but see discussion by Clark, *Contract Law in Ireland*, 3rd Ed (1992) at 364-6. The better view is probably that the contract is voidable.

[637] See Wylie, *Irish Land Law*, 2nd Ed (1986), para 25.06; Jones & Goodhart, *Specific Performance* (1986) at 177; but *cf* Jones & Goodhart at 24.

[638] *Fennelly v Anderson* (1851) 1 IR Ch R 706 at 709-11.

[639] On this see paras **1.20-22** *ante*.

[640] *Price's* case at 390 and cases cited by Buckley LJ.

where a plaintiff has fully carried out his obligations it is hard to see how the mutuality principle comes in at all.[641] In other cases the duty of one party to perform his obligations may depend on the other having performed his obligations or some specified part of them.[642] These usually are not truly *conditional* cases[643] but have mutual binding obligations from the start although the timing for performance varies. Although performance by the second party in time cannot be compelled until the first has performed to the agreed stage this is not the result of any principle of mutuality. The contract itself has negatived all idea of mutuality at the time the first party is to perform and in such a case the defence of want of mutuality fails.[644]

QUESTIONS OF TITLE

[9.74] In a vendor's action for specific performance it is a good defence to show that he has no title[645] unless the purchaser has unwisely agreed to a very restrictive special condition.[646] The position is similar if an enforceable undertaking to a local authority or other competent person or body prevents a vendor conveying.[647] Similarly if lawful action by a third party such as an order for sale obtained by a mortgagee prevents title being made.[648] In the absence of any express provision to the contrary, the vendor undertakes and is bound to show a good title to the property to be sold and to convey land corresponding substantially, in all respects, with the description contained in the contract.[649] A purchaser is normally entitled to insist that upon payment of his purchase money he gets a good clear title such as he could immediately present to any financial institution for a full loan on the security of the property.[650] Where a vendor expressly undertakes to make a good title the purchaser can refuse to complete by reason of the existence of a defect of title of which he was aware when he signed the contract and which the vendor has failed to remove.[651] The precise legal basis of a purchaser's right to a good title may not be absolutely clear but there is no doubt about its existence. It has been called "a right not growing out of the agreement between the parties, but which is given by law".[652] It has also been described as an implied agreement in the contract for sale and as a collateral right given by the law.[653] If the vendor fails to show good title in accordance with the contract the purchaser may rescind and recover his deposit.[654] The

---

[641] *Kirkland v Bird* (1968) 112 Sol J 440.
[642] Note example given and discussion by O'Connor LJ in *O'Regan's* case at 393-4 and discussion of the point and of *O'Regan's* case by Buckley LJ in *Price's* case at 390-2.
[643] See discussion of conditional contracts at paras **3.19-28** *ante*.
[644] *O'Regan's* case at 394
[645] *Kearney v Ryan* (1878) 2 LRI 61 (successful claim by purchaser for return of deposit).
[646] On such conditions generally see paras **9.78** *post*. O'Connor MR has said in *Re White & Hague's Contract* [1921] 1 IR 138 at 144 that "a purchaser may preclude himself by agreement from making any inquiry as to title". However, it is not clear how far an intending vendor can go towards excluding investigation of title altogether: see discussion of this by Wylie, *Irish Conveyancing Law* (1978) at para 10.040, 14.04.
[647] *McQuaid v Lynam* [1965] IR 564 at 568; *Lynch v Bradley* (HC) 22 August 1984, Barrington J, unrep at 17.
[648] *McLoughlin v Alexander* (1910) 54 ILTR 253 at 255.
[649] *Re Flynn & Newman's Contract* [1948] IR 104 at 112.
[650] *Per* Finlay in *Tempany v Hynes* (HC) 10 July 1975 at 17, *reversed* (1976) IR 101 on grounds not argued in the High Court: see discussion of this case at paras **11.02-12** *post*.
[651] *Re Flynn & Newman's Contract* at 111
[652] *Ogilvie v Foljambe* 3 Mer 53 at 64 approved by O'Connor MR in *Re White & Hague's Contract* [1921] 1 IR 138 at 145.
[653] *Re Geraghty & Lyons' Contract* (1919) 53 ILTR 57 at 58.
[654] *Re Flynn & Newman's Contract* at 112; *Re Clibborn & Horan's Contract* [1921] 1 IR 93 at 97; *Buckley v Dawson* (1854) 4 ICLR 211 at 215.

vendor is under a duty to disclose latent defects in title[655] and in the ordinary way if a purchaser before completion discovers such a defect he is entitled to raise an objection.[656] The vendor should try to remove the objection but may, depending on the circumstances, be entitled to rescind the contract under a rescission clause.[657]

[9.75] Lack of title may also be a defence if the vendor fails to show the *type* of title he has promised in a contract. Thus when a contract said that the property was "held by the vendors for ever in fee-farm" the court did not feel at liberty to force a leasehold title "for a long term of years now to come and unexpired" on the purchaser.[658] A promise of the interest of a lease for lives renewable for ever was not met when it turned out that the concurrence of a third person would be needed to enforce a renewal.[659] A vendor of a leasehold estate does not carry out his contract by offering proof of a possessory title.[660] The most he can convey is the right to hold possession of the lands during the residue of the term.[661] The same probably applies where a fee farm grantee's estate is sold[662] although if there is no re-entry clause or any other possibility of a re-entry by the grantor this kind of title should be safe enough. Sometimes possessory titles have been forced on purchasers but it has been said in a case involving a leasehold title that "it must be in a case which admits of indubitable evidence and leaves the purchaser subject to no risk."[663] The same judge also was inclined to accept that as a general rule a possessory title can be substituted for a documentary title though the question was still open whether "this is a proposition of universal application, no matter what the nature of the estate the subject of the contract".[664] Of course, where parties *contract for* a possessory title that is all the vendor need show.[665] The point about showing a different title from that offered in the contract cannot be taken to excessive lengths. It has been held that in a sale of property described as "your leasehold interest" the vendor met his obligations by showing good title to a long sublease; the contract did not "amount to an undertaking to convey a lease as distinguished from an underlease".[666]

[9.76] Normally a vendor who has a defective title at the date of the contract but can make it good before the agreed completion date, even later if time has not been made of the essence, is entitled to specific performance[667] unless, of course, some other ground for refusing it exists. The fact that the title is initially defective normally will not give a purchaser an immediate right to repudiate the contract.[668] He is bound to make his

[655] *Ie,* defects not visible from inspection of the property: see Wylie, *Irish Conveyancing Law* (1978) paras 10.025-8.
[656] *Peader Nolan Ltd v O' Meara* (HC) 2 October 1985, Carroll J, unrep at 7.
[657] On which see paras **10.34-42** *post.*
[658] *Re McDermott & Kellett's Contract* (1904) 4 NIJR 89 at 90.
[659] *Massereene v Finlay* (1850) 13 ILR 496 at 505.
[660] *Re Ashe & Hogan's Contract* [1920] 1 IR 159 at 169.
[661] *Ibid.* This point has been strengthened further by *Perry v Woodfarm Homes Ltd* [1975] IR 104 where the Supreme Court confirmed that there is no "parliamentary conveyance" to a squatter. See discussion by Wylie, *Irish Land Law,* 2nd Ed (1986), paras 23.15-19.
[662] *Mohan v Roche* [1991] 1 IR 560 at 568.
[663] *Re Ashe & Hogan's Contract* [1920] 1 IR 159 at 168.
[664] *Re Clibborn & Horan's Contract* [1921] 1 IR 93 at 100. He emphasised the difficulty of applying the proposition to leasehold estates.
[665] *Re McClure & Garrett's Contract* [1899] 1 IR 225.
[666] *Palmer v Coates* (1905) 39 ILTR 221.
[667] *McGirr v Devine* [1925] NI 94 at 97.
[668] *Murphy v Harrington* [1927] IR 339 at 344.

objections and requisitions and, if the vendor cannot or will not remove them, then the purchaser can repudiate.[669] It is important to note that there is a line of English authority to the effect that in a sale of land a purchaser can terminate the contract as soon as he discovers that the vendor does not have a good title to the property.[670] Some of these authorities were considered by Meredith J in *Murphy v Harrington*[671] and he concluded "It is clear that the reasoning in these cases only applies where the vendor has no title - where, if specific performance were granted, there would be no mutuality."[672] The modern view that mutuality is to be tested at the date of the hearing, not the time of the contract,[673] would seem to weaken this line of authority. The modern English position is stated by Goff LJ:[674]

> "It is true that where the vendor has no title the purchaser can on discovering the defect repudiate the contract forthwith in this sense, that thereby the vendor loses any right to specific performance, albeit he is able to make title before the date fixed for completion. This, however, is in my judgment a special right arising out of the difficulty of making title to land in England: see *Elliott v Pierson*[675] It does not affect the general principle that one should ordinarily look to the date of the hearing, and even in that case, unless the right to repudiate is exercised promptly, the vendor is allowed to put his title in order after the contract and claim specific performance. In that type of case I have no doubt that if both parties knew at the time of the contract that the vendor's title was defective and nevertheless contracted for a good title, the purchaser could not repudiate, at all events before the vendor had been allowed a reasonable time to perfect it."[676]

The latter part of that passage seems very much consistent with the two modern Irish decisions.[677]

[9.77] A formal contract usually provides a time limit for objections and requisitions but if an objection is serious or "goes to the root of the title" the vendor cannot bind the purchaser by a time condition.[678] When a defect in title is found then, unless the purchaser is entitled to repudiate at once and does so, the vendor should be given a reasonable time to cure the defect.[679] A vendor seeking specific performance does not need to have the property vested in his own name as long as he can compel the person in whose name it stands to convey it to the purchaser on the date on which the court directs completion of the sale.[680] When a person agrees to do something which he can do himself or get others to do the court requires him to do it or get it done unless the circumstances of a case make that highly unreasonable.[681] If an application to the court is necessary in order to make good title the vendor is likely to be expected to make it.[682] And, as we have seen earlier,

---

669 *Ibid.*
670 See Jones & Goodhart, *Specific Performance* (1986) at 62-7 and the detailed judgment of Megarry VC in *Pips (Leisure Productions) Ltd v Walton* 1981 EGD 1003; 43 P & CR 415.
671 [1927] IR 339 at 343-4.
672 At 344.
673 Para **9.70** *ante.*
674 *Price v Strange* [1977] 3 All ER 371 at 381-2.
675 [1948] Ch 452 at 455-6; [1948] 1 All ER 939 at 942.
676 *Cf* Buckley LJ at 389-90.
677 *McGirr's* case and *Murphy's* case.
678 *Re Carrige & McDonnell's Contract* [1895] 1 IR 288 at 296.
679 *Clegg v Wright* (1920) 54 ILTR 69 at 71-2.
680 *Northern Bank Ltd v Wilson* [1984] 16 NIJB at 16.
681 *Costigan v Hastler* (1804) 2 Schoales & Lefroy 583 at 598-601.
682 *Re Des Reaux & Setchfield's Contract* [1926] 1 Ch 178 considered by Meredith J in *Murphy's* case at 344.

there is usually an implied obligation on parties to make reasonable efforts to fulfil a condition of a contract[683] and each party is entitled to expect the other to be reasonable in taking such necessary steps are may be incidental to closing a sale.[684] A vendor plaintiff who, in reply to a proper requisition or objection, declines to do what is necessary to make good title, loses his right to specific performance.[685]

Restrictive conditions

[9.78] Formal contracts usually contain some restrictions on the right of the purchaser to investigate title. It is obvious that under an "open" contract the purchaser is entitled to a full investigation of title and no less obvious that the right to a full investigation may be cut down by conditions of sale.[686] It has been said that "a purchaser may preclude himself by agreement from making any inquiry as to title and specific performance may be enforced against him."[687] These are clearly valuable protections for a vendor whose title is defective. However, care must be taken by the vendor's solicitor in drafting a special condition and about the residual responsibilities on his client even when a restrictive condition is accepted.

[9.79] It is the general rule that, where a title is in fact defective, and the defect is, or ought to be, within the knowledge of the vendor, a condition against investigation will not prevent a purchaser from declining to complete unless that condition gives him some fair intimation or warning of the existence of the defect.[688] The vendor must fairly indicate what is the defect in his title to which the purchaser must submit and must take care that he is not guilty of any misrepresentation.[689] A condition will be misleading if it disguises the truth and puts the reader off the scent. One which "states, as though they were material, matters which are less material, and thereby distracts attention from the omission of what is more material" is misleading.[690] To bind the purchaser a condition must be fair and explicit and "the test of its being fair and explicit is whether it discloses all facts within the knowledge of the vendor which are material to enable the purchaser to determine whether or not he will buy the property subject to the stipulation limiting his right."[691] The condition must be clearly drafted because it will be construed in favour of the purchaser if it is ambiguous.[692] If the condition is ambiguous then, the title being bad, the vendor cannot get specific performance.[693] All the more so if the condition is a subterfuge or deliberately suppresses the true facts in relation to the defect it seeks to cover.[694] A clear condition, however, will enable a vendor to get specific performance despite the defect covered.[695] A misunderstanding about whether a vendor is left under the

---

[683] Para **3.26** *ante*.
[684] Para **3.27 ante**.
[685] *Maconchy v Clayton* [1898] 1 IR 291, at 307, 309, 310.
[686] *Re White & Hague's Contract* [1921] 1 IR 138 at 143.
[687] *Re White & Hague's Contract* at 144. But see discussion by Wylie, *Irish Conveyancing Law* (1978) at paras 10.040. 14.04.
[688] *Re Turpin & Ahern's Contract* [1905] 1 IR 85 at 103, 107.
[689] *Re Flynn & Newman's Contract* [1948]IR 104 at 112.
[690] *Re Lyons & Carroll's Contract* [1896] 1 IR 383 at 395.
[691] *Per* Cotton J in *Re Marsh & Earl Granville* 24 Ch D at 2 approved by Walker LJ *in Re Lyons & Carroll's Contract* at 397-8.
[692] *Re White & Hague's Contract* at 146.
[693] *Geoghegan v Connolly* (1858) 8 IR Ch R 598 at 60.
[694] *Boyd v Dickson* (1876) 10 IR Eq 239 at 254-5.
[695] *Re Furlong & Bogan's Contract* (1893) 31 LRI 191 at 194-5: registration pending in the Land Registry, vendor's right "incapable of being defeated"; see also *McGirr v Devine* [1925] NI 94 at 97-8.

normal obligation to deduce a good title or the purchaser must accept the title, whatever it is, may mean that there is not sufficient consensus for there to be a complete contract.[696] Even a contract by a purchaser to take such title as a vendor has does not relieve the vendor from the necessity of showing a bona fide title and producing the best title he can from the materials in his power.[697] The vendor will not, however, be required to make out any better title than he had at the date of the agreement.[698] A contract to take such title as the vendor has is a different thing from one which says nothing about title at all; in the latter case the interest sold is prima facie a freehold.[699]

Doubtful title

[9.80] A purchaser should not be compelled to take a title where there is a "reasonable decent probability of litigation".[700] A court will not force on a purchaser a title which would leave him to litigate points against judgment mortgagees.[701] There is authority for the view that an underlease, where the premises in it are comprised with others in an original lease under which the lessor has a right to re-enter for breach of covenant, so that the sublessee or his assignee might be evicted without any breach of covenant on his part, is bad title.[702] It seems otherwise if the property in the sublease is the same as that in the lease and superior lease.[703] Nor will a purchaser be forced to take property with a risk of an injunction restraining him from using it for the purpose for which he buys unless there is an express provision covering the point - *eg,* that he must get the necessary consent himself.[704] A liability to ejectment for forfeiture is a defect in title to which a vendor must call attention[705] and which will not be forced on a purchaser in the absence of a clear special condition requiring him to accept it. This is a matter of title; disrepair which may involve only an action for such damages for breach of covenant as are recoverable during the currency of the term[706] and, in the absence of a re-entry clause covering disrepair,[707] no risk of forfeiture is a defect in *subject-matter* and subject to the *caveat emptor* rule.[708] Where a vendor holds under a lease with a re-entry clause covering disrepair and fails to disclose a landlord's repairing notice to a purchaser a court may refuse specific performance on the ground that the vendor had not disclosed a material defect but it may also refuse a counterclaim for rescission and recovery of the deposit on the ground that

---

[696] *Gradwell v Maguire* (1872) IR 6 Eq 477 at 491-2, 493. See *Consensus* at paras **3.02-3** *ante* and defence of *No Contract* at paras **9.02-3**.

[697] *Keyes v Hayden* 1 WR 73 approved by O'Connor MR in *Re White and Hagues's Contract* at 145.

[698] *Molloy v Sterne* (1838) 1 Drury & Walsh 585 at 590; "for the longest term he could grant".

[699] *Swan v Miller* [1919] 1 IR 151 at 181.

[700] *Per* Alderson B in *Cattell v Corrall* 4 Y&C 228 quoted by Powell J *In Re Murphy & Griffin's Contract* [1919] 1 IR 187 at 204 and in *Re Walker & Elgee's Contract* (1918) 53 ILTR 22 at 24.

[701] *Tempany v Hynes* (HC) 10 July 1975, Finlay P, unrep at 16. On appeal, [1976] IR 101, the Supreme Court did not reject that point as a principle but held on grounds not argued in the (HC) that title was good: see Kenny J at 117.

[702] *Mulholland v Belfast Corporation* (1859) 9 IR Ch R 204 at 215 quoting Lord St. Leonards; *cf Geoghegan v Connolly* (1859) 8 IR Ch R 598.

[703] *Hayford v Criddle* 22 Beav 430 considered in *Mulholland's* case at 216.

[704] *Re Ashe & Hogan's Contract* [1920] 1 IR 159 at 165-6.

[705] *Re Flynn & Newman's Contract* [1948] IR 104 at 112; there was no forfeiture clause so the vendor was not in breach of his duty even though the landlord had written demanding that repairs be done. At 114 Kingsmill Moore J emphasised that he had formed no opinion whether an action by the vendor for specific performance would be successful.

[706] Discussed by Wylie, *Irish Landlord & Tenant Law*, paras 15.29-32.

[707] A very unusual omission nowadays.

[708] See Wylie, *Irish Conveyancing Law* (1978) at 5.03-4, 10.022-3.

the purchaser is bound by a clause to the effect that production of the last receipt for rent is conclusive evidence that all covenants have been observed and performed.[709]

[9.81] The court has power to make an order for specific performance which is conditional on the title being accepted; if a question arises on the title or the purchaser's right to reject it and claim damages in lieu of specific performance a separate issue can be tried if necessary.[710] In practice the court will consider and decide a wide range of issues of a title or conveyancing nature in a broad sense in an action for specific performance.[711] If two views on a point are open and a court leans in favour of there being good title there may yet be enough doubt to make it unreasonable to require the purchaser to accept the title.[712] If there is a serious doubt such as a difficult question of construction the court may be reluctant to force the title on the purchaser in a Vendor and Purchaser Summons[713] and may let the summons stand adjourned so that a construction summons may be issued and a decision given which will be binding on all interested parties.[714] The court may also adjourn an action for specific performance for a similar purpose[715] but this may not appeal as a very practicable way of settling an issue of the sort.[716] Obviously that will not be necessary if there is no real difficulty or doubt.[717] The modern tendency is to listen with less favour to a defence that title is too doubtful. It is the duty of a court hearing an action for specific performance, unless in very exceptional circumstances, "to decide the rights between the vendor and the purchaser even though a third party not a party to the action will not be bound by the decision".[718]

Acceptance of title

[9.82] A purchaser who is not bound to take his vendor's defective title may nevertheless decide to accept it with its defect. That he has this right is clear.[719] If he does so he must complete the purchase. It is well settled that in contracts for the sale of land where the vendor's estate turns out to be of a lower degree than that agreed to be sold, a willing purchaser is entitled to specific performance with compensation[720] although this is often modified by the terms of the particular contract.[721] If a right to compensation is validly excluded by the contract the purchaser will not get specific performance with

---

[709] *Beyfus v Lodge* [1925] 1 Ch 350 considered in *Re Flynn & Newman's Contract* at 111-2 but doubted in relation to the counterclaim by Jones and Goodhart, *Specific Performance* (1986) at 60 suggesting that where the facts justify the refusal of specific performance on the ground of non-disclosure or want of candour they also justify the setting aside of the contract.

[710] *O'Connor v McCarthy* [1982] IR 161 at 177.

[711] Eg *Dublin Laundry Co Ltd v Clarke* [1989] ILRM 29; *Crowley v Flynn* 1983 ILRM 513; *O'Connor v McCarthy* [1982] IR 161.

[712] *Crowley's* case at 516: held in fact good title not shown. See discussion by Jones and Goodhart *Specific Performance* (1986) at 65-6.

[713] On which see paras **8.53-9** *ante*.

[714] *Re Hogan & Marnell's Contract* [1919] 1 IR 422 at 428-9.

[715] *Wilson v Thomas* [1958] 1 All ER 871 at 879-80.

[716] See Jones & Goodhart, *op cit*, p 66 note 2. And see para **8.55** *ante* on third party rights and Vendor and Purchaser Summonses. *Cf Poole v Coates* (1842) 2 Drury and Warren 493 at 496-7.

[717] *Re Walker & Elgee's Contract* (1918) 53 ILTR 22 at 24.

[718] *Smith v Colbourne* [1914] 2 Ch 533 at 541; [1914-5] All ER 800 at 802 approved by the House of Lords in *MEPC Ltd v Christian-Edwards* [1981] AC 205 at 220; [1979] 3 All ER 752 at 757.

[719] *Re Geraghty & Lyons' Contract* (1919) 53 ILTR 57 at 58.

[720] *Swan v Miller* [1919] 1 IR 151 at 169 *per* Sir James Campbell C.

[721] As in *Molphy v Coyne* (1919) 53 ILTR 177.

compensation or "abatement".[722] A person who agrees to grant a certain interest which, it turns out later, he cannot give, normally must still convey, if required, as far as his interest in the property will permit.[723] If it turns out that he owns only part of the property he has agreed to sell the contract may be enforced in respect of that part.[724] An intending landlord who agrees to grant a lease in excess of his estate or powers may be required by the intending tenant to grant whatever lease he has power to grant together with compensation for the difference in value, if any, between what he agreed to grant and what he can grant.[725] Depending on the circumstances a defect may come within the arbitration provisions of the standard Law Society contract if that has been used.[726] When a purchaser is entitled to such compensation, whether or not under those arbitration provisions, he will be entitled to have his compensation paid by way of abatement of the purchase money and may delay closing until the amount has been agreed or fixed.[727]

[9.83] A purchaser may waive his right to investigate title and, in so far as he does so, he accepts the vendor's title and loses the right to rely on lack of title as a defence to a claim for specific performance. There may, of course, be an express waiver and that may be either absolute or conditional.[728] The question is more likely to arise in practice as an issue whether the conduct of the purchaser has amounted to a waiver of his right to investigate title further. Under standard conditions of sale any objection or requisition not made within an agreed time limit and not going to the root of the title is deemed to have been waived.[729] Taking possession on its own usually is not sufficient evidence of waiver but it has been described as a "very important consideration".[730] Even taking possession and doing some alterations may not necessarily be sufficient evidence of a waiver to prevent the purchaser rejecting the title.[731] A purchaser who is allowed into possession and works the land but is then dispossessed with some force by the vendor is very unlikely to be held to have waived his rights in relation to title problems.[732] However, a purchaser going into possession before completion must be very wary of the possibility of that being held to be a waiver of his rights in relation to title. The Law Society *General Conditions of Sale* do not deal with this point.[733] If a contract does provide for entry before completion the fact of entry is very unlikely to be evidence of waiver.[734] If there is no such provision a purchaser can protect his position by getting a letter from the vendor or his solicitor accepting that the relevant point is not waived though simply persisting with the point at

---

[722] *Molphy's* case; many such problems would now be covered by the arbitration provisions of General Condition 51 of the Law Society's standard conditions.

[723] *O'Rourke v Percival* (1811) 2 Ball & Beatty 58 at 64; the plaintiff failed because he dealt in fraud of a leasing power and/or he had gained an unfair advantage.

[724] *Ibid.*

[725] *Leslie v Crommelin* (1867) IR 2 Eq 134 at 141. *Cf Harnett v Yielding* (1805) 2 Schoales & Lefroy 549 where the plaintiff knew the intending landlord's title at the time of the deal: p 559-60.

[726] (1991) Ed General Conditions 33 and 51; note also 43-5.

[727] *Keating v Bank of Ireland* [1983] ILRM 295 at 299.

[728] *Townley v Bond* (1834) 4 Drury & Warren 240 at 261.

[729] See General Condition 17 of the Law Society's *General Conditions of Sale* (1991) Ed and consideration of a similar clause from Wylie, *Irish Conveyancing Law* (1978) Ed, at para 14.22.

[730] *Corless v Sparling* (1874) 8 IR Eq 335 at 340.

[731] *Boyd v Dickson* (1876) 10 IR Eq 239 at 253.

[732] Those events occurred in *Johnston v Johnston* (1869) IR 3 Eq 328. The court treated the defendant's resumed possession as ordinary possession of a vendor; waiver of title defects was not an issue.

[733] Note Wylie on a Northern Ireland clause *op cit* para 11.30. Note also implications for both parties considered at paras **11.23-5** *post.*

[734] *Bolton v London School Board* (1878) 7 Ch D 766.

issue in correspondence probably is good enough.[735] Acts suggesting ownership such as granting a lease[736] or a mortgage[737] are strong evidence of waiver. So is completing the purchase of part of property in sale without objection where the contract agreed on closing in two stages, provided for only one set of requisitions and the relevant title was common to the two parts of the property.[738] When a purchaser has accepted the title furnished by the vendor, by reason of waiver or otherwise, the question whether the title is in accordance with the contract no longer arises.[739] A waiver may cover just certain title matters leaving a purchaser free to investigate others.[740]

Title and the Statute of Frauds

[9.84] A written note or memorandum relied on to satisfy the Statute of Frauds need not state the estate or interest of the vendor in the property if the purchaser is prepared to take the interest which the vendor has.[741] So, if a vendor does not and cannot claim any greater interest than a tenancy and the intending purchaser is willing to accept that, the memorandum need not deal with it.[742] Of course, parties often deal on the basis that agreement on the title available is a material term. If an issue arises whether an oral contract, as distinct from any note or memorandum of it, needs express agreement on the precise title offered to be complete the purchaser's prior knowledge of the vendor's title may be a strong factor in reaching a conclusion that the oral contract was complete without any agreement on the nature of the title.[743] It would follow that the note or memorandum is sufficient without referring to the title.[744] Accordingly omitting to deal with questions of title does not necessarily afford a defence on the basis that an oral contract is incomplete or the note or memorandum relied on to satisfy the statute is insufficient.

MISDESCRIPTION

[9.85] Sometimes property or the title to it may be "misdescribed".[745] This sometimes arises where there are written contracts of a formal nature, typically using the Law Society's standard conditions, but in such cases the contract often contains provisions which cover issues of misdescription.[746] The parties will implement those provisions and usually no question will arise of the misdescription being a defence to a claim by either for specific performance. If a written contract is very informal or the party seeking specific performance relies on an oral contract and a note or memorandum to satisfy the Statute of Frauds he will think carefully about making any point similar to alleging

---

[735] As was done in *Rellie v Pyke* [1936] 1 All ER 345. J
[736] *Re Barrington* 3 LJ Bey 122.
[737] *Haydon v Bell* (1838) 1 Beav 337.
[738] *Peadar Nolan Ltd v O'Meara* (HC) 2 October 1985, Carroll J, unrep at 11.
[739] *Ibid.*
[740] *Corless v Sparling* (1874) 8 IR Eq 335 at 345.
[741] *Law v Roberts* [1964] IR 292 at 304-5.
[742] *Waldron v Jacob* (1870) IR 5 Eq 131 at 137.
[743] *Kelly v Park Hall School Ltd* [979] IR 340 at 347-8; on appeal at 351; this case was disapproved by the majority of the Supreme Court on "subject to contract" in *Boyle v Lee* [1992] 1 IR 555; [1992] ILRM 65.
[744] *Kelly's* case at 349-50; on appeal at 352.
[745] See the detailed consideration of misdescription by Wylie, *Irish Conveyancing Law* (1976), paras 10.032-8 and 10.046-9.
[746] Note the General Conditions mentioned in para **9.86** *infra*.

misdescription. Doing so might well assist a point by the defendant that the property in the alleged sale was not sufficiently stated or identifiable.[747] Success on that point could defeat the claim on the ground that there was not a complete contract or, if there was one, that the Statute was not satisfied. In certain cases a misdescription may overlap with title problems,[748] amount to innocent[749] or even fraudulent misrepresentation[750] or afford grounds for rectification[751] or rescission.[752]

[9.86] Many written contracts nowadays contain clauses entitling the purchaser (or indeed the vendor) to compensation for instances of misdescription and providing for arbitration if necessary.[753] Under the general law - *ie*, apart from any provision in the particular contract - a *vendor* is not entitled to compensation or an increase of price if a misdescription operates against him - *eg*, if more or better land is described in a contract than intended.[754] On suitable facts he may be able to get specific performance with rectification but the legal requirements for getting rectification and the onus of proof often cause difficulty.[755] The current Law Society's *General Conditions of Sale* (1991) Ed, provide that nothing in the memorandum, particulars or conditions shall entitle the vendor to require the purchaser to accept, or entitle the purchaser to require the vendor to assure (with or without compensation), property which differs substantially from the property agreed to be sold if the difference would materially prejudice the relevant party.[756] It also preserves the right of the purchaser to rescind or repudiate the sale where compensation attributable to a "material error" cannot be reasonably assessed.[757] Subject to those two points no "error" is to annul the sale or entitle either party to be discharged therefrom.[758] The word "error" is defined[759] to include "any mistake, omission, discrepancy, inaccuracy, mis-statement or mis-representation" in the memorandum particulars or conditions or in the course of any representation or negotiations leading to the sale, and whether in respect of measurements quantities or otherwise." With two exceptions[760] the purchaser is entitled to compensation by the vendor for loss suffered by him in his bargain relative to the sale as a result of an "error" communicated to him by or on behalf of the vendor. If the parties cannot reach agreement the issues may go to arbitration.[761]

[9.87] If a misdescription, though not proceeding from fraud, is in a material and substantial point, so far affecting the subject matter of the contract that it may reasonably

---

[747] On which see paras **3.09-10** and **5.34** *ante*.
[748] See paras **9.78-9 9.83-4** *ante*.
[749] Paras **9.16-23** *ante*.
[750] Paras **9.12-14, 9. 23**.
[751] Paras **10.15-24** *post*.
[752] Paras **10.25-33** *post*.
[753] As in *Geraghty v Rohan Industrial Estates* [1988] IR 419 (Law Society conditions of 1976); *Keating v Bank of Ireland* [1983] ILRM 295 (1978 conditions).
[754] *Re Lindsay & Forder's Contract* (1895) 72 LT 832.
[755] See paras **10.15-24** *post*.
[756] General Condition 33(*a*)(i).
[757] General Condition 33(*a*)(ii); this should not arise often.
[758] General Condition 33(*b*).
[759] By General Condition 33(*d*).
[760] (i) matters within General Condition 16(*a*) fixing purchasers with full notice of the actual state and condition of property subject to the vendor's duty under General Condition 15 to disclose certain easements etc; (ii) errors in plans furnished for identification only.
[761] General Condition 51.

be supposed that, but for such misdescription, the purchaser might never have entered into the contract at all, the contract is avoided and the purchaser is not bound to resort to a right to compensation.[762] Thus, an onerous right of way not disclosed by a vendor and of which the purchaser was not on notice would materially affect the contract from the purchaser's point of view and deprive the vendor of the right to an order for specific performance.[763] Where a contract referred to an advertisement the latter could be admitted in evidence to show that there is a misdescription in the contract.[764] Admitting the advertisement in evidence did not contravene the Statute of Frauds.[765] It is important not to confuse the principles or rules by which contracts are interpreted with those which guide the courts in enforcing or declining to enforce specific performance.[766] Where a vendor sues for specific performance he will fail, however clear the terms of his contract, including a condition to the effect that the property is believed and shall be taken to be correctly described and no compensation shall be allowed for misdescription etc, if the court feels that he has acted in such a way as to disentitle him to the relief.[767] Also, the court is less inclined to decree specific performance where there has been, *eg,* a misstatement as to area and the purchaser is barred from claiming compensation by a term in the contract than in cases where he is entitled to compensation.[768] A vendor having the benefit of a clause ruling out compensation for misdescription cannot get specific performance by unilaterally agreeing to allow compensation.[769] The relief may be obtainable if the parties have agreed, even in the course of the trial, to vary their contract by the introduction, in effect, of a clause providing for compensation.[770] It may also be granted where the vendor claims specific performance, the court would be disposed to refuse it unless the purchaser is willing to consent to a decree on terms of allowing compensation and both parties agree to that course.[771]

[9.88] If a misdescription or defect in title is not substantial[772] so that the purchaser will still get substantially what he bargained for he will not succeed in a defence to the claim for specific performance although he may be entitled to compensation.[773] This, of course, is subject to any provision in the particular contract and a clause barring compensation for misdescription will leave the purchaser without a right to specific performance *with compensation.*[774] The courts will not grant relief in respect of trivial misdescriptions or assumptions made by purchasers without reason. Thus, a "misnomer" such as describing as an "assignment" a deed which effected both an assignment and an appointment was held not to be such a misdescription as entitled a purchaser to be discharged from the

[762] *Flight v Booth* 1 Bing (NC) 370 considered in *Re Flynn and Newman's Contract* 1948 IR 104 at 109-10 and *Molphy v Coyne* (1919) 53
[763] *Molphy's* case at 179.
[764] *Thomson v Guy* (1844) 7 ILR 6 at 14, 15, Pennefather CJ *diss.*
[765] *Thomson's* case at 14, 16, Pennefather CJ *diss* at 12-13.
[766] *Molphy's* case at 181 referring to *Terry v White* 32 Ch D 14.
[767] *Ibid.*
[768] *Watson v Burton* [1956] 3 All ER 929 at 934.
[769] *Watson's* case at 937-8.
[770] *Watson's* case at 938 considering *Shepherd v Croft* [1911] 1 Ch 521 at 529.
[771] *Rutherford v Acton-Adams* [1915] AC 866 at 869.
[772] See examples at Wylie *Irish Conveyancing Law* (1978) para 10.037.
[773] *Stewart v Marquis of Conyngham* (1851) 1 IR Ch R 534 at 573; *Re Lewis decd* (1908) 42 ILTR 210 at 211; *McCann v Valentine* (1900) NIJR 28; *Hibernian Bank v Cassidy* (1902) 36 ILTR 156 at 157; *cf Martin v Cotter* (1846) 9 IR Eq R 351.
[774] *Molphy v Coyne* (1919) 53 ILTR 177 at 183-4.

contract.[775] It may not matter either that a document in the form of a lease is called an "agreement", especially where the contract agreed to sell the vendor's interest without defining whether it was legal. or equitable in nature.[776] A purchaser who is informed by particulars that the premises are in the occupation of tenants paying specified rents cannot complain if he discovers later that the tenure is greater than he had assumed without being misled by the particulars.[777] And if a purchaser knows when agreeing to buy what the true position is and that a description is incorrect he cannot rely on the misdescription to resist specific performance.[778]

---

[775] *Re Robb & Spillane's Contract* (1901) 1 NIJR 206 at 207.
[776] *Corless v Sparling* (1875) IR 9 Eq 595 at 600-1.
[777] *Clements v Conroy* [1911] 2 IR 500 at 524 529-30.
[778] *Dyer v Hargrave* (1805) 10 Ves 505; 1803-13 All ER 348 (purchaser sought specific performance with compensation and got compensation for defects of which he had not known); *cf Cobbett v Locke-King* (1900) 16 TLR 379.

Chapter 10

Some Other Reliefs

STRIKING OUT OR STAYING PROCEEDINGS FOR ABUSE OF PROCESS

[10.01] Negotiations do not always ripen into a contract.[1] If they break down a party who feels poorly treated or persuades himself to feel that way may issue proceedings for specific performance without considering too carefully whether he has an enforceable contract. This party is normally an intending purchaser who knows well the difficulty his proceedings and an associated *lis pendens*[2] will cause for the alleged vendor.[3] There is a real need for some control over this type of action. As Costello J pointed out:[4]

"A disappointed purchaser by instituting proceedings for specific performance and by registering a *lis pendens* against the land which he alleges he has purchased can effectively prevent a re-sale of the lands for a considerable time - perhaps extending over several years. Obviously substantial injustice could thereby result both to the owner of the land and to a subsequent innocent purchaser. In suitable cases the courts should be able to provide a speedy means for determining the issues between the vendor and the first purchaser. It seems to me that such a means is to hand. A vendor who is sued by a purchaser for specific performance may bring a motion (which is heard on affidavit) to stay or to strike out the proceedings and for an order directing the *lis pendens* to be vacated. In clear cases the court can so order; its jurisdiction arises in two ways."

Costello J then proceeded to consider one of the Rules of the Superior Courts[5] and an important inherent jurisdiction.[6] The alleged vendor may seek both types of relief. However the disappointed purchaser is likely to plead his case in such a way as to escape from the rule and force the vendor to rely on the inherent jurisdiction.

Possibly relief of similar effect could be obtained by an application for an order discharging a *lis pendens*.[7] However, it is very desirable to get rid of both the *lis pendens* and the related proceedings. The existence of proceedings capable of affecting land will be a major problem when the owner wants to sell it or raise money on its security even if a related *lis pendens* has been discharged. Conversely a subsisting *lis pendens* will attract queries even though the related proceedings have been struck out or stayed.

[10.02] Order 19, Rule 28 of the Rules of the Superior Courts may help in certain cases. This provides:

---

[1] See *Lynch v O'Meara* (SC) 8 May 1975, unrep at 4, 6.
[2] On which see paras **10.10-14** *infra*.
[3] See *Dorene Ltd v Suedes (Ireland) Ltd* [1981] IR 312 at 332-4.
[4] *Barry v Buckley* [1981] IR 306 at 307.
[5] See the next paragraph.
[6] Discussed in paras **10.03-5** *infra*.
[7] As in *Kelly v Kinneen* (HC) 29 April 1980, McWilliam J, unrep. See also *Dunville Investments Ltd v Kelly* (HC) 27 April 1979, Costello J, unrep. Discharging a *lis pendens* is, of course, a separate matter but that relief is often sought in the same motion which seeks to stay or strike out proceedings as the passage quoted from the judgment in *Barry's* case indicates.

"The court may order any pleading to be struck out, on the ground that it discloses no reasonable cause of action or answer and in any such case or in case of the action or defence[8] being shown by the pleadings to be frivolous or vexatious, the court may order the action to be stayed or dismissed, or judgment to be entered accordingly, as may be just."[9]

Although that wording does not expressly prohibit the admission of evidence on a motion under the rule to stay or strike out proceedings the court can only make an order under the rule when the pleading discloses no reasonable cause of action on its face[10] or the vexation or frivolity appears from the pleadings alone.[11] For this reason a party with a dubious claim usually can present it in such a way as to escape being caught by the rule. He is likely to plead facts which, if true, would support a good cause of action and therefore the pleading will not be struck out for simply failing to disclose a cause of action.[12] Nor will it appear *on the pleadings* to be frivolous or vexatious. The power of the courts to amend pleadings should also be kept in mind. If an application under the rule was otherwise likely to succeed but an amendment to the pleadings could, so to speak, save the pleading attacked and the action founded on it the court would be inclined to allow the amendment and not dismiss the action[13] unless the case was one where the relief would be given under the inherent jurisdiction anyway.

The inherent jurisdiction

[10.03] The court has an *inherent* jurisdiction to strike out or stay proceedings. This jurisdiction:

"is different from that directly arising from the Rules of the Superior Courts where a statement of claim discloses no cause of action or the proceedings constitute an abuse of the process of the court, where, pursuant to s 27, sub-s 5 of the Judicature Act (Ireland) 1877, the court may grant a stay of proceedings so far as may be necessary for the purpose of justice."[14]

On applications made to exercise the jurisdiction the court is not limited to the pleadings of the parties but is free to hear evidence on affidavit relating to the issues in the case.[15] It may be necessary "to adduce evidence in explanation of the pleadings".[16] If, for example, vexation is so established by undisputed facts which explain the nature of the claim made or pleading the court has inherent jurisdiction in the interests of justice to dismiss or strike out.[17] An action which cannot succeed is vexatious for that very reason and it would be an injustice to a defendant to allow it to continue.[18] In practice it seems

---

[8] This allows striking out a defence plea and is consistent with the probable position under the inherent jurisdiction; see para **10.03** *infra*.
[9] The identical former rule was considered by O'Higgins CJ in *McCabe v Harding* [1984] ILRM 105 at 108-9, Hederman J concurring and by Costello J in *Barry v Buckley* [1981] IR 306 at 307-8.
[10] *Barry's* case at 308.
[11] *McCabe's* case at 108-9.
[12] *Eg*, as in *Bond v Holton* [1959] IR 302 at 308, 310-11.
[13] *Sun Fat Chan v Osseous Ltd* [1992] 1 IR 425 at 428; *cf Bond v Holton* [1959] IR 302 at 308.
[14] *Per* McCarthy J in *Sun Fat Chan's* case [1992] 1 IR 425 at 428. Note that s 27(5) of the 1877 Act is primarily concerned with the cardinal principle of the Act that there should never be conflicting proceedings going on at the same time in two branches of the court.
[15] *Barry v Buckley* [1981] IR 306 at 308, approving Wylie's *Judicature Acts* (1906) at pp 34-37 where the author discusses s 27(5) of the 1877 Act very fully; *Stud Managers Ltd v Marshall* [1985] IR 83 at 86.
[16] *Per* O'Higgins CJ in *McCabe v Harding* [1984] ILRM 105 at 109, Hederman J concurring.
[17] *McCabe's* case at 109.
[18] *Ibid* at 110.

to be always a plaintiff who is caught by this inherent jurisdiction but, applying the same underlying logic, a defendant might be denied the right to defend an action in a plenary hearing if the facts are clear and it is shown that the defence is unsustainable.[19] This possibility could be useful if, for example, an intending purchaser threatens proceedings for specific performance but does not issue them; the owner of the land could begin proceedings to deal with that claim[20] and later consider applying to the court to have defence pleas struck out.

[10.04] Generally the courts should be slow to entertain an application to stay or strike out proceedings and grant the relief sought.[21] The jurisdiction should be exercised sparingly and only in clear cases but it is one which enables the court to avoid injustice,[22] particularly in cases whose outcome depends on the interpretation of a contract or agreed correspondence.[23] Experience has shown that the trial of an action may identify a variety of circumstances not contemplated at earlier stages in proceedings; it may appear at the early stages that the facts are clear and established but the trial itself may disclose a different picture. Subject to that qualification we may recognise the enforcement of a jurisdiction of this kind "as a healthy development in our jurisprudence and one not to be disowned for its novelty though there may be a certain sense of disquiet at its rigour".[24] It has also been described as "a jurisdiction necessary to be exercised on occasion to preserve a proper discipline in the conduct of litigation."[25] It should help if the court feels that on the hearing of the defendant's motion it has all the relevant facts and material which would be available on a plenary hearing of the plaintiff's action.[26]

The key question on an application of this sort may be whether there is "any element of reality" in the claim attacked[27] or it "lacks reality and is without foundation".[28] The application is likely to succeed if the claim attacked is "unsuccessful in law" even though it may be "not without merits".[29] Proceedings brought for improper reasons or for "an ulterior and collateral purpose" are specially vulnerable to being stayed.[30] If a court concludes that a claim is neither frivolous nor vexatious it should still consider whether the claim is so clearly unsustainable that it should be struck out.[31] Controversies such as whether a purchaser is able to raise the balance of the purchase price may be very difficult to determine on a motion to strike out or stay proceedings.[32] An issue which can be decided on documentary evidence filed in connection with the motion has a much better chance.[33] However, it may be necessary for the court to investigate fully the

---

19   *Per* McCarthy J in *Sun Fat Chan's* case at 428. He did not express any view on the decision in *Barry's* case as that had not been debated.

20   Eg, by seeking a declaration that no contract exists.

21   *Sun Fat Chan v Osseous Ltd* [1992] 1 IR 425 at 428.

22   *Barry v Buckley* [1981] IR 306 at 308.

23   *Stud Managers Ltd v Marshall* [1985] IR 83 at 86.

24   *Sun Fat Chan's* case at 428-9.

25   By O'Flaherty J in *O'Neill v Ryan* [1993] ILRM 557 at 558.

26   *McCabe's v Harding* [1984] ILRM 105 at 108.

27   *McCabe's* case at 109, *per* O'Higgins CJ, Hederman J concurring; cf Henchy J at 113.

28   *Ibid* at 110.

29   *Per* Henchy J in *McCabe's* case at 113. *Cf Dunville Investments Ltd v Kelly* (HC) 27 April 1979, Costello J, unrep at 3-5 where a *lis pendens* related to a claim to enforce a valid contract was vacated as specific performance of a prior contract had been decreed.

30   *McGinn v Beagan* [1962] IR 364 at 369 (debtor's summons stayed even though the debt was due).

31   *O'Neill v Ryan* [1993] ILRM 557 at 561 approving *DK v AK* (HC) 2 October 1992, Costello J, unrep.

32   *Stud Managers Ltd v Marshall* [1985] IR 83 at 86.

33   As in the *Stud Managers* case at 86-8.

circumstances in which an agreement was made and that would prevent a judge having the necessary degree of confidence entitling him to strike out proceedings.[34] In exercising this jurisdiction also the courts will take into account the results of possible amendment[35] and will be slow to shut out any argument, even at the stage of an appeal, which might save the action from an early demise.[36]

[10.05] The remedy of an order striking out or staying proceedings obviously is not limited to claims for specific performance. However, it has been said to be peculiarly appropriate to actions for the enforcement of contracts since it is likely that the subject matter would, but for the existence of the action, be the focus of another contract.[37] The need in practice for such a remedy is illustrated by the relatively high number of specific performance cases[38] found among applications to strike out or stay proceedings or to have a *lis pendens* vacated. Modern examples of the jurisdiction being exercised in specific performance cases are where an argument that a condition about planning permission was for the benefit of the purchaser alone failed,[39] an action depended on an alleged implied term giving the purchaser extra time to cope with planning problems,[40] a vendor had rescinded the contract and was perfectly entitled to do so,[41] an alleged vendor had stipulated that there would be no binding contract until a written contract was signed by both parties and the deposit paid[42] or the documents before the court did not disclose a sufficient memorandum to satisfy the Statute of Frauds and the plaintiff could not suggest that any other documents could constitute a memorandum.[43] It seems likely that many "subject to contract"[44] cases could also be dealt with now under the inherent jurisdiction. In *Boyle v Lee*[45] such an application was made and the High Court directed that issues be tried to determine the motion.[46] The plaintiff purchaser succeeded in the High Court but the judgments in the Supreme Court[47] have made it extremely difficult for parties to put up successful arguments in future against "subject to contract" or similar phrases.

Risk of liability for damages

[10.06] A party who brings or perseveres with an action which is likely to be struck out or stayed under the inherent jurisdiction should bear in mind that he risks liability in damages. Those could be substantial depending on the effect his proceedings have had. The test is not whether the action is, or is likely to be, stayed or struck out but is one quite

---

[34] *Lac Minerals Ltd v Chevron Mineral Corporation of Ireland* (HC) 6 August 1993, Keane J, unrep at 31-4. He considers the extent to which a court can take the surrounding circumstances into account in construing a contract at 28-30.
[35] *Sun Fat Chan's* case at 429.
[36] *Ibid.*
[37] By McCarthy J in *Sun Fat Chan v Osseous Ltd* [1992] 1 IR 425 at 429.
[38] A tiny proportion of total reported cases.
[39] *Sun Fat Chan's* case in the High Court recounted by McCarthy J in the report of the appeal, [1992] 1 IR 425 at 427-8, 429.
[40] *Ibid* at 429-30 - a different argument from that made in the High Court.
[41] *Stud Managers Ltd v Marshall* [1985] IR 83 at 87-8.
[42] *Barry v Buckley* [1981] IR 306 at 3.10.
[43] *Kelly v Kineen* (HC) 29 April 1980, McWilliam J, unrep at 10-11. This was an application to discharge *lites pendentes* but was decided on the basis that the claim for specific performance had to fail. Note reference to *Kelly's* case in *Barry's* case at 308.
[44] This topic is discussed in Ch 4 *supra*.
[45] [1992] 1 IR 555; [1992] ILRM 65.
[46] See judgment of Finlay CJ at 561-2 (IR); 67 (ILRM).
[47] See paras **4.22-5** *ante*.

likely to be met where proceedings are in fact struck out or stayed for abuse of process. The authorities establish[48] that a claim for damages at common law will lie for the institution or maintenance of a civil action if it can be shown that the action was instituted or maintained (*a*) without reasonable or probable cause, (*b*) maliciously,[49] and (*c*) that the claimant has suffered actual damage or the impugned action was one which the law presumes will have caused the claimant damage.[50]

As to reasonable or probable cause, the test to be applied by the court is an objective one and so the court must itself examine the facts and the legal principles applicable to them and then decide whether there were reasonable grounds for instituting or maintaining the action.[51] If the facts do afford reasonable and probable cause the proceedings were justified and usually it is not necessary to enquire further.[52] The belief of the plaintiff in the impugned proceedings in the merits of his case is usually not relevant to the question of reasonable and probable cause though it would be wrong to suggest that the belief could *never* come into that question.[53] An honest belief is unlikely to be a defence when there is a finding of malice and the belief was not reasonable in the circumstances.[54] Acting on favourable advice given by counsel usually is not conclusive that there was reasonable and probable cause and the court itself should consider whether the advice was correct.[55] However, the advice is likely to be a potent factor though its weight may vary according to factors such as the degree of experience of the counsel in the relevant area and the manner in which the case has been presented to him.[56] If the plaintiff misstated the facts to his legal advisers that would strengthen a claim that the proceedings had been instituted for an improper purpose.[57]

[10.07] Secondly, it is necessary to show also that the proceedings were instituted or maintained maliciously.[58] Malice means the presence of some improper and wrongful motive.[59] An intent to use the legal process in question for a purpose other than its legally appointed and appropriate purpose can amount to malice.[60] On this point the state of mind of the plaintiff in the impugned proceedings usually is important. Save in exceptional cases the "state of his belief goes only to malice, and not to reasonable and probable cause".[61] Where legal advice is obtained before proceedings are issued or while they are pending[62] the nature of that advice may be a highly material factor in considering whether the plaintiff had an improper motive; it may help to show that he was using the

---

[48]   *Dorene Ltd v Suedes (Ireland) Ltd* [1981] IR 312 at 316. Note the discussion in Ch 36 of McMahon & Binchy, *Irish Law of Torts* 2nd Ed (1990), esp their consideration of the *Dorene Ltd* case at p 682-3.

[49]   On this see next para.

[50]   See para **10.08** *infra*.

[51]   The *Dorene Ltd* case at 318.

[52]   *Tempest v Snowden* [1952] 1 KB 130 at 138-9; [1952] 1 All ER 1 at 4-6, approved by Costello J in the *Dorene Ltd* case at 318-9.

[53]   *Ibid*, approved by Costello J, *Ibid*.

[54]   *Cruise v Burke* [1919] 2 IR 182.

[55]   *Abbott v Refuge Assurance* [1961] 3 All ER 1074 considered in the *Dorene Ltd* case at 319.

[56]   *Abbott's* case at 1083-4, 1087; *cf* 1095

[57]   *Murphy v Kirwan* [1994] 1 ILRM 293 at 297 quoting Costello J.

[58]   The *Dorene Ltd* case at 319.

[59]   *Ibid*.

[60]   *Ibid*, citing *Pike v Waldrum* [1952] 1 Lloyds Rep 431 and a passage from the 16th Ed of Salmond on *Torts*; *cf McGinns v Beagan* [1962] IR 364.

[61]   *Per* Lord Denning in *Tempest v Snowden* [1952] 1 KB at 140; [1952] 1 All ER 1 at 6, quoted by Costello J in the *Dorene Ltd* case at 319.

[62]   As occurred in the *Dorene Ltd* case.

proceedings for some legally inappropriate purpose.[63] Thus, if counsel advises while an action is pending that he feels sure that it would fail if it went the full distance, the plaintiff in that action probably will be liable for persevering with it after receiving the advice[64] though not necessarily for having begun it.[65] Continuing with the action after getting that kind of advice may lead to a conclusion that the action has been kept going because of the pressure which the existence of the action and the associated *lis pendens* would exert on the defendant and to assist in negotiations,[66] both of which would be wrongful motives actuated by malice in the legal sense.

[10.08] The third and final ingredient[67] needed to succeed in an action for abuse of process is that the plaintiff has suffered damage as a result of the impugned proceedings.[68] In the absence of actual damage the claimant will have to show that the impugned action is one which the law regards as causing damage[69] or argue successfully that the law would presume that the plaintiff must have suffered some damage by being deprived of his ability to deal with his property as he wished.[70] It has been said that although an action does not give rise to an action for malicious prosecution inasmuch as it does not necessarily or naturally involve damage, there are legal proceedings which do necessarily and naturally involve damage.[71] Nevertheless it may be difficult to persuade a court that it should award damages for abuse of process unless actual loss is proved. Once actual loss is proved the court will not have to consider whether an action lies in the circumstances of the case without proof of actual damage.[72]

The plaintiff in an action for abuse of process would be wise to inform the defendant (ie, plaintiff in the abusing proceedings) of all losses which the plaintiff feels he is likely to suffer unless the impugned proceedings and any *lis pendens* are removed. That ought to help in relation to any difficulties about remoteness of damages.[73] Thus, in *Dorene Ltd v Suedes (Ireland) Ltd*[74] the defendant's solicitors gave a clear warning of a counter-claim for damages when agreeing to accept service of the summons and they followed that about three weeks later with full details of a substantial offer which their client was prevented from accepting by the *lis pendens*.

[10.09] Three further points may be noted at this stage. Firstly, it might be suggested that the defendant in the impugned action should apply to the court to have it struck out or stayed under the inherent jurisdiction[75] and so reduce the risk of it causing him loss.

---

[63] The *Dorene Ltd* case at 319.

[64] The *Dorene Ltd* case at 327-32. The position may depend on the firmness of the advice. In that case "Counsel's advice was quite unequivocal; he advised that Dorene's claim would not succeed": p 328.

[65] The plaintiff was not liable for *starting* the action as its solicitor gave bona fide advice that specific performance proceedings be instituted and "on balance" he was optimistic about the outcome: p 326. *Cf Murphy v Kirwan* [1994] ILRM 293 at 297 quoting Costello J.

[66] So found in *Dorene Ltd's* case: p 331; *cf Murphy's* case at 298.

[67] Of those noted at para **10.06** *supra.*

[68] *Dorene Ltd v Suedes (Ireland) Ltd* [1981] IR 312 at 319-20.

[69] *Ibid*, p 320.

[70] *Ibid* at 334.

[71] *Quartz Hill Gold Mining Co v Eyre* (1883) 11 QBD 674 at 691 approved by Costello J in *Dorene Ltd's* case at 317.

[72] The *Dorene Ltd* case at 320.

[73] On which see Ch 3 of McMahon & Binchy, *Irish Law of Torts*, 2nd Ed (1990); *cf* in contract Clark, *Contract Law in Ireland*, 3rd Ed (1992) at 453-61.

[74] [1981] IR 312 at 327.

[75] On which see paras **10.03-5** *supra.*

Certainly that step merits consideration. However, things often will not be clear enough in the early stages for that relief to be obtained.[76] This is obviously so when reasons why an action is being maintained improperly only come into being after it was commenced.[77]

Secondly, it is unnecessary for a party to show that the impugned proceedings have already been determined in his favour before he begins his action for damages for abuse of process. Such a requirement does exist in the tort of malicious prosecution.[78] However, separate torts of malicious prosecution and malicious abuse of the process of the court evolved during the 16th and 17th centuries.[79] It became clear also that the basis of the action was damage to the complainant and not injury to the public.[80] In *Dorene Ltd v Suedes (Ireland) Ltd*[81] the impugned claim was discontinued only six months after the counterclaim for damages for malicious abuse was delivered and the adverse opinion of counsel had been given.[82] No argument seems to have been made that the counterclaim should fail because it was brought before the impugned claim was determined.[83] The principles found by Costello J[84] strongly suggest that such an argument would have failed. In a modern English case[85] the Court of Appeal accepted arguments that there is a tort of abuse of process of the court established by *Grainger v Hill*[86] which must be distinguished from the tort of malicious prosecution and which does not depend on the impugned proceedings having terminated.[87]

Thirdly, an abuser is likely to lose the benefit of the professional privilege which normally prohibits disclosure of communications between a client and his legal adviser.[88] The principle underlying this privilege is that a person entitled to and consulting a lawyer should be able to place unrestricted and unbounded confidence in the professional agent and that the communications should be kept secret unless he consents to disclosure.[89] The privilege extends not only to advice sought and obtained in the expectation of or in preparation for actual or pending litigation but also to such communications with a lawyer as pass for professional communications in a professional capacity.[90] An exception was established in respect of communications criminal in themselves or intended to further any criminal purpose.[91] It became clear later that the exception covered all forms

---

[76] See the *Dorene Ltd* case at 333-4. See also McCarthy J in *Sun Fat Chan v Osseous Ltd* [1992] 1 IR 425 at 428.
[77] As in the *Dorene Ltd* case when counsel's advice was received.
[78] McMahon & Binchy, *Irish Law of Torts*, 2nd Ed (1989) at 676-8.
[79] *Dorene Ltd v Suedes (Ireland) Ltd* [1981] IR 306 at 315; *Speed Seal Products Ltd v Paddington* [1986] 1 All ER 91.
[80] The *Dorene Ltd* case at 315.
[81] [1981] IR 306.
[82] The counter-claim was delivered about a week after the advice. The date of delivery of the counterclaim is stated at p 313 and in the judgment at 330; getting the advice of counsel is covered by the judgment at 327-8.
[83] By discontinuance.
[84] Noted in para **10.06** *supra*.
[85] *Speed Seal Products Ltd v Paddington* [1986] 1 All ER 91 approving *Grainger v Hill* (1838) 4 Bing NC 212, 132 ER 769.
[86] (1838) 4 Bing NC 212, 132 ER 769.
[87] The *Speed Seal Products Ltd* case, headnote, item (2) and pp 97-8. This interlocutory appeal is wholly consistent with the thrust and result of the *Dorene Ltd* case.
[88] As occurred in *Murphy v Kirwan* [1994] 1 ILRM 293.
[89] *Bula Ltd v Crowley* [1994] 1 ILRM 495 at 497-8, considering *Smurfit Paribas Bank Ltd v AAB Export Finance Ltd* [1990] 1 IR 469; [1990] ILRM 588.
[90] *Bula Ltd's* case at 498.
[91] *R. v Cox* (1884) 14 QBD 153 at 167 approved in *Murphy's* case at 299.

of fraud and dishonesty.[92] The Supreme Court has stated recently the principle that professional privilege cannot and must not be applied so as to be injurious to the interests of justice and to those in the administration of justice where persons have been guilty of moral turpitude or of dishonest conduct, even though it may not be fraud.[93] Nothing could be more injurious to the administration of justice nor to the interests of justice than that a person should falsely and maliciously bring an action and should abuse for an ulterior or improper purpose the processes of the court.[94] Thus a person who sues for specific performance to obtain a commercial advantage by forcing the defendant to concede an unjustified claim so as to avoid the consequences of having to defend a High Court action is likely to lose the protection of professional privilege.

REMOVING A *LIS PENDENS*

The nature and effect of a lis pendens

[10.10] The law relating to *lis pendens* is of very long standing. The basic principle involved is that the law will not allow parties to litigation to give to others, pending the litigation, rights to the property in dispute so as to prejudice the opposite party.[95] The historical background has been noted by Kenny J:[96]

> "In the 18th and 19th centuries Chancery suits often continued for many years and,[97] as most of them related to land, the position of a purchaser, lessee or mortgagee of the property to which the action related presented a difficult problem. If a person acquired his interest from a defendant without notice of the proceedings, did he take it subject to the rights to which the plaintiff was subsequently declared to be entitled in the suit which might have been started many years before? The answer given in Ireland and England was that a person who acquired an estate or interest in relation to which a suit had been started when he got his title took it subject to the rights and liabilities which might be declared in the suit whether he had notice of it or not. This was based originally on the remarkable view that everyone knew of all the actions which were pending in the courts, and so took his interest with notice of them."

The underlying principle is not really one involving any doctrine of notice although, as we shall see shortly,[98] parliament introduced a provision that a purchaser or mortgagee is not affected by a *lis pendens* unless he has express notice or the *lis* is registered. Lord Cranworth explained the traditional position:[99]

> "It is scarcely correct to speak of *lis pendens* as affecting a purchaser through the doctrine of notice, though undoubtedly the language of the courts often so describes its operation. It affects him not because it amounts to notice, but because the law does not allow litigant

---

[92] *Murphy's* case at 299 approving a passage from *Crescent Farm (Sidcup) Sports Ltd v Stirling Offices Ltd* [1972] Ch 553.
[93] *Murphy's* case at 300.
[94] *Ibid.*
[95] *Mooney v Equity Bank Ltd* (HC) 22 May 1980, McWilliam J, unrep at 4; *Giles v Brady* [1974] IR 462 at 464.
[96] *Giles v Brady* [1974] IR 462 at 463-4.
[97] An Irish example cited by Kenny J is *Gaskell v Durdin* (1812) 2 Ball & Beatty 167; a bill seeking possession was filed in 1760 and the tenant's application for restoration was heard in 1812.
[98] Para **10.11** *infra.*
[99] *Bellamy v Sabine* (1857) 1 De G & J 566 at 578, approved by Kenny J in *Giles's* case at 466.

parties to give to others, pending the litigation, rights to the property in dispute, so as to prejudice the opposite party. Where a litigation is pending between a plaintiff and a defendant as to the right to a particular estate, the necessities of mankind require that the decision of the court in the suit shall be binding, not only on the litigant parties, but also on those who derive title under them by alienations made pending the suit, whether such alienees had or had not notice of the pending proceedings. If this were not so, there could be no certainty that the litigation would ever come to an end. A mortgage of sale made before final decree to a person who had no notice of the pending proceedings would always render a new suit necessary and so interminable litigation might be the consequence."[100]

[10.11] The doctrine of *lis pendens* must have worked considerable hardship because a purchaser or mortgagee who bought property in ignorance of a suit might find that the land was liable for claims established in an action which had been started many years before.[101] The justification for the rule apparently was to avoid delaying the progress of suits by having to join purchasers as new parties.[102] A purchaser put himself, to a great extent, in the power and at the mercy of the parties with whom he dealt, and with whom alone the court had to deal, and could not complain if the rights on which his own rights depended were not duly asserted or defended.[103]

Parliament intervened[104] by providing for a system of registration which did not alter the nature of a *lis pendens*[105] but provided that a purchaser or mortgagee would not be bound or affected by the *lis pendens* unless he has express notice of it or a memorandum or minute of it has been left with the appointed officer who must enter the particulars[106] in a book to be called "The Index to *Lis Pendens*" in alphabetical order by the name of the person whose estate is intended to be affected. To be effective the memorandum or minute should be registered within five years before execution of the conveyance to the purchaser or mortgagee.[107] Another statutory intervention gave the courts express power to vacate a *lis pendens* without the consent of the person who registered it if the relevant suit or proceedings is not being *bona fide* prosecuted.[108] Since the interventions by statute the object of registration of an action or proceeding as a *lis pendens* has been said to be "to prevent the parties to the proceedings from creating new rights inconsistent with the rights and equities asserted in the proceeding"[109] which still incorporates the same basic principle we have already seen.[110] It is important to note that there is no statutory requirement to specify any particular property in registering a *lis* and a claim over all the assets which a person or company owns is likely to suffice.[111] An intending purchaser or

---

[100] See also *AS v GS* [1994] 2 ILRM 68 at 71-3.
[101] *Giles v Brady* [1974] IR 462 at 467; *Re Kelly's Carpetdrome Ltd* [1984] ILRM 418 at 423.
[102] *Massy v Batwell* (1843) 4 Drury & Warren 58 at 68.
[103] *Ibid.*
[104] By the Judgments (Ireland) Act, 1844, the Judgment Mortgage (Ireland) Act 1850, the Lis Pendens Act, 1867 and s 21 of the Judgments Registry (Ireland) Act 1871: see discussion by Kenny J in *Giles's* case at 467-70.
[105] *Giles's* case at 463.
[106] Name, usual or last known abode and title trade or profession of the person affected, the court, title of cause, date of filing: see Wylie, *Irish land Law*, 2nd Ed (1986), para 13.165, esp fn 74 and cases cited. *Cf* Fitzgerald, *Land Registry Practice* (1989) at p 184 in relation to an entry on a folio.
[107] Section 5, Judgment Mortgage (Ireland) Act, 1850; see *Giles's* case at 467.
[108] Section 2, Lis Pendens Act 1867: see para **10.12** *infra.*
[109] By Naish C in *Re O'Byrne's Estate* (1885) 15 LRI 373.
[110] Para **10.10** *supra.*
[111] *Re Kelly's Carpetdrome Ltd* [1984] ILRM 418 at 423-4:

mortgagee must therefore check carefully to see whether the action related to a lis affects the property in which he is interested. It should also be noted that dealings by a person who is not a party to the litigation in respect of which a *lis* is registered are not affected by the doctrine of *lis pendens*.[112]

The test for vacating a lis pendens

[10.12] The test in deciding an application to have a *lis pendens* vacated is whether the action in respect of which the *lis* has been registered is being prosecuted bona fide.[113] A finding that it is not being prosecuted bona fide gives the jurisdiction to vacate it without the consent[114] of the person who registered it.[115] The phrase "bona fide prosecuted" in s 2 of the Lis Pendens Act 1867 covers both the institution and continuation of proceedings.[116] A claim is not being bona fide prosecuted if it is clear that the plaintiff will not obtain specific performance or his claim is "unsustainable"[117] This may apply even where the action is based on a valid contract. Thus where specific performance has been ordered in respect of an earlier contract having priority a *lis pendens* relating to a later contract has been vacated[118] though that decision did not affect the plaintiff's claim for damages or any rights he might claim in relation to the purchase price paid by the prior purchaser.[119] A claim for damages, however valid, normally will not justify the retention of a *lis*.[120] A claim to recover a deposit in reliance on a purchaser's lien[121] probably will[122] unless it is clear that the vendor has become entitled to forfeit the deposit.[123] A claim based on a statutory provision which, if successful, would affect an interest in land, does justify a *lis pendens*.[124] Since the court needs to be satisfied that the proceedings are not being prosecuted bona fide in order to direct the vacation of a *lis pendens* it is necessary to show that no issue of fact remains between the parties.[125] Thus, if the defence is that there has been rescission of the contract by consent that rescission must be "clear and unambiguous".[126] An intending purchaser who cannot point to a sufficient memorandum to satisfy the Statute of Frauds is likely to have his *lis pendens* discharged.[127]

Registration of a *lis* against a person who is not shown to have any interest in the relevant property cannot be allowed to continue.[128]A purchaser who has paid the entire purchase money and so left the vendor with no remaining beneficial interest in the

---

[112] *Mooney v Equity Bank Ltd* (HC) 29 April 1980, McWilliam J, unrep at 7 (the *lis* did not affect the defendant's right to sell as mortgagee).
[113] *Flynn v Buckley* [1980] IR 423 at 426-7, 429.
[114] Note the former doubt over the need for consent: para **10.13** *infra*.
[115] Section 2 of the Lis Pendens Act, 1867. See *Flynn's* case at 426, 429; *Culhane's* case at 13; *Dunville Investments Ltd v Kelly* (HC) 27 April 1979, Costello J, unrep at 3.
[116] *Culhane's* case at 13.
[117] *Dunville Investments Ltd v Kelly*, (HC) 27 April 1980, Costello J, unrep at 3, 4.
[118] The *Dunville Investments* case at 4-5.
[119] *Ibid* at 4.
[120] *O'Connor v McCarthy* [1982] IR 161 at 178.
[121] On which see para **5.04** *ante*.
[122] *Giles v Brady* [1974] IR 462 at 467, 470.
[123] As in *Stud Managers Ltd v Marshall* [1985] IR 83; p 88.
[124] *AS v GS* [1994] 2 ILRM 68 at 73 - a property adjustment order pursuant to the Judicial Separation and Family Law Reform Act, 1989 (on which see also paras **7.33, 7.37** *ante*).
[125] *Flynn v Buckley* [1980] IR 423 at 429.
[126] *Ibid*.
[127] *Kelly v Kineen* (HC) 29 April 1980, McWilliam J, unrep at 3, 10.
[128] *Carrigan v Carrigan* (HC) 12 May 1983, O'Hanlon J, unrep at 8-9.

property[129] is entitled to an order vacating a *lis pendens* registered against that vendor related to a subsequent action brought by some other person in relation to the land.[130] Vacation of a *lis pendens* has been ordered in specific performance cases where the vendor had lawfully terminated the contract and there was no new enforceable contract[131] and where there was an enforceable prior contract.[132] It has been held to be unnecessary on a vendor and purchaser summons where a mortgagee sold with priority and a plaintiff in a puisne claim against the land accepted that he could not claim any right to the lands as against the mortgagee.[133]

[10.13] Doubt existed formerly whether during the continuance of litigation in respect of which a *lis pendens* had been duly registered the court had jurisdiction to order that the *lis* be vacated without the consent of the party who registered it. It was held that there was no such jurisdiction.[134] The opposite view was also taken.[135] The issue underlying this doubt was whether the Lis Pendens Act 1867 applied to Ireland.[136] The doubt was resolved when the Supreme Court held that the 1867 Act did apply to Ireland and there was jurisdiction to vacate the *lis* without the consent of the party who registered it.[137]

[10.14] Issues involving *lites pendentes, eg,* concerning priorities or whether a vendor should take steps to have them vacated,[138] are often suitable to be heard on a vendor and purchaser summons.[139] It has also been considered convenient to decide an essential issue in claims for specific performance on applications to discharge *lites pendentes*.[140] Before passing from this topic let us note that a party with a *bona fide* claim for specific performance normally should protect his claim by registering a *lis pendens* and, in the case of registered land, arranging for the appropriate entry on the folio.[141] Our aim here has been to consider the removal of lites pendentes registered in connection with claims which are not prosecuted bona fide, not to discourage in any way the practice of protecting a bona fide claim with a *lis pendens*. The party seeking their removal is likely to consider also seeking an order striking out or staying the related proceedings, usually under the inherent jurisdiction.[142]

---

[129] On which see para **11.10** *post*.

[130] *Coffey v Brunel Construction Ltd* [1983] IR 36 at 43, 46.

[131] *Culhane v Hewson* [1979] IR 8 at 14.

[132] *O'Connor v McCarthy* [1982] IR 161 at 178; *Dunville Investments Ltd v Kelly* (HC) 27 April 1979, Costello J, unrep at 3-5.

[133] *Mooney v Equity Bank Ltd* (HC) 22 May 1980, McWilliam J, unrep at 8-9.

[134] *Giles v Brady* [1974] IR 462 at 469, approving *McDonnell v McDonnell* (1912) 46 ILTR 106; *cf Jolly v Taylor* (1912) 46 ILTR 106.

[135] *Culhane v Hewson* [1979] IR 8 at 13; *Dunville Investments Ltd* (HC) 27 April 1979 Costello J, unrep at 2-3.

[136] See the differing views of Kenny J in *Giles's* case at 468-9 on the one hand and of McWilliam J in *Culhane's* case at 11-13 and Costello J in the *Dunville Investments* case at 2-3.

[137] *Flynn v Buckley* 423 at 429. Note that *In Re Glencourt Investments Ltd* noted at [1979] IR 9 turned out to be of no assistance on this point: see *Flynn's* case at 427.

[138] As in *Mooney v Equity Bank Ltd* (HC) 22 May 1980, McWilliam J, unrep.

[139] We consider this type of summons in paras **10.00-00** *infra*.

[140] *Kelly v Kineen* (HC) 29 April 1980, McWilliam J, unrep at 10-11.

[141] See Fitzgerald, *Land Registry Practice* (1989) at 184.

[142] Considered at paras **10.03-05** *supra*.

RECTIFICATION

Mutual mistake

[10.15] The equitable remedy of rectification may be available where a mistake[143] has occurred in a written contract intended to represent what the parties have actually agreed. As Ball C explained:[144]

> "The jurisdiction of a Court of Equity to reform a settlement, in which it is established by evidence that error or mistake has occurred, is undoubted. Parol evidence will suffice, but it is obvious that when the claim for relief rests upon testimony exclusively, and is not supported by any written record of the intention of the parties, especially should time have elapsed since the deed was executed, much vigilance and caution are required on the part of the tribunal which is called upon to exercise the jurisdiction. Still if, after due deliberation, it arrives at the conclusion that the actual contract which was made between the parties differs from that expressed in the instrument, it is, in my judgment, as much bound to act as in any other case depending on testimony."

It is vital to be clear about what equity does and does not do. Rectification is concerned with defects in the recording, not in the making, of an agreement.[145] Courts of Equity do not rectify contracts; they may and do rectify instruments purporting to have been made in pursuance of terms of contracts.[146] The relief may be granted when parties have reached an agreement but an error is made in giving effect to their common intention in a written agreement.[147] An author has said "What is rectified is not a mistake in the transaction itself, but a mistake in the way in which that transaction has been expressed in writing".[148] Once a relevant mistake exists the modern position concerning the requirements for getting the relief of rectification is stated by Lowry LCJ:[149]

> "1.   There must be a concluded agreement antecedent to the instrument which is sought to be rectified; but
>
> 2.   The antecedent agreement need not be binding in law (for example, it need not be under seal if made by a public authority[150] or in writing and signed by the party if relating to a sale of land) nor need it be in writing: such incidents merely help to discharge the heavy burden of proof; and
>
> 3.   A complete antecedent concluded contract is not required, so long as there was prior accord on a term of a proposed agreement, outwardly expressed and communicated between the parties, as in *Joscelyne v Nissen*."[151]

---

[143] The relief of rectification is not limited to cases of mistake; para **10.24** *infra*. See discussion of the remedy by Wylie, *Irish Land Law*, 2nd Ed (1986), paras 3.162-5; Keane, *Equity and the Law of Trusts in the Republic of Ireland* (1988) in Ch 18. On the defence of mistake see paras **9.66-69** *ante*.

[144] *McCormack v McCormack* (1877) 1 LRI 119 at 124; see also p 126.

[145] *Irish Life Assurance Co Ltd v Dublin Land Securities Ltd* [1989] IR 253 at 260; *McD v McD* [1993] ILRM 717.

[146] *Per* James VC in *Mackenzie v Coulson* (1869) LR 8 Eq 368 at 375 approved by Griffin J in the *Irish Life Assurance Co* case at 260; *cf Monaghan County Council v Vaughan* [1948] IR 306 at 313.

[147] *O'Neill v Ryan (No. 3)* [1992] 1 IR 166 at 185.

[148] Snell's *Principles of Equity*, 28th Ed (1982) at p 610, approved by Murray J in *Moyola v Chichester-Clark* [1983] 9 NIJB at 17-18; *cf Young v Halahan* (1875) 9 IR Eq 70 at 78.

[149] *Rooney and McParland Ltd v Carlin* [1981] NI 138 at 146, approved by Griffin J in the *Irish Life Assurance Co* case at 263.

[150] On this point see also *Monaghan County Council v Vaughan* [1948] IR 306 at 315-7.

[151] [1970] 2 QB 86; [1970] 1 All ER 1213.

The jurisdiction, an equitable jurisdiction to alter the legal effect of an instrument,[152] is discretionary and it does not follow that it should be exercised in every case irrespective of circumstances.[153] It will be withheld, for example, if it would be a pointless exercise.[154] However, where a relevant type of mistake occurs and the principles identified by Lowry LCJ apply the normal result will be the granting of the relief.

[10.16] Lowry LCJ's statement of principles[155], while dispensing with the strait-jacket of complete antecedent formal contract, continues to insist on the need for communication and outwardly expressed accord between the parties.[156] It is in the light of this requirement that one must understand the phrase "common continuing intention" which means that the parties not only *have* the same intention but *are agreed* on it.[157] Accordingly the modern position is that a prior *contract* is not necessary but a prior and continuing common intention in regard to a particular provision with some outward expression of accord on it is needed.[158] Formerly it was thought that a prior *contract* had to exist.[159] It was said that "If the court comes to the conclusion that the parties have never entered into an agreement, it would be a contradiction in terms for it to say that it could reform the agreement".[160]

[10.17] The existence of that common continuing intention is not enough on its own. The party seeking relief must show that the common intention mistakenly left out of the document which he wants rectified was outwardly expressed and communicated between the parties.[161]

Denning LJ explained:[162]

> "...I am clearly of opinion that a continuing common intention is not sufficient unless it has found expression in outward agreement. There could be no certainty at all in business transactions if a party who has entered into a firm contract could afterwards turn around and claim to have it rectified on the ground that the parties intended something different. He is allowed to prove, if he can, that they *agreed something different* ...but not that they *intended* something different."[163]

It follows from the principles identified by Lowry LCJ that the party seeking rectification must show positively what the alleged common intention was.[164] Thus evidence directed at excluding "a significant area of land the subject of a CPO" from a deal lacks the

---

[152] As distinct from the contract: see cases cited at fn 146 *ante.*
[153] *Per* Kingsmill Moore J in *Lowndes v de Courcy* (SC) 9 April 1960, unrep at 18-19.
[154] *Noonan v O'Connell* (HC) 10 April 1987, Lynch J, unrep at 9.
[155] Quoted from Lowry LCJ in para **10.15** *supra.*
[156] *Per* Lowry LCJ in the *Rooney and McParland Ltd* case at 146.
[157] *Ibid.*
[158] See consideration of English cases by Lowry LCJ, *ibid* at 146-7 and by Griffin J in the *Irish Life Assurance Co* case at 262-3.
[159] *Lucey v Laurel Construction Co Ltd,* (HC) 18 December 1970, Kenny J, unrep at 10-11. Note discussion of this case by Griffin J in the *Irish Life Assurance Co Ltd* case at 261-2 pointing out that Kenny J did not appear to have been referred to *Joscelyne v Nissen.*
[160] *Per* Flanagan J in *Gun v McCarthy* (1884) 13 LRI 304 at 311.
[161] The *Irish Life Assurance Co. Ltd* case at [1986] IR 346.
[162] *Rose v Pim* [1953] 2 QB 450
[163] Approved by Griffin J in *Irish Life Assurance Co Ltd v Dublin Land Securities Ltd* [1989[IR 253 at 261; Lowry LCJ in *Rooney & McParland Ltd v Carlin* [1981] NI 138 at 145; Kenny J in *Lucey v Laurel Construction Co Ltd* (HC) 18 December 1970, unrep at 11.
[164] The *Irish Life Assurance Co Ltd* case at 263; *McD v McD* [1993] ILRM 717 at 722.

necessary precision, especially when there are two CPOs and the two combined do not cover the whole of the land intended to be excluded.[165] An agreement to sell ground rents in various estates together with so much of the surrounding or ancillary lands as the vendor believed to be of no value would be too imprecise.[166] When agents negotiating a deal for parties are unaware of the existence of a field it is impossible to show a prior accord which included the sale of that field.[167] In settling an action where it is intended that one party is to pay costs to the other it is essential that there is agreement for payment of the costs and on the exact terms of that agreement including a consensus as to the matters to be dealt with on any taxation.[168]

The common continuing intention must last until the parties make the agreement which is later sought to be rectified. "If one finds that, in regard to a particular point, the parties were in agreement up to the moment when they executed their formal instrument, and the formal instrument does not conform with that common agreement, then this court has jurisdiction to rectify, although it may be that there was, until the formal instrument was executed, no concluded and binding contract between the parties."[169]

Unilateral mistake

[10.18] As a general rule the courts only rectify an agreement in writing where there has been a mutual mistake - *ie,* where it fails to record the intention of *both* parties.[170] That was the original conception of reformation of an instrument by rectification.[171] Nowadays it will be ordered also when one party sees a mistake in the written agreement, knows that the other party has not seen it and signs the document knowing of those facts.[172] Rectification may be ordered when a party has entered into a written agreement by mistake, if he establishes that the other party with knowledge of that mistake concluded that agreement.[173] It has been said that a party who knows that the expression of an agreement is incorrect may not allege that there was no mutual mistake because the other party was not aware of that mistake.[174] It has been suggested also that, by what appears to be a species of equitable estoppel, if one party to a transaction knows that the instrument contains a mistake in his favour but does nothing to correct it, he (and also those claiming under him subject a possible issue about notice[175]) will be precluded from resisting rectification on the ground that the mistake is unilateral and not common.[176]

It was thought at one time[177] that rectification could not be granted to a party on the ground of unilateral mistake and that his remedy, if any, was rescission. We will discuss that subject shortly.[178]

---

[165] The *Irish Life Assurance Co Ltd* case at 264.
[166] *Ferguson v Merchant Banking Ltd* [1993] ILRM 136 at 141.
[167] *Rooney & McParland Ltd's* case at 147.
[168] *McD v McD* [1993] ILRM 717 at 722-3.
[169] *Irish Life Assurance Co Ltd v Dublin Land Securities Ltd* [1989] IR 253 at 260.
[170] *Per* Simonds J in *Crane v Hedgeman-Harris Co Inc* [1939] 1 All ER 662 at 664 in a passage approved by Griffin J in the *Irish Life Assurance Co Ltd* case at 262.
[171] The *Irish Life Assurance Co Ltd* case at 260.
[172] *Lucey v Laurel Construction Co Ltd* (HC) 18 December 1970, Kenny J, unrep at 10.
[173] *Per* Costello J in *O'Neill v Ryan (No 3)* [1992] 1 IR 166 at 185
[174] *Nolan v Nolan* (1957) 92 ILTR 94 at 99.
[175] On which see *Coates v McKenna* (1872) IR 7 Eq 113 at 120-1, 130; *Smith v Jones* [1954] 2 All ER 823 at 827-8. See also para **10.24** *infra*.
[176] Snell's *Equity*, 29th Ed (1990) p 630-1 citing *inter alia Monaghan County Council v* Vaughan [1948] IR 306.
[177] *Gun v McCarthy* (1884) 13 LRI 304 at 309-11; *Mortimer v Shortall* (1842) 2 Drury & Warren 417 at 424.
[178] Paras **10.25-33** *infra*.

[10.19] The conduct of a party against whom the rectification is sought on the ground of unilateral mistake must be such as would make it inequitable for him to object to the relief; it must be such as to affect the conscience of the party who has suppressed the fact that he recognised the presence of a mistake.[179] The knowledge of that party may have been such as to involve him in a degree of sharp practice.[180] The doctrine probably depends more on the equity of the position than on any measure of sharp practice and it seems to be unnecessary to prove sharp practice.[181] On the other hand, it may be somewhat over fastidious to shrink from applying the description of "sharp practice" to the conduct of a party who recognises that the other party is executing it under a mistake which can only be detrimental to him and deliberately suppresses his recognition of that fact.[182] In any event satisfying a court that in fact there has been sharp practice can only help to get the relief. Conversely, it will be very difficult to get rectification against a party who is free of any *mala fides*, improper conduct or sharp practice and who did not contribute to the mistake.[183]

Admissibility of evidence

[10.20] As a general rule, leaving aside any question of rectification for a moment, when a transaction has been reduced to writing by agreement of the parties no evidence may be given to prove the terms of the transaction except the document itself and extrinsic evidence is not admissible to vary the terms of the document.[184] Extrinsic evidence cannot be admitted to prove the *intention* of the parties at the time they executed the relevant document for the purpose of substituting that intention for the intention gathered by the court from the words used in the document.[185] Probabilities raised by surrounding facts may be taken into account, however.[186]

[10.21] In a few cases where rectification is sought the document sought to be reformed will afford sufficient evidence itself of the intentions of the parties to enable the court to rectify the mistake.[187] In this type of situation it is immaterial whether the court treats the instrument as if it was reformed or reforms it in an independent proceeding brought for that purpose.[188] The Privy Council has held in an Australian case that rectification may be granted even where the true meaning can be worked out by a process of construction.[189]

---

[179] *Per* Buckley LJ in *Bates & Son Ltd v Wyndham's (Lingerie) Ltd* [1981] 1 All ER 1077 at 1086; [1081] 1 WLR 505 at 515 in a passage approved by Keane J in *Irish Life Assurance Co Ltd v Dublin Land Securities Ltd* [1986] IR 332 at 353; *cf* Kingsmill Moore J in *Lowndes v de Courcy* (SC) 9 April 1960, unrep at 20.

[180] The *Irish Life Assurance Co Ltd* case at [1989] IR 261 considering *Riverlate Properties Ltd v Paul* [1975] 1 Ch 133; [1974] 2 All ER 656. *Cf Ferguson v Merchant Banking Ltd* [1993] ILRM 136 at 144.

[181] *Thomas Bates & Son v Wyndhams (Lingerie) Ltd* [1981] 1 All ER 1077 at 1086, 1090, 1091.

[182] The *Irish Life Assurance Co Ltd* case at [1986] IR 353.

[183] This may be inferred from material in the *Irish Life Assurance Co Ltd* case at [1989] IR 261, 265 and *Ferguson's* case at 144. *Cf Jameson v National Benefit Trust Ltd* (1901) 2 NIJR 19.

[184] *Macklin v Graecen & Co* [1983] IR 61 at 65-6.

[185] *Moyola v Chichester-Clark* [1983] 9 NIJB at 15 - a point agreed by counsel and noted by Murray J. And see Wylie, *Irish Conveyancing Law* (1978) para 15.19 and cases cited.

[186] *Lowndes v de Courcy* (SC) 9 April 1960, *Per* Kingsmill Moore J at 16. *Cf Rohan Construction Ltd v Insurance Corporation of Ireland Plc* [1988] ILRM 373 at 380-1

[187] *Fitzgerald v Fitzgerald* [1902] 1 IR 477 at 490, 491, 493, 495; *Re Davis's Estate* [1912] 1 IR 516 at 524-5: *cf Ex parte Rice* (1896) 30 ILTR 57; *Annesley v Annesley* (1893) 31 LRI 457.

[188] *Per* Porter MR in *Fitzgerald's* case at 484. Note the approach of the court in *Borrowes v Delaney* (1889) 24 LRI 503 at 512-3, 516-7. *Cf* discussion of correction of mistakes by construction by Lewison, *The Interpretation of Contracts* (1989) at paras 801-4.

[189] *Standard Portland Cement Co Pty Ltd v Good* (1982) 57 AJLR 151.

There is no doubt, however, that a deed may be rectified on oral evidence.[190] A court of equity may admit oral evidence but, it has been said, should not act upon doubtful evidence either in a suit to reform a deed or in a defence to a suit for specific performance.[191] A combination of oral and documentary evidence may also suffice.[192] The admission of oral evidence for this kind of purpose has been described as an "exception to the usual rule that parol evidence is inadmissible to contradict, add to or vary the terms of a written agreement."[193] However, the object of the evidence is really to show that there was a prior common intention which differs from the written document rather than to vary the terms of that document. Once it is alleged that the true agreement of the parties is different from that appearing in a written document the court is entitled and indeed bound to listen to the oral evidence.[194] That evidence is admissible even where a prior written agreement led to the agreement sought to be rectified.[195] However, the fact that there was a prior written agreement which the oral evidence contradicts may increase the burden of proof on the party seeking rectification.[196]

The onus of proof

[10.22] While there has been great variety in the language used by the courts the strong tendency has been to require a high degree of proof in order to get the relief. Ball C indicated that the onus of proof on a party claiming rectification of a written document is significantly greater than normal in civil proceedings.[197] Haugh J referred to it as "a very onerous burden" and even used the phrase "beyond all reasonable doubt".[198] In recent cases the burden has been described .as "heavy".[199] Another modern expression has been "convincing proof".[200] In one case Russell LJ said that "it is in our view better to use only the phrase 'convincing proof' without echoing an old fashioned word such as 'irrefragable' and without importing from the criminal law the phrase "beyond all reasonable doubt'.[201]

In principle, the burden of proof seems to be the normal civil one of the balance of probability.[202] However, the courts cannot be expected to close their eyes to the fact that in rectification cases the plaintiff is seeking to reform a *written* document which is sometimes quite formal and usually prepared with the benefit of professional advice. As Brightman LJ explained:[203]

---

[190] *Lowndes v de Courcy* (SC) 9 April 1960, unrep, *per* Kingsmill Moore J at pp 17-18; *Flood v Finlay* (1811) 2 Ball & Beatty 9 at 15; *McCormack v McCormack* (1877) 1 LRI 119 at 124; *Alexander v Crosbie* (1835) Lloyd & Goold, Temp Sugden, 145 at 149-50.
[191] *Fallon v Robins* (1865) 16 IR Ch R 422 at 428.
[192] *Mortimer v Shortall* (1842) 2 Drury & Warren 417 at 425.
[193] *Rooney & McParland Ltd v Carlin* [1981] NI 138 at 141-2.
[194] *Nolan v Graves* [1946] IR 376 at 386.
[195] *Gun v McCarthy* (1884) 13 LRI 304 at 308-9.
[196] *Nolan's* case at 388-9; *Alexander's* case at 149-50.
[197] *McCormack v McCormack* (1877) 1 LRI 119 at 124.
[198] *Nolan v Graves* [1946] IR 376 at 389.
[199] By Griffin J in *Irish Life Assurance Co Ltd v Dublin Land Securities Ltd* [1989] IR 253 at 259, 263; and Lowry LCJ in *Rooney & McParland Ltd v Carlin* [1981] NI 138 at 146 (in the second of his three principles).
[200] By Griffin J, *ibid* at 259, 260-1 ("convincing evidence"); Russell LJ in *Joscelyne v Nissen* [1970] 2 QB 86 at 98; [1970] 1 All ER 1213 at 1222.
[201] Quoted by Griffin J in *Irish Life Assurance Co Ltd's* case at 263.
[202] *Bates & Son v Wyndham's (Lingerie) Ltd* [1981] 1 All ER 1077 at 1085, 1090. *Cf* the onus of proof where fraud is alleged, para **9.11** *ante.*
[203] *Ibid,* 1090.

"The standard of proof required in an action of rectification to establish the common intention of the parties is, in my view, the civil standard of balance of probability. But as the alleged common intention ex hypothesi contradicts the written instrument, convincing proof is required in order to counteract the cogent evidence of the parties' intention displayed by the instrument itself. It is not, I think, the standard of proof which is high, so differing from the normal civil standard, but the evidential requirement needed to counteract the inherent probability that the written instrument truly represents the parties' intention because it is a document signed by the parties."[204]

Where one finds prolonged negotiations between the parties eventually assuming the shape of a formal instrument in which they have been advised by their respective skilled legal advisers the assumption may be very strong that the instrument does represent their real intention.[205]

Specific performance with rectification

[10.23] Although rectification is not to be regarded as a branch of the doctrine of specific performance[206] both are equitable remedies. The jurisdiction as regards both rectification and specific performance has been described as "delicate" and, on the basis of the case law, to be "exercised with discretion and care".[207] The Irish courts have accepted that there is jurisdiction to decree specific performance *with* rectification.[208] Previously difficulty had been felt over the Statute of Frauds and Sugden LC asked how he could admit oral evidence to make a contract conformable to the agreement of the parties if the court would have to reject the same evidence if adduced in an action to have the agreement executed.[209]

In England it has been held that the jurisdiction of courts of equity in this respect is to bring the written document executed in pursuance of an antecedent agreement into conformity with that agreement; when that is done, then, on principle, the instrument so rectified should have the same force as if the mistake had not been made in which case the Statute of Frauds would not be a defence to an action founded on it.[210] It has been pointed out that when the written instrument is rectified there is a writing which satisfies the Statute, the jurisdiction of the court to rectify being outside the prohibition of the Statute.[211] Apparently the signature needed to satisfy the Statute should be taken as affixed to the memorandum as rectified.[212] An alternative view has been that the rectified document only becomes effective as an instrument required by the Statute of Frauds

---

[204] Referred to by Keane J in *Irish Life Assurance Co Ltd v Dublin Land Securities Ltd* [1986] IR 332 at 351.

[205] *Crane v Hegeman-Harris Co Inc* [1939] 1 All ER 662 at 664-5 quoted by Griffin J in the *Irish Life Assurance Co Ltd* case [1989] IR 253 at 262.

[206] *Per* Russell LJ *Joscelyne v Nissen* [1970] 1 All ER 1213 at 1223 and expressing puzzlement at a suggestion by Cozens-Hardy MR in *Lovell and Christmas Ltd v Wall* (1911) 104 LT 85 that it should be so regarded.

[207] By Haugh J in *Nolan v Graves* [1946] IR 376 at 391.

[208] By clear implication in *Nolan v Graves* [1946] IR 376 at 398-9; *Black v Grealy* (HC) 10 November 1977, Costello J, unrep at 20. In *Rooney and McParland Ltd v Carlin* such an order was made at first instance (see p 140) but that was reversed for convincing reasons based on the facts: p 147.

[209] *Davis v Fitton* (1842) 2 Drury & Warren 225 at 233. *Cf Mortimer v Shortall* (1842) 2 Drury & Warren 417.

[210] *Craddock Bros v Hunt* [1923] 2 Ch 136; [1923] All ER 394, *per* Warrington LJ at 405; Lord Sterndale at 402, Younger LJ dissenting at 412-3. The majority decision was approved in *United States of America v Motor Trucks Ltd* [1924] AC 196.

[211] By Lord Birkenhead in *United States of America v Motor Trucks Ltd* [1924] AC 196 at 200-1 in a passage approved by Dixon J in *Monaghan County Council v Vaughan* [1948] IR 306 at 316.

[212] *Per* Sterndale MR in the *Craddock Bros* case at 402 (All ER).

when the order for rectification is made.[213] One might also have asked whether, for example, the Statute poses a problem when compliance with it is necessary but a material term[214] of the true contract or accord is not contained in or is wrongly stated by the document sought to be rectified and can be established only by the same oral evidence which proves the grounds for rectification. However, that point is covered by the example given by Lowry LCJ[215] in a passage approved by the Supreme Court[216] that the antecedent agreement does not need to be in writing and signed by the relevant party if relating to the sale of land.[217]

Some final points

[10.24] Some final points may be noted. Firstly, there is jurisdiction to rectify voluntary deeds[218] though the relief is unlikely to be ordered against a reluctant grantor or settlor.[219] Caution must be exercised also if the only evidence of intention is provided by the parol evidence of settlors.[220] The existence of this jurisdiction may be compared with the general rule that equity will not assist a volunteer. That rule affects claims for specific performance[221] so the jurisdiction to rectify voluntary deeds rarely will affect specific performance cases.[222] Secondly, though specific performance claims where questions of rectification arise seem to involve alleged mistake almost inevitably, the relief is not confined to mistake. Thus it may be appropriate where, *eg*, there has been fraud[223] or a person under a fiduciary duty has not explained an important matter properly.[224] Thirdly, a right to rectification is capable of being assured or transmitted[225] though it may be defeated by the defence of bona fide purchaser for value without notice.[226] An intending purchaser of land normally would not be bound to make enquiries about matters which might give rise to a right to rectification.[227] Fourthly, a party cannot get rectification or cancellation of an agreement simply because he did not know the legal consequences or because he did not know that a clause in it violated the law.[228] Fifthly, a claim for rectification may be defeated by normal defences of types used against claims for

---

[213] *Per* Haugh J in *Nolan v Graves* [1946] IR 376 at 398: he was satisfied that on the document he rectified the vendor would have the ordinary rights accruing to him under the contract that correctly represented the intention of the parties: p 399.

[214] On the material terms see paras **3.08-18** *ante*.

[215] *Rooney & McParland Ltd v Carlin* [1981] NI 138 at 146.

[216] *Irish Life Assurance Co Ltd v Dublin Land Securities* [1989] IR 253 at 263.

[217] But see Lord Sugden's query noted earlier in this paragraph.

[218] *Lowndes v de Courcy*, (SC) 9 April 1990, unrep, *per* Kingsmill Moore J at 18; *McCausland v Young* [1949] NI 49 at 123-4; *Fitzgerald v Fitzgerald* [1902 1 IR 477, esp Holmes LJ at 493; *Maunsell v Maunsell* (1877) 1 LRI 529 at 539-40; *cf Re Ottley's Estate* [1910] 1 IR 1 at 5-9.

[219] *McMechan v Warburton* [1896] 1 IR 435 at 439; Keane, *Equity and the Law of Trusts in the Republic of Ireland* (1988) at 18.10.

[220] The *Lowndes* case, *Per* Kingsmill Moore J at 18, 20.

[221] Paras **3.06-7** *ante*.

[222] See further on this jurisdiction Keane, *Equity and the Law of Trusts in the Republic of Ireland* (1988), para 18.10; Wylie, *Irish Land Law*, 2nd Ed (1986), paras 3.162-3.

[223] *Ball v Storie* (1823) 1 Sim & St 210 at 219; *cf Clark v Girdwood* (1877) 7 Ch D 9.

[224] *McCausland v Young* [1949] NI 49.

[225] *Blacklocks v JB Developments (Godalming) Ltd* [1981] 3 All ER 392 at 400; *Boots, The Chemist Ltd v Street* [1983] EGD 251 at 255.

[226] *Coates v Kenna* (1872) IR 7 Eq 113 at 120-1, 130; *Smith v Jones* [1954] 2 All ER 823 at 827-8; *cf* Holmes LJ in *Fitzgerald v Fitzgerald* [1902] 1 IR 477 at 493-4.

[227] *Smith's* case at 827-8.

[228] *Jackson v Stopford* [1923] 2 IR 1 at 11.

equitable relief, *eg*, acquiescence or laches[229] or, as we have just seen, the bona fide purchaser for value without notice. Cases must depend on their own facts and even the lapse of a long period of time will not necessarily defeat a claim especially if the parties have acted inconsistently with the incorrect document and consistently with the claim made for rectification.[230] Sixthly, it seems unlikely that negligence could be a good defence to a claim for rectification[231] though carelessness may, depending on the facts, make it difficult for the claimant to show the requisite prior common intention.[232] Negligence could affect a question of costs.[233] Finally the involvement of an agent in negotiations may also cause difficulties in proving the necessary common prior intention. A principal is deemed to receive information given to his agent but not communicated to the principal only if it was the agent's duty to pass it on.[234] Even if the principal is deemed to have got the information it does not follow that he is deemed to have assented to the inclusion of a proposed term in a deal.[235]

RESCISSION

[10.25] Rescission is another important equitable remedy.[236] It will be granted in the appropriate circumstances when the court considers it just and equitable to do so in order to restore the parties, at least substantially, to their respective positions before the matter relied on as the ground for rescission had its effect.[237] The object to be achieved by rescission in this equitable sense of the word is the restoration of *both parties* as nearly as may be to the position which each occupied before the transaction. The fact that the contract has been executed or the transaction completed is no bar to rescission unless by reason thereof *restitutio in integrum*[238] has become impossible.[239] Whether such *restitution* has become impossible or not is a matter for consideration and decision in relation to the facts of each particular case.[240] The primary purpose of all proceedings for rescission, as contrasted with that of actions for damages, is to restore the "status quo" and bring back the original position by undoing all that has intervened between it and the present.[241]

---

[229] *McCausland v Young* [1949] NI 49, at 88-95, *per* Andrews LCJ. See paras **9.47-51** *supra* for the defence of laches.

[230] *McCormack v McCormack* (1877) 1 LRI 119 at 125, 128 (36 years).

[231] *Monaghan County Council v Vaughan* [1948] IR 306 at 315.

[232] On that intention see paras **10.16-7** *supra*.

[233] *Eg*, as in *Young v Halahan* (1875) 9 IR Eq 70 at 82.

[234] Bowstead on *Agency*, 15th Ed (1985) at 412, approved in *Irish Life Assurance Co Ltd v Dublin Land Securities Ltd* [1986] IR 332 at 346. The High Court findings on agency are noted by Griffin J at [1989] IR 259-60 but the Supreme Court did not find a need to consider the extent to which the agent's knowledge should be imputed to the principal: p 264.

[235] The *Irish Life Assurance Co Ltd* case at [1986] IR 346.

[236] The relief is described as "an equitable one" by Henchy J in *Northern Bank Finance Corporation Ltd v Charlton* [1979] IR 149 at 197. See discussion by Keane, *Equity and the Law of Trusts in the Republic of Ireland* (1988) in Ch 17, Wylie, *Irish Conveyancing Law* (1978) at paras 12.56-73 and Snell's *Equity*, 29th Ed (1990) at 616-23.

[237] The *Northern Bank Finance Corporation* case at 197; *Cf* O'Higgins CJ at 183, Butler J concurring, Griffin J at 206-7 and Parke J at 213.

[238] *Per* Griffin J, *ibid* at 207; see paras **10.27-9** *infra*.

[239] *Per* O'Higgins CJ, Butler J concurring, *ibid* at 183; *cf O'Sullivan v Management Agency & Music Ltd* [1985] IR 351.

[240] *Per* O'Higgin CJ, *ibid*.

[241] *Per* Griffin J, *ibid* at 206 approving a passage in Spencer Bower & Turner, *Law of Actionable Misrepresentation*, 3rd Ed at para 249.

A right to rescission is therefore a good defence to an action for specific performance. The relief is much more than just a potential defence to such a claim; a party may rescind a contract or seek an order rescinding it without waiting for any other party to try to enforce it against him. Indeed he ought to move quickly in order to avoid the risk of losing the right to rescind.[242] It has been said that "An action or counterclaim for rescission is the usual form of proceeding for obtaining a judicial annulment of a contract induced by misrepresentation"[243] and of course that applies equally in all other cases where the remedy is available.

[10.26] Rescission is also an important remedy at common law.[244] Its meaning in that context is rather variable.[245] A judge has said that the term "rescission" in its strict legal sense is only applicable when the parties to a contract put an end to it by mutual agreement before it is broken.[246] A more widely used meaning is that where one party is in breach of an essential term of a contract the other party has the right to treat his own obligations under the contract as at an end in which event he is said to "rescind" the contract.[247] In this sense rescission is a volitional act of a party in taking advantage of the breach by the other party in order to terminate the contract in exercise of a right which the law recognises that he possesses.[248] The breach by the offending party may be regarded as a *repudiation* of the contract and the innocent party is then free to accept that the repudiation has brought the contract to an end or not to do so.[249] The repudiation need not be express but may be by conduct which makes quite plain an intention not to perform the contract.[250] Of course, not every striking of an attitude is a repudiation by conduct. Thus, an intending lessee does not repudiate an agreement for lease by refusing to execute a lease in a form which he *bona fide* contends was not in accordance with the agreement.[251] Delay in performing an obligation may be sufficiently serious to be treated as a repudiation.[252] The test whether an innocent party is entitled to treat a breach as a repudiation is to consider the effect of the breach on the contract as a whole and whether it would deprive the innocent party of substantially the whole benefit of the contract.[253]

This concept of rescission may lead to seeking the relief of a declaration that the contract has been validly rescinded rather than an order rescinding it.[254] From the date on which a rescission of this type takes place the parties are both freed from any further liability to *perform* the contract. However, an important difference from the equitable

---

[242] *Dillon-Leech v Maxwell Motors Ltd* (HC) 20 December 1983, Murphy J, unrep (recorded [1984] ILRM 624); *Bord Iaschaigh Mhara v Scallan* (HC) 8 May 1973 Pringle J, unrep; *cf Lutton v Saville Tractors Ltd* [1986] NI 327; *Mills v Healy* [1937] IR 437. See also para **10.33** below.

[243] By Griffin J, *ibid* at 206.

[244] Wylie, *op cit* paras 12.57, 12.63, 12.65-6; Clark, *Contract Law in Ireland*, 3rd Ed (1992), pp 218-21.

[245] See Wylie, *op cit* paras 12.04, 12.06, 12.56, 12.65.

[246] By Holmes LJ in *Maconchy v Clayton* [1898] 1 IR 291 at 310. *Cf* Fitzgibbon LJ at 307. See discussion of "Discharge through Agreement" by Clark, *Contract Law in Ireland*, 3rd Ed (1992), pp 407-11.

[247] *Robb v James* (1881) 15 ILTR 59 at 60. See discussion by Fitzgibbon LJ in *Maconchy's* case at 307; Buckley LJ in *Buckland v Farmer & Moody* [1978] 3 All ER 929 at 938-9 and Goff LJ, *ibid* at 942-3; Keane, *Equity and the Law of Trusts in the Republic of Ireland* (1988) at 17.01; Clark, *op cit* at 411-22 under heading "Discharge following from a Breach of Contract".

[248] *Re Atkinson & Horsells Contract* [1912] 2 Ch 1; [1911-13] All ER 893 at 896.

[249] *Industrial Yarns Ltd v Greene* [1984] ILRM 15 at 21.

[250] *House of Spring Gardens Ltd v Point Blank Ltd* [1984] IR 611 at 703-5.

[251] *Sweet & Maxwell Ltd v Universal News Services Ltd* [1964] 3 All ER 30.

[252] *Taylor v Smith* [1991]1 IR 142 at 155, on appeal at 171.

[253] *Ibid* at 155.

[254] *Re Clibborn & Horan's Contract* [1921] IR 93 at 100; *cf Commane v Walsh* (HC) 2 May 1983, O'Hanlon J, unrep at 4 (recorded at [1985] ILRM 166-7).

relief just discussed[255] is that the offending party usually will be liable in damages for his breach.[256] The general principle for the assessment of damages in this type of situation is compensatory so that the innocent party may be placed as far as possible in the same position as though the contract had been performed.[257] As we have seen,[258] the primary purpose of the equitable relief of rescission is the very different one of restoration of the *status quo* before the contract was made.

Another meaning of rescission covers a clause in a contract giving a party a right to terminate or "rescind" the contract or "rescind the sale".[259] Important examples are non-fulfilment of a condition precedent[260] or a vendor's right to rescind if the purchaser insists on certain matters.[261] In this type of case, like the last type just mentioned, the party exercising the right to rescind may seek a declaration that he has done so validly but, unlike the last type, there usually will not be any right to damages because the events leading to the rescission normally are not breaches of the contract.

[10.27] Equity traditionally has "followed the law".[262] Thus it has applied grounds sufficient in law to get rescission such as a breach going to the root of the contract[263] or fraud.[264] Equity did go further in certain respects. One very important difference is that equity has been much more ready to grant rescission for innocent misrepresentation. An order will be made for rescission of an executory contract if a statement made was wrong, even though made in good faith with no intention to mislead, the statement was material, it was made with the intention that the plaintiff would rely on it in making the contract and it was one of the factors which did induce him to enter into the contract.[265] At law an innocent misrepresentation did not authorise a rescission unless there was a complete difference in substance between what was actually taken and what was supposed to be taken.[266] Even in equity, however, rescission cannot be given for innocent misrepresentation after an executory contract has progressed to a completed transaction.[267] This principle is just as much applicable to the sale of a chattel or a chose in action as to the sale of real property carried out by a conveyance.[268]

[10.28] It is important to remember that a party who asserts and enforces his contract to the extent of getting an order for specific performance remains entitled to seek an order for rescission later if the other party still does not perform.[269] The reason is that the latter

---

[255] Para **10.25** *supra.*
[256] *Taylor's* case at 155.
[257] *Vandeleur v Dargan* [1981] ILRM 75 at 78.
[258] Para **10.25** *supra.*
[259] The last phrase is used in General Condition 18 of the 1991 Ed of the Law Society's *General Conditions of Sale.*
[260] See paras **3.20-28** *ante.*
[261] Discussed in paras **10.36-42** *infra.*
[262] See discussion of this maxim by Keane, *op cit* at paras 3.02-4.
[263] *Linehan v Cotter* (1844) 7 IR Eq R 176 at 179.
[264] *Thompson v Lambert* (1868) IR 2 Eq 433 at 438-9; *Re Moorehead's Estate* (1861) 12 IR Ch R 371 at 374.
[265] *Gahan v Boland* (HC) 21 January, 1983, Murphy J, unrep at 13-14; (SC) unrep at 2-3. *Cf Peilow v ffrench O'Carroll* (1969) 106 ILTR 29 at 44, 52. See further paras **9.15-21** *ante.*
[266] *Lecky v Walter* [1914] 1 IR 378 at 387; *Carbin v Somerville* [1933] IR 276 at 288. Note views of Keane, *op cit*, on *Lecky's* case at para 17.04.
[267] *Legge v Croker* (1811) 1 Ball & Beatty 506 at 514. See para **9.21** *ante.*
[268] *Lecky's* case at 386.
[269] *Croft Inns Ltd v Scott* [1982] NI 95 at 97; *Vandeleur v Dargan* [1981] ILRM 75 at 77. See also para **8.28** *ante.*

party has committed a breach of the contract of a repudiatory character which he has still not remedied.[270] The normal practice is to apply to the court to dissolve the order for specific performance and put an end to the contract.[271] If a purchaser has possession an order giving the vendor possession may be made at the same time as the order dissolving the contract;[272] the order for possession has been described as "a natural concomitant with an order rescinding the contract which the court had earlier ordered should be specifically performed".[273] It is possible at the same time to get an order also for forfeiture of a deposit and payment of interest until possession is given back.[274] The plaintiff coming back to court for relief of this sort must show that he remains willing and able to complete and the defendant remains in default.[275] If, for example, a vendor in this situation fails to deliver an abstract of title[276] or to deal with a requisition raised in relation to title he will not get rescission but the earlier order for specific performance is likely to stand.[277]

Rescission and restitutio in integrum

[10.29] There is a considerable difference also in the approaches of the common law and of equity to the question of *restitutio in integrum*.[278] To a greater or lesser, though always substantial, extent[279] this is a necessary ingredient for rescission. Lord Blackburn explained the difference:[280]

> "It is, I think, clear on principles of general justice, that as a condition to a rescission there must be a *restitutio in integrum*. The parties must be put *in statu quo*... It is a doctrine which has often been acted upon both at law and in equity. But there is a considerable difference in the mode in which it is applied in Courts of Law and Equity, owing, as I think, to the difference of the machinery which the courts have at command.
>
> But a Court of Equity could not give damages, and, unless it can rescind the contract can give no relief. And on the other hand it can take accounts of profits and make an allowance for deterioration. And I think the practice has always been for a Court of Equity to give this relief whenever by the exercise of its powers it can do what is practically just though it cannot restore the parties precisely to the state they were in before the contract".[281]

The High Court of Australia has stated that even though precise *restitutio in integrum* is not possible it is now sufficient if the situation is such that by the exercise of its powers including the power to take accounts of profits and to direct inquiries as to allowances proper to be made for deterioration it can do what is practically just between the parties and by so doing restore them substantially to the *status quo*.[282] In an older Irish case

---

[270] *Johnson v Agnew* [1980] AC 367 at 394; [1979] 2 WLR 487 at 493 approved by Hutton J in the *Crofts Inns Ltd* case at 97 and McWilliam J in *Vandeleur's* case at 77.
[271] *Ibid* (all three cases). See further para **8.28** *ante*.
[272] The *Croft Inns Ltd* case at 98; *McGuire v Conwell* (1932) 66 ILTR 213 at 214.
[273] By Hutton J in the *Croft Inns Ltd* case at 98.
[274] *McGuire v Conwell* (1932) 66 ILTR 213 at 214.
[275] *Bourke v Grimes* (1929) 63 ILTR 53 at 54, 55.
[276] The normal modern practice is simply to furnish title documents.
[277] *Bourke's* case (requisitions raised by court counsel).
[278] Discussed in this and the next two paragraphs.
[279] Usually rather less important in equity.
[280] *Erlanger v New Sombrero Phosphate Co* (1878) 3 App Cas 1218 at 1278-9;[1874-8] All ER 271 at 285-6.
[281] Those passages were approved by Griffin J in *Northern Bank Finance Corporation Ltd v Charlton* [1979] IR 149 at 207, He pointed out that the distinction noted by Lord Blackburn between the remedies at law and equity is no longer of importance as the High Court has full original jurisdiction and power to determine all matters and questions. *Cf* O'Higgins CJ at 183 approving passages from textbooks, Butler J concurring.
[282] *Alati v Kruger* (1955) 94 CLR 216 at 223-4.

Flanagan J said that it becomes a question whether the facts raise a sufficient equity to justify the court in making a decree for the rescission of the contract as executed.[283] In considering changes which have occurred in the property sold the court will also consider the extent to which they have been caused by the nature of the property itself or can be attributed to an act of the party seeking rescission.[284]

[10.30] The purpose of rescission of a contract[285] is the restoration of the *status quo ante* on the ground that the voidable contract is to be deemed wholly void *ab initio*.[286] When the agreed consideration has been given and cannot be undone a transaction cannot be set aside even on the ground of fraud because the parties cannot be put back into their original state before the contract.[287] And if a contract has been *partly* performed and that part cannot be undone there is no right to rescission.[288] If the parties can be restored substantially to their previous positions rescission may be available. As O'Higgins CJ explained:[289]

> "Where a fraudulent misrepresentation has induced a transaction the rule is that the person deceived has the right the rescind the entire transaction; but the right must be exercised *in toto* so that every part of the transaction, and everything given or obtained under it is cancelled or restored. The representee is not permitted to affirm part and rescind another part of the same transaction. The fact that the contract has been executed or the transaction completed is no bar to rescission unless by reason thereof *restitutio in integrum* has become impossible. Whether such *restitutio* has become impossible or not is a matter for consideration and decision in relation to the facts of each particular case."[290]

The principles involved may not be easy to apply in practice in all cases although normally there will be a right to damages if the representee is not entitled to rescission.[291] This remedy lies in the tort of deceit.[292] The issue, therefore, when there is difficulty about *restitutio*, is not whether the misled party has *any* remedy but whether he has the *particular* remedy of rescission.[293]

[10.31] However, the right to rescission is not lost just because it is impossible to restore the subject matter to the vendor in identical condition in which it was at the date of the contract where the alteration is due to the nature of the subject matter itself and cannot be attributed to any positive act or conduct of the purchaser.[294] It has been said that the

---

[283] *Gun v McCarthy* (1884) 13 LRI 304 at 310.

[284] *Carbin v Somerville* [1933] IR 276 at 288-90.

[285] In the equitable sense; the cases cited mainly involved fraud but the principles should apply also to rescission on other grounds.

[286] *Northern Bank Finance Corporation Ltd v Charlton* [1979] IR 149 at 198, Henchy J; *cf* Griffin J at 207 and Parke J at 213.

[287] *Hogan v Healy* (1876) 11 IRCL 119 at 124-5.

[288] *Smyth v Taylor* (SC) oral judgments, noted by McCarthy J in *Taylor v Smyth* [1991] 1 IR 142 at 167; see also Lardner J at 151-2.

[289] The *Northern Bank Finance Corporation* case at 183.

[290] The court decided by 3:2 that *restitutio* was not possible on the facts of that case.

[291] Wylie, *Irish Conveyancing Law* (1978) para 6.65-6; Clark, *Contract Law in Ireland*, 3rd Ed (1992) at 234-7.

[292] *Per* Henchy J in the *Northern Bank Finance Corporation* case at 197 and Griffin J at 207; also Palles CB in *Hogan's* case at 122. Deceit is considered by McMahon & Binchy, *Irish Law of Torts*, 2nd Ed (1990) at 664-73.

[293] *Per* Palles CB in *Hogan's* case at 122.

[294] *Carbin v Somerviile* [1933] IR 276 at 289

rule is that rescission cannot be enforced if events, which have occurred since the contract and in which the representee has participated, make it impossible to restore the parties substantially to their original position.[295] A representor who stands by and silently encourages acts of the representee cannot rely on them later as disentitling the latter to rescission.[296] The representee is under no obligation to spend any money to prevent property sold by fraudulent misrepresentation from deteriorating due to its inherent defects or in an attempt to make it what was sold.[297] Indeed if he does spend money on the property while insisting on the right to repudiate the contract for fraudulent representation he may not be able to recover that expenditure.[298] The representee must be not only willing but also *able* to make *restitutio in integrum*.[299] It follows that where fraudulent misrepresentation induces a contract with a third party[300] and the transaction is completed no form of rescission and restitution could restore, even substantially, the *status quo ante - ie*, the respective positions of the parties before the fraudulent misrepresentation was acted on to the purchaser's detriment.[301] The courts will be very wary of creating a wholly new factual and legal situation which would be incompatible with the mutuality and fairness inherent in restoring the *status quo ante*.[302]

Rescission in cases of mistake

[10.32 In *Monaghan County Council v Vaughan*[303] Dixon J, in contrasting rescission and rectification,[304] stated that where the parties contract under a mutual mistake of fact the agreement is liable to be rescinded at the instance of either party, since in such a case no contract came into being.[305] In a case of unilateral mistake one party is not ad idem with the other party or parties and there is therefore no real agreement between them; again rescission may be appropriate.[306] The circumstances in which a party can get rescission for unilateral mistake are fairly similar to those in which he can get rectification.[307] An obvious difference is that in a claim for rescission the plaintiff will not be trying to prove the common continuing intention[308] which is a feature of rectification cases. In a claim for specific performance with rectification[309] in which the plaintiff declined to seek rescission despite invitations from the courts to consider applying to amend the pleadings[310] Keane J found the following observations of Russell LJ[311] "peculiarly apposite":

> "Is the lessor entitled to rescission of the lease on the mere ground that it made a serious mistake in the drafting of the lease which it put forward and subsequently executed, when

---

[295] By Griffin J in the *Northern Bank Finance Corporation* case at 206.
[296] Based on a passage in Spencer Bower's *Law of Actionable Misrepresentation* (3rd Ed) approved by O'Higgins CJ in the *Northern Bank Finance Corporation* case at 183, Butler J concurring.
[297] *Carbin v Somerville* [1933] IR 276 at 290.
[298] *Carbin's* case at 289.
[299] The *Northern Bank Finance Corporation* case at 207.
[300] *ie*, a person other than the representor or his principal.
[301] The *Northern Bank Finance Corporation* case at 197, *Per* Henchy J.
[302] *Ibid.*
[303] [1948] IR 306 at 312.
[304] On which see paras **10.15-24** *supra*.
[305] Approved by Griffin J in *Irish Life Assurance Co Ltd v Dublin Land Securities Ltd* [1989] IR 253 at 260.
[306] *Per* Dixon J, *ibid*, approved by Griffin J, *ibid*.
[307] On which see paras **10.18-19** *ante*.
[308] Para **10.16** *supra*.
[309] The *Irish Life Assurance Co* Ltd case [1986] IR 332 at 352.
[310] Griffin J [1989] IR 253 at 260.
[311] In *Riverlate Properties Ltd v Paul* [1975] Ch133 at 140; [1974] 2 All ER 656 at 661 giving the judgment of the CA.

(*a*) the lessee did not share the mistake, (*b*) the lessee did not know that the document did not give effect to the lessor's intention, and (*c*) the mistake of the lessor was in no way attributable to anything said or, done by the lessee? What is there in principle, or in authority binding upon this court, which requires a person who has acquired a leasehold interest on terms upon which he intended to obtain it, and who thought when he obtained it that the lessor intended him to obtain it on those terms, either to lose the leasehold interest, or, if he wished to keep it, to submit to keep it only on the terms which the lessor meant to impose but did not? In point of principle we cannot find that this should be so. If reference be made to principles of equity, it operates on conscience. If conscience is clear at the time of the transaction, why should equity disrupt the transaction? If a man may be said to have been fortunate in obtaining a property at a bargain price, or on terms that make it a good bargain, because the other party unknown to him has made a miscalculation or other mistake, some high-minded men might consider it appropriate that he should agree to cure the miscalculation or mistake, abandoning his good fortune. But if equity were to enforce the views of those high-minded men, we have no doubt that it would run counter to the attitudes of much the greater part of ordinary mankind (not least the world of commerce) and would be venturing upon the field of moral philosophy in which it would soon be in difficulties."

That passage was accepted by Murphy J as a correct statement of the law in a later case where rescission *was* in issue.[312]

[10.33] In an older Irish case the opinion was given that "where there being a clear undoubted mistake by one party in reference to a material term of the contract which he entered into with another, and the other party knowingly seeks to avail himself of that, and seeks to bind the other to the mistake, the law of this court is, that it will not allow such a contract to be binding on the parties, but will give relief against it."[313] It may be that a unilateral mistake as to the amount of land included in a contract or its value will not give rise to a right of rescission in the absence of some abuse or sharp practice by the other party.[314] Rescission has been ordered where the party upholding the contract was "uncandid and dishonest" in seeking to do so and the court felt that if he had come there to enforce the contract his action would have been dismissed.[315] However, it may be arguable that a right to rescission depends on the general equity of the case without any need to prove sharp practice.[316]

A distinction may be drawn, at least in theory, between a contract which may be rescinded by reason of mutual mistake of the parties thereto and the avoidance of liability where it is established that there never was a consensus ad idem;[317] it has been said to be difficult to imagine a case in practice where there was no *consensus ad idem* to an apparent contract save in the context of some element of unilateral or mutual mistake.[318] Some older cases of unilateral mistake may suggest that a party against whom rescission is sought might be entitled to retain the bargain only by agreeing to a variation[319] to

---

[312] *Ferguson v Merchant Banking Ltd* [1993] ILRM 136 at 142.
[313] *Gun v McCarthy* (1884) 13 LRI 304 at 310.
[314] *Ferguson v Merchant Banking Ltd* [1993] ILRM 136 at 144.
[315] *Gun's* case at 311.
[316] *Cf* para **10.19** *supra* on the conduct of a party against whom rectification is sought.
[317] On which see paras **3.02-3** *ante*.
[318] *Ferguson v Merchant Banking Ltd* [1993] ILRM 136 at 142.
[319] Tantamount to rectification.

correct the mistake but, in so far as they may have supported that proposition, they should be regarded as wrongly decided.[320]

Other cases for rescission

[10.34] In practice the relief of rescission is most often sought in cases of fraud in its more obvious sense or its broad equitable sense and in cases of mistake. The relief is not confined to those types of case. Lack of title normally gives a purchaser the right to rescind[321] though usually he will have to make his objections or requisitions and give the vendor a reasonable chance to deal with them.[322] A vendor normally has a right of rescission if the purchaser cannot produce the necessary money to complete[323] and may have that right if the purchaser fails to pay the agreed deposit.[324] The current Law Society's *General Conditions of Sale* make it clear that failure to pay the agreed deposit in full is a breach of condition entitling the vendor to terminate the sale.[325] This is consistent with the stress laid by the Supreme Court recently on the importance of reaching agreement on a deposit and its amount.[326] Conversely a purchaser will be entitled to rescind if vacant possession is not available[327] unless some term of the contract cuts down his right to possession. Either party is likely to have a right to rescind if a condition precedent or subsequent is not fulfilled.[328] This type of situation and the rights of the parties in it are likely to be covered by carefully drafted special conditions[329] and time is likely to be "of the essence" for the condition to be met.[330] We have also noted that the relief of specific performance may be withheld in the exercise of the discretion[331] inherent in the remedy of specific performance[332] even where there has been no improper behaviour on the part of the plaintiff.[333] Equity may set aside a contract which is not equal and fair[334] and there may be an intermediate stage in which the court will not order a contract to be rescinded but, looking to the substantial justice of the case, will not order specific performance either.[335]

Loss of a right to rescission

[10.35] We have already seen that rescission usually is not available if the parties cannot be restored at least substantially to the *status quo*.[336] However a right to rescission which has come into being may be lost in certain circumstances. It will be unavailable if a bona

---

[320] See detailed consideration by Russell LJ in the *Riverlate Properties Ltd* case and Keane J's reference to that in *Irish Life Assurance Co Ltd v Dublin Land Securities Ltd* [1986] IR 332 at 353. *Cf* Flanagan J in *Gun v McCarthy* (1884) 13 LRI 304 at 309-10.

[321] Paras **9.78-81** *ante*.

[322] *Murphy v Harrington* [1927] IR 339; *McGirr v Devine* [1925] NI 94. And see para **9.80** *ante*.

[323] *Harris v Swordy* (HC) 16 June 1975, Kenny J, unrep at 7.

[324] *Morrow v Carty* [1957] NI 174 at 178-9.

[325] 1991 Ed, Condition 31.

[326] *Boyle v Lee* [1992] 1 IR 555;[1992] ILRM 65. See paras **3.12-14** *ante*.

[327] *Dickie v White* (1901) 1 NIJR 128; *Viscount Securities Ltd v Kennedy* (SC) 6 May 1986, unrep. And see paras **11.26-8** *post*.

[328] On such conditions see paras **3.19-28** *ante*.

[329] We look at rescission clauses in paras **10.36-44** *infra*.

[330] Para **3.28** *ante*.

[331] See paras **1.06-9, 9.37-8** *ante*.

[332] *O'Neill v Ryan (No 3)* [1992] 1 IR 166 at 96; *Conlon v Murray* [1958] NI 17 at 25.

[333] *Buckley v Irwin* [1960] NI 98 at 103.

[334] *Smelter Corporation of Ireland Ltd v O'Driscoll* [1977] IR 305 at 310-11.

[335] *Conlon's* case at 25.

[336] Paras **10.28-9** *supra*.

fide purchaser without notice of the relevant matters has bought the property.[337] Laches[338] may defeat a claim to set aside a transaction on the ground of undue influence[339] or improvidence.[340] Affirmation of the contract with full knowledge of the relevant facts precludes subsequent rescission.[341]

It is important to note that an invalid notice purporting to rescind a contract may itself be treated by the party getting the notice as a repudiation of that contract by the party giving it.[342] If the right to treat the contract as repudiated is not exercised quickly the party who served the invalid notice may be able to mend his hand but if he maintains his unjustifiable stance the right of the party given the notice to elect to treat the contract as repudiated is likely to be kept alive.[343] A party who wrongly maintains that the other party has been guilty of a repudiatory breach may be thereby in breach of the contract himself[344] and may find an order for specific performance being made against him as a result.[345] If difficulties arise over title a party who feels aggrieved by the other side's stance must be careful to take any steps such as making time of the essence or giving an opportunity to withdraw an objection which may be necessary in the particular case.[346] Whenever a right to rescind a contract accrues the party availing of it obviously must ensure that he actually does take the clear and definite step of rescinding it.[347]

RESCISSION CLAUSES

Purchaser insisting on objection or requisition

[10.36] If in a case not complicated by any fraud or unfair conduct on the part of a vendor a sale breaks down through his failure to make title the purchaser is entitled in the absence of any clause dealing with the point to the repayment of his deposit, usually with interest, and payment of the costs and expenses of investigating title.[348] If title shown is defective, a purchaser's objection is good and remains unanswered for a reasonable time, he has a right to rescind.[349] For the purpose of limiting the liability of vendors in the event of a sale breaking down it became customary to include in written contracts a condition enabling the vendor to rescind the contract if the purchaser made any objection or raised any requisition which the vendor was unable or unwilling to comply with. This type of condition was unpopular at first with judges of the Chancery Courts but it became recognised that with certain safeguards and restrictions, the condition should be accepted as a legitimate expedient by which vendors with defective titles could safely proceed to

---

[337] *Anderson v Ryan* [1967] IR 34 at 38 (exchange of motor cars).
[338] Discussed at paras **9.47-51** *ante*.
[339] *JH v WJH* (HC) 20 December 1979, Keane J, unrep at 30-31.
[340] *Ibid* at 32-38.
[341] *Royal Avenue Hotel Ltd v Richard Shops Properties Ltd* [1985] 6 NIJB 52 at 82.
[342] *Mills v Healy* [1937] IR 437 at 446, 447-8.
[343] *Ibid*, p 446, 448.
[344] *Taylor v Smyth* [1991] 1 IR 142 at 155-6; on appeal at 171.
[345] As in *Sweet & Maxwell Ltd v Universal News Services Ltd* [1964] 3 All ER 30.
[346] *Murphy v Harrington* [1927] IR 339 at 344-5; *McGirr v Devine* [1925] NI 94 at 97.
[347] *Hogan v Deasy* [1979] ILRM 71 at 74; *O'Mullane v Riordan* [1978] ILRM 73 at 77; *cf Commane v Walsh* (HC) 2 May 1983, O'Hanlon J, unrep at 5-6.
[348] *Per* Johnston J in *McMahon v Gaffney* [1930] IR 576 at 586.
[349] *Clibborn v Horan* [1923 1 IR 93 at 97; *cf Murphy v Harrington* [1927] IR 339 at 344-5; *McGirr v Devine* [1925] NI 94 at 97. See discussion of questions of title at paras **9.78-87** *ante*.

put their property on the market.[350] In more recent times conditions of the sort have been accepted as valid when they are used by the vendors for an honest purpose and not for trapping or tricking a purchaser and are relied on reasonably and not capriciously or arbitrarily.[351] A condition of this sort is not part of an "open" contract and is most unlikely to appear in a typical brief note which leads to an issue whether the Statute of Frauds is satisfied.[352] One almost always appears in formal written contracts and we turn next to the typical modern example of this.

The current Law Society condition

[10.37] The condition in the Law Society's present standard conditions reads:[353]

> "If the Purchaser shall make and insist on any Objection or Requisition as to the title, the Assurance to him or any other matter relating or incidental to the sale, which the Vendor shall, on the grounds of unreasonable delay or expense or other reasonable ground, be unable or unwilling to remove or comply with, the Vendor shall be at liberty (notwithstanding any intermediate negotiation or litigation or attempts to remove or comply with the same) by giving to the Purchaser of his Solicitor not less than five working days notice to rescind the sale. In that case, unless the Objection of Requisition in question shall in the meantime have been withdrawn, the sale shall be rescinded at the expiration of such notice."

That precise wording[354] was considered recently by the Supreme Court[355] Finlay CJ identified these four main principles applying to the exercise by a vendor of the right to invoke such a clause:

> "The first of those principles is that it must be shown if the vendor is to exercise his right in availing of the clause that he was acting reasonably, not arbitrarily, not capriciously. Secondly, it must be shown that the vendor in entering into the contract in the form in which it was concluded between him and purchaser had not been reckless. Thirdly, it must be shown that the purchaser was at the time of the invocation of the clause by the vendor persisting in the objection or requisition concerned and, fourthly, it must be shown that at the time of the invocation of the clause and the purported rescission of the contract, the contractual obligations were surviving at that time."[356]

The modern clause is similar in substance to conditions in use for a very long time[357] but clearly care must be taken in considering any decided case to see whether any difference in the wording in that case from the clause being considered could affect the position. For example, a feature of the current Law Society clause absent in some older clauses[358] is the *locus poenitentiae* giving the purchaser a chance to withdraw his point and this may be a factor in considering the reasonableness of a vendor's use of a rescission clause.[359] In

---

[350] *McMahon's* case, *ibid*.

[351] *Ibid*, p 586-7.

[352] On which see Ch 5 *ante*, esp paras **5.12-21**.

[353] *General Conditions of Sale*, 1991 Ed, condition 18.

[354] It could have been the identical clause 18 in the 1988 Ed.

[355] *Williams v Kennedy*, 19 July 1993, unrep.

[356] At 10-11. There was no dispute about the principles applying. Other principles existed but were not relevant to the case. The court only had to consider the first two principles of the four noted.

[357] Johnston J noted in *McMahon's* case at p 586 that one was considered by a court as far back as 1827.

[358] Eg, *Re Starr-Bowkett Building Society and Sibun's Contract* (1889) 42 Ch D 386; *Re Dames and Wood* (1885) 29 Ch D 626.

[359] Considered by Murphy J in *Lyons v Thomas* [1986] IR 666 at 679.

the modern version just quoted there are four stages leading to the actual use of the right to rescind - *ie*, the making of the requisition or objection, the vendor's unwillingness to satisfy it, the purchaser being told of the unwillingness and the purchaser falling to withdraw his point.[360]

Reasonable use of the clause

[10.38] It is vital to remember that a contractual right of rescission of this sort must be exercised reasonably and in good faith, not arbitrarily or capriciously.[361] A headnote writer has summarised a judgment thus:[362]

"A condition giving the vendor the right to rescind in the event of his unwillingness to comply with an objection to the title must not be considered as giving him an arbitrary power to annul the contract; some reasonable ground for his unwillingness must be shown. Before a vendor will be allowed to rescind, he must satisfy the court that he entered into the contract in ignorance of some material fact or document, or under some mistaken notion that he was entitled to sell and could make a title; there must be no failure of duty on his part, no element of shortcoming, and he must have omitted nothing which the ordinarily prudent man, having regard to his contractual relations with other persons, is bound to do".[363]

In his judgment in the same case Cozens-Hardy LJ said:[364]

"It is not enough for the vendor to say: Here is a contract which, as a matter of construction, entitles me to rescind this contract. The answer is 'No, you must look at all the circumstances; are they such as to entitle you to put an end to that Contract of Sale which, in form and in fact, you have entered into?'."[365]

[10.39] The text of the standard Law Society condition[366] might seem at first sight to give the vendor a lot of scope for rescission though the need to prove grounds of unreasonable delay or expense or other reasonable ground cuts it down considerably. That requirement fits in well with the general approach of the courts. However, the courts also require that the vendor does not act unreasonably, capriciously or in bad faith. Viscount Radcliffe, giving the opinion of the Privy Council, explained the position as follows:[367]

"... It is plain enough that, so far as the terms of the contract go, the respondent is within its rights. Clause 3(3)[368] is as much a part of the various undertakings and stipulations that make up the total nexus of the parties' agreement as any other of its clauses, and it is in fact a stipulation that was included in the draft put forward by the purchaser. If a vendor, having stipulated for or been conceded such a right, is to be precluded from asserting it in any particular context, it must be by virtue of some equitable principle which enures for the protection of the purchaser; and it is not in dispute that courts of equity have on

---

[360] *Duddell v Simpson* (1866) 2 Ch App 102 at 109.
[361] *Royal Avenue Hotel Ltd v Richard Shops Properties Ltd* [1985] 6 NIJB 52 at 82; *cf Kennedy v Wrennel* [1981] ILRM 81 at 82-3.
[362] *Re Jackson & Haden's Contract* [1906] 1 Ch 425.
[363] Approved by Costello J in *Kennedy v Wrennel* [1981] ILRM 81 at 82. See also discussion by the CA in *Baines v Tweddle* [1959] Ch 679; [1959] 2 All ER 724.
[364] At 425.
[365] Approved by Costello J in *Kennedy's* case at 82.
[366] Set out in para **10.37** *supra*.
[367] *Selkirk v Roma Investments Ltd* [1963] 1 WLR 1415 at 1422; [1963] 3 All ER 994 at 999.
[368] The rescission clause: the relevant words were "... which the vendor shall be unable or unwilling to remove or satisfy...".

numerous occasions intervened to restrain or control the exercise of such a right of rescission in contracts for the sale of land, despite what, on the face of the contract, its terms seem to secure for the vendor.

[369]"It does not appear to their lordships, any more than it did to the learned judge who tried the action, that there is any room for uncertainty as to the nature of the equitable principle that is invoked in these cases. It has frequently been analysed, and frequently applied, by Chancery judges, and, although the epithets that describe the vendor's offending action have shown some variety of expression, they are all related to the same underlying idea, and their variety is only due to the fact that, as each case is decided according to the whole context of its circumstances and the course of conduct of the vendor, one may illustrate more vividly than another some particular aspect of that idea. Thus, it has been said that a vendor, in seeking to rescind, must not act arbitrarily, or capriciously, or unreasonably. Much less can he act in bad faith. He may not use the power of rescission to get out of a sale 'brevi manu', since by doing so he makes a nullity of the whole elaborate and protracted transaction."[370]

Breach of duty by party seeking to rely on rescission clause

[10.40] Another important point to bear in mind is that a party may not be able to avail of this type of rescission clause if he is in breach of a duty which he owes to the other party. For example, a vendor is under a duty as to accuracy of statement in relation to a description in a contract made with a view to an intending purchaser acting on it as correct.[371] If he fails in that duty by, *eg*, being reckless in the formulation of the contract, he cannot rely on the rescission clause even though the shortcoming on his part is less than fraud or dishonesty.[372] An intending vendor is also under a duty to satisfy himself before he signs a contract for sale that he will be in a position to convey what he is contracting to sell.[373] Again, if he falls short in the duty he may not avail of a rescission clause.[374] By entering into a contract recklessly and without ascertaining that he has a title to sell he loses his entitlement to do so.[375] However he may be able to protect himself by fair special conditions which set out clearly the difficulty which a purchaser must accept.[376] Thus, if the title is irregular and defective but still amounts to a good "holding" title and the contract covers the position carefully the vendor will be able to rescind if the purchaser insists on a better title than the vendor can provide.[377]

[10.41] Duties of vendors which may prevent them relying on a rescission clause are not limited to matters of title or the terms of the contract. Fraud will clearly have that effect.[378]

---

[369] From here to the end of the quoted text was approved by Murray J in *Royal Avenue Hotel Ltd v Richard Shops Properties Ltd* [1985] 6 NIJB 52 at 84-5. It seemed to him that all the pejorative terms used by Lord Radcliffe applied to the vendor's "deplorable" attempt to rescind the contract.

[370] Approved by Murphy J in *Lyons's* case at 677-8.

[371] *Molphy v Coyne* (1919) 53 ILTR 177 at 184.

[372] *Ibid*: on the facts no recklessness.

[373] *Kennedy v Wrennel* [1981] ILRM 81 at 82-3 quoting Romer LJ in *Baines v Tweddle* [1959] Ch 679;[1959] 2 All ER 724.

[374] *Kennedy's* case at 83.

[375] *Nolan v Driscoll*, (HC) 25 April 1978, McWilliam J, unrep at 5.

[376] See paras **9.82-3** *ante*.

[377] *Re Commins and Hanfy's Contract* (1905) 5 NIJR 111 112, 113; *cf McMahon v Gaffney* [1930] IR 576 at 581-2, 587-8.

[378] *Molphy v Coyne* (1919) 53 ILTR 177 at 184; *cf Re Commins and Hanafy's Contract* (1905) 5 NIJR 111.

Failure to make reasonable efforts to obtain a necessary consent is likely to prevent reliance on a rescission clause though much can depend on the wording of the clause dealing with the consent.[379] Breach of the duty to take proper care of the property pending completion[380] will prevent the use of a rescission clause in order to escape liability to compensate the purchaser.[381]

Some other factors

[10.42] Other factors may prevent or restrict the use of rescission clauses of the type we are now discussing. They will not be available to deal with requisitions raised by court counsel after an order for specific performance is made where issues of title remain outstanding.[382] The requisitions in this situation are not made on behalf of the purchaser and have been described as "necessary to enable the plaintiff (vendor) to enforce his decree".[383] It seems that if by agreement of the parties a purchaser spends money on the property sold over and above that which a rescission clause contemplates being returned to him if the vendor uses it the latter cannot enforce the clause.[384] A rescission clause usually will not cover something the subject of a collateral contract and so a party cannot rely on the clause to get out of what he agreed to do by that contract.[385] And a vendor may not take an unfair advantage of it by delaying its exercise while he negotiates for a sale to a third party.[386] Nor can he rely on one when the purchaser has made an objection which goes to the root of the title.[387]

Rescission for failure to meet a condition

[10.43] If parties agree that a certain matter is to be a condition of their contract[388] and provide for a right of rescission if the condition is not met the court normally will respect what the parties agreed upon.[389] The court cannot substitute an alternative provision of its own for that made by the parties themselves.[390] However, there normally will be a duty on the parties to try to fulfil conditions[391] and failure to fulfil that duty is likely to prevent reliance on a rescission clause.[392] In the case of a right to rescind because a condition has not been met by a certain time a party who waives the particular time limit normally keeps the right to insist on compliance with the condition but may have to fix a new date or give the other side a reasonable time to fulfil the condition.[393]

---

[379] *Royal Avenue Hotel Ltd v Richard Shops Properties Ltd* [1985] 6 NIJB 52 at 81. Note discussion of conditions by Murray J at 78-81. See consideration of the duty to try to fulfil conditions at paras **3.26-7** *ante*.

[380] On this duty see paras **11.12-13** *post*.

[381] *Lyons v Thomas* [1986] IR 666 at 681-2.

[382] *Bourke v Grimes* (1929) 63 ILTR 53 at 54, 55.

[383] By Murnaghan J in *Bourke's* case at 55.

[384] *Lucey v Laurel Construction Co Ltd* (HC) 18 December 1970, Kenny J, unrep at 13-14.

[385] *Kennedy v Wrennel* [1981] ILRM 81 at 82-3.

[386] *Smith v Wallace* [1895] 1 Ch 385.

[387] *Coyle v Central Trust Investment Society Ltd* [1978] ILRM 211 at 215 (vendor tried to enforce clause for forfeiture of deposit and re-sale).

[388] See discussion of conditional contracts at paras **3.19-28** *ante*.

[389] *Crean v Drinan* [1983] ILRM 82 at 87.

[390] *Ibid.*

[391] See paras **3.26-7** *ante*.

[392] *Royal Avenue Hotel Ltd v Richard Shops Properties Ltd* [1985] 6 NIJB 52 at 81.

[393] *McKillop v McMullan* [1979] NI 85 at 92-3.

Rescission clauses generally

[10.44] We have just looked at two particular types of rescission clauses[394] but many other types may be agreed by parties.[395] For example, the current Law Society *General Conditions of Sale* provide that failure to pay the deposit in full is a breach of condition entitling the vendor to "terminate the sale".[396] Another important type of clause is one providing that if a purchaser fails in any material respect to comply with conditions of sale his deposit shall be forfeited and the vendor may re-sell.[397] The vendor may not rely on that type of condition when the purchaser has made an objection which goes to the root of the title.[398]

It is essential, of course, that the term relied on as giving a right to rescind is an agreed term. A party cannot rescind on the basis of a condition which he has tried to impose unilaterally.[399] Nor will a court exercising an equitable jurisdiction allow a party to escape his obligations by an unreasonable and unilateral act as by trying to impose an unreasonably short time limit.[400] Rescission has been described as "a drastic operation" and the onus of establishing the facts giving rise to the right to rescind is on the party relying on it.[401] If, for example, a clause allows rescission on the ground of difficulty, delay or expense in complying with a requisition, the vendor must be able to prove such difficulty, delay or expense in order to rely on the clause.[402] The right to rescind must also be exercised within a reasonable time.[403] This applies just as much where the rescission is made under an express term of a contract as where it is based on *eg*, a material misrepresentation.[404] However, parties may spend considerable time in trying to improve the title but, depending on the circumstances, the vendor may be able to limit a time for the purchaser to accept the title he *can* make and to rescind in the event of refusal.[405] The right to rescind may not be used to defeat a claim by a purchaser to compensation to which he is lawfully entitled[406] or because a purchaser's requisition has been upheld by a court decision.[407]

---

[394] Meaning here simply clauses under which parties may, depending on the circumstances, have a right to terminate the contract. Note the different meanings of "rescission" discussed at para **10.26** *supra*.

[395] See discussion by Wylie, *Irish Conveyancing Law* (1978) paras 12.56-73 and 14.27-35.

[396] *General Condition* 31; this is consistent with the importance placed by the Supreme Court on a deposit in *Boyle v Lee* [1992] 1 IR 555; [1992] ILRM 65 (see paras **3.12-14** *ante*).

[397] *General Condition* 41 of the Law Society's conditions, 1991 Ed.

[398] *Coyle v Central Trust Investment Society Ltd* [1978] ILRM 211 at 215.

[399] *Moynihan v Crowley* [1958] IJR 21 at 24.

[400] *Kelly v Park Hall School* Ltd [1979] IR 340 at 352.

[401] *Royal Avenue Hotel Ltd v Richard Shops Properties Ltd* [1985] 6 NIJB 52 at 81.

[402] *Re Weston and Thomas's Contract* [1907] 1 Ch 244 considered by McWilliam J in *Nolan v Driscoll* (HC) 25 April 1978, unrep at 5.

[403] The *Royal Avenue Hotel Ltd* case at 82; *Ker v Crowe* (1873) 7 IRCL 181.

[404] The *Royal Avenue Hotel Ltd* case at 82-4 citing case law and the 25th Ed (1983) of *Chitty on Contracts*.

[405] *Nolan's* case at 5-6; title held sufficient.

[406] *Lyons v Thomas* [1986] IR 666 at 681-2.

[407] *Re Quigley and McClay's Contract* [1918] 1 IR 347.

Chapter 11

From Contract to Completion

THE PURCHASER AS BENEFICIAL OWNER

[11.01] Judicial opinion in Ireland and England has been unanimous in holding that when a vendor and a purchaser enter into a valid and enforceable contract for the sale of property, supported by payment by the purchaser of part of the purchase price, the vendor becomes a constructive trustee for the purchaser of a beneficial or equitable estate in the property.[1] The only area of disagreement is the extent of that estate.[2] Has the purchaser the entire beneficial estate in the property or only a part of it corresponding to the portion of the purchase price he has paid? On either basis the vendor still has a substantial interest in the property. Save where the contract provides otherwise, he is entitled to remain in possession until the purchase money is paid and, as such possessor, he has a common law lien on the property for the purchase money; even if he parts with possession of the property he has an equitable lien on it for the unpaid purchase money; and he is entitled to take and keep for his own use the rents and profits up to the date fixed for completion.[3] If he hands over possession he has the right to regain it if the contract is not completed.[4] And if a purchaser is let into possession without completing his contract[5] but is dispossessed later by the vendor, even in circumstances which do not enjoy the approval of the court, the vendor's resumed possession is likely to be treated as the normal possession of a vendor between contract and completion.[6]

Tempany v Hynes

[11.02] The key modern Irish case is *Tempany v Hynes*[7] in which a company gave two debentures as security. The lender appointed the plaintiff to be receiver of all the property charged. The receiver had power to sell or concur in selling the assets charged and he agreed to sell the relevant property. Between the date of his appointment and that of the contract for sale two judgment mortgages were entered on the folios as burdens affecting the interest of the registered owner. The defendant bought the property and paid a 25% deposit. After the contract but before completion of the sale two more judgment mortgages were registered. The plaintiff got releases of the pre-contract mortgages.[8] The

---

[1] *Per* Henchy J in *Hamilton v Hamilton* [1982] IR 466 at 484.
[2] *Ibid* referring to Wylie, *Irish Land Law* and *Irish Conveyancing Law*; *Coffey v Brunel Construction* [1983] IR 36 at 43, *per* Griffin J.
[3] *Per* Henchy J in *Tempany v Hynes* [1976] IR 101 at 109. The full passage is set out in para **11.07** *infra*.
[4] *Re Strong* [1940] IR 382 at 402. Another part of that sentence from *Re Strong* was disapproved by Kenny J in *Tempany's* case at p. 116 in a passage quoted at para **11.06** *infra*.
[5] This is discussed at paras **11.23-5** *infra*.
[6] *Johnston v Johnston* (1869) IR 3 Eq 328 at 334.
[7] [1976] IR 101. *Tempany's* case was applied in *Murnaghan Bros Ltd v O'Maoldomhnaigh* [1991] 1 IR 455 at 458 (one third interest) and *Viek Investments Ltd v Revenue Commissioners* [1991] 2 IR 520 at 525 (over 98%); *cf Waterford Glass (Group Services) Ltd v Revenue Commissioners* [1990] 1 IR 334 at 337.
[8] This turned out to be unnecessary as the *ratio* of the majority judgment caught the pre-contract mortgages: see para **11.08** *infra*.

defendant refused to complete unless he was paid enough money to clear the post-contract mortgages. Finlay P refused specific performance[9] as he felt that to force the title on the purchaser and leave him to fight out an issue with the post-contract judgment mortgagees would be to force upon him a doubtful title.[10] The Supreme Court unanimously ordered specific performance though there are important differences between the judgments of Kenny J (with which the Chief Justice agreed) and Henchy J.

[11.03] As we shall see, the receiver's appointment was vital to Kenny J's judgment.[11] He rejected the view that once a contract was signed the vendor ceased to have any beneficial interest in the property:[12]

> "The first argument for the plaintiff was that when the contract for sale was signed on 26 February, 1974, the company became a trustee for the defendant who became the owner of the entire beneficial interest in the lands and that the company did not own any estate or interest on which the two judgment mortgages of 22 May and 1 July, 1974 could operate; it was submitted that those judgment mortgages would be removed from the folio on the registration of the transfer to the defendant."

> A vendor who signs a contract with a purchaser for the sale of land becomes a trustee in the sense that he is bound to take reasonable care of the property until the sale is completed, but he becomes a trustee of the beneficial interest to the extent only to which the purchase price is paid. He is not a trustee of the beneficial interest merely because he signs a contract. This is made clear by Lord Cranworth in *Rose v Watson*:[13]

>> 'There can be no doubt, I apprehend, that when a purchaser has paid his purchase-money, though he has got no conveyance, the vendor becomes a trustee for him of the legal estate, and he is in equity, considered as the owner of the estate. When, instead of paying the whole of his purchase-money, he pays a part of it, it would seem to follow, as a necessary corollary, that, to the extent to which he has paid his purchase-money, to that extent the vendor is a trustee for him; in other words, that he acquires a lien, exactly in the same way as if upon payment of part of the purchase-money the vendor had executed a mortgage to him of the estate to that extent.'[14]

> Until the whole of the purchase money is paid, the vendor has in my opinion a beneficial interest in the land which may be charged by a judgment mortgage."

Further support for Kenny J's view comes from Lord Westbury LC in *Rose v Watson*:[15]

> "When the owner of an estate contracts with a purchaser for the immediate sale of it, the ownership of the estate is, in equity, transferred by that contract. Where the contract undoubtedly is an executory contract, in this sense, namely, that the ownership of the estate is transferred, subject to the payment of the purchase money, every portion of the

---

[9]   (HC) 1974 No 3937P unrep.
[10] At p 16. The effect of the receiver's appointment is not discussed in his judgment so presumably the point was not opened to him. Henchy J noted that the point was "not dealt with in the High Court": [1976] IR 101 at 111; likewise Kenny J at 117.
[11] See para **11.08** *infra*.
[12] At p 114-5.
[13] (1864) 10 HLC 672.
[14] At 683-4. *Cf* Lord Westbury at 678.
[15] At p 678. *Cf* Lord Cranworth at 683-4.

purchase money paid in pursuance of that contract is a part performance and execution of the contract, and, to the extent of the money so paid, does, in equity, finally transfer to the purchaser the ownership of a corresponding portion of the estate."[16]

[11.04] The claim in *Rose v Watson*[17] was to enforce a purchaser's lien[18] where he had successfully resisted a claim for specific performance on the ground of representations inducing him to enter into the contract.[19] Under the contract he had paid a 10% deposit and some interest payments. After the contract the vendor mortgaged the property. The mortgagee gave the purchaser notice of the mortgage but did not attempt to interfere with the contract at all thus leaving the purchaser still bound to perform that contract.[20] It was held that the mortgage, "being made subsequently to the contract of sale, and, of course, subject to that contract, conveyed to the Appellants only that which the vendor was entitled to under that contract."[21] In a modern Irish case, *Re Kelly's Carpetdrome Ltd*,[22] a company paid a 25% deposit with money provided by another company before mortgaging the property to a bank. The company which provided the deposit money was held to have a 25% beneficial interest in the property in priority to the bank.[23] In neither of those cases did the person who paid the deposit proceed with the purchase to completion so no issue arose what the position would have been between him and the mortgagee if he had paid all the purchase money.

[11.05] Reverting to the *Tempany* case, Kenny J criticised[24] judicial and textbook statements which, in his words, "have stated that from the date of the signature of the contract (whether the whole or any part of the purchase money has been paid or not) the purchaser is the owner of the entire beneficial interest in the land." He moved to an Irish case of 1916:

"This issue arose in *Kissock and Currie's Contract*[25] which was a decision of the Court of Appeal in Ireland in which a judgment mortgage had been registered against a vendor[26] between the date of the contract for sale by him and its completion. The sale was closed without any payment being made to the judgment mortgagee. A subsequent purchaser[27] objected to the title because he maintained that the judgment mortgage was valid and this claim was upheld. Sir Ignatius O'Brien LC said at p 388 of the report: 'I think that, from the point of view of the judgment creditor ...his debtor had an interest in land after the date of the contract for sale and until completion,[28] capable of being affected by the judgment'. If this case was correctly decided, as I think it was, the principle underlying

---

[16] That passage is quoted with approval by O'Byrne J giving the majority judgment of the Supreme Court in *Re Strong* [1940] IR 382 at 402.
[17] (1864) 10 HLC 672.
[18] On which see para **5.04** *ante*.
[19] Reported in the name of *Myers v Watson* at (1851) 1 Sim NS 523.
[20] *Per* Lord Westbury at 681 and Lord Cranworth at 684. In fact he got out of it on the ground of the representations.
[21] *Per* Lord Westbury at 681.
[22] (HC) 29 November 1983, Costello J, unrep.
[23] At p 15.
[24] [1976] IR at pp 114-5.
[25] [1916] 1 IR 376.
[26] *Ie* the *previous* vendor who had sold to Kissock.
[27] The purchaser, *Currie*, in the reported case.
[28] The words "until completion" possibly might be taken as meaning that the interest of the vendor lasted only until completion - *ie*, was "transient". If that were so, O'Brien LC could hardly have decided as he did. Kenny J certainly did not take them that way in *Tempany's* case.

it disposes of the puzzling concept[29] in some of the other cases that such a judgment mortgage is valid when registered but ceases to be effective when the sale is completed because then the vendor's interest is deemed to have passed to the purchaser from the date of the contract. I prefer the principle stated by Lord Cranworth."

Kissock's case was itself a split decision. O'Brien LC[30] examined the law before the enactment of any legislation on judgment mortgages:[31]

"The operation of a contract upon judgments before the new law seems to have stood thus: a contract for sale would prevail over a subsequent judgment-creditor in equity, but the creditor would have a legal right under his judgment, and he would have an equitable right to have so much of the purchase-money required to pay his debts as remained unpaid; to the extent of the money paid before his judgment, he would be bound in equity. But if the purchaser paid any part of the purchase-money to the exclusion of the judgment creditor, after he had notice of the judgment, he would still be bound to that extent by the debt."

Dissenting Cherry LCJ said:[32]

"It is argued that, until the purchase-money is paid, some shadow of an interest remains vested in the vendor, which may be affected by the judgment mortgage; but I do not think that this is so. The most that the vendor could retain would be a lien for unpaid purchase-money, and that has never, so far as I am aware, been held to be an estate or interest in the lands which can be captured by a judgment-mortgage."

Accordingly the majority judgment in *Kissock's* case[33] clearly supports the majority judgment in *Tempany's* case; the minority judgment in the older case probably goes further in the opposite direction than Henchy J who accepted in the later case that the vendor had a "substantial interest"[34] even though it would not "survive the completion of the sale and the registration of the defendant as full owner".[35] It is worthy of note that Kenny J drew a distinction[36] between the vendor's trusteeship in the sense of having to take reasonable care of the property pending completion and in the sense of holding the beneficial interest in the property.[37] In the latter sense it is limited by the proportion of the purchase price paid but there is no such limitation on the duty to take care which derives from the fact that the purchaser has a significant interest in the property and is usually precluded from the occupation and control of the property until actual completion.[38]

---

[29] The concept could be less puzzling if Kenny J had accepted Henchy J's view that only a *transient* interest of the vendor was affected: see para **11.05** *infra*.

[30] With whom Moriarty LJ concurred.

[31] At 386 quoting a passage from Sugden's *Vendors and Purchasers*.

[32] At 391.

[33] Note the discussion by Keane, *Equity and the Law of Trusts in the Republic of Ireland*, para 5.16 including the suggestion that it should be treated as having been reversed *sub silentio* by *Re Strong*.

[34] [1976] IR 101 at 109.

[35] At 111.

[36] In the second para of the extract quoted in para **11.03** *supra*.

[37] See discussion by Murphy J in *Lyons v Thomas* [1986] IR 666 at 675-6. Note Kenny J's emphasis of "the beneficial interest" in *Tempany's* case at 115.

[38] *Per* Murphy J in *Lyons's* case at 676.

[11.06] Kenny J continued in *Tempany's* case:[39]

> Counsel for the plaintiff relied on a passage in the judgment of O'Byrne J in *In re Strong*[40] at pp. 401-402 of the report. It reads:
>
>> 'Under the general rules of law and equity, apart from the provisions of the Local Registration of Title (Ir) Act 1891, the position, as between a purchaser of lands, who has paid his purchase money but has obtained a conveyance, and a judgment debtor [*sic*] who has registered his judgment as a mortgage affecting lands, seems to be quite clear. Where a contract is entered into for the sale and purchase of lands the vendor becomes a trustee for the purchaser and the latter becomes owner in equity of the lands subject to certain rights of the vendor to secure payment of the balance of the purchase money and to regain possession of the lands should the contract not be completed.'
>
> The first sentence is dealing with the position of a purchaser who has paid the whole of the purchase money and has not got a conveyance when a judgment mortgage is registered against the vendor; the purchaser then takes the lands free of the judgement mortgage. The second sentence deals with the position after a contract for sale has been signed and no part, or part only, of the purchase price has been paid. The second sentence is, in my view, incorrect. The structure of the two sentences suggests that the second is explanatory of the first: it is not.[41] It is re-stating the view of Lord Cairns and of Jessel MR which I do not accept and which is not consistent with what Lord Cranworth said."

He concluded (on this argument):[42]

> "At the date when the two post-contract judgment mortgages were registered on the folios, the deposit only had been paid and they therefore affected whatever beneficial interest the company had in the lands. Therefore, I reject the argument that, because a contract for sale had been signed, the vendor company had no beneficial interest in the lands which could be affected by the post-contract mortgages."

[11.07] Henchy J considered the same main point:[43]

> "When a binding contract for the sale of land has been made, whether the purchase money has been paid or not,[44] the law (at least in cases where the parties proceed to the stage of conveyance)[45] treats the beneficial ownership as having passed to the purchaser from the time the contract was made: *Gordon Hill Trust Ltd v Segall*.[46] From then until the time of completion, regardless of whether the purchase money has been paid or not, the vendor, in whom the legal estate is still vested, is treated for certain purposes (such as the preservation of the property from damage by trespassers) as a trustee for the purchaser. But, coupled with this trusteeship, there is vested in the vendor a substantial interest in the property pending completion. Save where the contract provides otherwise, he is entitled to remain in possession until the purchase money is paid and, as such

---

[39] At 115-6.

[40] [1940] IR 382.

[41] The first sentence referred to the purchaser as having "paid his purchase money" and the second mentioned the "balance of the purchase money" so indeed they do contemplate different situations.

[42] At 116.

[43] Page 109-110.

[44] This indicates the view that even if no money at all has yet been paid the purchaser is regarded as the beneficial owner.

[45] This phrase seems to let in the possibility that making a binding contract does not *necessarily* transfer any beneficial ownership.

[46] [1941] 2 All ER 379.

possessor, he has a common law lien on the property for the purchase money; even if he parts with possession of the property he has an equitable lien on it for the unpaid purchase money; and he is entitled to take and keep for his own use the rents and profits up to the date fixed for completion. It is clear, therefore, that between contract and completion the vendor has a beneficial interest in the property which is capable of being charged by a judgment mortgage:..."

He then said that when a judgment mortgage is registered as a burden affecting the interest of a registered owner after an enforceable contract has been made to sell the land, what becomes affected thereby is "the transient beneficial interest of the registered owner". Since a judgment creditor (by registering his judgment as a judgment mortgage) could not acquire any greater estate or interest in the land than the registered owner has at the time of such registration, all that could pass to the judgment creditor here was[47]

"the interest in the land which the registered owner had after the making of the contract to sell, namely, an interest which would pass out of existence once the sale had been completed, the purchase money paid and the purchaser registered as full owner."[48]

[11.08] Kenny J considered a second argument that the appointment of the receiver by the debenture holder effected an equitable assignment to the debenture holder of all the property subject to the floating charge. He decided that point in favour of the plaintiff:[49]

"In my opinion the claim of the debenture holders in relation to the lands in the three folios ranks before the rights of the four judgment mortgagees and the vendor has shown a good title to all of the lands in the three folios. When the transfer from the plaintiff and the company to the defendant, the mortgage debenture and the appointment of the receiver are produced to him, it will be the duty of the registrar of titles to cancel the entries of the four judgment mortgages which appear on the folios without proof of the payment of any sum in respect of any of them."

That passage is the *ratio* in the majority judgment. It is interesting to note that it caught the pre-contract judgment mortgages as well as the two registered after the contract. Henchy J did not need to consider the point as he held that the vendor was entitled to succeed on different grounds.[50]

[11.09] Kenny J did not deal with Henchy J's point that the vendor's interest which would be affected by the judgment mortgage was only a transient one or with a point that s 71(4)(c) of the Registration of Title Act 1964 had the effect of making the purchaser's rights under his contract override the judgment mortgagee's rights.[51] The latter was a "statutory recognition" of the conclusion reached in *In re Murphy v McCormack*[52] and *In re Strong*[53] that the unregistered right of a purchaser for value from the registered owner was not subject to a judgment mortgage registered against the registered owner after the

---

[47] [1976] IR 101 at 110.
[48] It followed, in his view, that if the defendant completed the purchase and became registered as full owner he would be entitled to have the post-contract judgment mortgages cancelled from the folios.
[49] At p 117, O'Higgins CJ concurring.
[50] His conclusion is at p 111 and his *ratio* is considered at para **11.05** above.
[51] At p 110-1.
[52] [1930] IR 322.
[53] [1940] IR 382. Note consideration of that case by Costello J in *Re Lynch, Monahan and O'Brien Ltd* (HC) 14 October 1986, unrep at 5-7.

contract to sell. And it would seem that the a purchaser's right to specific performance is an "unregistered right" within s 71(4)(*c*).[54]

[11.10] Where the *entire* of purchase money has been paid pursuant to a binding contract the purchaser becomes entitled to the entire beneficial interest in the land on the basis of either judgment in *Tempany's* case[55] and the vendor becomes a bare trustee for him.[56] A vendor who has received all the purchase money may be said to have a "bare legal estate".[57] Whilst different views have been expressed as to the time when, and the extent to which, the beneficial interest passes to the purchaser before the entire purchase-money has been paid, there has at all times been unanimity that, where the purchase money has been paid in full, the entire beneficial interest is vested in the purchaser.[58] At the other end of the scale, if none of the purchase money has been paid pursuant to the binding contract, the majority decision in *Tempany v Hynes*[59] means that the purchaser has not yet any beneficial interest in the property. However, he still has his right to insist on specific performance of his contract unless the fact that no purchase money has been paid involves a breach of the contract sufficient to entitle the vendor to get out of the deal[60] or some other defence succeeds.[61] Of course, in many cases there is a dispute on major issues - *eg*, whether a contract exists at all or whether the Statute of Frauds is satisfied - and the alleged vendor will not accept any part of the purchase price; in this kind of situation the non-payment of any part of the purchase money cannot be a breach of the contract if one is proved to exist.

[11.11] The main difference of opinion in *Tempany v Hynes* was summarised thus by Henchy J in *Hamilton v Hamilton*:[62]

> "In *Tempany v Hynes* I expressed the opinion that a purchaser, whether he has paid part of the purchase price or not, becomes the equitable or beneficial owner of the whole estate. That view, however, did not prevail in that case. Mr. Justice Kenny (with whom the Chief Justice concurred) considered that the equitable or beneficial estate becomes vested in a purchaser only to the extent to which the purchase price is paid. Unless and until a different conclusion is reached by a full court, that majority opinion must be taken to be the law."

In the same case O'Higgins CJ[63] stated[64] that *Tempany v Hynes* dealt only "with the transient interest of a vendor, pending the due completion of the sale by the payment of the purchase money, in the property contracted to be sold".[65] It had no application to a

---

[54] See also Keane, *Equity and the Law of Trusts in the Republic of Ireland* at para 5.16.
[55] On the principles explained by Kenny J in para **11.02** above. *Cf Re Lynch, Monahan and O'Brien Ltd* (HC) 14 October 1986, Costello J, unrep at 5.
[56] *Coffey v Brunel Construction* [1983] IR 36, *per* O'Higgins CJ at 40 and Griffin J at 43, 46, Hederman J concurring with both; *Re Strong* [1940] IR 382 at 402; *McLean v McErlean* [1983] NI 258 at 265, 271.
[57] *McLean v McErlean* [1983] NI 258 at 265, 271. *Cf Re Scarlett* [1958] NI 28 at 42.
[58] *Per* Griffin J in *Coffey's* case at 43.
[59] [1976] IR 101.
[60] *Eg*, under condition 31 of the Law Society's, *General Conditions* (1991) Ed, failure to pay the deposit in full may entitle the vendor to "terminate the sale".
[61] See Ch 9 *ante* on defences.
[62] [1982] IR 466 at 484. See also discussion of *Tempany's* case by Murphy J in *Lyons v Thomas* [1986] IR 666 at 675-6.
[63] Who had concurred with Kenny J in the *Tempany* case.
[64] At p 476.
[65] This is interesting as it is close to the minority judgment of Henchy J in *Tempany's* case.

case where the vendor defaulted and was liable to a decree for specific performance.[66] The position in Northern Ireland seems similar to the minority view of Henchy J. In *Re Scarlett*[67] it was held that the purchaser, who had only paid a deposit, had acquired an equitable interest in the land when the vendor died and "this interest was so extensive as to leave the testator no beneficial interest which could be accounted an estate in lands[68]." In England the predominant view seems to be that once a specifically enforceable contract for the sale of land is made the purchaser becomes the owner of the land in equity and the vendor becomes a constructive trustee of the land for the purchaser, subject in each case to their respective rights and duties under the contract.[69] However, the vendor's trusteeship has been said to be "progressive"[70] and it has been said of the vendor: "The vendor is not a mere trustee; he is in progress towards it, and finally becomes such when the money is paid, and when he is bound to convey".[71] Those last views would seem compatible with the approach of Kenny J in the *Tempany* case.

[**11.12**] The present Irish position - ie, the majority judgment in *Tempany's* case - is attractive to a large extent. The idea that a purchaser should own the beneficial estate to the extent to which he has paid his purchase-money is fair and reasonable. It has the weighty support of the House of Lords decision in *Rose v Watson*[72] where Lord Cranworth felt that such a principle was "founded upon such solid and substantial justice" that he could "rejoice" that the Lords were able to lay down that rule.[73] It is consistent with what equity does in certain other cases. We see it, for example, in cases where one person has contributed to the cost of property which is in the name of another.[74] It also fits in comfortably with events which may happen after contract - eg, payment of a purchase price by instalments or, moving in the opposite direction, the forfeiture of a deposit. There seems to be no difficulty in principle about a purchaser increasing his share of the beneficial ownership in accordance with the amount of instalments paid. If a deposit is validly forfeited it ceases to perform its second role as a part payment of the purchase money[75] and there is no difficulty about the notion that the purchaser then loses his beneficial interest in the property.

[**11.13**] There is a second important point of difference in the judgments in *Tempany's* case. The minority judgment held that the interest of the vendor ceases to exist when the sale is completed, the purchase price paid and the purchaser registered as full owner.[76] This is attractive. It would seem to follow that anything affecting the vendor's transient

---

66 At 476.
67 [1958] NI 28 at 42. In *McLean v McErlean* [1983] NI 258 the entire purchase money had been paid and the main issue was whether the purchaser could rely on the Statute of Limitations (Northern Ireland) 1958.
68 For the purposes of s 16 of the Charitable Donations and Bequests (Ireland) Act 1844.
69 Snell's *Equity*, 29th Ed (1990), p 195, 463. But *cf* Jones & Goodhart, *Specific Performance* (1986) at 217-9.
70 Jones & Goodhart, *op cit*, p 217.
71 *Per* Plumer MR in *Wall v Bright* (1820) 1 Jac & W 494 at 503.
72 (1864) 10 HLC 672.
73 At 684.
74 We touch on this at paras **7.30-1, 7.35** *ante*. See discussion of implied trusts by Wylie, *Irish Land Law*, 2nd Ed (1986) at paras 9.045-8 and constructive trusts at paras 9.059-60; also Keane, *Equity and the Law of Trusts in the Republic of Ireland*, paras 12.12-16 and Ch 13.
75 On which see para **3.11** *ante*. If the vendor is entitled to forfeit the deposit this normally means that the contract has gone.
76 *Per* Henchy J in *Tempany's* case at p 111. *Cf* O'Higgins CJ in *Hamilton's* case at 476.

interest and not having priority over the purchaser's claims - primarily his right to specific performance should not affect the purchaser after completion of the purchase and his registration as owner.[77] But this is not the law; if Kenny J had accepted it he would surely have decided differently on the first point argued.[78] The need for registration as owner to enable an instrument to operate to transfer land is a feature of the Registration of Title Act 1964[79] but does not affect the principle that a purchaser who has a binding contract and has paid the purchase price has become the beneficial owner.[80] That need does not arise in cases of unregistered title though the purchaser will obviously do searches and effect registration in the Registry of Deeds in order to protect his priority. In those cases the vendor's interest in the land terminates when the purchase price has been paid in full and the duly executed purchase deed is delivered.[81] In *Re Strong*[82] it was accepted in argument that, in the case of land outside the Land Registry, a judgment mortgage registered after payment of the full purchase money though before conveyance would not affect the land sold as the vendor no longer had a beneficial interest in the land once he was paid. That, of course, did not govern a situation in which part only of the purchase money was paid when the judgment mortgage is registered.

VENDOR'S DUTIES TO PURCHASER

[11.14] When a binding contract has been made and some of the purchase money paid the vendor owes the duties of a trustee to the purchaser. This trusteeship has been described as "unorthodox"[83] and is limited by the fact that until he has been paid in full the vendor himself still has valuable rights in the property[84] even though the purchaser has a share in the beneficial ownership commensurate with the proportion of the price already paid and a right to insist on specific performance if necessary. A very important departure from the normal incidents of a trust is that in this case the vendor/trustee has his own legitimate interest to protect, *ie*, the receipt of the purchase money, to protect. Also important is the fact that the property will be restored to him in the event of the contract being rescinded for any reason.[85] As trustee the vendor may not impose a restrictive covenant for his own benefit unless a fresh agreement is made.[86] Nor may a vendor bind the purchaser by a post-contract deed altering the legal position relating to the property without his consent unless he has provided for that in the contract.[87] It may be a vendor's duty to keep houses properly tenanted as far as he reasonably can when

---

[77] And Henchy J held that he would be entitled to have the post-contract judgment mortgages cancelled from the folios: *Tempany's* case at 111.

[78] See para **11.06** *supra*.

[79] Section 51(2) of the Registration of Title Act 1964. See consideration by O'Higgins CJ in *Coffey v Brunel Construction* 1983 IR 36 at 40 and by Griffin J at 44.

[80] *Coffey's* case, *per* O'Higgins CJ at 40 and Griffin J at 45.

[81] On *delivery* of a deed see Wylie, *Irish Conveyancing Law*, paras 16.118-25 and note that delivery as an "escrow" is not a real delivery.

[82] [1940] IR 382 at 395. *Cf Coffey's* case.

[83] By Murphy J in *Lyons v Thomas* [1986] IR 666 at 676. *Cf* "qualified trusteeship" in *Malone v Henshaw* (1891) 29 LRI 352 at 359.

[84] Note the rights set out by Henchy J in the first passage quoted at para **11.07** *supra*.

[85] Pointed out by Murphy J in *Lyons v Thomas* [1986] R 666 at 676.

[86] *Gilmurray v Corr* [1978] NI 99 at 103-4, affirmed by CA: note at 106. And see para **3.31** *ante*.

[87] *Johnston v Morris* (HC) 7 December 1978, McWilliam J, unrep at 6-8.

they would become a burden to the purchaser if left empty.[88] On the other hand, granting tenancies on unfavourable terms is likely to be a breach of trust.[89] The vendor is bound, until possession is given to the purchaser, to manage and preserve the property in sale with the same care as a trustee would exercise in regard to the property subject to his trust[90] and the purchaser is entitled to get what he contracted to buy.[91] A vendor who neglects the property is likely to have to pay the cost of making good that neglect.[92] When that kind of claim succeeds in a specific performance action the purchaser will be entitled to a credit for that cost on closing.[93] It would not be open to a vendor to try to use a rescission clause in the contract for the purpose of trying to avoid that right.[94] If it is shown that the property sold has been damaged between the date of sale and the time when the purchaser gets possession, the onus of proof is shifted to the vendor and it is for him to establish, if he can, what portion of the damage pre-existed the sale and what portion could not have been prevented by the exercise of due care and forethought on his part.[95] The vendor also has a duty to preserve the property from trespassers.[96] He is not an insurer[97] but must take reasonable steps to prevent damage by trespassers[98] or by the elements.[99] Of course he must not damage the property himself.[100] When a mortgagee sells and the mortgagor damages the property the resultant loss falls not on the purchaser but on the mortgagee who will have a remedy against the mortgagor for what that is worth.[101] If a vendor sells a property to a second purchaser he may be accountable as a trustee to the first purchaser for the proceeds of sale[102] though usually the first purchaser can get an order for specific performance binding both the vendor and the second purchaser.[103] And taking a step in relation to planning matters which can prejudice the purchaser may be a breach of trust.[104] In addition to duties arising from a vendor's status as a trustee there will be a general duty on both parties to try to fulfil conditions of a contract[105] and each party has the right to expect the other to be reasonable in taking such steps as may be necessary towards completing a sale.[106]

---

[88] *Malone v Henshaw* (1891) 29 LRI 351 at 359-60. The position of a vendor's tenants with statutory renewal rights is considered by Barrington J in *Neville v Slattery Estates Co Ltd* (HC) 15 February 1984, unrep at 4-5; he considers an unauthorised letting made by the *purchaser* at 7-12. In practice nowadays most purchasers may prefer that no new tenants be let into occupation.

[89] *Abdulla v Shah* [1959] AC 124 at 132.

[90] *Bank of Ireland v Waldron* [1944] IR 303 at 306, 308.

[91] *Connolly v Keating (No 2)* [1903] IR 356 at 360.

[92] *Neville v Slattery Estates Co Ltd* (HC) 15 February 1984, Barrington J, unrep at 18-19; *Lyons v Thomas* [1986] IR 666 at 685-6.

[93] *Ibid.*

[94] *Lyons v Thomas* [1986] IR 666 at 681-2. On rescission clauses see paras **10.36-42** *ante.*

[95] *Bank of Ireland v Waldron* [1944] IR 303 at 308, *per* Overend J.

[96] *Per* Henchy J in *Tempany v Hynes* [1976] IR 101 at 109.

[97] We consider the question of risk at paras **11.18-20** *infra.*

[98] *Clarke v Ramuz* [1891] 2 QB 456 *Cf Viscount Securities Ltd v Kennedy* (SC) 6 May 1986, unrep; a trespasser left spoil on the property.

[99] *Treacy v Dwyer Nolan Developments Ltd.* [1979] ILRM 163 at 165. *Cf Smyth v Smyth* (1903) 37 ILTR 82; this involved a court sale and the basis of the decision may have been that the storm damage occurred one day before the chief clerk's certificate was filed: see para **3.60** *ante.*

[100] *Cumberland Consolidated Holdings Ltd v Ireland* [1946] KB 264 at 269. *Cf Connolly v Keating (No 2)* [1903] 1 IR 356.

[101] *Re Dwyer* [1901] 1 IR 165 at 167.

[102] *Lake v Bayliss* [1974] 2 All ER 1114 at 1117-8; [1974] 1 WLR 1073 at 1076. The consideration for the first contract was unusual.

[103] See para **8.13** *ante.*

[104] *Sinclair-Hill v Sothcott* (1973) 226 EG 1399 (withdrawal of application for permission).

[105] See para **3.26** *ante.*

[106] Paragraph **3.27** *ante.*

[11.15] An important duty of a vendor is to use reasonable care to preserve the property in a reasonable state of preservation and, as far as may be, as it was when the contract was made.[107] He is bound to take reasonable care of the property until the sale is completed.[108] He is normally not liable in respect of physical defects in the property at the time of the contract; the maxim *caveat emptor* applies.[109] Also the Law Society standard conditions will deem the purchaser to buy with full notice of the actual state and condition of the subject property.[110] The duty of reasonable care extends to protecting the property from damage by trespassers.[111] If a vendor is out of possession[112] but is warned about trespass he ought to take steps to prevent further trespass.[113] A vendor normally is not under any obligation to engage professional house minders to protect vacant premises pending completion of a sale although this is a point which parties might wish to cover in a special condition.[114] Depending on the circumstances he may be well advised to cut off services such as water, gas and electricity[115] and, if it is right that the services should be disconnected, the charges for reconnection would be borne by the purchaser.[116] Normally the vendor should not cut off services without consulting the purchaser. Inspection at frequent and regular intervals may also be desirable.[117] A vendor should be careful about storing combustible materials in the property as it may need to be protected and fortified with all the care and diligence which a prudent property-owner would exercise to prevent wrong-doers gaining access.[118] Particular care may need to be taken about leaving licensed premises vacant.[119] It is important to remember that there will often be a duty to *consult* the purchaser.[120] Indeed finding out what are the purchaser's wishes and implementing them as far as practicable is usually a safe course for a vendor save that he will bear in mind also the possibility of the contract going off with the result that he regains the entire beneficial ownership of the property. If a purchaser offers an indemnity against loss his wish is virtually a command.

[11.16] A purchaser may be guilty of contributory negligence, especially if he has access to the property and fails to do what he reasonably ought to do.[121] A wrong is defined by the Civil Liability Act 1961 as meaning "a tort, breach of contract or breach of trust...,"[122]

---

[107] *Per* Coleridge CJ in *Clarke v Ramuz* [1891] 2 QB 456 at 459, approved by Murphy J in *Lyons v Thomas* [1986] IR 666 at 674-5. See also *Re Dwyer* [1901] 1 IR 165 at 167, *Malone v Malone* (HC) 9 June 1982, Costello J, unrep at 14 and *Harris v Swordy* (HC) 16 June 1975, Kenny J, unrep.

[108] *Tempany v Hynes* [1976] IR 101 at 114, *per* Kenny J; *Malone v Malone* (HC) 9 June 1982, Costello J, unrep at 14.

[109] On this see Wylie, *Irish Conveyancing Law* (1978), paras 5.03, 5.11-12.

[110] *General Condition* 16, (1991) Ed, subject to certain obligations of disclosure. A similar condition was applied by Kenny J in *Harris v Swordy* (HC) 16 June 1975, unrep at p 7.

[111] *Tempany's* case at 109; *Bank of Ireland v Waldron* [1944] IR 303 at 306. *Cf Viscount Securities Ltd v Kennedy* (SC) 6 May 1986 where a trespasser left spoil on the property.

[112] Eg, a mortgagee with carriage of sale but not possession, as in *Bank of Ireland v Waldron* [1944] IR 303, or an owner living abroad as in *Lyons v Thomas* [1986] IR 666.

[113] *Bank of Ireland v Waldron* [1944] IR 303 at 306; *Lyons's case* at 682-5.

[114] *Lyons's* case at 683.

[115] As in the circumstances of the *Lyons* case: p 683.

[116] *Lyons's* case at 685.

[117] *Ibid*, p 683. Murphy J did not go the whole way with the purchaser about the steps which should be taken to preserve the property.

[118] *Bradley v Donegal County Council* (HC) Cir App, 14 November 1989, unrep, O'Hanlon J who held that the property *was* secured sufficiently.

[119] *Mulrooney v Regan* (HC) 30 June 1978, McWilliam J, unrep at 6.

[120] *Malone v Henshaw* (1891) 29 LRI 352 at 361.

[121] We consider the purchaser *in possession* before completion in paras **11.23-5** *infra*.

[122] Section 2.

which is broad enough to cover claims of the sorts we have just been discussing, and accordingly damages recoverable by a purchaser may be reduced in proportion to the extent to which they were caused by his own negligence or want of care.[123] If he knows of damage to the premises he will be under a duty to inform the vendor of it.[124] Of course, the purchaser is not yet in possession of or entitled to interfere with the premises and thus there is little he can do with the premises. This factor will be taken into account in assessing the degree of contributory negligence.[125]

[11.17] The purchaser should be careful that he does not waive his claim by taking his purchase deed. The acceptance of a conveyance may be sufficient evidence of waiver if the purchaser knew or ought to have known of the facts.[126] But, while this is the general rule, the inference of waiver will not arise if other facts show that the claim is not meant to be waived.[127] It is important to remember also that the contract itself may merge in a conveyance so that the parties lose their remedies under the contract and have to rely on rights under the purchase deed.[128] This also depends on the intentions of the parties[129] so a party who wants to rely on a term of the contract after taking his conveyance should make it clear that the contract is not intended to merge in the conveyance. A contract, however, will not merge in an order for specific performance.[130] It remains in force and, if the defendant fails or refuses to comply with the order for specific performance, the plaintiff may either apply to the court for further orders to enforce the contract[131] or accept the repudiatory breach, ask the court to dissolve the order for specific performance and enjoy the normal remedies for breach of contract[132] and the opportunity to forfeit the deposit.

RISK

[11.18] If property is damaged between contract and completion one party, normally the purchaser, can often get compensation from the other. It is important, however, to remember that property can suffer damage without there being an effective remedy against anyone. Weather damage may occur without either side being at fault although a vendor retaining possession will be liable if the damage is due to his want of reasonable care.[133] Vandalism is an increasing problem nowadays. If vandals damage property which is held to have been sufficiently secured by the vendor, the purchaser probably will have

---

[123] *Lyons v Thomas* [1986] IR 666 at 682; the purchaser was a "frequent trespasser" on the premises post-contract: p 684.
[124] *Lyons's* case at 684.
[125] In *Lyons's* case 10% of the blame was apportioned to the purchaser: p 685.
[126] *Connolly v Keating (No 2)* [1903] 1 IR 356 at 360.
[127] *Ibid.* The purchaser had raised a requisition which was understood to cover the relevant claim: p 362.
[128] *Adair v Carden* (1892) 29 LRI 469 at 481; *Re Otway's Estate* (1862) 13 Ir Ch R 222 at 235.
[129] See Wylie, *Irish Conveyancing Law* (1978) para 19.03; note that *General Condition* 48 of the Law Society's, *General Conditions of Sale* (1991) Ed, preserves all obligations designed to survive completion of a sale and all warranties in the conditions which have not been implemented by the purchase deed and are capable of having effect after completion.
[130] *Vandeleur v Dargan* [1981] ILRM 75 at 76-7.
[131] See paras **8.25-8** and **3.55-6** *ante*.
[132] *Johnson v Agnew* [1980] AC 367 at 493, approved by McWilliam J in *Vandeleur v Dargan* [1981] ILRM 75 at 77.
[133] *Treacy v Dwyer Nolan Developments Ltd* [1979] ILRM 163 at 165. *Cf Smyth v Smyth* (1903) 37 ILTR 82; this involved a court sale and the basis of the decision may have been that the storm damage occurred one day before the chief clerk's certificate was filed: see para **3.60** *ante*.

to complete the deal without any compensation or abatement of the price.[134] Where vandals cause damage and the vendor is liable for failing to take proper care of the property the purchaser may be guilty of contributory negligence, especially if he has access to the property, and suffer a proportionate reduction in his compensation.[135] Even if the damage is caused by someone with an interest in the property a claim against him may be of little value sometimes and the loss may have to be suffered by one of two innocent parties.[136] If one party has to compensate the other for damage to the property the one who pays or allows an abatement obviously suffers a loss. Normally this will be the vendor but, if the purchaser has been let into possession prior to completion[137] so that he has control of the property,[138] it would seem that the vendor's duty to take reasonable care of it ends and the purchaser would then owe such a duty to the vendor. A vendor who is careless about his duty to the purchaser is unlikely to be able to invoke a rescission clause in a contract in order to escape liability due to his default.[139] Those are some of the reasons why the parties should consider carefully who is bearing the risk of the property deteriorating and cater for that risk as best possible including getting insurance cover and making sure that grounds do not arise which would allow the insurer to repudiate liability.[140] Both vendor and purchaser have every incentive to take precautions. As we have seen,[141] between contract and completion each has a substantial interest in the property. A vendor can never be absolutely certain until actual completion that the entire beneficial ownership of the property will not revert to him. It seems clear enough now that the doctrine of *frustration* can apply to a contract for the sale of land[142] and, if it does occur, the vendor will be left with the subject matter of the contract. That would leave any loss caused by post-contract damage with him so this is another reason why he needs insurance protection.

[11.19] The traditional position is that gains and losses other than income, rents and profits[143] which arise between contract and completion belong to or are borne by the purchaser. As Sugden LC explained:[144]

"... a purchaser in common cases is the owner of the estate from the time of the contract, and from that period must bear any loss, and is entitled to any benefit; and this applies as well to damage to the property, *eg*, by fire, as to the interest in the property, for example, the death of the life for which it was holden. So as to profit, for an accidental improvement of the property would belong to the purchaser as well as an additional interest by the dropping of a life, where the reversion was the subject of the sale."[145]

---

[134] *Bradley v Donegal County Council* (HC) Cir App, 14 November 1989, O'Hanlon J, unrep at 6-8.
[135] *Lyons v Thomas* [1986] IR 666 at 682-5.
[136] *Re Dwyer* [1901] 1 IR 165 at 167-8 (damage by defaulting tenant purchaser).
[137] On which see paras **11.23-5** *infra*.
[138] The fact that the purchaser is precluded from occupation and control is a major factor in the duty of care of a vendor while he retains possession: *Lyons v Thomas* [1988] IR 666 at 676.
[139] *Lyons's* case at 677-82.
[140] *Eg*, problems are likely if property is vacant for long.
[141] On the basis of *both* judgments in *Tempany v Hynes* [1976] IR 101.
[142] In *Neville & Sons Ltd v Guardian Builders Ltd* (SC) 27 July 1994, Blayney J, unrep the Supreme Court held that a contract for the grant of a licence including the right to build houses had not been frustrated. Specific performance was ordered. No submission was made in either the SC or the HC ([1990] ILRM 601) that the doctrine of frustration could not apply. Frustration is discussed at paras **9.59-65** above.
[143] Which normally belong to the vendor: para **11.21** *supra*.
[144] *Vesey v Elwood* (1843) 3 Drury & Warren 74 at 79.
[145] *Cf Enraght v Fitzgerald* (1842) 2 Drury & Warren 43; *Vincent v Going* (1841) 3 Drury & Warren 75. But note the Law Society condition considered in the next para.

That passage may now be applied as if the words "to the extent that he has paid for it" appeared after "contract"[146] but that does not affect the points which Lord Sugden was making. The central point is that gains and losses become part of the property. If the deal goes through the gains and losses will be the purchaser's. If the contract goes off and the property reverts to the vendor any gain or loss becomes his. Thus, if property is damaged by fire post-contract but the purchaser has a good defence to an action for specific performance the loss falls on the vendor.[147] These points about the incidence of risk are, of course, subject to any claim that either party can make about breach by the other of a duty to use reasonable care to maintain the property in a reasonable state of preservation and that duty in turn is subject to any special bargain negotiated between the parties.[148]

[11.20] The current Law Society *General Conditions of Sale* largely shift the risk from purchaser to vendor:

"Subject as hereinafter provided, the Vendor shall be liable for any loss or damage howsoever occasioned (other than by the Purchaser or his Agent)[149] to the subject property (and the purchased chattels) between the date of sale and the actual completion of the sale BUT any such liability (including liability for consequential or resulting loss) shall not as to the amount thereof exceed the purchase price."[150]

The liability imposed on the vendor does not apply to inconsequential damage or insubstantial deterioration from reasonable wear and tear in the course of normal occupation and use not materially affecting value.[151] Nor does it apply to damage occasioned by operations reasonably undertaken by the vendor in his removal from and vacation of the property provided that the same are so undertaken with reasonable care.[152] And any loss or damage resulting from a requirement, restriction or obligation imposed by a competent authority after the date of sale[153] is also excluded.

The modern condition may be contrasted with a typical former condition which provided:

"The property shall as to any damage from whatever cause arising after the date of the sale be at the sole risk of the Purchaser and no claim shall be made against the Vendor for any deterioration or damage unless occasioned by the Vendor s wilful neglect or default."[154]

"Wilful default" in that context means no more and no less than a formula by which the Courts of Chancery describe an intentional (as opposed to an unconscious or accidental)

---

[146] In the light of the majority judgment in *Tempany v Hynes* [1976] IR 101: see para **11.03** *supra*.
[147] *Simmons v Pennington* [1955] 1 All ER 240 (vendor let insurance lapse).
[148] *Lyons v Thomas* [1986] IR 666 at 676.
[149] There is no expressed requirement of showing that the purchaser or his agent was guilty of negligence or breach of duty.
[150] *General Condition* 43, (1991) Ed. Note the position under the general law at para **11.19** *supra* and also a typical former condition noted a few lines below.
[151] Condition 44(*a*).
[152] Condition 44(*b*).
[153] This is defined in Condition 2 as meaning the date of auction, if the sale was by auction, and otherwise the date on which the contract became binding on the vendor and the purchaser.
[154] This is Condition 26 of the 1978 Ed and was considered in *Lyons v Thomas* [1986] IR 666 at 676-7, *Bradley v Donegal County Council* (HC) Cir App, 14 November 1989, O'Hanlon J, unrep and *Neville v Slattery Estate Co Ltd* (HC) 15 February 1984, Barrington J, unrep at 18-19 and by Wylie, *Irish Conveyancing Law* (1978) at para 11.32.

negligent act or omission.[155] "Default" must involve either not doing what you ought or doing what you ought not, having regard to your relations with the other parties concerned in the transaction; in other words, it means the breach of some duty you owe to another or others.[156] "Wilful", as explained by Bowen LJ in *Re Young and Hortson's Contract*:[157]

"... is a word of familiar use in every branch of the law, and although in some branches of the law it may have a special meaning, it generally, as used in Courts of Law, implies nothing blameable, but merely that the person of whose action or default the expression is used is a free agent, and that what has been done arises from the spontaneous action of his will. It amounts to nothing more than this, that he knows what he is doing, and intends to do what he is doing, and is a free agent."

POSSESSION

Vendor in possession pending completion

[11.21] Save where the contract provides otherwise the vendor is entitled to retain possession of the property until the purchase money is paid.[158] This principle is adopted by the current Law Society *General Conditions of Sale*.[159] When a purchaser fails to comply with an order for specific performance the vendor may apply to the court to rescind the earlier order and give him back possession if he has parted with it.[160] The order giving back possession is a "natural concomitant" with an order rescinding the contract which the court had previously ordered to be specifically performed and there is no reason in principle why an order for possession should not be made if the vendor appears entitled to possession instead of compelling him to bring separate proceedings.[161] If a vendor gives the purchaser possession pending completion and later takes back possession, even using force for that purpose, his resumed possession is likely to be treated as the normal possession of a vendor.[162] The vendor is also entitled to take and keep for his own use any rents and profits up to the date fixed for completion.[163] The vendor in possession is never entitled to interest unless there is some very unusual provision in the contract but, if his own default causes delay for which he must compensate the purchaser, he is entitled to set off the interest which the purchaser has saved due to the delay up to the level of extinguishing the claim by the purchaser.[164]

---

[155] *Per* Murphy J in *Lyons v Thomas* [1986] IR 666 at 677. See also *Re Postmaster-General and Colgan's Contract* [1906] 1 IR 287 at 294-7.

[156] *Per* Parker J in *Bayley-Worthington and Cohen's Contract* [1909] 1 Ch 648 approved by Costello J in *Northern Bank Ltd v Duffy* [1981] ILRM 308 at 309-10.

[157] (1885) 31 Ch D 168 at 174, approved by Costello J in *Northern Bank Ltd v Duffy* [1981] ILRM 308 at 314.

[158] *Per* Henchy J in *Tempany v Hynes* [1976] IR 101 at 109 and Moriarty LJ in *Re Kissock & Currie's Contract* [1916] 1 IR 376 at 392.

[159] *General Condition* 27. Note the vendor's right under *General Condition* 25(ii) to elect to take rents and profits less outgoings in lieu of interest when completion is delayed by default of the purchaser.

[160] *Croft Inns Ltd v Scott* [1982] NI 95 at 98.

[161] *Per* Hutton J in the *Croft Inns* case at 98. There seems to be a similar practice in England: Jones & Goodhart, *Specific Performance* at 208.

[162] *Johnston v Johnston* (1869) IR 3 Eq 328 at 334; the use of force met the "censure" of the court.

[163] *Tempany's* case at 109.

[164] *O'Brien v White-Spunner* [1979] ILRM 240 at 242. See para **11.28** *infra*.

[11.22] A purchaser normally is not entitled even to access to the property before completion. A wise vendor may agree some form of access if there is a good reason for it. It is possible, for example, that a vendor who will not let his purchaser's intending mortgagee or subpurchaser inspect the property cannot complain about resultant delay by the purchaser.[165] Generally a purchaser should not interfere with the property before he is entitled to possession. If the purchaser makes an unauthorised subletting before becoming entitled to possession the vendor is entitled to an account of the rents[166] and to delay completion of the sale until an accurate account is forthcoming.[167] If he trespasses on the property before completion he may make himself guilty of contributory negligence if the premises are deteriorating and he fails to take appropriate action such as leaving the premises secure after he has been there or sending specific information to the vendor about what he found.[168]

Purchaser in possession pending completion

[11.23] Of course if the vendor gives the purchaser possession before completion things may change radically. A vendor should think long and hard before he allows his purchaser into possession. From a purely practical viewpoint giving possession removes much of the purchaser's incentive to get his money together to complete the deal. The expense and inconvenience of having to sue for possession may also discourage the vendor from taking as firm a line as he ought. However, sometimes the balance of advantage may favour letting the purchaser in, especially if the vendor has to leave the premises vacant otherwise and a risk of trespass or deterioration is seen. If he does let in the purchaser much will depend on the nature of the possession given. A common practice in Ireland is to have the purchaser sign a caretaker's agreement having put the balance of the purchase money on deposit with the interest normally going to the vendor on completion. An advantage of the caretaker's agreement is that the vendor can use a summary District Court procedure to recover possession if necessary.[169] When the caretaker's agreement is terminated the purchaser has no right by virtue of the contract to remain in possession because, in the absence of an express stipulation to that effect, a purchaser is never entitled to possession before the contract is completed.[170] Sometimes a purchaser is let in on a caretaker's agreement when parties are still only in negotiation;[171] this seems very undesirable as the parties have not even established their basic agreement. A purchaser let into possession as a caretaker cannot be said to be entitled to the rents and profits and so will not be normally liable for interest.[172] This is why parties make an express agreement in many cases that the purchaser must put the balance of the purchase money on deposit. Sometimes access for the purchaser to the property may be arranged for one reason or another, *eg*, to arrange for work to be done after completion or to measure for carpets and curtains. In such cases it is important to make it clear that the access is given by permission only and is limited to the agreed purposes. On this basis the possession of the property remains with the vendor.

---

[165] *Schindler v Pigault* (1975) 30 P & CR 328.
[166] *Neville v Slattery Estates Co Ltd* (HC) 15 February 1984, Barrington J, unrep at 10-11.
[167] *Ibid.*
[168] *Lyons v Thomas* [1986] IR 666 at 684-5. See para **11.16** *infra.*
[169] On which see Wylie, *Irish Landlord and Tenant Law*, paras 3.15, 27.42.
[170] *Gowrie Park Utility Society Ltd v Fitzgerald* [1963] IR 436 at 439.
[171] As in *Davies v Hilliard* (1965) 101 ILTR 50 (negotiations towards a tenancy).
[172] *O'Byrne v Robinson* [1955/6] IJR 46 at 48.

[11.24] It is important to bear in mind some possible consequences of giving the purchaser possession before completion. One which the purchaser must consider carefully is that equity will imply a term that he must pay interest on the unpaid balance of the purchase money unless there is express agreement to the contrary or something in the circumstances to negative such circumstances.[173] This is so even though the delay in completion may be due to the vendor's wilful default.[174] Without such an implied agreement the purchaser would get an unfair benefit. Either he would be paying the agreed price less the value of interest on the unpaid balance for the period of delay or he would be getting free accommodation. The principle involved has been said to be that the purchaser who gets the full benefit of his bargain cannot rely on the non-execution of a conveyance, not affecting his immediate beneficial enjoyment, as an answer to a claim for interest.[175] The act of taking possession is an implied agreement to pay interest "for so absurd an agreement, as that the purchaser is to receive the rents and profits, to which he has no legal title, and the vendor is not to have interest, as he has no legal title to the money, can never be implied."[176] The parties may, of course, vary these principles by agreement but clear words would be needed to oust them altogether.[177] If the vendor gives the purchaser possession but then dispossesses him there is no liability for further interest.[178] The *rate* of interest is not necessarily the rate specified in the contract as applying if the purchaser delays completion[179] and, obviously, a purchaser who gets possession by agreement before completion is not thereby in default. In fixing rates of interest in specific performance actions or court sales the court is not confined to any court rate.[180] The courts are well aware that if the purchaser can pay the vendor a lower rate of interest than a bank would charge it will be in his interest to delay completion of the sale for the longest possible period.[181] Another possibility is that the purchaser who goes into possession before completing may become liable for a rent[182] or for use and occupation. A purchaser given possession in connection with a contract which is unenforceable by action due to lack of writing seems unlikely to be held to be under an implied obligation to pay rent for the property.[183] If he gets possession pursuant to a contract which is later rescinded he may escape liability for use and occupation during the period between the entry and the rescission but probably will become liable if he stays on after rescission.[184]

---

[173] *Greene v Quinn* (1940) 75 ILTR 107 at 109; *Beresford v Clarke* [1908] 2 IR 317 at 319-20; *Johnston v Johnston* (1869) IR 3 Eq 328 at 334.

[174] *Greene's* case at 109. However, in *O'Byrne v Robinson* [1955/6] IJR 46 the fact that the purchaser got possession as a caretaker defeated the submission that he should pay interest even though the vendor was in default: p 48.

[175] *Per* Gibson J in *Beresford v Clarke* [1908] 2 IR 317 at 319. This case concerned an agreement for a new tenancy with a fine; the purchaser was given possession paying the rent while a title defect was cured; he had to pay interest on the fine.

[176] *Per* Grant MR in *Fludyer v Cocker* (1805) 2 Ves 25 at 27, approved by Romer J in *Re Priestley's Contract* [1947] 1 All ER 716 at 721.

[177] *Re Priestley's Contract* at p 723.

[178] *Johnston's* case at 334.

[179] In *Greene's* case interest was awarded at the "usual" 4% rate though the contractual default rate was 6%.

[180] *Law v Roberts (No 2)* [1964] IR 306.

[181] *Law's* case at 307.

[182] If a tenancy were held to be created: the risk of the former Rent Restrictions Acts applying to a tenancy could have been serious: see Wylie, *Irish Conveyancing Law* (1978) para 11.27. See also *Francis Jackson Developments Ltd v Stemp* [1943] 2 All ER 601 where the purchaser got possession on signing a letter by which he agreed to pay "for occupation and use" a "sum equivalent to" interest at a certain rate on the balance of the purchase money.

[183] *Corrigan v Woods* (1867) IR 1 CL 73 at 75.

[184] *Markey v Coote* (1876) IR 10 CL 149.

[11.25] There are other possible consequences of the purchaser being given possession. The duty of the vendor in relation to the preservation of the property[185] will be affected in accordance with the degree of control the purchaser gets over the premises and the chance of the purchaser being held responsible in whole or in part will increase. In the usual case where the vendor retains possession his duty to the purchaser in relation to the preservation of the property depends to a large extent on the fact that the purchaser is normally excluded from the occupation and control of property until he completes the sale.[186] The giving or acceptance of possession may be a sufficient act or part performance to take a case out of the Statute of Frauds.[187] Delay may cease to be a bar to a claim for specific performance.[188] And taking possession may be evidence of acceptance of the vendor's title.[189]

Purchaser's possession on completion

[11.26] On an open contract a purchaser is entitled to possession on paying his purchase money.[190] That means real and complete possession free from any continuing use by the vendor or interference by a trespasser. As Lord Greene MR explained in *Cumberland Consolidated Holdings Ltd v Ireland*:[191]

> "Subject to the rule *de minimis* a vendor who leaves property of his own on the premises on completion cannot, in our opinion, be said to give vacant possession, since by doing so he is claiming a right to use the premises for his own purposes, namely, as a place of deposit for his own goods inconsistent with the right which the purchaser has on completion to undisturbed enjoyment...
>
> Occupation by a person having no claim of right prevents the giving of 'vacant possession', and it is the duty of the vendor to eject such a person before completion... The reason for this, it appears to us, is that the right to actual unimpeded physical enjoyment is comprised in the right to vacant possession. We cannot see why the existence of a physical impediment to such enjoyment to which the purchaser does not expressly or impliedly consent to submit should stand in a different position to an impediment caused by the presence of a trespasser."[192]

If there is such an impediment to enjoyment the purchaser would still get the right to possession in law. However, what he bargains for is not merely the right in law, but the power in fact to exercise the right.[193] For the vendor to be in default the impediment must be one which substantially prevents or interferes with the enjoyment of the right of possession of a substantial part of the property.[194] Thus, a large quantity of spoil[195] left on land was a sufficient impediment.[196] So was a trespasser who had built a shed on the land and refused to move.[197] An attempt to make a letting of meadows would be inconsistent

---

185 See paras **11.14-15** *supra*.
186 *Lyons v Thomas* [1988] IR 666 at 676.
187 See paras **6.10-11** *ante*.
188 See paras **9.42-70** above on laches.
189 Wylie, *Irish Conveyancing Law* (1978) paras 14.72, 14.75.
190 *Bank of Ireland v Waldron* [1944] IR 303 at 305.
191 [1946] KB 264 at 270; [1946] 1 All ER 284 at 287.
192 Approved by Griffin J in *Viscount Securities Ltd v Kennedy* (SC) 6 May 1986, unrep at 5. *Cf* Walsh J at 14-15.
193 *Per* Lord Greene, *ibid*.
194 *Ibid*. In an old case cited in an Editorial Note in the All ER it was held that there may be no vacant possession when beer was left in a cellar: *Savage v Dent* (1736) 2 Stra 1064.
195 C. 3,000 cubic metres costing £10,000 to £12,000 to remove in 1983.
196 The *Viscount Securities* case *per* Walsh J at 15.
197 *United Yeast Co Ltd v Cameo Investments Ltd* (1975) 111 ILTR 13.

with giving vacant possession.[198] And a vendor must get rid of a squatter[199] or a tenant[200] unless, of course, he has contracted to sell subject to the tenancy.[201] In England it has been held that rubbish filling two thirds of the basement of a warehouse[202] and substantial furniture left in a house[203] prevented vendors from giving vacant possession. Difficulties of this sort may not be confined to purely physical matters. Thus, in the purchase of a farm the goodwill of the vendor's family may be essential to the enjoyment of possession.[204] And a local authority notice limiting the occupation of property can mean that there is a failure to give vacant possession in the sense of the right to occupy and enjoy the property.[205]

[11.27] The current Law Society *General Conditions of Sale* provide that, subject to any provision to the contrary in the particulars or in the conditions or implied by the nature of the transaction, the purchaser is entitled to vacant possession on completion.[206] The phrase "or implied by the nature of the transaction" is unclear.[207] It may not go so far as to let a vendor rely on circumstances which, for example, might put an intending purchaser on notice of the presence of tenants and of their rights.[208] It is therefore important to spell out clearly in any contract any restrictions which are agreed to be placed on the purchaser's right to vacant possession.

[11.28] Where there is delay in giving a purchaser possession, which is not due to any defect in title,[209] he is entitled to compensation for the period he is kept out of possession in breach of contract.[210] This compensation may take the form of an occupation rent to be paid by the vendor.[211] If the purchaser saves interest by reason of the delay he must set that off against the damages to which he is entitled.[212] But if the interest exceeds the damages the vendor is not entitled to any balance because giving him that would enable him to profit by his own wrong.[213] Where the sale is delayed by the vendor's default the general rule is that the vendor, instead of getting interest, must be satisfied with the interim rents and profits but he does not lose both ways.[214]

---

[198] *Guerin v Heffernan* [1925] 1 IR 57 at 68.
[199] *Dickie v White* (1901) 1 NIJR 128.
[200] *Re Postmaster-General and Colgan's Contract* [1906] 1 IR 287 at 292 (affirmed at 477). *Cf Irish Land Commission v Macquay* (1891) 28 LRI 342.
[201] *Hibernian Bank v Harrington* (1912) 46 ILTR 27 - purchaser buying "with possession subject to the court tenancy" entitled to possession only from the last gale day of the year.
[202] The *Cumberland Consolidated Holdings* case.
[203] *Norwich Union Life Insurance Society v Preston* [1957] 2 All ER 428.
[204] *Guerin v Heffernan* [1925] 1 IR 57 at 62-6.
[205] *Topfell Ltd v Galley Properties Ltd* [1979] 2 All ER 388 at 390.
[206] *General Condition 2.*
[207] It did not appear in the 1976 Ed considered by Wylie, *Irish Conveyancing Law* (1978), paras 10.078, 10.110.
[208] If a purchaser knows that persons are in occupation he is likely to be deemed to know of their tenancies and all rights attaching to them: *Healy v Farragher* (SC) 21 December 1972, unrep at 8-12; *Carroll v Keayes* (1873) IR 8 Eq 97; cf *Clements v Conroy* [1911] 2 IR 500.
[209] The rule in *Bain v Fothergill* (or *Flureau v Thornhill*) is likely to limit severely a party's damages due to title defects without fraud or bad faith. See Wylie, *Irish Conveyancing Law* (1978) paras 12.78-83 and the detailed discussion by the HC and SC in *McDonnell v McGuinness* [1939] IR 223 and by O'Connor MR in *Kelly v Duffy* [1922] 1 IR 62.
[210] *Bank of Ireland v Waldron* [1944] IR 303 at 305.
[211] As was done in *Law v Roberts (No 2)* [1964] IR 306.
[212] *O'Brien v White-Spunner* [1979] ILRM 240 at 242-3.
[213] *Per* Leech VC in *Esdaile v Stephenson* (1822) 1 Sim & St 122 in a passage approved by McWilliam J in *O'Brien's* case at 242.
[214] *Per* Wilberforce J in *Re Hewitt's Contract* [1963] 3 All ER 419 at 422, [1963] 1 WLR 1298 at 1302 approved by McWilliam J in *O'Brien's* case at 242.

Index

Agistment "lettings"

SOF, 5.06

Agreement

agent, by, 3.32-3, 3.35
charge, for, SOF, 5.06
lease, for, see **Lease, Agreement for**
mortgage, for, SOF, 5.06
to make contract, 4.04, 4.16-18
"up to a point", 4.17

Annuity, 1.25

Arbitration

arbitrator's power to order SP, 1.24
staying proceedings, 1.24

Auction, 3.45-53

bid, agreement not to, 3.51, 9.09
bids as offers, 3.45
deposit, 3.49
enquiries at, 3.50, 3.53
injurious falsehood by *purchaser*, 3.50
"knocking down", 3.45
misrepresentation by *purchaser*, 3.50
"puffer", 3.46
reserve, 3.45-5, 3.51
Sale of Land by Auction Act 1867, 3.46
stakeholder, 3.49
SOF, 3.47, 3.65
vendor's right to bid, 3.46, 3.51-2

Auctioneer, 3.45-53

agent of both parties, 3.47
authority to sell by other method, 3.48
 to sign for parties, 3.47
care, duty of, 3.52
contract, no guarantee there will be, 3.52
court sales, in, 3.62
duty to persons attending, 3.53
 to purchaser, 3.53
 to vendor, 3.52
information given by, 3.53
"knocking down", 3.45
negligent misrepresentation, 3.53
note in book, 5.17
"puffer", 3.46
statements by, 3.53

trade usage, 3.48
witness, signing as, 3.47, 5.28

Bain v Fothergill, rule in,

hardship, 9.40

Bankruptcy

act of, 8.15, 8.18
effect on contract, 8.15, 8.17
lease, agreement for, 3.17
Official Assignee, 8.15-8
 disclaimer by, 8.17
 vesting in, 8.16
relation back, 8.15, 8.18
rescission of contract, 8.17

Boyle v Lee

agreement to agree, 4.21
cases overruled by, 4.24-5
deposit, 3.12-14
striking out, 10.05
"subject to contract", 4.01, 4.22-5

Building contracts

certainty, 1.11, 1.21-2
interlocutory injunctions, 1.22
possession available, 1.21
supervision by court, 1.12
when SP available, 1.21-2

Business use

part performance, 6.01, 6.10

Caretaker

District Court, 11.23
purchaser as, 11.23

Caveat emptor

physical defects, 11.15

Certainty

building contracts, 1.11, 1.21-2
contract, of, 1.11
mandatory interlocutory injunctions, 2.16
severable term, 1.11

Chattels, 1.25

SOF used as, 6.01, 9.08-9

Fraudulent misrepresentation, 9.12-15

agent, 9.15
context, importance of, 9.13
defence to SP, 9.12-15
duty to correct wrong impression, 9.13, 9.15
distinctions from innocent, 9.22
inducing cause, 9.14
principal and agent, 9.15
repudiation, 9.14
separate cause of action, 9.12
two meanings, 9.13

Frustration, 9.59-65

accrued rights, 9.63
bases of doctrine, 3 possible, 9.61
change in law, 9.65
changed circumstances, 9.61
compulsory purchase, 9.65
entire contract going, 9.63
essential thing continuing, 9.60
event contemplated, 9.61-2
impossibility of performance, 9.60, 9.64
intervening illegality, 9.61
just and reasonable, 9.61-3
leases, 9.59, 9.65
mutual expectation destroyed, 9.60, 9.62
present position, 9.59
presumed common intention, 9.61
principles from case law, 9.61
rare application, 9.59
  risk, 11.18
self-induced, 9.64

Gains and losses, 11.19

"Gazumping", 5.02

Gift, 3.06

intended, 3.07
perfection, 3.06

Hardship, 9.38-41

balancing, 9.40
change of circumstances, 9.38, 9.40
damages, 9.40

discretion of court and, 1.08
exceptional defence to SP, 9.38
existing at date of contract, 9.38
Mareva injunctions, 2.20
operating with other factors, 9.41
third parties, of, 9.39-40

High Court

constitutional points, 8.02-3
costs, 8.05
forwarding from Circuit Court, 8.08
full original, 8.02
President, as party, 8.14
procedure, 8.04
remitting to Circuit Court, 8.03
summons, 8.04
V&P jurisdiction, 8.04, 8.54

Hiring premises, 1.17

Husband and wife

advancement, 7.30
agreements, 7.30
Judicial Separation and Family Law
  Reform Act 1989, 7.33
mother in the home, 7.32
wife contributing,
  furniture, 7.31
  improvements, 7.31
  mortgage repayments, 7.31
  purchase, 7.30
"working wife", 7.39

Ignorance of law

illegality, 9.49
rectification, 10.24

Illegality, 9.48-55

change in law, 9.51
connected act or contract, 9.50
contract partly illegal, 9.50
court cannot aid, 9.48
court cannot ignore, 9.53
defence to SP, 9.48-55
fraud on public, 9.54
fraud on revenue, 9.48
illegal contract completed, 9.52
indirect breach of law, 9.50

test for, 10.12
vendor with no interest left, 10.12
V&P Summons, 10.14

Loan

contracts for, 1.19
giving agreed security, 1.19
pointless orders, 1.13
subject to, 3.25

Locus standi

purchaser with binding contract, 2.07,
    8.13

Lord Cairns' Act, 1.28-31

Malice

abuse of process, 10.07
malicious prosecution, 10.09

Mareva injunctions, 2.18-20

Material terms, 3.08-18

access, 3.05, 3.10, 3.18
agreement for lease, 3.16-7
closing date, 3.15
completion, reasonable time, 3.15
consensus on, 3.08
contract,
    including disputed, 3.03
    misstating, 3.03
    omitting, 3.03
deposit, 3.11-14
    paid under former deal, 3.18
expenditure of money, 3.17
fines, 3.17
guarantees, 3.17
indemnities, 3.18
leaseback, 3.18
note or memorandum,
    draft documents, 5.13
    including terms not agreed, 5.13
    subsidiary, 5.13
    terms to be evidenced, 5.12
part performance and, 6.05
parties, 3.09, 5.12
    SOF, 5.12
physical layout, 3.05, 3.10

possession, date of, 3.15
    vendor retaining part, 3.15, 3.18
price, 3.08-9, 5.12, 5.35
    downpayment, substantial, 3.09
    instalments, 3.09
    "luck penny", 3.09
    method of fixing, 3.08
    SOF, 5.12
property, 3.05, 3.09-10, 5.12, 5.36
    SOF, 5.12
rates, 3.18
rent, 3.17, 5.36
residence, right of, 3.18
stock, 3.18
SOF, 5.12
stamp duty, 3.18
"subject to contract", 4.06
subjective test, 3.10, 5.12
submission to, 5.14
tax losses, 3.18
tenancies, 3.13
title, 9.84
vendor, 3.09
    one of two or more co-owners, 3.09
waiver, 5.14
water rights, 3.18

Maxims of equity, 9.37

Memorandum, see Note or
Memorandum

Merger

contract in conveyance, 11.17
    in order for SP, 11.17

Minors

FHPA, 7.28
mutuality, 9.73

Misdescription

compensation, 9.86-8
defence to SP, 9.85-8
Law Society conditions, 9.85
SOF and 9.87

Misrepresentation

purchaser, by, at auction, 3.50

361

lis pendens, 10.14
parties, 8.12
pleadings, 8.54
procedure, 8.54
served while completion notice running,
    8.34, 8.59
SP outside scope, 8.58
third parties, 8.55
title, 8.56-7
validity of contract outside scope, 8.58

Vesting orders

compulsory purchase, 3.67
Trustee Act 1893, 8.26

Vexation, 10.02-3

Volunteer, 3.06
rectification, 10.24

Wages and salaries, 2.12

Waiver

conditions, 3.29
    time for, 3.29
contract as whole, 3.30
covenants, 3.17
fines, 3.17
right to investigate title, 9.83
SOF and, 3.30, 5.14

term of sole benefit of party, 5.14
vendor's duty, claims for breach of, 11.17

Warranty

damages for breach, 8.50-1

Water

rights as material term, 3.18

Ways and wayleaves

material term, 3.18
SOF, 5.06

Wilful default

interest, 8.45
risk, 11.20

Will

contract to leave property by, 1.25

Witness

auctioneer signing as, 3.47, 5.28
solicitor signing as, 5.28

Writing

note or memorandum, 5.17

Year

contract performed within, 5.11
    SOF, 5.11